Putin Confronts
the West

ALSO BY RENÉ DE LA PEDRAJA
AND FROM McFARLAND

*The Russian Military Resurgence: Post-Soviet Decline
and Rebuilding, 1992–2018* (2019)

*Free Trade and Social Conflict in Colombia, Peru and Venezuela:
Confronting U.S. Capitalism, 2000–2016* (2016)

*The United States and the Armed Forces of Mexico,
Central America and the Caribbean, 2000–2014* (2014)

Wars of Latin America, 1948–1982: The Rise of the Guerrillas (2013)

Wars of Latin America, 1982–2013: The Path to Peace (2013)

Wars of Latin America, 1899–1941 (2006)

Putin Confronts the West

The Logic of Russian Foreign Relations, 1999–2020

René De La Pedraja

McFarland & Company, Inc., Publishers
Jefferson, North Carolina

LIBRARY OF CONGRESS CATALOGUING-IN-PUBLICATION DATA

Names: De La Pedraja Tomán, René, author.
Title: Putin confronts the West : the logic of Russian foreign relations, 1999–2020 / René De La Pedraja.
Other titles: Logic of Russian foreign relations, 1999–2020
Description: Jefferson, North Carolina : McFarland & Company, Inc., Publishers, 2021 | Includes bibliographical references and index.
Identifiers: LCCN 2021001040 | ISBN 9781476684994 (paperback : acid free paper) ∞
ISBN 9781476642406 (ebook)
Subjects: LCSH: Russia (Federation)—Foreign relations—21st century. | Russia (Federation)—Politics and government—1991– | Russia (Federation)—Foreign relations—Western countries. | Western countries—Foreign relations—Russia (Federation) | Putin, Vladimir Vladimirovich, 1952—Influence.
Classification: LCC DK510.764 .D44 2021 | DDC 327.470182/109051—dc23
LC record available at https://lccn.loc.gov/2021001040

BRITISH LIBRARY CATALOGUING DATA ARE AVAILABLE

ISBN (print) 978-1-4766-8499-4
ISBN (ebook) 978-1-4766-4240-6

© 2021 René De La Pedraja. All rights reserved

No part of this book may be reproduced or transmitted in any form or by any means, electronic or mechanical, including photocopying or recording, or by any information storage and retrieval system, without permission in writing from the publisher.

Front cover image © 2021 Shutterstock

Printed in the United States of America

McFarland & Company, Inc., Publishers
Box 611, Jefferson, North Carolina 28640
www.mcfarlandpub.com

To Beatriz and Jaroslav

Acknowledgments

The acknowledgments I provided in *The Russian Military Resurgence* apply equally to this volume. In bringing this project to completion, Charles L. Perdue, the acquisitions editor at McFarland & Co., played an essential role when he recognized the need for this companion volume to complete the story of my previous book.

The History Department at Canisius College has remained supportive of my scholarly endeavors. Mark Gallimore diligently reviewed many chapters in this book, and he felt readers needed to be aware of the context behind Russia's clashes with the West. He was the first to encourage me to pursue what at first seemed a quixotic project. Bruce Dierenfield kindly took time away from his own writing to scrutinize several of the chapters in this book. Dave Devereux has made valuable suggestions about word choice. A special thanks goes to Stephen Maddox, who has generously shared his expertise on the fascinating history of Russia.

My wife Beatriz did not hesitate to support a project that seemed to have no end in sight. As in previous volumes she has read every line and drawn all the maps. Her participation is all the more meaningful for me because health reasons almost deprived me of her invaluable collaboration. Her full recovery has made me appreciate how indispensable was her assistance I took for granted in my previous books. My son Jaroslav has continued to provide support for the book in numerous ways.

I appreciate the time and effort all the individuals devoted to improving the text. Any deficiencies that remain are solely my responsibility.

Table of Contents

Acknowledgments   vi
Preface   1

Part I. The Age of Illusions

1. The Collapse of an Empire   5
2. Turmoil and War in the "Near Abroad"   15
3. The West and the First Chechnya War   28
4. The New Architecture for Relations with the West   33
5. Ukraine: Deceptive Calm   43
6. The Turning Point: Kosovo   51

Part II. From Acquiescence to Resistance

7. The Second Chechnya War and Islamic Radicalism   61
8. Bridges to the West   69
9. Russia and the U.S. Invasion of Iraq   76
10. Seeking Friendships   81
11. Russia in the Middle East   89
12. The West on the Offensive   96
13. Response to the Color Revolutions   105
14. Skirmishes with the West   113
15. Countdown to Collision   120
16. The Five Day War with Georgia   128
17. The Response of the West to the War   140
18. Friends in the Caucasus   147

Part III. Russia Ascendant

19. A Foreign Ministry for a World Power   157
20. The Reset in U.S. Relations with Russia   165
21. The Reset in the Near Abroad   172

Table of Contents

22. Growing Divergences with the West	181
23. Crisis in Ukraine	190
24. Reprisals Over Ukraine	204
25. Russia on the Offensive	211
26. The Russian Diplomatic Campaign	221
27. The Rollercoaster of U.S.-Russia Relations	229
Chapter Notes	237
Annotated Bibliography	279
Index	281

Preface

Russia has for centuries appeared to the West as a country impossible to understand. This widespread myth has generated the tendency to see Russia not just as mysterious but as inherently dangerous. Thus, by default the country has fallen into playing the role of the "other"—at least a rival and many times the enemy.

The purpose of this book is to show readers that Russia in its foreign relations has been no more inscrutable or enigmatic than most Western countries. This volume forms part of the larger topic of "post–Soviet Russia in the world" and is the continuation and the natural complement to the author's previous *The Russian Military Resurgence: Post-Soviet Decline and Rebuilding, 1992-2018*. While the books may be read independently of each other, the readers who study both will obtain the deepest and most complete understanding of the role Russia has played in the world since the fall of the Soviet Union in 1991.

The single most important foreign issue of post–Soviet Russia has been its relationship to the "West," a convenient designation to group the U.S., NATO, the European Union (EU), and Japan. Even though these four components have not always agreed on all the tactics nor have they all confronted Russia simultaneously, they have consistently pursued a common hostile strategy toward Moscow. Other studies have discussed extensively the policy debates among the component parts of the West, but this book takes a novel approach by concentrating on Russia's responses.

Ultimately these Western nuances have not mattered because they have not modified the fundamental strategy of striving to deprive Russia of any influence on issues beyond its borders.

The concentration on the hostility from the West means that Russia's relations with other parts of the world, most notably the countries of Asia, Africa, and Latin America, enter into the narrative only when directly touching upon the West. The Middle East has been different, and the book provides a more extensive account of the increasing Russian involvement in that traditionally turbulent region.

The availability of the diplomatic cables of the U.S. via Wikileaks has provided the opportunity to examine events otherwise remaining in secrecy for decades. But this dependence on U.S. records raises the question of their usefulness and even validity for the reconstruction of Russia's foreign relations.

The overwhelming majority of cables demonstrate that U.S. diplomats tried to report accurately on Russian events. And in the few cases when diplomats refused "to speak truth to power," the results were major crises such as the outbreak of hostilities in the Five Day War with Georgia in August 2008. The U.S. diplomatic cables do have the major limitation of being strongly biased against Russia. The author believes that after filtering out the inherent bias in the documents, it is possible to reconstruct an accurate picture. The diplomatic cables usually separated the actual narrative from the opinion or interpretation, in this way assisting scholars in the pursuit of truth.

Two outside checks also exist to verify the validity of these diplomatic cables. The Russian Federation is no longer the closed society of the Soviet Union, unpublished reports have become available in Russia, and some have even reached prestigious institutions in the United States such as the Hoover Archives in Stanford, California. Whenever available, those unpublished Russian materials have confirmed the narrative in the U.S. diplomatic cables.

Also, a vigorous press in Russia and renewed Western media coverage in the last decade have produced considerable reporting and even occasional revelations. Although usually lacking the detailed reporting on negotiations, the press often confirmed the basic story contained in the U.S. diplomatic cables.

The above considerations have convinced the author that the accounts in these chapters are solid and will stand the test of time. The author faced the choice of having to wait decades until all the secret documents of the governments concerned became public or to offer readers this first draft of history based on the treasure trove of U.S. diplomatic documents. The decision for readers is whether to proceed reading the text right now or to stop and wait at least several more decades for the appearance of an ideal book.

Resolute readers who proceed will see that the material in this book corresponds to the three main periods in the foreign relations of Russia since 1992. The first part covers the years of the Boris Yeltsin administration, when many Russians naively believed that total submission to the demands of the West was the best policy for the country. The "Age of Illusions" brought major setbacks and finally forced Russia, in 2000, to adopt a defensive stance. But by then the decline in the 1990s had been so precipitous that the Kremlin usually lacked the means to confront the assaults coming from the West.

In the third stage underway by 2008, "Russia Ascendant," the country felt sufficiently strong not just to repulse the Western attacks but also to take the offensive. The return to the ranks of world powers meant that Russia could use its newly recovered strength to shape the world even in the face of bitter Western opposition.

Part I

The Age of Illusions

1

The Collapse of an Empire

When Russia was weak in the 1990s and beyond, we did not take Russian interests seriously. We did a poor job of seeing the world from their point of view, and of managing the relationship for the long term.—Secretary of Defense Robert M. Gates[1]

Farewell to Communism

The Loss of Fourteen Soviet Republics (the "Near Abroad")

Moscow's direct rule over the other fourteen Soviet republics helped to shape Soviet foreign policy. Three factors were most influential. First was the strategic value of most of those territories, and in effect they constituted the first line of defense against any invasion of Russia. Second was the presence of a large number of ethnic Russians in many of the fourteen Soviet Republics. In Moldova and to a large degree in the Baltic Republics the ethnic Russians had come after World War II; they had been present in Belorussia, Kazakhstan, and Ukraine for centuries. Similar to the ethnic Russians were other nationalities, most notably the Abkhazians and the Ossetians, who insisted on remaining under the rule of Moscow.

Third was the existence of natural resources in the fourteen non–Russian republics, such as Azerbaijan and Kazakhstan. This third factor provoked less controversy, because after the collapse of the Soviet Union the Russian Federation inherited the overwhelming majority of those riches. Moscow did have concerns over the Western intrusion into the oil fields of Central Asia and the Caspian Sea and over the routes for gas and oil pipelines. Still, the conclusion remained valid that the Russian Federation did not feel the need to resume control over the natural resources of the other fourteen former Soviet republics.

It is not an exaggeration to state that the struggle with the West over the nature of the links with the other Soviet republics has been the principal preoccupation of Russian foreign policy. This concentration on the affairs of the "near abroad" (the collective name for the other fourteen Soviet republics), at times prompted the U.S. to dismiss Russia as "regional" rather than a world power. Even if Moscow had kept all or some of the Soviet republics under its rule, the shift from state ownership and a single party Communist system to private property and an open political system meant a dramatic and fundamental change in the foreign relations of Russia after 1991.

The End of Communist Ideology

With the fall of the Soviet Union, the driving force in foreign policy ceased to be a universal dogma. Fierce disputes over the correct way to reach Socialism damaged relations with other countries and were responsible for the Sino-Soviet split of the 1960s. In response to Chinese requests, Mikhail Gorbachev ended the arcane quarrel with Beijing, and once Communist dogma disappeared as a factor in foreign relations, the path was open to forge close ties with China under the presidency of Vladimir Putin. The insistence on imposing the Soviet way as the "correct" path to Socialism caused friction even with such loyal allies as Cuba and Vietnam. Although during the Cold War that tension remained little known in the West, it discouraged other countries in Asia, Africa, and Latin American from adopting the Soviet way to Socialism.[2]

Without ideology, the justification to support the Communist regimes in Eastern Europe vanished. During the Cold War the Kremlin devoted time and resources to prop up the Eastern European regimes, but that effort stopped even before the Soviet Union ended in December 1991. In many ways the attention the Kremlin lavished on the Eastern European countries passed after 1991 to the fourteen former Soviet republics comprising the near abroad.

One of the revelations after the collapse of the Soviet Union was that the Communist Party had been giving secret subsidies to its foreign counterparts. Observers often wondered how Communist parties without members and no visible means of support were able to survive in many countries into the 1980s. The fall of the Soviet Union halted these subsidies, and never again has the Kremlin funded foreign Communist parties.[3]

Not just Communist parties but also national liberation movements ceased to receive funds. Under Nikita Khrushchev the Soviet Union had publicly announced its support for peoples seeking independence from colonial powers. But by 1991 this policy had exhausted its potential because very few places in the world still remained under colonial rule. By then the national liberation movements either became separatist revolts inside a new country or in other cases were factions seeking to use a civil war to gain control of the government. The Russian Federation discontinued its support for those groups and thus removed a source of friction in the relations with the West.

Atheism

An integral part of the ruling dogma had been atheism, a necessary component of its materialist philosophy. The Communist Party persecuted all forms of religion and discriminated against those holding religious beliefs. This hostility to God carried over into foreign policy, and Communists urged foreigners to persecute religion and to abandon the belief in any God. The anti-religious campaign, however, was never complete even inside the Soviet Union. In a bizarre contradiction, while the Communist Party persecuted religion, the KGB quietly supported and even financed the Orthodox Church and Islamic institutions. The Soviet government often had to moderate its atheism and anti-religious policies in its relations with foreign countries, in particular those in the Middle East.[4]

With the collapse of the Soviet Union, the Russian Federation no longer had to carry the ideological baggage of atheism, and relations with foreign countries could improve without any religious constraints. Removing the atheist barrier had little effect on foreign relations during the 1990s when Russia was in dire straits. Once Russia began its recovery in the early twenty-first century, the Kremlin was able to capitalize on its religious openness to improve relations with Catholic states in Latin America and with the Muslim countries of the Middle East and Asia.

Ideological Propaganda

Last but no less significant, the Russian Federation rejected the Soviet approach of promoting and praising the benefits of Socialism. On the contrary, during the 1990s Russia, with the fervor of a recent convert, denigrated Socialism and preached the benefits of capitalism to anyone willing to hear. If before 1990 Communism had been the cure for all the problems of any country, after 1991 capitalism became the new idol to be worshipped. This missionary zeal to destroy Socialism had as one of its unfortunate consequences the initial Russian support for the Western campaign against Serbia when the former Yugoslavia began to disintegrate. Boris Yeltsin's government was determined to eliminate Socialist influence in the world, and the Communist ideas of Serb leaders made them prime targets for destruction. This anger against Serbs paralleled the hostility toward Cuban leaders, who refused to abandon Communism.[5]

The financial meltdown of August 1998 in Russia forced a revision of this almost fanatical belief in capitalism. The Kremlin once again concluded that the state was essential for the success of the economy. In its foreign relations Russia was ready to collaborate with official enterprises in other countries. And the Kremlin realized that Russian state firms were also a very useful instrument to pursue foreign policy goals. The stage of doing missionary work for either Communism or capitalism was over, and Russia concentrated on crafting measures to deal with the specific issues in its relations with foreign countries.

The Descent: 1991–1992

After the failed coup attempt of August 1991, the Soviet Union for all practical purposes ceased to function and was unable to pursue an effective foreign policy. Prior to the coup attempt, a power struggle had raged between Boris Yeltsin and Mikhail Gorbachev, the titular head of the Soviet Union. After August 1991 real power was in the hands of the winner Yeltsin, who, in a glaring omission, did not remove Gorbachev from office. The months slipped by, the Soviet Union disintegrated, and the fifteen constituent republics saw the opportunity to break free from Moscow's rule.

For Gorbachev foreign relations had been one of his priorities, but not for Yeltsin. The latter was typical of the provincial and parochial Russians who showed little interest and had scant knowledge of the world outside their country. However, Yeltsin was a consummate politician, who remained well attuned to the feelings of his Russian constituents. During his presidency, whenever the Russian people expressed strong passions about a particular foreign policy issue, Yeltsin did then stand up and try to uphold the country's role in the world, but it was often too late to do anything.

Once public opinion on a foreign policy issue subsided, Yeltsin resumed his usual indifference to international affairs. Harmful as this attitude turned out to be for Russia during his presidency, even worse came from his tendency to give away for nothing many of the rights of the country. Time after time what the tsars and the Communists had accumulated over decades and sometimes centuries, Yeltsin gave away in a day and sometimes in a few minutes. The key to this behavior lay in his isolationist sentiment. Giving away non–Russian territories was a natural response for Russian isolationists, whose attitude in part represented a rejection of the seventy years of internationalism that the Communists tried to instill in the minds of Soviet citizens.

When it became clear after the failed August coup of 1991 that Yeltsin was going to replace Gorbachev, who by then had become the darling of Western audiences, the valid concern spread in the West about the future direction of Russian foreign policy. In countless speeches and even in several books, Gorbachev had proclaimed lofty principles to disguise his abject submission to the demands of the West. Although Yeltsin never formulated such artificial pronouncements, he rarely reversed his predecessor's policies. Once the West realized that it was going to be business as usual with Yeltsin, a sense of relief set in.[6]

The disintegration of the Soviet Union was advancing so fast that the West fell behind in increasing its demands. Moving goal posts forward has been a favorite diplomatic tactic of the U.S., but the speed of events overtook even Washington. The independence of the three Baltic Republics was the minimum ultimatum of the West, with that of Ukraine being second on the wish list. As it became clear that more of the fifteen former Soviet republics were going to become independent countries, the West made new claims but had never expected all of the Soviet republics to become independent so suddenly. The conventional wisdom was that at least some of the Central Asian republics would remain part of the Soviet Union.

With Moscow dumping independence on several of the former Soviet republics, the West began to realize that the opportunity to fulfill a secret and long-held fantasy was approaching. Ever since the entry of Russia into the world stage in the late seventeenth century, the appearance of this new power became a matter of great anxiety to Western capitals. What European countries most resented was that Russia became the arbiter in the balance of power. The tsars overcame most Western fears, but the open goal of the Communists to seek world domination proved too much to ignore. The secret wish to dismantle or eliminate the "Eurasian hegemon" gained force.

The sudden independence of the fifteen former Soviet Republics left the West behind and scrambling to shape an appropriate policy to further its goals. The response consisted of two fundamental elements. First, the West declared the borders of fourteen of the former Soviet republics to be inviolable; any attempt by Moscow to reestablish control over those territories received full condemnation as a blatant violation of international law and of all the principles of the post–World War II settlement. But what about the fifteenth of the former Soviet republics, the new country born on 25 December 1991 and soon to adopt the name of the Russian Federation? Here a different policy was at play: its borders could be altered or broken as the West so desired.

Gorbachev performed his assigned role to the hilt, and among other rewards received the Nobel Peace Prize. The buffoonish Yeltsin did not achieve similar recognition, but during almost all his presidency the West gave him every possible benefit of the doubt and at key moments provided crucial support to keep him in power. This assistance of course did not come for free, and was a continuation of the practice of having someone in the Kremlin who would strive to cooperate with the West.

Diplomatic Withdrawal

First Yeltsin had to take control of the foreign policy machinery of the Soviet Union. As the first popularly elected president of the Russian Socialist Republic (one of the fifteen Soviet republics), Yeltsin already controlled a small foreign ministry composed of under 240 officials. In November 1990 he appointed Andrei Kozyrev to be his foreign minister. The functions of this small agency were insignificant and in numbers could not match the Foreign Ministry of the Soviet Union, which had at least 3,700 officials. After the August 1991 failed coup attempt Yeltsin should have taken over all the Soviet ministries and agencies (and in the process probably saved Russian rule over some of the

Central Asian republics), but he was slow to act. He waited until 18 December 1991 to issue the decree transferring the Soviet Foreign Ministry to the Russian Foreign Ministry.[7]

The decree also placed the embassies, consulates, missions, and any assets of the former Soviet Foreign Ministry under Russian control. Kozyrev remained in charge, and he became the first foreign minister of Russia when the Soviet Union came to an end on 25 December 1991. Questions arose over whether the young Kozyrev could direct such a large agency, but his total loyalty to Yeltsin and his stated desire to follow the West on all policy matters meant that his tenure was safe, at least during the initial years.[8]

The first task of Kozyrev was to eradicate the Communist influence from the Foreign Ministry. Because this agency had played a marginal if not insignificant role in the failed August 1991 coup attempt, the Foreign Ministry at the beginning escaped the purges taking place in other parts of the Russian bureaucracy. The dismissal of senior generals had been widespread in the Ministry of Defense, to cite one example, but nothing comparable occurred at the Foreign Ministry. Kozyrev required all employees to apply again to preserve their positions, and around 800 were not rehired. The purge was political, and the main goal had been to remove those officials associated with the Communist Party.[9]

The total number of personnel fell below three thousand but the number of officials in Moscow increased because the economic crisis in Russia was worsening and the food lines becoming longer. The government was unable to pay salaries not just to troops but also to diplomats stationed abroad. Some embassies went so far as to sell material possessions in order to feed their staffs. Many employees, facing hunger abroad, returned home to try to survive with the help of relatives and colleagues. Recognizing the inevitable, the Foreign Ministry closed 10 embassies, 14 consulates, and other missions in countries of Africa, Asia, and Latin America; Russia was abandoning its role as a world power and retreating to the still expensive status of a regional power.[10]

Only after August 1992 did the Foreign Ministry reassign 400 of the returning diplomats to the new missions in the fourteen former Soviet republics, the "near abroad." Moscow was reduced to struggling to retain some influence over former territories. It thus came as a surprise that Kozyrev in one of his first foreign trips decided to travel to Africa, when Russia was in the process of withdrawing from that continent. In reality the visit was understandable once its goal became clear: he had come as a debt collector to try to extract from rich Angola at least the partial repayment of the large loans the Soviet Union had granted. The other stops in South Africa and Egypt during Kozyrev's trip were window dressing to disguise the new role of Russian diplomats as debt collectors.[11]

Military Withdrawal

Money also ended the close relations between Vietnam and Russia. The Soviet Union had extended loans and deployed military advisers and technical personnel to Vietnam, and in appreciation for this assistance, Hanoi authorized Soviet military personnel to operate the former American base at Camranh Bay. The U.S. had spent a small fortune constructing this massive complex, and its conversion into a Soviet base was the final humiliation for Washington from the Vietnam War. Independent Russia no longer could afford to maintain uniformed personnel at Camranh Bay, and disputes arose with Hanoi over how to pay for the military and technical advisors. By early 1992 Russia was well on the way to withdrawing from Vietnam, a country that because of its fear of China, had no choice but to seek restoration of ties with the United States to gain a strategic partner.[12]

Foreign Minister Kozyrev shared Yeltsin's intense dislike for Communists, and the foreign policy of independent Russia in its initial years mimicked the strong anti–Communism of the West. The major exception was China, which whether Communist or not, was too large to antagonize; both Yeltsin and Kozyrev continued the gradual improvement of relations with the Communist giant to the south, but the full development of Sino-Russian relations had to await the Vladimir Putin presidency in the twenty-first century.[13]

Little Cuba was a different matter, and here Kozyrev could display his anti–Communist credentials. The Russian Foreign Ministry stated on 18 January 1992 that Cuba needed to "bend over backwards" to meet U.S. demands,[14] or in other words to abandon its struggle for independence and to surrender to Washington. The U.S. played the game of moving goal posts in negotiations with Cuba; as soon as Havana accepted a U.S. request, then even harsher demands appeared on the table. Washington wanted nothing less than the repeal of the Cuban Revolution or regime change, and because the country did not comply, in February 1992, in a stunning reversal, Russia voted against Cuba in the U.N. Human Rights Commission.[15]

Russia had lost all interest in playing a significant role not just in Latin America but also in Asia and Africa. Moscow by rapid steps was dismantling its empire and the retreat did not stop at Eastern Europe. Russian troops were the last remnant of the Kremlin's influence in that region, but the withdrawal from Eastern Europe was still not complete when Russia became an independent country on 25 December 1991. At the start of 1992 the Yeltsin administration had still not removed Russian troops from East Germany and Poland. Wealthy West Germany agreed to pay for the construction of living quarters in Russia for the soldiers stationed in East Germany, and as soon as the facilities were finished, the last units were scheduled to return home.[16]

The situation in Poland was more complicated. Soviet troops had been present in Poland since 1945, unlike in Czechoslovakia and Hungary. They became well established in Poland, and officers even acquired properties for retirement. The over 50,000 Russian soldiers demanded compensation or quarters similar to those West Germany was building in Russia, but Poland lacked the means to make those payments. Moscow lacked the funds to pay their salaries, so Russian diplomats did not have much leverage to delay their withdrawal.[17]

The Three K's

Even before the last Russian units left Eastern Europe, the West had set its eyes on more ambitious targets. The second basic principle of policy toward the Russian Federation was that its borders were not sacred. The West saw that for the first time in centuries the fantasy of dismantling Russia had a chance of becoming a reality.

Karelia

The first test case was Karelia, a large stretch of land north of St. Petersburg and extending all the way to the White Sea. After its defeat in World War II, Finland ceded this territory to the Soviet Union. In early February 1992 private groups appeared in Finland demanding its return, and polls showed overwhelming support for this proposal. The advocates claimed that once the half a million expelled Finns reclaimed their homes, the area could become very prosperous and yield abundant produce for St. Petersburg.[18]

Whatever the merits of the argument

for returning Karelia, the Finnish government was hesitant to raise the issue with the Russian Federation. Friendship with Russia was much more important than any slice of territory, no matter how tempting. Citizens sometimes revived the claims, but the Finnish government refused to be the battering ram to make the initial breach in the borders of the Russian Federation. The West sympathized with the dilemma of Finland and for the moment left Karelia pending until a more propitious time.[19]

Kaliningrad

No such hesitation constrained Lithuania, and its officials made claims to the Russian enclave of Kaliningrad. At a time when the most pressing task for Lithuania was to make sure that Boris Yeltsin lived up to his promise to withdraw Russian troops from the country by 1994, to stoke the fire with territorial demands was risky. The West stepped in and dampened the enthusiasm of Lithuania. Kaliningrad posed a real threat to NATO, and for the military alliance eliminating this Russian enclave was high on the list of priorities. But Lithuania was premature in stating its claims, and the topic belonged to the future once Russia was prostrate and helpless.[20]

Kurile Islands

Just as with Karelia, the West kept Kaliningrad ready for use during an opportune moment. In contrast an impatient Japan pressed its case for the return of the four main southern islands of the Kurile in the Pacific Ocean. In the San Francisco Peace Treaty of 1951 Japan had renounced all claims to the Kurile Islands, but some loose ends remained unsettled.[21]

Under promises of generous foreign aid, Tokyo lured Boris Yeltsin to visit Japan. For the Japanese, even if Yeltsin did not return the territory, just a statement from him that the four main southern islands did not belong to Russia would at last give Tokyo the first shred of evidence to justify the claim.[22] Until 1993 Yeltsin had been very generous in giving away Soviet territory, and that was how the other fourteen former Soviet republics had been able to obtain independence. He had not hesitated to abandon Russian interests in Central and Eastern Europe, because those countries had never been part of the Russian heartland. But the Kurile Islands were different because they were inside the Russian Federation.

Also, after the expulsion of the Japanese settlers in 1945, all the Russian inhabitants were passionate about keeping the islands under Moscow's rule. Here Yeltsin faced two hurdles: he had to give up territory of the Russian Federation and then he had to expel Russian citizens from the islands. Even Mikhail Gorbachev had rejected the Japanese claim, and Yeltsin hesitated to reverse the decision of his predecessor.

As Yeltsin wrestled with this issue, preparations were far advanced for a trip to Japan in 1992. What saved the Kurile Islands for Russia was the nationalistic backlash over events taking place halfway around the world, in Transnistria. The struggle of Russian speakers to preserve their culture against the Rumanian majority evoked nationalistic sympathies across Russia, and the political antennae of Yeltsin made him support the rebels. He could not do otherwise with the Kurile Islands. He postponed his trip to Japan to October 1993, and during his visit he refused to give up the islands. Japan has continued to insist on their return, but to no avail.[23]

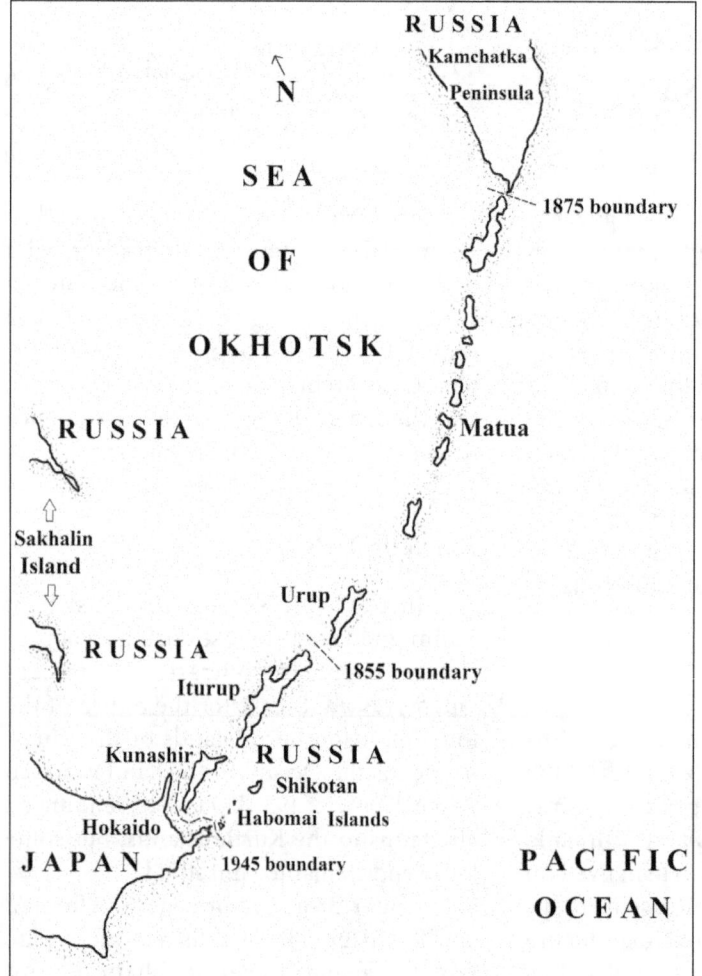

The First Stirrings of NATO

The failure of the three K's (Karelia, Kaliningrad, and Kurile Islands) to make any breach in the borders of the Russian Federation was an initial setback for the West. The U.S. and European governments desisted from pushing harder on the three K's because trying to fragment the

Russian Federation risked great dangers. Since 1991 Russia had been in an economic meltdown, and the population noticed that after the fall of the Soviet Union the food lines were longer. Hunger was widespread, officials went unpaid, and crime was rampant. Western countries began to fear that criminal organizations and terrorist groups might acquire chemical weapons, nuclear materials, and strategic missiles. The disintegration of Yugoslavia and the outbreak of bloody ethnic strife in the Balkans foreshadowed a much worse conflagration in Russia. The West faced the real risk of the sudden implosion of Russia with the inevitable flood of millions of refugees scrambling to reach Western Europe and the United States. When Russia was most vulnerable to disintegration, the West hesitated to push hard out of fear of triggering terrifying consequences for the world.

The temporary abandonment of plans to dismember the country reinforced the arguments for creating a strong barrier against Russia. This "containment 2.0" was the strategy of surrounding the Russian Federation even more than NATO had ever been able to accomplish during the Cold War. The task was even harder because after 1989 friendship had replaced the hostility of China. Unless the West could somehow detach China from Russia, the chances of encircling and isolating Russia were slim at best.

Conference for Security and Cooperation in Europe (CSCE)

The aging Cold War warriors defended NATO as a treasured relic from the past. In April 1990 the Foreign Minister of Czechoslovakia, Jiri Diensthier, proposed expanding the Conference for Security and Cooperation in Europe (CSCE) until it replaced both NATO and the Warsaw Pact. CSCE had played a major role in defusing tensions during the Cold War because almost all European countries were members. The West was receptive to the enlargement of the functions of CSCE but did not want this organization to replace NATO and the dying Warsaw Pact. The disbandment of the Warsaw Pact on 1 April 1991 removed the urgency to expand the functions of CSCE. The West also made clear to the countries of Eastern Europe that the sole options were NATO and the European Community (the European Union after November 1993).[24]

The strengthening of CSCE was useful but was not urgent or even necessary because of the vigorous role the United Nations assumed after the collapse of the Soviet Union. With Russia voting almost always with the West in the Security Council, the possibilities of expanding the UN role were immense. Even an amendment to the UN Charter could have included CSCE as a specialized agency. Because a treaty had not established CSCE, bringing the organization under the UN mantle was also an easy way to fill that legal vacuum. But these and other valid alternatives fell by the wayside for a West determined to impose NATO on the countries stretching between Western Europe and the Russian Federation.

Conventional Forces in Europe Treaty (CFE)

Moving all at once the former Soviet Bloc countries into NATO was too abrupt a change, and the West preferred a gradual transition. A first step came with the signing of the Conventional Forces in Europe Treaty (CFE) in Paris on 19 November 1990. By this agreement, the Soviet Union accepted parity in conventional forces between the Warsaw Pact and NATO. For example, the treaty limited the military alliances to 20,000 tanks and 20,000 artillery pieces, and similar ceilings existed for other weapons. In addition the treaty restricted the ability of Russia to move troops along its flanks; this "flank" regime made impossible any rapid buildup of its forces near the borders. The treaty also mandated rigorous inspections on both sides to assure compliance.[25]

The treaty was already a brilliant victory for the West, and then the disbandment of the Warsaw Pact on 1 April 1991 shifted the military balance even more against Russia. Without firing a shot, the West had gained such a significant military superiority that many observers believed that NATO was headed to oblivion. The most logical alternative was to match the end of the Warsaw Pact with the abolishment of NATO as an anachronism of the Cold War. Although the press discussed this possibility, Western officials had no intention of ever sacrificing their cherished military alliance.[26]

In the greatest blunder of late Soviet and Russian diplomacy, the Kremlin failed to insist on iron-clad treaty guarantees against the eastward expansion of NATO. The oversight was unexplainable, when Soviet diplomacy for decades had pressed hard for the neutralization of Germany and other areas of Europe. The only lasting legacy of that approach was the recognition of the neutrality of Austria in 1955, a country bordering on non-aligned Switzerland.[27] Because Finland and Sweden already enjoyed de facto neutrality, for the first time in history the creation of a large swath of neutral territory stretching from the Baltic Sea to the Black Sea was a real possibility. The dream of lasting peace for Western Europe seemed to be within reach.

To the world's great loss, both Mikhail Gorbachev and his successor Boris Yeltsin forgot about the neutralization of large segments of Europe and instead cast Russia into the arms of the West. To be fair to Gorbachev, the George H.W. Bush administration made repeated promises to the Soviet Union that NATO would not expand to the east. In a memorable statement, on 9 February 1990 Secretary of State James Baker told Gorbachev and Foreign Minister Shevardnadze that "there would be no extension of NATO's jurisdiction for forces of NATO one inch to the east."[28] In reality Baker had been referring only to West Germany, but because later Gorbachev accepted the reunification of Germany and the entry of the former East Germany into NATO, both Baker himself and other Western officials concluded that the Kremlin had given the green light to the eastward expansion of NATO.

The "one inch to the east" statement poisoned U.S.-Russian relations for decades. Nothing could excuse the failure of both the Soviet Union and the Russian Federation to have insisted on treaty guarantees while the leverage of Russian troops in Central and Eastern Europe existed. Whether the choice was between the ideal alternative of neutralization or a formal treaty agreement banning NATO from expanding did not matter. What remained striking was the colossal blunder of Russian diplomacy.[29]

As mentioned before, Yeltsin cared little about issues outside the Russian heartland and was more than willing to give the West a free hand to shape the post–Cold War order. And in a fatal weakness, Yeltsin craved recognition and acceptance from the West. Not facing any Russian resistance, the U.S. was free to expand NATO to the east, but the George H.W. Bush administration declined to enlarge NATO. This policy was almost certain to continue during a second presidential term. But the election in November 1992 brought Bill Clinton to the White House. The incoming administration was ready to expand NATO eastward.

2

Turmoil and War in the "Near Abroad"

It is very well [...] that Russia plays a defining peacekeeping role in the space of the former Soviet Union.—General Dmitry Volkogonov[1]

The formal end of the Soviet Union on 25 December 1991 intensified the armed clashes already starting in many of the former Soviet republics. Some ethnic groups concluded that to extract the maximum benefit from the disappearance of the Soviet Union, they had to take direct action. Fierce combat began in South Ossetia in January 1991 and spread across most of the Caucasus. Conflict also engulfed Moldova in March 1992.

The Structural Defect

The end of the Soviet Union on 25 December 1991 dumped on the world a problem of colossal consequences. The two main architects of the collapse of the Soviet Union—Mikhail Gorbachev and Boris Yeltsin—never had an idea of the forces that they had unleashed and did not understand the true nature of the problem. Commentators were quick to point out similarities with the recent breakup of the colonial empires of Britain and France but the closest analogy was almost two centuries away in the New World.

Between 1810 and 1825 Spain lost its territories in America with the exception of the islands of Cuba and Puerto Rico. New republics occupied the space of the former colonial empire, but they lacked clear and rational boundaries because the administrative divisions existing had served the purposes of empire and not the needs of the new states. Wars broke out, and border clashes became a characteristic of the region. After two centuries of conflict, the majority of disputes have been settled, but even today minor territorial quarrels persist.[2]

The main lesson after two centuries of struggle in Spanish America was that the administrative units of an empire were not always suitable for the new countries. The ill-defined inherited boundaries made finding agreement difficult, and sometimes countries resorted to war to settle their territorial claims. This happened in a region having the essential similarities of language and religion. In the multiethnic Soviet Union, the presence of peoples speaking different languages and having diverse religions created problems of an even greater magnitude than in Spanish America. The transfer of territories among the Soviet republics was indispensable to reflect the needs of ethnic groups, but both Gorbachev and Yeltsin refused to make adjustments to the borders of the former fifteen Soviet republics.[3]

The lessons from the disintegration of the Spanish Empire meant nothing to a West determined to splinter the Russian Federation into mini-states. For the West the first step was to refuse to consider any changes in the borders of the former fourteen non–Russian Soviet Republics. After independence in December 1991, any apparent infringement of the territories of the new republics brought swift condemnation to Moscow.

This intolerant policy toward any attempt by the Kremlin to modify the borders did not mean a guarantee for the territorial integrity of the Russian Federation. Whenever the possibility emerged of taking lands away from the Russian Federation, as the previous chapter showed, the West welcomed and applauded those initiatives and often encouraged them. The stated goal of preventing the return of a Eurasian hegemon required striking at Russia any time the opportunity appeared to cut off even a small slice. The twin goals of extirpating Russian influence in the former Soviet Republics and preventing any return of Moscow's influence were already apparent in the early cases in Transnistria and the Southern Caucasus.

Moldova and Transnistria

As the briefest and least bloody of the armed clashes, Moldova is the starting point for this chapter. On 27 August 1991 Moldova, one of the Soviet republics, proclaimed its independence. However, in the eastern part of the country the Russian minority feared absorption into Rumania and organized Transnistria as a separate entity loyal to Moscow. Attempts to find a negotiated solution failed, and an impatient Moldova sent troops into Transnistria on 2 March 1992.[4]

The almost quixotic resistance of Transnistria caught the imagination of the Russian people, and volunteers traveled to defend the country. Russian public opinion was so in favor of the rebels that the politically astute Boris Yeltsin proclaimed Russian support for the separatist region. The West expected larger Moldova to crush the rebel region and had not realized that the Russian Fourteenth Army had not disintegrated as had happened to Soviet forces stationed in other Soviet republics. Although numbering less than 14,000 soldiers, the Fourteenth Army supported the Transnistrians, even in defiance of direct orders from Moscow. Yeltsin, afraid to anger domestic nationalists, tolerated the independent policy of the Russian troops. In an attempt to halt the support for the separatists, the Defense Ministry appointed General Alexander Lebed as the new commander of the army, but he intensified the support for Transnistria.[5]

The turning point came on 3 July 1992 when massed artillery barrages of the Fourteenth Army shattered a Moldovan offensive. General Lebed bluffed about launching an invasion to reconquer all of Moldova. The threat worked, and a panicky Moldovan government agreed to a ceasefire on 21 July, which among other clauses authorized the presence of Russian troops on the Transnistrian side. The halt in hostilities has lasted until the present, yet the search for a final settlement to the dispute has proved elusive.[6]

On the map Transnistria appears as a sliver of territory between the Ukrainian border and the Dniester River. Most of the large factories and power plants of Moldova are located in this area, and these enterprises were the principal reason why so many ethnic Russians had emigrated to the region during the Soviet period. The output from these manufacturers went to Russia, and the region generated the electricity for the rest of Moldova. In addition, during the Soviet period Moldova had been an agricultural breadbasket for Russia.[7]

After the ceasefire of July 1992, the first task for diplomats was to negotiate agreements about the free passage of goods

2. Turmoil and War in the "Near Abroad"

and persons across both countries. Many of the inhabitants who lived on one side of the border also worked, went to school, and bought produce in the other country. Moldovans needed free passage across Transnistria to reach their traditional markets at Odessa in Ukraine. Moldova made the very important concession of allowing the use of its official seals and customs documents for products originating in Transnistria and headed for export markets other than Russia. By 1996 negotiators had succeeded in reaching accords on the commercial, social, educational, and personal links between the two countries.[8]

Russian Troops

No progress occurred on the two interrelated issues of the reincorporation of Transnistria into Moldova and the presence of Russian troops. Transnistria saw the presence of Russian troops as the only real guarantee of its independence, while Moldova insisted on their withdrawal. To pressure Moscow, Western powers invented the accusation that Transnistria was a ploy to reestablish the Russian empire. Western diplomacy exerted pressure on the weak Yeltsin administration. Moscow complied and in 1995 deactivated the Fourteenth

Army and reduced its status to that of a brigade.⁹

At the 1999 November OSCE summit in Istanbul Moscow showed its good faith by promising to withdraw its last troops and the remaining arsenals by 2001. But because Transnistria had not been a party to that agreement and had not even been invited to the Istanbul summit, its leader Igor Smirnov refused to abide by its terms. When Moscow ordered its troops to abandon their barracks and to remove the weapons from the arsenals, waves of protesters impeded the movements of the soldiers. In an extreme case of defiance, women lay flat on the railroad tracks and blocked the passage of the trains. The West, with its selective attitude toward repression, was impatient to see the Kremlin use force to clear the path no matter what the human cost and the toll of lives.¹⁰

The "general will" of the Russian people was to support Transnistria, and not even the Kremlin dared order Russian troops to fire on defenseless civilians. After years of patient persuasion, the Kremlin removed most of the large Soviet-era arsenals in Transnistria, in exchange for maintaining a token force and providing financial support for the separatist region. Even after the deactivation of the brigade in 2002 and the reduction of the number of Russian soldiers to 1200, Ukraine still feared Russian encirclement both on its western and eastern borders. Western diplomats pointed out that the force was too small to launch any major invasion. From a military perspective that conclusion was true but overlooked the critical role the small contingent could play in triggering a much larger Russian response, as later happened in Georgia in 2008. Although the West increased the diplomatic pressure and made sure that no country recognized the independence of Transnistria, the dispute remained unresolved.¹¹

The Caucasus: Georgia, South Ossetia, and Abkhazia

Tsar Peter the Great, in one of his lesser known campaigns, defeated the Persians and captured Baku, the capital of Azerbaijan, in 1723. His conquest marked the start of Russian involvement in the southern Caucasus. After his death in 1725, Russia abandoned this distant conquest and pulled back the border to the Terek River. Only a century later, in 1828, did tsarist control extend over the nationalities of Armenia, Azerbaijan, and Georgia.¹²

Tsarist rule was on the verge of completing its first hundred years when the Russian Revolution of 1917 brought the collapse of the empire and the start of a Civil War lasting until 1921. Foreshadowing what happened again in 1991, in 1918 the three main nationalities in the Caucasus took advantage of Russian weakness to proclaim their independence. However, in both instances the elimination of Russia left a power vacuum too big for the new republics to fill. No different than what the U.S. did later, Britain—able to draw on its presence in Persia and its empire in India—attempted to fill the void in authority. Britain stationed garrisons in the region and established a protectorate over the Southern Caucasus.

The Bolsheviks (Communists) emerged victorious in the Russian Civil War. British officials believed that Armenia, Azerbaijan, and Georgia could block the southern advance of the revolutionary Red Army. Winston Churchill disagreed, and in a clear warning to NATO advocates of the twenty-first century, he argued that arming Azerbaijan and Georgia for that purpose was "like using a piece of putty to stop an earthquake."¹³ The majority of British troops withdrew from the Caucasus by mid–October 1919. Two British battalions remained at Batumi, and they too left in the summer of 1920. No longer fearing opposition from London, the Bolsheviks proceeded to reestablish Russian rule in the area north of Persia and Turkey.[14]

By the end of 1920 the Red Army completed establishing Moscow's control over both Azerbaijan and Armenia. In early 1921 Bolshevik forces entered Georgia but faced strong resistance from the local population and from Turkish troops. To overcome this local resistance, a fourth nationality, the Abkhazians, proved decisive. They remained a pillar supporting Moscow during the entire period of Soviet rule in Georgia.

With the formal establishment of the Soviet Union in January 1924, Moscow adopted the formula of creating separate republics for most of the nationalities in the vast country. But these national republics were window dressing, and a powerful repressive apparatus kept the locals in fear of the central state and preserved stability in the region. After 1985 when the reforms of Mikhail Gorbachev undermined the authority of the Soviet Union, the nationalities regained the freedom to hate and attack each other. Without the strong repressive apparatus of the central state, nationalities fell into a state of war and turned into a reality the nightmarish scenario of British political writer Thomas Hobbes.

First Blood in the Caucasus: South Ossetia

Disturbances and protests had been rising in number and intensity in the Caucasus ever since Mikhail Gorbachev began to restructure the Soviet Union in 1985. Tensions seemed strongest in Abkhazia, but the first region to experience savage violence was tiny South Ossetia. The South Ossetians lived among ethnic Georgians, intermarriage between the two groups had been extensive, and many South Ossetians were more fluent in Georgian than in their native language. But the Georgian nationalist leader was the firebrand Zviad Gamsakhurdia, who went so far as to condemn intermarriages with Ossetians. He also began to carry out his promise to expulse all Ossetians.[15]

South Ossetia pleaded with Moscow to resume its traditional role of protecting nationalities in the Caucasus. But a Soviet Union in a free fall was in no condition to prevent "ethnic cleansing," so the South Ossetians in desperation organized their own self-defense militias. Volunteers flocked from the Caucasus to help the tiny region, and Ossetians bought weapons from starving Soviet troops often in exchange for food.

Unlike Abkhazia where war started on a specific date, South Ossetia drifted into combat. Tensions had been building during late 1990s and erupted into street violence in the capital of Tskhinvali in January 1991. The Ossetians were tough fighters and they drove out the Georgians but not before the latter had wrecked irreparable damage to many cultural symbols in the city. The Georgians applied for the first time in Tskhinvali their policy of erasing all traces of other ethnic groups; in South Ossetia the fierce resistance of the locals halted that cultural genocide before the Georgians could complete their task.

The Georgians used their control of the surrounding hills and three of the four routes into Tskhinvali to harass traffic and to deprive the city of electricity and natural gas. In another escalation Georgians expelled Ossetians from surrounding villages, and the Ossetians reciprocated by the expulsion of Georgians from Tskhinvali. The consequences of the war went beyond the immediate region, and over 100,000 Ossetians living in other parts of Georgia had to flee.[16] These expulsions and the attempted cultural genocide made impossible any reconciliation with Georgia.

The introduction of Soviet troops and uniformed policemen brought a temporary calm, but sporadic outbursts continued to occur along the roads in March 1991. The election of Gamsakhurdia as president of Georgia in May 1991 sparked renewed violence when the new president tried to regain control of South Ossetia. The locals lived up to their reputation of being fierce fighters, and the military setbacks they inflicted on the Georgians discredited Gamsakhurdia. Revolts against his rule broke out in December, and after days of protests and rioting, the once idealized president fled for his life to Russia on 6 January 1992.[17]

The end of the Soviet Union on 25 December 1991 converted the war in South Ossetia into an international dispute among independent countries. When Eduard Shevardnadze became the provisional ruler on 6 March 1992 he agreed to a ceasefire. On 15 June 1992, Ruslan Khasbulatov, who was the chair of the Russian parliament, threatened Georgia with war. Russian army units took aggressive measures and Russian helicopters even attacked a Georgian military column. At this moment President Boris Yeltsin on 22 June telephoned Shevardnadze to propose a meeting to defuse the crisis. The Georgian president knew that he had a weak hand to play and accepted the Russian conditions. By the terms of the Sochi agreement of 28 June 1992 another ceasefire went into effect and created a peacekeeping force composed in equal parts of Russian, South Ossetian, and Georgian troops.[18]

War in Abkhazia

The military weakness of Georgia had been the fundamental reason for the failure to crush the rebels in South Ossetia. Ethnic Georgians outnumbered the 97,000 Abkhazians by around 3 to 1, and the provisional government of Eduard Shevardnadze expected a quick victory to bring electoral benefits in upcoming elections. To launch the invasion of Abkhazia on 14 August 1992, Shevardnadze used the pretext of the need to protect the railroad line stretching through Abkhazia from the Russian border through Georgia and then to Armenia. The unopposed entry emboldened the invaders to push beyond their initial objective of the southern town of Gali. The advance reached Ochamchira, and on 18 August 1992 the Georgians took full control of Sukhumi, the capital of Abkhazia.[19]

Vladislav Ardzinba was the leader of the local Abkhazian authorities, and he had done everything possible to avoid a clash with Georgia in order to spare his people the danger of destruction. He was a historian and a university professor, and Abkhazians had turned to him in their greatest moment of need and placed their fate in his hands. He scrambled to organize militias for the defense of the capital, but small arms and Molotov cocktails could delay the advance of the large Georgian armored columns for only a few hours. He ordered his government to withdraw to the west into Gudauta, a city that became the provisional capital of Abkhazia.[20]

Georgian troops then made an amphibious landing to the west at Gagra and caught the unprepared Abkhazians by surprise. The capture of this port on 22 August cut off the rebels from the direct supply route to Russia and also trapped the remnants of the resistance between the large Georgian garrison at Sukhumi and the troops at Gagra. The moment was ripe to strike a final blow against the Abkhazians huddled around Ardzinba at Gagra, but in a major strategic blunder, the Georgians failed to launch the final offensive.[21]

In Sukhumi the Georgians burned museums, libraries, and archives. They also destroyed significant buildings, statues, and any other signs of the Abkhazian culture. The Georgians targeted the houses of Abkhazians for burning, and soon a wave of refugees was fleeing from the smoldering ruins of the capital city. Likewise in Gagra, the occupation forces set on fire private homes. The Georgians also committed acts of torture, murder and mutilation, while rapes and the threat of sexual terror traumatized Abkhazian families.²²

On 25 August 1992 the Georgian commanders announced that 100,000 Georgians stood ready to die in order to annihilate the 97,000 Abkhazians. And in April 1993 in a chilling manifestation of the principle of "economy of force," a Georgian minister stated that only the young Abkhazians (15,000 in number) needed to die in order to deprive that nation of any descendants and thus to assure its extinction. In a diabolical twist, the Georgian occupiers tracked down old Abkhazians for execution, so that no elders were left alive to try to fill from their memories the huge gaps left by the destruction of archives and libraries.²³

The Georgian threats of extermination transformed the war into a national struggle for survival. Abkhazians formed a united front around Ardzinba and were determined to do everything to save their culture. The rampage, the atrocities, and the genocide—both cultural and biological—precluded any reunification with Georgia. In an early indication of where the sympathies of the West lay, foreign media, except for that of Russia, paid little attention to the barbaric atrocities the Georgians were inflicting on the Abkhazian victims.²⁴

Outnumbered and outgunned, the Abkhazians stood no chance of defeating their invaders. Historian Ardzinba asked for outside help, and he succeeded in rallying volunteers from the North Caucasus. Here Ardzinba was playing a dangerous balancing act, because although the majority of his people were Christians, he knew that the Muslims of Russia, in particular the Chechens, provided the bulk of the volunteers. Ardzinba ordered the attack against Gagra on 1 October. It took ferocious fighting over several days until the rebels were able to take the town on 8 October 1992; in the process they captured armored vehicles and artillery. The victory also reopened the routes to Russia for both volunteers and supplies.²⁵

The political fragmentation in Georgia prevented Shevardnadze from making any military response to the loss of Gagra, and this pause gave diplomacy a first chance to settle the conflict. President Boris Yeltsin had made frantic phone calls to both rulers to end the fighting, but to no effect. The horrific scenes on television had made the Russian people sympathize with the Abkhazians. But Moscow did not want to create a precedent for other minorities inside the Russian Federation or encourage the looming defiance of Chechnya.²⁶

The creation of a peacekeeping force was one way to halt the fighting, but the West, already bogged down in the quagmire of the former Yugoslavia, had no desire to deploy peacekeepers into Abkhazia. At this early stage of the conflict, Russia opposed the introduction of any peacekeepers from countries outside the former Soviet Union, but at the same time Moscow was reluctant to send Russian peacekeepers. However, the real obstacle to any halt to the conflict was the Georgian insistence that Abkhazia return Gagra as a precondition to any talks between the two sides on the future status of the region.²⁷

Ardzinba was not about to give up Gagra, and sensing the futility of negotiations, he used the captured weapons and vehicles to launch an offensive that sent the Georgians reeling back to the Gumista River by the end of 1992. In effect, the rebels were poised to begin the assault on Sukhumi, an operation that just a few months before had seemed to be a fantasy. Moscow was so eager to end the war that it reversed its previous position and accepted the presence of foreign troops in a peacekeeping force. The gesture proved meaningless, because the West still did not want to participate in any peacekeeping operation.²⁸

In March 1993 Ardzinba launched attacks on Sukhumi, incessant combat raged over the capital, and the Abkhazian leader sensed that this was the year to decide the

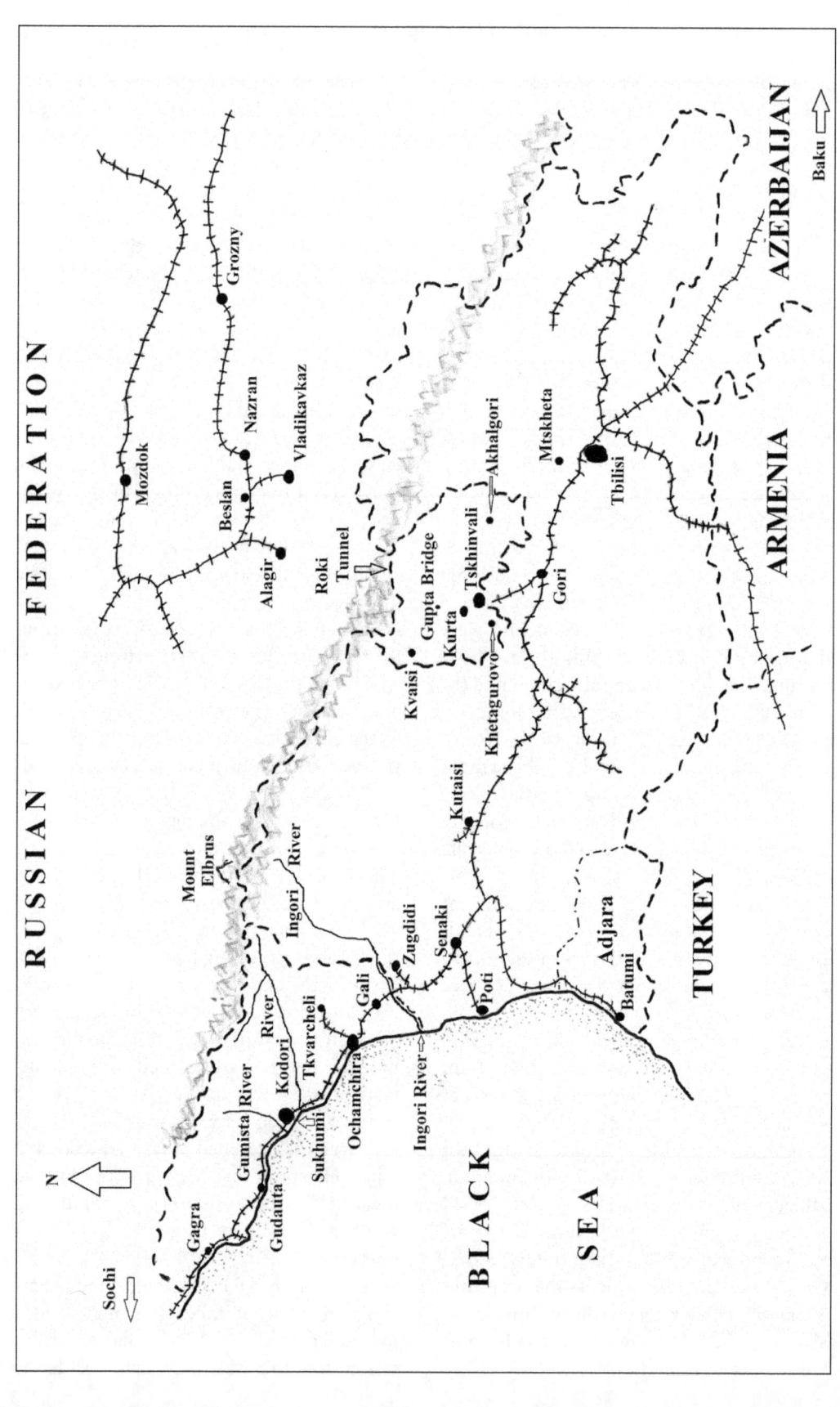

fate of the region.²⁹ He went to great lengths to court Russians. Even Americans admitted that he was an "articulate, well-informed, and an impressive spokesman for his cause."³⁰ And in contrast to Shevardnadze who in his Moscow visits was passive, Ardzinba "had been visiting everyone in Russia."³¹

With Abkhazian forces pressing hard on Sukhumi in August 1993, Georgia joined Russia in requesting U.N. peacekeepers. However, the U.S. and Western powers, still stuck in the Yugoslavian mess, were reluctant to make this commitment. All sides felt the need to have better information, and as first step, the U.S. joined the other members of the Security Council in August to create the United Nations Observer Mission in Georgia (UNOMIG) composed of about 150 observers. The duration of UNOMIG was for two years, after which the Security Council had to renew its term.³² Russia pointed out the inadequacy of UNOMIG because "the mission had been very badly conducted and had spent more time sitting and eating (like time-serving bureaucrats) than on making initiatives to settle the conflict."³³

To rally the defenders of Sukhumi, Shevardnadze went in person to the besieged capital, but to no avail. He was fortunate in being able to escape alive when on 27 September 1993 the Abkhazians liberated their devastated capital. No Georgian forces remained to block the rebels, who three days later reached the Ingori River, the traditional southern boundary. Bent on revenge, the Abkhazians expelled Georgians from the city, and once again countless refugees left either aboard Russian warships or fled to the border. The expulsion of Georgians had already begun upon the recapture of Gagra on 8 October 1992. Almost 200,000 Georgians fled, and this mass departure meant that the Abkhazians were no longer a minority in their own country but at last became the majority.³⁴

The final campaign came only in April 1994 when the Abkazians occupied the entire Kodori River valley. Russia was pressuring Ardzinba to halt the offensive, but the U.S. wanted Russia to do nothing less than to force him to abandon all the territorial gains and to convert Abkhazia into an obedient region subject to Tbilisi. At this time both the U.S. and Russia opposed the independence of Abkhazia, but Moscow wanted much more autonomy for the region than the U.S. was willing to consider.³⁵ And if Ardzinba would somehow renounce independence, "his own people would cut off his head and throw his body into the sea. And they would replace him with someone who would adhere more closely to their wishes. The Abkhazi were a stubborn people, and proud of it."³⁶

Nothing Russia said could persuade the U.S. to drop its opposition to an U.N. peacekeeping force in Georgia. Later in 2008 the U.S. came to regret this stubbornness. Russia, deprived of any other alternative, negotiated a ceasefire agreement on its own on 14 May 1994. Under its provisions, Russia deployed about 2,000 peacekeepers in the border, repeating the formula it had used in South Ossetia to defuse the crisis.³⁷

Failure in diplomacy did not deter Georgia from infiltrating small armed teams into southern Abkhazia in early May 1998. After the first clashes, Abkhazia expelled most of the ethnic Georgians still residing in the Gali region. The expulsion of an additional 30,000 Georgians (who had been spared in 1994) deprived the guerrillas of a base of support, and once again Georgia suffered another military defeat.³⁸

The Caucasus: Armenia and Azerbaijan

The Soviet Union

The outbreak of combat in South Ossetia in early 1991 surprised most observers who until then had expected armed

clashes to occur in Armenia. On 20 February 1988 Nagorno-Karabakh issued a public declaration demanding its transfer to Soviet Armenia; up to that time the region, with its capital of Stepanakert, had been administered from the Azerbaijan capital of Baku. For the first time in recent Soviet history, the public heard about a topic the ruling Communist Party had kept secret. Armenians held massive rallies, and workers showed their support by going on strike in local factories; the resulting shortages of key parts caused bottlenecks in numerous plants across the Soviet Union.[39]

Just eight days after the Nagorno-Karabakh region had asked for the transfer, a bloody massacre occurred in Sumgait, a town not far from Baku. On 28 February 1988 Azerbaijanis burned and looted the apartments and other properties of Armenians. The angry mobs also beat, raped, and murdered many Armenian civilians. It took the authorities a day to restore control over a devastated Sumgait.[40]

Such violent outbreaks had been very infrequent in post–Stalin Soviet Union and had always been brutally suppressed. But the Politburo took no measures other than to reject the request of Nagorno-Karabakh for transfer to Soviet Armenia.[41] For the first time in two centuries, the Armenians, who had always looked to Russia as their defender, experienced "the deep feeling of betrayal" and felt abandoned.[42]

After the 20 February 1988 declaration in Stepanakert, Azerbaijanis began to flee from southern Armenia, while after the Sumgait massacre Armenians likewise left Azerbaijan. In a curious action, Armenians and Azerbaijanis quite often agreed to exchange the ownership of apartments in their respective regions. But these exchanges were the final expression of the cooperation fostered between the two peoples under Soviet rule, and by 1992 both sides reverted to savage ethnic cleansing.[43]

The Sumgait massacre, reinforced by later attacks, created a feeling of national crisis among the entire Armenian population. The citizens were still traumatized by the memory of the Armenian genocide during World War I, and they believed that the Azerbaijanis were intent on completing the extermination of the Armenian nationality. So in the looming confrontation, while the Azerbaijanis concentrated on the expulsion from their territory of the Armenians, for the latter what was at stake was the very survival of the nationality otherwise facing extinction.[44] Neighboring Georgia declared independence on 9 April 1991 and Azerbaijan on 30 August, but for Armenia any premature declaration of independence raised the additional risk of an invasion from Turkey. Armenia waited until 23 September 1991 to take the momentous decision.[45]

For Armenia the declaration of independence was a bitter recognition that war was inevitable. In an impressive show of national will, the Armenians had been rallying to the defense of their country since the Sumgait massacre. The conviction of dying with arms in their hands rather than suffering another genocide was widespread, and many Armenians rushed to serve in volunteer militia units. The odds were overwhelming: Azerbaijan was bigger, possessed a much larger population, and inherited more weapons from its Soviet arsenals. Azerbaijan had twice the artillery, four times the armor, and ten times the amount of ammunition.[46]

Facing such dire threats, the country needed decisive leadership. In 1990 the historian Levon Ter-Petrosyan became the country's first non–Communist ruler and he was elected the first president on 16 October 1991. It was quite revealing that in both Abkhazia and Armenia at the moment of their greatest peril the two countries sought leadership from distinguished scholars who studied the past.[47] During the last agonizing months of the Soviet Union Boris Yeltsin tried to broker a peace. But the mediation efforts came to a fiery end on 20 November 1991 when Armenians forces, by accident, shot down a helicopter carrying negotiators.[48]

War in Nagorno-Karabakh

November 1991 was also significant because that month marked the start of the withdrawal of the 11,000 Soviet soldiers who until then had formed a buffer between the Armenians and the Azerbaijanis in Nagorno-Karabakh. By March 1992 the last of the troops had departed, but they left behind almost all their equipment and weapons. The Azerbaijanis decided to squeeze Nagorno-Karabakh into submission, and they seized Khojali, with its landing field near Stepanakert. But fierce Armenian resistance foiled the attempts to capture Stepanakert, even after the Azerbaijanis began to use in February 1992 "Grad" multiple rocket launchers against the civilians.[49]

The turning point came on 26 February 1992, when on the anniversary of the Sumgait massacre, Armenian militias overwhelmed the defenders of Khojali and by the next day controlled not just the town but the vital air field. By a coincidence Armenia possessed twice as many helicopters as Azerbaijan, and over the coming months brave crews dared fierce anti-aircraft fire to bring much needed supplies to Stepanakert. The Armenian forces extended their control around Khojali until by April it was safe for cargo planes to land at the air field. By May 1992 the Armenians also had broken the blockade on Stepanakert and gained control of the dirt path to Armenia. Contributions from the Armenian diaspora made possible building the new Lachin road linking the homeland with Nagorno-Karabakh. And to make the victory complete, the defeated Azerbaijani troops fled in disorder and abandoned many weapons, which proved very useful to outfit poorly armed Armenian units.[50]

The West and Russia had been trying

to stop the fighting and chose CSCE (Conference for Security and Cooperation in Europe) in February 1992 as their preferred instrument. CSCE on 24 March 1992 convened the warring parties to a conference in Minsk to settle the dispute, but both sides ignored this appeal and insisted on seeking final victory on the battlefield. This ill-fated conference has still not convened.[51]

The frontline stabilized in mid–1992, and president Ter-Petrosyan was using up his political capital in a strenuous effort to persuade the country to accept the CSCE peace process. But the prospects for an acceptable peace agreement collapsed when new rulers who were determined to resume hostilities came to power in Baku. A new Azerbaijani offensive regained some towns during the second half of 1992, but the military effort lost momentum by the start of 1993, and the front line settled into sporadic skirmishing. The Armenian worry that Turkey might intervene on the side of Azerbaijan vanished when during 1993, the Kremlin made known its opposition to any Turkish involvement.[52]

Intense internal divisions plagued the Azerbaijani military, unlike the Armenian side which by 1992 had finished converting the militia units of 1990 into a formal hierarchal command structure. Many times the Azerbaijani abandoned well-defended positions, and the war was never very popular. The average Azerbaijani citizen wanted to drive out Armenians from his neighborhood but was not eager to fight in the distant region of Nagorno-Karabakh. Desertions were frequent, and units sometimes refused to fire on Armenians. It was not uncommon for Azerbaijani units even to fight against each other in the struggle of rival factions for power. And in another contrast with Armenia, Azerbaijan lacked a core of competent officers. Armenia had been among the few non–Slavic republics to be well represented in the Soviet officer corps, while Azerbaijani conscripts usually ended up in the Soviet construction battalions and possessed few if any combat skills.[53]

To provide basic training for its officers, Azerbaijan brought in former American and European servicemen. The government bought new equipment and also reestablished the Soviet system of conscription to replenish the depleted ranks of defeated units. The new president Heidar Aliyev launched the second big offensive of the war on 17 December 1993.[54]

Once again the Azerbaijani offensive began well but then turned into a rout when Armenian forces blocked most of the supply routes of the attackers. The demoralized Azerbaijani forces could not stop the counterattack in the spring of 1994, and soon Armenia gained control of the remaining towns in Nagorno-Karabakh. Even before the Armenians reached a town, rumors of their imminent arrival set in motion the second biggest wave of migration of the war, and at least half a million Azerbaijanis left both Armenia and Nagorno-Karabakh. The largest population transfer in the Caucasus had occurred, with at least a million persons in total (counting the Armenians who had escaped in previous years) having to abandon their homes.[55]

Azerbaijan threw raw battalions of green troops in a desperate attempt to stem the tide. But each new Azerbaijani attack racked up huge casualties and facilitated additional Armenian advances. The proverbial David had defeated Goliath, and Baku had to abandon the demand for a return to the *status quo ante bellum*. Azerbaijan looked to Western diplomats for a solution, but they too lacked any leverage to compel Armenia to retreat.

At this moment Russian diplomat Vladimir Kazimirov conveyed to the Azerbaijanis the message from President Yeltsin that they had to accept the front line (or "line of contact"). Afterwards both sides could discuss the status of Nagorno-Karabakh as part of a broader settlement in the conference CSCE had two years earlier tried to convene at Minsk. Azerbaijan accepted the ceasefire agreement and the war ended on 12 May 1994. But when it came time to approve a second agreement on having Russian troops as peacekeepers, Azerbaijan delayed. How could this reversal have occurred? The reason was simple: the U.S. did not want Russia to increase its presence in the Caucasus. The American support was all that Azerbaijan needed to evade the second agreement. President Yeltsin, basking in the glow of having ended a war and sensing opposition from the West, unwisely let the matter drop.[56]

The Search for Peace

Armenia had won the war but at a staggering cost. Intense winters and shortage of electricity brought tremendous suffering to a country whose borders with Turkey and Azerbaijan remained closed. The only link with the outside world was the dilapidated railway running through Georgia. Citizens lined up for long lines lasting 24 hours to purchase bread, and the establishment of ration coupons in March 1992 somewhat ameliorated the food shortages. In a major reprisal, Azerbaijan made the pipeline carrying the oil for export bypass Armenia to deprive that country of any transit royalties.[57]

In late 1997 President Ter-Petrosyan attempted to remedy the desperate economic situation of Armenia by negotiating a partial withdrawal from Nagorno-Karabakh in exchange for the lifting of the economic blockade. Just like in 1992, he wanted the Organization for Security and Cooperation in Europe (the new name of CSCE), to facilitate an agreement between the two countries. He realized that the Armenian victory had been almost a miracle. Once Azerbaijan rebuilt its military, tiny Armenia could not hope to prevail against its richer and larger neighbor. But when in a long newspaper article of November 1997 he expounded his views, the proposal stunned the Armenian people. They had fought and sacrificed for so long and were not about to exchange for a bowl of food what they had bought with their blood. Here was a clear case of a ruler going against Jean Jacques Rousseau's "General Will." Almost every family in the country had lost a loved one in the war, and nobody could accept the prophetic view of Ter-Petrosyan that Armenia could not defend Nagorno-Karabakh. The people, the political parties, and the military united to topple Ter-Petrosyan on 3 February 1998, and the next day Robert Kocharian became the provisional president and later in March won a new election.[58]

The population was determined to suffer any economic hardship to save Nagorno-Karabakh. After 1996 renewed Russian investment in Armenia restored prosperity to the country, and the years of hardship in the 1990s became only a distant memory. And for Armenians the Russian takeover of the economy was a small price to pay to preserve their nationality against the threats from Azerbaijan and Turkey.[59]

Yerevan became perhaps the closest ally of the Kremlin. Armenia was among the first to join the Collective Security Treaty Organization in May 1992 even when Russia stressed that the agreement applied only to the boundaries of Soviet Armenia and not to the disputed territories. Armenia fell into a false sense of security and even went so far in August 1994 as to hand control over the routes from Iran and Turkey to the Russian border guards of the Federal Security Service.[60]

3

The West and the First Chechnya War

Everyone can begin a war at his will but not finish it.—Niccolò Machiavelli[1]

After the end of the Soviet Union on 25 December 1991, the new Russian Federation faced many challenges abroad. At home the economic problems were massive, but they did not seem to pose a threat to Moscow's authority. The absence of open warfare reinforced the impression that Chechnya was just another Byzantine political dispute. Not until the start of hostilities in December 1994 did Western powers realize that Chechnya was the first real revolt against Russian rule.

The Road to Independence

After the war began in Chechnya, scholars and journalists strove to reconstruct the origins of that crisis, but until that moment, Western media and even diplomats had provided little coverage of what was happening in a tiny corner of the immense Russian Federation. Just as with many of the problems facing the Russian Federation, Mikhail Gorbachev created the crisis in Chechnya. In the Caucasus the *nomenklatura* or Communist party ruling class was weakest in Chechnya. The ethnic Russian members depended on Moscow's support to rule the region. When in September 1991 Gorbachev abandoned the Chechen *nomenklatura*, he left an opening for a former Soviet air force general, Dzhokhar Dudayev, to come to power.[2]

Dudayev, a native of Chechnya, was elected to be its first president, and in one of his first actions, he proclaimed the independence of Chechnya on 1 November 1991. Thus Chechnya joined the "parade of sovereignties" of the fifteen Soviet republics proclaiming their independence, but its constitutional situation was different. Chechnya had always formed a part of the Russian Socialist Republic and had never gained the status of a Soviet republic.

Should other regions inside the Russian Socialist Republic decide to seek independence, another "parade of sovereignties" could well ensue and lead to the disintegration of the country. Sensing this danger, Boris Yeltsin, the president of the Russian Socialist Republic, ordered the national police to restore control over Chechnya. The units were landing in Grozny airport on 9 November when Gorbachev countermanded the order and aborted the operation.[3]

Twice Gorbachev had taken actions indispensable to make possible the revolt in Chechnya. But what worried most Yeltsin about this second action was the power play by Gorbachev. After meetings with leaders of many Soviet republics, Yeltsin agreed to abolish the Soviet Union on 25 December. The task of subduing rebel Chechnya became the responsibility of the new Russian Federation.

Yeltsin suffered from an inability to stay focused on one issue for a long time.

3. The West and the First Chechnya War

The Russian president, dazzled by the attention foreign leaders bestowed on him after 25 December, ignored the simmering issue. Dudayev, when he was most vulnerable to being overthrown, benefited from another stroke of good luck. The former Soviet general knew that he was so weak because he lacked an armed force. He could count on many volunteers in that region with a long history of violence but possessed only small arms for the police.

To secure weapons for his supporters, he first stopped attempts to remove the Soviet-era arsenals from Chechnya. Then he took advantage of the collapsing discipline in the former Soviet bases to acquire not just armored vehicles and artillery but also aircraft. The disintegration of Soviet forces also hastened the departure of former Soviet troops. Dudayev had been demanding their removal, and his armed followers surrounded Russian bases. Desertions and corruption plagued most units, and a reluctant Defense Ministry ordered the withdrawal.[4]

The departure on 8 June 1992 of the last Russian troops made Dudayev the ruler of a region enjoying *de facto* independence. His three main tasks were to establish a responsible structure of government, to bring a minimal level of prosperity, and to obtain international recognition for his regime.

His rule soon revealed two somewhat contradictory characteristics. He was very authoritarian and eliminated other political groups by turning into a dictator. Paradoxically, he was also a weak ruler, and most of the region slipped out of his control and into the hands of war lords. He had been too slow to take possession of all the Soviet arsenals, and war lords took control of many weapons. By 1994 his rule did not extend far beyond the capital, and most of Chechnya drifted into lawlessness in a glaring example of a "failed state."[5]

Chechnya became a haven for illegal activities, and corruption was rampant. The country became famous for fraudulent oil deals. Many of the petroleum deals had an international dimension, and they further discredited the image of Chechnya abroad. Because corruption, lawlessness, and poverty were also rampant across the Russian Federation, for Western observers Chechnya was indistinguishable from the prevailing pattern of malaise.

Dudayev attempted to carry out an independent foreign policy, but his actions backfired. He antagonized the U.S. and Western countries by proclaiming support for Saddam Hussein of Iraq. Chechnya had an international boundary with Georgia to the south, but Dudayev angered its government by giving refuge to deposed Georgian ruler Zviad Gamsakhurdia. Dudayev had neither gained any international support for the independence of Chechnya nor consolidated a strong and prosperous state.[6]

The West and the Russian Military Campaign

The failings of the Dzhokhar Dudayev regime offered the Kremlin an opportunity to restore its authority over the breakaway region. By early 1994 the worst of the fallout from the collapse of the Soviet Union seemed to be over, and the Yeltsin administration felt capable of assuming new burdens. Chechnya had been under economic blockade since 1992, but the restrictions had failed to remove Dudayev from power. The rampant corruption then existing on the Russian side made the economic blockade ineffective. The Russian government was unpopular, and a quick victory in Chechnya seemed an easy way to improve the chances of Yeltsin in the presidential elections of 1996.[7]

By early 1994 the Kremlin decided to intervene in Chechnya but not with military force. In a first attempt, opposition groups tried to overthrow Dudayev. Russia distributed weapons and money to war lords, but the fragmented Chechen opposition could not mount a real challenge. In a second effort in November 1994, Russian mercenaries came to reinforce the opposition forces. The operation ended in complete failure on 26 November 1994, and irrefutable evidence—including captured Russian citizens—confirmed that Moscow had staged the operation. The disclosure of the Russian involvement panicked Moscow into an emotional reaction, and already on 28 November Russian planes were bombing Grozny and other points in Chechnya.[8]

One of the proponents of the invasion was Defense Minister Pavel Grachev who made the infamous statement that two airborne divisions could win victory in two hours. With considerable difficulty the first units crossed the border into Chechnya on 11 December 1994, and the march toward the capital took longer than expected.[9] The slow advance coincided with the previously scheduled visit of Vice President Al Gore, who had come to Moscow on 14–16 December to reassure the Russians about the expansion of NATO. When asked about the ongoing operation, both in private and in public the Vice President "stated that the U.S. hoped the matter of Chechnya would be ended with minimal bloodshed and through negotiations [...] and emphasized this was an internal Russia matter."[10]

U.S. officials realized that they had blundered in letting Gore make this statement. Here Russia was providing the opportunity to apply pressure, yet the U.S. government threw away the leverage. In classical diplomacy nothing is free, everything is about *quid pro quo*. The U.S. did not have to worry for long over its mistake, because of the Russian debacle in Grozny on New Year's Eve. In the worst battlefield disaster since World War II, three Russian columns attempted to storm the Chechen capital and suffered horrendous and humiliating losses. Gruesome street combat lasted for weeks, and relentless aerial bombarding and artillery shelling reduced large sections of Grozny to rubble.[11]

Even before Russian troops gained control over most of Grozny by late January 1995, the U.S. government sought to extract the maximum benefit from the Russian predicament. President Bill Clinton in a letter to Yeltsin urged Russia to seek a solution through negotiations. Instead the military solution that Russia adopted made the U.S. "deeply distressed over the growing cost in human life, including among civilians."[12]

The concern for lives might seem touching, but the real reason was more practical. The Yeltsin administration was starting to realize that it had been bamboozled over NATO expansion, and that despite earlier assurances, the U.S. was determined to have the military alliance extend all the way to the borders of the Russian Federation. And the Chechnya crisis gave the U.S. a pressure point to keep Russia on the defensive while more countries of the former Soviet bloc entered NATO.[13]

However, U.S. officials realized that they could not press too hard on the Chechnya button, because also at stake was the pro–Western government in Russia. Right on the firing line was Foreign Minister Andrei Kozyrev, who was already under tremendous criticism for being such a pliant tool of the West. Foreign diplomats followed the rule of talking with Kozyrev only in a very small groups to extract the maximum concessions from him.[14]

In reality the U.S. did not have to press Kozyrev or Yeltsin very hard on Chechnya. Yeltsin was an extreme example of the craving many Russians felt to gain Western acceptance, and he was desperate to have foreign leaders attend the Victory in Europe annual parade in Moscow on 9 May 1995 to celebrate the 50th anniversary of the defeat of Nazi Germany. The incongruity of having a victory parade while the Russian army was bogged down in combat did not bother Yeltsin, who should have cancelled the event and concentrated on winning the war.[15]

Several Western leaders threatened not to attend the V-E parade if Russia did not end the bloody military campaign, and Clinton himself remained ambivalent until the end about confirming his attendance. In the end, Yeltsin capitulated to their demands in order to have their presence for the show he dreamed about. Clinton in his letter of 6 January 1995 wanted a role for the Organization of Security and Cooperation (OSCE), and Russia accepted on 11 April the creation of an "OSCE Assistance Group in Chechnya." By accepting the OSCE presence, Russia converted the Chechnya War from an internal to an international issue.[16]

The entry of OSCE into the conflict still did not satisfy the European leaders threatening to boycott the V-E parade if the war was still raging, so in another capitulation, Russia declared a ceasefire on 21 April 1995. Although several war lords signed the ceasefire, the majority of officials of the Dudayev regime refused to participate.[17]

The Russian military was close to defeating the rebels in early April. Had not the obsession to please Western leaders forced an abandonment of the last stages of the offensive, Russia was poised to win a complete military victory by the summer of 1995. Dudayev and his remaining officials were on the run, the rebels were short of ammunition, and defections were widespread. The Russian army was tracking down the last of the rebel leaders in the southern mountains of Chechnya when news of ceasefire on 21 April shattered the troops' will to fight. Both the soldiers and the officers felt they were little more than cannon fodder in some sick game Moscow officials were playing. The personnel sank into indifference, corruption, and in extreme cases even reached arrangements with the rebels to reduce casualties.[18]

The ceasefire was scheduled to end on 12 May, but already on 30 April Dudayev rejected its terms, even before the V-E parade celebration. Combat had never stopped, and the expiration on 12 May was a mere formality. The arrival of the OSCE mission led to the signing of a new ceasefire on 31 July, but compliance was no better than for the original one of 21 April, and by early October combat was widespread.[19]

The Last Stage of the War

Guerrilla operations became the norm during the rest of 1995. Because the April–May ceasefire had given the rebels a breathing space to recover their forces and to resupply, the war was certain to last for years. The Chechens, who remembered the Soviet failure in Afghanistan, were sure that Moscow would soon tire of the war and depart. The relentless media coverage of the savage war also exerted enormous pressure on the Kremlin to accept the independence of Chechnya as the only possible solution.[20]

Political and international restrictions deprived Russia of the opportunity to impose a military solution on Chechnya. The most important political constraint came in 1996, when Yeltsin faced the major hurdle of his reelection. After another attempt at a military solution in early 1996 failed because of the rebel revival, the Yeltsin administration decided to sacrifice Chechnya for the sake of electoral victory. A major obstacle disappeared when in a rare success, a missile strike killed Dudayev on 21 April. Yeltsin held deep grudges against the rebel ruler, instead the Russian president was more than willing to negotiate with other Chechen leaders.[21]

The fear that the candidate of the Communist Party might win the presidential election of 16 June 1996 persuaded the West to support Yeltsin. Foreign governments stopped pressuring Yeltsin over Chechnya, and the media reduced its negative coverage of Chechnya. The Western strategy was successful, and although Yeltsin did not win the 16 June election by the required 50 percent margin, he easily won the run off on 3 July.[22]

Yeltsin understood that the Western tolerance about Chechnya was temporary, and after his reelection he wanted to bury this crisis. His appointment of General Alexander Lebed to be in charge of Chechnya policy was decisive, and the general was able to bring momentum to the negotiations OSCE intermediaries had been conducting since January 1996.[23]

The large rebel attack on Grozny in early August finished convincing Yeltsin on the need to negotiate a withdrawal from Chechnya. Although Russian troops remained in control of part of the capital and were confident of recapturing the rest, the Russian president had long since lost the taste for this war and was psychologically defeated. The stumbling block in the negotiations was the juridical status of Chechnya. The rebels demanded *de jure* independence, while Russia insisted on *de facto*. Squaring this circle seemed impossible until OSCE negotiators remembered the formula used in New Caledonia of deferring to a later date the final solution. For New Caledonia a referendum in 20 years would decide the fate of that territory, for Chechnya the referendum would be in five years, after Yeltsin's second term expired.[24]

Both sides signed the Khasavyurt Agreement on 31 August 1996 ending the war. Russian forces began a slow withdrawal from Chechnya, and the last units departed on 5 January 1997. The pending business was the requirement to hold the referendum on the political fate of Chechnya no later than 31 December 2001.[25] Implementing this mandate was political suicide for whoever was Yeltsin's successor, while any attempt to repeal the Khasavyurt Agreement meant strong opposition from the West.

4

The New Architecture for Relations with the West

When the Cold War ended, international relations lost the tools that superpower rivalry had provided for conflict management. Yet new mechanisms for ensuring stability in a situation that had changed radically were not created in their place.—Russian Foreign Minister Igor S. Ivanov[1]

You will see, when I am gone, the imperialist powers will wring your necks like chickens.—Joseph Stalin[2]

The need to modify Cold War institutions to serve the post–Soviet world was not obvious to the West. The U.S., savoring its supposed "triumph" in the Cold War and "the end of history," believed that few if any changes were needed. In contrast, Russia advocated for expanding existing channels and for creating structures to guarantee peace and stability. Russian officials were excited about the illusion of creating a new world order.

The European Bank for Reconstruction and Development

The realization started to dawn that it was going to take the combined efforts of all existing international financial institutions just to stabilize the economic situation in the former Communist countries. In this critical juncture, the creation of a new institution focused on developing the private sector in the former Communist countries appeared to be a reasonable proposal. On 29 May 1990 in London the founding states signed the agreement creating the EBRD, "the first self-consciously political and European international institution of the post–Cold War world."[3]

The legislatures of the member states appropriated the funds for EBRD. Delegations of legislators also doubled up as representatives of their countries to the Parliamentary Assembly of the Council of Europe. To assure easy communication, the EBRD signed a cooperation arrangement in September 1992 with the Parliamentary Assembly of the Council of Europe, the oldest European integration institution. The match offered a public forum for the bank to publicize its activities among European legislators. The resolutions of the Parliamentary Assembly also provided political guidance for the bank's lending and investment activities.[4]

The Soviet Union, although a founding member of EBRD, had lacked any voice in the deliberations leading up to the creation of the bank. This was one of the most important legacies of the process: the role of the Soviet Union was to obey the decisions the West made about the charter and other aspects of the bank.⁵ In effect, the Soviet Union entered EBRD "in an apprentice capacity"⁶ because the country was so far behind the rest of the world. The rampant Eurocentrism bordered on arrogance.

The disappearance of the Soviet Union in December 1991 did not mean that the U.S. was ready to support the new Russian Federation. At the EBRD's first annual meeting in April 1992, the U.S. once again refused to authorize extending loans out of other member's contributions. The Russian Federation could only borrow to the limit of its contribution to the bank. In effect, the restrictions placed on loans meant that EBRD could do little to accomplish its principal goals of promoting the private sector and supporting an open political system in Russia. Advice, training, and guidance were the main activities in Russia of EBRD during its early years, while major loans went to the small countries of Eastern Europe.⁷

When the Russian economy went into a freefall, even the U.S. at last admitted that to avoid disaster EBRD needed to help other international financial institutions. In 1993 the U.S. agreed to contribute to the creation of the Russia Small Business Fund within EBRD. Another major donor was Switzerland, and with this solid financial backing the Russia Small Business Fund began operations in 1994 and became one of the most successful programs of the bank.⁸

By the end of the 1990s one-third of EBRD lending had gone to Russia, and its operations there were the largest for the bank. In accordance with its ideological mandate, 85 percent of the funds went to the private sector, and the rest went to infrastructure projects having the state as the only possible partner. The Russia Small Business Fund provided 800,000 loans, including those to create private banks whose task was to disburse loans to other small businesses.⁹ EBRD was having considerable impact in spreading Western practices and ideas across small and medium businesses. But to make Russia resemble Europe was a daunting task requiring the help of additional institutions.

The European Union

The experience with the establishment of the European Bank for Reconstruction and Development anticipated the policy of the European Union toward Russia. In a nutshell, Western powers discussed and defined the needs of Russia, provided the bulk of the funds, and imposed the policies. The coincidence that the Russian Federation came into existence on 25 December 1991 just a few months before Western European countries signed the Treaty of European Union on 7 February 1992 created the impression that for the first time in history, almost the entire European space was available for reshaping. The prospects of a new world order filled many in Europe with tremendous enthusiasm and fueled illusions inside Russia.

The entry into force of the Treaty of European Union on 1 November 1993 made possible membership for the Central and Eastern European countries, but from the start Russia posed a problem of a different magnitude. The country was a natural market for many EU products, and the prosperity of Europe required ready access to the energy sources and raw materials of Russia. Despite these compelling reasons, EU dragged its feet during 1992, and not even frequent entreaties from Moscow could budge the Western European countries to come to a decision about relations with Russia.¹⁰

The U.S. had the preponderant voice in all the agreements discussed in this chapter, and the same was true for the EU even though the U.S. was not a member. The failure of EU to reach a consensus about Russia opened the door for U.S. involvement. Washington's earlier goal of dismembering Russia gave way to fears of the country collapsing into chaos and having its nuclear warheads fall into the wrong hands. The economy of Russia had to be stabilized at all costs. After Foreign Minister Andrei Kozyrev asked the U.S. on 25 February 1993 to encourage EU members to prepare a trade agreement, U.S. pressure persuaded the EU to take action.[11]

The Western European countries revealed their approach with the "Joint Political Declaration on Partnership and Cooperation between the Russian Federation and the European Union" of 9 December 1993. In this declaration, the EU invited Russia to join the family of European nations and promised to help transform and modernize the country. The EU asked Russia to adopt European political and economic principles in exchange for material rewards. Both sides wanted "the creation of a favorable climate for domestic and foreign private investment." In appreciation of Russian measures, the EU already had taken steps to allow the entry of many Russian goods into member countries duty free. The greatest reward for good behavior was yet to come when the EU promised to establish a free trade area with Russia.[12]

The Joint Declaration was full of references to mutual cooperation through "a deeper understanding between their peoples" and painted an idyllic picture of harmonic relations. President Boris Yeltsin and his Foreign Minister Andrei Kozyrev believed this rhetoric and supported the idealistic enthusiasm of this Declaration. The flowery language on the sharing of mutual principles concealed the absence of the voice of Russia and confirmed the Europeans' attitude of superiority evident during the creation of the EBRD.[13]

Negotiations led to the "Agreement on Partnership and Cooperation" signed on 24 June 1994. This second text was harsher than the Joint Declaration because in the intervening period the bad economic situation of Russia had turned for the worse in 1994. If in 1991 Russia welcomed the fait accompli of the EBRD as necessary to obtain development aid, in 1994 a suffering and sometimes starving Russia had no choice but to accept the conditions of the EU.[14]

The assumption that Russia was so backwards meant that only the strictest adherence to the guidance of the EU offered the country any chance to escape from its dismal situation. The EU held the commanding position, and a weak Russia could only obey Brussels. The long text did establish the regulations for economic integration between the two sides in a wide variety of commercial activities. Buried in other clauses was the real Russian desire to establish a free trade area, a possibility the EU postponed into the future.[15]

To provide instructions to Russia, the agreement created a council (renamed the Permanent Partnership Council in 2003). But before any of its clauses could enter into force, the start of the First Chechnya War in December 1994 halted the process of ratification. Principles could not stand in the way of profits, and in the interim agreement of 17 July 1995, the EU authorized the immediate implementation of all clauses pertaining to trade, customs, and property. After the end of the First Chechnya War in August 1997 the member states completed the ratification, and the Agreement on Partnership and Cooperation entered into force on 1 December 1997. It was valid for ten years, and after 2007 the agreement has renewed on an annual basis.[16]

The Council of Europe

Founded in 1949, the Council of Europe, the oldest of the European integration institutions, had the task of providing the ideology for the entire continent. A Committee of Ministers was the governing body of the new Council, which was advised by a Parliamentary Assembly

(PACE) consisting of deputies from the legislative bodies of each of the member states. The most notable innovation came with the establishment of a European Court of Human Rights in 1952. At the beginning the activities of the Court focused on inter-state disputes rather than appeals from ordinary citizens, as became the norm starting in the 1990s. The Council of Europe, located in Strasbourg, enjoyed great prestige even before the collapse of the Soviet Bloc, and the former Communist countries sought membership in this by then respectable institution.[17]

Among the first acts of the new Russian Federation was to send observers to the Council of Europe in January 1992, and the Parliamentary Assembly granted them "special guest" status the next month. On 7 May 1992 Moscow filed the application for admission into the Council of Europe. Russia expected great benefits from the Council, and these hopes became more urgent when the Kremlin failed to transform the Conference on Security and Cooperation in Europe (CSCE) into a new trans-Atlantic security structure.[18]

The illusions of the Russian elites did not find echo inside the Council of Europe. The countries of Eastern Europe and those of the near abroad became member states, but the Kremlin saw with dismay the Russian application suffer a humiliating delay of over two years. The country underwent an excruciating ordeal in the admissions process. The real reason for the delay was that over a third of the officials in the Secretariat of the Council of Europe signed a petition demanding that under no circumstances should Russia ever become a member.[19]

The insolent bureaucrats refused to consider Russia to be a part of Europe. The officials in the Council of Europe revealed a streak of arrogance when they assumed the authority to determine who qualified to be considered European. When the Russian invasion of Chechnya in December 1994 marked the start of a long war, the horrific images of combat provided a great excuse to suspend the admission process on 2 February 1995.[20]

For over a year an intense debate raged in the institution about whether Russia should be admitted at all. The progress the country had made in democratic practices and the rule of law was immense compared to the Soviet period but inferior to the level already existing in most Western European states. The Kremlin wanted guidance to advance along this path and its pleas finally wore down the opposition of the skeptical member states. So even though the Chechen War was still raging, the Council of Europe moved toward welcoming Russia into the organization. A final consideration in favor of admission came with the realization that if Boris Yeltsin lost the presidential elections, the Communists would return to power and reverse all the progress achieved so far in Russia. The country became a member state on 28 February 1996, but by that date the Council of Europe was in no condition to satisfy many of the original expectations of the Kremlin.[21]

Since the 1980s a three-fold division of labor emerged among European integration institutions. National security matters were the primary responsibility of NATO, while economic issues remained the prerogative of the European Union; everything else fell under the jurisdiction of the Council of Europe. And in the few instances when NATO could not fulfill security functions, such as in peacekeeping and military observer missions, it was a rival organization, the CSCE that provided the services rather than the Council of Europe. On economic issues the EU expanded its field of action and squeezed out the Council of Europe; only in the European Bank for Reconstruction and Development has the Parliamentary Assembly of the Council of Europe remained an influential voice. Otherwise, the EU became the principal if not sole authority on economic and financial matters. And in a direct challenge "the EU has invaded the Council of Europe's holy of holies—the sphere of protection of Human Rights and national minorities."[22]

Russia soon realized that the Council of Europe was losing its importance. But the accession process had been so bruising, and the other member states were so keen on scrutinizing the new member to detect any signs of inappropriate behavior, that in a major mistake, the Kremlin decided to keep a low profile. Rather than trying to push the organization into new directions, Russia deferred to the preferences of the major European powers. No doubt existed that membership in the Council of Europe had been a hollow and expensive victory for Russia, because the country ended up paying a disproportionate share of the organization's dues.[23] Membership in the Council of Europe turned out to have little more than symbolic value.

START I and START II Nuclear Disarmament Treaties

When building a relationship with the European Union and the Council of Europe, at first glance Russia did not have to deal with the United States. However, even though the U.S. was not a member state of those two organizations, it still exerted enormous pressure. Whether through proxies such as Britain or a shifting cast of client states, the U.S. exercised so much influence that at times the Europeans could resemble puppets of Washington.

No matter how much Russia caved in to requests from Washington, nothing could ever satisfy a U.S. Congress unable to let go of the Cold War hostility. Since the fall of the Soviet Union the recurrent pattern has been of the U.S. Congress passing or threatening to pass legislation hostile to Russia should any presidency consider adopting a more moderate policy. Bashing Russia has remained a very effective campaign tactic in U.S. elections.

The START I Treaty was a rare example of sanity prevailing in U.S.-Russian relations. George H.W. Bush and Mikhail Gorbachev signed the START I Treaty on 31 July 1991. The U.S. Congress was in no rush to vote on ratification, but the irrefutable benefits for both sides overcame the latent hostility, and the treaty entered into force on 5 December 1994. In one of the largest arms reductions measures in history, the treaty limited both countries to a maximum of 6000 nuclear warheads and no more than 1600 "delivery vehicles," for the most part intercontinental missiles. Both countries opened their facilities for inspection to assure mutual verification and also destroyed considerable amounts of weapons and nuclear warheads.[24]

The benefits of START I sparked a new round of negotiations culminating in START II. The new proposal set the limit of nuclear warheads of each side at a maximum of 3,500. Bush and Yeltsin signed the new agreement on 3 January 1993, but ratification of START II proved elusive.[25] Nonetheless, the progress on the nuclear disarmament treaties suggested that the opportunity existed to improve the security of Europe.

From CSCE to OSCE

For Russia CSCE (Conference on Security and Cooperation in Europe) offered the best opportunity to replace both the Warsaw Pact and NATO. After the end of the Soviet Union the illusion of creating a new transatlantic alliance became popular in Russia. CSCE was attractive to Moscow because the organization operated on the principle of consensus, so that in effect Russia possessed a veto power resembling that on the Security Council in the United Nations.[26]

The U.S. realized that CSCE needed to

go beyond its traditional function of hosting periodic meetings. The U.S. joined other countries on 21 November 1990 to sign the Paris Charter which gave the Conference the authority to have field offices. In November 1993 Vienna became the headquarters for the organization. But the U.S. had already blocked efforts to transform CSCE into a replacement for NATO, and Washington made it clear that the only game in town for Europe was the military alliance. Dynamic officials at CSCE, unlike the more passive staff of the Council of Europe, continued to press for a more active role.[27]

The outbreak of wars in the Caucasus and in the former Yugoslavia provided the opportunities to expand CSCE. In the Nagorno-Karabakh conflict between Armenia and Azerbaijan, both belligerents wanted observation missions but not from NATO or the UN. A similar situation appeared in the former Yugoslavia. This created a niche for the CSCE to satisfy by providing military observers, and even the U.S. came to recognize the convenience of enlarging the capabilities of CSCE. But Washington continued to prefer NATO and believed that giving new duties to CSCE meant taking them away from the military alliance.[28]

The new observer functions of CSCE did revitalize the institution, and its new headquarters in Vienna became a center for diplomatic activity. The original name no longer expressed the enhanced functions of the institution, and the members adopted the new designation of Organization for Security and Cooperation in Europe (OSCE) on 1 January 1995. But under whatever name, it was clear that Russia had suffered a setback in its attempts to assign a wider role to OSCE in the relations with the West.[29] And over the years whenever Russian delegates tried to raise broader security issues, the European countries rallied behind the U.S. to block any discussion. Ironically, the principle of consensus that had so worried the U.S. about OSCE proved very convenient to stop any Russian efforts to make the institution serve a prominent role in international relations.

The Expansion of NATO

Russia could not afford to ignore NATO, because the West already made the decision not to abolish that military alliance even after the rival Warsaw Pact had ceased to exist on 1 April 1991. In effect, NATO became the first military alliance in history to lack a clear opponent, but that absence did not prevent the U.S. from shaping a new mission for the Cold War organization: "The long-term goal is to establish NATO as a central pillar of a Europe-wide system of cooperative security, continuing to maintain the security of its own members while projecting security and stability eastwards."[30]

The decision to conserve NATO did not require immediate action on accepting new member states. A hasty decision to expand to the east was not in the West's interest, because only on 28 October 1992 did the last Russian troops evacuate Poland, and Russian garrisons were still present in the Baltic Republics.[31] As late as July 1993, the new Bill Clinton administration maintained a moderate position: "at an appropriate time, we may choose to enlarge NATO membership. But that is not now on the agenda."[32]

The West did not want to act on NATO enlargement until Russia made up its mind about joining the military alliance. Any indication of Russia's willingness to enter was sure to trigger a major policy debate. But first the West needed to wait until the Kremlin adopted a firm position. "The popular impression is that Russia is dead set against any expansion of NATO. In fact, Russian views on this question are in flux. Yeltsin is still on the record as favoring Russian membership in a transformed NATO over the long-term."[33]

The waiting period ended when Russia gave an unexpected reply. On 25 August 1993 during an official visit to Poland, Yeltsin startled his hosts by stating that Poland was free to join NATO. It was hard for Western diplomats to believe the statement, but later Yeltsin made the same comment about the Czech Republic. Final confirmation came in a letter from Yeltsin repeating his announcement but with the sole qualification that this was not the ideal solution.[34] It was hard to imagine Russia committing a worse blunder in foreign relations.

U.S. officials and President Clinton interpreted the statements from Yeltsin as the green light for NATO expansion. But before the U.S. could start accepting new members from the former Soviet Bloc countries, an unforeseen internal obstacle almost derailed the process.

To the surprise of many, the Pentagon did not want to bring new members into NATO. Two successive secretaries of defense—Les Aspin and William Perry—likewise opposed expansion, and so did the new Chairman of the Joint Chiefs of Staff John Shalikashvili, himself born in Poland and fluent in several Slavic languages. The American public expected massive cuts in military spending after the Cold War, but this goal was impossible to achieve with NATO expansion. Only at huge expense could the U.S. hope to bring the equipment and training of the former Communist countries up to NATO standards.[35]

Since late 1991 all former Soviet Bloc countries in Europe had been clamoring for NATO membership. The three strongest candidates, Hungary, Poland, and the Czech Republic, presented their applications on 6 May 1992. Once Yeltsin gave his approval on 25 August 1993, these countries lobbied extensively to persuade the Clinton administration. U.S. voters of Eastern European origin were their most effective tool. Prospects for the Democratic Party were not good in the November 1994 congressional elections, and politician Clinton believed that welcoming Eastern European countries into NATO meant gaining popularity among many voters.[36]

The turning point came in January 1994 when Clinton was on a European tour. While in Prague, he announced in front of a gathering of Eastern European leaders "that now the question is no longer whether NATO will take in new members, but when and how."[37] This policy statement went beyond anything under discussion inside the U.S. government and also caught European governments by surprise. Clinton had made the decision almost on the spot in response to the requests of Eastern European countries.

The ostensible purpose of the trip had been to rally support for "Partnership for Peace," a new NATO program U.S. diplomats had crafted to satisfy the main concerns of the Pentagon. Nobody doubted that the armed forces in Eastern Europe were in deplorable condition and in need of a long period of remedial work. The Eastern European countries welcomed the Partnership for Peace but had the major fear that it might trap them in a minor role. To ease that worry, Clinton stated that this program was not "a permanent holding room" and instead was the major step on the way to full membership.

The clarification removed the concern of the Eastern Europeans but opened the question of Russian membership. The U.S. had taken the road of separating the path of the Eastern Europeans from that of Russia, but this two-track approach risked serious Russian opposition. The easiest way to disguise the latent decision to include the Eastern Europeans but to exclude Russia was to persuade Yeltsin to enter the Partnership for Peace program. The reality of NATO expansion was becoming too obvious to hide from the Russian public, and American diplomats struggled in vain throughout 1994 to gain Russian acceptance for this fig leaf.

The Baltic States and G8

Clinton did not yet push for Russian acceptance of the Partnership for Peace because he first wanted to obtain something much more important from a pliable Yeltsin. Russian garrisons were still in the Baltic Republics, and Clinton wanted their removal. Here the decision was no longer about withdrawing troops from the Soviet Bloc countries but from the former republics of the Soviet Union. The withdrawal of the Russian military from the Baltic Republics was the first step to eventual entry into NATO. This revived "containment" policy evoked strong opposition from the Russian public. But Yeltsin, in an attempt to remain in the good graces of the West, had promised the president of Estonia that Russian troops would depart from the Baltic Republics by the end of August 1994.[38]

Clinton searched for weak spots and confirmed that Yeltsin's craving for acceptance from the West provided a great opportunity. Clinton had promised U.S. support for Russia's entry into many international organizations, but he realized that the most significant for Yeltsin was Russia's admission into the exclusive club of the G7. The vanity of Yeltsin craved the group photographs of himself standing next to the world's most powerful leaders. In reality, the meeting of heads of state were meaningless, so Clinton was surprised when the U.S. Treasury and other member states of G7 opposed Russian membership. It turned out that parallel to the well-publicized gatherings of the G7 heads of state, the Finance Ministers had their own quiet meetings to transact important business. The Finance Ministers opposed the participation of Russia because they spent most of their time talking about the economic collapse of that country.[39]

Clinton satisfied the U.S. Treasury by securing an initial arrangement that allowed Yeltsin to attend the meetings of the heads of state but excluded Russian officials from the secret meetings of the Finance Ministers. Clinton thus had in place a quid pro quo of classical diplomacy: in exchange for the withdrawal of Russian troops from the Baltic Republics in late August 1994, Russia began the accession process into the G-7, which later became the G8.

The deal was disastrous for Russia for two main reasons. To satisfy his personal vanity, Yeltsin sacrificed the interest of over a million ethnic Russians living in the Baltic Republics. Second, Yeltsin failed to demand a treaty guaranteeing the neutrality of the Baltic Republics or at least prohibiting their entry into NATO. The only concession that Russia obtained was that the 10,000 Russian veterans living in Estonia would receive permanent residence. Yet even to obtain this crumb Clinton had to make a personal appeal to the president of Estonia.[40]

An announcement on 10 July 1994 finalized the agreement. The withdrawal of Russian troops from the Baltic Republics made possible for the first time the later expansion of NATO into the territory of the former Soviet Union and was an immense diplomatic triumph for the U.S. And on a personal level, Clinton consolidated his role as the dominant partner in what became known in the media as the "Bill and Boris show." Criticisms not just from the media, but also from Congress, and even from even inside the White House claimed that Clinton was spending too much time on Russia and even coddling Yeltsin, when in reality the American president would have been a fool not to milk his Russian counterpart.

The dominance Clinton had acquired over Yeltsin reached the extreme with U.S. insistence on Russia joining the Partnership for Peace. This program was a mechanism to fast track the Eastern European countries into NATO while still retaining the illusion that Russia could one day join the military alliance. Once the U.S. decided to accept the Eastern European countries ahead of Russia, it was a foregone conclusion that the alliance would become anti–Russian. Although a few countries, such as Hungary, were starting to seek friendly relations with Russia, most of Eastern Europe did not differentiate Russia from the Soviet Union.[41]

Public criticism of the Partnership for Peace was mounting in Russia, and Yeltsin was reluctant to join the program. On a visit to Moscow to watch the V-E parade, Clinton forced the Russian president to accept the program. At this moment Clinton showed his absolute dominance by telling Yeltsin that "you don't have to sign anything yourself" but had to tell Foreign Minister Kozyrev to sign the Partnership for Peace agreement later that month.[42]

The two episodes of the withdrawal of Russian troops from the Baltics and the Russian signing of the Partnership for Peace agreement confirmed that Yeltsin was incapable of resisting the decisions of the U.S. about NATO expansion. Yeltsin was continuing the tradition of Mikhail Gorbachev of accepting all the demands of the West. However, only a small minority in Russia supported this give-away policy, and resistance was growing to the election of Yeltsin to a second term. Much as he wanted to please the West, his political instincts told him that he had to look tougher in foreign relations. But because he did not want to damage his reputation in the West, Yeltsin could not do it himself and needed to delegate the unpleasant task.

Mission Impossible for Yevgeny Primakov

On 12 January 1996 Boris Yeltsin appointed Yevgeny Primakov to be the new foreign minister of Russia. Even though the discontent with his predecessor Andrei Kozyrev had been intense during the previous year, the Russian president could not bring himself to fire the loyal subordinate because both men shared the illusions about the benefits of friendship with the West. Only when the political survival of Yeltsin was in danger in the 1996 elections did the president turn to Primakov.[43]

At that time Primakov was the head of the Foreign Intelligence Service (FIS) the approximate equivalent of the CIA. He had earlier become popular with the Russian public when in November 1993 in an unprecedented step he released to the public a secret FIS report predicting NATO expansion and warning of the serious consequences for Russia.[44]

Yeltsin, with his usual naiveté, believed that Primakov could restore Russia's world status at least sufficiently to assure the re-election. But the problem was that the Kozyrev-Yeltsin team during the initial years of the Russian Federation had given away most of the bargaining chips in exchange for almost nothing. And to accentuate Russian weakness, the First Chechnya War, raging since December 1994 had given the West additional leverage over Moscow. The longer the war lasted, the greater the pressure the West could bring against Russia.

Clinton tried to reassure Yeltsin that relations with the West were on a sound track, and the American president proudly pointed to the stationing of Russian military officers for the first time at NATO headquarters as the start of a new era of cooperation with the Kremlin.[45] But Yeltsin needed more than cosmetic changes for his political survival, and fellow politician Clinton complied by halting any steps toward NATO expansion until after the Russian presidential elections. U.S. and European officials were in a rush to admit new members from the former Soviet Bloc and complained about this unbearable delay. One of the sacred principles of NATO has been that no outside power could have a veto over admitting members, and here Russia, without asking for it, acquired a temporary veto. With France's support the U.S. was able to impose a pause on the process of admitting new members.[46]

Primakov used this pause to try to reduce the damage from NATO expansion. One proposal was to divide NATO into separate political and military components: any state could join the political side, but only the original members remained in the military alliance. This alternative meshed with previous plans of the Russian Foreign Ministry to create a new trans-Atlantic security structure, but the West opposed the idea. Another Primakov proposal was to limit NATO expansion to adjacent members, but this second idea had no more success than the first one.[47]

The U.S. deflected these and other proposals of Primakov to make NATO expansion tolerable to Russia, but once Yeltsin won the presidential runoff election on 3 July 1996, the gloves came off. In a brutal and blunt conversation with Primakov in Moscow on 15 July, presidential envoy Strobe Talbott laid out the facts of life:

> If by red line you mean that you are not prepared to accept the Baltic States' and Ukraine's eligibility for NATO membership in the future, then we have got a collision of red lines, yours and ours. We will be at an impasse if not in a train wreck. In other words, one of our red lines is now and will continue to be that no country is going to be ruled out of eligibility, certainly not by some other country.[48]

In effect the U.S. had delivered an ultimatum about a policy that has not changed until the present. Primakov was too seasoned a diplomat even to attempt a reply and referred the matter to future conversations and turned to discuss another topic. And when Yeltsin against all hope clung to the interpretation that the admission did not apply to the former Soviet republics, Clinton in a meeting in March 1997 told the Russian president that he was completely wrong.[49] The U.S. ultimatum had trapped Russia in a corner.

The West was too clever to let Russia go away empty-handed. Several countries, in particular Hungary and also France, were already uncomfortable with the harsh attitude toward Russia.[50] In 1997 Turkey also voiced its concerns through American diplomats: "Turkey's view was that all thinking about Europe must include Russia as an integral and important component of the whole."[51]

The original position of the West had been to push ahead with NATO expansion and to ignore Russia altogether. However, for the sake of maintaining unity within the military alliance, the West modified its harsh position and accepted the insistent request of diplomats to create a new channel of communication with Russia. The result of negotiations was the signing of the Founding Act of 27 May 1997 in Paris, France. The Founding Act established a Permanent Joint Council to meet twice a year at the level of foreign ministers and every month at the level of ambassadors.[52]

The idea of having officials on both sides hold regular meetings seemed beneficial, but in practice NATO members met prior to the meeting with Russia to agree on a common position. The Permanent Joint Council became another venue to repeat the views of each side. NATO went ahead with its expansion plans and announced on 8 July 1997 that the Czech Republic, Hungary, and Poland had been accepted for the final stage of the membership process in the military alliance. Russian citizens struggling to survive in a collapsing economy barely noticed and were already resigned to the inevitable.[53]

The first meeting of the Permanent Joint Council on 26 September 1997 gave the Yeltsin administration the opportunity to celebrate its partnership with the West and to reinforce the false idea that the West took into account Russian views. Additional confirmation came with Russia's accession to the G-7, which became the G-8 after the Denver summit of June 1997. Official media emphasized the prestige that membership in that exclusive club was supposed to bring to Russia.[54] The West was pleased to see that at least for the moment trinkets had sufficed to placate Russia.

5

Ukraine: Deceptive Calm

The Ukrainians expect all the advantages of the Soviet Union, such as low energy prices, while enjoying the advantages of independence.—Russian Foreign Minister Andrei Kozyrev[1]

A different leader, a different time, who knows?—British scholar Andrew Wilson[2]

After the end of the Soviet Union on 25 December 1991, Ukraine became an independent country. In a glaring difference with the other Soviet republics, Ukrainians believed they had a right to preferential treatment from Moscow. They felt that they were entitled to compensation if not reparations for the immense damage the Soviet Union had inflicted on Ukraine. Boris Yeltsin was among the Russians who felt guilty about Soviet treatment of Ukraine and were sympathetic to claims for compensation.

The more widespread view among Russians was that Ukraine was a brother who deserved maximum support. At the moment of independence almost all Ukrainians knew Russian, and almost half of those who called themselves Ukrainian claimed to speak only Russian. For its part Moscow was seeking to establish an intimate relationship with Ukraine, similar in nature to what was taking shape with Belarus. But as the first section shows, the new leadership of Leonid Kravchuk wanted to break free from the Kremlin.

The Start of Relations with Ukraine

The stark divergence between the goals of Moscow and Kiev were evident even before the formal end of the Soviet Union on 25 December 1991. While an idealistic Boris Yeltsin wanted to replace the Soviet Union with a loose confederation under the name of the Commonwealth of Independent States, the stern Leonid Kravchuk would have none of it. Yeltsin believed that the former Soviet Republics did not need individual armies, because the existing Soviet armed forces were more than adequate to cover the military requirements of this new Commonwealth. Kravchuk disagreed and blocked this proposal so dear to Yeltsin. At the same time the Ukrainian president plotted to take control of the close to one million Soviet military personnel stationed in Ukraine. In brilliant undercover operations, Ukrainian personnel seized the three Soviet military districts without having to fire a shot. Moscow suffered in a week a greater loss of troops than it had ever experienced during the worst defeats of World War II.[3]

This humiliating and shameful disaster made possible the establishment of a new Ukrainian military, and a powerless Moscow watched the units within the three Soviet military districts shifted their allegiance to Kiev. Exceptions did occur, and during 1992 many individuals and sometimes even whole detachments abandoned

Ukraine and returned to Russia. The Black Sea Fleet remained loyal, and Moscow also retained control over the strategic nuclear warheads in Ukraine.[4]

Nuclear Warheads

Prior to the end of the Soviet Union, the Soviet General Staff withdrew tactical nuclear weapons from Ukraine but lacked the time to dismantle nuclear warheads on the strategic missiles. Physical presence did not give Kiev actual control over the nuclear warheads, because the Kremlin possessed the launch codes. The original intent of Kravchuk was to make his country a nuclear power, and because the code mechanisms came from Ukraine, Kiev explored deactivating the codes. The danger of an accidental nuclear explosion was too great and forced the abandonment of the plan.[5]

For the first and last time in Russian-Ukrainian relations, the Kremlin enjoyed full support from the U.S. Not just Ukraine, but also Belarus and Kazakhstan possessed nuclear weapons, and in the Lisbon protocol of 1992 the three countries agreed to their removal. Belarus and Kazakhstan implemented the non-proliferation agreement, but Ukraine was slow to comply.[6]

Kravchuk tried to obtain something in exchange for the removal of the nuclear warheads. As compensation, Russia was willing to provide fuel for the nuclear reactors in Ukraine but Kravhcuk also wanted a guarantee for the territorial integrity of Ukraine. The U.S. pressured Ukraine to sign because of the fear that lack of maintenance of the launch mechanisms might trigger another Chernobyl-style accident. After Kravchuk lost his bid for reelection in July 1994 and the more sympathetic to Russia Leonid Kuchma became the new president, the Kremlin agreed to sign the Budapest Memorandum on 5 December 1994. The U.S., Britain, Ukraine, and Russia confirmed the denuclearization of the country and also recognized the borders ("territorial integrity") and security of Ukraine. The Memorandum was not a treaty and was never ratified by the legislatures of any country, so its six clauses did not create binding legal obligations. The last of the nuclear warheads left Ukraine in 1996.[7]

The Black Sea Fleet

The major consolation prize for Russia in the Ukrainian debacle was the Black Sea Fleet. Its commander Igor Kasatonov refused to recognize the authority of Kiev and remained loyal to Moscow. To try to eliminate this fly in the ointment of his otherwise huge victory over the Soviet armed forces, Kravchuk demanded that Yeltsin remove the admiral from command, but this power play was too transparent for even the Russian president to miss and he refused the request.[8]

The Ukrainian president then tried to steal the command from under Admiral Kasatonov. Just as he had done with the ground forces, Kravchuk pushed hard for the sailors to take the oath of loyalty to Kiev, but with little effect. In July 1992 two incidents almost sparked bloodshed. In the first one Ukrainian forces seized the commandant's office, but Kasatonov sent loyal marines to regain control. The admiral remained in command of the Fleet until January 1993 and by then its sailors and officers were committed to Russia. In the second incident, one warship raised the Ukrainian flag and sailed for Odessa. Aircraft and warships of the Black Sea Fleet soon were in hot pursuit and fired warning shots, but the runaway ship reached Odessa harbor.[9]

Both sides signed an agreement in Moscow on 17 June 1993 calling for an equal split of the vessels. The allocation of ships was supposed to begin in September 1993 after both countries established basing rights for the Russian share of the fleet. In a staggering surrender, Moscow abandoned

all claims to the many naval bases along the Black Sea littoral of Ukraine except for Crimea. But this appeasement did not satisfy the Ukrainians, who refused to recognize Russian rights to the naval base at Sevastopol.[10]

Crisis in Crimea

The hostility of Leonid Kravchuk toward Russia made reaching an agreement about the Black Sea Fleet or about anything else impossible. His conversion from a Communist bureaucrat to fiery Ukrainian nationalist had been complete, and he rejected anything that smacked of cooperation with Moscow. He had been responsible for shattering the illusions of Boris Yeltsin about creating a Commonwealth of Independent States to succeed the Soviet Union. He blocked the proposal for a single military force and also the idea of a single citizenship for all inhabitants of the former Soviet Union. Kravchuk also opposed the creation of any parliamentary body—even if composed of delegates from the existing legislatures—for the region of the former Soviet Union.[11]

Kravchuk made few changes to the existing state structure of the Soviet period. At most he renamed a few existing agencies, and he adopted the required state symbols of a flag, a coat of arms, and a national anthem. His most important innovation was to impose the Ukrainian language as the sole medium for conducting official business. He also began removing Russian from the educational system, and in Western Ukraine instruction in Russian ceased for most school children.[12]

For Kravchuk the Ukrainian language was essential for the nationalist project. He justified official preference for Ukrainian as necessary to overcome centuries of repression. The new policy clashed with the desire of many inhabitants to use Russian, the common language throughout the country. Resentment against the language policy was widespread in southern and southwestern Ukraine, and in Crimea the intense anger posed an open challenge to Kiev's authority.[13] The episode served as a trial run for the world famous operation of 2014.

Since 1990 the peninsula had been trying to reduce its ties with Kiev and to increase links with Moscow. In this stage of experimentation, Kiev, Moscow, and Simferopol engaged in substantive negotiations about the future of Crimea. But then the sudden end of the Soviet Union in December 1991 aborted the process.[14]

The Constitutions of 1992

Until April 1992 negotiators still had a good chance of reconciling the demands of Kiev and Simferopol. What the pro–Russian groups in essence were seeking was a "condominium," an arrangement for sharing sovereignty. Precedents existed in colonial territories, and in Europe Andorra was a model.[15]

The possibility of finding a peaceful solution through negotiations ended when Ukrainian extremists gained control of the Kiev parliament and on 29 April 1992 reduced the powers of the Crimean government. The Simferopol parliament replied with "The Act on the State Independence of the Crimean Republic" on 5 May and the next day adopted a new constitution. This 6 May 1992 Constitution weakened the authority of Kiev in the peninsula and made possible close ties with Russia.[16]

The Ukrainian parliament repudiated "The Act of State Independence of the Crimean Republic" on 13 May and demanded amendments to the Crimean constitution. The peninsula seemed headed for a violent clash, had not the war in Transnistria right on Ukraine's western border urged caution. The Kremlin had opposed the revolt in Transnistria, but the Russian Fourteenth Army on its own supported the separatist region. Nobody could rule out the possibility that the Russian Black Sea Fleet might join with the separatists in Crimea and confront Kiev with a full-blown revolt.[17]

When Simferopol realized that neither the Kremlin nor the Russian Black Sea Fleet had any desire to support an armed revolt, Crimean leaders were left with no choice but to negotiate an agreement with a Kiev also eager to end the clash. On 25 September 1992 the Crimean parliament adopted most of the amendments Kiev had wanted for the 6 May Constitution, and this action defused the crisis. The amended text still retained some of the ambiguity of the original, and in a major concession Kiev allowed the Crimean conscripts to fulfill their military service in the peninsula. This practice came to play a decisive role in the events of early 2014.[18]

The Confrontation of 1994

The refusal of the Kremlin to support Crimea reduced the options for Simferopol. The illusion of a prosperous future had lured many inhabitants to vote for the independence of Ukraine in the referendum of 1 December 1991 by the small margin of 54.7 percent. Most inhabitants seemed more concerned about economic wellbeing than about political loyalties. But as Ukraine went into an economic free-fall in 1992, the illusions of prosperity evaporated and the population felt duped by the promises of Ukrainian politicians.[19]

In still another maneuver designed to restrain separatist tendencies, pro–Kiev legislators promoted a bill to create the new position of president of Crimea. The Simferopol parliament passed the law in September 1993 and the Ukrainian parliament approved the law. It was, however, "a high-risk strategy" that could play into the hands of pro–Russian separatists.[20]

Six candidates ran in the presidential election of 16 January 1994. The pro–Russia vote was split among several candidates, and first-place winner Yuri Meshkov received 38.5 percent of the vote. With no candidate having reached the 50 percent threshold, a runoff election was necessary, but the outcome was never in doubt, because in the first round the pro–Russian candidates had in total received 52 percent of the vote. But Kiev was shocked to see than in the second round of 30 January 1994 Meshkov received 73 percent of the vote. The results were similar in the elections for the Simferopol parliament on 27 March 1994, when the pro–Russian deputies received 67 percent of the vote; the lower percentage was because of party lists and quota seats.[21]

The votes in the presidential election of 30 January 1994 were the best indicator of the strong Russian sentiment. Three-quarters of the population wanted to restore links with Russia, and Kiev had to take extraordinary measures if it wanted to avoid the image of being an occupier holding a colonial territory by force. For his part the winner Meshkov was realistic about his prospects in office and was leaning toward what could have meant a "condominium" status for the region with both Russia and Ukraine holding sovereignty. His early measures called for granting Russian passports to inhabitants of Crimea, the recognition of dual-citizenship, the replacement of the worthless Ukrainian currency with the Russian ruble, and placing Crimea under the time zone of Moscow.[22]

Meshkov, an attorney by profession, had first been elected deputy to the last Soviet parliament of Crimea in 1990 and had become the embodiment of pro–Russian feelings. He moved Crimea into the Moscow time zone, but before embarking on any other major restructuring, he needed to know how far the Kremlin was willing to support him; for any trilateral talks to succeed, all parties had to participate.[23]

Meshkov, after his election to the presidency, went on a trip to Moscow, and to his utter dismay the Kremlin showed almost no interest in Crimean matters. In a final insult, Boris Yeltsin declined even to see the Crimean leader, who for the rest of his life held the Russian president in deep contempt. On a practical level, the refusal meant that Russia was not coming to the negotiating table. Meshkov was left alone to defend the will of the Crimean people against the impositions of Kiev.[24]

Both in bilateral negotiations and on the ground, the balance of power favored Kiev. Kravchuk sent military and police reinforcements to Crimea as part of the strategy to take control of all security agencies. Because local police remained loyal to Meshkov, Kravchuk began by setting up a parallel police structure. A showdown almost turned bloody when forces loyal to Kiev seized the main police headquarters in Simferopol on 18–19 May. The attempt provoked so much anger that a defiant Crimean parliament on 20 May voted to reestablish the 6 May 1992 Constitution.[25]

Crimea was on the verge of a direct confrontation with Kiev, and Meshkov made another desperate appeal to Moscow for support, but his plea was ignored. In the face of the refusal of Russia, the Crimean parliament retreated and dropped its plan to restore the 6 May 1992 Constitution. Kiev won the showdown and pushed its advantage by gaining control of the police forces in Crimea during the summer of 1994. The situation was favorable for Kiev, because a power struggle between the Crimean parliament and Meshkov weakened the separatists.[26]

Meshkov had been a great organizer of the pro-Russia movement but as ruler of Crimea he faced an impossible situation. After a few months the inhabitants regarded his presidency as incompetent on economic matters. The increase in the price of bread reduced his popularity, and the ineffective response to epidemics during the summer eroded support. The Crimean parliament and Meshkov clashed over economic policy during the rest of 1994, and the divided separatists could not oppose Kiev.[27]

The disappointment with Meshkov was overwhelming, and in desperation the inhabitants placed their hopes in the next election for president of Ukraine. Voters believed that Leonid Kuchma was sympathetic to the pro–Russian sentiments in Crimea. In the runoff of 10 July 1994 people overwhelmingly voted for him in Crimea, where he received almost 90 percent of the vote, the highest percentage anywhere in Ukraine. Thanks to this massive majority he was able to win the nationwide election but with the narrow margin of 52 percent of the vote.[28]

The overwhelming vote for Kuchma in Crimea also reflected the realization that separation from Ukraine faced huge economic hurdles. The North Crimean Canal brought water from the Dnieper River, and Kiev threatened to ruin crops by shutting off the supply. Hydroelectric plants in Ukraine also provided most of the electricity for Crimea, and by a flick of a switch Kiev could plunge the region into darkness. Two-thirds of the regional budget came from the mainland, and the peninsula did not have available any other sources of revenue. Seeking a face-saving way out of the impasse, leaders in Crimea turned to OSCE to broker a negotiated solution.[29]

Kuchma welcomed the mediation of OSCE as one more way to show the Kremlin that he was eager to find a peaceful solution. On the ground, however, he was ruthless, and in September 1994 he authorized the seizure of the last police stations still under the control of Meshkov in Crimea. The policemen had been working without pay and put up no resistance.[30]

The Kremlin, with excessive optimism, regarded the election of Kuchma as a great opportunity to improve relations with Kiev. As part of a larger policy to obtain sympathetic treatment for Russian concerns, the Kremlin declined to pressure him on Crimea or on anything else. Moscow ignored the demands of Crimea and of Russian nationalists in order to achieve the larger goal of converting Ukraine into a strong ally like Belarus and Kazakhstan. And Russia, although recovering from economic collapse faster than Ukraine, still lacked the resources to assume the huge expense of rescuing a bankrupt Crimea.[31]

The Kremlin supported the efforts of OSCE to find an arrangement acceptable to Crimea and Kiev. Ukraine was in the process of writing its first post–Soviet constitution, and OSCE was able to make sure that in the majority of clauses its terms coincided with those in the local constitution. The start of the First Chechnya War in December 1994 eliminated any last chance of Russian intervention. Kuchma and the Ukrainian parliament plotted to destroy the separatist movement once and for all. As a preparatory move, Kiev increased its police and military detachments in Crimea.

When everything was in place, Kuchma and the Ukrainian parliament struck hard on 17 March 1995. Kiev abolished the May 1992 Crimean Constitution, the Crimean presidency, and any Crimean laws curtailing the authority of Ukraine. And in a final ultimatum, Kiev warned the Simferopol parliament to comply or else face suspension. That same day troops arrived in Meshkov's office and stripped him of his telephones, his cars, and his fifteen bodyguards. The abolition of the office of the Crimean presidency left Meshkov powerless, but without any arrest order against him, he stayed in the presidential suite in the sixth floor of the parliament building.[32]

The Crimean parliament rushed to gather and the next day on 18 March 1995 asked for protection from President Yeltsin and the Russian Duma. Meshkov sent a similar appeal to Moscow and also to the international community, but a bankrupt Russia mired in the First Chechnya War was in no condition to help. When the Crimean president with great emotion appealed for the inhabitants to come to a public protest, the turnout was minimal. Meshkov remained languishing in the sixth floor of the parliament building. Sometime after May 1995 soldiers dragged him from his office and put him on a plane bound for Moscow.[33]

The question remained whether Ukraine would use its reestablished authority to win the hearts and minds of the people or just treat the peninsula as a distant and neglected colony. The abrupt expulsion of former president Meshkov suggested that Kiev was not interested in real reconciliation. The OSCE mediation helped to disguise the tremendous defeat the people of Crimea had suffered but was not a long-term solution. Under no circumstances could Ukraine assume that separatist feelings had faded in Crimea.[34] Even more dangerous was the conclusion that the Kremlin would always ignore the desperate pleas of Crimea.

The Friendship, Cooperation, and Partnership Treaty

The last unfinished business over Crimea concerned the Black Sea Fleet, but the Kremlin had always wanted a broad agreement going beyond that single issue. Russia had been engaged in negotiations with Ukraine since 1993 over a Friendship, Cooperation, and Partnership Treaty, but because Ukraine wanted to break its economic ties with Russia, no agreement had been possible. The situation changed on 10 July 1994 after the election of Kuchma, and not just because he was supposed to be pro–Russian. Ukrainian officials and oligarchs were reaching the harsh conclusion that economic independence from Russia if not impossible and least was unattainable for many decades. The logical alternative was to negotiate a treaty as favorable as possible to Ukraine and still acceptable to Russia.[35]

The indispensable prerequisite for the Friendship treaty was to reach a compromise about the Black Sea Fleet and its bases. A major obstacle to solving this issue was the prohibition in the Ukrainian Constitution against the presence of foreign troops. Because no treaty could include clauses granting bases to foreign countries, the solution was to sign three separate executive agreements on 28 May 1997. According to their terms, Ukraine retained 18 percent of the original ships of the Black Sea Fleet. Russia agreed to pay an annual rent for installations in Crimea; in still another major appeasement, Russia agreed to rent specific facilities within Sevastopol rather than the entire city. Clauses also stipulated limits on the number of personnel and airplanes Russia could deploy in Crimea until 2017, when the agreements were set to expire.[36]

The agreements over the Black Sea Fleet cleared the last obstacle standing in the way of a comprehensive arrangement. President Boris Yeltsin came to Kiev to sign the Friendship, Cooperation, and Partnership Treaty on 31 May 1997. This treaty was a major victory for Kuchma, because Russia recognized the territorial integrity and borders of Ukraine. The treaty was supposed to create strong bonds between both countries, when in reality it marked the high point of cooperation. Routine expressions and tired clichés comprised a text devoted to economic, trade, cultural, scientific, and transport issues. Only in three places did the treaty mention geographic locations in Ukraine. If the few references to OSCE are ignored, the treaty could have been signed between any two countries in the world. The Friendship and Cooperation Treaty, the formula classical diplomacy offers to enhance peaceful relations between countries, turned out to be a hollow and meaningless document.[37]

The treaty did not satisfy Russian legislators, who concluded that Yeltsin had given away too much to Ukraine in exchange for very little. Ratification of the treaty in the Russian parliament proved to be a long and arduous process and was not completed until 1999. Both Russian and Ukrainian nationalists were opposed to the Friendship and Cooperation Treaty, and even prior to its entry into force questions arose over whether it could be the foundation for a long and peaceful relationship between the two countries. In particular the question of the future of Crimea was too obvious to ignore, although almost no one seemed to worry about a similar problem among the less vocal ethnic Russians in Eastern Ukraine.[38] The far from groundless hope existed that intense trade and material interests could overcome the ethnic and language tensions.

6

The Turning Point: Kosovo

> *NATO's attack on Serbia in 1999, ignoring Russia's objections and bypassing the United Nations, was by far the single greatest act and the single most important factor in eroding the trust that served as the basis of Russia's relations with the West.*—U.S. diplomat William H. Hill[1]

The disintegration of Yugoslavia began in the early 1990s when many of its constituent ethnic groups demanded independence. The weakening of the central government in Belgrade gave the nationalists the opportunity to establish their own mini-states after years of turmoil and armed combat. In 1920 Yugoslavia had been the West's attempt to accommodate the many conflicting demands for independence from ethnic groups too intermingled to permit easy separation.

The failure of this experiment in Yugoslavia did not prevent NATO from plunging into the volatile Balkans. In 1998 all that remained to solve was the status of the province of Kosovo in Serbia. The issue was not just about the political future of a forgotten corner of Europe. Serbia in 1914 had triggered the start of World War I. Unpredictable events characterized the turbulent Balkans, and who could guarantee that history would not repeat itself in Serbia?

The West and Kosovo

Kosovo was not immune from the disintegration of authority in Yugoslavia, and rebel attacks against local police began in the early 1990s. The Kosovo Liberation Army began an organized campaign against the police in 1996, but the rebels could not have much of an impact, because just like many would-be rebel movements, they lacked weapons. The situation changed in March 1997 when in a vain attempt to halt disorder in Albania, the government opened its arsenals. The distribution of over 600,000 weapons of all types to Albanians provided the opportunity for Kosovo rebels at last to acquire a formidable armament. Late in 1997 a widespread campaign began in Kosovo directed not just at authorities but against Serbian civilians to force them to flee. The real terrorists were the rebels, and when the Serbs reacted with brutal repression, soon thousands of refugees of both sides fled the zone to escape reprisals. In an example of selective morality, the West proved sympathetic to the plight of the civilians of Kosovo and not of the Serbians. NATO threatened to begin a bombing campaign in October 1998 if Serbia did not withdraw its troops.[2]

Serbian president Slobodan Milošević accepted some of the demands of the West and agreed to withdraw his forces from one-third of the territory Serbia held in Kosovo. NATO postponed its bombing campaign, and Serb forces withdrew from territory then occupied by the rebels. Even

more harmful for Serbia was the decision by Milošević to authorize the entry of observers from the Organization for Security and Cooperation in Europe (OSCE). These teams reported atrocities on the Serbian side and helped to shape opinion in the West. The media enjoyed unrestricted access to the region and reported rampant destruction and fleeing refugees. Most impactful were the graphic scenes CNN brought to television screens across the world. This coverage hardened the will of NATO to take action against the demonized Milošević.[3]

Civil wars are always savage affairs and even more so if they are also ethnic in nature. On top of that combustible mixture, the religious fanaticism of Muslim Albanians against Christian Serbs added a crusader's zeal. Although many Europeans wondered whether they were backing the right side, in the 1990s the West was sympathetic to the Islamic rebels, but after the 9/11 terrorist attacks support for Islamic groups faded.[4]

Nobody doubted the brutality of the war in Kosovo, but what Russia found perplexing was the selective nature of Western sensitivities. When Georgians ravaged Abkhazia in 1992 and started ethnic cleansing, the West paid almost no attention. NATO could intervene in Kosovo on humanitarian grounds but Russian involvement in Abkhazia for the same purpose was unacceptable. This contradiction worried even Georgia, afraid that this precedent justified Russian support for the independence of Abkhazia.[5]

The West could not support independence for Kosovo if it wanted to avoid setting a precedent for many other regions in Europe just waiting for a sign to start a revolt. The Russian Foreign Minister Igor Ivanov asked "don't you understand we have many Kosovos in Russia?"[6] The recent Russian defeat in the First Chechnya War demonstrated the power of nationalist movements, and the Kremlin was concerned about the possible disintegration of the country.

Other European countries, in particular Spain, were also worried about setting a precedent for supporting the independence of any restless region. The formula was attractive: start a revolt, provoke the occupiers into launching a savage repression, have atrocities filmed and broadcast to the world, and then have the West come to the rescue to defend the separatist region. For those who dreamed of creating still another mini-state, the temptation was hard to resist. The risk of disintegration in Europe was large, because most countries contained minority groups. The multiplication of ethnic mini-states meant returning Europe to the tribalization existing before the Roman Empire.

To calm these fears, the U.S. opposed the independence of Kosovo as a tactical move to maintain the unity of the Western alliance. The U.S. wanted to force Milošević to remove all Serbian authorities from Kosovo but with the province remaining a part of Serbia. This claim if not downright duplicitous was at best disingenuous. The U.S. demands made independence inevitable, but the U.S. disguised that outcome.[7]

The Western European countries began to have serious misgivings about an armed intervention in Kosovo; in particular they wanted United Nations authorization for any action. Because Russia held a veto in the Security Council, the U.S. had to labor hard to forge a consensus with the Europeans to take action without UN approval. Secretary of State Madelaine Albright, a ferocious Cold Warrior, took the lead in persuading both Europeans and doubters within the U.S. government to support a NATO bombing campaign against Serbia.

By this time the media had demonized Milošević to such a degree that the West welcomed his removal from office. Cold Warriors claimed that the departure of that tyrant would make possible an age of peace and stability in the turbulent Balkans. Secretary Albright also wanted to affirm the relevance and power of NATO, an understandable view coming from a Cold Warrior. In a perverse twist, she tied the commemoration of the 50th anniversary of NATO to the bombing of Serbia; to celebrate the organization's creation she needed a massive demonstration of firepower more spectacular than any fireworks display.[8]

Neither the rebels nor the Serbs could prevail in 1998, and to try to break the stalemate, Serbia was preparing to launch a major offensive early in 1999. Whether this final Serb effort would be more effective that previous ones remained a moot point, but for the Clinton administration stopping the impending advance gave a convenient pretext to unleash a bombing campaign.[9]

The Kremlin was resigned to the inevitable and only asked to delay the bombing until after Prime Minister Yevgeny Primakov returned from a visit to Vice President Al Gore. While the Russian official was aboard a plane headed to Washington, D.C., Gore explained that the bombing campaign was set to start in a few hours on 24 March 1999; NATO had kept the hour secret so that the Russians could not give any advance warning to the Serbs. Primakov cancelled the trip and had his plane make a U-turn back to Moscow.[10]

President Bill Clinton on 24 March 1999 telephoned Boris Yeltsin to say that "the Europeans have decided we have to launch airstrikes against military targets in Serbia soon."[11] Yeltsin countered with an impassioned and truthful warning that if the West proceeded with this strike, "our people will certainly from now have a bad attitude with regard to America and with NATO." He had devoted his entire presidency "to try and turn the heads of our people, the heads of the politicians towards the West, towards the United States [...] and now to lose all that." And he made his final plea: "I ask you to renounce that strike."

In the most important consequence, the bombing marked the end of close ties between Clinton and Yeltsin. In protest over the start of the bombing on 24 March 1999, Russia curtailed almost all cooperation and meetings with NATO and reduced its staff at Brussels headquarters to a skeleton level.[12]

The fiery bombing campaign against Serbia made come true the wish of Secretary Albright for a fitting celebration for the 50th anniversary of NATO. She was unperturbed about the irony of using the defensive military alliance to attack a weak country. She was not alone in thinking that the bombing campaign would be over in a few days. The conventional wisdom was that once Milošević saw the bombardment destroy his forces in Kosovo, he would accept the harsh conditions NATO insisted on imposing.[13]

To everyone's surprise, that did not happen and as the days turned into weeks of bombing, no end seemed in sight. NATO planes soon ran out of obvious military targets and on 2 April bombed the first civilian installations in downtown Belgrade. NATO soon was hitting trains, bridges, refineries, and power plants across Serbia to force Milošević to accept the Western ultimatum. After the war it was learned that the Serbian military was well prepared and had protected its principal units. Instead, nobody could doubt the massive damage that the bombing was inflicting on civilian areas. Pentagon spin doctors emphasized the precision of the air campaign, but the CNN cameras broadcast a different story. Here television backfired on the West, because rather than images of brutalities against defenseless rebels, the screen showed inhabitants being pulverized by relentless bombing. Each bomb that fell on a civilian target in Belgrade weakened the will of the West to sustain the campaign and also embittered the Russian viewers who saw the same images on their televisions.[14]

Russia lobbied hard for a pause in the bombing as the best way to bring Milošević to the negotiating table, but the West maintained its traditional position of exerting the maximum military pressure on an opponent—in this case Serbia—until it first accepted all the conditions. In a conversation on 25 April Yeltsin raised for the first time the threat of using nuclear weapons to stop the bombing. Clinton saw right through this bluff and ignored it, but mentioning nuclear weapons revealed how close the clash over Kosovo came to spiraling out of control.[15]

The air campaign was not achieving the desired results, and NATO put into motion a backup plan of sending troops on the ground to drive the Serbians out of Kosovo. The bombing had failed to stop the ethnic cleansing, and on the contrary Serbian forces intensified their efforts to expulse the hostile inhabitants. In preparation for an invasion, NATO members sent troops to Greece, Albania, and North Macedonia. At that time nobody could have guessed the unexpected role these troops later played in ending the crisis.[16]

As NATO forces rumbled into position, the bombing of the Chinese embassy in Belgrade on 7 May revealed the dangers of the air campaign. The Chinese protested the attack and joined with Russia in calling an end to the air strikes. The U.S. and its allies had been receiving constant warnings from pro–West individuals in Russia that the continued bombing of Serbia promised to wreck all the past improvement in relations. But sending in NATO troops to replace the bombing campaign did not seem by itself a very soothing alternative.[17]

A series of moves misled the West into believing that relations with Russia would not suffer. The first indication came on 14 April 1999 when Yeltsin named the former Prime Minister Victor Chernomyrdin to be the special envoy on Serbia. The appointment of this pro–Western official came at the suggestion of Vladimir Putin, who in one of his first forays into foreign relations, concluded that Kosovo was a losing proposition for Russia. Putin felt that Russia had a better chance of extricating itself from the Kosovo mess if Chernomyrdin was in charge of the principal negotiations with Serbia.[18]

When Yeltsin dismissed Primakov from office on 12 May 1999, this second action also confirmed the optimism of the West. The Prime Minister had been considered too sympathetic to state enterprises, and his removal signaled that no return to Socialism was possible. The real reason for the dismissal of Primakov was because Yeltsin was looking for a successor. The Prime Minister was older than the president and unsuitable to be the heir apparent.[19]

Yelstin was also worried about protecting his legacy. He believed that having gained formal admission to the exclusive G-7 club of world leaders, which then became the G-8, was one of his most important achievements. The G-8 was scheduled to meet at Cologne, Germany, on June 18, and Russian negotiators had to secure a ceasefire so that Yeltsin could participate in that meeting. Yeltsin, just as his predecessor Mikhail Gorbachev, attached enormous significance to having photographs taken standing next to Western leaders.[20]

The West concluded that it had a winning hand and pushed hard to make Russia accept a UN resolution forcing Serbia to capitulate. If Yeltsin wanted to be received at the G-8 meeting, Russia was going to have to pay a humiliating price. Chernomyrdin hoped to soften the terms by having a neutral person participate in the negotiations, but he was outmaneuvered when the U.S. proposed the Finnish President Martti Ahtisaari as the candidate. Chernomyrdin agreed, but his hope of a sympathetic person turned out to be unfounded, and the Finnish President endorsed the NATO demands.[21]

Both men went to Belgrade to deliver the ultimatum and they expected Milošević to delay or even reject the terms. Chernomyrdin and Ahtisaari were surprised to have the Serbian ruler accept the ultimatum. On 3 June the Serbian parliament ratified the agreement, but NATO continued the air strikes. The U.S. insisted that Serbian forces first had to start their withdrawal from Kosovo before NATO would halt the bombing; only at that moment would the Security Council approve the UN resolution.[22]

The terms of the UN resolution were so favorable to NATO that Russian ambassador to the UN Sergei Lavrov made a last-ditch effort to mitigate its most outrageous clauses. An arrogant U.S. became impatient with this delaying tactic, and an angry Clinton telephoned Yeltsin telling him to order the obstruction at the United Nations to stop. For the last time a Russian president overruled the diplomats at the UN, and the Security Council approved the resolutions on June 10; on that day NATO suspended its air strikes on Serbia.[23] The West had won a resounding victory in Kosovo and the crisis seemed to be over.

Crisis with Russia: The Pristina Dash

The rather sudden acceptance by Slobodan Milošević of the terms offered on 1 June had surprised participants and observers. Indications abound that Russian officers in the military attaché's office informed Milošević that Russia was preparing to undertake an operation to save at least something for Serbia in Kosovo. A team of 18 intelligence commandos had been in Kosovo since May to survey the ground for a possible operation. The outrage against the West reached a fever pitch inside the Russian military, and it was easy to find generals willing to participate in the scheme. The plotters kept the foreign ministry and most senior commanders in the dark about the operation, but this was not a rogue group. Cognizant of their oath of obedience, sympathizers in the Kremlin brought a simplistic version of the proposal to Boris Yeltsin at a moment when he was angriest and drinking too much. Without analyzing the proposal, the Russian president gave his authorization.[24]

The operation rested on a solid premise that if Russian forces occupied territory in Kosovo, then the Kremlin could at last achieve its goal of having its own sector in Kosovo. Russian diplomats would then be in a position to negotiate the partition of Kosovo, the only reasonable long-term solution. But even the most superficial and hasty glance confirmed that the operation stood no chance of success and could provoke a major confrontation between Russia and the United States.[25]

No major Russian combat units were in the area, and in contrast NATO was already deploying tens of thousands of soldiers and considerable equipment in neighboring countries. The planners of the operation expected to even the odds by flying in airborne troops from Russia into the Pristina airport in Kosovo. Sending inadequate number of soldiers and then waiting for reinforcements to arrive to turn the tide has been a frequent source of military disasters, and it was far from sure that Russia could pull off the risky maneuver.[26]

The only unit available to seize the Pristina airport was a battalion of Russian soldiers forming part of peacekeeping forces in Bosnia. On June 11 at 0400 the unit of 186 soldiers left its base and headed for Serbia. The battalion crossed the border at 1030 and was slowed down by cheering crowds. Serbian police struggled to clear the roads so that the convoy could continue its trip. CNN was broadcasting images of jubilant crowds greeting the convoy. The thirty armored vehicles made good time racing across Serbia and into Kosovo province. At 0400 hours on 12 June, about 24 hours after the departure from their base in Bosnia, the Russian troops took control of the Pristina airport, ahead of the rebels. They had won the race to seize the airport, and NATO forces did not enter Kosovo province until after 0530.[27]

By a fortuitous circumstance, the first NATO troops to arrive in the vicinity of Pristina airport were 600 British paratroopers. In another stroke of good luck its commander was the calm General Mike Jackson, who was also fluent in Russian. General Jackson struck up a relationship with the Russian general and the two men even drank whiskey together. Both men were not sure what this small Russian detachment was supposed to do in the middle of the thousands of soldiers NATO was pouring into the region. The Russian general believed that his troops were supposed to form part of the peacekeeping forces in Kosovo under the command of the British general. The explanation was convincing for General Jackson, who established a perimeter around the Russian battalion; when more NATO troops arrived he deployed these units to take control of the roads leading from Kosovo to Serbia.[28]

The Russian battalion was surrounded, and the promoters of the operation did not want to accept the military reality that they had rushed the battalion into a trap. Russia wanted to recover a favorable position by airlifting reinforcements, but such a movement faced huge obstacles. In Russia Ilyushin-76 cargo planes loaded with airborne troops were waiting for the flight clearances from neighboring countries to depart for Kosovo from Russia. The decisive struggle was over airspace, but an impatient Supreme NATO Commander Wesley Clark wanted the war to start right away on the ground.[29]

General Clark was a character straight out of the movie *Dr. Strangelove,* and he was obsessed with driving the Russians out of the airport even if this meant an armed clash. He ordered General Jackson to take control of the runways, but the British commander refused by stating that "I am not going to start World War III for you."[30] General Jackson consulted British cabinet officials, who supported his position. French paratroopers were not far away, but Paris had pulled them out of this mission. Using his four-star rank, a frustrated General Clark then ordered the nearest American force, a unit of Apache helicopters, to take control of the Pristina airfield. Its commander responded that he needed authorization from the Pentagon. By the time the authorization worked its way through the chain of command, weather conditions in Kosovo had made flying impossible, and the mission had to be postponed.

An outraged General Clark returned to his office in Brussels.[31]

The real battle took place in the air. Hungary, already starting to lean toward Russia, approved the request to fly over its airspace, but Ukraine was suspicious and delayed. Meanwhile the U.S. pressured Hungary to repeal the authorization, and its government announced the need to suspend the permission pending further review. Ukraine tried to satisfy both Russia and the U.S. by granting permission but only for 72 hours. By the time the open period expired, Hungary could not complete its review and thus the air space of Ukraine and Hungary was closed. Russia tried to secure overflight permission through Rumania and Bulgaria, but forewarned American diplomats were able to block those routes.[32]

Meanwhile the situation of the Russian battalion in Pristina was becoming desperate. The soldiers were hungry and were running out of water, and British General Jackson ordered his men to provide a water truck and to share their rations with the Russians. What had seemed as a brilliant maneuver to outflank NATO had turned out to be one more humiliating defeat for Russia. Yet the operation—the equivalent of Primakov turning his airplane around—raised spirits among the Russian public and kept alive the hope that one day the country could regain its rightful place among the international community.[33]

The Kremlin had every right to oppose the NATO intervention but should have stayed away from any cooperation with Western powers. Russia was learning the hard way that it had "a voice in but not a veto over NATO decisions"[34] and in such a situation why even bother to engage in negotiations? Cooperation with the West brought no benefits and many setbacks not to mention humiliation. It was time for Russia to reevaluate its relations with the West and to draw the appropriate conclusions from the Kosovo episode.

The End of the Age of Illusions

Kosovo finished shattering the dream that the West would accept Russia as an equal partner. The United States held the view that Russia had "lost" the Cold War and Washington was free to dictate terms to the loser. Western Europe was less harsh on Russia but its attitude was perhaps even more arrogant than that of the U.S. Western Europe was willing to share its civilization with a primitive Russia in great need of a colonial overlord. But before Western Europe could accept Russia as a full partner, the country had to abandon all its distinctive national characteristics and become just like Europe.

Each Russian citizen experienced the disillusionment with the West at a different moment in the 1990s. The appointment of Yevgeny Primakov as Foreign Minister in January 1996 reflected the loss of faith in the West by a significant group of Russians, although a majority still believed cooperation was possible. The U.S. insistence on expanding NATO was the next step weakening pro–Western feelings in Russia. The breaking point came with the NATO bombing of Serbia in 1999. Afterwards the majority of Russians came to accept the hostile nature of the West. Pro-Western political parties in Russia refused to recognize this new reality, and they crippled their chances of any widespread popularity by insisting on pursuing the anti–Russian positions that the West demanded.[35]

After Kosovo, Russia never again embarked on another quixotic adventure like the Pristina Dash. At the same time, the Russian military was not up to the task of facing the West, and the process of reforming the institution became a high priority for the Kremlin. The Kosovo crisis also closed the debate between proponents of nuclear forces over conventional forces. Nuclear weapons had not stopped NATO and only conventional forces could act as a deterrent.

The main task in the 2000s was to reconstruct the economy, and once resources were available, Russia could revitalize its military. A prerequisite for economic growth was a strong centralized government under new leadership and able to restrain the oligarchs of the 1990s.

Officials who had stood out during the Kosovo crisis were on track to rise to high office. A good example was ambassador to the United Nations Sergei Lavrov. He had done almost the impossible to defend Russian interests at the Security Council, and he was the logical choice to become Foreign Minister in February 2004.

The most famous case was Vladimir Putin, who had been one of the first to realize that Russia needed to extricate itself from the Kosovo crisis. Within his subordinate position he labored to return sanity to Russian foreign policy and was instrumental in finding a face-saving formula. His realistic assessment of Russia's weakness did not mean that he had abandoned hopes about a return to world power status.

The consequences of the Kosovo Crisis were profound for Russia and marked a turning point in its foreign relations. The West and in particular the U.S. were slow to realize how much circumstances had changed. On the contrary, most American officials clung to the naïve belief that Russia was desperate to cooperate with the U.S.

Bill Clinton, like his predecessors, worried about his legacy. American presidents wanted to see their actions have lasting impact on the world, and Clinton exceeded those expectations. His two most lasting legacies in foreign relations were the expansion of NATO and the military campaign in Kosovo. Those two actions shaped the nature of relations between the West and Russia during the early decades of the twentieth century.

The West, rather than reflecting on the need to reverse course in its policies of hostility toward Russia, entered into the twenty-first century determined to push harder at every favorable moment. But the opportunities to weaken Russia were fast disappearing, because the age of illusions about Western intentions had come to an end.

Part II

From Acquiescence to Resistance

7

The Second Chechnya War and Islamic Radicalism

> *The current Government of Russia diplomatic line on Chechnya perhaps can be summed up as telling outsiders nicely that there is no need to butt in.* —U.S. Embassy in Moscow[1]

Failed State and the Radicalization of Chechnya

The departure of the last Russian troops from Chechnya on 5 January 1997 "represented an unparalleled victory in modern Chechen history: the country was free from Russia military presence for the first time since the mid-nineteenth century."[2] The new country proceeded to choose a replacement for President Dzhokhar Dudayev, who had died in the war against Russia.

The combat hero and war lord Shamil Basayev had been the favorite but received only 24 percent of the vote in the presidential elections on 27 January 1997. Instead in a stunning upset Aslan Maskhadov—who had been the army commander of Dudayev—won with 59 percent of the vote. An indignant Basayev rejected the voting results and all Western principles.[3]

Maskhadov had a chance to consolidate his position and to prepare Chechnya for full independence in 2001. The public wanted the new president to restore Soviet-era institutions and to return order and stability to Chechnya. Maskhadov soon learned that he faced the same obstacles as his predecessor Dudayev. War lords continued to rule the countryside, and just like Dudayev before the Russian invasion of December 1994, the authority of the new president did not extend beyond Grozny, the capital. The downward spiral continued, and by the end of 1997 "Chechnya became one of the worst examples of a failed state."[4]

Without any links to Russia, the economy deteriorated and many inhabitants lost their jobs. War lords obtained income from kidnappings, and lawlessness characterized the region. The Chechens wanted to escape their economic distress, but Maskhadov could not offer any solution. War lords clashed over control of the remaining resources in the region. Maskhadov himself suffered four assassination attempts and was in constant fear for his life. Open Civil War broke out in July 1998, and the president put down the revolt of an Islamic fundamentalist group. In that month Gudermes suffered artillery duels in bitter fighting between rival groups.[5]

Maskhadov crushed the defiant Islamists and, after escaping another assassination attempt, he decided to seek foreign assistance for Chechnya. He had already taken a first step in August 1997 during a visit to Tbilisi when he tried to repair relations with Georgia. He apologized for the earlier Chechen support for Abkhazians in their war of independence, but Georgia did not go beyond encouraging friendly contacts along their common border.[6]

Much more important for Maskhadov was his trip to the U.S. in August 1998. The visit to Washington, D.C., was decisive for the Chechen leader, because it represented his last chance to secure Western support for a secular Chechnya. Maskhadov had come at the invitation of a moderate Islamic group and not of the U.S. government. His real goal was to secure U.S. support, and during his visit he pleaded his case in congress and with officials in the Commerce Department, USAID, and the State Department. The Pentagon, despite the U.S. military presence in the Middle East, showed no interest in meeting with him.[7]

Maskhadov needed economic assistance to save his economy, and he also wanted international recognition for an independent Chechnya. U.S. officials explained that he first had to secure Russian approval before Chechnya could obtain any international recognition. Some economic assistance was possible, but only after the release of the many foreign hostages in Chechnya. Because Maskhadov did not control the war lords holding the hostages, he could not deliver on the *quid pro quo* and did not qualify for U.S. aid.[8]

He returned empty-handed from the U.S. trip, and while he was away, rival war lord Basayev had created a parallel power structure. Basayev persuaded other war lords to adopt Islamic fundamentalism. He enjoyed support from wealthy Arabic donors who were paying for Islamic training camps. The unemployed youth were brainwashed to follow jihad and to adopt Islamic extremism. In response, Maskhadov decided to forestall the opposition by being the first to proclaim Sharia law. On 3 February 1998 Sharia law went into effect in Chechnya, and this all-absorbing body of law deprived the legislature of any meaningful role.[9]

Basayev dismissed the enactment of Sharia law as an insincere ploy. Already in September 1998 he was casting eyes at neighboring Dagestan, another Muslim region in Russia. Some disputes had arisen in Dagestan between the traditional followers of Islam and a minority of extremists who wanted to follow the example of Chechnya.[10] In this internal dispute among religious factions, Basayev saw the opportunity to launch a bigger project "to replace Russian rule in the region with a Pan-Caucasus Islamic entity."[11]

The "Pan-Caucasus Islamic entity" moved Basayev closer to fulfilling his intention of creating a Caliphate for the Caucasus. Anticipating victory, he entered into negotiations with the Taliban of Afghanistan for the purpose of securing international recognition for a soon-to-be-proclaimed new Islamic Caliphate in the Caucasus.[12]

The exchange of gunfire at the Dagestan border with Chechnya became so intense, that Russian police dug trenches along the frontline. The Kremlin found this situation intolerable and ordered the Ministry of Interior to tighten security along the border. Russia had been trying to impose a blockade to prevent smuggling and kidnappings, but with little success. The border was just too long and rugged to patrol, and a more practical solution was for Russian forces to reoccupy the territory up to the Terek River Valley, for long the traditional southern border of tsarist Russia. This northern third of Chechnya consisted of relatively flat terrain suitable for tank deployments; in addition the population was pro–Russian and opposed the demands of Islamic radicals. The shortened border facilitated controlling trade with Chechnya.

The preparations for a partial Russian occupation of northern Chechnya were not yet ready when Basayev acting on his own invaded Dagestan. His intention was to use that region as a base to proclaim to the world the creation of a new Caliphate of the Caucasus. He assumed the title of "emir" and led a force of 1,500 militants across the border on 7 August 1999 near the Botlikh area. He had overestimated the sympathy for his cause and ran into fierce resistance from militias. The inhabitants were attached to their traditional Islamic practices, dating back to the Arab conquest of the eight century, and were not about to allow more recent converts to Islam dictate how they should practice their religion.[13]

Officials at Dagestan had been clamoring for Russian troops, but the soldiers were slow to arrive. By the time the Russian soldiers reached their positions, the Chechen militants had fortified themselves in houses outside Botlikh; because building structures in this harsh mountainous climate took decades, the officers did not want to shell these hard to replace houses. The Dagestani had no hesitations and demanded that the Russians open fire and shatter the houses sheltering the invaders. The artillery barrages smashed the Chechens, and the ferocious resistance from moderate Muslims finished driving out the invaders. But the boldness of the Chechen radicals forced the Kremlin to reexamine its plans for Chechnya.[14]

The Russian Invasion and the Response of the West

The Chechens had attacked Dagestan before the preparations for the Russian occupation of northern Chechnya were complete. For the Kremlin It was an easy decision to hasten the preparations and to execute the Russian operation ahead of schedule. By taking control of the northern third of the country, Russia avoided the savage and destructive land campaign of the First Chechnya War and also hoped to gain grudging acceptance from the West.[15]

The original plan to advance only as far as the Terek Valley became untenable in September, after a string of apartment bombings left hundreds of civilians dead across Russia. These terrorist attacks set off a wave of hysteria in Russia similar to what swept the United States two years later after the 9/11 attacks. In both countries the perpetrators had been Islamic radicals, and the angry public clamored for a strong and forceful response. The Russian military, for its part, wanted to avenge the humiliating defeat it had suffered in the First Chechnya War.

The emotional pressure to expand the operation proved irresistible, and the Kremlin decided to occupy all of Chechnya. However, the Russian military had not recovered from its precipitous decline since the fall of the Soviet Union and was in no condition to conduct the operation. The last-minute expansion of the offensive stretched the capabilities of the Russian military to the breaking point. Aerial bombardment began on 22 September 1999, and that same day the artillery situated next to the northern third of Chechnya opened fire on rebel positions.[16]

The land campaign started on 30 September, but more important had been the attraction campaign of the Ministry of Interior police and the Federal Security Service. As part of their intelligence functions, these agencies had been quietly approaching Chechen war lords and their subordinates; the goal was to persuade as many as possible of the rebels to switch sides and join the Russian effort. These often frustrating and difficult conversations required patience and time to yield results, but even if they failed, at least the agents identified the rebel groups who should be the main targets for the Russian military offensive.

The Russian forces rolled across northern Chechnya and encountered few pockets of resistance. On 5 October 1999 troops had reached the Terek Valley, and already some units were pushing south of the river into friendly villages. However, the campaign had not been a cakewalk, and over 155 soldiers died in the combat and hundreds more were wounded. Because civilian casualties and property damages were very modest, Russia felt comfortable in allowing in this first stage of the war the presence of both Russian and foreign correspondents, who followed the relentless Russian advance to the Terek River.[17]

Western powers had condemned the invasion even before it began. The Europeans were very harsh in their criticism of Russia, and they insisted that no military solution was possible for this Islamic revolt. The U.S. also joined in placing blame upon Russia.[18]

The Kremlin expected this criticism and was making sure that the Second Chechnya War not a repeat of the first one. Just like Defense Ministry was trying to compensate for the glaring weaknesses of the Russian military, so the Kremlin attempted to minimize the hostility of the West. Everyone knew that the excessive media coverage of the First Chechnya War had given a tremendous boost to the rebels, and Moscow was determined to prevent this from happening again. Correspondents could follow the swift and Russian advance across the northern third of Chechnya in September 1999, but once the savage combat began south of the Terek River, the Defense Ministry prohibited any independent television coverage and also blocked the entry of NGOs. Foreign correspondents for their part were afraid to enter into Chechnya, because the lawlessness made them easy targets for kidnapping and even murder by the criminal gangs of war lords.[19]

The Kremlin did not impose censorship on the newspapers, and those Russian journalists who somehow sneaked into the region filed reports published weeks or even months after the fact. The controls over the media resembled those the U.S. had imposed during the Vietnam War and were never as extreme as those Britain applied during the Malaya insurgency. Without a daily stream of gory images on television to feed the anti–Russian hysteria, it became harder in the West to rally criticism against the military offensive in Chechnya.

The West sought to bypass the controls on the media by seeking to obtain reports from international agencies, but here again Moscow controlled all the cards. Under extreme pressure Russia had authorized the presence of the "OSCE Assistance Group" in 1995, but the lawlessness in the region after the end of the first war made its functioning impossible. Fearing for the lives of its personnel, the Group shifted its base to Moscow in 1998 and thus lacked a permanent presence on the ground when the war resumed in September 1999. Then it was an easy matter to block the return of OSCE on the grounds that Moscow could not guarantee the safety of its members.[20]

Showdown in Istanbul

Keeping OSCE out of Chechnya was important not just to dry up the flow of information but to prevent any "internationalization" of the war. From the start the Kremlin argued that this was an internal matter not requiring the involvement of foreign countries. The West insisted on the return of OSCE to Chechnya because the presence of this international organization undermined Moscow's argument. In many meetings Secretary of State Madelaine Albright brought up the matter with Russian officials who ignored her requests.[21]

In similar deadlocks in the past during the Boris Yeltsin administration, President Bill Clinton had used his ascendancy over the Russian president to attain U.S. goals. A familiar pattern had repeated itself over the years with Yeltsin first opposing the U.S. in public and then in private caving in to the demands of Clinton. The unexpected showdown came at OSCE summit in Istanbul. As expected, Yeltsin opened the public meeting on 18 November 1999 with the predictable statement that Chechnya was an internal matter and with harsh comments about countries who tried to intervene in Russian internal affairs.[22]

The language had been very virulent but still within the range of past performances. When Clinton began a public rebuttal, an angry Yeltsin took off his headphones and seemed ready to start pounding on the table as his predecessor Nikita Khrushchev had once done at the United Nations. Yeltsin was starting to get up to leave in the middle of Clinton's speech when words whispered by a Russian diplomat avoided a public spectacle.[23]

The most shocking development was yet to come at the private meeting between the two leaders. Clinton dismissed the public meeting as theater for domestic consumption, and then he proceeded to extract approval as he had always done before. But this time Yeltsin began an even harsher attack against those who wanted to meddle in Russian internal affairs. After Kosovo Yeltsin at last stood up and defended Russian interests. He had experienced a discovery and with a sense of bitterness realized that for all these years he had been played for a fool, but not this last time.[24]

In reality Yeltsin was preparing the ground for his successor, who faced the immense task of repairing Russia's status as a world power. It turned out that Yeltsin's virtuoso performance at the Istanbul summit in November 1999 was his swan song on the international arena. To everyone's surprise he announced his retirement on 31 December 1999 and appointed as acting president Vladimir Putin. The Chechnya issue was in the hands of a new individual, who won on the first round the election for president on 26 March 2000.

International Organizations and Chechnya

The succession process in Russia did not delay the efforts in the West to intervene in Chechnya. Western powers assumed that the Chechen rebels were not fanatical Islamic radicals and were rational individuals amenable to arguments. Beginning with a resolution of the Parliamentary Assembly of the Council of Europe on 4 November 1999, Western powers on many occasions demanded an immediate ceasefire and the start of negotiations to reach a political solution. The International Monetary Fund joined the campaign by halting its loans to Russia in early December 1999. Negotiations were appropriate among civilized peoples but not when dealing with the first waves of the Islamic radical onslaught appearing in many parts of the word. The West did not heed the clear warning of January 2000 when the Taliban of Afghanistan became the only country ever to have recognized the independence of Chechnya. U.S. officials even went so far as to meet with Chechen representatives in January and February 2000.[25]

The Europeans were the most emphatic in condemning Russia for its use of force and were threatening economic sanctions. The Europeans were drifting into the dream of creating peace and harmony across a violent world and saw the Chechnya War as a clear violation of international law and fundamental human principles. The European Union took the lead in taking action against Russia over Chechnya. In January 2000 the European Union imposed mild sanctions on Russia and threatened to take even harsher measures if Russia did not halt its campaign against the rebels. The ineffectiveness of these measures and a backlash from business groups persuaded the European Union to abandon any reprisals and to resume dialogue with the new Putin administration in May 2000.[26]

From the start the U.S. response had been less forceful because two groups struggled to shape policy toward Chechnya. In the late Clinton administration it was becoming hard to ignore the many intelligence reports reaching Washington about the growing threat from the spreading Islamic radicalization. The evidence indicated that Chechnya was a small part of this Islamic movement. It made sense for the U.S. to support Russia in its war against the Chechen rebels and as part of the global effort to halt the march of Islamic radicalization.[27]

The second group was the traditional Cold Warriors who saw the revolt of Chechnya as an opportunity to weaken Russia and start its disintegration into mini-states. The Cold Warriors had also been the driving force behind the expansion of NATO, and they dreamed at the least of encircling the Russian Federation with NATO member states. The Cold Warriors enjoyed substantial support in the U.S. Congress. It has been very easy for influential Americans to arouse anti–Russian feeling in the U.S. Congress.[28]

The struggle between the pro–Russia supporters and the Cold Warriors over control of U.S. policy slowed Washington's response to the Second Chechnya War and left the path open for indignant Europeans to take the lead. After the European Union lost interest in the matter, other bodies took up the struggle. The refusal of Russia to accept the November 1999 call of the Parliamentary Assembly of the Council of Europe for an immediate ceasefire was the breaking point. In reprisal, this body on 6 April 2000 stripped the Russian delegation of its voting rights. Russia saw this drastic action as another example of double standards, because that same body had refused to condemn NATO bombing of Serbia.[29]

The Europeans also pursued a parallel effort in the UN Human Rights Commission and obtained a similar resolution on 25 April 2000. This resolution was most unusual because the UN Commission went beyond its jurisdiction of human rights to demand an immediate ceasefire and the start of negotiations with the Chechen rebels; the U.S. despite initial reluctance, did vote for the European resolution which passed 27 to 7. The resolution in the UN Human Rights Commission and the stripping of Russian voting rights in the Parliamentary Assembly seemed like major setbacks for Moscow but were in reality the high point of the campaign over Chechnya. An early indication that the campaign over Chechnya had peaked came on 27 June 2000 when the Committee of Ministers of the Council of Europe refused to consider the expulsion of Russia.[30]

Russia ignored the resolution of the UN Human Rights Commission. The U.S. used this non-compliance as the reason to request a strong condemnation of Russian actions in Chechnya. The Russian veto blocked any action in the Security Council and in the General Assembly the U.S. lacked the votes to pass a resolution. And when in October 2000 the U.S. asked the members of the European Union to introduce the General Assembly resolution asking Russia to comply with the demands of the UN Commission on Human Rights, the attempt gained little support. The failure to achieve anything demoralized the Europeans, and "some have explained the European Union's lack of resolve as Chechnya fatigue."[31]

In a major setback for the anti–Russian campaign, the Parliamentary Assembly of the Council of Europe restored the voting rights to the Russian delegation on 25 January 2001.[32] Seeing the European front collapsing, the incoming George W. Bush administration took a harsher line on Chechnya than its predecessor. Secretary of State Colin Powell pressed the Russians hard in his meeting of 11 May 2001 and reaffirmed the Western cliché that "a military solution to the conflict is not possible."[33] Powell demanded that the OSCE Group gain entry to Chechnya, because "the time is right for pushing the Russians for concrete action." But Russians associated OSCE with the humiliating Khasavyurt Agreement of 31 August 1996 ending the First Chechnya War, so compliance with the U.S. request was impossible. Rather than just say no to U.S. demands, Russian officials promised to discuss steps to assure the safety of OSCE officials once the Kremlin authorized their return to Chechnya.³⁴

Control over the media and the end of conventional warfare were draining the energy from Western efforts to intervene in Chechnya. Russia controlled all important centers in the country and the flat northern terrain; only in the southern mountainous region did the rebels still offer scattered resistance. Without shocking images it was hard to impact television viewers, and the dull published accounts of guerrilla raids could not grab the attention of a majority of readers.

The U.S. could still do a lot of damage to Russia even without European cooperation. Bill Clinton promised to suspend American assistance but did not make any cuts. In contrast, his successor George W. Bush had spoken during the presidential campaign of imposing harsh economic sanctions. The Kremlin still had two weak spots. The recovery from the 1998 August economic crisis was still not complete, and Russia needed more time to return to a stage of prosperous growth. U.S. sanctions could well dampen and at least delay economic recovery and deter foreign investment. On the military front, the Russian army was winning but still required several years to achieve a complete victory. Russian troops and police still suffered from many weaknesses and sometimes lacked the abundance of equipment, such as helicopters, that their Soviet predecessors in Afghanistan had possessed. Should the U.S. decide to provide funds and modern weapons to the Chechens, the insurgency could well drag on indefinitely.³⁵

President Putin realized that given the weaknesses of the Russian army, it was imperative to keep the U.S. out of the conflict. He was the first to realize that with no clear victory in sight, Russia was going to have to sacrifice many things to make sure that the U.S. stayed at least neutral about Chechnya. He sensed that the opportunity lay in the emerging struggle against Islamic fundamentalism. Not just U.S. agencies but also Russian intelligence were monitoring the increasing radicalization of Islamic groups across many countries, and it made sense for the U.S. to accept Russia as an ally in this new struggle.

On 9 September 2001 Putin telephoned Bush to report that the Taliban had assassinated a pro–Russian leader in Afghanistan and that this act formed part of a larger Islamic offensive set to take place across the world. In addition, Putin reported that his intelligence services believed some spectacular action was imminent over the next few days but that no further details were available. On 11 September when Islamic terrorists struck the Pentagon in Washington, D.C., and the Twin Towers in New York City, Putin was the first leader to phone the White House to express his solidarity and support.³⁶

The 9/11 attacks pushed President Bush into the camp of those officials who since the late Clinton years had been urging close collaboration with Russia everywhere against the Islamic threat. In effect, the 9/11 attacks knocked the wind out of Western efforts to intervene in Chechnya against Russia. But the logic of cooperation with the U.S. on the war against Islamic radicals likewise imposed obligations on Russia in the usual format of a *quid pro quo*. The most serious concession was Russian acceptance of U.S. bases in the former Soviet republics of Central Asia. Once the 9/11 terrorist attacks were traced back to the Taliban in Afghanistan, it was inevitable that the U.S. would strike back. But any campaign against Afghanistan had a greater chance of success if U.S. forces could establish bases in the former Soviet republics of Central Asia. At a contentious meeting in Sochi on 22 September 2001 Putin overruled the objections of his generals to the entry of U.S. forces into Central Asia. In reality the Russian generals enjoyed little credibility because of their failure to deliver on their promises of a quick and easy victory in Chechnya.³⁷

With the U.S. supporting the campaign in Chechnya, Russia gained the opportunity to reduce the involvement of other parties in the war. The first step was to restrain OSCE, an organization requiring consensus for its activities. When in December 2002 the vote came to extend the life of the OSCE Group in Chechnya, Russia expressed its opposition and thereby excluded this organization from playing a role in the war.³⁸

The end of Western efforts to intervene in Chechnya came at the showdown in the UN Commission for Human Rights in April 2003. Twenty-two countries co-sponsored a resolution accusing Russia of human rights violations. The draft was milder than the one of 2000 but still demanded that Russia allow the entry of media into the region. A fierce struggle ensued behind the scenes over the resolution. The U.S. had refused to be one of the co-sponsors, and although it voted for the resolution, American diplomats did not lobby to secure its passage. In a sharp reversal from the vote in 2000, the resolution received only 15 votes in favor and lost by a vote of 21 against.³⁹

Skirmishing over Russia's role in Chechnya was far from over, but the opportunity to pressure the Kremlin declined fast after the last Chechen offensive in 2004 ended in failure. In 2005 Chechnya became one of the safest places in Russia. And to the consternation of many in the West, Russia did find a military solution for Chechnya. As the issue receded from world attention, the Kremlin recovered the freedom to expand its relations with the West, as the next chapter reveals.

8

Bridges to the West

In the months prior to the attacks of September 11, the U.S.-Russia and NATO-Russia relationships were stuck somewhere between friend and foe. [...] After September 11, however, there was a dramatic improvement in relations between the U.S. and Russia as well as between NATO and Russia.—Hilary Driscoll[1]

Russia Turns to the West

U.S. support for the Russian effort to crush the revolt in Chechnya was only the beginning of cooperation between the two countries. In a first sign of goodwill, Vladimir Putin told George W. Bush that Russia was cancelling its naval maneuvers in the Pacific so as not to distract the U.S. military. Putin also announced the start of intelligence sharing with the West on terrorist and Islamic groups.[2]

Once the U.S. confirmed after the 9/11 attacks that the Al-Qaeda militants had trained in Afghanistan, a military strike against the Taliban government was inevitable. Russia offered to share detailed tactical information on Afghanistan with the U.S. military and intensified its support for the Northern Alliance, the only armed opposition group still resisting the Taliban in that country. Because of the legacy of the Soviet-Afghan War, the Kremlin ruled out the participation of Russian ground troops in Afghanistan. In reality the Russian military, already bogged down in Chechnya, was in no condition to assume another commitment.[3]

Washington appreciated the Russian cooperation but had additional requests to make. When the time came for American troops to enter Afghanistan, supporting them posed a logistical nightmare. The Kremlin gave the U.S. permission to ship non-lethal supplies and equipment across Russia to Afghanistan. The request did not extend to lethal items because the U.S. hoped to establish support bases near Afghanistan in the former Soviet republics of Central Asia. The Russian military and most Kremlin officials considered Central Asia to be their backyard and were angry about having Americans bases in the region. But these were the same generals who in late 1999 had argued for a quick and easy victory if Russian troops moved south of the Terek River in what turned out to be the quagmire in Chechnya. At a contentious meeting in Sochi on 22 September 2001, Putin overruled the objections of his generals. When Putin brought the matter before the Duma, at first only the pro–Western parties supported the establishment of the American bases in Central Asia. But once the rest of the political parties realized that the Kremlin had already made the decision, they too acquiesced.[4]

Putin saw the 9/11 attack as providing Russia with a great opportunity to reach out to the West, and he was determined to make the most of the moment. In a surprise decision, on 17 October 2001 Russia announced the closing of its naval base of Camranh Bay in Vietnam and the listening post in Lourdes, Cuba. Both facilities had

69

long since lost any military value, but they remained as a symbol of Moscow's commitment to those two regimes. The abandonment of always loyal Cuba was cruel when its government had been one of the few to side with Russia on the resolutions about Chechnya in the U.N. Human Rights Commission.[5]

Some years later Putin recognized that abandoning Cuba had been a mistake, and Russia made amends with generous compensation for one of its most loyal allies. But in the months after 9/11, the Kremlin was trying to promote stronger bonds with the West, and as part of this campaign toned down its criticisms about the entry of the Baltic Republics into NATO. Poland, Hungary, and the Czech Republic had already joined the military alliance in March 1999, and Russia resigned itself to membership for the rest of Eastern European countries.[6]

The admission of the Baltic Republics was a different proposition because NATO was entering the territory of the former Soviet Union. The threat for Russia was immediate, because for the first time since the expulsion of the Nazi invaders in 1944, St. Petersburg was once again within range of hostile fire. And NATO flaunted its intention to welcome other former Soviet republics into the military alliance. The Cold Warriors saw the opportunity to encircle Russia with hostile states, in effect to achieve at last the strategy of containment the West had failed to complete during the struggle against the Soviet Union.

The only way that Russia could have stopped the admission of the Baltic Republics into NATO was to launch a preemptive military operation such as the seizure of ports and crossroads to choke those countries into submission. But the Russian military was in no condition to carry out any major operation while stuck in the quagmire of Chechnya. Also, the Russian economy was still too weak to withstand the crippling blows of financial sanctions.

Accepting the entry of the Baltic Republics into NATO as inevitable, the Kremlin nevertheless hoped that this bitter pill could be sweetened by reaching out to the West. History provided an easy precedent, when Bill Clinton had delayed the entry of Poland, Hungary, and the Czech Republic into NATO until after the reelection of Boris Yeltsin; the West could have extended the same courtesy to Putin until after his reelection.

NATO also needed to give assurances that membership did not mean halting compliance with the standards that the Organization for Security and Cooperation in Europe (OSCE) established for protecting the rights of ethnic Russians in the Baltic Republics. This did not happen, and Russian minorities in Estonia and Latvia saw their status fall to that of second-class residents. The West believed that preventing the wholesale expulsion of the Russian minorities from the Baltics had been more than adequate compensation.[7]

In later years Russians complained that the cooperation had been a one-way street with the West taking a lot and giving very little. This conclusion does not explain why the West refused to seize this once-in-a-lifetime opportunity to build solid and lasting bonds with Russia. Policy makers in the U.S. have been divided between those who favor improving ties with Russia and the Cold Warriors who want confrontation. When the Kremlin made conciliatory moves toward the West, the establishment fell into paralysis over how to respond. The lowest common denominator was to support the Russian campaign in Chechnya against Islamic radicals, as the previous chapter explained. But going beyond grudging support on Chechnya proved impossible, and the months slipped by without any other goodwill gesture to Russia.

What brought Russia and the United States together was the 9/11 attack, but then the world was left waiting for months and years for Islamic radicalism to strike another big blow. Intelligence and police agencies were able to block the isolated terrorist groups existing under the loose banner of Al-Qaeda. The failure of Islamic radicalism to launch new attacks in the years after 9/11 diminished the urgency in the West to form an alliance with Russia. The Kremlin for its part knew what weak cards it held and contrary to speculation in the West, did not ask the *quid pro quo* of halting NATO expansion as the price for Russian support in the fight against Islamic radicalism.[8]

The desire of Russia to cooperate in the struggle against Islamic terrorism had created an environment favorable to improving relations with the West. By a stroke of good luck, the timing could not have been better for the entry into force of the Open Skies Treaty.

Open Skies Treaty

The treaty established complex rules for the member countries to conduct aerial surveillance over their territories. The treaty dated back to 24 March 1992, and the U.S. Senate approved it on 3 November 1993. But without Russian participation, the treaty was meaningless. To sway a skeptical Russia to ratify the treaty, the main signatories pledged a favorable interpretation of its clauses. Sweetening the pill worked, and after a sufficient number of ratifications by member states, the treaty entered into force on 1 January 2002. The staff for the program found a congenial home inside the headquarters in Vienna of OSCE (Organization for Security and Cooperation in Europe).[9]

Organizing and carrying out the flights already posed a substantial challenge. Adverse weather conditions over Russia frequently forced the postponement of many missions. The first Russian overflight over the U.S. took place in August 2002, and the first U.S. plane flew over Russia in December of that year. The Open Skies program reached 500 completed flights in 2008; about 10 percent were U.S. missions. In a special ceremony in front of the imperial palace in Vienna, the release of 500 balloons celebrated a rare success story in cooperation between the West and Russia.[10]

The U.S. was not satisfied with this accomplishment and was looking for any pretext or incident to pounce on Russia. When in 2006 Latvia asked for a suspension of flights over its territory for one month, Russia—in keeping with the spirit of the treaty—had not raised any objection, even though the reason for the suspension was a meeting of NATO ministers in that country. But when in April 2008 Russia asked for a one-week delay in overflights because a rare combination of religious holidays had created a shortage of hotel rooms for visiting crews, the U.S. saw the opportunity to embarrass Russia for having violated the treaty. This unexpected outburst caught by surprise those few Russian diplomats who still believed in the benevolent intentions of the West. Angry Russian diplomats considered the Western comments to be proof of a "double standard" and called the statements "over the top, unfair, and harsh."[11]

Russia made arrangements so that the delayed flights could take place a little later, and the public uproar subsided. But the U.S. could not savor for long its having scored propaganda points against Russia because the disturbing news came that Britain intended to abandon its flights in the Open Skies program. The only suitable British airplane for the missions was the Andover, but it had reached the end of its lifespan and was nothing more than a "bucket of bolts flying in formation."[12] Britain did not possess a replacement plane, and did not want to lease a substitute plane, such as the Swedish Saab.

The unstated underlying reason for

Britain's withdrawal was that the Open Skies flights had lost all military and intelligence value, because Russia no longer posed any armed threat to the West. At that moment even Britain understood the reality, but the Cold Warriors in the U.S. could not allow its loyal ally to break from the accepted view that Russia posed a significant military threat. The U.S. worried not only about the cancellation of the British flights but also over the concern that if other countries likewise ceased to fear Russia, then all the quotas of flights over that country would be lost. The Cold Warriors in the U.S. needed to be inciting fears to keep the many skeptical Europeans following the anti–Russian line.[13]

Nuclear Weapons

At the start of 2002, the ratification process for START II seemed hopeless. This proposed treaty reduced the nuclear warheads to 3,500, a number lower than the maximum of 6,000 warheads allowed under START I. The proposed treaty also limited the number of delivery vehicles, in particular the intercontinental ballistic missiles (ICBMs), and also prohibited the deployment of "multiple independently targetable reentry vehicles" (MIRVs). With great enthusiasm George W.H. Bush and Boris Yeltsin signed the treaty on 3 January 1993, but by the time the son of the American president occupied the White House in 2001, the treaty had still not entered into force. The U.S. Senate took its time, and on 26 January 1996 ratified the treaty. On the Russian side a series of unfortunate events delayed ratification. A major obstacle came in April 1999 when the Russian legislature postponed consideration of the treaty because NATO began to bomb Serbia. Approval for the treaty at last came on 14 April 2000, but the Russian legislature added the provision that ratification was contingent on U.S. adherence to the 1972 Anti-Ballistic Missile Treaty.[14]

This condition left the treaty in legal limbo, because the U.S. Senate did not like to have its authority constrained by any foreign country. For its part, Russia had never been satisfied with START II because many of the country's nuclear warheads were deteriorating and the cost of maintaining the 3,500 old ones was much higher than for the U.S. with a modern arsenal. The Kremlin wanted to reduce the number of warheads, so when George Bush proposed that both leaders announce additional reductions, Vladimir Putin saw an opportunity to reach a deal.[15]

The Kremlin was suspicious of personal promises between heads of states, because even if written down and given the lofty sounding term of "executive agreements," they still could be abandoned at a moment's notice. Instead a treaty promised a more lasting situation, and even if repealed, a process of months or even years would ensue before the treaty was no longer in force. Because Bush was obtaining everything he wanted in the deal, he was open to writing a new agreement, one of the briefest of major treaties in recent times. In five clauses and 500 words, the two sides signed the Strategic Offensive Reductions Treaty (SORT) on 24 May 2002. The new treaty lowered the number of "deliverable" nuclear warheads to a maximum of 2,200, with the reduction taking place over a period of ten years. Riding on the wave of U.S.-Russian cooperation after 9/11, the treaty sailed through the U.S. Senate to obtain unanimous ratification. Approval in the Russian Duma proved harder because by then the U.S. invasion of Iraq had aroused considerable anger throughout the world. The treaty squeaked by with the minimum requirement of two-thirds of the votes on 14 May 2003.[16]

The treaty entered into force on 1 June 2003, but already critics were busy denouncing its lack of enforcement mechanisms and its exclusive focus on "deliverable" nuclear warheads. The criticisms were unfair, because SORT was an amendment to START II whose book-long text contained all the details that any legal eagle could want. An almost unheard of and possibly unique event in international relations had occurred: two countries adopted a binding amendment to a proposed treaty (START II) that never entered into force.[17]

On 13 June 2002 the U.S. announced its withdrawal from the 1972 Anti-Ballistic Missile Treaty. Adherence to this treaty had been the condition the Russian Duma had placed for ratification of START II. Promptly the next day on 14 June Russia announced its withdrawal from START II. Diplomats on both sides scrambled to do damage control and pointed to the still not ratified SORT bill signed just the month before on 24 May 2002, which seemed to be a better treaty because of the larger reduction in nuclear warheads. Both countries realized that the abandonment of START II could send a chilling message to the world that the two nuclear superpowers did not want to reduce their arsenals. The Bush and the Putin administrations both worked hard to obtain legislative approval for SORT, and their efforts paid off when the treaty entered into force less than a year later on 14 May 2003.[18]

At least on the surface the damage from the abandonment of START II had been patched up, but both countries realized that the existing arrangement of START I plus SORT was inadequate to meet the changed circumstances in the world. Negotiations began on a new treaty, but as so often happened when a sense of urgency was lacking, no concrete results were forthcoming. As the years passed by, the need to do something became more pressing, because START I was set to expire on 5 December 2009. And by then the task of finding a replacement treaty for START I became the responsibility of another U.S. administration.

The Problem of NATO

Towering over all issues of relations with the West was NATO. The entry of Poland, Hungary, and the Czech Republic in March 1999 did not slow the drive to expand the military alliance, and the Cold Warriors pressed hard to bring many new states into NATO as soon as possible.[19] The establishment of the NATO-Russia Permanent Joint Council in 1997 had been a sop to Moscow and had "given Russia zero influence over the alliance's actions."[20] Instead the West used the Council to attack Russia over its Chechnya policy. Hostility to NATO intensified in Russia except in the shrinking pro–Western political parties.[21]

Shortly after taking office in 2000, Vladimir Putin raised with Western leaders the possibility that Russia might become a member of NATO. This idea was very controversial inside Russia, but before he could try to secure domestic acceptance, he needed the wholehearted approval of the West. German Chancellor Gerhard Schröder supported Russian entry, while British Prime Minister Tony Blair was sympathetic and insisted that whether this or another proposal, the West needed to find new mechanisms to placate Russia.[22]

Putin was reviving in 2000 the proposal that Mikhail Gorbachev had made three times to the George H.W. Bush administration in 1990; this time the Russian president hoped that George W. Bush would be more supportive than his father had been. Sensing a favorable climate, the Policy Planning Staff of the State Department proposed that NATO invite Russia to join. This agency was not some rogue group of disaffected bureaucrats but represented the view that Russia needed to be accepted as a full partner in all institutions if world peace had any chance of becoming a reality in the foreseeable future. As confirmation of this view, former Secretary of State James Baker published an article urging that the West offer Russia the possibility of joining NATO.[23]

These ideas plunged the Cold Warriors into paranoia, but they had not been idle and were ready with a counterblow. Standard operating procedure over the decades has been the ploy of using a spy scandal to derail even the slimmest chance of improving relations with Russia. In March 2001 the revelation that Robert P. Hanssen had been a spy inside the FBI triggered the expulsion of 50 Russian diplomats on the questionable argument that they all had participated in handling this single mole. Moscow retaliated with the same number, until both sides agreed to halt the expulsions before there was nobody left in either country's embassies.[24]

The resulting spy hoopla made Russia unacceptable to the American public for entry into NATO, but European countries did not stop their campaign on behalf of Russian membership. The new Prime Minister of Italy, Silvio Berlusconi, became the most forceful advocate for Russia, and he went so far as to clamor for Russian entry not just into NATO but also into the European Union. Critics then and later demonized Berlusconi in an attempt to portray his pro–Russian policy as somewhat insane, when in reality he was espousing the prevailing public opinion in Italy. After Germany, Russia had become the second most important trading partner for Italy. The ties between Russia and Italy were even stronger because of the close friendship between Berlusconi and Putin.[25]

Berlusconi was impatient to bring Russia into NATO, and in a preemptive move to prevent that possibility, the Cold Warriors proposed to create a new body to replace the ineffective Permanent Joint Council and to welcome Russian generals and a large diplomatic staff including an ambassador into NATO headquarters in Brussels. In reciprocity, Russia offered to accept the presence of NATO generals and officials in a facility in Moscow. The offer was too much for the Cold Warriors.[26] "The Russian proposals are intended to operate in the context of a more general integration of Russia into NATO activities and its structure than we and allies can envision or support," and the proposal was dismissed as reflecting "the persistence of a Soviet-style perspective in Russian Foreign Ministry thinking."[27]

Russian entry into NATO never had a chance, because "many participants in this process impose one more condition for membership that Russia can never satisfy— namely that the candidate not *be* Russia."[28] Berlusconi, realizing that the West was not yet ready to grant full membership to Russia in the military alliance, decided to support the establishment of a NATO-Russia Council as a first step toward the ultimate goal of full integration into European institutions. He believed that the frequent contact of Russian officials with their NATO counterparts in Brussels and Moscow was favorable to the creation of personal bonds among officials of both sides, just as he had done with his close friend Putin.

This intimate and constant contact with Russians worried the Cold Warriors who were in no rush to conclude the negotiations. Repeated messages from Berlusconi to Bush to accelerate the negotiations persuaded the American side to drop their objections to what was after all a harmless arrangement. The original intention had been to sign a new agreement in the scheduled Prague Summit of November 2002, but Berlusconi knew that Putin could not attend a summit announcing the expansion of NATO. As an incentive to conclude the talks ahead of schedule, Berlusconi offered the bait of paying for a huge production in Rome to celebrate the signing of the treaty on 28 May 2002. Italy spared no expense to put on a grand spectacle, and the ceremony was a huge success. For Berlusconi this new agreement was supposed to be just the first of many more arrangements to link Russia closer to Europe.[29]

Berlusconi had done everything he could at that moment to recognize the place Russia already held in the world stage. After the celebrations in Rome, it was time to bring Russia back to earth with the bad news. First of all, after an initial period of optimism, the new NATO-Russia Council turned out to have the same flaws of its predecessor. Western countries resumed their practice of meeting beforehand to form a common front against Russia in the new Council.[30]

Second, the West proceeded with plans to admit the Baltic Republics into NATO. Italy blocked their entry but it also wanted to bring Rumania and Bulgaria into the alliance. To overcome the resistance to the entry of Rumania and Bulgaria, Italy compromised by accepting the admission of the Baltic Republics. In what has been named "The Big Bang," at the Prague Summit of 21 November 2002 NATO announced that the Baltic Republics, Bulgaria, Rumania, Slovakia, and Slovenia were next in line to become members of the military alliance. The Prague Declaration ratified the intention of NATO to receive additional members in the future. Western leaders wanted Putin to assist the ceremony, but this was like rubbing salt in the wound, and only the Russian Foreign Minister attended to report on events.[31]

The admission of the Eastern European countries was not a major concern for Russia, but the entry of the Baltic Republics raised alarm bells in Moscow. Russia had given many warnings about NATO expansion but had been helpless to respond. Ukraine had been first country to conclude that Russia was too paralyzed to react. The dangerous assumption that Russia was a pliant paper tiger was spreading across NATO members and even in Georgia. And as long as Russia had a weak military and a struggling economy, the conclusion remained valid, as Kremlin officials well realized. But these weaknesses did not mean that Russia lacked any influence on world affairs, and the episode of the U.S. invasion of Iraq showed for the first time that Russia could not be taken for granted.

9

Russia and the U.S. Invasion of Iraq

Punish France, forgive Russia, ignore Germany.—Condoleezza Rice[1]

Iraq remained an unstable country in the Middle East ever since the Gulf War of 1991. Its ruler, Saddam Hussein, had survived the Western invasion, but at the price of having to comply with many burdensome conditions—including on-site inspections. While the dictator tried to reduce compliance, the Western allies insisted that he fulfill every one of the requirements. A cat-and-mouse game lasting throughout the 1990s ensued, and at times it seemed that a new war might break out this time with the explicit goal of overthrowing Hussein.

Hussein was one of several secular rulers in the Middle East, and he used savage force to remain in power. He destroyed the emerging Islamic fundamentalism and any other challenges to his rule. Hussein also opposed the ayatollahs of Iran. Nobody doubted that Hussein's totalitarian regime was brutal, but his goals did coincide with Western efforts to block the spread both of Islamic fundamentalism and of the ayatollahs of Iran.

Iraq was under severe economic sanctions, and the restrictions on oil exports provided Russian firms with great opportunities. After the fall of the Soviet Union the general retreat of Russia from the Middle East made even more valuable the commercial ties with Iraq. Russian companies found ways to reap huge profits in Iraq, while the bribing of key officials yielded many lucrative contracts in Iraq. When the Russian economy was collapsing in the 1990s, Iraq became an attractive alternative. The economic links of Russia with Iraq were so important, that U.S. diplomats—prone to facile Marxist interpretations—reduced Russia's Iraq policy to purely commercial considerations.[2]

From the end of the Gulf War in 1991 to early 2003 many Russians came to Iraq to earn salaries and fulfill contracts. The Russian government had many advisers scattered across the Iraqi ministries, and officials of both military intelligence (GRU) and the Foreign Intelligence Service (SVR) possessed extensive networks of informants across the country. The messages coming from these many sources was that Iraq offered perhaps unique opportunities for Russian firms to reap profits; nobody reported concerns about Islamic radicals because Hussein had been very thorough in eradicating this threat.

This reality on the ground did not prevent the George W. Bush administration from reaching the false conclusion that Iraq had been involved in the 9/11 attacks. Other books have described in great detail the tortuous and flawed process leading to the irresponsible and baseless accusation that Hussein had acquired weapons of mass destruction. Since at least the 1960s the U.S. State Department has prepared summaries of information on major issues of the day for sharing with allies and sometimes with other countries. These summaries saved other governments the labor of procuring the information at their own cost but almost always contain an implicit slant justifying the U.S. position on a particular issue: no "free" information exists. But the American and Russian reports differed in substance.[3]

Numerous informants and Russian spy satellites confirmed that Iraq did not possess any weapons of mass destruction. Russia had been sharing its intelligence on Islamic radicals since 9/11, and nothing resembling weapons of mass destruction appeared on the radar screen. Had a real threat existed, the initial Russian responses to 9/11 indicated that the Kremlin was ready to support the use of force against Iraq.

The U.S. insisted on an immediate invasion of Iraq to topple Hussein and destroy his weapons of mass destruction. Tony Blair, the British Prime Minister, supported the Bush administration, while both Germany and France seemed sympathetic. The U.S. wanted approval from the UN Security Council for the use of force against Hussein, but Russia was not eager to return to the Cold War role of always being the naysayer. The Kremlin gained some time when Western allies insisted on giving diplomacy a real chance to defuse the looming crisis.[4]

Weeks before the UN Resolution came to a vote, already Russia had been the first country to make its position on Iraq crystal clear. In a meeting in Moscow of 16 October 2002 between Silvio Berlusconi and Vladimir Putin, the Russian president stated that "there were two red lines he could not cross: an automatic trigger for the use of force, and unilateral action by the U.S. without international sanction."[5]

Russian approval was no longer essential for the U.S. invasion, because the situation had changed since the Gulf War of 1991. In that earlier conflict, the U.S. had to consult Mikhail Gorbachev, the last ruler of the Soviet Union, not out of courtesy, but because Soviet troops still faced NATO. The U.S. strategy against Hussein in 1990 had required moving troops out of Europe for deployment against Iraq, but in 2003 the Russian military was in no condition to pose any threat to NATO. The end of the Cold War provided the freedom to deploy the most powerful military in the world as the U.S. saw fit without needing the approval of any country or combination of countries.

The Defiance of Europe

The U.S. was angry with the Russian resistance but regarded it as just an opening gambit and still hoped to persuade a reluctant Kremlin to join what was called "the coalition of the willing." Proof for this optimistic interpretation came when Russia on 8 November 2002 voted for Security Council Resolution 1441 calling for Iraq to dismantle its weapons of mass destruction. The Kremlin had gone along with the resolution in a show of unity with the Western allies even though Russia itself lacked any evidence that Iraq possessed those weapons. However, Russian diplomats had been careful to block amendments to the resolution that would have authorized the U.S. to invade Iraq unilaterally. For his part, Saddam Hussein misplayed his cards and lashed out against Russia. In a fit of rage at the Kremlin for having supported the resolution, he cancelled the huge contract Iraq had awarded over the West Qurna oil fields to Lukoil, one of the Russian energy giants.[6]

France having a veto in the Security Council and Germany holding one of the rotating seats in that body had been reluctant to support U.S. policy, and they became even more skeptical when U.N. inspectors on the ground in Iraq could not locate mass destruction weapons either nuclear or of any other type. France and Germany were still willing to defer to the senior ally and its more impressive intelligence-gathering apparatus. The situation changed when France received photographs of Iraq from its first spy satellite. Because until then Iraq had not been a priority for France, it had taken some time to position the satellite over the region. Once the photographs started to pour in, analysts tied the images to the reports from agents on the ground and reached the irrefutable conclusion that Hussein lacked any weapons of mass destruction. France shared the information with Germany, and Chancellor Gerhard Schröder realized the significance of the evidence. But when France made an attempt to share the intelligence with the U.S., arrogant American officials dismissed the evidence as distortions, errors, or plain hoaxes.[7]

For the European powers, accustomed to follow the U.S., the decision to defy Washington was difficult and traumatic. France and Germany dreaded being the sole members voting against the U.S. resolution. They believed that the U.S. could once again pressure the rotating members of the Security Council to vote in favor of the invasion of Iraq. Already the U.S. had bullied the candidate states for NATO membership to sign a letter supporting the proposed invasion of Iraq, and the U.S. was exerting similar pressure on other members of the Security Council.[8]

France and Germany were terrified about having to defy the U.S., and in desperation they remembered that Russia could be their salvation. Once again Western Europe was repeating the historical pattern of calling on Russia when a dire emergency materialized. France and Germany knew that Russia was opposed to the use of force against Iraq, but they feared a "mini-Yalta" with the U.S. bargaining away something in exchange for Russian support over Iraq. In reality the fear was groundless, because one of the guiding principles of the Vladimir Putin administration has been not to sacrifice principles or friends.

The U.S. came to recognize that Russia could not support a Security Council resolution authorizing the use of force against Iraq but believed that with proper encouragement Russia might take the "Chinese option" of abstaining, thereby leaving France alone to hang in the wind as the sole "traitor." The U.S. decided to make a full-court press to secure UN approval, and as part of that campaign, Secretary of State Colin Powell went in person to make a memorable presentation before the Security Council on 5 February 2003. And in a visible confirmation about the veracity of the claims Powell was making in his speech, he had sitting right behind him CIA director George Tenet.[9]

For some time it seemed that the presentation of Powell had been the high point of his long and distinguished career. Later it became clear that had been the worst moment of his career and also one of the most humiliating moments in U.S. diplomacy. In what ranked as the worst intelligence failure since the Pearl Harbor attack of December 1941, Powell claimed that the world needed to take immediate action to prevent Hussein from launching his weapons of mass destruction. Russia had watched with amusement this outrageous presentation and concluded that nothing had changed.[10]

French president Jacques Chirac and German Chancellor Gerhard Schröder were not so sure, and fearing that the U.S. diplomatic offensive might make Russia waver, they decided to invite Putin to their capitals to insist on the arguments against the Iraq invasion. For the Russian ruler the visits were unnecessary because he had decided already by October 2002 to oppose the invasion, but sensing a rare opening among Western powers, he went anyway. His goals were twofold. First because Russian attempts to dissuade the U.S. from launching a military operation had met with no success, he wanted to see if France and Germany could help him persuade the

U.S. to abandon its mad adventure. Second, he hoped to develop closer ties with France and Germany, in the hope that those countries could deliver what the U.S. had failed to do in several issues vital for Russia. Postponing the expansion of NATO was the highest priority for Russia, but a close second was negotiating a free trade agreement with the European Union. The U.S. had done little on other major issues such as membership in the World Trade Organization and increasing foreign investment in Russia, two areas in which Germany and France could play decisive roles.[11]

After a brief visit to Berlin on 9 February 2003 to solidify ties with German Chancellor Schröder, Putin then travelled the next day to the French capital, "where Chirac arranged for a welcome perhaps unseen for any Russian leaders since Tsar Alexander I's triumphant visit following the defeat of Napoleon."[12] The French president shut down half of Paris and spared no expense to impress his Russian guest. In their talks the two leaders reaffirmed their positions, and Putin achieved his first goal of securing French support to try to persuade the U.S. to abandon its suicidal course. The German chancellor flew in to sign a tripartite declaration opposing the U.S. intention to invade Iraq.[13]

After days of expectation, Russia realized that Washington was not going to heed France and Germany. Putin decided to take another approach to abort the U.S. invasion. Iraq did not have weapons of mass destruction but did have Saddam Hussein as the ruler, and if Russia could persuade him to leave power, the justification for the invasion crumbled. To accomplish this goal, on 22 February Putin entrusted former prime minister Yevgeny Primakov with the task of going to Baghdad to deliver the news to Hussein that he had to resign. The Russian emissary, who was also a former foreign minister and an expert on the Arab world, carried out his secret mission. He delivered the message to Hussein who refused the offer; after four hours in Baghdad Primakov returned to report the failure of his mission to Putin.[14]

With no success in Baghdad, Putin decided to make one last appeal to the U.S. and sent his chief of staff, Alexander Voloshin, to talk to anyone willing to listen in Washington, D.C. Voloshin was an excellent candidate for the mission, although Primakov would have been even better. But the Kremlin knew that U.S. officials dismissed the former prime minister as "a friend of Saddam Hussein," and were unwilling to listen to anything he said. Primakov had been willing to share his lifetime of expertise on the Arab world with the Americans, but the label of "friend of Saddam Hussein" made him toxic. Historically U.S. officials complain that Russians refuse to talk, when so often the blame lies on Americans who do not want even to ask the questions, much less to listen.

The Bush administration, still hoping to win at least a Russian abstention on a Security Council authorization to use force, made all its senior officials available to meet with Voloshin. Beginning with the CIA Director it was clear that U.S. wanted to persuade the Russian representative rather than hear his arguments. One of the crudest ploys was the attempt to link Saddam Hussein with the Chechen rebels as a way to convince Russia to support the invasion of Iraq. Russia knew well that the claim that secular Hussein was somehow supporting the Islamic fundamentalists of Chechnya was preposterous in the extreme.[15]

When the Chechnya gambit did not work, the U.S. Secretary of Commerce turned to an even baser argument. Although it has been a hallowed tradition in the U.S. to denounce Marxism as obsolete and irrelevant, U.S. officials have a tendency to apply Marxist motivations to the actions of other countries. In a crude attempt at bribery, the Secretary of Commerce promised Voloshin that after the invasion Russia would receive oil concessions and preserve its commercial advantages if the Kremlin supported the operation.

After hearing Voloshin report on the failure of his mission, Putin concluded that Russia, in union with France and Germany, had done everything possible to deter the U.S. from its suicidal course. However, Putin was not certain that Iraqi diplomats had dared to deliver this message to Saddam Hussein, and to make sure that the Iraqi ruler knew what was coming, the Russian president sent one last mission to Baghdad. This time Putin asked the speaker of the Duma, Gennady Seleznyov, to convey the sad news to Hussein. As if talking to a terminal patient, Seleznyov explained that there was nothing else that Russia could do to save Hussein. The Iraqi ruler seemed resigned to his fate but predicted that the invasion meant the start of a long struggle for control of the country's resources and its oil deposits.[16]

The American steamroller for the war proceeded forward without interruption, and just a few hours after bombs had begun to fall in Iraq on 24 March 2003, the White House was surprised to receive a telephone call from Putin. The Russian ruler showed a genuine concern for the plight of the American president, and the phone call expressed sympathy for the predicament the U.S. found itself in and which resembled his own when he had launched the Second Chechnya War. The conversation contained the subliminal message that the American president was going to suffer because the U.S. establishment and its intelligence community had misled him. Bush appreciated the call as coming from someone who had been in a similar predicament and could express sincere sympathy.[17]

Putin knew that the Iraq War was the new reality, and that Russia needed the U.S. to continue working together on many other pressing issues. Neither the Iraq War not the waning Second Chechnya War should be obstacles to improving U.S.-Russian relations. What Putin could not have foreseen was that the U.S. unilateral invasion of Iraq had set a very valuable precedent for Russia. When starting in 2014 American female diplomats in hysterical speeches more suited for a cheap soap opera than to the UN Security Council denounced the Russian reunification with Crimea, Russia could refer to the unjustified U.S. invasion of Iraq. The moment of anguish in 2003 turned out to be the best gift possible for Russia during the struggle over Crimea.

10

Seeking Friendships

Relations with European nations are Russia's traditional policy priority. The main goal of Russia's foreign policy in Europe is to build a stable and democratic system of pan-European security and cooperation.—Russian Foreign Policy Concept[1]

The Kremlin hoped that its opposition to the Iraq War meant the start of close ties with France and Germany. But the temporary alliance turned out to be a one-shot affair, and once the urgency of trying to stop the Iraq War passed, relations with Europe returned to business as usual. France bore the brunt of the blame for having tried to block the Iraq War. Silly denunciations of France such as boycotting its wines and giving French fries the new name of "Freedom" fries sheltered Russia from U.S. anger.

Having France as a shield did not mean progress on many issues important to Russia. The NATO-Russia Council proved to be ineffective and was the high mark of collaboration with Russia. Basic steps toward closer economic relations, such as the admission of Russia into the World Trade Organization and the transformation of the Partnership and Cooperation Agreement of 1994 into a free trade zone with the European Union, languished in limbo.

The refusal to go beyond the Partnership and Cooperation Agreement of 1997 erected a wall around Russia and also accentuated the differences with the Western European economies. Instead, had Russia been part of a free trade zone, any association agreements of the European Union with the former Soviet republics would have raised few concerns. Technical commissions and not the rampaging crowds of Ukraine in 2014 could have resolved the minor differences.

In the wide arc stretching from Norway to Turkey the Kremlin strove to improve bilateral relations. The biggest disappointment was Bulgaria. Despite deep historic ties dating back to the nineteenth century and widespread popular sympathy for Russia, Western powers manipulated the Bulgarian government into taking measures hostile to the Kremlin. Relations with Norway warmed during the first decade of the twenty-first century, but this hopeful trend was waning even before the country succumbed to anti–Russian hysteria after the Ukrainian crisis of 2014. But positive results came from countries such as Finland, Hungary, and Turkey.

Keeping Finland Neutral

In contrast to Norway, a member of NATO, Finland was not part of that military alliance but was a member of the European Union. In 1995 Finland, Austria, and Sweden were the last three countries to enter the EU without any expectation of later becoming members of NATO. Subsequent admissions into EU have come with the understanding that those countries would join NATO after a few years. Treaty clauses stipulated the neutrality of Austria (and also of Switzerland), while tradition was the main basis for the neutrality of Finland and Sweden. The possibility of Sweden joining NATO has surfaced after the Ukrainian crisis of 2014, but so far the country has preferred to preserve its traditional neutrality.

Independence from the tsars came to Finland during the Russian Revolution of 1917. The Russo-Finnish War of 1939–1940 proved that in spite of desperate and heroic resistance, the Finns could not defend themselves from Russia. A terrified Finland became an ally of Nazi Germany during World War II, but with the defeat of the Axis powers, Finland was at Russia's mercy. With remarkable foresight, Soviet leader Joseph Stalin decided against annexation and preferred to keep Finland as a buffer state with the West. Modest territorial adjustments in the Karelia region and the payment of compensations satisfied the Soviet Union.[2]

For the U.S. the conflicted history with Russia offered hope of making Finland a member of NATO. The Finns, however, always confronted the geographic reality that they could see Russia with their own eyes but the U.S. was far away across the ocean. When Vladimir Putin became president on 1 January 2000, he made close relations with Finland a high priority. He visited the country at least once a year, and he made sure that other senior Russian officials also came. In contrast, the U.S. almost never sent anyone of a rank higher than ambassador.[3]

Having Putin's ear meant that the often sluggish Russian bureaucracy was fast to respond to issues of concern to Finland. One example was Moscow allowing the Finns to ship out forest products through the Saimaa Canal, which formed part of the territory Russia acquired after World War II. On another economic issue, Russia suspended duties on exports of round wood, a vital input for Finland's paper industry. As an additional sweetener, Russia encouraged Finnish companies to bid on the colossal construction projects of the 2014 Sochi Olympics. Reciprocal measures cost Helsinki almost nothing; for example, Finland authorized using its territorial waters for laying the North Stream gas pipelines to Germany (Sweden also granted similar permission to Gazprom).[4]

A traditional function of the Finnish president after World War II has been to serve as the guarantor of good relations with Russia. Finnish officials were delighted to have Russian figures, and in particular Putin, talk to them not just about bilateral topics but also about global issues. For a small country, these visits gave a glimpse into world crises not otherwise available and, because Putin always welcomed comments from his hosts, Finland gained a sense of having a voice. In contrast, Finland realized that joining NATO meant falling into the ranks of the numerous uninfluential minor member states.[5]

Putin also counted on the Finns, who were good note-takers, to share his remarks with Western powers, and in this way Finland found itself courted by Western diplomats to learn about Russian views.[6] One of Putin's first foreign trips as president was to Finland. Because he was new on the international scene, he strove to make a good impression on his hosts: "Putin was able to name all 26 Finnish-Russian Border Crossings (including the four under construction) which even the Finns could not have done without notes."[7] However, in later foreign trips the Russian president restrained his erudition so as not to embarrass less-gifted world leaders.

The U.S. invasion of Iraq in March 2003 made Finland hesitant to join NATO. The war became so unpopular in Europe, that any credibility the U.S. might have enjoyed vanished. In the elections of 2006 and 2007 NATO membership returned to the political arena, but the Finns decided to conserve their traditional neutrality.[8] The Kremlin was pleased to see the failure of the U.S. campaign to acquire another NATO member state. Even when anti–Russian hysteria swept large parts of Western Europe after the Ukraine crisis of 2014, Finland maintained its traditional neutrality.

Hungary: Surprising Reversal

When the presidents of Finland, Hungary and Russia gathered on 19 July 2007, the summit was a minor diplomatic coup. Estonia, Finland, and Hungary had been holding meetings since the collapse of the Soviet Union to defend the cultural identity of Finno-Ugrian peoples. The majority of the population of Europe belongs to the Indo-European language family, but Finno-Ugrian is the next largest language family. The incident over the Bronze Soldier Statue had strained the relations of Russia with Estonia, and the Kremlin offered to host the summit in one of its republics speaking a Finno-Ugrian language. President Vladimir Putin was the gracious host, and both Finland and Hungary attended to strengthen their ties with Russia.[9]

The ties with Finland were long, but the tilt of Hungary toward Russia was unexpected. The brutal Soviet invasion of Hungary in 1956 seemed to guarantee very hostile anti–Russian policies. Hungary was one of the first three countries of the former Warsaw Pact to join NATO in 1999, and on 1 May 2004 the country became a member of EU. But just a few years later, to the dismay and shock of U.S. diplomats, Hungary drifted toward the Russian side on almost all issues.[10] What accounted for this remarkable reversal?

President Vladimir Putin first buried the past when he apologized in public for the Soviet invasion of 1956, and the Hungarians were satisfied with the apology. Unlike in Estonia with the incident over the Bronze Soldier Statue, a movement to have a referendum on removing the statue of Soviet victory in World War II from the center of Budapest fizzled out. Despite having many survivors alive, the 1956 Soviet invasion faded into history.[11]

Hungary was the country in Europe most dependent on natural gas for its energy needs, and over 80 percent of that gas came from Russia. Hungary strove to fill the resulting trade imbalance by exporting consumer goods to Russia. Gazprom acquired control of the principal distribution facilities in the country, and later Hungary authorized the South Stream pipeline to pass through its territory. This last step was very significant, because South Stream was under Russian control, while the West wanted the countries of the region to support the rival EU pipeline project of Nabucco.[12]

Other Russian firms invested in Hungary, and they purchased important stakes in key companies. However direct investment in the Hungary remained comparable to that of other foreign countries and thus did not make citizens fear a Russian takeover of their economy.[13]

Another factor driving Hungary toward Russia was disenchantment with the EU. By 2007 among Hungarians existed "considerable antipathy toward the European Union." Hungarian minorities inside other European countries continued to suffer ill treatment. Opinion surveys confirmed the widespread prevalence of these views, and in an attempt to maintain citizens loyal to the European idea, the EU lavished funds on Hungary. By 2016 financial contributions to the country were four times larger than revenue collections for the EU. On a longer perspective, Hungary's disillusionment was an early warning of deep-seated mistrust of the Western European project.[14]

U.S. diplomats lived trapped in the past of the 1956 invasion, and with consternation they saw their dreams of having Budapest lead the anti-Russian offensive dissipate. Arrogance was also at play, because the U.S. could not accept the silence of Hungary or much less the country becoming a "neutral ally." U.S. diplomats were outraged that Budapest was "inclined to give Russia the benefit of every doubt."[15] A turning point came when former Prime Minister Yevgeny Primakov made an unofficial visit to Budapest to promote economic ties in his role of president of the Russian Chamber of Trade and Industry. Prior to his arrival he made on 25 May 2007 comments critical of U.S. policy in an interview to a Hungarian publication, but during his visit Hungarian officials did not question those statements. In another perceived insult, Budapest did not even bother to inform the U.S. Embassy about the Primakov visit, much less consult about its appropriateness.

After the Primakov visit, the U.S. ambassador, as if dealing with a banana republic, complained to the Hungarian Prime Minister Ferenc Gyurcsany, who "frankly admitted that the Government of Hungary had completely missed the downturn in U.S.-Russian relations."[16] But the Prime Minister did not apologize, and although he promised closer coordination, the implicit message was that Hungary was not going to comply with U.S. demands.

A sulking U.S. plotted how to get Hungary back in the team of the anti-Russian choir. The policy of waiting seemed to have paid off when in January 2008 Budapest supported the independence of Kosovo. A later chapter will show how divided Europe has been on this issue, but Hungary did take the precaution of explaining its decision to the Russian ambassador.[17] It was the turn of Moscow to accept an adverse decision.

Despite the exception of Kosovo, Hungary remained sympathetic to Russia. In July 2008 the foreign minister explained "that our focus is on implementing our interests, especially those of our business community."[18] These economic concerns influenced a Hungary already predisposed to take Russia's side during the Five Day War with Georgia, which broke out just the next month. Both NATO and the EU took action against Russia, but Hungary gave weak support and was among the countries trying to delay and reduce the reprisals. U.S. and Western diplomats were livid over the refusal of Hungarian officials to join the chorus of voices making anti-Russian statements to the media during August 2008.[19]

Hungary's ties with Russia remained close, and even the wave of anti-Russian hysteria after the crisis in Ukraine of 2014 did not change the relationship. Although Hungary was too small to keep NATO and EU from taking hostile actions against Russia, at every opportunity it joined other countries to minimize sanctions and to push for their repeal. The coincidence of national interests on most issues between Hungary and Russia resulted in the construction of a long-term relationship.

Breakthrough in Turkey

The most important diplomatic success for Russia after the fall of the Soviet Union came in Turkey. The country possessed a thriving economy, a large population, and a strategic location. Turkey was a member of NATO, and during the Cold War had played the role of keeping the Soviet Union bottled up in the Black Sea. With great perception, the Kremlin realized that the West did not accept Turkey despite its membership in NATO.

Unlike Hungary and Finland, Turkey was a Muslim nation, but this did not pose an insurmountable hurdle. Russia had a large Muslim minority and was sensitive to Islam.[20] Economic factors were also very strong, but their role should not be exaggerated. Despite Russia having the strongest economic ties with Germany, these commercial links have not been able to influence Germany's foreign policy to a comparable degree. Two outside events occurred that made Russian economic ties much more important to Turkey than they were to Germany.

After a long and agonizing period of years of uncertainty and anxiety, most Turks came to the harsh conclusion that the EU did not want the country to become a member. The application process was also demeaning, because arrogant Europeanists imposed on Turkey a whole set of often humiliating requirements in order to assimilate into the secular West. Many of these changes required modifying not just legislation and the constitution but also the entire way of life for the country in economic, social, and even cultural realms.

The decisive break with the U.S. came during the U.S. invasion of Iraq in 2003. U.S. war plans called for using Turkey as a staging base for launching the northern part of the invasion of Iraq: While U.S. troops advanced north from the Persian Gulf, a large army was supposed to march south from Turkey. The U.S. already had forces stationed in Turkey, but in accordance with the NATO charter, each member state had to give permission to use its territories for offensive operations against a third country. When the U.S. requested permission to use Turkish soil to launch the northern part of the invasion of Iraq, Ankara refused.[21]

The subsequent U.S. fiasco in Iraq confirmed the wisdom of the Turkish refusal. The 9/11 attacks had generated considerable sympathy for the U.S. in Turkey just like in many other countries, but that goodwill evaporated with the invasion of Iraq. Across Turkish society and the government, a huge debate still ongoing began about whether the country should remain tied to the West or should instead turn to Russia.[22] The most pessimistic voices believed that "it will take 100 years to overcome the half a millennium of bad blood between the two countries."[23]

The two economies complemented each other. Having about half the population of Russia, Turkey was better poised than any European country to become an economic partner. Russia supplied most of the natural gas to Turkey. After both countries completed the Blue Stream pipeline in the Black Sea in 2003, this direct link lowered delivery costs for gas. In addition, Russia also provided about one-third of the oil for Turkey, even though many other suppliers were available. Trade in other products was brisk, and Russia became Turkey's second largest trading partner, after Germany. Turkish construction companies were involved in rebuilding Moscow and were active in other regions of Russia as well. Many of the contracts for building the infrastructure of the 2014 Sochi Olympics went to Turkish firms. To enhance commercial ties, Turkey pressed for the accession of Russia into the World Trade Organization and into the Organization for Economic Cooperation and Development.[24]

Turkey became a favorite destination for Russian tourists, who came to outnumber the Germans, until then the most numerous. The proximity of Turkey to some parts of Russia and the low cost of living made the country very affordable to Russians of modest income who otherwise could not afford the high expenses of vacations to Western Europe. Turkey offered welcoming people, delicious food, historical and archeological sites, and many beaches. Medical tourism for procedures cheaper than in Russia was also important. Russian tourists were present in large numbers almost everywhere in Turkey.[25]

U.S. diplomats adopted a crude Marxist explanation for Turkey's rapprochement with Russia. The Turkish government, unlike the German, had not resisted the pressures for closer political ties with Russia. The coincidence of interests with Russia turned out to be not just economic but also political and strategic. Both the U.S. and the EU liked to lecture Turkey on what it needed to do to meet Western standards. The tone was often condescending and even arrogant, and this incessant carping irritated the proud Turks. In an updated variety of neo-imperialism, the West demanded complete adherence to its demands.

Instead Russian leaders and diplomats refrained from commenting on domestic issues or civil-military affairs and remained non-judgmental.[26] A certain anxiety preceded meetings with Western officials who complained about Turkish internal affairs; instead, when dealing with Russian representatives, the Turks knew that they could concentrate on the specific issues at hand. In one of many examples, Turkey as a Muslim country was experiencing the Islamic conservatism sweeping through the Middle East. Ankara rejected Islamic fundamentalism but wanted to soften the harsh secularism necessary at the time Kemal Atatürk founded the Turkish Republic. Russia with its large Muslim minority understood the drift of Turkey toward a more traditional Islam, in contrast to a materialistic West trapped in sterile secularism.[27]

Sensing an opening, Russia sent high-level delegations to Turkey and received return visits from senior Turkish officials, starting with the prime minister in 1999. Because Turkey had been a member of NATO since 1952, some observers dismissed these visits as a waste of time for the Kremlin. The skeptics appeared to be right when in July 2000 the Turkish Prime Minister compared the Russian offensive in the Second Chechnya War to the actions of Adolf Hitler against the Jews. These insults did not dismay Kremlin officials who labored to present a true picture. The calm diplomacy paid off when Turkish officials reversed their position and starting in late 2001 condemned the Chechen rebels as terrorists and Islamic extremists.[28]

The threat from Islamic extremism was one of the many strategic issues the two countries needed to discuss. Turkey had no hesitation, because the fear of an invasion from the Soviet Union—the main reason for belonging to NATO—disappeared when the successor state of the Russian Federation no longer shared a common land border with Turkey. Additional reassurance came when Russia declined to establish a protectorate over Adjara in August 2008. And Turkey also was angry at Georgia for having stripped the Adjara region of its autonomy. Among the strategic topics to discuss with Russia, the most important was the Black Sea and NATO.

Black Sea and Straits Convention

The Montreux Convention of 1936 codified the rules for warships passing through the Bosporus and staying in the Black Sea. The signatories recognized that Turkey, the country with the longest coastline in the Black Sea and control of both sides of the Straits, had the final decision on the entry of warships of non-littoral nations and the duration of their stay. Except in wartime, merchant ships of any country enjoyed freedom to come, leave, and loiter in the Black Sea without restrictions. Instead for warships of non-littoral nations, the Montreux Convention placed strict limits on their tonnage and the duration of their stay. And as the final arbitrator, Turkey could at any moment suspend passage of warships, even if no wartime situation existed.[29]

During the Cold War the Montreux Convention was a powerful tool to limit Soviet access to the Mediterranean, although the U.S. never ratified the treaty. After Bulgaria and Rumania became NATO members in 2004, Washington planned to convert the Black Sea into another barrier choking the Russian Federation. The next step was for Ukraine and Georgia to become members of the military alliance and thus almost squeeze Russia out of the Black Sea. Once Azerbaijan joined NATO, the U.S. could project its power even as far as the Caspian Sea.[30] This broader strategy depended on acquiring full control over the Black Sea, but here NATO member Turkey proved to be an insuperable barrier. The Turkish military insisted that only littoral states could participate in naval operations in the Black Sea and excluded NATO.[31]

The Vladimir Putin Visits to Turkey of 2004 and 2009

The implicit alliance between the two countries gained a big boost from the visits of Vladimir Putin to Turkey in 2004 and 2009. The 2004 state visit was the first trip in history by a ruler of Russia to Turkey. The scale of the deployment was huge, and the motorcade in Ankara came to number 150 cars. Along with representatives of state enterprises came hundreds of private Russian businessmen. Putin held long meetings with the leaders of Turkey, and he struck a cordial relation with then Prime Minister Recep Tayyip Erdogan. Both Putin and Erdogan, as rising stars, were the center of attention. The visit ended in a sinister tone for the West, when the Russian Defense Minister and the commander of the Russian navy stayed behind for an extra day to discuss military cooperation with their Turkish counterparts.[32]

Turkey reciprocated with visits to Moscow, and the pattern emerged of the leaders and high officials of two countries meeting to discuss the bilateral issues.[33] The U.S. was slow to realize that Turkey was drifting away, in part because in the sprawling Turkish bureaucracy, pro–U.S. officials handled contacts with American diplomats.

U.S. reliance on its Cold War ally seemed well placed when Ankara supported the independence of Kosovo. This major success for Washington did not disturb a Kremlin well aware of the intense domestic pressure Erdogan was under to recognize Kosovo. Likewise, Ankara shared U.S. concerns about Russia's withdrawal from the Conventional Forces Treaty (CFE). Turkey revealed its real attitude by its coolness toward giving a MAP (Membership Action Plan) to Georgia and Ukraine at the Bucharest meeting of NATO in April 2008. Turkey said it was willing to go along with a consensus, and Georgia described the Turkish position as a pretext to avoid having to say no.[34]

The Kremlin knew better and saw its patience rewarded when Turkey refused to condemn Russia during the Five Day War. The conflict was still raging when Erdogan proceeded with his scheduled trip to Sochi. Ignoring U.S. efforts to isolate Russia after the war with Georgia, Turkey was also trying to delay any NATO reprisals against Russia and was among the first pressing for the return to business as usual in the relations of the military alliance with Russia. No wonder that for U.S. officials the Turkish reaction "smacked of appeasement."[35]

Another momentous visit finished sealing the strong ties between Russia and Turkey, but this time in 2009 Putin was coming not as president but as prime minister. As the U.S. Embassy reported "Russian Prime Minister Putin's August 6 visit to Ankara resulted in a flurry of deals and media frenzy, further heightened by the last-minute participation of Italian Prime Minister Berlusconi."[36] Both Putin and Berlusconi loved to spring surprises, and the unexpected arrival of the Italian Prime Minister found almost all the personnel of the Italian Embassy away on summer vacation. As soon as the Italian Premier learned that Putin was coming to Ankara, he could not resist the opportunity to board a plane to visit his friend.

The excuse for Berlusconi's last-minute trip was to ratify Italy's commitment for the

South Stream gas pipeline over the West's Nabucco gas pipeline. The U.S. in 2008 had blocked the route for South Stream through Bulgaria, and the Russian response was years of patient diplomacy to gain the support of Turkey and also to sign up Greece, Italy, Austria, and Hungary. South Stream bypassed a Ukraine no longer able to play the extortion card of syphoning off gas supplies destined for other countries in Europe.[37]

Turkey did not need South Stream for its own gas consumption, because it was well supplied through the already existing Blue Stream. Another agreement signed during the 6 August 2009 visit called for the construction of Blue Stream II, a parallel pipeline making possible supplying natural gas to Israel, Cyprus, and other countries in the region. Economic links had become important to both countries, and Russia came to surpass no longer just individual countries but the entire EU as the most important trading partner of Turkey.[38]

On almost all issues the Kremlin and Ankara came to agree, and the rare differences did not impede the growth of deep ties. Russia had gained an indispensable ally in Turkey, whose membership in NATO survived as an anachronism from the Cold War.

11

Russia in the Middle East

Russian activism is fundamentally aimed at raising Moscow's profile on the international stage. By positioning itself as a "bridge" between the West and the Muslin world, the government of Russia seeks [...] improved relations with the Muslim world, including greater access to Middle Eastern markets.—U.S. Embassy Moscow[1]

Overview

With Russia collapsing during the grim years of the 1990s, the country could not play a meaningful role in the Middle East or, for that matter, anywhere else in the world. Russian diplomats could do nothing to prevent the U.S. from imposing its will on the Middle East.[2]

The Second Chechnya War precluded any major foreign policy initiatives in the Middle East, yet in a paradox that same conflict persuaded the Kremlin to seek closer ties with the region. The reason behind this move was the urgent need to halt any assistance from Islamic countries to the fundamentalist Chechen rebels. After patient diplomatic work, Turkey came to the conclusion that it was in its best interests to support Russia in the Chechnya War. Similar conversations also persuaded Iran and Saudi Arabia to adopt the same pro–Russian policy.[3]

The countries of the Middle East supported Russia in Chechnya because they too faced challenges from Islamic fundamentalists. Leaders in the region also began turning to Russia for advice and were nostalgic for the years of the Soviet Union when an alternative to the West had existed. The Iraq invasion of March 2003 when the U.S. acted with impunity confirmed the need for a counterweight. The visit to Moscow in 2003 of Crown Prince Abdullah bin Abdul Aziz al Saud—later King of Saudi Arabia—was the formal invitation for Russia to return to the Middle East.[4]

Egypt

The defeat of the Chechen rebels in 2005 opened for Russia the possibility of resuming a meaningful role in the Middle East. Egypt had once been a close ally of the Soviet Union and seemed the logical starting place to revive the Russian presence. In many ways Vladimir Putin was following his fellow citizens who in droves flocked to Egypt; over 90 percent of the revenue Egypt earned from Russia consisted of tourist dollars. In spite of the large sums tourists spent in the country, Russian exports to Egypt were larger than imports by more than $200 million dollars, and none of the exports were petroleum-related.[5]

President Putin came to Egypt on 26–27 April 2005 in a visit that "will be remembered more for its ceremonial and nostalgic aspects than for substantive agreements or strategic realignments."[6] It was not just that the tight U.S. grip on Egypt prevented improving the relationship with Russia. President Hosni Mubarak adopted the policy of trying to diversify his country's foreign relations, but the slow-moving Egyptian bureaucracy proved incapable of rising to the occasion. Russia came ready to sign major cooperation agreements, but the sloppiness and tardiness of the Egyptian bureaucracy blocked action. The Russians felt insulted but as consummate diplomats hid their feelings.

Egypt was far from lost to Russia in spite of the disappointing results from the Putin visit. President Mubarak was embarrassed and tried to make amends by taking frequent trips to Moscow to consult on the many pressing issues of the Middle East. Relations with Egypt grew stronger, and a real blossoming came in the late 2010s.[7]

Algeria

Despite the disappointments of the April 2005 Egypt visit, substantive results came the next year when President Putin visited Algeria on 10 March 2006. The moment was very propitious: relations with France, the former colonial ruler, were at a tense point, and Algeria was looking for support from another world power. Unlike European countries, Russia had never been a colonial power in the region and did not need to explain messy historical episodes from the past. Russia was the natural choice for arms supplier, and during the March 2006 visit Algeria signed contracts to purchase weapons worth as much as seven billion dollars.[8]

The sum at first glance was too much for Algeria to pay, but Russia offered the sweetener of cancelling the large Soviet-era debt. This sufficed to clinch the deal, and soon factories in many remote parts of Russia hummed with activity fulfilling the orders. For a few years Algeria took third place after China and India as the largest market for Russian weapons. The magnitude of the deal set off alarms in bordering Morocco, and in a subsequent trip to that country, Putin in person reassured the king that the Russian weapons could be used only for defense. Other Middle Eastern countries followed the example of Algeria and also wanted to acquire similar armament. Libyan ruler Muammar Qaddafi was one of the last to order Russian weapons; although he had maintained close ties with the Soviet Union, he was too slow in jumping on the Russian bandwagon, a delay that later turned out to be fatal for him.[9]

Despite the importance of arms sales, commerce in general was the driving force in relations with the Middle East in the 2000s. Russia ran up huge trade surpluses because the country possessed in abundance many of the products the region needed. In contrast to European countries, the Middle East did not need to purchase oil and gas from Russia; even the few unfortunate countries in the region without deposits obtained fuel from wealthy neighbors who sometimes even offered price discounts. As another step to facilitate economic exchanges, in 2006 Russia opened in ten Arab countries chambers of commerce such as the Russo-Moroccan and the Russo-Tunisian business councils. An invaluable person in setting up these councils was former Prime Minister Yevgeny Primakov, an Arab scholar with many years of diplomatic postings in the region. Typical of the problems facing the Russo-Tunisian Business Council was the huge trade imbalance: the country imported $357 million in grains, metals, and some petroleum but exported to Russia just $10 million in olive oil, zinc, and dates. In Morocco the situation its Business Council faced was even more extreme when imports from Russia resulted in a trade deficit of one and half billion dollars.[10]

In contrast to the relationship with Arab states in the Mediterranean, the ties with the Gulf States were complex, as was the case in Abu Dhabi. At least 10,000 Russians lived in that Gulf state, and they had their own Russian-language school for children. Present in the United Arab

Emirates were 450 Russian companies, including an unspecified number of firms linked to the Mafia. Tourism from Russia was also important, but a seamy aspect was the role of Abu Dhabi in the sex trade. Russian women were in high demand in the Middle East, and through kidnapping they sometimes ended up in prostitution. Gold and diamonds comprised 40 percent of Russian exports to Abu Dhabi, followed by 20 percent machinery and 10 percent foodstuffs. Official recognition of the economic importance of the United Arab Emirates came on 10 September 2007 when Putin became the first Russian president to visit Abu Dhabi.[11]

Trade with the Middle East gave a powerful boost to the economic recovery of Russia and encouraged the Kremlin to increase its involvement in the affairs of the region. The autocratic nature of most regimes meant that increasing the volume of trade often hinged on the whim of a ruler. Sometimes a sharp increase in Russian exports was the result of a single favorable deal with one country. But the Russians were far from being mere suppliants, and in a phenomenon exceeding the expectations of the Kremlin, starting in October 2006 a series of Middle Eastern visitors made a virtual pilgrimage to Moscow. Prime Minister Ehud Olmert of Israel was the first to visit Putin, and then other Middle Eastern rulers also came to make their views known to the Kremlin. President Mubarak and the foreign ministers of many Arab countries joined the parade, and their visits confirmed that Russia had returned and was again playing an active role in the turbulent affairs of the region.[12]

The West was not pleased with the return of Russia to the Middle East, but the U.S. tied down in the Iraq quagmire lacked the freedom to take countermeasures. For its part, the Kremlin stated "that Russia would not take advantage of U.S. difficulties in Iraq and wished the U.S. success in stabilizing the country."[13] Rather than support the anti–U.S. insurgency in Iraq, Russia quietly reestablished its naval presence in the Mediterranean. The U.S. watched with dismay while Russia revived its abandoned naval base at Tartus in Syria. But it was not so much the reappearance of warships showing the Russian flag that explained the popularity of Moscow among Middle Eastern countries.

During the Soviet period, the pro–Arab policy in the Middle East had not been as beneficial to the Kremlin as might seem at first glance. In contrast, the Russian Federation decided to engage all parties in the region. This was easiest to accomplish with Turkey but harder with Iran. At the insistence of Putin, Russia maintained close and amicable relations with Israel but at the same time kept contacts with arch-enemies of Israel such as Hezbollah and Hamas. A first presidential visit to Israel in 2005 confirmed the strong links with Russia, and President Putin, who had a strong attachment to Russian Jews, always supported close economic ties with Israel. As a result, Russia was the only country with open channels of communication with almost all the players in the Middle East.[14]

Russia's position in the Middle East was already well established before the Five Day War with Georgia in August 2008. The smashing Russian victory in the war sent panic waves throughout the West, but the reaction in the Middle East was of respect and admiration. Russia was not just a valuable economic partner but also a military power in its own right. An obvious immediate benefit was intensified interest in acquiring Russian weapons, but the response went much deeper. In an unexpected benefit from the creation of the Russia Today television channel, its Arabic version was swamped after the Five Day War with messages from viewers who were delighted that "Russia was back" as a power in the Middle East.[15]

Another attractive factor was the refusal of the Kremlin to intervene in the

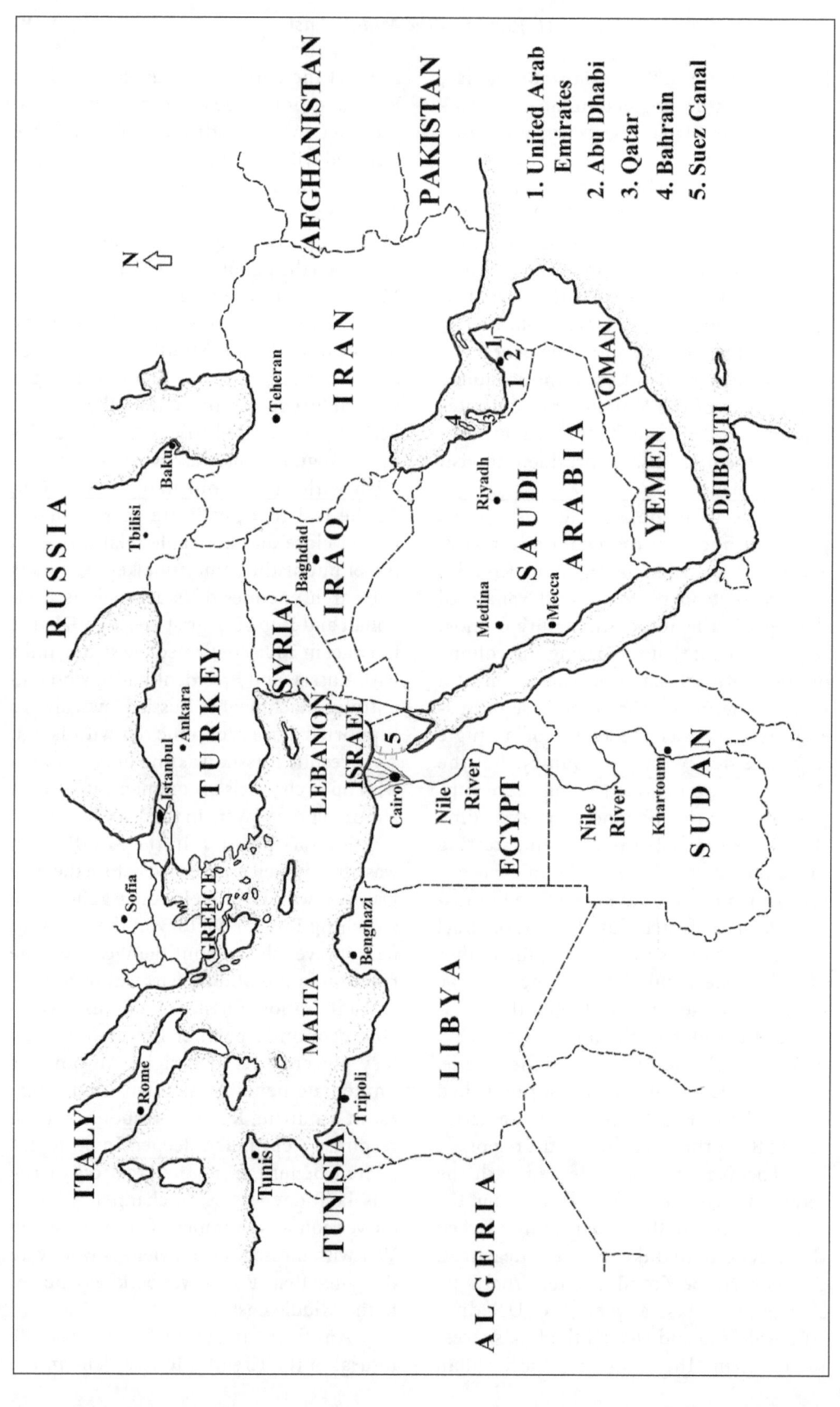

domestic affairs of countries, an attitude that contrasted with the insistence of Western countries on lecturing local rulers on how to conduct their internal affairs. This tolerant attitude helped Russia to nurture its relationship with Saudi Arabia. Its princes knew that Moscow never was telling them how to run their country, in contrast to the United States. This reassurance was important in trying to build relations between Russia and Saudi Arabia. In spite of a visit by President Putin, Saudi Arabia still was hesitant to support the simple matter of Russia's entry into the World Trade Organization. Saudi Arabia had a tendency to sign deals, such as one with Russian Railways to build track, and then to abandon them. The same happened with arms purchases, first announced and then postponed. In contrast to the large Russian investments in the United Arab Emirates, Saudi Arabia attracted little Russian capital, and only a few hundred Russians resided in the kingdom, compared to 35,000 American citizens.[16] Saudi Arabia turned to Russia not so much to diversify its foreign relations as out of fear that the Kremlin was moving too close to Iran. In reality, Russian relations with Saudi Arabia were almost as difficult as those with Iran, as the next section shows.

Iran: Difficult Ties

Among the most important foreign policy challenges for the United States was Iran, a country sharing that distinction with Afghanistan, Iraq, and North Korea. The Iranian Revolution of 1979 marked the start of the U.S. obsession with Tehran. In contrast, already in the late 1980s Moscow lost interest in Iran, and the last direct link ended in December 1991 when the collapse of the Soviet Union eliminated the common border between the two countries. During the grim 1990s Iran disappeared from Russian foreign policy.[17]

The fear of Iran was so strong in the U.S. that the paranoia made analysts believe that a convergence of interests was sure to produce a strong alliance between Tehran and Moscow. Yet Iran did not reciprocate the Kremlin's interest in improving relations. During the Cold War the ayatollahs called the U.S. the "Great Satan" and the Soviet Union "the little Satan," and this underlying hostility still lingered. And not just the desire to create a theocratic society motivated Iranian leaders who seemed to live in a bygone age. Iran aspired not just to pursue an independent foreign policy but also to become a major regional power in the Middle East. When India with a population of over a billion and considerable resources has been struggling to become a regional power, the burden was unbearable for a smaller Iran.[18]

Tehran made few efforts to improve ties with Russia, and the Kremlin gravitated toward the Western position on Iran's nuclear program. In 2003 President Putin communicated through his friend Italian Prime Minister Silvio Berlusconi the decision of Russia not to help Iran with the construction of nuclear reactors.[19] But at the same time, the war in Chechnya was still a real threat, and Moscow did not want to antagonize the religious fanatics too much out of fear that "Iran could retaliate by stirring up serious trouble and instability in sensitive areas, including even inside Russia, with its increasingly significant Muslim population."[20] The trade with Iran consisted 90 percent of Russian exports of agricultural and industrial products. Iran became an important market for many Russian businesses, because unlike other countries, it did not need to import gas and petroleum.[21]

Russia's repeated efforts to improve ties with Tehran hit a wall, to the point that in 2007 President Putin was "quite frustrated" and "exasperated" with Iran.[22] With no other alternative available, Russia agreed to join the West in imposing a first round of sanctions against Iran.²³ Russia still opposed extreme measures such as the plan during the late Bush administration to launch a wave of air attacks to try to destroy Iranian nuclear installations. In an attempt to forestall Western strikes, on 16 October 2007 Putin visited Tehran, the first Russian ruler to do so since World War II. "The visit of the Russian president breaks up the front of countries, which oppose Iran [...] for this very reason it is very harmful."²⁴

Western sanctions on Iran hurt the economy and helped boost Russian exports. Even though Iran was not a major trade partner, Russia did not want to lose one of its important export markets for non-petroleum products.²⁵ Anti-Russian feeling spread in Iran when the Kremlin voted with the West in the International Atomic Energy Agency. On the other hand, "the Iranian opposition was also condemning Russia for working with the Iranian government."²⁶

After bursts of intermittent activity, Russian engineers in 2010 completed the Bushner nuclear reactor which went on line in 2011. At the same time, Moscow supported ever tougher sanctions on Iran for trying to build nuclear weapons. The stubborn refusal to cooperate with Russia left Iran alone in the world stage without any powerful advocate.²⁷ In contrast, the goodwill and supportive actions of the Kremlin made the rest of the countries of the Middle East regard Russia in a favorable light. And Syria soon was in desperate need of a powerful ally.

Syria: A Deepening Relationship

After Anwar Sadat ended Egypt's alliance with the Soviet Union in 1976, Hafez al-Assad of Syria remained the Kremlin's last close ally in the Middle East. The collapse of the Soviet Union ended these close ties, and Syria was left adrift during the 1990s. Already in 1999 Russia was starting to make a small comeback when a Syrian-Russian Permanent Commission on Economic Cooperation began to function. Seven Russian companies were involved in 25 projects in Syria in the areas of irrigation, mineral prospecting, and petroleum facilities. And just like in Soviet times, Syrians again came to Russia to study technical careers.²⁸

When al-Assad died in 2000 and his son Bashar al-Assad came to power, the West saw an opportunity to restore its influence over Syria. The U.S. and former colonial power France seemed to be close to winning over the new ruler, but then Syrian involvement in the war in Lebanon derailed the process. Even after Damascus withdrew Syrian troops from Lebanon, nothing satisfied a West feeling betrayed by al-Assad and determined to remove him from office. Western sanctions hit Syria hard, and al-Assad saw his regime in danger of collapse.²⁹

A similar dilemma had faced Libyan ruler Muammar Qaddafi, who decided to seek Western support. Qaddafi left a secondary role for Russia, and by the time he realized in 2009 that only the Kremlin could save him, it was a classic case of too little too late. The opposite reaction came from al-Assad who intensified his ties with Russia and just left the door open to the West for a possible reconciliation. He also improved Syrian relations with Iran, in the hope of attracting the attention of Saudi Arabia that opposed all Iranian influence.³⁰

The U.S. embargo on spare parts grounded the Syrian civilian airline, and Damascus regretted not having from the start acquired a fleet of Russian commercial planes. A ministerial group had been holding annual meetings since 2003 to improve trade relations between Russia and Syria, but the annual gatherings accomplished little. When Russia agreed to cancel Syria's Soviet-era debt, Syria reciprocated at the 2006 ministerial gathering by trying to do everything possible to increase the economic links. That same year al-Assad also authorized Russia to rehabilitate the Tartus and Latakia naval facilities on the coast of Syria. A first indication of interest had come as early as 1999, when Russia began to establish ship repair facilities in Tartus. But the naval installations had remained abandoned since the collapse of the Soviet Union, and it took dredging and refurbishing to make them operational again in 2006.[31]

The Kremlin wanted authorization because the Russian navy was desperate to find a home base once the lease on Sevastopol in Crimea expired in 2017. The facilities in Syria also had the additional symbolic value of being the only ones outside the former Soviet Union. One of the requirements to be a world power is for a country to have military installations beyond its borders, and Russia, with its bases in Syria, was just barely satisfying this condition.[32]

A cornered Syria lavished contracts to Russian companies and granted other economic incentives to try to persuade the Kremlin to support the regime. Damascus feared additional sanctions from the United Nations, and only Russia with its veto in the Security Council could stop those crippling measures. In amicable meetings the Kremlin explained that its support could not be "bought" with contracts no matter how lucrative. Russia was trying to show the Middle Eastern countries that it was a reliable and loyal partner who remained true to its friends.[33]

As the first decade of the twenty-first century came to a close, Qaddafi in Libya was having difficulty weaning himself from the West, and Iran insisted on maintaining an independent policy. In 2006 al-Assad was the first ruler to realize that a close alliance with Russia could guarantee the survival of a Middle Eastern regime. Unlike Qaddafi, who took too long to abandon the West, the Syrian ruler never came to regret his decision.

12

The West on the Offensive

For two years Putin had sought a new relationship with the United States through his friendship with Bush, but Russia had received little return on the investment.—Steven Lee Myers[1]

Fiasco in Transnistria

When Vladimir Vorodin became the president of Moldova on 4 April 2001, he made reunification with the separatist region of Transnistria his highest priority. He was from that region (his mother still lived in the rebel area), and in the past he had been pro–Moscow and spoke Russian like a native. He believed that he had the best opportunity to obtain the withdrawal of Russian troops from Transnistria and to reunify the region with Moldova.[2]

His initial enthusiasm for seeking an agreement encountered strong opposition from Igor Smirnov, the president of Transnistria. Vorodin pleaded with Russian diplomats to force the separatist leader to comply. Because the Russian diplomats could not budge Smirnov, Vorodin by January 2003 reached the erroneous conclusion that the Foreign Ministry in Moscow was the real obstacle to reaching an agreement with Transnistria.[3]

Up to this moment the Organization for Security and Cooperation in Europe (OSCE) had been in charge of the negotiations, and Vorodin sought its approval on 1 February 2003. Once OSCE headquarters gave its support, the Moldovan president went on a goodwill visit to Moscow. He asked Vladimir Putin to appoint a special representative from the Presidential Administration to negotiate a settlement, in this way bypassing the Russian Foreign Ministry. The task of the presidential representative was to hammer out a new constitutional arrangement for Moldova to make possible reunification with Transnistria.[4]

The high point of Vorodin's visit of February 2002 was the splendid reception the Moldovans hosted in their Moscow embassy. As an indication of the lengths the Moldovans were willing to go to impress Putin, they placed two hundred meters of red carpet from the sidewalk where Putin stepped down from his official vehicle all the way to the reception hall in the embassy several floors up. In spite of the outlandish efforts during the visit, no official announcement appeared about the appointment of a new presidential representative to Moldova.[5]

The delay reflected Russia's need to examine its entire strategic situation. Two concerns preoccupied the Kremlin. First the West insisted that a precondition for ratifying the amended version of the Treaty on Conventional Armed Forces in Europe (CFE) was that Russia first withdraw its troops from Moldova and Georgia. This concern assumed an extra urgency when in 2002 NATO invited Bulgaria, Rumania, Slovakia, Slovenia, and the Baltic Republics to join NATO. Unless the West ratified the new CFE, then NATO gained the opportunity to station forces right on Russia's borders.[6] The second concern was the ongoing Chechnya War. Moscow was in a weak position and was willing to sacrifice foreign commitments in order to save the Russian Federation from disintegration.

As part of global withdrawal, Russia had already abandoned its installations in Cuba and Vietnam. Pro-Russian regimes survived in those countries, and the Kremlin expected that a suitable agreement would likewise protect the rights of ethnic Russians in Transnistria. Unlike in the rest of Eastern Europe, the Moldovan Constitution prohibited the country from joining any military alliance. This clause appealed to a Kremlin no longer having to worry about NATO membership for Moldova. At the same time, success in Transnistria promised not just to earn goodwill from the West but also offered a blueprint for reaching a similar settlement in Georgia.[7]

A stumbling block since the 1990s had been the refusal of President Smirnov to allow the removal of the large stores of weapons and ammunition of the former Soviet Fourteenth Army in Transnistria. The frontline position of Moldova in any conventional war with NATO had meant that ammunition depots and arsenals were not just for the supply of the Fourteenth Army but for other units in the former Soviet military district. In the past local women blocked the tracks to prevent the departure of the ammunition trains, but in March 2003 Transnistria authorized the removal of the huge stocks of military equipment and weapons. Trains began rolling, and the evacuation was expected to be finished by the end of 2003.[8]

This major breakthrough convinced President Vorodin that Moscow could overcome the resistance of Smirnov. However, the Kremlin also insisted that Russian troops stay in the region for at least a decade. But for the West the withdrawal of Russian troops was a non-negotiable demand and formed an essential part of its core policy of driving Russian behind its borders. The OSCE representative responded "We cannot stand idle and allow Russia to pressure Moldova [...] more than anything else, Russia needs to know that this issue is important to its major European and North American partners."[9]

A reminder of the indispensable role Moscow played came when, on 16 June 2003, a small detachment of lightly armed Transnistrian soldiers appeared to halt the loading of 125 mm tank shells aboard a train. Large piles of the dangerous ammunition remained stranded in the box cars and across the train station. Everyone knew that the well-armed Russian troops would never use force against the locals, who did authorize the return of the 125 mm shells to supply depots.[10]

The Kozak Memorandum

Vorodin pleaded one more time with the Kremlin to appoint a special presidential representative and to bypass the Foreign Ministry. Sometime in July Putin complied and appointed Dmitry Kozak to negotiate a troop withdrawal from Transnistria but protecting at the same time the rights of ethnic Russians. This was a tall order or almost a mission impossible for constitutional law expert Kozak, who warmed up to the challenge. He did have a trump card to play to secure the approval of Smirnov to any agreement: "Russia has a lot of compromising information about Smirnov and his family, but it was held by other ministries and not in the hands of the Ministry of Foreign Affairs."[11]

Whether because of the *kompromat* or economic pressure, the resistance of Smirnov crumbled. Trying to put the best face forward, he declared that "We are allies of Russia. When the Russian Federation has a position that will be our position."[12] In reality, the Kozak mission was already doomed because vicious envy had produced bitter opposition from the foreign affairs bureaucracy of the West. A high OSCE official "appeared particularly resentful of Voronin's request to bring someone new like Kozak into the process."[13] Western diplomats were incensed to have a new kid on the block be the one to find a solution.

As late as September 30, Transnistria continued to resist reaching an agreement, and in order to secure an acceptable formula, Kozak proceeded in two steps. He released the first fifteen articles of his agreement of what came to be known as the Kozak Memorandum on 18 November. As a constitutional expert, he struggled to find a solution to satisfy the complete rejection of Moldova to any federalist formula while protecting the rights of the minority in Transnistria. With the federalist option unacceptable, the only alternative left was to establish veto authority over the central government. According to this formula, the upper chamber of the legislature gained the authority to block any legislation harmful to Transnistria. Because the Kozak Memorandum guaranteed representation for the Russian minority in the upper chamber, in effect Transnistria gained a veto over Moldovan state actions.[14]

President Vorodin did not waste much time on the constitutional niceties, because he was among the few to realize the true meaning of the Kozak Memorandum. With excitement he exclaimed "Russia has decided to give up Transnistria!"[15] The Kozak Memorandum was nothing less than one more step in Russia's withdrawal from the strategic commitments of the former Soviet Union. Much as the Kremlin tried to disguise the reality, in essence it was a humiliating confession of Russia's weakness.

Everyone understood that making this new arrangement work in Moldova was going to be hard but not impossible. Smirnov demanded that Russian troops stay in Transnistria indefinitely, but Moldova insisted on a total withdrawal. A patient Kozak negotiated the compromise of 2020 as the deadline for the departure of the last Russian troops. On 23 November Russian diplomats completed the final version of the Kosak Memorandum. To make the final text of the agreement acceptable to Moldova, the trains resumed the removal of military equipment in November, an indication of Moscow's intentions to complete the withdrawal.[16]

The Putin Visit

To disguise its humiliating withdrawal, the Kremlin planned to announce the successful resolution of the conflict at OSCE headquarters. To maximize the favorable publicity and to earn the most goodwill, the Kremlin scheduled a presidential visit to Moldova. At Chisinau, Putin intended to sign the agreement in the company of both Smirnov and Vorodin. A diplomatic triumph trumpeted in the media served to mask another Russian setback, when in reality Russia was offering the West a bloodless victory on a silver platter.

Western diplomats were livid, and they denounced the Kozak Memorandum as unworkable for Moldova. OSCE officials were incensed that they had been left out of the negotiations and did not want Russia to receive all the credit for having brokered a deal. As soon as the draft of the Kozak Memorandum of 21 November became public, the messages and the phone calls to President Voronin poured in from Western countries. NGOs—the convenient tool of the West—called for a massive rally on 23 November to protest the agreement, and already on 21 November crowds gathered in Moldova to express their anger. Additional outside stimulus came from the massive television coverage of the unfolding Rose Revolution in Georgia.[17]

Most inexcusable was the behavior of the chair of OSCE. This organization is supposed to act only with the consensus of all its members, and it was correct in stating that the organization could not support the Kozak Memorandum because of the absence of consensus among members. But the chief of OSCE directed words to Voronin "sharper and blunter than the somewhat veiled message of this public statement."[18]

President Vorodin, without even the fig leaf of OSCE support, was under heavy domestic and Western pressure to reject the Kozak Memorandum. Western powers that had been so outraged when Russia tried to influence Moldova had no hesitation about applying massive pressure on Vorodin to reject the agreement. For several days the Russian embassy in Chisinau had been busy organizing the coming presidential trip, and preparations were well advanced for the signing ceremony on 25 November. Already a Moldovan military band practiced playing the Russian national anthem—not an easy task because of its opera-like musical composition.[19]

The pressure proved unbearable to Vorodin, who caved in to the demands of the West. In Moscow the airplane to take the Russian president to the signing ceremony was getting ready for departure, and a large contingent of reporters was boarding their separate plane to cover the events in Chisinau. Shortly before 6:00 a.m. Vorodin picked up the telephone and called his Russian counterpart to say that Moldova could not sign the agreement.[20]

The news fell like a bombshell in Moscow, and the entire staged presentation fell apart. Putin was angry at this last-minute reversal and for years resented the U.S. role in torpedoing the peace plan. No damage control was possible, even though the West without reason fretted for several years about the revival of a "Kozak II." Any settlement for Transnistria was dead, and all that remained was to draw lessons from this botched diplomatic episode.[21]

The European Union assumed the role of spokesperson to express Western displeasure. In a conversation with the Russian Chargé in Brussels, an official "reminded the Russian that the EU wants to have an agenda with Moscow to discuss frozen conflicts, and the EU wants Russia to be predictable and not launch unilateral surprises like the Kozak Plan."[22] Lecturing any sovereign state in this way was insulting, and Russia rejected the sermon.[23]

The anger of the West lacked any rational explanation, when the only cost was to let Russia reap the fleeting fame from the agreement. The West, by considering unacceptable a deadline of 2020 for the withdrawal of Russian troops, made possible their indefinite presence.[24] The Kozak Memorandum had been the last real opportunity to settle this dispute. Once Russia regained control of Crimea in 2014 the remoteness of Transnistria vanished, and warplanes were just a few minutes flying time away. The Russian Defense Ministry proudly has been displaying images of the 1,200 soldiers engaged in maneuvers and training in the separatist republic.

Historical perspective also reveals that the Kozak Memorandum was the last time Russia offered to abandon any of its overseas commitments. Russia tried appeasement one last time on a much smaller scale over the Adjara crisis in Georgia, but by then Moscow was no longer willing to abandon an entire region, and nothing similar to the Kozak memorandum ever appeared for the separatist republics of Abkhazia and South Ossetia. Russia was slowly moving from acquiescence with Western demands to resistance.

The Color Revolutions

Good luck gave Russia an unexpected victory in Transnistria. The final stage of this episode coincided with the outbreak of the Rose Revolution in Georgia. The televised images of the crowds in Tbilisi stimulated the protestors in Moldova to take to the streets. The Kremlin failed to realize that the nearly simultaneous demonstrations in Moldova and Georgia marked the start of the process later baptized as the "Color Revolutions."

Georgia: The Rose Revolution

Moscow believed that the Rose Revolution was an internal affair not posing a challenge—much less a threat—to Russia. In the last years of the presidency of Eduard Shevardnadze, Moscow proved accommodating to the rising wave of Georgian nationalism and expected to continue placating any new ruler. The economic ties between both countries were so strong that Russia could not imagine that many Georgians were willing to assume the high costs of complete independence from their northern neighbor.

Over the years the Shevardnadze regime became very unpopular. Although he was personally honest, his associates and relatives engaged in widespread corruption and illegal practices. Greedy officials channeled into their own pockets funds allocated to the army and police, while the authority of the government eroded.[25]

Shevardnadze lacked the political skills to create and maintain a governing structure. In contrast to most Soviet-era political leaders, he did not know how to concentrate power in his hands as leaders in other former Soviet republics had done. During the Soviet period the Communist Party had provided the governing structure, but without any similar organization, Shevardnadze saw power slip from his hands. To his credit, he realized his weakness and made known his intention not to seek reelection in the next presidential contest.

His decision not to run panicked his supporters who wanted to cling to their lucrative benefits. The key test for any future presidential contender was the parliamentary election of 2 November 2003. With the stakes being so high, massive voter fraud took place before, during, and after Election Day. When the electoral commission announced that pro-government parties were winning, the first demonstrators gathered to protest in Tbilisi on 5 November.[26]

At this initial stage a prompt offer by the government to rerun the fraudulent election could have weakened the opposition, but Shevardnadze did nothing. Western NGOs had taught opposition groups how to organize mass mobilizations, and all that the protesters needed was a rallying cry. The demand for the resignation of Shevardnadze proved more than adequate to incite citizens to take to the streets to express their pent-up frustration at the corrupt regime. And the leader who best captured the public mood was the young rising star Mikheil Saakashvili, who preferred to be called "Misha."[27]

The demonstrators adopted the rose as their symbol, and they held daily protests in Tbilisi demanding the resignation of Shevardnadze. The several thousand protestors remained peaceful and stayed within a small area in downtown Tbilisi. The opposition did not need huge crowds because almost the whole country supported the movement.[28]

The turning point came on 22 November when the president convoked the new members for the first session of parliament. Just as he was addressing the legislators, the crowds broke into the building and took control of the assembly. The unpaid police melted away, and the bodyguards of the president rushed him to safety. The shaken Shevardnadze instinctively sought protection by telephoning Vladimir Putin.[29]

The Russian President and his team happened to be dining at one of Moscow's popular Georgian restaurants. Not yet realizing that the hand of the West was behind the protests, the Kremlin reasoned from analogy that the unfolding Rose Revolution resembled an earlier movement in Armenia that resulted in a change of government in 2002 but without any impact on relations with Russia.[30]

During the last years of Shevardnadze relations with Russia had been deteriorating. The Kremlin was disappointed with the Georgian president for not having forged closer ties with Russia, so when the telephone call interrupted Putin at dinner, no one among those present cared to rescue Shevardnadze. Many Russians still blamed the Georgian president for having contributed to the fall of the Soviet Union. The Kremlin was not willing to launch a massive military intervention to save his collapsing regime.[31]

Putin could not ignore the request for help and in response he sent Foreign Minister Igor Ivanov to Tbilisi. The choice was not accidental because Ivanov had Georgian ties and could understand but not speak that language. Upon his arrival on 23 November, he negotiated an agreement with opposition leaders that called for a rerun of the parliamentary elections and also moved up the date of the presidential elections to January 2004. Shevardnadze accepted the agreement, and Ivanov, believing that his tasks was finished, left for Adjara to tie up the last loose end of securing the approval of the local political boss Aslan Abashidze.[32]

When Ivanov disembarked from his plane at Adjara, Abashidze asked him "What on earth have you done? Shevardnadze has resigned!"[33] It turned out that once Shevardnadze saw that Russian troops were not coming, he realized his regime was doomed. As long as Ivanov was at his side, the Georgian President retained the illusion that Russia might still intervene. But when the Foreign Minister left, despair gripped Shevardnadze, who then resigned. Ivanov had been assigned a mission impossible, but the way he mishandled the political transition made not just him but Russia look bad and out of touch. This botched mission helped persuade Putin to appoint a new foreign minister in February 2004.

At first glance Russian interests did not seem to have suffered harm. The Rose Revolution made Misha the most popular figure in Georgia, and he coasted to an overwhelming victory in the presidential election of 4 January 2004.[34] The Rose Revolution seemed to have been just one of those periodic outbursts that rocked the countries of the turbulent Caucasus, and the Kremlin still did not realize the real threat that the "Color Revolutions" posed. But in the last quarter of 2004, a wake-up call came from Ukraine.

Ukraine: The Orange Revolution

Leonid Kuchma, during his two terms, maintained proper relations with Moscow, although the simplistic label of "pro–Russian" was far from accurate. The Ukrainian president tried to extract the most from both the West and Russia without antagonizing either side. Toward the end of his second term, Kuchma decided to select his successor. To the bafflement of both Ukrainian politicians and the Kremlin, he chose Viktor Yanukovich, a former governor, who besides having many personal defects, was a bad campaigner and a poor speaker.[35]

The Kremlin also had serious doubts, but Putin felt that Russia had no choice but to support the candidate of Kuchma. The Kremlin put all its resources behind Yanukovich. The most important asset was Russian-language television whose coverage extended across the country and in some regions provided all the television channels. Russian political operatives also came to help Yanukovich, but they were soon dismayed by the ineptitude of his campaign and tried to warn the Kremlin of the impending defeat.[36]

The Russian responses had been too little and too late, because both NGOs and Western governments had been anticipating the October 2004 elections for years. Whether it was USAID, EU, or NGOs (often financed with government funds), Western organizations had been preparing to elect their candidate to the presidency. Independence had not brought benefits to the population and on the contrary, Ukraine was in a downward spiral just at the time that Russia was recovering from the disastrous 1990s.[37]

Western efforts to make Russia responsible for the dismal situation in Ukraine diminished the appeal of Yanukovich. To regain the lead, he appealed to the feelings of Russian speakers in Eastern Ukraine and in Crimea. By playing the ethnicity card, he introduced into the political debate a very dangerous element. His advantage diminished when, under mysterious circumstances still not clear today, the opposition candidate Viktor Yushchenko fell ill from a supposed poisoning on 5 September. He went abroad for treatment and was out of the campaign during his convalescence of two weeks. His followers were not dismayed and spread the accusation that the Kremlin had ordered him killed even though conclusive evidence never appeared. When he returned to campaign with a disfigured face, supposedly the result of the poisoning, he became a hero among the voters of western Ukraine and Kiev.[38]

To try to save Yanukovich, Putin, in his only foray into the electoral politics of Ukraine, made a three-day visit to Ukraine in late October on the eve of the election. While he avoided announcing his support for Yanukovich, his presence reaffirmed the view that closer ties with Russia were indispensable for Ukraine to escape its deteriorating situation. Putin stood by Yanukovich in a public ceremony in an open sign of support, but in spite of all the Kremlin's efforts, Yushchenko came in first place in the 31 October 2004 election.[39]

The lack of a majority forced a runoff on 21 November, and this time rampant voter fraud characterized the election. Each side used every available trick to pad the votes in its favor, yet in spite of the massive fraud, Yanukovich was able to eke out a margin of victory a few decimal points higher than Yushchenko. These results were of doubtful validity, and it was confirmed that on average voter fraud had been twice as high in the regions supporting Yanukovich. The voter results showed the polarization of the country into pro–Western and pro–Russian supporters, and in this sense the runoff election of 21 November 2004 was the opening act in the fragmentation of Ukraine, a process still ongoing at the present. In western Ukraine almost the entire population voted for Yushchenko, while the opposite happened in eastern Ukraine and in Crimea with the overwhelming majority of voters casting their ballots for Yanukovich. In a revealing insight into the later revolt in 2014, the pro–Russian feelings were stronger in Donetsk and Lugansk than in Crimea and Sevastopol.[40]

Putin congratulated Yanukovich on his victory, but the West did not want to accept the defeat. Huge crowds, soon numbering over 200,000, gathered in Maidan Square in Kiev. While the anger was real, the preparations for mass protests had been taking place since the summer. In what became a trademark of this type of protest, demonstrators camped in the square and their tents became the most visible symbol; a whole complex of mess halls, water supplies, and sanitary facilities appeared almost overnight in Maidan Square.[41] Just like in Georgia, outgoing president Kuchma refused to send the police or much less the army to drive out the protestors. In Georgia it was clear that the uniformed personnel would not use force against the peaceful demonstrators, but whether the police would have heeded the order to clear the square in Kiev remains an open question.

The demonstrators minimized anti–Russian expressions and preferred to frame their struggle as one in favor of democratic practices, human rights, and against the rampant corruption of the Kuchma regime.

For special events the number of protestors rose to close to a million, but as one scholar with insight noted "the demonstrations in Ukraine needed to be huge precisely because the demonstrators did not enjoy the enormous, almost even unanimous, reservoir of support that those in Georgia the previous year had enjoyed."[42]

Under immense pressure, Kuchma accepted a Supreme Court decision calling for a third round of elections. This time many safeguards made impossible any large-scale voter fraud. The election of 26 December 2004 gave Yushchenko a victory with a margin of three percent and confirmed that the pro–Russian half in the east and south was distinct from the rest of the country. When Yushchenko took office on 23 January 2005, he faced the enormous task of having to overcome the huge divide between the east and the west.[43] For the Kremlin the whole episode had been a disaster, yet Ukraine was not the last blow.

Kyrgyzstan: The Tulip Revolution

The high water mark for the Color Revolutions was Kyrgyzstan. Askar Akayev had been the president of the country since independence from the Soviet Union in December 1991, but over the years he lost touch with a population composed of rival ethnic groups. He came from the north, and southerners resented the overrepresentation of northerners in the government. Institutions deteriorated and corruption became rampant. His children exploited the government to their benefit. Discontent surfaced when protests erupted in March 2002, and this first challenge proved a trying experience for a government that with great difficulty restored order.[44]

Kyrgyzstan also had the distinction of being the only country to have in its territory American and Russian bases. Just outside the capital Bishkek was the Manas air base, which the U.S. leased since 2001. For its part, Russia operated several facilities in the country. The rent for the Manas base was very important for the Akayev family and became a major source of funds for corruption. The U.S. found dealing with Askar Akayev to be difficult, and not just because he was always asking for increases in the rent payments.[45]

European countries either had low-level diplomatic representation or none at all, and only Germany had its own embassy at Bishkek. In this partial diplomatic vacuum, the U.S. embassy, American NGOs, and to a lesser degree OSCE came to play a disproportionate rule inside Kyrgyzstan. The U.S. ambassador was on the lookout for any opportunity to bring to power a pro–American regime.[46]

The Constitution did not allow Akayev to run for reelection after his term expired in late 2005, but the parliament could remove that restriction if the government won a large majority in the legislative elections earlier in that same year. Another clause in the Constitution also required candidates for parliament to win not just a plurality but a majority (over 50 percent) of the votes; if not, then the two candidates with the highest number of votes went into a runoff. In the election of 27 February 2005, most of the pro–Akayev candidates received the largest number of votes for the 75 seats in the parliament. However, only 33 candidates reached the 50 percent threshold and thus the rest of the races went into the runoff scheduled for 13 March. The massive fraud caused tremendous anger, and groups of protestors started to appear across the country.[47]

Voter fraud allowed pro–Akayev candidates to win the runoff election on 13 March. NGOs confirmed that the election had been stolen and also mobilized people to take to the streets. The U.S. ambassador was open in his support for the protests. The rallying cry was the demand for the resignation of Akayev, just like in Georgia the demand had been the resignation of Eduard Shevardnadze.[48]

In Bishkek the anti-government forces struggled to bring several thousand protestors into the streets, but in the south in cities such as Jalalabad the simplest appeal sufficed to gather crowds numbering over 50,000. Just like the protests of the Orange Revolution aggravated the ethnic division in Ukraine, so in Kyrgyzstan the Tulip Revolution intensified the rivalry between the ethnic groups in the south and those in the north.[49]

The first two Color Revolutions had been peaceful, but violence and destruction came to characterize the Tulip Revolution. In Kyrgyzstan acts of violence multiplied after the runoff election of 13 March when many individuals went on a rampage of looting, arson, and killing against other ethnic groups. Lighting the match of a Color Revolution was threatening to detonate the powder keg of ethnic tensions in Kyrgyzstan.[50]

The president later claimed he should have sent the police and army against the demonstrators as soon as the protests started, but his authority was crumbling, and police units were already defecting. An attempt on 20 March to have the police repress the protestors in Jalalabad and Osh backfired and outraged the crowds. The next day a wave of protestors overran government offices in those two cities, and soon after armed rebels gained control of the southern part of the country.[51]

The disintegration of authority still did not persuade Akayev to abandon the presidency, and he refused on 22 March to negotiate a solution. The next day the rebels gained control over two-thirds of the country and were isolating the government in the capital district of Bishkek. When protestors organized a rally in Bishkek, the local police arrested over 200 and sent dozens more badly bruised citizens to the hospital.[52]

This botched operation inflamed passions, and a large number of protestors prepared for an even larger rally to protest the police beatings. In the morning of 24 March NGOs helped to mobilize a crowd numbering over 15,000 in the central square to demand the resignation of the president. At the same time, other individuals spread across the city to loot, burn, and destroy. The situation was turning ugly and was headed to a bloodbath. Key officials were no longer willing to oppose the demonstrators, and later that same day Akayev and his family fled to safety in Moscow where he sought asylum.[53]

The whirlwind of events caught the Kremlin by surprise. Until then Moscow believed that the Color Revolutions were a European phenomenon not supposed to occur in the authoritarian regimes of Central Asia. Yet the U.S. was able to create the conditions favorable for the Tulip Revolution without having to direct the process. The elections of 10 July 2005 brought the southerner Kurmanbek Bakiyev to the presidency.[54]

The new president wanted closer ties with the U.S., but he could not break the strong links of Kyrgyzstan with the Russian economy. At least half a million citizens worked in Russia, and their remittances were indispensable for the survival of the country. The U.S. tried to extend its influence even though Russia in public downplayed the incident in an attempt not to have another point of contention with Washington.[55] In Kyrgyzstan, the coming to power of a pro–Western regime had been a case of imperial overreach on the part of the U.S, as even a cursory glance at a map of the region revealed. With the U.S. war in Afghanistan turning into a quagmire, it was inevitable that at some time in the future Russia would have the opportunity to restore its position in Kyrgyzstan and to overturn the temporary U.S. ascendancy.

13

Response to the Color Revolutions

The Color Revolutions had a significant impact on both U.S.-Russia relations and Russia's relationships with the former Republics of the Soviet Union. —Lincoln A. Mitchell[1]

The Rose Revolution in Georgia at first seemed just another example of the chronic instability affecting that former Soviet republic, but then the Tulip Revolution in Kyrgyzstan revealed a more widespread phenomenon. The reelection of Vladimir Putin to a second term on 14 March 2004 did reassure Russian ruling circles, but the outbreak of the Orange Revolution in Ukraine on 21 November 2004 once again revived the concerns that something similar could happen in Russia and return the country to the chaos and weakness of the 1990s.

Controlling NGOs

The Orange Revolution in Ukraine shocked the Kremlin. Considerable efforts to elect a pro–Russian candidate had not stopped Western NGOs (Non-Governmental Organizations). These organizations distributed ideological content and mobilized citizens. In the near abroad the weakness of local institutions made the NGOs very influential. The money NGOs received to spend in the former Soviet republics had a greater impact than even larger expenditures in Western countries.

Inside Russia NGOs spread, with their numbers climbing to 160,000 in 2006. The overwhelming majority of NGOs engaged in issues of local interest. A distinct category was NGOs receiving foreign financing. Post-mortems of the Orange Revolution showed that those NGOs receiving foreign financing led the protests and had mobilized the population to carry out regime change. These NGOs also used the social media to achieve their political goals.[2]

The international outcry was immediate when the Duma, the lower house of the Russian parliament, passed a bill requiring that NGOs report foreign funds and giving the government the authority to close NGOs it considered harmful. On 23 December 2005 and on 27 December the Federation Council, the upper house of the Russian parliament, passed the same bill.[3]

A moment of suspense followed because President Vladimir Putin delayed signing the bill. In a final curious twist the president signed the bill into law on 10 January 2006, but the decision was not made public until a week later when the official text appeared published on 17 January. Even then the new law did not go into effect until 90 days later to give NGOs time to prepare for the new reporting requirement.[4]

U.S. diplomats followed its implementation in excruciating detail, while NGOs pressed for diplomatic intervention by foreign powers. Those hopes for delay vanished when the Federal Security Service (FSB) revealed on 22 January 2005 that of four British diplomats and one Russian caught spying, at least one diplomat had been transferring funds to twelve NGOs. The operation also cast suspicion on the British Council at St. Petersburg, which was facing tax-related legal accusations.[5] A separate measure came when the president signed a law "On Countering Extremism," on 28 July 2006, which gave the government additional powers to outlaw hate groups and skinheads. Although the concern existed that the law against extremism might stifle public debate, most human rights groups supported the measure.[6]

The fears that the laws on extremism and the NGOs might begin an era of repression proved unfounded. The government used its new powers to shut down groups supporting the Chechen rebels. The prime example was the Dutch NGO engaged in preparing cases of human rights abuses during the war for appeals to the Council of Europe.[7]

At the same time, the Kremlin concluded that the threat of a Color Revolution inside Russia had been exaggerated. By 2007 foreign diplomats noted that NGOs could still influence the political agenda. The U.S. Embassy continued to recommend funding these organizations through channels such as USAID.[8] The relative quiet of NGOs during the War with Georgia in August 2008 suggested that they were harmless, in reality the Kremlin had been lulled into a false sense of security lasting until the rude awakening of the events of late 2011 and early 2012.

Restraining the Organization for Security and Cooperation in Europe (OSCE)

OSCE had made possible the great success the NGOs achieved in the Color Revolutions. OSCE conferred an air of legitimacy on NGOs, and at the operational level provided support, advice, and information. The primary culprit in OSCE was one of its semi-autonomous branches, the Office for Democratic Institutions and Human Rights (ODIHR).[9]

After the collapse of the Soviet Union, OSCE found a new field for action in the conflicts raging in the former Yugoslavia and the near abroad. OSCE observers were an acceptable alternative to countries rejecting the presence of United Nations personnel. But when in November 1999 President Bill Clinton pressured Boris Yeltsin to allow OSCE to enter Chechnya, the attitude of many Russian officials turned hostile, and Foreign Minister Igor Ivanov denounced OSCE as a tool to spread Western control.[10]

The organization expanded to provide the observer missions in both Chechnya and in the former Yugoslavia. However, when it became clear that the OSCE observer mission was complicating the Russian victory in Chechnya, the Kremlin blocked the renewal of its presence at the end of 2002.[11]

The ruling principle of OSCE was unanimity. Observer missions required unanimous approval both for their creation and termination, and in practice this meant that once established they could function forever. The first step Russia took was to make sure that all missions in the future were of fixed duration and not indefinite, and thus they required unanimous approval for renewal. But existing missions, such as observers to elections in Russia and other countries of the near abroad, were another matter. In order to restrain these ongoing missions, the Kremlin threatened to reduce its payments by asking for an assessment similar to that used for UN dues.[12]

Russia wanted a charter in order to end a legal anomaly of OSCE. Unlike other major international institutions, OSCE has operated without the authority of a formal treaty. The executive branches of governments signed and implemented the founding agreements, which have never received approval from their respective legislative bodies. The U.S. was sympathetic to solving this juridical problem but not at the price of giving any member a complete veto power over all of OSCE's activities. OSCE has remained in this legal limbo and no compromise has appeared as Europe heads into the 2020s.[13]

Double standards when monitoring elections also bothered Russia. The elections in Afghanistan and Iraq were rife with errors, yet OSCE was harshest in criticizing elections in Belarus and Ukraine with fewer problems. Russia denounced a fixation of OSCE toward Eastern Europe and the near abroad. In a glaring contrast, when the OSCE at last agreed to monitor elections in the U.S., it sent only sixteen observers but claimed that seventy observers were inadequate to monitor the Russian parliamentary elections of 2 December 2007.[14]

Russia also complained about the failure of OSCE to achieve accords with the hostile parties in Georgia. According to Foreign Minister Sergei Lavrov, the Border Monitoring Operation (BMO) in Georgia was "overly expensive" and "not useful."[15] Russia blocked the renewal of BMO at the end of 2004.[16]

In 2005 "Russia had sensed it had gone too far in bashing the OSCE" and was backtracking by trying to find a more suitable role for the organization.[17] Russia was comfortable discussing many international issues in OSCE meetings because it was not alone and could count on the support of at least a dozen other countries. In this more relaxed atmosphere diplomats could do their real work of coming up with creative solutions.[18]

Russia proposed bringing for discussion at OSCE meetings "military issues, including Euro-Atlantic security, NATO enlargement, Conventional Forces in Europe (CFE) and security in Eastern Europe," but Western powers rejected the proposal. In bodies such as the NATO-Russian Council, Moscow was isolated, and the gatherings gave the impression of ganging up on Russia. It was standard operating procedure for the U.S., NATO, and the EU to align their positions prior to any meetings with Russian officials.[19] "While U.S.-EU unity in OSCE never guarantees success, its absence almost guarantees failure on key issues" explained a U.S. diplomat with a tinge of regret, and then he went on to state that once the organization lost its "ability to further U.S. goals and interests" then it "should be wrapped up."[20]

After President Putin denounced in his Munich Speech of 10 February 2007 the attempts of Western countries to take over OSCE, Russian diplomats started to hint that Moscow might depart from the organization, something very easy to do for any member state because no treaty governed its existence. However, by September 2007 Foreign Minister Lavrov concluded that the benefits of staying in OSCE outweighed the costs of leaving.[21]

Moscow was able to make sure that OSCE no longer took any major action hostile to Russian interests. As relations between the West and Russia deteriorated during the 2010s, both sides agreed on the need to preserve OSCE as one of the last remaining channels for effective interaction.[22] Russia concluded that additional measures were still required to block Western intervention in the near abroad.

Strengthening the Collective Security Treaty Organization (CSTO)

After the collapse of the Soviet Union, a variety of agreements and organizations appeared all having the common goal of facilitating ties among the former Soviet republics. One of these new organizations was the Collective Security Treaty Organization (CSTO). Russia sponsored the establishment of this body in 1994 along with the other founding members of Armenia, Belarus, Kazakhstan, Kyrgyzstan, and Tajikistan. Georgia later joined but withdrew in 1999; Uzbekistan also left but returned in 2006.[23]

After the Color Revolutions, the Kremlin decided to strengthen CSTO. Russia already financed a small staff in Moscow and its director was always a Russian. In 2003 the appointment of General Nikolay Bordyusha, a former army general with considerable intelligence experience, brought for the first time an influential official to head CSTO.[24]

The war in Afghanistan gave a boost when Russia used the organization to obtain speedy approval for sending assistance and arms to government forces fighting Islamic extremists. CSTO also provided an institutional framework for training soldiers and police of member states in Russia, and the organization hosted its first military exercises in 2008. CSTO also offered discounts on Russian arms sales to the member states.[25]

The treaty creating CSTO contained a clause similar to NATO's article 5 guaranteeing that the other member states would come to the rescue of any country attacked. This guarantee was fundamental for Armenia, because as its defense minister explained, the Russian 102nd Division stationed at Gyumri near the western border was all that deterred the Turkish Third Field Army from overrunning the country. On 25 February 2010 Moscow expanded on that guarantee when head of the CSTO Bordyuzha stated that the member states enjoyed the protection of Russia's nuclear umbrella.[26]

The obvious need to fight against the traffic in illegal drugs was an incentive for cooperation on internal security. The real reason for reviving CSTO was to prepare the member states to resist any future Color Revolutions. Russia wanted to educate member states about the techniques the West was using to carry out regime change in the former Soviet republics. Russia sought to enhance the prestige of CSTO by seeking to cooperate with NATO. However, U.S. officials refused and ridiculed the organization as "a pitiful attempt to recreate a Warsaw Pact–like structure."[27]

The Media Offensive

Russia Today

An anti–Russian slant characterized Western media coverage of the Color Revolutions. Even before Russian officials realized that the country needed its own channels to make its voice heard abroad. A global news network had become a requirement for world power status comparable to the possession of nuclear weapons, aircraft carriers, and a permanent seat in the UN Security Council.[28]

Mikhail Lesin, a Russian advertising entrepreneur, had been trying to persuade the Boris Yeltsin administration to finance a television network for foreign viewers. Not until the second presidency of Vladimir Putin did Lesin's repeated pleas receive attention. In early 2005 the government provided half of the funds to create the not-for-profit Russia Today television network and at the urging of the Kremlin, Russian banks provided the rest of the funds. The first year's budget was small compared to the sums ten times larger BBC spent to broadcast to television audiences across the world.[29]

Lesin hired the journalist Margarita Simonyan to be the chief editor. Even though she was only 25 years old, she had experience in the U.S., and native fluency in English. From its Moscow studio Russia Today began its first live broadcast in English on 10 December 2005, and television transmissions in Arabic began in 2007 and in Spanish in 2009. The studio in

Moscow always had the latest digital and broadcasting equipment and was ahead of the technological capabilities of domestic television stations.[30]

It was not easy to make Russia Today available to viewers. A first niche came from hotel chains eager to provide their guests with news from home. But getting into the cable services proved tougher because not many viewers were willing to pay for the subscription. Russia Today, just like the Fox network in its early years, had to pay the cable networks to distribute its programming. In the initial years programming concentrated on events taking place in Russia, the news most appealing to Russian immigrants.[31]

The catalyst for change at Russia Today came with the Five Day War of August 2008. It was the only Russian network broadcasting in English on events in Georgia, and its viewership jumped when people scrambled to find any news about the war. In spite of the best efforts of Russia Today, tiny Georgia still won the media war, and the Kremlin struggled to explain to the world that Russia had been attacked.[32]

Simonyan decided that Russia Today needed to change its focus from Russian to global news. The priority shifted to collecting impactful stories from across the world. To reflect the changes, in 2009 the network assumed its designation of RT. And at the suggestion of a British publicist, the network adopted the slogan of "Question More."[33] "Instead of celebrating Russia" RT decided to "turn a critical eye on the rest of the world, particularly the United States."[34]

As part of the restructuring, Simonyan established RT America in 2010. A studio opened in Washington, D.C., to produce and broadcast content for distribution inside the United States. RT made the programs appealing to the American public by hiring well-known hosts such as Larry King to anchor the programs; young, promising journalists also filled the air waves.[35]

On 30 October 2015 RT UK began broadcasts in Britain, and its incisive reporting made it the most watched foreign news broadcast in the country. RT also began that year transmission in German and in 2017 RT added the French language. The web site in Spanish became very popular in Latin America, and RT was on the forefront of making available its coverage in smart phones and other platforms. RT has been nominated for several Emmy awards.[36]

The effect that all the broadcasting of RT had on the public remained unclear. This question became important during the U.S. presidential election of 2016, when Hilary Clinton and the Democrats blamed their electoral defeat on RT and in particular on Simonyan. The alternative news, controversial guests, and heated debates appealed to viewers, but figures on rankings have remained almost non-existent. Less direct indicators such as RT having the largest number of subscribers in YouTube have been misleading, because RT has bought many disaster and accident videos that attract many non-political viewers. In the internet RT also made available stories and news Americans would otherwise not have heard.[37]

The Public Relations Offensive

Western media was still portraying Russia in negative terms or at best ignored the country. To try to improve the image, the Kremlin hired two Western public relations firms, Ketchum in the United States and GPlus for Europe. Ketchum had the burdensome obligation of having to file under the Foreign Agents Registration Act, but the firm had already provided similar services to other governments, so it already knew the routine. The firm concentrated its efforts in three main areas.[38]

The PR firm produced daily media summaries of reports about Russia. This service duplicated what Russian diplomats and agencies such as RIA Novosti were already doing, but the Kremlin wanted this duplication. Second, Ketchum devoted most of its efforts to the core activity of contacting journalists, academics, and even officials. This outreach effort could take many forms, such as lunch invitations, providing information, meetings, and even conferences. Reporters rushing to meet a deadline knew that by contacting Ketchum they could obtain quotes, information, and even leads to other sources.

The Kremlin paid Ketchum well for its services but was surprised that the firm submitted no bills for planting stories in the news. The Kremlin wanted to know how much it cost to place an article or opinion piece in prestigious newspapers such as the *Wall Street Journal*. The practice of paying journalists was widespread in Russia and in Latin America. In Africa a complex procedure evolved of governments paying not to publish an article after having read a draft. Here Ketchum played an educational role as it explained to a surprised Kremlin that payments were not the way to influence journalists.

The third area for Ketchum was to help stage major news events taking place in the United States. Russian diplomats already knew this procedure, but visiting officials with little exposure to the West needed a lot of coaching. Ketchum handled contacts with the press to make sure that the visit by a top Russian official received the maximum positive coverage.

GPlus, the European public relations firm, had the hard task of trying to improve the media practices of the Kremlin. What Russian diplomats in the U.S. found sensible if not indispensable, high officials in Moscow considered strange and unnecessary. GPlus explained that it was important for officials and mandatory for press officials to talk and mingle with Western reporters at informal gatherings or lunches. And here it was not the allure of a good free meal that attracted Western journalists, but the possibility of gaining insights into stories, and perhaps a tidbit or two of inside information. Over time it became acceptable for unnamed Kremlin officials to leak facts and sometimes even stories to the media.

Journalists with the official statements in English and quotes from unnamed sources were set to write their stories. However, the Russian tradition of detailed press briefings followed by questions did not appeal to Western journalists, who ceased to attend by 2008. To hide their absence, a press Kremlin official asked a Russian journalist to pretend to be a foreigner by asking a question in fluent English.[39]

Lake Valdai International Discussion Club

In the public relations campaign, at first Russia had been copying and adapting Western models. RIA Novosti came up with the novel idea of organizing an annual forum where journalists, commentators, and scholars could hear notable Russian figures. The first forum was at Lake Valdai, and this beautiful site gave the name for the annual event taking place later in other regions in Russia and lasting sometimes as long as ten days. The featured speakers for the first meeting in 2004 were business leaders and cabinet ministers, so the surprise was complete when President Putin made an unexpected appearance and stayed for hours to discuss and take questions from the participants.[40]

This discussion club has often been the site for important announcements on domestic and foreign issues. Western participants wished that their home countries staged similar events, but Valdai has remained unique in the world. The Kremlin often has been disappointed to see that attendance did not always mean favorable coverage. Nevertheless, Valdai contributed to normalizing relations with Russia after the Five Day War with Georgia in 2008.

The Institute of Democracy and Cooperation

In October 2007 President Putin announced the creation of the Institute of Democracy and Cooperation with headquarters in Moscow and branches in Paris and New York City. The Institute was supposed to be a channel for dialogue between Russia and the West over the issues of democratic practices, human rights, religious freedom, and ethnic minorities.[41] As the U.S. Embassy in Moscow noted, "this not-quite nongovernmental organization is a novel step in Russia's expanding outreach efforts."[42]

The public relations firm of GPlus coached the directors of the two branches on how to handle Western media. Historian Natalia Narochnitskaya headed the Institute in Paris, and this former Duma deputy hired British intellectual John Laughland to be its director. The Paris branch hosted panels, issued reports, and made statements on issues of the moment. The Institute became one more fixture in the vibrant intellectual life of the French capital.[43]

The Institute in New York operated out of the 20th floor of a Manhattan skyscraper offering panoramic views. Under the direction of Andranick Migranyan, an Armenian-Russian former professor of the Moscow State Institute of Foreign Relations (MGIMO), the New York branch organized panels, hosted events, and partnered with similar American institutions.[44]

The publicity firms hired by the Kremlin registered under the Foreign Agents Registration Act (FARA), but at least during the early years of the Obama "reset," the U.S. government proved lax on enforcement and the Institute escaped official scrutiny. But when the Obama administration decided to lash out at Russia over the annexation of Crimea, the Institute was an easy target. The New York office had not attracted adequate private funding and failed to match the publicity achievements of the Paris branch. A cost-benefit analysis showed that the New York office had not lived up to expectations, and in June 2015 it shut down and director Migranyan returned to Moscow.[45]

TASS

The news service of the government was ITAR-TASS. In 2008 the Five Day War with Georgia found ITAR-TASS unprepared. Its reporting was almost all in Russian, and the language barrier prevented the diffusion of its press releases among Western media. A first step was to provide its news services in the main foreign languages of the world, including English, Spanish, French, and Arabic. The news service also reopened many news bureaus closed after the end of the Soviet Union and expanded the number of its correspondents inside Russia and abroad. The revitalization of the organization called for a new name, and in September 2014 ITAR-TASS returned to the simpler TASS designation of the Soviet period.[46]

Sputnik

The news organization RIA Novosti and Voice of Russia overlapped in functions. RIA Novosti targeted both domestic and foreign audiences, but Voice of Russia had only international listeners on radio. In response to the word-wide interest in news about Russia after the reunification with Crimea, the Kremlin on 10 November 2014 inaugurated a new agency, Sputnik, to convey information to foreign audiences. Sputnik took over the international services of RIA Novosti (its domestic services passed to a new agency Rossiya Segodnya) and also merged with Voice of Russia.[47] Margarita Simonyan, the chief editor of RT, expressed the reason behind the choice of this word: "I thought that is the only Russian word that has a positive connotation, and the whole world knows it."[48]

Sputnik, in its initial years, could not broadcast from the United States. Legislation prohibited foreign ownership of stations in the United States, and Sputnik struggled to lease air space from domestic owners. However, by relying on satellites, Sputnik was able to transmit a wide variety of radio programs in English. The radio programs were also available on the internet.[49]

The internet and not radio was turning out to be the real platform for Sputnik. The agency provided online news in over 30 languages and also offered its wire services in English, Spanish, Chinese, and Arabic. News flashes to computers and portable telephones across the world became the main channels for Sputnik to communicate with viewers. Photojournalists took captivating pictures for these news flashes accompanied by catchy and brief text captions. Sputnik, just like RT, also began to pursue the possibilities of reaching audiences in the United States through the many portals of social media.[50]

14

Skirmishes with the West

Seen from Moscow, the old Iron Curtain, running through the center of Europe, was being replaced with a new one, much closer to home.—British journalist Angus Roxburgh[1]

Damage Control in Ukraine

The Orange Revolution of December 2004 had been a victory for the West and a major setback for Russia. The Kremlin for the first time confronted the real possibility of losing its influence over Ukraine. On 24 January 2005 Yulia Tymoshenko became the first prime minister for the administration of recently elected president Viktor Yushchenko, the coalition that had made possible the Orange Revolution was determined to reduce Russian influence in the country. But the strong hostility between the prime minister and the president paralyzed the government. On 8 September Tymoshenko, just eight months after having taken office, resigned and plunged the country into political confusion.[2]

The self-destruction of the Orange Revolution was a relief for Moscow already in January 2006. Gazprom signed a favorable deal with Kiev, and for the first time Ukraine agreed to pay world prices for gas imports. No bloc or party had emerged as the dominant force in the country, and Russia did not detect any direct challenges to its vital interests. And although President Yushchenko continued to talk about Ukraine's entry into NATO, his government was too weak to take any action.[3]

It was not just good luck that had favored Russia. Taking a page out of the activists of the Orange Revolution, the Kremlin supported Viktor Yanukovych's efforts to hire American campaign consultants. Among these was Paul Manafort, later famous during the Donald Trump years. These American consultants were decisive in making possible the victory of Yanukovych's followers in the 2006 parliamentary elections. As a result, in a remarkable reversal of fortune, he became prime minister on 4 August 2006, barely a year and a half after the Orange Revolution had blocked his presidential bid.[4]

The new prime minister promised to improve relations with Russia, yet he was far from a Russian puppet. He continued to state that integration into Europe was inevitable for Ukraine, which first had to complete the long admission process into the World Trade Organization. Afterwards would come membership in the EU and much later in NATO.[5]

Yanukovych was a politician determined to consolidate his grip on power. Instead of going on vacation in August 2006 as the president did, Yanukovych devoted himself to enlarging the bureaucracy under his direct control. Well aware that his real base of support was in Eastern Ukraine, he selected followers from the Donetsk region to fill the overwhelming majority of positions.⁶ These appointments reinforced the deep bonds already existing between Donetsk and Yanukovych, a relationship that came to have tremendous significance in the events of 2014.

Everything indicated that Ukraine was starting to regain stability. In the political realm Yanukovych's tenure as prime minister promised him success in the presidential election of 2010. To prevent this outcome, his fierce opponent President Yushchenko took the unprecedented step of dissolving the Ukrainian parliament in the early days of April 2007 and convoking new parliamentary elections. When the election took place on 30 September, the results were far from conclusive, and Ukraine returned to a pattern of political uncertainty. With no other alternative available, President Yushchenko reconciled himself with Yulia Tymoshenko, such was his determination to drive Yanukovych from office.⁷

Forming a coalition from the competing parties in the new legislature did not prove easy, and only on 18 December 2007 did she become the new prime minister of Ukraine. Despite holding a slim two-vote majority in the parliament, she stayed in office until 4 March 2010. However, the slim margin meant that the government could take little action to halt the deteriorating economic situation in Ukraine.⁸

Weak Economy

Business confidence declined, in spite of all the efforts of Ukrainian authorities to make the country attractive to Western investors. The political instability also frightened Russian investors, who already owned assets worth over a billion dollars in Ukraine. In a major legacy from Soviet times, Russia was often the main if not sole market for many Ukrainian firms. But with the increased risks of doing business in Ukraine, many Russian companies stopped making investments or tried to avoid the country.

The best-known example was state-owned Gazprom, which concluded that relying on pipelines through Ukraine to supply gas to Europe was too risky. Gazprom, after the Orange Revolution, sought to establish alternative routes, beginning with North Stream to Germany through the Baltic Sea and Blue Stream through the Black Sea to Turkey. These pipelines were under construction in 2007, but Moscow did not push for a speedy completion.⁹

With the economy in Russia booming and its domestic market expanding, many private Russian firms saw little need to invest in risky Ukraine. The dependence on Ukraine for nearly 20 percent of the components for Russian defense industry made the Kremlin begin a process of shifting production to Russia. In another consideration, the high demand for Russian products meant that Ukraine ran trade deficits with its northern neighbor.¹⁰

For Russia the political chaos in Ukraine was not the ideal situation but was acceptable. Once the anti–Russian feelings of the Orange Revolution diminished, the Kremlin could work even with the more pro–Western Tymoshenko. And the prospects were good that Yanukovych could redeem the defeat of 2004 by winning the presidential election in 2009.¹¹

Georgia after the Rose Revolution: The Spy Crisis

After the Rose Revolution, the Kremlin held the hope that relations with Georgia would improve. Although the Rose Revolution is often regarded as the start of the downward path to collision with Russia, in reality the deterioration of relations was well advanced under the previous president, Edouard Shevardnadze.

The new president, Mikheil Saakashvili, or "Misha" as everyone called him, started off well on 10 February by making Moscow his first foreign stop. He handled himself sloppily, but President Vladimir Putin attributed the erratic behavior to the new leader's youth and inexperience. In reality Misha knew exactly what he wanted, and the day after his inauguration in January 2004 he promised to restore the territorial integrity of Georgia. In subsequent announcements he reiterated his goal of bringing Abkhazia and South Ossetia under the control of Tbilisi. This open and public defiance was in stark contrast to the quiet approach of Shevardnadze, who had always taken pains not to antagonize his powerful neighbor to the north.

Adjara

President Putin was willing to dismiss the provocative statements of the Georgian leader but the crisis over Adjara in April 2004 was a different matter. Misha issued an ultimatum to the local political boss Aslan Abashidze to give up his power over that autonomous region. The situation had an international dimension, because Turkey was a signatory to the treaty of 1921 guaranteeing the autonomy of Adjara, while Russia maintained a base at the small port of Batumi. Turkey agreed to stay out of the conflict after Georgia promised to respect the autonomy of Adjara, but the Kremlin had not yet made up its mind.[12]

Abashidze was an unconditional supporter of Russia, and the Kremlin was most reluctant to lose this valuable ally. But Russia was still bogged down in the Second Chechnya War and did not know yet that victory was coming later that same year. The Kremlin still distrusted the capabilities of its armed forces and did not believe that another military campaign simultaneous with the Second Chechnya War was possible. Reports that the Georgian military was in bad condition had reached the Kremlin, but Putin preferred to err on the side of caution. The Russian leader told Misha: "OK Mikheil Mikheilovich, we helped you on this one, but remember well, there will be no more free gifts offered to you, on South Ossetia and Abkhazia."[13]

Putin repeated this story many times to Western officials, who showed no gratitude because they considered the annexation of Adjara to be only one small one step in the drive to encircle the Russian Federation with NATO members. The crisis seemed to be over on 5 May when the Russian Foreign Minister Igor Ivanov flew with Abashidze to Russia. However, a few months later, when Saakashvili dismantled the autonomy of Adjara, Turkey felt it had been tricked and in response lost interest in supporting the territorial integrity of Georgia.[14]

South Ossetia and the U.S.

The loss of Turkish support did not worry Mikheil Saakashvili, who was already implementing his scheme to bring South Ossetia under Georgian control. Misha believed that he could repeat the Adjara maneuver. As a first step to intimidate the South Ossetians, on Independence Day, 26 May 2004, in Tbilisi, he reviewed the parade of the new tanks and military hardware Georgia had been purchasing abroad. Then on 31 May he shut down the Ergneti market south of Tskhinvali. He stationed troops along the border with South Ossetia to prevent smuggling, but the campaign was just a fig leaf to disguise the troop preparations for a military offensive.[15]

The Russia Foreign Ministry told Misha not to launch an invasion, but he ignored the warnings from Moscow and instead went to Washington to receive its blessing. However, the visit did not turn out as Misha expected. Secretary of State Colin Powell was direct: "don't get yourself into a situation that may overwhelm you and think that we are going to race in to rescue you from any difficulties you get into."[16] A stunned Misha went back to Georgia and ordered his troops to withdraw from the border with South Ossetia.

Misha in no way abandoned his plans to reincorporate South Ossetia by force, and he considered the blunt warning from Secretary of State Powell to be but a bump on the road. When Condoleezza Rice became the next Secretary of State, Misha was sure that at last U.S. diplomacy would carry out the expressed wishes of President George W. Bush to support Georgia in every way possible. The President himself came to Georgia on 10 May 2005 to give thanks to Misha in person for having sent troops to both Afghanistan and Iraq. The American president was just one of many U.S. politicians who made the mandatory pilgrimage to Georgia, where they all fell under the spell of Saakashvili, who displayed his fluency in English. The Georgian president was so enamored of the U.S. that English was almost the official language inside the government; in an ironic twist, the decades-long resentment over Russian displacing the native Georgian gave way to a rush to impose English.[17]

Upper Kodori Gorge

This aping of the U.S. bothered Moscow, but a much more serious provocation came on 4 July 2006 when Georgian troops seized the Upper Kodori Gorge in Abkhazia. Russia restrained the rebels from launching an operation to retake the territory, but when Moscow requested a UN Security Council resolution condemning the Georgian invasion, the U.S. rushed to defend its client state and refused to support the action on the ground, saying that any warnings should be done in private. The U.S. was acting like a parent who refuses to have anyone else reprimand their spoiled child.[18] In reality, the occupation of the Upper Kodori Gorge was just one more step in the West's main goal of trapping Russia behind its borders.

The Georgian president was aware of the limitations of his army, but not wishing to recognize the weak combat capabilities of his citizens, he decided to make up for their warrior skills with shiny and brand new weapons. Because Georgia supplied troops for both Afghanistan and Iraq, the Bush administration showered weapons on this ally and provided excellent and extensive training for Georgian soldiers, who, however, still did not seem very competent to foreign observers. Despite the American largesse, Saakashvili wanted more, in particular the heavy weapons indispensable to compensate the obvious deficiencies of Georgian soldiers. He was trying to mimic the "Shock and Awe" tactics of the American military to win a quick and easy victory over the separatists in Abkhazia and South Ossetia. Close allies of the U.S. such as Bulgaria and the Czech Republic consulted Washington about the exaggerated quantities Georgia was purchasing of powerful offensive weapons, such as heavy artillery and multiple rocket launchers. The Bush administration adopted the policy that Misha could have all that he wanted, on the assumption that the more toys he received, the better his behavior.[19]

The Kremlin remained unsure about the response to make. The provocative Georgian actions came to the attention of Azerbaijan, which saw in Georgia an example to follow and in Saakashvili a leader to imitate. The whole Russian position in the Caucasus was starting to crumble, and for a while Moscow could count only on the loyalty of Armenia and the separatist republics of Abkhazia and South Ossetia.[20]

Spy Crisis

Georgia triggered the Spy Crisis when it arrested 11 of its own citizens and four Russian officers on 27 September 2006. The Russian Foreign Ministry stated that the four arrested officers belonged to the Russian units still stationed in Georgia. It cannot be confirmed whether any of the four were military intelligence officers of GRU as Georgia claimed.[21] The arrested officers did not have diplomatic status, and Georgia prepared a public trial. This spectacle infuriated the Kremlin, but it wisely restrained its response. Intense pressure from the U.S. and NATO members persuaded Georgia to deport the four officers on 4 October, but the incident left a bad legacy.[22]

European NATO members were outraged by the way Georgia had treated the four detained Russian officers. To try to counter the negative publicity, Georgia released a video of the supposed spying activities, but the blurry televised images lent themselves to contradictory interpretations. In Moscow the idea spread even among the media that the Spy Crisis of 27 September was a direct response to NATO's decision to begin an Intensified Dialogue (ID), the first formal step in a country's process to enter than military alliance; the next step was the Membership Action Plan (MAP).[23]

The separatist republics accused Georgia of staging the Spy Crisis as a pretext to launch an invasion, and they suspended all talks with Tbilisi. Their termination of these conversations was the clearest indication that no peaceful outcome to the status of Abkhazia and South Ossetia was ever going to be possible.[24]

In response Russia hastened the closing of the last two Russian bases inside Georgia. In a prior statement in May 2005 both countries expressed their willingness to dismantle the bases by the end of 2008, but the hostility in Georgia to Russian servicemen persuaded the Kremlin to speed up the withdrawal. Russia handed over the Akhalkalaki base to Georgia and withdrew from the Batumi base by the end of the summer of 2007.[25]

The arrest of the four officers unleashed a wave of anti–Georgian actions in Russia. Overzealous officials expulsed at least 600 peaceful Georgians, and private Russian citizens harassed persons of Georgian ethnicity in different ways. The Kremlin halted these vengeful actions and to its immense credit did not allow their repetition under the much more serious circumstances of war in August 2008. Nevertheless, the harassment persuaded many of the over half a million Georgians living in Russia to take out citizenship in their adopted country.[26]

On 3 October 2006 the Kremlin imposed an economic near-blockade on Georgia, even though Tbilisi had released the four detained Russian officers on 2 October. Russian officials announced travel warnings to citizens considering visiting the country and stopped issuing entry visas to Georgians. Russia suspended all rail, air, road, sea, and mail connections with Georgia. The Kremlin also threatened to halt the remittances Georgians working in Russia sent home to their relatives. The negative impact on the Georgian economy loomed large, so U.S. diplomacy pressed Russia to reduce and repeal these harsh measures. As was already the traditional pattern, the U.S. wanted to normalize relations between the two countries by applying maximum pressure on Russia and ignoring Georgia that once again escaped scot-free. When Russia proved slow to respond to U.S. pressure, the official position became that the sanctions were beneficial to the West by driving Georgia to seek closer economic and political ties with EU.[27]

Russia also issued a direct, clear, and final warning to Georgia. When the Georgian Foreign Minister came to Moscow to try to obtain the lifting of the economic blockade, both Foreign Minister Sergei Lavrov and Russian Security Council Secretary Igor Ivanov on 1 November 2006 told him

> that Russia believes Georgia is planning to start violence. If that happens, Russia will respond with direct force. If that means confronting the whole international community, so be it. Russia will not care what damage it does to its relations with the U.S. or Europe; a Georgian initiation of hostilities will mean direct Russian military response.[28]

This statement accurately predicted Russia's actions during the August 2008 War with Georgia. But once again Misha believed that with the NATO umbrella moving closer over his country, he had gained the opportunity to lash out with impunity at his powerful neighbor to the north.

Missile Defense and the First Sanctions

The unilateral U.S. withdrawal from the Anti-Ballistic Missile (ABM) Treaty in December 2001 was a matter of deep worry for Russia. The Kremlin felt that this action foreshadowed the deployment of a missile defense intended to nullify Russia's second-strike nuclear capability. Initially the fears proved premature, and not until 2004 did the U.S. designate sites in the Czech Republic and Poland for the anti-missile installations.[29]

The Kremlin was angry, and U.S. briefings in November 2005 failed to calm Russian fears. The unconvincing justification American diplomats peddled around the world was that these missile defenses were needed to deter rogue states such as Iran and North Korea. But once these installations were operational, nothing prevented the U.S. from pointing them against Russia.[30]

The arrangements to install these weapons required considerable time, and Washington hoped that the protracted delays would calm Russia. The actual implementation could not begin because the U.S. first had to overcome opposition within NATO. Many European countries did not want to antagonize Russia, and several years passed without any action on the proposed missile defense.[31]

Arms Sales and the First Sanctions

While American diplomats struggled to hammer out a consensus with NATO allies about missile defense, another issue came to cloud relations with Russia in 2006. As part of the process of reviving its economy, the Kremlin promoted the sale of Russian weapons to foreign countries. The U.S.-financed projects of the 1990s for defense conversion were a thing of the past, and Russian diplomats promoted arms exports across the world.

Russia could no longer afford to give away weapons for free as the Soviet Union had done with its allies, so requiring payment limited the number of countries able to acquire Russian weapons. The West resented that Russia continued to sell weapons to China after the Tiananmen Square episode of June 1989, and France opposed Russian arms sales to the former French colonies of Algeria and Syria. For the U.S. the breaking point came when Russia signed big arms deals with Venezuela in July 2006.[32]

In retaliation, on 28 July 2006 the U.S. imposed sanctions on two Russian arm exporters—Rosoboronexport and Sukhoi—for supposedly having violated a non-nuclear proliferation law. So as to avoid singling out Russia, the U.S. decree also targeted two firms from India, two from North Korea, and one from Cuba, but the damage was already done, because Sukhoi had not signed any deals with Iran in years.[33] The sanctions "constituted a personal offense to Putin" who felt "deeply offended."[34] The Russian president promised to take up the matter at his next meeting with George Bush in November 2006, and later that same month the U.S. lifted the sanctions on Sukhoi after the firm provided information clarifying its sales.[35]

In the first days of November 2006, Russian diplomats learned that the U.S., rather than repealing the sanctions on Rosoboronexport, intended to extend them to three other Russian firms engaged in selling weapons abroad. In spite of Russian protests, the U.S. went ahead and adopted the sanctions on 28 December 2006, but they did not go into effect until they were published in the *Federal Register* on 5 January 2007. The American action was very insulting, because just after Russia voted on 23 December 2006 for UN Security Council sanctions on Iran over its nuclear weapons program, here was the U.S. taking punitive actions against Russia.[36]

An early example of the sloppiness typical in U.S. sanctions against Russia came when the Treasury Department targeted the individual Aleksandr Safanov, but Russian agencies, try as they might, could not uncover any information on that individual or even locate him. The name was widespread in Russia and often was used as a pseudonym to disguise the real owners of a firm. So in other words the U.S. was trying to punish a phantom or front entity.[37]

On a different level was Rosoboronexport. This official agency handled arms exports and also controlled the firms, both private and state-owned, producing the items. The sanctions prohibited any U.S. financial institution from lending money or in any way facilitating the arms sales of the targeted entities. The way Rosoboronexport operated was that as soon as it was sure that the foreign buyer was committed to making a purchase, then the Russian firm went abroad to borrow the entire cost of producing the items; these sums then became the working capital for the individual arms factories.[38]

The Bank of New York and several European banks provided the lowest rates for the loans, but U.S. sanctions closed access to American financial markets. Transactions in the "Euro" zone were not affected, but those in the "dollar" zone in Asia and the Middle East imposed higher costs on Rosoboronexport as it secured alternate lenders and made currency conversions. The estimated loss of profits for the Russian firm was about 1 to 2 percent—still leaving a wide margin of at least 98 percent.[39]

Just as it had done with Sukhoi, the U.S. Treasury offered the possibility of lifting the financial sanctions on Rosoboronexport if it provided detailed information on its arms sales. The firm, however, declined, because it felt that its market would suffer if potential customers knew that the U.S. government had access to proprietary and confidential information. The debate inside the Kremlin about whether to continue assuming the additional costs was not resolved until on 31 October 2007 when President Putin categorically announced that Russia will not accept interference in its arms sales. Russia remained committed to observing international agreements and Security Council resolutions but otherwise retained the right to decide to what countries to sell weapons.[40]

The dispute over the sanctions against Russian arms exports was still raging in late January 2007 when the United States announced it was proceeding with the construction of a missile defense system in the Czech Republic and Poland. These two nearly simultaneous blows proved too much for Putin, and he "finally lost patience with the Americans [...] I have had enough!"[41] This reaction was out of character for the Russian president, who already had a well-earned reputation for being cool and calm, even at times icy, under the most difficult circumstances. Only his closest aides knew about his anger with the U.S., so nobody in the West realized that on his way to the security conference in Munich, he was preparing to vent not just his but the world's frustration at the United States.

15

Countdown to Collision

Russia is a country with a history that spans more than a thousand years and has practically always used the privilege to carry out an independent foreign policy.—Munich Speech of Vladimir Putin

The Munich Speech of Vladimir Putin

When the president of Russia accepted the invitation to attend, for the first time, the annual Munich Conference on Security Policy, nobody expected any major pronouncements. However, indications of a major shift in Russian policy already were evident. Previously the Russian ambassador to the U.S. Yuri Ushakov in an interview had taken a tough tone, and as recently as 1 February 2007 Foreign Minister Sergei Lavrov stated that for Russia the U.S. was the "most difficult partner."[1]

Already in the home stretch of his second term, the president offered reflections at the international reunion on 10 February 2007. The conference format gave him considerable flexibility "to say what I really think about international security problems."[2] Just this admission was very revealing, because it confirmed that other opinions existed inside the Russian government. The Kremlin was not divided or fragmented, because on some issues it had nor or might not need to take a formal position. Putin's real goal was to communicate the philosophy underlying the rationale behind specific responses of the Russian government to the Western actions.

When he heard a Western defense minister state that not just the UN but also EU, and NATO could authorize the use of military force in the world, he could not let this statement pass without a rebuttal. First of all, he pointed out that for many states military action had become the new normal, when in reality "the use of force should be a really exceptional measure." Second, the Russian president emphasized over and over that "the use of force can only be considered legitimate if the decision is sanctioned by the UN" but not by other organizations such as EU and NATO. By highlighting the indispensable role of the UN, he was attacking the recurrent practice of Washington since Cold War days of turning to other organizations—in a few cases some almost unknown—to obtain a fig leaf to justify U.S. military intervention. The implicit message was that if the UN served as a gate keeper to military actions, the use of force was sure to decline in relations among states.

To make sure than no one misunderstood to whom he was referring, Putin stated that "one state and, of course, first and foremost the United States, has overstepped its national borders in every way." In the case of the Iraq invasion, the unilateralism went to extremes when the U.S. created its own little coalition when no existing international organization was willing to authorize the invasion of Iraq.

The Munich speech, however, was not a declaration of hostility against the United States and was more an appeal for Washington to modify its policy. The American public had already tired of the military intervention in Iraq and the real possibility existed of preventing another manifestation of unilateralism. The challenge for other world powers and not just for Russia was to move the United States into the channels of multilateralism and to recognize the supremacy of the UN over military interventions. He cited several examples of cooperation with the U.S. and agreed with "our European partners to the effect that Russia should plan an increasingly active role in world affairs." Unilateralism had thrived with the collapse of the Soviet Union, and the obvious way to return to multilateralism was for Russia to return to the world stage.

Secretary of Defense Robert Gates replied with gracious remarks to Putin's broadside and pledged U.S. cooperation in solving international problems, so at least at the Munich conference no fireworks erupted. But how was Washington to respond to the direct attack on its post–Soviet foreign policy? And what did it mean for the future of U.S.-Russian relations? A voice from the past provided the best analysis of the Munich speech. At the Gorbachev Foundation, Andrey Ryabov and the former Soviet ruler Mikhail Gorbachev explained that "Putin was proposing an agenda for cooperation, but warning that the lack of respect for Russia's interests would inevitably lead to confrontation."[3]

The Munich speech made a profound impression on several European countries, because Putin had expressed openly what they hesitated to say. Hungary and Greece felt that his speech reenergized the discussions at the 28 February 2007 meeting of the NATO-Russia Council. However, the U.S. was quick to dampen down any possibility of a meaningful dialogue. Even worse, the U.S. saw the Munich speech as an unfortunate rant by an individual rather than the expression of serious concerns held by many countries in the world. Not everyone in the West ignored the message, and at least *Time* magazine recognized Putin's vision by declaring him the "Person of the Year" for 2007.

The U.S. has a tradition of ignoring the major personality flaws of foreign leaders as long as the individuals remain pro-American. From Pancho Villa to Manuel Noriega, the U.S. courted unsavory characters in Latin America. The Bill Clinton administration put up with Boris Yeltsin's drunkenness and buffoonery as the necessary price to pay to extend U.S. supremacy over most of the former Soviet bloc. The general attitude was that foreign leaders should be cut some slack for having a bad day; perhaps Putin got up on the wrong side of the bed or his breakfast pancakes had been lumpy. U.S. officials regarded the Munich speech as an eccentric oddity, and their main preoccupation was to prevent a similar outburst from spoiling the mood at the upcoming Bucharest Summit of April 2008. An always graceful Putin was more than willing to provide reassurances to foreign diplomats because he knew that mere repetition was ineffective.[4] Once again he was confirming the lesson from the country's thousand-year history, that foreigners were accustomed to ignore the words coming from Russia.

The Munich speech shows that President Putin was under no illusion that the U.S. would change its behavior. But then why did he make these remarks if he knew they were ineffective? In reality the principal reason to give his speech was to regain ground on the ideological struggle with the West. Chapter 1 explained that after the fall of the Soviet Union, Russia lacked any ideological way to question or much less to stop the march of Western principles. The Bush administration repacked Western ideas into the seductive "Freedom Agenda," and the Kremlin lacked any ideological alternative. The Munich speech helped fill this void by denouncing the evils of unilateralism, and revealing that Russia once again could offer a valid alternative to the West to bring prosperity and peace to many countries.

The Bronze Soldier Statue Incident in Estonia

As the Soviet bloc disintegrated, angry crowds removed, tore down, or destroyed many monuments and statues related to Communist rule, but those of purely Russian significance most of the time escaped unharmed. A clear line existed, however, with the memorials commemorating the defeat of Nazi Germany. World War II had been such a traumatic and defining moment for the Russian population that anything related to the heroic struggle against Nazi Germany acquired not just mythical but also sacred dimensions. When proposals appeared to remove the World War II monuments located in prominent sites, a Russian outcry was inevitable. Only in Austria, with its neutral status, and in Hungary, with its growing ties to Russia, did circumstances preclude taking any action to offend Moscow.

In Estonia a weak administration was determined to demonstrate its power by removing the Bronze Soldier, a statute located close to the main government buildings. The plan was to move the memorial to a military cemetery, in spite of the protests from Moscow and the objections of ethnic Russians living in Estonia. Authorities initiated the operation by placing a fence around the memorial before dawn on 26 April 2007. That same night a crowd of young Russians numbering at least 1,500 gathered outside the monument to prevent its removal. Estonian officials in anticipation of disturbances had brought police from the entire country to arrest almost all the protestors.[5]

It was ironic to reflect that Mikhail Gorbachev made possible the collapse of the Soviet Union by refusing to order the arrest of the protestors in the Baltic Republics in 1991. Instead in 2007 the mass arrest of pro–Russian demonstrators in Estonia evoked no anguished cries from the West about human rights, and NGOs remained silent. Angry Russian youths established a blockade around the Estonian embassy in Moscow, and sometimes they even hurled bricks at the windows of the embassy.[6]

EU officials quietly negotiated a solution to end the clashes outside the Estonian embassy. In exchange for the departure of the Estonian ambassador, the Russian protestors agreed to lift their siege on 4 May 2007. President Putin in his speech during the 9 May Victory Parade limited himself to denouncing countries that "belittle" and "desecrate" monuments commemorating the Soviet victory in World War II.[7]

Another Russian response turned out to be a first in world history. Estonia was one of the most digitally connected societies in the world but on 27 April its computers experienced disruptions. "The initial attacks were technically unsophisticated and seemed more like a cyber riot than a cyber war," and consisted of barrages of spam to e-mail accounts and cyber-vandalism.[8] On 30 April the attacks multiplied and became more harmful. The web sites of the Estonian government crashed one after another because of Distributed Denial of Service (DDS) attacks. Then on 3 May the hackers' focus shifted to the private sector, and in particular to banks. Financial institutions were much better prepared to face the security threats to their accounts and their customers, but the ferocity of the assault found the private sector vastly outgunned.[9]

The only way to save the banks was to close all foreign links, but at the huge costs in many missed financial transactions and money transfers. So while the banks escaped with their accounts relatively unharmed, the financial cost had been substantial. The cyber war also shut down the web sites of the leading newspapers, and this absence of information left the population confused and anxious. Additional pressure came when Russian authorities at this moment decided to introduce new revisions and sanitary safeguards on trade with Estonia but without imposing anything resembling a blockade. The goal was to harass and annoy Estonian businesses and also to encourage customers to use the facilities and services on the Russian side of the border.[10]

The cyber war reached its highest level on 9 May, VE day, and then tapered off afterwards. The last major attack occurred on 15 May when "bots" crashed the site of one Estonian bank for 30 minutes. By early June the attacks returned to the nuisance level existing before 27 April.

Everything indicated that private Russian individuals had carried out the Cyber War, and the most respected group of digital experts in Estonia said privately "that no smoking gun incriminating Moscow has turned up and likely won't. The use of bots, proxies, and spoofing tactics makes it extremely difficult to determine with any certainty the origin of the attacks."[11] Despite this conclusion, "the government of Estonia believes it has enough circumstantial evidence to link Moscow with the attacks" and foreshadowing the Obama administration years later, accused the Kremlin.

Estonia had been trying to free itself from dependence on Russia, but the economic ties were too advantageous for both countries to let this dispute harm business for long. The disruptions in traffic on the border disappeared, and by early September 2007 relations between the two countries were normalizing. Estonia had suffered serious economic losses and paid a high price for the sake of removing one statue.[12] Whatever plans other countries had to remove Soviet statues faded, so although the Bronze Soldier did not return to its original location, Russia could be considered to have emerged largely victorious from this clash. Not until the outbreak of the crisis in Ukraine in 2014 did another former Soviet republic dare to topple statues.

Conventional Forces in Europe Treaty (CFE)

"In the beginning was the Word," was how Vladimir Putin described his Munich speech in a press conference at Amman during a goodwill trip to the Middle East. And continuing the analogy to the Bible, "now we have said our word and hope attitudes toward it will be positive."[13] He did not have to remind his audience that the Word in St. John's gospel was so powerful because it introduced the eventful ministry of Jesus Christ.

On 26 April 2007, the same day of the start of the crisis with Estonia over the Bronze Soldier Statue, Putin delivered his final address to the Russian parliament. He announced that it was "expedient to declare a moratorium on Russia's implementation of the Conventional Forces in Europe Treaty until all NATO members, with no exception ratify it."[14] Rather than a moratorium, he could have announced Russia's complete withdrawal but did not do so because he wanted to give the West one last chance to save this treaty hanging in limbo since 1999.

The announcement caught many Western countries by surprise; for example "the French reaction was to register 'incomprehension.'"[15] Russian diplomats explained that "Russia just cannot live with the current Treaty any longer, and that Russia is at the end of its tether."[16] What had caused the Kremlin to turn against CFE?

The treaty was a legacy of the final years of the Soviet Union and the majority of its clauses reflected altogether different circumstances. It had been revised in 1996 and amended in 1999 to try to take into account the entry of former members of the Warsaw Pact into NATO. Thirty countries signed the "Agreement on Adaptation of the CFE" in 1999, but only four—including Russia—had ratified the revised treaty. Not a single NATO state had ratified the agreement, which imposed a very strict inspection regime on Russia. The essence of the agreement consisted of limiting the number of tanks, heavy artillery, and armored combat vehicles each country could deploy within Europe.[17]

Russia never reached those ceilings and the real complaint of the Kremlin was the "flank" regime. The Adapted Treaty of 1999 sharply limited the number of heavy weapons Russia could deploy in the military districts in St. Petersburg and the Caucasus. The ferocious rebel resistance at the start of the Chechnya War pushed Russia to exceed the limit of heavy weapons in the Caucasus. The Bill Clinton administration used this violation as a pretext not to submit the revised CFE treaty for ratification to the U.S. Senate. In reality the U.S. was using CFE as leverage to force Russia to desist from its campaign to reestablish control over Chechnya.[18]

The U.S. goal for wanting to limit Russian deployments near St. Petersburg became clear when the three Baltic Republics joined NATO. This enlargement was unsound from a military perspective, because war games confirmed that Russia could overrun those three countries. NATO needed to have the "flank" regime in place to prevent the Kremlin from doing in the Baltics what it had done in Chechnya.

The end of major operations in Chechnya reduced the need for heavy weapons in that war, and Russia was able to state in July 2002 that it was back in compliance with the ceilings in CFE for the Caucasus and requested ratification of the Adapted Treaty. The West replied by placing new conditions, such as the withdrawal of Russian troops and heavy weapons from Transnistria, Abkhazia, and South Ossetia. In reality only in Transnistria did the troops still have some Soviet-era heavy weapons, but even there the quantities were well below the ceilings of the CFE for the "flank" requirement. The number of Russian soldiers was very small in these three regions. The Western demand to withdraw from Abkhazia and South Ossetia was outrageous, because international agreements with implicit UN authorization authorized the presence of lightly armed Russian peacekeepers in these two separatist regions.[19]

Russia refused to accept this blackmail, and in response NATO states postponed the ratification of the Adapted CFE. Years passed without any action until on 26 April 2007 Putin at the annual address to the Russian parliament declared a moratorium. The legislative process to repeal the treaty normally consumed months, and clever Western diplomats saw the opportunity to engage in endless negotiations to lure Russia into prolonging the duration of the treaty. In a final warning in June 2007, the Kremlin showed its determination by denying the requests to carry out the routine inspections under the CFE treaty. Angry diplomats of countries that had never ratified the treaty had the impudence to denounce Russia for these refusals.[20]

Nobody in Russia questioned the need for the moratorium, and all that was left was for the bill suspending the CFE treaty to wind its way through the legislative channels. On 7 November the Duma passed the bill, and the upper house also gave its approval. President Putin signed the bill into law, and effective on 12 December 2007 Russia suspended any participation in the CFE. The country regained the liberty to deploy its conventional forces across the vast expanse of its territory.[21] Conspiracy theorists saw in the repeal a first preparation for the Five Day War with Georgia in August 2008, when on the contrary the Kremlin saw in the freedom to deploy troops a deterrent to prevent Georgia from starting hostilities. Rational leadership in Tbilisi should have seen in the abrogation of CFE one more warning against taking rash actions, but as the next chapter shows, the state of mind of Georgia was far from sane.

Kosovo—Again

The consequences of the collapse of Yugoslavia in the early 1990s have continued to have an impact on relations between the West and Russia. The Pristina episode of 1999 almost led to war between NATO and Russia, and afterwards finding a formula for Kosovo proved elusive. By 2004 most Western countries advocated independence for Kosovo as the best solution, while Serbia and Russia preferred to maintain the status quo of this region. Because international peacekeepers prevented the outbreak of violence among ethnic groups, nobody sensed a rush to find a permanent solution.[22]

Serbia was intransigent and refused to accept the independence of Kosovo. As long as Serbia could count on support from Russia, any negotiated solution was impossible. The solution to the Kosovo crisis lay through Moscow but the U.S. refused this path and the Europeans were rather skeptical.[23]

France and Austria, as early as 2005, urged negotiating with Russia as the only way to solve the Kosovo crisis. A long laborious consultation ensued among European countries over whether to engage in bargaining with Moscow over Kosovo, and after several years still no consensus emerged, because negotiating with Russia as an equal was anathema to U.S. officials. Through their contacts Russian diplomats found out about the draft proposal and in March 2007 they reacted indignantly. Russia was not "looking for a 'swap' in another region or a horse-trade on another issue [...] Lavrov had been clear: Russia had a principled difference with the U.S. over Kosovo."[24]

The firm Russian refusal outraged many European countries, and Italy—no longer governed by pro–Russian Prime Minister Silvio Berlusconi—was the harshest in its response and demanded immediate independence for Kosovo: "in the end there must be recognition, because the EU cannot let Russia impose its will on Europe."[25] But countries such as Bulgaria and Greece were opposed to independence for Kosovo. Ukraine was worried about the impact on Transnistria. The most important holdout was Spain, because it feared creating a precedent for its restless province of Catalonia.[26]

The U.S. applied pressure on the dissidents and hoped to secure consensus by the end of 2007. Dissatisfied with the slow pace of progress on Kosovo, the new French president Nicolas Sarkozy decided to take a more direct approach. He sent his Foreign Minister Bernard Kouchner on the mission impossible of threatening Russia into compliance. France was accustomed to brow-beating its former African colonies, but such a policy stood no chance of success against a world power.[27]

Kouchner went to Moscow for a two-day visit in September 2007. He offered the usual vague carrot of seeking "a close relationship with Russia" but also warned that if Russia did not comply with French demands, that "the Sarkozy government would be more vocal on human rights and on the situation in Chechnya."[28] Foreign Minister Kouchner was the last Western official to try to use Chechnya as leverage against Russia, but he was beating a dead horse because that war had been over for three years. He also met with human rights organizations and made a visit to the newspaper which employed Anna Polikovskaya before the journalist's tragic death. By these actions the French Foreign Minister only confirmed Russian fears that

NGOs were mere tools of Western powers to effect regime change.

Foreign Minister Lavrov, often condemned to bear the impertinent comments of Western officials, took the attacks with grace. In the joint news conference with his French counterpart, the Russian Foreign Minister Lavrov called his counterpart a friend from past diplomatic engagements and waxed eloquently on the long bilateral relationship with France.

By January 2008 the U.S. felt that a clear majority of Western countries were willing to support the independence of Kosovo. Attention shifted to trying to prepare for possible Russian responses. The Kremlin insisted on having the Security Council approve any solution, but the U.S. once again decided to bypass that international body and to create its own group of followers.

The one big holdout was Spain, which had almost gained the opportunity to have a major impact on world affairs. Help for Spain came from an unexpected source when Georgia pleaded for delaying the independence of Kosovo as long as possible; Georgia correctly pointed out that the West was creating the perfect precedent for Russia to recognize the independence of the separatist republics of Abkhazia and South Ossetia. Most European countries likewise feared setting a precedent, but their obsession with preventing Russia from imposing its will drove them to recognize the independence of Kosovo.[29]

Should the Kremlin respond to the independence of Kosovo by recognizing the separatist republics in Georgia, then the West was ready with a large range of countermeasures. In the reprisals appeared for the first time the goal of "Russian isolation" a prominent element of later Western responses to the Kremlin. Another possibility was to boycott the 2014 Sochi Olympics. The West did not like to host international sporting events in Russia and was on the lookout for any excuse to boycott the Sochi Olympics of 2014.[30]

Russia refused to budge on the independence of Kosovo and promised to veto any attempts to secure membership for the new country in the United Nations and OSCE. In a big disappointment for Moscow, Turkey supported the independence of Kosovo, and a Turkish firm was producing nine tons of flags for the new country. Russia understood that the large Muslim population in Kosovo made the Turkish recognition inevitable, but still this was a bitter pill to swallow.[31]

On 17 February 2008 Kosovo unilaterally declared its independence, and the West stood ready to respond to Russian measures. The days passed with nothing but the predictable verbal condemnations. Then President Putin at a press conference announced that Russia "would not ape Western actions" and just because the West "took a stupid and illegal decision" did not mean that Russia had to act in the same way.[32] The Duma previously received a request from the separatist republics in Georgia to recognize their independence, and the Kosovo declaration persuaded the Russian legislature to schedule hearings on these frozen conflicts, including Transnistria.

The Duma held hearings on 13 March 2008, but this was far from a forceful action. Western diplomats accurately concluded that the Kremlin wanted to keep alive the possibility of responding, but that for the moment no action was imminent. The division among European countries was clear although muted. Kosovo has remained until the present in a diplomatic limbo and has not escaped the status of a frozen conflict. The West rushed to make Kosovo a member of the World Bank and the International Monetary Fund on 29 June 2008, but Russia has prevented Kosovo from joining the UN and OSCE.[33]

Despite the ambiguous outcome in Kosovo, the West insisted on proceeding with independence in the face of strong Russian objections. Once again the West had demonstrated its determination to ignore the views of Moscow. The arsenal of countermeasures the West had readied remained unused in the face of the weak Russian response. Did this mean that Russia would never react? The Kremlin had done everything over Kosovo short of drawing "red lines"; the decision to support Serbia in 1914 led to World War I, and Russia was determined not to repeat that blunder. Russia had specified "red lines" only about NATO membership for Georgia and Ukraine, but the failure to mount even a modest response to Kosovo independence suggested in a Chinese analogy that Russia was nothing but a "paper tiger." Was it safe to conclude that a clawless bear was unwilling and unable to respond if the West crossed the red lines of Georgia and Ukraine?

16

The Five Day War with Georgia

> *While Russia was not interested in an armed conflict [...] if Georgia was determined to precipitate hostilities, Russia would respond.*—Deputy Foreign Minister Grigory Karasin[1]

The declaration of independence of Kosovo in February 2008 certainly pointed Georgia toward a confrontation with Russia, but in contrast to the opinions of many Western observers, this war was from predetermined or inevitable. According to a prevailing view, Russia was determined to seek revenge for its humiliation over the independence of Kosovo. Nothing could be further from the truth, and as this first section shows, Russia was the only country striving to prevent Georgia from starting a war.

The Failure of Diplomacy: The Bucharest Summit of April 2008

In the specific case of Abkhazia, the Kremlin was under considerable domestic pressure to recognize this separatist region. Russia declined to take this route but did want to express its displeasure by lifting on 6 March 2008 Russia the 1996 economic sanctions against Abkhazia. This blockade had been in place as part of the measures to try to prevent a return to combat by any side inside Georgia. Abkhazians suffered hunger and other deprivations while the blockade lasted.[2]

By lifting sanctions but not recognizing Abkhazia, Moscow had crafted a finely tuned response that showed Russian diplomacy at its best. But additional measures proved necessary when the Kremlin learned that at the scheduled NATO summit at Bucharest of 2-4 April 2008, the U.S. and Eastern European countries were preparing to extend a Membership Action Plan (MAP) not just to Georgia but to Ukraine as well. On 13 March 2008 the Duma unanimously passed a non-binding resolution urging the executive branch to recognize the independence of Abkhazia and South Ossetia and also of other frozen conflicts such as Transnistria.[3]

The Bucharest Summit of 2-4 April 2008

Russia did not know that President George W. Bush decided in the last days of February to offer MAP for Georgia and Ukraine as the first step for entry into NATO. He was determined to complete the expansion of the military alliance, and once Georgia and Ukraine joined, the Black Sea became a NATO lake capable of squeezing Russia out of its vital trade routes through the Bosporus. Russia had, for years, and most notably Vladimir Putin in the recent Munich speech of 2007, expressed total opposition to an expansion which Secretary of State Condoleezza Rice supported with enthusiasm.[4]

Bush hoped to make the expansion tolerable to Russia by drawing on his long friendship with Putin; in Western media it has become a cliché to say that Putin constantly bamboozled a naïve Bush, when in reality it was the American who betrayed the trust of the Russian. But Bush first had to secure the approval of German chancellor Angela Merkel. Germany and other countries such as Spain realized that extending MAP to Georgia and Ukraine without any warning was an insult to Russia and could probably provoke hostile reactions. Russia has been Germany's most important trading partner, and Chancellor Merkel did not want anything to endanger her country's prosperity, so she correctly blocked granting MAP to Georgia and Ukraine. But the Eastern Europeans in union with the U.S. and the unexpected ally of France, under its new president Nicolas Sarkozy, still demanded action.[5]

In a decisive meeting with the Eastern Europeans in which paradoxically all spoke Russian as their only common language, an exasperated Merkel accepted a contradictory compromise. The Bucharest Summit rejected granting MAP to Georgia and Ukraine but declared in the communiqué of 3 April that they "shall become members of NATO." A NATO meeting of Foreign Ministers later that same year in December would finally grant the two countries the MAP, and real membership in the military alliance was inevitable after several years. Not surprisingly, Georgia was ecstatic about its virtual acceptance into NATO.[6]

The next day, on 4 April, Putin arrived for the closing session at Bucharest; he became the first and last Russian president ever to attend a NATO summit. He went through the formalities and respected his promise to Bush not to give a second Munich speech. He clutched to the refusal to grant MAP status as a life raft for Russia, but the president, just like the Foreign Ministry, realized that the country suffered a major defeat.[7]

Russia's Efforts to Prevent War

If Russia had been the aggressive country typically portrayed in Western media, the Kremlin would have responded to the Bucharest decision by launching invasions of both Georgia and Ukraine to prevent their admission into NATO. But in spite of regarding the setback as a "stunning blow" and being angry "that the U.S. had gotten everything it wanted," the Kremlin concluded that "the best Russia could hope for was to slow the pace of expansion."[8]

Russia recovered from the defeat at Bucharest and realized that it still had a few diplomatic cards to play. A treaty requirement for admission into NATO has been that an aspiring country could not be involved in a territorial dispute with any of its neighbors. As long as the separatist regions of Abkhazia and South Ossetia existed as independent entities, then at least according to the treaty articles, Georgia could not become a member of NATO.

Immediately upon Putin's return from the Bucharest summit, he issued a statement on 4 April that Russia promised to provide economic, financial, and humanitarian assistance to Abkhazia, and also to embark on projects such as the restoration of the transportation infrastructure. The statement gave the impression of being a response to the Bucharest summit but in reality was in reply to the reports that Georgia was planning to launch invasions of Abkhazia and South Ossetia.[9]

Russian media on 15 April reported that the Kremlin intended to open "offices" in Abkhazia and South Ossetia for the purpose of providing services to the at least 90 percent of the population which held Russian passports. The offices were supposed to open by 18 April, but the U.S. and other

Western powers furiously protested and condemned them as the equivalent of having embassies and thus openly recognizing the independence of those separatist republics.[10]

In response to this outcry, the Kremlin reversed course and suspended plans to open the offices in the separatist republics. Instead, Putin issued "Instructions" to government officials to "promote economic, social, cultural, and educational ties" with Abkhazia and South Ossetia; the Instructions also ordered regional offices in bordering regions to provide consular services for Russian citizens residing in the separatist entities.[11] In retrospect, the Russian reversal was a mistake because it confirmed the assumption in Tbilisi that the U.S. would always be able to protect Georgia from its northern neighbor.

Georgia, however, was not satisfied completely with the weak U.S. protest over the "Instructions." Tbilisi halted talks over Russian accession into the World Trade Organization (WTO). Georgia had come to have a veto power over Russian accession because the only outstanding issue blocking WTO membership was the failure to negotiate an agreement over the transit of merchandise on the common border. Georgia demanded that Russia repeal the "Instructions" but the Kremlin rejected the blackmail.[12]

Russian intelligence confirmed that Georgia was planning to launch a military operation to regain control over Abkhazia and South Ossetia. After the war it has become commonplace to put all the blame on the volatile president of Georgia, Mikheil Saakashvili, and he does bear the primary responsibility. But an attitude of preferring to use force to settle disputes already existed within large sectors of the government. The Russians had detected this hostility, but in a noteworthy lapse, the U.S. Embassy failed to report any aggressive tendencies.[13] The oversight was not caused solely by an extreme case of "clientelitist," when an American embassy becomes a captive advocate of the local government, and actually represented the desire to supply Washington with only what it wanted to hear.

Georgia, since the Rose Revolution of November 2004, enjoyed tremendous U.S. support and had become a pet project of President Bush, who included the country in his now-forgotten "Freedom Agenda" for the whole world. Because American diplomats dismissed all Russian reports that Georgia was planning to attack as baseless fear mongering, the Kremlin took more direct actions on the ground to deter Georgia from launching an attack. By the agreement of 14 May 1994 Russia had the right to station up to 3000 peacekeepers equipped only with small arms. Russia had never reached that threshold and over the years deployed no more than 2000 from the regular army. On 29 April 2008 Russia announced that it was filling the full complement of 3000 with elite airborne forces. The airborne troops for the first time brought heavy weapons, in this case ten 122 mm artillery pieces.[14]

Russia warned the U.S. constantly that the American client state was out of control and preparing to start a war. While the few practitioners of *Realpolitik* in the Kremlin welcomed a Georgian attack as the best and simplest way to settle the dispute, the majority of Russian officials felt that their armed forces were not yet ready for a war against Georgia. The formidable arsenal Georgia had acquired through its spending spree of arms purchases abroad argued for leaving the military solution as a last resort.[15]

Georgia on the contrary became more determined to take military action. Three events influenced the Georgian attitude. First of all, the return of colorful Silvio Berlusconi to be the ruler of Italy had for all practical purposes deprived Georgia of any chance of receiving a Membership Action Plant (MAP) at the December meeting of the Foreign Ministers. The Italian Prime Minister, a true ally of Russia and a personal friend of Putin, persuaded Germany to delay NATO membership for Georgia and Ukraine. Saakashvili learned that Germany in June regretted the promises made at the April summit and was no longer willing to support a MAP for either country.[16] Lastly, on 7 May Dmitry Medvedev was inaugurated as the new president of Russia, after Putin stepped down because of the two-term limit in the Russian Constitution. Outwardly Medvedev appeared more pro–Western and possibly also weaker than Putin and thus less likely to take forceful action against Georgia.[17] Saakashvili concluded that the window of opportunity to get away with a seizure by force of the separatist regions was fast closing for Georgia.

Russia for its part was following a two-track policy. At one level, it hoped that the increased presence in Abkhazia would deter Georgia. At another level, Russian diplomats pressed hard for Georgia to sign a "non-use-of-force" pledge, a euphemism for the largely discredited older term of "non-aggression pact." Russia made repeated efforts to enlist U.S. and Western support for the non-use of force agreement but to no avail. A stubborn U.S. was doing everything possible to try to stop Berlusconi and Merkel from blocking a MAP offer to Georgia at the December NATO meeting.[18]

A disappointed Russia learned to its surprise that the deployment of the elite airborne forces to Abkhazia had failed to persuade Georgia to abandon its plan to launch an invasion. Russia had reached the limit of troops allowed under the 1994 agreement and needed to find a way around the restriction. On 31 May the Kremlin announced the ingenious solution of sending a railway battalion of around 400 soldiers to rebuild the railroad line running from Russia through Abkhazia to Armenia. Because these were not combat troops, they did not fall under the 3000 limit.

Georgia was outraged by the railway battalion and Saakashvili threw many a temper tantrum but to no avail. Unlike the earlier reversal over opening Russian offices in Abkhazia, this time Moscow stood its ground and refused to recall the railway battalion. Only after completing the rehabilitation of the network of tracks did the railway battalion withdraw on 4 August, just days before Georgia launched its attack on South Ossetia.[19]

Once Georgia realized that Russia was not walking away from Abkhazia, Saakashvili realized that the original plan for a simultaneous invasion of Abkhazia and South Ossetia was no longer militarily feasible. Georgia reduced its invasion plans to occupying only South Ossetia, where Russia had not reinforced its small peacekeeping detachments. The Russian General Staff considered the enclave indefensible and ruled out sending any troops. But a message had to be sent, and in a final warning, four Russian fighter jets deliberately flew over South Ossetia; such a violation of supposedly Georgian airspace had never before taken place. Georgia refused to realize that they were a final clear warning that the Russian air force was ready to engage in combat action if Georgia attacked South Ossetia.

The Kremlin pressed Georgia hard to sign the no-use-of-force agreement and hoped that the visit of Secretary of State Condoleezza Rice might at least persuade Saakashvili from taking the path of war. In retrospect, the visit of the Secretary of State on 10 July 2008 was the last opportunity to avert the outbreak of war. It is hard to believe that she was not informed of all the military preparations of Georgia. She failed to deliver a blunt warning message and only recommended but did not insist that Saakashvili sign the non-use-of-force agreement.[20]

For the Secretary of State Tbilisi had been one more stop in her world tour, and she failed to realize that her real mission was to prevent the outbreak of war. She left Saakashvili with the mistaken impression that he was free to seize South Ossetia quickly and then present Russia and the world with a fait accompli. Diplomacy was over and all that was left was to finalize the details for the invasion of South Ossetia.

Georgia hosted military exercises named "Immediate Response" for NATO and non-members in July, and Russia in reply organized the military maneuvers "Caucasus 2008" for August. Saakashvili decided to wait until the Russian troops finished their exercise and returned to their bases deep inside vast Russia. The Georgian president did not know that news of the impeding invasion had reached Moscow, and that as a precaution, the Russian General Staff retained two battalions from the Caucasus 2008 maneuvers just north of the Roki Tunnel, the lifeline into South Ossetia.[21]

The Georgian president gave the order to launch the offensive into South Ossetia on the night of August 7 at 11:30 p.m. The war began when Georgian artillery pounded the capital of Tskhinvali and left in ruins many civilian neighborhoods.

International Law and the Military Conflict in Georgia

The term international "law" is unfortunate and in many ways inaccurate, because what jurists and scholars really are talking about are practices, customs, and traditions; a superficial resemblance puts international law closer to the observations anthropologists make about isolated tribes and cultures. Yet the association with texts, such as treaties, agreements, and conventions makes hard abandoning the term of "law." And the existence of court cases and the proliferation of international tribunals since the twentieth century reaffirms the "law" aspect and makes dropping the term highly unlikely.

In reality, international law more resembles a continuum or range. At one end are the "hard" and legal texts, which supposedly have universal validity. Yet even here, such sacrosanct principles as the immunity of diplomats have come under fire, most notably during the Iranian hostage crisis of 1979 when Tehran used American diplomats as bargaining chips to obtain the unfreezing of financial assets. The range then proceeds to widely accepted practices probably codified in agreements and then to more informal understandings valid for only some regions or a small number of countries. And always is the future, where international law lags behind in trying to develop practices and texts to meet new and ever changing circumstances.

Aggression and Illegal Acts of War

The *Report of the Independent Fact-Finding Mission on the Conflict with Georgia* embodies widespread European views.[22] The Fact-Finding Mission detailed and elaborated the European position on the war articulated by French president Nicolas Sarkozy: Georgia was guilty of aggression while Russia was guilty of having employed disproportionate force to repel the attack. For both the French president and the Fact-Finding Commission, the urgent priority was to bury the war in the past, and the easiest way was to blame both sides.

For the first part of the pre-established narrative, the Fact-Finding Mission in accordance with "hard" international law had no choice but to condemn Georgia for starting the Five Day War. Over several days Georgia planned and implemented the preparations for a lightning offensive to seize control of all of South Ossetia. On the night of ⅞ August 2008 the massive shelling Georgia unleashed left most parts of the capital Tskhinvali in ruins. The Georgian army used not only artillery but also large numbers of GRAD multiple rocket launchers. International law considers illegal the use of these very inaccurate rocket launchers in dense urban areas, so Georgia was the aggressor and also utilized disproportionate and illegal force to try to gain control of Tskhinvali.

The Fact Finding Mission confirmed that the Russian peacekeepers in South Ossetia had not taken any provocative action to justify the Georgian onslaught. The Russian peacekeepers holed up in their compound possessed only small arms and thus lacked the means to launch artillery barrages or take any substantial military action. The categorical condemnation of Georgia should have ended any discussion about who started the war, yet this conclusion of the Fact-Finding Mission tends to get lost or ignored. At least in the United States, talking heads and pundits on television continue until today to condemn Russia for attacking Georgia. Even American diplomats in their robot-like condemnations of Russia in the United Nations cannot resist citing Georgia as a victim of Russian aggression.

Conduct of War

By condemning Georgia for using GRAD multiple rocket launchers against civilians, the Fact-Finding Mission paradoxically opened a line of argument to criticize the Russian conduct of the war. The assumption in the West was that Georgia had been the victim, but unless the Fact-Finding Mission found something—anything—to condemn Russia, then the inevitable conclusion was that Georgia needed to be punished and its leaders dragged to an international tribunal for condemnation as war criminals.

Along ceasefire lines in the world, such as in the India-Pakistan border, armed inroads result in a fierce military response until the invaders are pushed back behind the frontier line. This return to the *status quo ante* has been possible when a clear dividing line existed, but that was not the situation in South Ossetia. A wedge of Georgian villages isolated Tskhinvali in the north, and nothing resembling a border line existed to separate the intermingled villages and neighborhoods.

In many ways Russia has never recovered from the shock of having been attacked for the first time since the Nazi invasion of 22 June 1942. Being in a state of trauma affected the Russian rulers and commanders who almost to the end of the war were in a state of ignorance about what was going on in the battlefield. For all practical purposes Russian troops only knew what their spotters and observers could see with optical equipment. It is well known that Georgian drones reported in detail all movements of Russian troops, who lacked the means to shoot down the drones and did not have any drones of their own. Aerial reconnaissance was useless, because although the Russian possessed complete control of the air, the coordination with ground troops was deficient. The tragic result was that all but one of the Russian airplanes shot down during the war was because of friendly fire; in such a chaotic situation the Russian airplanes were in no condition to report on Georgian movements.

The Russian General Staff took only one precaution before the war. In response to repeated warnings from the South Ossetians of an impending Georgian attack, the Russian high command decided to leave two battalions near the northern entrance of the Roki Tunnel. These units had participated in the just concluded Caucasus 2008 military maneuver and rather than returning them to their distant home bases, keeping them nearby provided ready reinforcements; however, the force was too small to take on the entire Georgian army.

After Georgia began its shelling of Tskhinvali on the night of August 7–8, these two battalions rushed down the Roki Tunnel to try to protect the vulnerable Russian peacekeepers. This force together with the Ossetian militias won the first battle of Tskhinvali and sent the initial wave of Georgians reeling in retreat. But before the battlefield situation could stabilize, a second wave of Georgian troops arrived to try to capture the city from the west. The 2nd Brigade had come from its base in Senaki and caught by surprise Russian commanders who were in the dark about the movements of Georgian forces.

On 9 August the arriving Georgian brigade was on the verge of capturing not just Tskhinvali but also the Russian peacekeepers, who would make great bargaining chips to negotiate a final peace settlement. In an unexpected benefit from the Second Chechnya War, Chechens loyal to Moscow in the Vostok and Zapad battalions were the nearest troops available for combat in South Ossetia. When these seasoned warriors reached Tskhinvali late in the afternoon of August 9, in ferocious street-by-street fighting they stopped the Georgian troops, who then fled in a panicky retreat.

With Georgian units appearing out of nowhere, Moscow and commanders did not know what else to expect. In desperation officials scrambled to send all available units to South Ossetia and to Abkhazia. Although airborne units (without their heavy weapons) were starting to arrive, to complete the deployment required at least a week. A sense of urgency gripped Moscow when it learned that the Russian peacekeepers had almost been captured.

Most worrisome, Georgian artillery continued to pound Tskhinvali, and Russian commanders prudently interpreted the shelling as preparation for a new Georgian ground attack. The Fact-Finding Mission and—in accordance with the mandate of President Sarkozy—interpreted international law to condemn Russia for having used disproportionate force. The implication was that Russia should have halted all operations and patiently suffered the nonstop shelling coming from Gori.

When small Russian forces made a weak movement toward Gori and encountered no resistance, they were afraid of being lured into a trap and halted the advance. When reinforcements arrived to mount a full offensive against Gori, and by the time the Russians reached Gali, the Georgians, including President Saakashvili, who had come to rally his demoralized troops, had fled the city in a panicky rush.

Meanwhile, under pressure from Abkhazians to launch an offensive on their sector, Russian airborne patrols crossed the border into Georgia expecting to clash with the 2nd Brigade at Senaki. To the surprise of the patrols, they entered a void and encountered no resistance. The main Russian forces, which until they had been waiting for their heavy weapons and tanks to arrive, now rushed deep into Georgia riding trucks and any lightly armored vehicles.

The war had another unexpected impact on the Kremlin. As the battlefield reports came in, it was becoming evident that the disintegrating Georgian army had been nothing more than a paper tiger. The Georgians were no Chechens, who had fought the Russian army to a standstill, and in the war with Georgia the Chechens were fighting on the side of Russia. Moscow had to shift in a few hours from having to repulse the aggressor to having to decide the fate of the aggressor. This stunning development caught everyone by surprise and was still hard to accept and the Kremlin needed some time to process the new situation. Meanwhile Russian troops were streaming across Georgia, cutting the country in half at different points, and blockading on land and water the Black Sea coast.

For the Fact-Finding Mission, committed to a nineteenth-century view of static warfare, Russia should have stopped all military operations immediately to maintain a "symmetrical" response. That it did not do so showed that never in its wildest dreams had Moscow ever considered the possibility of waging and winning a war with Georgia. The Foreign Ministry and the General Staff did not have ready formulas to apply in case of a victory. It was understandable that the Kremlin required a few days to decide what to do, and indecision among officials made hard forming a consensus.

Since independence Georgia had been a constant problem for Russia, and it made sense to try to take advantage of this victorious war to find a solution for the Caucasus that went beyond South Ossetia and Abkhazia. Here was the opportunity for Russia to regain the Adjara region bordering on Turkey and also to establish a direct link with close ally but land-locked Armenia. At the very least Moscow needed to impose iron-clad treaty obligations on Tbilisi not to threaten or interrupt the trade routes of Armenia with Russia and other countries; the question of the Armenian minorities in Georgia also called for a solution.

Moscow reaffirmed the key principle of its foreign policy of never annexing by force people who did not want to belong to Russia. The Kremlin was committed to stop any separatist attempts inside its borders but would not force or annex unwilling peoples; so while indications exist that the smashing Russian victory had persuaded many Georgians to accept rule from Moscow once again, this option was never on the table. Adjustments to the borders were another matter; in particular it was in Russia's interest to gain control over at least part of the pipeline passing through Georgia. Officials in Moscow were so caught up on trying to decide what to do about Georgia, that only at the last moment did they realize that airborne units were fanning out across the country and detachments were racing to see who would be the first to hoist the Russian flag over Tbilisi. The orders to halt reached the forward patrols just short of the defenseless Tbilisi international airport.

The Nicolas Sarkozy Missions to Russia

Sarkozy I

The precipitating factor in the Russian decision to halt the military advance in Georgia was the trip of French President Nicolas Sarkozy. He sensed the divisions and indecision inside the Kremlin, and with unusual skill played the card of a non-existing Western position to pressure President Dmitry Medvedev to accept a ceasefire. Sarkozy came also as president of the European Union. Even more important, the U.S. delegated to France the task of salvaging favorable terms from the debacle in Georgia.

In retrospect the decision to delegate the task to Sarkozy appeared as an astute move, when in reality Washington lacked other options. Secretary of State Rice had betrayed the confidence of Foreign Minister Sergei Lavrov when she revealed his preference for removing Saakashvili from office as the only way to guarantee peace in the Caucasus. By scoring a few propaganda points she hoped to hide her blame for having failed to restrain Saakashvili during her trip to Tbilisi in July.[23]

The French president eagerly assumed the task of mediator among the warring parties. But while the Bush administration wanted first an immediate return to the *status quo ante bellum* and then the gradual reincorporation of Abkhazia and South Ossetia into Georgia, Sarkozy realized that the two separatist republics were irretrievably lost.

The appearance of Sarkozy came at a most opportune moment for President Dmitry Medvedev, who welcomed the participation of the French president as an opportunity not just to bring the war to an end but also one more attempt to bring Russia closer to Europe. Sensing an opening, Sarkozy agreed to come to Moscow but only on the condition that a ceasefire enter into force by the time he arrived. Although Medvedev complied with the request, in the ceasefire order he still left Russian troops considerable freedom not just to advance but also to eliminate any hostile Georgian formations. On 12 August 2008 at 1400 hours Russian artillery delivered its last barrage, while the Russian air force made its last bombing run around that time. The Russian armed forces declared the official end of active combat operations at 1500 hours.[24]

Outwardly Sarkozy accomplished his first objective of stopping the war, but once he reached Moscow he learned that Russian troops were still on the move although no longer heading toward Tbilisi. After heated negotiations in Moscow, he reached a vague agreement on six principles. He and Medvedev announced the news to the world in a press conference late on 12 August. The text authorized Russian peacekeepers to "take additional security measures" until international monitoring could take place, avoided any mention of the territorial integrity of Georgia, and called for "an international debate on the future status of south Ossetia and Abkhazia."[25] In many ways the 12 August 2008 agreement, although far from settling the dispute, was a Russian victory, yet Sarkozy and his team considered it also a victory and celebrated on board their airplane as they headed for Tbilisi to sell the agreement to Saakashvili and indirectly to the Americans.[26]

The Americans were not pleased, but having ruled out a military intervention, there was nothing the U.S. could do but swallow the bitter fruits of its failed policy in Georgia. When Saakashvili and his associates saw the six principles, their first reaction was to tear up the agreement. But then for the first time since Colin Powell in 2004 a Western leader talked bluntly to the Georgian president: "Where is Bush? Where are the Americans? They are not coming to save you. No Europeans are coming either. You are alone. If you don't sign, the Russian tanks will be here soon."[27]

Saakashvili agreed to sign but wanted to make several changes to the text, and in heated discussions Sarkozy narrowed down his request to just one: dropping the word "status" from the sixth principle on negotiations about the future. Medvedev made the serious mistake of accepting the change. At first sign dropping the word "status" did not change anything on the ground so the Russian side could be excused for not realizing the significance of the modification. However the consequences were lasting, because the change made harder finding a definite solution to Abkhazia and South Ossetia. In an immediate consequence, the dropping of a single word meant that the six principles, rather than a non-negotiable agreement, were subject to revision, modification, and even repeal. Thus the seemingly minor change opened the door for an attempt at the renegotiation of the six principles in a separate trip by Sarkozy in the future.

Sarkozy II

Historical perspective shows what event came next, but the protagonists at that time did not yet know that the financial crisis was about to erupt and plunge the world into the Great Recession. The changing economic conditions of Russia and the West modified their negotiating positions.

Sarkozy and the French were premature in their celebration of the 12 August accord. Soon it became clear that the Russians and the separatist regions were in no rush to implement the six principles. The French foreign minister explained that at most the Russians were complying with three of the principles. An optimist might find solace in the Kremlin's repeated intention to follow the six principles at some moment, and at first glance the disagreement seemed to be just a matter of timing or how fast to implement the 12 August accord.[28]

Four events, however, seemed to reinforce the position of Western officials, in particular the Americans, who felt that Sarkozy had been duped in Moscow. First of all, Russian troops stayed in their forward positions and in effect they were slowly strangling the Georgian economy by making more expensive and difficult the transport of goods from the Black Sea ports to the rest of the country. That the Russian troops were also safeguarding deliveries to ally Armenia did not enter into the equation of these anti–Russian hardliners.

Second, Russian troops had occupied some additional territory after the 12 August accord, but in almost all cases the territory involved had been rather minor. The big exception had been the Akhalgori district of South Ossetia. A major reason why the French had considered the trip a brilliant success was that they believed that the 12 August agreement prevented Russian forces from occupying this district forming about a fourth of the surface area of South Ossetia. Keeping Akhalgori under Georgian control meant that the negotiations to bring South Ossetia back under Tbilisi's control still stood some chance of success. But when Russian troops occupied the district without encountering any resistance, the possibility of using Akhalgori as a bargaining chip vanished.[29]

Third, the attempts of the U.S. and its Western allies to use the United Nations to force the separatist regions to return under Georgian control had run into firm Russian opposition. Unable to manipulate the UN, both the U.S. and Western countries had no choice but to turn to Sarkozy to try to secure the full implementation of the 12 August accord.

Last, the Kremlin's decision to recognize the independence of Abkhazia and South Ossetia on 26 August gave an added urgency to seeking compliance with the 12 August accord. This recognition meant that Russia no longer supported the territorial integrity of Georgia. While it was becoming clear that the return of the separatist republics to Georgian control was impossible, the withdrawal of Russian troops from the rest of the country still seemed a reachable goal. And even more disturbing aspect of the Russian recognition of independence was that Medvedev declared for the first time that Moscow was determined to protect the rights of Russian citizens in the world. The statement did not seem relevant or applicable to Georgia because the Abkhazians and South Ossetians were not ethnic Russians even though over 90 percent of them had applied for and received Russian passports.[30] Medvedev's often overlooked statement about protecting Russian citizens looked to the future and was an early warning about ethnic Russians in Ukraine.

The real urgency to settle the matter came from the U.S. Washington had long lived with the illusion that as the supposed "winner" of the Cold War, it was entitled to dictate the fate of countries. But for the first time since the collapse of the Soviet Union in December 1991, Russia had openly defied U.S. wishes, and the aggressive Bush administration could not accept the new situation in Georgia.

The best option for a response came from the huge ego of French President Nicolas Sarkozy. The U.S. pressured the European allies to take reprisals against Russia and spread the message that the Russians had duped the French president. What Sarkozy could not stand was being held up to ridicule because he had been outsmarted at the game of diplomacy, in which France has excelled. But Washington knew that even the French president needed additional arguments to convince Moscow. In his next trip to Moscow, Sarkozy had at his disposal the powerful threat of economic sanctions against Russia. The U.S. promised its own reprisals and believed that Europeans could be persuaded to take devastating measures; while Sarkozy was not so sure that the European Union would rally behind anything more than symbolic measures, his hurt ego made him very willing to wave the threat of sanctions as a bluff to force the Russians to comply with the 12 August accord and even to extract more concessions.[31]

The second Sarkozy mission had four broad goals. The first and most important was to obtain the withdrawal of Russian forces back to the positions the peacekeepers had held prior to the war. Russian forces since 12 August patrolled Georgian territory, established checkpoints, and in general maintained a firm grip over the country. In accordance with classical diplomacy, the Kremlin wanted to use this military presence as a bargaining chip to force Georgia to accept the loss of the separatist republics and to obtain the removal of Saakashvili from office.

The second goal was to finish creating the "international mechanism" stipulated in point 5 of the six principles of the 12 August accord. As an emergency measure but not as the final "international mechanism" Russia accepted the deployment of OSCE monitors to Georgia. Sarkozy's task was to secure access for the OSCE team to the disputed regions.

The third more ambitious goal was to create "one and only one international mechanism [...] and one to which Russia is not a third party."[32] That Russia would agree to give up the peacekeeper status it had enjoyed since the early 1990s in the separatist republics was unrealistic.

The fourth goal was the real driving spirit behind the Sarkozy trip to Moscow and that was to reaffirm the right of the West to approve any Russian action in the future. As a high-ranking French diplomat expounded, "the primary European and Allied interest is to establish a new international dynamic permitting the rest of the international community to regain some control over Russia's actions."[33] Or in other words, the dangerous bear was on a rampage and had to be put back into its cage.

Even as late as the first days of September 2008, the possibility of obtaining a full withdrawal of Russian forces back to the pre-war boundaries of the separatist republics seemed like a "non-starter" to European diplomats. Moscow dismissed the EU's September 1 threat to suspend talks on a Partnership and Cooperation Agreement as predictable and complained of fatigue over the EU using that threat. It seemed that the second Sarkozy mission was headed for failure even before the French president flew to Moscow.[34]

In reality, the situation almost changed between the EU statement of 1 September and Sarkozy's arrival on 8 September. Russia became the first country to feel the effects of the world financial crisis even before it began with the bankruptcy of Lehman Brothers on 15 September. The Russian economy had been strong in August but after September 1 the first downswings made the country vulnerable to economic sanctions.

Russia wanted to keep the so-called "buffer zones" as leverage to obtain an agreement recognizing the loss of the separatist republics, but by early September the occupation became a wasting asset because Tbilisi would never agree as long as it enjoyed the support of the West. In retrospect the decision to halt the advance on the Georgian capital on 12 August had been a mistake, because Moscow threw away the opportunity to dictate a victor's peace along the lines of classical diplomacy. Nothing on the ground prevented Russia from resuming the offensive, but the huge world outcry and condemnation of Russia as the aggressor showed that the window of opportunity for a military solution had expired.

Thus, by the time Sarkozy arrived on 8 September, Russia was willing to accept the withdrawal of its troops from the buffer zones in exchange for some concessions. But for Sarkozy, the withdrawal was just the first of his long list of demands, and he came with "a take it or leave it attitude, very American in style and very confrontational [...] the atmosphere during the negotiations was quite charged and at times became openly hostile. Sarkozy at one point grabbed Foreign Minister Lavrov by the lapels and called him a liar in very strong terms."[35]

Sarkozy achieved his first goal, and on 8 September in a press conference the French president proudly stated that "on October 15 there must no longer be a single Russian soldier anywhere other than where he was before August seventh."[36] As far as the second and third goals, he convinced Russia to accept the presence of the OSCE monitors and to have an EU team of 200 observers be the primary "international mechanism" for supervising the ceasefire. Because Russia had no say in the activities of the EU, Sarkozy seemed to have achieved his goal of depriving Moscow of any role in the "international mechanism."

These were tough terms for Russia to accept, and "in order to get the deal done, Sarkozy had at one point when they reached an impasse threatened to storm out of the talks and go home."[37] But as far as the fourth goal of gaining some control over Russia's actions, the second Sarkozy mission fell far short. Moscow refused to repeal its recognition of Abkhazia and South Ossetia, and Western diplomats came to the conclusion that a Cyprus-style stalemate was the probable, as has in fact has been the case until the present.

American diplomats were calling for deadlines and sanctions if Russia did not complete the withdrawal of its forces, but once the world financial crisis began with the bankruptcy of Lehman Brothers on 15 September, any desire in the West to impose economic sanctions on Russia evaporated. The financial crisis inaugurated the Great Recession, and as Western countries scrambled to save their tottering economies, Georgia soon faded as a focus of attention.

It is instructive to reflect on the crucial role of timing. Had the second Sarkozy mission taken place one week later after the start of the world financial crisis, the negotiating position of the French president would have been much weaker; it is not inconceivable that the second Sarkozy mission might not have taken place and the six principles of 12 August would have remained as the sole guide for settling the dispute. But once the financial crisis struck the West, the position of Russia slowly became stronger, and Moscow realized that it had given away too much in the 8 September accord. The opportunity to make some corrections was coming, but first Russia had to deal with the response of the West to the war.

17

The Response of the West to the War

The key priority is establishing international arrangements as soon as possible to deny Russia a pretext for maintaining its presence in Georgia.—French Diplomat[1]

The West ruled out military intervention in the war between Russia and Georgia. Britain, France, and Germany, were completely opposed, while already in the first days of the war U.S. officials stopped pressing for a military response. The logistics of such a move were formidable because the Montreux Convention limited the tonnage of warships entering the Black Sea. During the Cold War NATO member Turkey had been the bulwark to contain restrain the Soviet navy, but in an ironic reversal the country now was keeping NATO out of the Black Sea.[2]

No chance existed of repeating the Crimean War of 1854–1856 and the West turned to non-military means to try to restore Georgian control over Abkhazia and South Ossetia under the direct rule of Georgia. The guns were not yet silent when on 11 August 2008 NATO members held their first meeting after the start of the war and failed to agree on a response. The U.S. labored hard to secure a consensus over the coming weeks but no common front against Russia emerged.[3] No less significant, U.S. diplomats also began pressing levers of influence inside Russia to try restore at least the status quo ante bellum.

Inside Russia

Almost instinctively the U.S. turned to NGOs and social media inside Russia to bring public pressure on the Kremlin to withdraw its troops from Georgia. But by the time the West launched its campaign to persuade Russians to go out on the streets to demand a withdrawal from Georgia, the TV images of the horrendous and savage Georgian shelling of Tskhinvali were already deeply etched in the minds of the public. The TV stations over the next weeks and months repeated the newsreels and updated them with scenes of destitute Ossetians struggling to survive among the ruins.[4] Here for the first time since the treacherous Nazi invasion of 22 June 1941, a foreign power had attacked Russia, and this sense of being the innocent victim galvanized Russian nationalism.

Online users were overwhelmingly and passionately on the side of the Kremlin. In addition, bloggers and hackers on their own unleashed a cyberwar against Georgia on a much larger scale that what hit Estonia the previous year in the Bronze Soldier incident. Private Russian hackers caused more damage to Georgia than all the destruction that the Russian military had inflicted with conventional weapons. For the U.S., the Russian internet, rather than an ally, in this case turned into a powerful tool to support the Kremlin.⁵

Such was the nationalist fervor that when the U.S. turned to NGOs to mobilize anti–Kremlin protests, almost unanimously the responses were negative. Indicative of the reaction was the attitude of the sometimes anti-war Committees of Soldiers' Mothers. One of its leaders stated that "the only criticism of Russia's conduct on the South Ossetia conflict is that it waited too long to help the [Russian] peacekeepers."⁶ This respected organization had made a name for itself by challenging the Kremlin over the abuses conscripts suffered, but now its support for Russia's policy was complete. And as the frosting on the cake, even Mikhail Gorbachev, that tragic figure from the Soviet past, joined fellow Russians in denouncing the Georgian invasion.

The war with Georgia united Russia in a way not seen before since World War II. Nothing that the West could do had any chance of shifting public opinion. On the contrary, the more the West condemned Russia, the greater became the disillusionment among the Russian public and in particular its intelligentsia. The lingering illusion that the West really cared about Russia had largely died out after the Kosovo incident of 1999, but a sizeable segment of the population still believed that the intentions of the West were not hostile. The rush of the West to support Georgia finished opening the eyes of Russians, and at last a majority of the population came to accept the view that they were alone against a hostile West.⁷

A sure formula for success in U.S. electoral campaigns has been to label the other candidate or the opposition party as being anti–American. That Western advisers have not understood the applicability of this principle to Russian politics may be excused, but this absence has been inexplicable for Russian opposition leaders. The pattern of invasions across its history has made its nationalism much stronger than in the U.S., yet a few Russian opposition parties foolishly agreed to condemn the excessive use of military force during the Georgian War. Nobody dared to question the initial Russian response, but when opposition figures adopted the Western attitude that Russia had used excessive force, the double standard or even hypocrisy was too blatant to ignore. NATO had savagely bombed Belgrade and other civilian targets in Serbia to obtain compliance over Kosovo, but if Russia did a minuscule fraction of that bombing in Georgia, then it was excessive.⁸

The inevitable outcome was that the Russian opposition political parties shrank into insignificance because of their refusal to support the troops. The opposition parties made themselves irrelevant by assuming the anti–Russian label. The attempt of the West to mobilize Russian internal protests against the Kremlin's policy in Georgia had been a failure. The defeat had been so complete that the Russian government failed to realize that the structure of NGOs and other anti–Russian assets was still in place, and given the right circumstance, could roar back into action, as later happened in 2012.

The Kremlin's Solution

As early as 14 August 2008, Foreign Minister Sergei Lavrov for the first time stopped mentioning "territorial integrity," the formal legal term that meant recognizing the Soviet-era boundaries in their entirety. Up to the start of the war Russia routinely repeated its support for the territorial integrity of Georgia, but the statement of Lavrov suggested a profound shift. Prior to the war "a vast majority of the population" of South Ossetia and of Abkhazia obtained Russian passports and thus acquired a claim to Russian citizenship.⁹ Placing all these citizens under the control of Tbilisi was political suicide, and continuing to talk about the territorial integrity of Georgia no longer fit the vastly changed circumstances the war had created.

Abkhazia had regained the Upper Kodori Valley and was trying to extend its control along the entire length of the Ingori River. South Ossetia destroyed the Georgian villages and expelled the Georgian minority from most of the region. In Moscow the initial belief among experts was that Moscow would honor South Ossetia's repeated request to reunite South Ossetia with North Ossetia inside Russia and to recognize the independence of Abkhazia. But the Dmitry Medvedev administration felt that annexing even one of the two regions opened Russia to the accusation that the real intent of the war all along had been to acquire territory in the manner of the tsars.[10] In reality, any action the Kremlin took faced inevitable condemnation from the West. In retrospect the Medvedev administration could have simplified matters by holding plebiscites under international supervision so that the inhabitants could decide on their political future.

The issue of the inevitable annexation to Russia went on hold when separatist leaders from Abkhazia and South Ossetia came to Moscow to request protection on 14 August.[11] What the leaders were asking for was a variation of the "protectorates" of the European colonial system. Domestic affairs remained under the control of local leaders, while Russia provided military and economic support, including free movement of goods and people across the borders.

Many Russian nationalists wanted the annexation of the two separatist republics. As a compromise, the Duma (lower chamber) and the Federation Council (upper chamber) on 25 August unanimously approved a resolution urging President Dmitry Medvedev to recognize the independence of Abkhazia and South Ossetia. In an attempt to seek a future accommodation with the U.S., he sent a very mild letter on 26 August to President George W. Bush announcing the decision to recognize the two states and putting the blame for the war on Georgian ruler Mikhail Saakashvili. Pundits claimed that the recognition was a response to the declaration of independence by Kosovo in February 2008 but the letter to Bush very diplomatically did not mention Kosovo at all.[12]

The West on the Offensive

Moscow's recognition of the independence of Abkhazia and South Ossetia on 26 August persuaded most Western countries to take strong action to prevent Russia from reclaiming any territories of the former Soviet republics. Already in late August the U.S. diplomats in Vienna pressured Austria not to engage in talks about the South Stream pipeline because they were "inconsistent with the requirements of the situation in Georgia and vis-à-vis Russia."[13] The U.S. expected similar reprisals to be just the start of tough action, but when the European Union meet on 1 September, the deep divergences among member states postponed taking any action to impose economic sanctions on Russia. The most the U.S. could obtain was the suspension of negotiations on a new version of the 1997 Partnership and Cooperation Agreement.[14]

The U.S. also wanted to expel Russia from the NATO-Russia Council, the coordinating body established in May 2002, but the Kremlin preempted that measure by announcing on 21 August that it was suspending all military cooperation with NATO countries.[15] For their part, the European allies were not willing to expel Russia from the Council. The most that the U.S. could obtain was a declaration of "no business as usual," but the allies rejected the view that "it is not possible to use the NATO-Russia Council structures and procedures during this time."[16]

The Kremlin's investment in the Collective Security Treaty Organization (CSTO) paid off when on 5 September it was the only international body to condemn Georgia as the aggressor. However, the organization was not a rubber-stamp for Russia as many in the West believed, and CSTO left up to the individual member states to decide whether to recognize the independence of Abkhazia and South Ossetia. The U.S. needed something—anything—to retaliate. The U.S. senate had been considering approval of the civilian nuclear cooperation agreement with Russia, a treaty beneficial to both countries, but on 8 September 2008 the Bush administration killed the agreement by withdrawing it from the senate.[17]

The U.S. did not even hesitate to undermine the Open Skies Treaty as a way to punish Russia. This treaty provided for overflights of member territories, and ever since it went into force in January 2002, had been one of the most successful agreements between the West and Russia. When Georgia announced that it would not allow any flights over its territory, the Western members supported the request, but when Russia stipulated in late August that Open Sky planes could not deviate in the slightest from their flight plans because of the fear of accidental shootings, Western countries seized the opportunity to denounce Russia for "a breach of its treaty responsibilities."[18] When Russian repealed the restrictions on 15 September, the uproar subsidized, and the Open Skies program resumed its normal operations.

Before the U.S. could come up with other reprisals, the Kremlin decided to placate EU members by supporting the German proposal to have an investigative commission determine the causes of the war. Germany and other countries wanted to know for sure who had started the war before embarking on an expensive round of sanctions. The Russian Foreign Ministry was not enthusiastic about the investigative commission because in the past similar supposedly neutral bodies became instruments to condemn the Kremlin. Nevertheless, the gamble seemed reasonable, and the ready availability of an abundance of videos, photographs, testimonies, and captured documents depicting how Georgia started the war by opening a murderous and sustained shelling of Tskhinvali on 7 August seemed to preclude a hostile ruling.[19]

Russia had been most vulnerable during the month of September, because its economy started to feel the financial crisis of 2008 before it had impacted the West. Once the financial crisis of 2008 reached the West, countries became more receptive to accepting the overwhelming evidence that Georgia had been the aggressor. The European countries were the first to lose any interest in damaging their profitable trade with Russia. An early indication that the danger to Russia was dissipating came in late September when the Council of Europe, after visiting the site of the war, declined to deprive Moscow of its voting rights in the Parliamentary Assembly of that organization. The Assembly played an important liaison role with Russian legislators, and the Council of Europe concluded that keeping channels open to Moscow was more important than any punitive action. The favorable result in the Council of Europe was an early reflection of the successful outreach campaign on the part of Russian diplomats.[20]

The Russian Diplomatic Campaign

In diplomatic campaign over Georgia the most important country for Russia was Turkey because of its control of the entrance to the Black Sea. A previous section traced the growing rapprochement between Turkey and Russia since the last years of the twentieth century, and the

Kremlin did not want the war with Georgia to affect that relationship. A military consideration was also fundamental. Although Turkey was a NATO member, as long as it enforced the serious limitations on the entry of warships into the Black Sea, Russia was free to act with impunity. The Kremlin's decision not to seize Adjara with its minor port of Batumi also eliminated any possibility of Turkey having again a land border with Russia.

Ankara appreciated Russian reluctance for annexations, and when Prime Minister Erdogan visited Moscow just a few days after the war was over, he showed no intention of taking harsh actions against Russia. The Kremlin worked hard to extend every possible courtesy to Erdogan during his visit; Prime Minister Putin joined the talks between the Turkish Prime Minister and President Medvedev. "Russian protocol was impressive, with Russian authorities closing the Moscow airport road to facilitate Erdogan's short-notice travel."[21]

The recognition of the independence of Abkhazia and South Ossetia on 26 August set off a new round of frantic activity lasting until early October. Even before Russia launched a diplomatic campaign to secure recognition by other countries of the independence of Abkhazia and South Ossetia, U.S. officials were already engaged in a well-financed campaign to block that move. The earlier competition over the independence of Kosovo repeated itself; and just like Russia had blocked U.N. membership for Kosovo, so the U.S. did the same for Abkhazia and South Ossetia.

The "country count" became the scene of fierce competition, and the U.S., with considerable experience on pressuring reluctant allies and banana republics, had the clear advantage and took the lead. But while in the initial weeks Russia could not get any country to recognize Abkhazia and South Ossetia, the U.S. did not have much success in obtaining condemnations of Russia. And Moscow scored a big success when India declared that it was not taking sides in this dispute.[22] By September 3 Russia moderated its goals: "Russia's President, Prime Minister and Foreign Minister fanned out [...] in a full-court press to enlist support for its decision to recognize the Georgian breakaway regions' independence."[23]

Not able to compete everywhere with the inducements and threats the U.S. routinely employed, Russia decided to concentrate its diplomatic efforts on the near abroad and on sympathetic countries such as Turkey. The Kremlin understood that China could not openly support the independence the separatist republics out of fear of creating a precedent for its own ethnic regions, yet Beijing did reject Georgia's direct appeals to condemn Russia. China limited itself to endorsing the Kremlin's steps to bring peace to the region.[24]

The dry spell came to an end when Nicaragua became the first country after Russia to recognize the separatist republics. The action took U.S. diplomats by surprise, because they had done their due diligence in both informing and threatening the Nicaraguan government. But here the legacy of the Soviet Union proved helpful to Moscow: Daniel Ortega was grateful to the indispensable support the Soviet Union had provided to the Nicaraguan Revolution. In traditional societies these debts are sacred, and President Ortega wanted to repay the Kremlin by stating in an emotional speech on 2 September that his country was recognizing the independence of Abkhazia and South Ossetia.[25]

The Kremlin enjoyed plenty of time to savor the spontaneous Nicaraguan action, because a year had to pass before another country—Venezuela—recognized the separatist republics. A handful of other countries also recognizing Abkhazia and South Ossetia, but by the middle of September the Russian Foreign Ministry gradually withdrew from this high-stakes poker game. The U.S. had won the "country count," but even if Russia had been the winner, the situation would have resembled at best the situation of Kosovo, a country in international limbo despite having secured recognition from many countries. The Kremlin could not afford to waste its scarce resources on persuading countries to recognize Abkhazia and South Ossetia when other consequences of the war with Georgia demanded attention.[26]

By September 10 the Russian priority had become the return to "business as usual" at least with the European countries and possibly also with the United States. A clear example of the new policy came with the visit of Sergei Lavrov to Poland on 10–11 September. The Foreign Minister explained to his Polish counterparts that Russia wanted to leave behind the emotional histrionics during the Georgian War and was ready to engage on mutually beneficial trade relations between the two countries. To other European countries Russia also dangled the possibility of improving cooperation on trade and other economic issues.[27]

The diplomatic offensive gained time for the Kremlin, even though the European countries—under strong U.S. pressure—were skeptical about the Russian promises. But when on 15 September the world financial crisis began with the collapse of Lehman Brothers, the onset of what became the Great Recession soon weakened any desire of the Europeans for a confrontation with Russia. The power relationship between the West and Russia drastically changed, as each country scrambled to cope with the devastating effects of the world economic crisis.

One by one the European institutions—always in defiance of strong U.S. pressure—resumed normal contacts with Russia. The EU was the first, and it resumed negotiations over the Partnership and Cooperation Agreement with Russia. As one French official explained, "the EU cannot put is relations with Russia on hold indefinitely."[28] By then the Council of Europe was the only institution still criticizing in public Russian actions in Georgia, but this was risky because Moscow contributed 12 percent of its budget. By the end of October the Council of Europe likewise softened its tone.[29]

The U.S. attempt to use OSCE against Russia ran into the European refusal to adopt any harsh measures. At NATO the U.S. believed it had full control, but the European countries were already clamoring in October for a resumption of meetings of the NATO-Russia Council. Europe needed Russia's cooperation in so many areas that any idea of abolishing this Council was inconceivable. By the end of October NATO was again engaging with Russia. The U.S. made a last desperate attempt to keep the contacts to the bare minimum, but much to its regret could not stop relations from returning to the pre-war "business as usual,"

At the same time, the bargaining position of the West over Georgia deteriorated. Russia had given away too many things in the Sarkozy-Medvedev agreement of 8 September, but once the Great Recession ensued, avoiding full compliance with its harsh terms was easy for the Kremlin. Russian troops with heavy weapons allowed UN and OSCE observers to arrive, but just some meters down the road poorly armed separatist militias blocked the path. For the rest of the year European and American diplomats complained to their Russian counterparts who claimed to lack authority over the separatist officials. And when the mandate for the OSCE mission expired on 31 January 2009, Russia blocked the renewal.[30]

Russia remained open to negotiating another mandate for OSCE under new conditions reflecting the reality on the ground, an approach the West rejected. The United Nations Observer Mission in Georgia (UNOMIG) was also set to expire in February 2009. In contrast to previous years when Russia had to struggle to find enough votes to renew the mandate, the

West all of a sudden was extremely eager to preserve UNOMIG. Both sides needed more time to renegotiate the agreement, and the UN Security Council on 13 February 2009 approved a temporary extension until June 15. But when it became clear that the West wanted to use the renewal of UNOMIG to reestablish Georgian control over the separatist republics, Russia vetoed the request on 15 June. The end of UNOMIG left the EU mission as the only international group in Georgia as international observers, but because the separatist republics refused entry to the observers, its functions were harmless if not meaningless.[31]

As early as November 2008 any European desire to take reprisals against Russia had vanished, yet the U.S. did not stop badgering allies such as Japan to make a tardy condemnation of Russian actions over Georgia. The European countries wanted to concentrate all their resources on coping with the Great Recession, and it was time to bury Georgia as a dispute between the West and Russia.

And there was nobody better than the colorful Silvio Berlusconi to proclaim this reality. In the early 2000s as prime minister he had extended cover to his friend Vladimir Putin while Russia was vulnerable during the Second Chechnya War. When Berlusconi returned as prime minister in 2008, it took him a while to gain control over the pro–U.S. Italian foreign policy establishment. He announced his new policy in a press conference on 12 November when Berlusconi absolved Russia of all blame for the Georgia war and blamed the U.S. for having instigated this regional conflict. American diplomats with resignation observed that "the latest comments are a culmination of a string of inflammatory and unhelpful comments in support of Putin that began shortly after Berlusconi took office this year."[32]

The Italian Prime Minister was expressing in public what other European leaders did not want to state to avoid hurting American sensibilities. The divisions within the West were too big and massive for the U.S. to patch up, and as the Bush administration entered into its final months, Russia returned to "business as usual" with the European countries. Meanwhile in the United States the search for a less confrontational alternative led to the formulation of the policy of "reset" under the Obama administration as a way to avoid the need for sanctions sure to hurt the American economy as much as Russia.

18

Friends in the Caucasus

Medvedev and Putin have been united and firm in their desire to reestablish Russian influence in the Caucasus.—Presidential advisor of Azerbaijan[1]

Restoring control over Chechnya had never been the sole interest of Russia in the Caucasus. Even before the defeat of the Chechen rebels in 2004, the Kremlin sought to neutralize U.S. and NATO incursions into the three former Soviet republics in the Caucasus. While loyal Armenia strove hard to intensify its ties with Russia, Georgia in sharp contrast moved toward the West. Between the two extremes of Armenia and Georgia was Azerbaijan, where Russia faced stiff competition from the West.

Azerbaijan: Restraining the West

The Second Chechnya War was still raging in Chechnya when in January 2001 Vladimir Putin made the first presidential visit to Azerbaijan since Leonid Brezhnev's days. President Heidar Aliyev and Putin enjoyed a cordial friendship because both men had been KGB officials for decades. After Heidar died in December 2003 the close ties continued when his son Ilham became the new ruler of Azerbaijan. In many ways the links became even stronger, because not only had Ilham lived 17 years in Russia but he also maintained close family and commercial ties with major Russian businessmen. Personal ties have always been very important in the Caucasus, and the friendship between the Heidar family, Putin, and Russian businessmen facilitated increasing Russian influence in Azerbaijan.[2]

Unlike Christian Armenia and Georgia, Azerbaijan was a Muslim country. In sharp contrast with Chechnya, secularism was strong in Azerbaijan. Despite its border with Iran, both the elite and most inhabitants rejected the theocracy of Iran and opposed converting their country into an Islamic Republic. The result was that Azerbaijan felt "sandwiched between two elephants in Iran and Russia," and for a while flirted with the idea of breaking from its geographical trap by turning to the U.S. and NATO.[3]

It was not just wishful thinking that fueled dreams of making Azerbaijan an independent regional power. Baku had been an oil producer since the nineteenth century, and although output declined during the Soviet period, Western companies felt that the application of new technologies promised to extract more crude from old fields and for the first time to exploit the deposits under the Caspian Sea. But was the oil competitive with output from other parts of Russia and the rest of the world? And even if it was, how could the crude come from Azerbaijan without having to pass through Russia?

Western oil companies concluded that

exporting crude was feasible if a separate pipeline could reach the Black Sea. However, Turkey opposed increasing the number of oil tankers passing through the already crowded shipping lanes in the Bosporus and offered instead the sensible alternative of having the pipeline extend all the way to the Mediterranean at the port of Ceyhan. Even though the oil companies liked the idea of a Mediterranean terminus, they still needed several years to assemble the financing for the then second longest oil pipeline in the world. Engineering and political obstacles delayed the start of the project, and only in September 2002 did construction begin. Baku-Tbilisi-Ceyhan (BTC) delivered its first crude to the Mediterranean in July 2006. A simultaneous project built a parallel pipeline to transport gas into western Turkey.[4]

Part of the reason the project was so expensive and took so long to build was that the pipeline did not follow the most efficient path and instead snaked around Armenia by a longer route, passing exclusively through Georgia. Baku demanded this detour in order to punish Armenia for its continuing occupation of the Nagorno-Karabakh region, but another goal was to bypass Russia. When the Baku-Tbilisi-Ceyhan project was in its infancy, the Boris Yeltsin administration, still living under the illusion that whatever the West wanted was in the best interests of Russia, failed to take steps to block the pipeline, a neglect that the Kremlin later came to regret.[5]

Once the pipeline was operational, the oil revenues flowing into Azerbaijan created a mirage of prosperity. The government of Ilham Aliyev believed that the oil wealth would last forever and went on a spending spree. Baku purchased many weapons in preparation for an offensive to wrestle control of Nagorno-Karabakh from Armenia, and these acquisitions triggered an arms race with its neighbor.[6]

Baku also for the first time embraced a nationalistic project. The government began to support the revival of the Azerbaijani language in an attempt to displace Russian, until then the lingua franca of the Caucasus. In July 2007 the authorities cancelled the contracts to broadcast Russian television in Azerbaijan. In a break with the tradition since the Soviet period, officials diverted most students away from Russia and instead sent them to Western universities to earn their degrees. But when the graduates returned home, they found few jobs waiting for them, because oil exporting countries tend to suffer from the "Dutch Disease," a tendency for petroleum to stifle all other economic activities.[7]

With unemployment at record levels, most Azeri turned to two traditional solutions. Since Soviet times the rich soils and warm climate converted the region into a garden supplying fruits and vegetables for Russia even during the frigid winter months. And the inhabitants followed the produce to Russia, and they became the principal vendors at markets throughout European Russia (the Chinese played a similar role in the Far East). At least 2 million Azeri lived in Russia, many of them as illegal immigrants. Thus, the struggle of the citizens to survive contrasted with the superficial image of the shiny new buildings appearing in the Baku skyline.[8]

Russia launched a charm offensive to try to restore its deteriorating influence in Azerbaijan. President Putin visited Aliyev at least twice a year, and many Russian delegations likewise came trying to improve ties with Baku. But the glitz of the West proved irresistible to the Azeri leader. It may seem hard to believe in the light of later events that Azerbaijan was following in the footsteps of Mikheil Saakashvili in bordering Georgia.[9]

The original goal for Azerbaijan was to join both NATO and the EU, but that membership required breaking with Russia. Ilham concluded that his father had been too generous with Russia and proceeded to restrict previous agreements.[10] Azerbaijani officials welcomed NATO membership for Georgia but felt Saakashvili was too abrasive in antagonizing Moscow. The conclusion in Baku was that "once NATO accepts Georgia, they will accept us."[11] In July 2008, just a month before the outbreak of the Five Day War, the calibrated policy was that "Azerbaijan always tries to stay a step behind Georgia on issues related to Euro-Atlantic integration, letting the Georgians test the waters in terms of Russia's response."[12]

It is amazing to see how quickly a war can change attitudes, and just several weeks after the end of the Five Day War of August 2008, Azerbaijani officials stated "that the Russian invasion of Georgia is the beginning of a new era."[13] The war itself had been costly for Azerbaijan, and just the disruption of railroad traffic through Georgia represented losses of over a billion dollars. For weeks thousands of railroad wagons with cargoes often rotting remained abandoned on both sides of the border. Even though the pipeline to Turkey suffered no interruption, close hits by the Russian artillery sent the reminder that Moscow could stop the flow of oil at any time and thus plunge Azerbaijan into a catastrophic situation.[14]

The Five Day War taught the lesson that Western countries came and went, but that Russia was always going to be in the Caucasus. The first to experience this changed situation was Vice President Dick Cheney, who in his previously scheduled visit to Baku in September 2008 received a cold and sometimes disrespectful reception from Azerbaijani officials.[15] In meetings with Western diplomats President Ilham Aliyev "has criticized Saakashvili and stated in no unclear terms that Georgia is not a model for Azerbaijan."[16]

Azerbaijan needed to return toward Moscow, but President Aliyev was slow to make this course correction. When Russia in August 2014 imposed an embargo on fruits and vegetables from the European Union the measure benefited Azerbaijan, whose farms scrambled to meet the shortfall of fresh produce in Russian markets. The opportunities for profitable relations with Russia suggested deepening the ties with the northern neighbor, but the mirage of oil wealth precluded joining the Eurasian Economic Union. Slowly Azerbaijani officials came to the realization that the oil and gas deposits in the Caspian Sea did not match the exaggerated expectations of the 1990s. The Russian success in blocking the Western-backed Nabucco gas pipeline to southern Europe showed that Azerbaijan could not expect a repetition of the profits from the Baku-Tbilisi-Ceyhan oil pipeline. The hesitation of Azerbaijan to become an ally of Russia contrasted with the firm loyalty of Armenia to Moscow.

Armenia: Staunch Ally

Despite considerable political turbulence in Armenia after its independence from the Soviet Union in 1991, the alliance with Russia has remained the bedrock of the Armenian state. However, periodic popular protests and political upheavals in 1998, 2004, 2008, 2011, and 2018 made the Kremlin question the stability of Armenia.[17]

Surrounded by hostile neighbors, this landlocked country clings to Russia as a life raft. Christian Armenia borders on the south with the Islamic Republic of Iran and to the west with Muslin Turkey. Most dangerous were the tensions to the east over the disputed region of Nagorno-Karabakh. The natural lifeline should be Christian Georgia, but this country to the north sometimes has acted more like an enemy. With nowhere else to turn to guarantee its survival, Armenia embraced Russia as its savior.[18]

Armenia, a member of the Collective Security Treaty Organization (CSTO) practically has outsourced its defense to Russia. The guards of the Federal Security Service

(FSB) patrol the borders with Georgia, Iran, and Turkey, and Russian detachments provide security for Yerevan International Airport. Ever since the fall of the Soviet Union Russia maintained the 102nd Base (originally the 102nd Division) at Gyumri next to the Turkish border and not far from Georgia. The majority of its soldiers have been Armenians who volunteer to serve in the Russian army. Armenia hosts a network of Russian air defenses and a sizeable number of Russian airplanes in its airfields. The Russian military served as the real deterrent against the Turkish Third Field Army, which was otherwise free to overrun Armenia.[19]

The Russian security presence was indispensable for the survival of Armenia. The cost of supporting an army capable of defending the country from its powerful neighbors was simply prohibitive and surpassed the human resources of the small population.

Defense has been the essential foundation in Armenia's relations with Russia but economic ties have been equally important. Almost all the trade of Armenia has been with Russia, and the single most important export to the northern neighbor has been a local brandy. Over a thousand Russian firms operate in Armenia, and they control the energy sector, not just gas but also power utilities and a nuclear plant. Of the largest 800 firms, at least 500 belong to Russians. This investment from Russia has been indispensable to keep the country prospering. Visa-free travel has facilitated personal and business links. The economic relationship with Russia has been beneficial to Armenia, and in some years the country has enjoyed double-digit economic growth.[20]

The biggest obstacle to increasing trade not just with Russia but with other countries has been the geographical isolation of landlocked Armenia. Travel through hostile Azerbaijan is impossible, and its ally Ankara kept the Turkish border and the key railroad closed to all traffic. Because the route through Iran suffers from many restrictions, Georgia and its vital railroad links has remained the sole commercial route with the outside world; even airplane flights had to use Georgian airspace. The only direct railroad to Russia passed through rebel-held Abkhazia, but war in 1992 left that track damaged. This blockage forced Armenia to divert all its cargo to the port of Poti in Georgia. Yerevan's constant pleas to Moscow to repair the segment through Abkhazia in order to reestablish the direct rail link with Russia came to contribute to the outbreak of the Five Day War with Georgia in August 2008.[21]

In contrast to Tbilisi, Yerevan was very careful not to do anything to upset its northern neighbor. The FSB routinely recorded the conversations of Armenian officials who pretended not to be aware of the eavesdropping. They learned to be careful in their discussions, and if secrecy was indispensable, the Armenian officials moved sensitive meetings into foreign locations.[22]

Armenia was very successful in attracting investments from Russia and Western countries. The refugee camps of the 1990s disappeared when Armenians either found local employment or else migrated to Russia and the United States. The large diaspora in Russia and in the United States, besides sending remittances home to relatives and providing most of the tourist revenue, also helped to lobby foreign governments.[23] One senior Armenian diplomat revealed that "the secret of success is Armenia's policy of complementarity, which aims to balance Euro-integration and friendly engagement with Russia."[24]

The display of military power during the Five Day War with Georgia of August 2008 confirmed that Russia had returned as a world power and that it could overrun the entire Caucasus at any moment. "The Armenian government has seemed as if it were excited to help Russia in this campaign, proving itself to the Kremlin" and applauded the use of Russian jets based in Armenian airfields against Georgia.[25] But despite this enthusiastic support, the refusal of the Kremlin to redraw boundaries so as to give Armenia access to the Black Sea through a Russian protectorate over Adjara dashed Armenian illusions. Moscow's failure to demand guarantees from Tbilisi for transit rights to Armenia was very disappointing.

The Russian military tried to avoid damaging the transportation infrastructure, but segments of the railroad suffered damage. Cargoes heading from Poti to Tbilisi and to Armenia were backed up in the port and many wagons remained abandoned along the railroad track. In areas under Russian occupation, the troops expedited shipments to Armenia, but the Georgians in those segments under their control favored train convoys headed to Azerbaijan over those for Armenia. Once Russian troops withdrew, Georgia rebuilt those segments of track leading to Tbilisi and then to Azerbaijan but left for last the branch line heading to Armenia. When Yerevan sent its railroad engineers to speed up the repairs, Georgia promptly returned them and enjoyed the fleeting revenge of having Armenia suffer food and fuel shortages. The threat of Georgia closing the border persuaded Yerevan not to recognize the independence of Abkhazia and South Ossetia, yet the government placated Moscow by eliminating from all future official statements any reference to the "territorial integrity" of Georgia.[26]

By 11 September 2008 the railroads were once again operating, but the shortages Armenia suffered compelled the country to take some painful and even wrenching decisions. Much as Armenians wanted a direct land link to Russia—and perhaps even a return to its rule—the Kremlin refused to restore the tsarist borders. This disappointment—almost like a lover whose partner does not want to take the relationship to the next level—did not mean a break with Moscow because Armenia had no other protector. But it forced the country to consider the repeated suggestions to do something that all Armenians previously considered a heresy and unpardonable: the restoration of relations with Turkey.

Armenia was worried that its interests might suffer because of the close ties between Turkey and Russia. Russian officials, who avoided commenting on domestic matters, did feel free to make suggestions to Turkey about its foreign policy. Russia recommended restoring relations with Armenia, and the Turks were receptive to the idea. However, Turkey remarked that its willingness to overcome the hostility of the past stood no chance of success first because of the total Armenian recalcitrance and second because Ankara had tied any opening of the Turkish border with Armenia to the solution of the Nagorno-Karabakh territorial dispute with Azerbaijan.[27]

Expecting a Turkish refusal, the Armenians, under considerable Russian pressure, agreed to talks. When the Turks not only agreed to converse but began to take confidence-building measures to reassure Armenia about their good intentions, a baffled Yerevan could not believe what was happening. Yerevan clung to one last barrier: Armenia refused to sacrifice Nagorno-Karabakh. Armenians, often unfairly accused of being too much in love with money, here bluntly stated that Nagorno-Karabakh was more important than any profitable trade deal. Negotiations seemed to have reached a dead end, until Russia once again intervened.

President Putin personally told President Recep Tayyip Erdogan that it was time to overcome the weight of the past. If Turkey no longer held grudges against Armenia, then why was it letting a small country like Azerbaijan dictate its foreign policy?

Turkey did not really need Azerbaijan, and if Baku in reprisal decided to shut off oil and gas shipments, Russia, through the Blue Stream pipeline, was more than willing to make up for the shortfall, and if necessary at a lower price.[28]

When Azerbaijan learned that Turkey was no longer insisting that Nagorno-Karabakh be a condition for a rapprochement with Armenia, Baku was livid and did suspend some gas shipments to Turkey but later relented. On 10 October 2009 Turkey and Armenia signed a treaty reopening their border to trade. Armenian, Turkish, and Russian businessmen were excited about the prospects of active commerce, and even the state Russian Railways, which provided service in Armenia, expected a boom in traffic between Armenia and Turkey.[29]

Both Russian and Armenian officials had been so busy dealing with Turkey that they failed to notice the mounting resentment of Georgia against Armenia in early 2010. Georgian officials believed that "Armenians want everything while offering nothing," because they "believe Georgia is in a position of weakness after the war with Russia, which has left the country in a fragile psychological state."[30] Georgia in the waning years of the Mikheil Saakashvili presidency wanted to reaffirm its power and felt it was time "to teach Armenia a lesson by shutting the border."

A Georgian official proudly stated to the U.S. Ambassador that "We could close the border in one day," a statement that panicked American diplomats and sent them into damage-control mode. The same aggressive and militaristic attitudes that had plunged Georgia into the disastrous war with Russia in 2008 were still present in the country in 2010. Any closing of the Georgian-Armenian border was an immediate *casus belli* for Russia, which was obligated under the Collective Security Treaty Organization to save Armenia from hardship and shortages of food and fuel. The last thing Washington wanted was to give Russia the perfect excuse to finish dealing with Georgia. Apparently neither the Kremlin nor Yerevan ever found out about this threat from Georgia. Panicky American diplomats scrambled to force Tbilisi to abandon any plans to close the border with Armenia and thus avoid a resumption of hostilities with Russia.

Armenia, without any oil deposits, knew that its survival as a country depended on Russian support. Armenia had been a founder of CSTO and also in 2015 joined the Eurasian Economic Union, two moves that pleased the Kremlin. Yerevan had been subtle in its relations with the West and used its diaspora more effectively than Baku's to influence foreign countries. In particular, the Armenian lobby in the U.S. had been petitioning Washington to pressure Turkey to lift its economic blockade against Armenia. Instead the sole instrument that Azerbaijan possessed to regain Nagorno-Karabakh by peaceful means was the Turkish blockade of Armenia.[31] When on 10 October 2009 the foreign ministers of Armenia and Turkey signed protocols restoring trade on the border, for Azerbaijan to see "that Turkey is willing to give up this leverage while gaining nothing on Nagorno-Karabakh is seen as an outright betrayal" of a country sharing the Muslim religion and a similar Turkish language.[32]

In reality, Ankara was under intense domestic pressure to restore trade with Armenia, and already many Turks were traveling by the long route around Georgia to do business with Armenians. The Turkish border regions next to Armenia had languished since the economic blockade of 1994 and wanted to recover their former prosperity. The turning point came when President Putin asked Erdogan to separate the trade blockade from the Nagorno-Karabakh dispute. An additional bonus for Russia was that Turkey put the blame for the reversal of its policy on the U.S., thereby further eroding the reputation of Washington.[33]

War Over Nagorno-Karabakh

After expending tremendous diplomatic capital, Russia was furious with the refusal of Armenia to normalize relations with Turkey. Armenia failed to realize that the deal with Turkey was the last opportunity to negotiate a favorable agreement over Nagorno-Karabakh. A snubbed Turkish President Erdogan responded by fostering strong ties with Azerbaijan, and soon Turkey was providing weapons to Azerbaijan and military training to Azeri officers. An outraged Ilham Aliyev decided to try a military solution in April 2016, but when five days of combat showed little progress on the battlefield, he accepted the ceasefire proposal of Vladimir Putin. Armenia did not see the attack of April 2016 as a final warning and instead sank into a false sense of security.

Azerbaijan had never recovered from the trauma of its shocking defeat in the 1990s. How could a poor and small Armenia have achieved such a smashing victory over a large and better armed foe? President Aliyev believed that his troops had lost because of the disorganization and chaos reigning in his country. A close admirer of Vladimir Putin, Aliyev sought inspiration in the campaign to restore order to Russia and went beyond to take the next step of creating an authoritarian system in Azerbaijan. Aliyev believed that his authoritarian rule could convert the nationalism of his people into a decisive victory to solidify his regime for decades to come.

In contrast, Armenia since the 1990s had embarked upon a quixotic crusade to create a model democratic government. Popular upheavals overthrew governments, Byzantine disputes divided the population, and the country fragmented into around 20 political parties each claiming to be the true democratic expression. While bitter quarrels over the nature of an Athenian-like democracy consumed Armenians, the military suffered neglect.[34]

The clash of April 2016 had been a trial run for Azerbaijan, but Aliyev delayed the final offensive when a new prime minister came to office in Armenia in 2018 and offered the hope of a peaceful solution. Once again negotiations stalled, and Armenia believed the matter was not urgent, despite mounting indications of the massive rearmament by Azerbaijan. Besides buying weapons from Russia, Aliyev obtained attack drones in secret purchases from Israel. He also had his officers receive extensive training in Turkey.[35]

The stage was set for the decisive confrontation between the autocratic Azerbaijan and one of the systems in the world closest to ancient Athenian democracy. Occasional artillery shelling had been taking place along the "line of contact" of 1994, and Azerbaijan used the pretext of a violent Armenian rocket barrage on 27 September 2020 to launch the long-prepared offensive to drive out the Armenians "like dogs" from the Azerbaijan lands as Aliyev boasted.[36] The claim seemed premature, and the offensive bogged down to a war of attrition during the first four weeks. The slow progress emboldened the Armenian prime minister to claim that the Azeri offensive had failed. All the time massive artillery barrages and "suicide" drones had been pulverizing with great precision the heavy weapons and armored vehicles of the Armenians.[37]

The breakthrough came on 18 October when Azerbaijan captured an old bridge on the Iranian border and embarked on the unexpected push on the southern front. Armenian defenses crumbled, and in desperation Yerevan called up reservists to halt the advance but to no avail. When Azerbaijan captured Shusha, the Armenian army pressed its prime minister to seek a truce because no further resistance was possible. Azeri soldiers were fast approaching Stepanakert, the capital of Nagorno-Karabakh, and it seemed that Aliyev was going to retake all the disputed territories by force.

An authoritarian regime had won a striking victory over a democratic system.[38]

Good luck ran out for Aliyev when his forces by mistake shot down a Russian helicopter and killed two of its crewmembers on 8 November 2020. The craft had been on a routine trip over Armenian air space and near the Azerbaijani enclave to the west far from the zone of combat. This attack on Armenia proper was a *casus belli* and required Russia to come to the aid of its ally under the Collective Security Treaty Organization. The terms of this treaty applied only to Armenia proper and not to the disputed territories.[39]

In an all-night negotiating session, Russian diplomats and President Putin imposed a solution on both warring parties. The Kremlin had tired of Armenia's refusal over decades to negotiate a solution to Nagorno-Karabakh and was not about to reverse the battlefield victories of Azerbaijan. By the agreement of 9 November, both sides kept their existing positions and agreed to the entry of 1,960 Russian peacekeepers with armored vehicles. Russia assumed control of the Lachin road to assure the supply of Stepanakert and the Armenian enclave but not the delivery of any armament. The agreement also forced Armenia to evacuate all Azerbaijani territories outside Nagorno-Karabakh.[40]

The agreement had just been signed when Russian peacekeepers began arriving aboard Ilyushin-76 planes, and the swift deployment reminded both parties of who was the real military power in the region. A jubilant Aliyev had won so much, that he could savor the victory and the huge surge of popularity for his regime. In victory parades and demonstrations, the uniformed president broadcast his triumph and confirmed that his authoritarian approach was the key to defeat a faction-ridden Armenia torn by internal quarrels.[41] But the real winner was Russia that once again reaffirmed its position as the dominant power in the region. Armenia and Azerbaijan relearned the lesson that they needed to remain friends of Russia.

PART III

Russia Ascendant

19

A Foreign Ministry for a World Power

> *The Ministry of Foreign Affairs of the Russian Federation carries out work for the direct implementation of the foreign policy course approved by the President of the Russian Federation. The Foreign Ministry of Russia coordinates foreign policy activities pursued by federal executive authorities and monitors them.*—Russian Foreign Policy Concept[1]

Once the abysmal situation of the 1990s ended, Russia undertook the difficult task of reconstructing its economy and its institutions after 2000. The rise in world petroleum prices gave a tremendous boost to oil and gas exports, while the mineral riches of its vast territory contributed to the revival of industry. Defense production became one of the country's largest exports, and foreign investment contributed to the expansion of the civilian sector.

In a situation not occurring since tsarist times, grain production and exports steadily rose during the twenty-first century. Starting in 2016, Russia became the world's largest exporter of wheat. A combination of foreign technology and wise governmental policies converted agriculture into a productive sector of the economy. No less significant was the struggle to halt the decline in population. Doomsayers had predicted the near extinction of the Russian people. Instead a decline in death rates, an increase in fertility, and immigration from the near abroad gradually reversed the population decline after 2000.

Russia encountered many obstacles when trying to make changes in its legal system and the army, yet even in those problem areas positive results appeared after 2010. The Russian military joined the ranks of the leading armed forces of the world, but was the Foreign Ministry contributing to the resurgence of a world power?

The Foreign Ministry

The Russian Foreign Ministry struggled to find a role after the collapse of the Soviet Union in December 1991. This difficulty might seem hard to understand, because, just like its counterparts abroad, the institution was supposed to conduct the foreign relations of the country. But there lay the obstacle, because during the Soviet period the Foreign Ministry exerted little influence on international relations.

After the end of Soviet Union, the Foreign Ministry, just like the military, had to recreate itself. Even though the emergence of a new Russian military required over twenty years to accomplish, its essential mission of defending the country was never in doubt. The challenge for the Foreign Ministry was to find meaningful functions within the new governmental structure emerging in post–Soviet Russia.

The Soviet Union

The Foreign Trade Ministry was in charge of economic relations with foreign countries. This institutional distribution of functions was not typical in the West. For example, the French Foreign Ministry and the U.S. State Department have devoted most of their activities to promoting business and economic relations with other countries. Instead, in the Soviet Union the existence of the Foreign Trade Ministry deprived the Foreign Ministry of any major role in economic matters.

The authority of Soviet diplomats over political and military relations was even weaker, because during the Soviet period three institutions curtailed the role of the Foreign Ministry. At least half of the personnel serving abroad belonged either to military intelligence (GRU) or KGB, and a popular witticism claimed that the diplomats existed only to provide cover for the personnel of the intelligence agencies. The Foreign Ministry resented the presence of so many intelligence officials performing most diplomatic functions abroad. In the embassies and missions, the ambassadors and senior diplomats were no less angry about being in the dark about the activities of KGB and GRU. In an additional insult, the security service, on the pretext of conducting counterintelligence, recruited diplomats to inform on their colleagues. As a result, the spy agency knew everything that the ambassador and the other senior diplomats were writing, saying, and planning.[2]

The third institution squeezing the Soviet Foreign Ministry was the International Department of the Central Committee of the Soviet Communist Party. This Department was the real foreign ministry, because it received and answered the key messages from both intelligence officials and diplomats. On major questions the International Department consulted with the Politburo for the final decision. In an attempt to bolster the nominal status of the diplomatic service, Joseph Stalin assigned one of the Seven Sisters, those huge and imposing buildings erected in Moscow during his rule, to be the headquarters of the Foreign Ministry.[3]

The only real privilege for the diplomats had been the tradition since Stalin's days of having the foreign minister be a member of the Politburo, the powerful ruling body of the Soviet Union. Although KGB and GRU were the real power in foreign relations, the Communist rulers realized that for public relations purposes diplomats, whether ambassadors and foreign ministers, should be the visible face for the West. Having the foreign minister be a member of the secretive and even mysterious Politburo gave substance to the claim that he possessed real authority. But in reality, he was aware that he hung on air and lacked any real power. In a revealing example, Andrei Gromyko opposed the Soviet invasion of Afghanistan in December 1979, but when he realized he was the last holdout, he agreed to support that doomed adventure.[4]

Gromyko kept quiet about his frustrations, but other diplomats and even ambassadors became demoralized once they realized that other than drab routine duties, their real mission was to provide cover for intelligence officers. Without an independent and meaningful role, many diplomats turned to alcoholism and consumerism, while others sometimes harassed female employees and engaged in bizarre sexual practices. Some diplomats also secured appointments for unqualified relatives. Ambassadors—all of whom were members of the Communist Party—realized that they could guarantee their immunity from prosecution by using official funds to purchase expensive gifts for members of the Central Committee of the Communist Party. After the death of Stalin members of the Communist Party could be tried only by their peers, and KGB could do little more than report the nepotism, corruption, and depravity occurring among some senior diplomats.[5]

Self-policing by the Communist Party was ineffective in the Foreign Ministry, but persuaded almost all diplomats not to abandon the regime. Although in 1979 one ambassador escaped to the West, much more numerous were the defectors from the intelligence agencies during the last decades of the Soviet Union. The Politburo concluded that overlooking the personal flaws of its representatives abroad was a small and necessary price to pay to keep them loyal to Moscow.[6]

The immunity that Communist Party members enjoyed from investigation by KGB contributed to the disillusionment not just of its officers but also of the majority of honest diplomats who saw that their complaints about rampant corruption, nepotism, and sexual intimidation went largely ignored. The realization spread in the late 1980s that the cause of the problem was the Communist Party itself and that no solution was possible without the removal of this corrupt and harmful Party. Among Soviet citizens the belief was almost universal that officials stationed abroad lived a pampered life, so when diplomats in late 1990, first in Geneva and then in other embassies such as New York, Paris, and Vienna, resigned from the Communist Party, this action had a profound impact on public opinion. Resignations from the Communist Party were already rampant inside the country, but to see diplomats abroad and those in the Foreign Ministry also leaving was one more blow hastening the collapse of the Soviet Union.[7]

The Russian Federation

On 18 December 1991 Boris Yeltsin issued a decree abolishing the Soviet Foreign Ministry and transferring its personnel and assets to the already existing Russian Foreign Ministry until then composed of only 270 employees. The personnel numbers of the new ministry of the Russian Federation rose to 3,000, 700 fewer than the 3,700 of the Soviet Foreign Ministry.[8]

The disappearance of the Soviet Union on 25 December 1991 made possible substantial changes in the structures of the new Russian government. Although on economic matters the Foreign Trade Ministry remained the predominant agency, in other areas the Foreign Ministry succeeded in expanding its influence. The greatest opportunity for an enhanced role came from the abolishment of the Communist Party. At the Foreign Ministry about 700 of the officials closest to the Communist Party lost their jobs in 1992, a mild purge compared to the Bolsheviks, who had replaced almost all the personnel of the Foreign Ministry in 1917. Without the stifling weight of the Communist Party, the Foreign Ministry could start to resemble its Western counterparts. Almost as important, the rivalry with the military declined, because the Foreign Ministry continued to operate without interruption after December 1991 but in contrast the military remained in legal limbo. Not until 7 May 1992 did the government formally establish the Russian armed forces, but by then it was too late to reverse the deterioration of that institution. Military intelligence (GRU) likewise declined in quality. Russian diplomats faced less rivalry from a weakened GRU, which, however, still retained a strong presence in major embassies and in important missions.[9]

The fragmentation of KGB into several new agencies reduced the influence of intelligence officers over the direct conduct of foreign relations. KGB had exercised enormous control over diplomats because, unlike GRU, which was stationed only at the embassies and missions, KGB officials were present both abroad and at the headquarters of the Foreign Ministry. The situation changed after 1991 when the functions of KGB most affecting the Foreign Ministry passed to two separate agencies, each with a distinct jurisdiction. The Foreign Intelligence Service (SVR) became an approximate equivalent of the CIA and inherited the agents of the former KGB at embassies, consulates, and missions across the world. The SVR retained many of the overseas police functions of the former KGB, and under the guise of counterintelligence, kept diplomats under surveillance. Because the SVR was one of the few agencies after the disappearance of the Soviet Union to have survived with an adequate budget, apparently at the insistence of Boris Yeltsin, it did have ample funds to recruit informants among embassy employees and diplomats.[10]

In Moscow the successor agency to KGB was the Federal Security Service (FSB), an organization patterned after the FBI in the United States. Its exact function inside the building of the Foreign Ministry remains unclear, and the FSB did not seem to have a presence. External security for the mammoth building (one of the Seven Sisters) has remained in the hands of the uniformed police of the Ministry of Internal Affairs (MVD). American diplomats suspected that just like during the Soviet period many meeting rooms and offices were bugged with electronic listening devices. The FSB may well have taped some conversations with foreign diplomats, and it is not inconceivable that its agents may have recruited diplomats and employees to inform on conversations with foreigners. During the 1990s the low salaries in the Foreign Ministry made recruitment feasible but infrequent because the Yeltsin administration was not generous in funding the FSB.[11]

The creation of the Department for New Threats and Challenges in the early 2000s provided an opportunity for bringing FSB personnel into the Foreign Ministry. The deputy foreign minister of counterintelligence came over from FSB in 2015 after a long and distinguished career at the security agency. But this new department since early in the twenty-first century has also been hiring many new graduates from the Moscow State Institute of International Relations (MGIMO), so these could not have been former FSB officials. And in a break from the pattern in the rest of the ministry, the New Threats Department had a "surprisingly high number" of women.[12]

In general, the Foreign Ministry has remained a male bastion, and in 2009 of 4,500 diplomats and 5,000 support personnel about 15 percent were females. The women predominated in secretarial and clerical positions, with only a small number being diplomats. This gender imbalance came about more by accident than by deliberate design. In the 1990s high inflation eroded official salaries, and employees sought to find better paying jobs in the private sector, a difficult task because the economy was collapsing. Educated women entering the labor force in the 1990s preferred to pursue lucrative positions in business rather than ill-paid positions in government agencies such as the Foreign Ministry. A similar phenomenon was taking place in the military, where officers with marketable skills tried to find employment in the private sector, or at least moonlighted at odd jobs in order to support their families.[13]

Diplomatic skills transferred easier into the private sector than military abilities, so the lure of private jobs has remained strong at the Foreign Ministry. Even when in the 2000s salaries started to keep up with inflation, the gains were offset by having to live in Moscow, by then not just the costliest city in Russia but also one of the most expensive in the world. And during the 1990s, salaries at the Foreign Ministry were so low for junior diplomats that their wives often earned ten times as much. Promotions did not close the gap, and even wives selling cars earned salaries several times higher than those of their husbands at mid-level diplomatic positions.

Since the 1990s these economic realities concentrated the recruitment of diplomats to the Moscow region. Only citizens of independent means who owned apartments or were married to wives with well-paid jobs could afford to live in Moscow. In contrast, the Communist Party had pursued a policy of affirmative action toward minorities, and citizens of the other fourteen Soviet republics could aspire and not just dream of becoming diplomats. After the collapse of the Soviet Union, all that was left of those attempts to bring diversity to the diplomatic corps was a few subsidized apartments owned by the Foreign Ministry, but these went to well-connected diplomats probably from St. Petersburg.[14]

The few Muslims on the staff had entered the Foreign Ministry during the Soviet period, and as they aged their replacements from the Islamic community were nowhere in sight. So although the Foreign Ministry pursued policies sympathetic to Middle Eastern countries, it failed to harness the potential of the large Muslim minority living inside Russia. In contrast, after 2010 the military was aggressive in recruiting Muslims and other minorities for all levels. The revitalized armed forces also offered better economic conditions and opportunities for promotion. The prestige of working in the Foreign Ministry was high but after the successful war with Georgia polls showed that the military had become one of the most admired institutions in Russia.[15]

Even before the smashing victory over Georgia, the military had been regaining influence within the government. Since 1992 the Foreign Ministry had been trying to play a greater role in weapons sales but suffered a major setback when President Vladimir Putin on 16 August 2004 issued a decree creating the Federal Service for Military-Technical Cooperation as part of the Ministry of Defense. This new Service authorized sales of arms abroad and coordinated its activities with twenty other agencies, one of which was the Ministry of Foreign Affairs. Final authority remained in the hands of the president, and the Foreign Ministry saw its limited influence over military exports diluted even more. In contrast, the approval of arms sales constituted a major function of the U.S. Department of State and other Western counterparts.[16]

The Diplomatic Career Path

In spite of the competition from the military after 2010, the Foreign Ministry remained an attractive career option for Russian citizens living in Moscow. As in the Soviet period, the first step for students wishing to enter the Foreign Ministry or the Trade Ministry was to enroll in the Moscow State Institute of International Relations (MGIMO). This had been an elite institution for children of the Communist Party and in the 1990s became a preferred destination for many families of the new Russian elite. Admission to this prestigious university was very competitive; over half of the entering students expressed their intention to join the Foreign Ministry and a sizeable percentage wished to join the Trade Ministry.

The lure of higher pay persuaded most graduates to choose jobs in the private sector and in large commercial firms. Only a minority remained true to their original calling and entered the Foreign Ministry or the Trade Ministry. Those still wanting to pursue a diplomatic career accounted for three-fourths of diplomats, and the percentage of MGIMO graduates was even higher for those holding senior positions in the ministry. Not all the students joined the Foreign Ministry upon receiving their degrees, and many pursued graduate studies at the Diplomatic Academy. In spite of its title, the same selection process was at work inside this Academy as at MGIMO, with most of the graduates taking employment in the private sector in either Russian or foreign companies. While a degree from

MGIMO was an informal prerequisite for holding high positions in the Foreign Ministry, attendance at the Diplomatic Academy was optional.[17]

The one-fourth of diplomats who were not alumni of MGIMO had followed one of two possible paths. A first group comprised those who had intended to become academics in such fields as history and "super-hard" languages. A second group were those with technical degrees, such as engineers who provided the specific skills the Foreign Ministry needed to conduct its negotiations or to provide its administrative support services. The individuals in these two groups often had advanced degrees such as a Ph.D. and were always highly knowledgeable in their fields. Once they transitioned into the diplomatic community, their opportunities to rise to senior positions in the Foreign Ministry were the same as the graduates of MGIMO.[18]

The most career-savvy went from MGIMO or the Diplomatic Academy to the Foreign Ministry, with the goal of making themselves attractive to future employers in the private sector. These junior diplomats, many of them women, might spend five to ten years in the Foreign Ministry, and once they acquired adequate skills, contacts, and experience, they then moved to well-paying positions at Russian or foreign corporations. Diplomatic service could also be a springboard for senior posts in the government. The most famous was Yevgeny Primakov, whose long diplomatic career in the Middle East culminated in his being appointed twice as prime minister of Russia. Dmitry Peskov, the Kremlin press secretary, and Yuri Ushakov, a former ambassador to the United States, were some of the diplomats who entered the presidential administration.[19]

The new hires normally spent their initial years at the Foreign Ministry in order to become familiar with the routines of diplomacy, but this practice often suffered modification for both personal and institutional reasons. New hires with independent means or with wives earning high salaries were content to stay in the vibrant life of Moscow for as long as possible, in part so as not to lose the wife's job. On the opposite economic spectrum were poor individuals who struggled to pay the rent on their cramped and very expensive apartments in Moscow. Their goal was to obtain a foreign posting as soon as possible so that they could accumulate enough savings from their overseas allowances to buy an apartment for the inevitable return to Moscow at a later stage of their careers.[20]

The number of new hires wishing for assignments in Western Europe and North America was always higher than the available positions. Even though the embassies at those places were the largest in the diplomatic service, junior officials could expect to spend five or more years waiting for a vacancy to open. The situation was ideal for those who wanted to stay as long as possible in Moscow, but for those without the means, the long delay could mean leaving the diplomatic service in order to obtain a job elsewhere with decent pay. By contrast, new hires whose language skills were needed in hard-to-staff embassies or in hardship posts could find themselves assigned overseas in six or fewer months, not adequate time to absorb the routines of diplomatic practice.

Russian embassies and consulates, just as in the Soviet period, preferred to employ spouses and children of diplomats for administrative duties rather than import private citizens from Russia or hire locals. This family priority could be beneficial and boost income, provided that Russian language schools existed for the children of diplomats. All the large missions possessed secondary schools, and the medium-sized embassies had at least primary schools, but in the small embassies or consulates the school at most extended only up to the fourth grade and might not even exist.[21]

Knowledge of languages played the

determinant role in the entire career of diplomats. Students who intensified their language training in secondary school may not have always realized that they were taking a major and perhaps the most important decision affecting the rest of their lives. In contrast to the U.S. Foreign Service which had no language requirement for entry, everyone entering the Russian diplomatic corps had to be conversant in two foreign languages, with one of them being English. Students of MGIMO acquired a mastery of both spoken and literary English that few native speakers could match. Cases of Russian diplomats preferring to speak only in English were frequent. Although some of the older diplomats might still betray a slight Russian accent when speaking in English, the young hires with easy access to the internet and English-channel television attained near native speaking fluency.[22]

No rigid principles existed on the choice of the second language, but some patterns were evident. Slavic languages were considered too similar to Russian and too easy to qualify for the second choice and almost always precluded promotion higher than the departments dealing with Eastern European countries. Neither was Spanish a frequent choice, in spite of Russia's close relations with Cuba, Nicaragua, and Venezuela. Despite the limited demand, the Foreign Ministry always possessed adequate numbers of diplomats fluent in Spanish. In stark contrast, the United States, with a large population of native Spanish speakers, has struggled to fill the many openings requiring Spanish proficiency.[23]

French was the second most popular language for Russian diplomats, and it was the indispensable requirement for those seeking assignments to any of the prestigious agencies of the United Nations and the European bodies such as EU and OSCE. And as in the United States, the hardest slots to fill were those requiring "super-hard" languages. The Foreign Ministry could never attract enough speakers of Farsi, Arabic, and Hindi, despite offering almost certain promotions and salary increases within their geographic department and the missions abroad. A major reason why the Foreign Ministry hired academics was to fill the shortages of diplomats with working knowledge of these "super-hard" languages.[24]

The Foreign Ministry based its hiring, posting, and promotion policies on the language skills of the individuals. Because all were expected to know English well, it was the second language that most differentiated individuals from the rest of the diplomats. So those fluent in Chinese could expect to spend their entire careers in the missions and offices dealing with China. In an important difference with the U.S. Foreign Service, the Russian Foreign Ministry did not provide the opportunity learn or cover the cost of studying foreign languages. Despite many on-the-job opportunities and incentives the U.S. State Department provided to learn foreign languages, American embassies and consulates suffered from a shortage of personnel proficient in local languages.[25]

Inevitably, a certain superficiality emerged among American diplomats who did not linger long in one language or culture, in marked contrast to their Russian counterparts fluent in two languages who spent their whole lives dedicated to the study of the history, politics, literature, and culture of the host countries. Only in countries speaking a rare Asian or African language did Russian diplomats encounter the same barriers as their American counterparts. The disadvantage was more apparent than real, because just like American diplomats, the Russians enjoyed the luxury of piggybacking on the widespread presence of English across the globe. The best example was India. Which of its dozens of languages should Russian diplomats learn, and why should they even bother when English sufficed to transact all business with New Delhi? And for small, poor countries, English substituted well for any little-known local language.

Language proficiency marked out the career paths of Russian diplomats. The new hires began work in the Foreign Ministry, and after a year or two, they went on their first postings to an embassy, consulate, or mission. After a period of three to five years, the junior diplomats either left for another embassy in their geographic area of expertise or came back to their original department in the Foreign Ministry. This first homecoming was decisive, because after having spent several years in Moscow, they then returned to the field as senior diplomats holding important rank. In the hard-to-staff areas they might even receive their first ambassadorial appointment to a small or insignificant country. Based on their performance in this second tour in the field, the most successful diplomats returned to Moscow, either as head or deputy of a geographic department.

The significance of these appointments was that those heads or deputies of the geographic departments were on track to rise to the highest positions. Those individuals could then aspire to be chargés d'affaires, ministers, and ambassadors at prestigious places. The most important appointments were at the UN, the United States, Western Europe, Japan, and China. Holding these senior positions signified the culmination of a long successful career then capped with a well-earned retirement. But here already a clear separation appeared between those dealing with major powers and those diplomats in the hard-to-staff areas. The latter had already held high positions in those marginal countries, and after their second tour in Moscow they could expect to repeat their previous posting abroad. Diplomats stationed in minor countries initially advanced rapidly but then reached a plateau and watched their careers stagnate. It was the successful ambassadors with postings to major countries who were first in line to reach the rank of deputy foreign ministers.

In comparison to the U.S. Foreign Service, the Russian diplomatic corps numbered at most a third. Yet in spite of its modest size, the Foreign Ministry provided good diplomatic services for Russia.[26] Out of the wreckage of the Soviet Union the Foreign Ministry adapted to the new circumstances and acquired the capability to conduct the foreign relations of a world power. In shaping the policy toward other countries, the Foreign Ministry also became an influential voice but never to the degree of its Western counterparts.

20

The Reset in U.S. Relations with Russia

Alas! How should you govern any kingdom, that knows not how to use ambassadors?—William Shakespeare.[1]

The Barack Obama Administration

The inauguration of Barack Obama on 20 January 2009 marked the start of another effort to improve relations with Russia. In the previous attempt after 9/11, President Vladimir Putin took the initiative in trying to cooperate with the U.S. In 2009 the Obama administration baptized its initiative the "reset." In a televised meeting with Foreign Minister Sergei Lavrov on 6 March 2009 Hillary Clinton opened a box containing a gadget with a button labeled "reset"; both officials were supposed to press the button to symbolize the start of a new relationship. In one more indication of the proverbial weak language skills of the State Department, the Russian word in the button was not "reset" but "overload"; like a teacher explaining to a pupil, Lavrov said "you have it wrong."[2]

In a trip to Moscow in July 2010, Obama expected to electrify the public as he had done in European capitals and in Cairo but was disappointed. "Obamamania just did not infiltrate Russia. The student audience for his major public speech looked rather bored."[3]

The red line for the Kremlin was NATO membership for Georgia and Ukraine; everything else could be negotiated to find a compromise. The reset was able to advance not because of the personal chemistry between Dmitry Medvedev and Obama but because Georgia and Ukraine receded from view. The U.S. stated that NATO membership for those two countries was a distant goal.

Because the Obama administration never rejected NATO membership for Georgia and Ukraine, this dark cloud remained lurking. But where the light was shining, the Kremlin and the Obama administration were free to make substantial improvements in their relations. Progress took place in four main areas.

New START Treaty

The first was the signing of a New START treaty on 8 April 2010. This treaty—ratified by the U.S. Congress and the Russian parliament—reduced the number of strategic nuclear warheads of each country from 2,200 to 1,550 and also limited the number and type of "delivery vehicles." The treaty provided verification procedures and brought considerable savings in the costs of maintaining the two largest nuclear arsenals in the world.[4]

Afghanistan

For the Obama administration, another priority was Afghanistan, and here

Russia was more than willing to help the U.S. in the war against the Taliban. The U.S. increased its troop strength in Afghanistan, but this "surge"—as it came to be called—required the delivery of large quantities of supplies, weapons, and equipment to American troops. The U.S. had relied on Pakistan until this moment to provide the logistical access, but militant Islamists in that country were blocking, targeting, and even destroying the trucks and trains taking supplies to U.S. forces in Afghanistan. Pressuring the Pakistani government to protect the lifeline put at risk the survival of that fragile regime.[5]

And to make things worse, Kyrgyzstan was threatening to close the Manas air base, an important staging area and a stop in the route bringing non-lethal supplies across Russia to American forces in Afghanistan. The U.S. believed that Russia was pressuring Kyrgyzstan to close the Manas air base as part of the "Great Game" of empire in Central Asia. The Kremlin's position was that the U.S. could have bases in Central Asia as long as needed for the war against Islamic extremists. Russia persuaded Kyrgyzstan not to close the base, and the Russians confirmed that the threat to close had been just a ploy of the Kyrgyz to extract higher rent payments from the U.S.[6]

Support for the U.S. base in Manas formed part of the larger question of using Russian space to transport supplies and equipment to Afghanistan. On 6 July 2009 Obama and Medvedev signed an agreement giving the U.S. the right to use all facilities in Russia to move both lethal and non-lethal cargoes to Afghanistan. Having to separate the two types of cargoes delayed and made more expensive the deliveries; instead the freedom to mix both lethal and non-lethal cargoes saved both time and money. A bitter enemy of Islamic extremism, Russia was more than pleased to make this positive contribution to the U.S. war in Afghanistan.[7]

Iran

The most pressing issue for the U.S. was Iran. The Obama administration was determined to stop the nuclear weapons program of the country but to make sanctions effective needed the full support of all major powers. Russia did not see the need for sanctions and concentrated on improving relations with Iran. But by April 2009 Moscow was receiving indications that the country was advancing in its nuclear program. Sensing an opening, U.S. officials shared satellite photographs and top secret materials proving that Iran was making fast progress on its program to acquire nuclear weapons.[8]

Because Russia hesitated to turn against Iran, the U.S. believed that Tehran was Moscow's ally. Relations with Iran were complex and leaned more toward subdued tensions. At the heart of the Russo-Iranian relationship was the refusal of the Ayatollahs to seek an alliance with Moscow. Tehran insisted on going it alone and unlike Syria, never accepted the need to have a world power as its sponsor or patron. The overwhelming evidence of Tehran's deception persuaded Russia to vote on 9 June 2010 for the Security Council resolution 1929 imposing harsh sanctions on Iran over its nuclear program.[9]

The U.S. and Western Europe imposed additional financial sanctions on Iran. "We had not briefed the Russian government on our intentions to go beyond UN Security Council 1929. We reasoned that if we did, the Russians would back away from the Security Council Resolution."[10] The Russians were angry at this "bait and switch," but the Kremlin kept its complaints within private channels and did not make any public criticisms.

Missile Defense

The Bush administration had decided to establish a missile defense system against

Iran and North Korea. In 2004 the U.S. selected the Czech Republic and Poland as the site for the installations. The Kremlin opposed the proposal on the grounds that the missile defense could also target Russia. Disregarding the objections, the Bush administration entered into talks with the Czech Republic and Poland to acquire facilities for the missile defense system.

It was clear that ratification of the New START treaty was not going to be possible if the question of missile defense remained unsolved. To break the deadlock over New START, the Obama administration announced in September 2009 the abandonment of plans to establish a missile defense in the Czech Republic and Poland. A major reason for the change had been the political opposition within those countries. Moscow welcomed the move but still inserted a reservation in the New START treaty that if the U.S. resumed plans to install the missile defense, Russia could exceed the limit established in the treaty for the nuclear warheads. This provision was necessary to convince the Russian legislature to ratify the treaty.[11]

The missile defense proposal remained a vexing issue, and at one moment Medvedev threatened to deploy medium-range missiles in the Russian enclave of Kaliningrad if the U.S. resumed plans to deploy the missile defense system. By then the Obama administration had already decided that both the New START treaty and Russian support for sanctions on Iran were more important than the missile defense in Eastern Europe. In addition, the missile defense was flawed and a waste of taxpayers' money. The system was so bad, that even after the end of the reset, the Obama administration did not hesitate to cancel the proposal in March 2013. But the damage had already been done, and from 2001 to 2013 the U.S. missile defense plan consumed time and energies all better devoted to other pressing issues.[12]

To promote other joint projects, both countries created a presidential commission on U.S.-Russian relations. The new body looked for opportunities to develop partnerships in the areas of business, economy, education, and culture. The commission organized 18 groups to strengthen the ties between both countries at the official, private, and personal level.[13]

European Security Treaty

Despite the significant degree of cooperation with the Obama administration, President Dmitry Medvedev knew very well that progress had been possible only by tiptoeing around the red line of NATO membership for Georgia and Ukraine. Georgia was a non-issue, because it could not join as long as NATO respected its own founding charter that disqualified for membership those countries involved in a territorial dispute. The real struggle was over Ukraine.[14] Russian officials spoke about "the danger posed by a western Russian tug-of-war over Ukraine, warning that Russia will never give it up" and that Ukraine could be "the potential death knell of U.S.-Russian intentions to restart the bilateral relationship."[15]

Since the fall of the Soviet Union Moscow on repeated occasions proposed the two complementary alternatives of reliance on OSCE rather than NATO for security in Europe and neutralization of Eastern European countries and the former Soviet republics. Austria, Finland, Moldova, Sweden and Switzerland were neutral states, but the West rejected extending neutralization or "Finlandization." The West insisted on incorporating the non-neutral countries west of Russia into NATO, and by 2009 only Georgia and Ukraine were not members.[16]

The major reason why the U.S. felt that Ukraine could still become a member of NATO was the belief among Cold Warriors that weakness had forced Russia to engage in the reset. According to this viewpoint, the New START treaty and the transit agreement for Afghanistan showed that Russia was too feeble to oppose U.S. requests. But the anti–Russia paranoia was still strong, and Cold Warriors continued to attack the Obama administration for giving away too much to Russia. Vice President Joe Biden, the leader of the hard liners, came to the rescue of reset by claiming that the Russians "have a shrinking population base, they have a withering economy, they have a banking sector and structure that is not likely to be able to withstand the next fifteen years [...] and they are clinging to something in the past that is not sustainable."[17]

The Kremlin dismissed Biden's comments as intended for domestic political consumption and proceeded to elaborate an alternative system for relations between the West and Russia. The intellectual challenge was daunting, because the Presidential Administration and the Foreign Ministry had to come up with a proposal to bridge the abysm separating the NATO solution of the West with Russia's need for a neutral zone. In February 2009 and before the American reset, Russian diplomats were telling their Western counterparts that a new security architecture was in the works. Indeed, these Russian feelers were a major reason why the Obama administration felt confident about launching the reset in the first place.[18]

In March 2009 Russian diplomats stated that Medvedev was working on a proposal "intended to address the gaps and failures in European security, which NATO, the OSCE, EU, CSTO, and individual nations cannot satisfactorily guarantee."[19] These comments were most unwelcome for Western diplomats who did not want to modify the existing architecture.

In several statements President Medvedev had pointed out the deficiencies in the existing architecture, and in a speech on 5 June 2009 he announced that Russia was preparing "a new pan–European security treaty." In order to avoid springing a surprise such as the Kozak Memorandum of 2004, Russian officials discussed with Western counterparts possible ideas for inclusion and reported that a draft treaty was taking shape. Although many officials at the Foreign Ministry felt that the text was still not ready for public discussion, President Medvedev decided to release the draft treaty on 29 November 2009. The Kremlin explained that this was a work in progress and that the text needed inputs from other countries and institutions before the final language was ready for submission to the legislatures of each country.[20]

The European Security Treaty was a lost opportunity. The proposed treaty was trying to prevent a repetition of the Five Day War with Georgia of August 2008. This example was appropriate, because the conditions that led to the war with Georgia remained latent in Ukraine and even in other countries of the near abroad. What was ingenious about the draft was the way it integrated NATO into the new treaty without requiring the abolishment of that military alliance; a supplementary treaty to be signed with NATO provided channels to enhance cooperation and trust with Russia. The main treaty offered peace for all of Europe by establishing innovative mechanisms to prevent tensions from turning into war as happened with Georgia. The treaty was filling some of the gaps the drafters of the United Nations Charter had left unaddressed.[21]

The proposed treaty in effect was doing what the West should have done after the collapse of the Soviet Union. Medvedev was offering the West an elegant alternative to renewed confrontation between NATO and Russia. Vladimir Putin, then prime minister, saw no harm in the proposal, but suspecting the outcome, he maintained his distance. The Collective Security Treaty Organization (CSTO) embraced the proposal which seemed to be off to a good start.

The Medvedev draft proposal found a receptive audience in Western European countries such as France, Germany, and Italy, which remembered well the ravages of two world wars. For the Western Europeans, the promise of guaranteeing peace was too seductive to resist. The proposed treaty formed a capstone to the existing security architecture and meshed with the obligations under NATO and the UN.[22] As a Russian diplomat pleaded, "No one can have anything to lose from this and everyone will be a winner."[23] And with both France and Britain retaining veto power in the Security Council, their strategic interests were never at risk.

In contrast the NATO members from Eastern Europe, with the exception of Hungary, condemned the draft. They were outraged by the supplementary treaty that limited NATO military deployments in countries that joined the military alliance after April 1997. The Czech Republic, Poland, and Rumania denounced the Russian proposal and even went so far as to demand that each country reject the document in strong public statements.[24]

In spite of the tough talk from most Eastern European countries, the U.S. had the final word. As Prime Minister Putin suspected, the U.S. response was predictable, and American diplomats saw the text as a ploy "to reestablish Moscow's role as a great power [...] foundering on the tension between progressive European ideals and Russia's instincts to protect state sovereignty."[25] Although "the draft is clumsy and tendentious," American diplomats agreed with the Biden interpretation that it was a sign of Russian weakness and saw in negotiations the opportunity to extract concessions from Moscow.

Highest priority for the United States was to revive the moribund Conventional Forces in Europe Treaty (CFE), which Russia abandoned in 2007. By shifting the negotiating focus into the CFE and into the safe forum of OSCE, the U.S. could advance its goal of weakening Russia. All that American diplomats had to do was to pretend interest in Medvedev's proposal and then use that sympathy as leverage against Russia. The subtle negotiation game proved too difficult for Secretary of State Hillary Clinton to comprehend, and on 29 January 2010 she rejected the need for a new treaty and directed Moscow to negotiate adjustments within the existing agreements on OSCE and the NATO-Russia Council.[26]

For all practical purposes the Clinton rejection killed the Medvedev proposal. The intellectual significance of the proposed treaty was great, because it represented a partial retreat from the principles of Putin's Munich speech of 10 February 2007. The swift U.S. rejection confirmed better than anything else Washington's commitment to unilateralism. The Munich speech remained the antithesis to U.S. policy and the guiding principle for Russia.

Cheeseburger Summit and Spies

The Obama administration concluded that the unwelcome treaty proposal had been one bump in the road similar to obstacles during the negotiations for New START agreement and missile defense. Nevertheless, the idea of giving something to Russia as a way to keep the momentum on the reset going forward seemed advisable. In particular, the U.S. needed to convey the message that it did not regard Russia as an enemy.

No better way came to show this attitude when in May 2010 the U.S. lifted the sanctions on Rosoboronexport and three other Russian arms firms. The U.S. had taken that action in 2006 over groundless concerns that those Russian companies were helping Iran's nuclear program. When the Kremlin supported harsh UN Security Council sanctions on Iran, it made sense to repeal reprisals against Russia. For good measure, the U.S. already had abrogated the almost forgotten sanctions dating back to 1999 on two other Russian firms also accused of helping Iran. For the first time since 1999, no Russian firm faced any sanctions. In addition, in May the Obama administration named Michael McFaul, a Russian scholar from the inner circle of the White House and not a diplomat, to be the next ambassador to Moscow.[27]

The above measures persuaded the Obama administration that it had placated Russia and that the reset could continue moving forward. But because the U.S. also allowed Russia to complete the sale of the S-300 anti-aircraft defense system to Iran, hardliners in Washington began to fear that the Obama administration was capitulating to Russia.

The atmospherics of relations with Russia were good, and the two countries seemed to have achieved a rapport inconceivable during the last years of the Bush administration. To emphasize the amicable relations, Obama invited Dmitry Medvedev for a state visit to the United States for June 2010. The two young attorneys had already developed a close relationship in previous meetings, and the trip promised to bring them closer. Medvedev went on a tour of Silicon Valley to confirm his support for a digital world, and high point of the state visit came when he and Obama sat down to eat cheeseburgers at a famous fast-food place on 24 June 2010. The image of the two leaders chatting at the informal gathering like two old friends went round the world and fueled the illusion of cooperation between the two superpowers.[28]

The visit came to be known as the "Cheeseburger Summit" and it promised to be the first of many more chummy gatherings. But the FBI, which liked to play the role of "spoiler," had other plans. On 11 June 2010 the agency informed the White House (just as it later did in 2018 before the Donald Trump meeting with Vladimir Putin in Helsinki), that it planned to arrest 12 Russian spies but was extending the courtesy of delaying the move so as not to disrupt the conduct of foreign relations. The FBI offer was disingenuous at best, because the whole point of the arrest was to remind Americans that the Russians could not be trusted. The political motive to hurt Obama in the mid-term elections was obvious, while the FBI needed to justify its huge expenses of supporting the idle staffers assigned to counterintelligence.[29]

The media loves spies, and once the FBI began carrying out their arrests on 27 June, the public feasted on stories about the spy ring. By then one of the suspects had left the country, but if it had been a true spy "ring" all of them would have been tipped off to flee between 11 June (if not earlier) and 27 June. Eight of the spies were couples, one of the couples was from Peru, and another one claimed to be Canadian. The alleged mastermind of the spy ring was the later famous Anna Chapman, a dashing and pretty red hair soon called the Russian Matta Hari.[30]

The best the FBI could come up to describe the spy ring was the label of a big sleeper cell. But rather than targeting political and military objectives, the supposed spies lived in suburbia and blended in with locals. One worked at a travel agency, and Chapman used her beauty and charm to promote a successful career in real estate and to increase her net worth to over 2 million dollars. None of the arrested individuals had gone through the many years of rigorous training required of real Russian spies. Many were little more than informal "contacts," who provided tidbits of information to Russian officials in the same manner as U.S. citizens do when talking with American diplomats abroad. Others were at most paid informants, but their labor seemed pointless because almost all that they were supposed to have reported came from public sources and none of the information was classified so that they could not be charged under the espionage laws.

The spy ring kept an eye on wealthy Russian émigrés perhaps for tax purposes or to try to uncover indications that their wealth came from corruption at home.[31]

A spy swap a few days later exchanged the 11 Russians with 4 Americans held on similar charges in Russia, and in this way both governments defused a crisis generated by overzealous subordinates trying to protect their countries from unfounded fears.[32] But staging a spy crisis was not going to derail the Obama reset. A divergence on foreign policy could set back relations with Russia, but in 2010 no real confrontation loomed on the horizon. The hidden time bomb was Ukraine, and once Washington rejected Medvedev's European Security Treaty proposal, a clash was inevitable. But as the next chapter shows, a combination of unusual circumstances made possible the postponement of a confrontation over the near abroad.

21

The Reset in the Near Abroad

There can be no question of the West giving Russia carte blanche in the near abroad.—U.S. Embassy, Tbilisi[1]

The problems discussed in the previous chapter were so important that it was easy to see why the Obama administration failed to realize that the vital issues for Russia were Georgia and Ukraine. The Kremlin drew red lines against NATO and EU expansion in those two countries, but the George W. Bush administration disregarded the warning.

The Five Day War decided the fate of Georgia, even though until the present a stubborn U.S. has refused to accept the outcome. The Obama administration scored a success in the reset by allowing this conflict to fade from public view. Ukraine was different, because the clash of the U.S. and Russia over that country seemed inevitable, as did happen in 2014. But by a series of coincidences Ukraine receded into the background and the Obama administration could claim another success in its reset.

Georgia: Defusing Tensions

OSCE, UN, and EU

It might seem paradoxical that an essential step for restoring a semblance of normalcy to Georgia was to end the presence of foreign observers. Of the three agencies involved, the first to go was the Organization of Security and Cooperation in Europe (OSCE). Member states blamed the observers for having failed to prevent the outbreak of the Five Day War, and as a result their mission expired on 31 December 2008.[2]

OSCE had focused more on South Ossetia, while the United Nations Observer Mission in Georgia (UNOMIG) concentrated on Abkhazia. UNOMIG was a legacy of the 1991–1992 Georgian invasion of Abkhazia, and Russia had to exert tremendous pressure to secure its renewal. But in early February 2009, it was the Western powers who in a remarkable reversal pleaded with Russia to renew the observer mission.

The unexpected turn caught Russian diplomats by surprise, but sensing a trap, on 13 February they accepted a "technical" extension only until 15 June. The Abkhazians meanwhile lobbied Russia hard to prevent the return of UNOMIG. When the final vote came on 15 June 2009, Russia vetoed the resolution for the renewal of UNOMIG for another year.[3]

The United Nations High Commissioner to Georgia held the rank of ambassador and headed a small staff. Western powers pressured the UN Comptroller to continue funding the position, but the official explained that such a substantial expense in the budget required Security Council authorization. Once the UN High

Commissioner departed, the UN lost any direct role.[4]

The EU monitors were the last remaining officials who satisfied the requirement stipulated in the Sarkozy-Medvedev Agreement for an "international instrument." In practice, the EU monitors never began to function. Neither Abkhazia nor South Ossetia allowed the entry of the EU monitors. Over the next few years they faded from view, yet the EU still maintained a large staff in Tbilisi.[5]

Coup Attempt and Military Maneuvers

Since April 9 protests had taken place on a daily basis in Tbilisi; these street demonstrations expressed the widespread anger at President Mikheil Saakashvili for having plunged the country into a disastrous war. The sometimes violent demonstrators were trying to repeat the pattern of the previous "Color Revolutions" but before the movement could reach a critical mass, a battalion stationed near Tbilisi mutinied on 5 May 2009 and prepared to overthrow the government. The coup attempt then collapsed and the conspirators were arrested without any loss of life.[6]

Saakashvili denounced Moscow for having tried to carry out regime change. Although the Kremlin had always stated that his removal from office was a prerequisite for guaranteeing peace in the region, in reality no evidence ever appeared supporting these accusations. The street demonstrations fizzled out by the end of May.[7]

The failed coup attempt had been one more scare in the often turbulent Caucasus, and no less provocative was Georgia's decision to host military exercises for NATO and non–NATO members from 6 May to 1 June. Russia pressured countries not to participate, and Kazakhstan, Moldova, and Serbia cancelled their attendance. The staging of similar NATO exercises had been a precipitating factor in the Five Day War, and just like in 2008, Russia countered with its own maneuvers called "Caucasus 2009" involving over 12,000 soldiers, armored vehicles, and artillery pieces. Spokesmen for the Russian Defense Ministry stated that many of the units in Caucasus 2009 had participated in the victorious Five Day War and implied that they were ready to resume combat.[8]

Tensions were rising in Georgia, and something was needed to defuse an explosive situation. A partial solution came with the release of the *Report* from the EU's Fact Finding Mission on the Conflict in Georgia. Russia with misgivings and Georgia under pressure from the West had agreed to cooperate with this Mission headed by the distinguished Swiss diplomat Heidi Tagliavini. The *Report* recognized that Georgia had started the war by carrying out an unprovoked and criminal shelling of civilian population.[9]

Most Western countries were suffering from "Georgia fatigue" and were no longer talking about reprisals by the end of 2008. The U.S. did not like the *Report*, so American diplomats blocked a key appointment to Tagliavini, whom they considered "inappropriate" even though she had been named "Switzerland's outstanding diplomat."[10]

Maritime Dispute

Sooner than anybody had expected, the time came to decide whether the U.S. and the West were determined to confront Russia over the separatist republics. Turkey, the home of a large Abkhazian diaspora, was the second most important trading partner after Russia. With the closure of land routes to Turkey after the Five Day War, many Abkhazian-owned ships sailed between the two countries. Georgian patrol boats began to detain Abkhazian vessels trading with Turkey. The ship owners had to pay huge fines and in some cases had their vessels confiscated. What Georgia was trying to do was to repeat the maneuver of 2006 when it had seized the Upper Kodori River as the first step toward the recovery of the separatist region. In 2006 the U.S. defended the invasion, and Georgia expected the same support in 2009.[11]

Russia was determined to protect Abkhazian shipping. The Foreign Ministry restrained the Black Sea Fleet and the Russian air force from using the Georgian patrol craft as target practice and urged a proportional response. The Federal Security Service (FSB) in charge of maritime security deployed its coast guard boats to escort the Abkhazian vessels. The Georgian boats stopped bothering Abkhazian shipping and the U.S. advised Georgia to avoid any incident.[12]

Russia met this sign of U.S. goodwill with its own suggestion to Abkhazian vessels to avoid the undisputed territorial waters of Georgia off Batumi and Poti. However, Georgia could not resist making one last act of defiance, and in July 2010 its patrol craft seized an Ukrainian vessel carrying a cargo of wheat in Abkhazian waters. The clear lesson was that any ship needed to coordinate its movements with the FSB to obtain escorts to Abkhazian ports.[13]

U.S. Acquiescence

The decision by the Obama administration to stop Georgian attempts to intercept maritime shipping prevented a revival of hostilities in Abkhazia. The U.S. decision reflected a broad evaluation of the post-war Caucasus. Russia had emerged as the dominant power in the region, and the U.S. could do little to reverse this new reality. The Bush administration had been guilty of imperial overreach by trying to enter into Georgia.

Hardliners and the inveterate Cold War warriors in Washington wanted to rebuild Georgia's military by once again sending the latest and most powerful weapons to the defeated country, but such a policy bordered on madness. All the conditions were present to use the existing front lines as the base for a formal treaty to end the crisis, but Washington never found the political will to accept the limits of American power. Rather than annexing most or all of Georgia, Russia adopted a moderate interpretation of the territorial claims of the separatist republics. For example, in Abkhazia the entire Ingori River made the best natural frontier boundary with Georgia, but by the time the Abkhazians asked for this frontier line, Russia did not want to go far beyond the Soviet boundary along the southern half of the river.

No matter how fair Moscow had been in dealing with Georgia, nothing could hide the fact that for the first time the United States was forced to accept a situation not to its liking. Since 1992 the West had imposed on Russia many adverse decisions, and until the Five Day War a weak Kremlin had not been able to mount any serious opposition.

Ukraine: From Antagonism to Cooperation

The situation in Ukraine was more explosive than in Georgia. Ethnic Russians in Ukraine, many already having taken out Russian passports, were unhappy with Kiev, and in Crimea inhabitants were even asking for reunification with Russia.[14]

The fervent desire of many inhabitants to return to Russian rule clashed with the huge cost of taking Ukraine out of its economic mess. In a telling comparison, the per capita income of Poland and Russia had been similar in 1990, but in 2013 the per capita of Poland was three times larger. The Ukrainian economy was locked in a downward spiral while the Russian economy grew and prospered after overcoming the financial crisis of August 1998. Over three million Ukrainians came to Russia in search of jobs, and remittances to relatives back home were a major source of income for the country.¹⁵

Just as with Georgia, events came to a head at the Bucharest Summit of 1–4 April 2008. At that meeting NATO declined to offer a Membership Action Plan (MAP) for Georgia and Ukraine but stated that the two countries eventually shall become members of the military alliance. This attitude alarmed Moscow, and in response the Duma passed a nonbinding resolution on 4 June stating that if Ukraine received a MAP from NATO, then Russia would repeal the treaty recognizing the boundaries and the territorial integrity of the country.¹⁶

Germany detected the potential for conflict behind the Duma resolution, and in a trip to Kiev, Chancellor Angela Merkel decided to backpedal. She told Ukrainian officials they would have to wait many years—she refused to give a specific number—before Ukraine could expect to receive a MAP. She believed that she had halted the downward spiral in relations with Russia, but history is full of surprises, and the war broke out not in Ukraine but in Georgia.¹⁷

The most logical lesson from the Five Day War was that Russia should not be provoked into using its military. The Russian red lines were real for both Georgia and Ukraine, and the West should respect them. But the Bush administration drew the wrong lesson and concluded that the Five Day War "provides new impetus to moving Ukraine into MAP and toward NATO membership" and was the way "to give a strong boost to Ukraine's territorial integrity."¹⁸

The defiant Bush administration still expected the meeting of NATO foreign ministers in December 2008 to grant MAP to both Georgia and Ukraine, but the U.S. allies were hesitant. According to its own charter, NATO could not accept Georgia as a member because of its unresolved territorial disputes, and the military alliance had never granted a waiver on this prerequisite. To bring Ukraine down to earth, Silvio Berlusconi, who had resumed the post of prime minister of Italy, visited Kiev to convey to President Viktor Yushchenko the message that MAP was out of the question for Ukraine. Berlusconi stated that Ukraine should concentrate first on acquiring EU membership before thinking of joining NATO.¹⁹

NATO and EU membership receded into the background when the vital issue of supplying natural gas to Ukraine during the winter captured the West's attention. Russia shipped gas to Ukraine at favorable prices but still higher than the prices the region had enjoyed during the Soviet period. Kiev subsidized the cost to consumers, an expense that bankrupted the treasury. Ukraine was unable to pay for the imports, and once before, in January 2006, Gazprom had suspended deliveries.²⁰

In response to the non-payment of debts, Gazprom again halted shipments on 1 January 2009. When Kiev retaliated by syphoning gas from the pipelines for its own consumption, European countries suffered gas shortages. Although Russia agreed to resume shipments on January 19, the gas crisis gave great urgency to completing alternate pipelines such as North Stream through the Baltic Sea and Blue Stream through the Black Sea. The U.S. and most European countries did not want to deprive Kiev of its major bargaining chip with Moscow and tried to block these pipelines.²¹

In spite of Western diplomatic efforts to try to force Russia to provide free gas to Kiev, the two gas cut-offs of 2006 and 2009 had a major effect on Ukrainian voters. No matter how much those living in western Ukraine wanted to join Western European institutions, only Russia could provide the gas for the cold winters. The impression was that during 2008 and 2009 most Ukrainians, and not just Russian speakers, concluded that President Viktor Yushchenko and his Prime Minister Yulia Tymoshenko had become too hostile toward Moscow.

This subtle shift in attitude was fundamental for the looming presidential campaign in 2009. Although six serious candidates competed on 17 January 2009, the failure of any one to win a majority forced a runoff for 17 February 2009. The candidates were all pro–Russian in varying degrees, with the exception of the incumbent Yushchenko, who "was not only eliminated but abjectly humiliated" by coming in last place.[22] Among the pro–Russia candidates, Victor Yanukovych won the most votes and Yulia Tymoshenko came in second place.

In 2004–2005 direct involvement in the Ukrainian elections had backfired on Russia and led to the Orange Revolution and the hostile Yushchenko presidency. This time, rather than supporting any of the two candidates, "the more striking phenomenon has been Moscow's public even-handedness."[23] The strategy paid off, and two days after the 7 February 2009 runoff almost complete voting results showed Yanukovych, the most pro–Russian candidate, winning with a margin of 3.5 percent or almost 900,000 votes.[24] Ukrainian voters had participated in the most important election in their country's independent history. Tymoshenko lost because the disillusioned supporters of the 2004–2005 Orange Revolution did not turn out in sufficient numbers to vote for her.[25]

Upon taking office, Yanukovych learned that the government was so bankrupt that the International Monetary Fund (IMF) refused to extend bailout funds until the treasury first paid off $2 billion in debts. Russia lent the $2 billion and thus opened the way for Kiev to receive the funds from the IMF. However, Yanukovych knew that by the time winter arrived, the subsidies to keep domestic gas prices low would once again bankrupt the treasury.

The only thing Ukraine possessed to bargain for gas was the Sevastopol naval base. In the Kharkov agreement signed between Yanukovych and Dmitry Medvedev on 21 April 2009, Russia guaranteed to supply gas at a 30 percent discount in exchange for an extension of the lease on Sevastopol until 2042. The Ukrainian and Russian parliaments ratified the agreement.[26]

Moscow wanted to bring Ukraine into the Eurasian Economic Union of the former Soviet republics. The task did not seem too hard, because Ukraine already enjoyed many tariff benefits in the trade with its most important economic partner. Russian orders revived the military industry, whose factories had been in decline since the end of the Soviet Union. Moscow was very interested in the Antonov cargo planes manufactured in Ukraine and ordered 160. The Russian navy also began to put orders for warships in the Ukrainian shipyards, which had built the largest vessels for the former Soviet Union.[27]

Moscow also strengthened military cooperation and for the first time invited Ukrainian officers to observe Russian maneuvers such as Vostok 2010 in the Far East. The Russian Defense Ministry also diverted repair work to Ukrainian facilities. The goal was to intensify military cooperation and to make Ukraine a member of the Collective Security Treaty Organization (CSTO). But because after the Orange Revolution Russian firms and stage agencies had been distancing themselves from Ukraine, reversing course was not easy. The Kremlin felt frustrated that projects of cooperation with Ukraine dragged on and proved hard to execute.[28]

When the Obama administration took office, the concern was that "Ukraine is shaping up as a key challenge in U.S.-Russia relations."[29] But by stepping back behind the red lines of Russia, the Obama administration removed the fundamental barrier blocking the development of good relations with Moscow.[30] Good luck had allowed the U.S. to avoid having to consider proposals on the neutralization of Ukraine or even on its partition. The U.S. did not even have to worry about the plight of Russian speakers inside Ukraine.[31]

Central Asia

The Tulip Revolution of March 2005 in Kyrgyzstan intensified the previous anxieties of the Kremlin about its position in Central Asia. The entry of U.S. forces into the region worried those who felt that the real goal of the West was to encircle Russia with NATO bases.[32] But as long as the Second Chechnya War lasted, Putin concluded that he had no choice but to accept an American presence in Central Asia as the price for U.S. non-interference in the Caucasus.

Uzbekistan

Half of the population of the former Soviet republics in Central Asia lived in this one country, which was under the authoritarian rule of Islam Karimov. Since 2002 the U.S. maintained a base at Karshi Khanabad, not far from the northern border of Afghanistan, and the facility played a useful role in the campaign against the Taliban. Karimov welcomed the lucrative rent payments and supported the U.S. war against Islamic extremism because he regarded them as a threat to his authoritarian rule.[33]

As a precaution, Karimov also arrested many citizens suspected of being Islamic extremists, even though many were just critics of the government. Among those arrested in June 2004 were 23 local merchants from Andijon, in eastern Uzbekistan. They were kept in prison and their trial took place early in May 2005. Outside the courthouse protesters gathered to demand the liberation of the prisoners, and over the coming days the size of the crowd increased. On the night of 12 May armed men broke into the prison to liberate the accused; in the ensuing confusion hundreds of inmates also escaped. The former prisoners and the crowds then went into a rampage of destruction and also broke into many government buildings in Andijon.[34]

President Islam Karimov was determined to prevent another "Color Revolution" from taking place in Uzbekistan. He flew down from the capital of Tashkent to Andijon and gave orders to quell the disturbances. Late in the day on May 13 the authorities restored order but at the cost of at least several hundred killed and many more wounded.[35]

No doubt existed that Islamic fundamentalists played a major role, but whether they masterminded and directed the uprising as the Uzbek government claimed has remained unclear. The refusal of President Karimov to allow an inquiry led the EU and NATO to place sanctions on his regime. The EU put 12 officials involved in the repression on a no-visa list, placed an arms embargo on Uzbekistan, and threatened additional reprisals.[36]

The Pentagon and Secretary of Defense Donald Rumsfeld wanted to preserve the U.S. base and argued against placing any sanctions on Uzbekistan, but the Bush administration began to move to the EU position. Karimov felt betrayed, because he had welcomed the Americans to counterbalance the influence of the Kremlin. He had been one of the first to denounce Putin for wanting to revive the Soviet empire, but the American condemnation of the Andijon repression demonstrated that the U.S. was not willing to support him in a time of need.[37]

The Kremlin, without having to lift a finger, was handed the opportunity to restore Russia's influence in Uzbekistan on a silver platter. All Russia had to do was to reaffirm its traditional policy of non-interference in the internal affairs of any country. China also stated its support for Karimov, who no longer felt that the lucrative rent payments justified the U.S. presence. In July 2005 he gave the U.S. six months' notice to abandon the base at Karshi Khanabad.[38]

The U.S. had lost in Uzbekistan but Russia was not responsible for this American setback. The Kremlin knew all about Karimov's efforts to reduce Russian influence to the minimum and had no illusions about having gained an ally. To bypass the arms embargo and to obtain Russian weapons at lower prices, Uzbekistan joined the Collective Security Treaty Organization in December 2006, but it was clear that this was a marriage of convenience not destined to last. Karimov knew that as long as he did not threaten or betray the Kremlin, he had nothing to fear from Russia.[39] This simple lesson proved impossible to learn for another Central Asian ruler whose luck was about to run out.

Kyrgyzstan

In the last year of the Bush administration, Russia was again feeling threatened and encircled by the West. The proposal to station missile defense batteries in the Czech Republic and Poland, the plans to extend NATO membership to Georgia and Ukraine, the attempt to make the Black Sea into a NATO lake, and the push of the West into the Caspian Sea all aroused deep anxiety in the Kremlin.[40]

The Five Day War with Georgia in August 2008 had still not made felt its consequences, and Russia still feared a NATO push through Georgia and into the Caspian Sea. After the Obama administration took office on 20 January 2009 Russia realized that the U.S. no longer was interested in making Georgia a NATO member and pushing into the Caspian Sea. And when the pro–Russian Viktor Yanukovich was elected president of Ukraine on 14 February 2010, the danger of a Western encirclement receded.

President Putin since 2002 had conditioned Russian acceptance of the U.S. role in Central Asia to the prosecution of the war in Afghanistan against the Taliban; the corollary was that once the Islamic threat disappeared in a distant future, then Russia was willing to pressure for an end to the U.S. presence in Central Asia. However, the outbreak of unexpected disturbances in Kyrgyzstan compelled the Kremlin to assume an active role for the first time.

The Tulip Revolution of 2005, even more than the other "Color Revolutions" in Georgia and Ukraine, failed to live up to the expectations of better conditions and democratic practices. The rebel Kurmanbek Bakiyev emerged as the ruler of the country, yet he turned out to be more corrupt and ruthless than the regime he had helped to overthrown during the Tulip Revolution.[41]

Disillusionment with Bakiyev turned into frustration and anger. Already in June 2005, one year after the Tulip Revolution, citizens began protests. The U.S., after having sponsored the Tulip Revolution, became a major contributor to the corruption through the rent payment for the Manas base. This installation was crucial to the war effort in Afghanistan and its significance increased with the loss of the base at Karshi Khanabad in Uzbekistan in 2005. Russia counterbalanced the U.S. presence by opening several small bases in Kyrgyzstan, which became the only country ever to have hosted military installations of these two world powers.[42]

Angry citizens with no other channel to express their frustrations participated in larger and more violent demonstrations. In March 2010 the capital city of Bishkek experienced the largest riots so far, and with difficulty the government restored order. But after the riots Moscow learned that President Bakiyev had stolen Russian funds earmarked for social and construction projects, and on top he lied about his schemes. An angry Kremlin felt betrayed and exposed to ridicule. For the first time in the history of the Russian Federation, Moscow staged a coup against a foreign government, and soon officials of the Federal Security Service (FSB) and other Russian security agencies were busy with preparations. The protestors with Russian support held a massive demonstration in Bishkek on 7 April 2010, and when authorities restored order, 87 citizens were dead and hundreds more wounded. The massive demonstration had been just the final push to provoke the collapse of the regime; that same day Bakiyev resigned and fled.[43]

A pro–Russian interim administration came into office, and subsequent regimes have made sure to remain on favorable terms with Moscow while never threatening the lucrative U.S. base at Manas. The crisis itself was not over yet, because the sudden collapse of Bakiyev caught his many supporters in the south by surprise. In mid–May crowds took to the street in southern Kyrgyzstan. The disturbances spread and in early June 2010 turned violent.[44]

An outburst of ethnic violence ensued in the south. In the cities of Osh and in Jalalabad crowds went on a rampage of looting, burning, and raping against the wealthy Uzbek minority. Half a million Uzbeks left in panic to escape the fury of the mobs.[45] The horrific images of death and desolation filled television screens across the world, and in response Secretary of State Hillary Clinton asked Russia to deploy troops to restore order in Kyrgyzstan.[46] The Kyrgyzstanis were making both official and private appeals for Russia to annex the country. Most of the Central Asian republics had been an expensive burden on the Soviet Union, and Moscow was not interested in annexation.[47]

Secretary Clinton offered a UN resolution authorizing the entry of Russian troops into the country to stop the ethnic cleansing in the south, but Moscow declined to intervene. Meanwhile, Russian agents reported that the ethnic violence had been a one-time explosion of decades-long repressed anger. Russia concentrated on equipping and transporting Kyrgyzstani forces into the south, and as they completed their deployment, the violence subsided and order returned to the region.[48]

22

Growing Divergences with the West

Moscow is willing and able to offer advice from the sidelines and is always ready to encourage dialogue, but it lacks both the capacity and the leverage needed to independently broker a resolution to the most pressing conflicts.—U.S. Embassy Moscow[1]

The effort to create a free trade zone in the near abroad was another initiative Russia took without the approval of the West. The U.S. and the EU found the proposal so unrealistic that they did not even bother to try to block it. By the time the free trade zone for the near abroad became a concrete reality after 2008, it was too late for the West to strike back.

The West opposed the strong ties between Russia and Syria. For Moscow, Syria was the first real foreign policy foray outside the former Soviet Union since the fiasco in Kosovo. The rivalry over Syria also marked the end of the "reset" in foreign relations with the United States. The growing independence of Russia prompted the West to seek a solution in "regime change."

Eurasia: From Community to Economic Union

The West has labeled the different attempts to create a single economic space among the former Soviet republics as nothing more than a power play to resurrect the Soviet Union. The need for a single economic space was real, but it was the president of Kazakhstan, Nursultan Narabayev, who first proposed the idea in a lecture he gave at Moscow State University in March 1994. He realized that the landlocked Central Asian countries could never prosper without easy access to the routes, resources, and markets of the Russian Federation.[2]

Under the prodding of President Narabayev, Kazakhstan, Belarus, and Russia signed a Customs Union Treaty in 1995, but it was just another meaningless piece of paper. This first attempt failed because Boris Yeltsin had still not abandoned the illusion of creating the Commonwealth of Independent States (CIS) among all the former Soviet republics.[3]

The CIS has survived until today as a periodic meeting of the heads of state of most of the former Soviet republics, but without any real functions. The official agenda has been dull, although heads of state do conduct useful private conversations outside the formal meetings. With the coming to office of Vladimir Putin in 2000, Russia sidelined the CIS. A decisive step came with the signing of a treaty on 10 October 2000 for the establishment of the Eurasian Economic Community. The founding members, besides the trio of Belarus, Kazakhstan, and Russia, were Kyrgyzstan and Tajikistan.[4]

The Eurasian Economic Community

became the nursery for projects to integrate the member states, and a big success came in 2003 when Ukraine decided to enter a "single economic space" in 2003. The enthusiasm was short-lived, because as a result of the Orange Revolution in 2004 Ukraine withdrew from the agreement. Russia for its part had been hesitant, because of the high upkeep cost of the organization. For Western observers the preponderance of Russian citizens in key positions was proof of a desire to extend influence. Moscow was more worried about having to pay such a large part of the bill in return for very little.[5]

World Trade Organization

In October 2007 the original trio of Belarus, Kazakhstan, and Russia agreed on a two-year process to create a Customs Union, which Western observers expected to fail. The fear existed that the entry into force of the Customs Union was in conflict with the membership applications of the three countries for the World Trade Organization (WTO). Any hesitation disappeared when the Great Recession of late 2008 struck. As countries across the world scrambled to find solutions to overcome the economic crisis, the presidents of the three member states signed an agreement on 19 December 2009, creating for the first time a real Customs Union.[6]

The Customs Union came into existence on 1 December 2010, and in accordance with the treaty, customs officials disappeared from the border with Belarus on 1 July 2010 and from the border with Kazakhstan on 1 July 2011. The tariff-free movement of goods among the three countries has continued until today.[7]

Russian accession into WTO proved difficult, because Georgia insisted on having its customs guards staff the entry points in the separatist republics of South Ossetia and Abkhazia. A deadlock on WTO membership seemed inevitable, when Switzerland negotiated a compromise. Russia accepted having a private Swiss firm enforce customs regulations at the three border crossings. U.S. corporations saw many profit opportunities in the Russian market and wanted WTO accession. The Obama administration, in what can be considered the last episode of the reset, pressured Georgia to drop its objections.[8]

On 9 November 2011 Georgia and Russia signed the agreement handing over control of border customs to the Swiss firm. After the proper ratifications, Russia joined the WTO on 22 August 2012, thereby completing 18 years of negotiations, the longest admission process of any country until then.[9]

Eurasian Economic Union

With the WTO hurdle out of the way, the path was open to integrate the member states of the Eurasian Economic Community. The process culminated on 1 January 2012 with a new set of accords creating a "single economic space." The goal was to introduce the "Four Freedoms" for the three economies, so that goods, capital, services, and people could move without any restrictions. The Eurasian Economic Community was following the previous path of Western European integration and had outgrown the term "Community" as being too narrow.[10]

An agreement on 10 October 2014 abolished the Eurasian Economic Community and established a new Eurasian Economic Union in its place. The agreement entered into force on 1 January 2015 among the three founding members of Belarus, Kazakhstan, and Russia. Armenia had participated in the negotiations, and it too became a member on 2 January 2015, followed by Kyrgyzstan on 8 May 2015.[11]

The Eurasian Economic Union has been a success. A major accomplishment has been facilitating the free flow of labor from the former Soviet republics into Russia. The economy of Belarus has benefited the most, followed by that of Kazakhstan. The advantages for Russia were real, but because of its vast economy, less in percentage terms than for the other countries.[12]

The existence of the Eurasian Economic Union helped Russia withstand the sanctions the West imposed after the crisis in Ukraine of 2014. The Union helped Russia advance on the path of import substitution rather than the exclusive reliance on oil and gas revenues to pay for imports. The protectionist fears that the Eurasian Economic Union might lead Russia to turn inward were unfounded, and in a first breakthrough, the organization signed a free trade agreement with Vietnam on 30 May 2015. The accord went beyond tariffs and also included provisions granting Russian firms the same right to operate in Vietnam as local firms.[13]

The Eurasian Economic Union gained additional international recognition when it signed a free trade agreement with China on 17 May 2018. Because China and the EU are the two largest trading partners of Russia, the Free Trade agreement was a major diplomatic triumph for the Eurasian Economic Union.[14]

The Arab Spring: Libya and Syria

The Arab Spring found Syria relying on Russia for support but Bashar al-Assad still was trying to repair relations with the West. He did not realize that the West found him obnoxious and was eager to see him go. In December 2010 the mass uprising in Tunisia marked the start of the Arab Spring. A wave of protests, riots, and revolts swept the Middle East. The rulers who weathered the storm best were the hereditary monarchies but secular republics struggled to survive the passions the outpouring of pent-up hatred. The president of Tunisia fled on 14 January 2011, and the high point of the Arab Spring came with the resignation of Egyptian President Hosni Mubarak on 11 February 2011.

Libya and Muammar Gaddafi

After the collapse of the governments in Tunisia and Egypt, Libya rose in revolt. The anger of the rebels was directed against Muammar Qaddafi, who had ruled the country since 1969. The rebels gained control of eastern Libya and its key city of Benghazi, but relentless bombing by Qaddafi's air force prevented them from reaching the capital, Tripoli, in the western part of the country. The U.S. and European countries had never accepted Qaddafi, who also made some enemies in the Arab world because of his sometimes eccentric behavior. His relations with Russia were better, but his maverick streak kept him from forging close links. Russia was sympathetic to him but was not committed to his survival.

The media was replete with calls for intervention on the side of the rebels. The Obama administration had assimilated the lessons from the Bush fiasco in Iraq and was reluctant to intervene in still another Middle Eastern country. The Obama administration shifted the responsibility to the UN Security Council. A different attitude came from Vice President Joe Biden, who represented the hawkish wing of the administration and the foreign affairs bureaucracy. The only possible holdout was Russia, and Biden traveled to Moscow to encourage President Dmitry Medvedev to support a Security Council resolution authorizing the use of force against Gaddafi. The resolution called for the establishment of a "no-fly zone," but the vague and flexible wording could justify any military action in Libya.[15]

The Russian Foreign Ministry opposed the resolution. Prime Minister Vladimir Putin had serious objections and afterwards condemned the Security Council resolution in very harsh terms. Medvedev did not share these concerns, and he felt that the improved cooperation with the U.S. during the first three years of his presidency called for making a gesture of good will. The European countries, in particular France and Italy, were also pressuring Medvedev, who instructed the Russian delegation to the Security Council to abstain from this vote.[16]

On 17 March 2011 the Security Council adopted the resolution on Libya, and just two days later NATO launched a ferocious air campaign to cripple Gaddafi. Once again the West manipulated humanitarian concerns about avoiding a dreadful slaughter to justify regime change. Without air power, Gaddafi's forces could not stop the rebel advance, and soon the regime was disintegrating. On 20 October 2011 rebels captured and beat Gaddafi, and his gruesome death (eerily reminiscent of Saddam Hussein's savage execution) was just one step in the turmoil. Many of the pro–Western rebels turned out to be Islamic extremists, and the struggle with these fanatics added another layer of complexity to the civil war.[17]

Rather than the striking foreign policy success Vice President Biden wanted, the Western intervention in Libya resembled more an "Iraq II" and became an embarrassing fiasco for the Obama administration. The hardliners had made a mess of Libya but they failed to learn the lesson about the dangers of intervention in the volatile Middle East. And going beyond the mandate of the UN resolution again angered Russia. The Kremlin felt deceived because the U.S. had pulled another "bait and switch" just as happened after the UN 1929 resolution on Iran.[18]

Syria and Bashar al-Assad

Events in Libya left the Kremlin feeling betrayed by the West. When the next test came in Syria, Moscow was determined to prevent an "Iraq III." Russia had important economic and business interests in Syria, and the country hosted the only Russian military bases outside of the territory of the former Soviet Union. The Kremlin also considered Bashar al-Assad to be a bulwark against the instability and the Islamic extremism sweeping the Middle East. Unlike Gaddafi, Bashar al-Assad did not hesitate to become a close and loyal ally of Russia.

At first Syria seemed to have escaped the worst of the Arab Spring. But demonstrations began in earnest on 18 March 2011 and continued almost every day throughout most of the cities in Syria. The southernmost city of Daraa was the hotbed of the opposition, and when the authorities used force to disperse the crowds, the protests turned into an armed insurrection. For a while the West believed in the imminent fall of the regime.[19]

Just as in Libya, the Syrian warplanes halted the advance of the rebels and gained time for the regime to consolidate its forces. Because the army and police were not adequate to garrison all posts across the country, the government concentrated its troops and abandoned other regions, such as the Kurdish region in the northern strip of the country bordering on Turkey. The strategic withdrawal of troops saved al-Assad but exposed the country to a long and arduous campaign in the future when the regime attempted to reassert its authority.

During the summer of 2011 many indicators suggested that the regime al-Assad was on the verge of collapse, even with its use of warplanes to try to hold back the rebels. By early August "the Russian leadership has accepted that the regime of Syrian President Bashar al Assad is unsalvageable."[20] Even more striking "the Iranians are drawing similar conclusions about the ability of the Syrian regime to survive." The rebels were so sure of victory that they promised Moscow not to remove Russian bases from Syria; for its part "Washington secretly offered to guarantee the survival of its base there."[21]

Given the track record of U.S. assurances, in particular the 1991 promise not to extend NATO east from Germany, Moscow could not trust the guarantee. Nevertheless, during the summer of 2011 the real possibility existed that both Russia and the West could stay out of the Syrian civil war. Letting the struggle play out and allowing the stronger contestant to emerge the winner seemed the safest course to follow. But by the fall of 2011 the al-Assad regime revealed an unexpected resilience and showed no signs of imminent collapse. The West had been willing to stay out of the war as long as the rebels seemed to be winning, but once their offensive stalled, the calls for Western intervention on their behalf intensified.

Convinced that the third time would be the charm, the West decided to intervene militarily by repeating the formula of the no-fly zone. The usual horrific scenes appeared in Western media to justify the intervention against a barbaric and savage regime. The shocking television images persuaded world public opinion to condemn the Syrian regime, and in this supercharged atmosphere European powers presented a resolution to Security Council calling on al-Assad to step aside. The U.S. assigned to Moscow the role of persuading the Syrian ruler to go into exile as the only way to escape crushing sanctions on Syria. Russia refused to be the errand boy and joined China to veto the resolution on 4 October 2011. The battle lines were in place for ten years of rivalry between the West and Russia over Syria.[22]

The West imposed additional sanctions on Syria and also provided support for the rebels. And Russia increased its assistance to al-Assad to allow the regime to survive. The foreign support each side received made possible a long and bloody civil war. The rebels suffered from two major weaknesses. First, they were fragmented into warring groups, and should they defeat al-Assad, Syria was sure to turn into another chaotic Libya. A second disadvantage of the rebels was the mounting spread of Islamic fundamentalism. These extremists had been present since the start of the uprising in April 2011, but by 2013 they had become the majority of the rebels and displaced the more pro–Western groups.[23]

Russia had changed its position from supporting the West over Libya early in 2011 to defying the West in Syria later in that same year. The reset in relations between Russia and the U.S. drowned in the sands of Syria during 2011, although its last gasp came only in 2012.

The West's Last Try: The White Revolution

After the first Russian veto over Syria on 4 October 2011, Western governments turned to NGOs to unleash another Color Revolution. Russians were content to enjoy the order and prosperity the country had been experiencing since 2000, but many idealists dreamed of an ideal political system.[24]

For the West it was a good moment to strike a blow, because Russia was vulnerable during the transition from the four-year presidency of Dmitry Medvedev to the six-year term of his successor. Many assumed that he would run for reelection, while others speculated on who would be his successor. The suspense came to an end on 24 September 2011 when Vladimir Putin spoke before the convention of the political party named United Russia and on television stated that he would be its candidate for the next presidential election. The announcement did not come as a complete surprise as insiders had predicted this possibility. Putin also explained that he and Medvedev had agreed to swap positions years before. He promised to appoint Medvedev to the post of prime minister once Putin resumed the position of president of Russia.[25]

Western observers were outraged over this revelation but Russians not so much, and opinion polls showed strong support for Putin. For Western critics the event smelled of a return to the Politburo, and they saw the unanimous approval by the convention as a revival of the Communist Party congresses of the Soviet Union. And the fact that the legislature had extended the presidential term to six years meant that Putin could stay in office until 2024. Despite all these criticisms, everything indicated that without Western interference the political transition in 2012 would have been peaceful. The United States knew that the Russian NGO law of 2005 had not crippled those organizations still able to inflict serious harm on the Kremlin.[26]

When Washington tried to activate the NGOs in 2008 to protest Russia's involvement in the Five Day War with Georgia, the U.S. learned that Color Revolutions were ineffective against nationalistic feelings. But this limitation was not present in late 2011 and early 2012. Thus NGOs were free to whip up the opposition against the regime, although in many ways their task was impossible, because "no other regime was as well prepared as Russia to respond to a Color Revolution."[27] The police and security services had studied the Color Revolutions and adopted techniques to prevent the rallies from turning into an uprising. The television channels either belonged to the state or to supporters of the regime, and most of the print media was pro-government. The one gap in the defensive system was social media, and opposition groups used the internet to mobilize followers.

Just like in most of the Color Revolutions, a disputed parliamentary election triggered the wave of protests in Russia. Party operatives did not realize they were repeating the same mistake, and in a misguided attempt, they stole many votes in the election of 4 December 2011 to give United Russia about 49 percent of the votes for the parliament. Both the government and the opposition agreed that voter fraud had occurred, but they differed on the extent, and the electoral commission accepted only 10 percent of the complaints as valid. The fraud worried Putin, who ordered the installation of web cameras in all the polling places in Russia, so that everyone could observe the voting taking place in the presidential election of 4 March 2012.[28]

The response did not satisfy opposition groups, because they demanded a rerun of the elections just like happened in the Color Revolutions. On 5 December opponents used social media to ask disgruntled citizens to gather for a rally in Moscow, and over 5,000 showed up to protest. Well-trained police dispersed this unauthorized meeting and arrested over 300 protestors. The next day another 2,000 demonstrators appeared, only to be dispersed again by the police. The opposition groups changed tactics and filed for permission to hold a public meeting on Saturday 10 December at Bolotnaya square in Moscow, and the authorities granted the permit.[29]

Organizers claimed to be able to summon 60,000 protestors, but in a first disappointment, only 25,000 showed up at Bolotnaya square on 10 December 2011. The demonstrators demanded new parliamentary elections and also the resignation of Putin. The police presence was enormous, and the number of uniformed personnel equaled that of the protestors who had adopted white as the symbol for their color revolution. By late afternoon the protest was dying down, and when the authorized time expired at 6:00 p.m., the police cleared the square and made sure that no one attempted to set up camps. In this and later rallies, the police seized any tents, one of the most powerful weapons of the Color Revolutions. The protestors obtained authorization for a second rally on 24 December in Sakharov Avenue, and this time almost 80,000 participated and then left.[30]

The Kremlin knew that the U.S. was behind the protests and resented the comments of Secretary of State Hillary Clinton expressing support for the White Revolution. The U.S. presented a resolution to the UN Security Council in support of the demonstrations in Russia. The double veto of China and Russia stopped the resolution on 4 February 2012 and deprived the White Revolution of international recognition.[31]

The West had timed the vote on the UN Security Council resolution to coincide with the high point of the protests. On 4 February 2012 as many as 100,000 protestors braved the freezing temperatures of -20 °C to return to Bolotnaya square. The protestors remained peaceful and their leaders promised not to use violence. Just as the event was ending the police once again cleared the square and made sure that no tents or any other habitable facility remained in place. A major reason why the government authorized the rallies was to let the protestors vent their anger in a cathartic effect and also to exhaust them in the cold weather.[32]

The protests of 4 February 2012 did not translate into votes in the presidential election of 4 March 2012. In accordance with the forecasts of independent polling firms, Putin cruised to victory with 64 percent of the vote and avoided the need for a runoff. It was hard to make accusations about voter fraud when anybody could watch the election process unfold at the polling sites through the web cameras. In a counter argument, critics claimed that many citizens still believed that they lived in the Soviet Union and that the web cameras were surveillance tools to make sure that voters cast their ballots for the official candidates. This argument reinforced the myth about the continued existence of the so-called *Homo sovieticus* or mindless individuals who did what the state told them to do. According to this belief the survival of *Homo sovieticus* also accounted for the small size of most rallies and for the lack of endurance of protestors who drifted away.[33]

The fatalism, if not spreading apathy, was already evident in the 6 May 2012 rally to protest Putin's inauguration the next day. Organizers expected one million citizens to mobilize, but at most 20,000 showed up at Bolotnaya Square. The number could have been higher had not police barricades blocked the bridges leading to the square. Unlike in previous rallies, extremists including anarchists predominated and when they tried to become violent, the authorities saw an opportunity to end the protest. Police targeted key individuals for detention and later in the evening carried out hundreds of arrests until the crowd dispersed.[34]

The inauguration of Putin the next day signaled the end of the White Revolution. Organizers tried to convoke one large protest, but because they lacked authorization, police had the perfect excuse to arrest anyone wearing white ribbons. In an additional deterrent the police rounded up demonstrators for service in the army. A few small protests still took place in other parts of the country, but by early June complete calm returned to the country.[35]

Very efficient police tactics had not been the main reason for the defeat of the White Revolution. Although the protestors ranged from the young to the old, they did not share any common ideological views. Communists and far left people alternated in the crowds with free-market fanatics and extreme Russian nationalists who wanted to revive the Soviet Union. At the 4 February 2012 rally—the largest of all— urban middle class youths were a majority and could have provided a cohesion lacking in the opposition. However, the privileged urban middle-class young people still remained a minority within the population of the country. Also, these urban youths were more concerned with sending an anti–Establishment message consisting of "do not take us for granted" rather than fighting hard to overthrow of the government.[36]

In a crucial difference, the demonstrators never possessed the emotion and intensity of those who had participated in the August 1991 coup attempt. After the collapse of the Soviet Union, the passionate nationalist groups who had most fiercely opposed the August 1991 coup no longer formed part of the Russian Federation.[37]

The Kremlin knew that the West had exploited weaknesses inside Russia and took additional precautions. The legislature required NGOs receiving funds from abroad to register as a foreign agent and also placed strict limits on the activities of those organizations. On 18 September 2012 the Kremlin closed the offices of USAID, an official American agency, which the government blamed for contributing to the unrest. The legislature gave officials the authority to impose huge fines on organizers of unauthorized rallies and gatherings and also authorized the government to close social media whenever those networks threatened peace and order.[38]

The Magnitsky and the Dima Yakovlev Acts

In spite of the failure of the White Revolution, the Obama administration felt its investments in NGOs had been worthwhile. The protests kept Russia on the defensive for almost four months and generated tremendous negative publicity against the Kremlin. The U.S. Congress did not want to let up the pressure. The opportunity to strike another blow at Russia came with the repeal of the Jackson-Vanik Law, a Cold War relic. This 1974 law prevented granting Permanent Normal Trade Partner (PNTP) status to the Soviet Union until the Kremlin granted Jews the right to emigrate. After the fall of the Soviet Union the law became pointless, because anyone could leave the successor Russian Federation, and in addition Moscow later negotiated visa-free travel with Israel.[39]

Both Washington and Moscow neglected the Jackson-Vanik Law until Russia entered the WTO in August 2012. Moscow was in no rush to seek a repeal, because the failure to grant the status of Permanent Normal Trade Partner hurt U.S. business once Russia became a member of WTO. U.S. business groups lobbied hard to obtain the repeal, but legislators demanded the quid pro quo of imposing visa bans and asset confiscation on Russian officials accused of involvement in the mysterious death in prison of Russian whistleblower Sergey Magnitsky. Congress offered Obama the simultaneous deal of repeal of Jackson-Vanik and passage of the Magnitsky bill.[40]

Obama despaired of any better alternative and, not imagining any serious repercussions, he signed the Magnitsky Act into law on 14 December 2012. This hostile measure galvanized the Russian legislature into action over an unexpected topic. For years the large number of adoptions by U.S. families of Russian orphans had raised concerns among nationalists in the country. In a most egregious example, an American family with a commercial mentality of "full satisfaction or a full refund" returned an adopted child to Russia. The most shocking case was Dima Yakovlev, who died because of ill-treatment at the hands of his American family. Because over 60,000 abandoned children had found loving American households, the Kremlin for years had blocked proposals to limit the adoptions, but the nationalist outrage in Russia over the Magnitsky Act was unstoppable. On 21 December 2012 the Russian legislature passed the Dima Yakovlev Act, banning all adoptions of Russian children by U.S. citizens.[41]

Angry American parents directed their rage at the U.S. Congress, and the Obama administration could only remind the public of the harmful consequences that happened whenever the American legislature tried to micromanage the complex relations with Russia. At the same time, the role of the Magnitsky Act in ending the Obama reset with Russia should not be exaggerated. The sharp disagreement over the Syrian civil war was the real cause of the end of the Obama reset. The Magnitsky Act and the Dima Yakovlev Act were significant because they poisoned the atmosphere, but bad relations did not necessary mean confrontation. All the U.S. had to do was to reduce its involvement in Ukraine, but self-restraint proved impossible for a West insistent on driving Russia back behind its borders.

23

Crisis in Ukraine

The Crimea is Russia. It is a simple fact of life.—Deputy Foreign Minister Alexander Grushko[1]

Russia's disillusionment with the West, not only with the U.S. but also with the EU, was total.—Richard Sawka[2]

The new Obama administration concentrated on the reset with Russia and left relations with Ukraine to the European Union (EU). The new president of Ukraine, Viktor Yanukovych, tilted toward Russia but not too much. He was playing the latest round in the traditional Ukrainian game of milking both the West and Russia; even if a president favored one side, he still offered some compensation to the other side.

With an eye to his reelection in 2015, Yanukovych prepared to compensate the West for the pro–Russian measures he had taken early in his term. He saw the opportunity when in 2011 the EU offered to negotiate an Association Agreement.[3]

The Unraveling of Ukraine

The Association Agreement with the EU

Specialized committees worked in near secrecy to resolve a myriad of details affecting the economies of Ukraine and the EU. But when after three years of consultations the text became public, it became clear that the Association Agreement had been a political ploy to keep Russia out.[4]

Against all hope, Moscow proposed trilateral negotiations as a way to create a vast free trade zone. An arrogant EU rejected the Russian suggestion and even told Moscow to stay out of this matter, because the EU—in a copy of NATO attitude—was not going to let any third country dictate its bilateral policies.[5]

The EU negotiated an Association Agreement that imposed all the obligations of membership but without the benefits. Ukraine had to renounce the many advantages of its economic ties with Russia in exchange for the possibility of benefits in the future. The text of over 900 pages contained only a small part of the obligations the EU imposed on Ukraine. The country also became responsible for fulfilling the hundreds of thousands of pages of regulations Brussels had promulgated for its member states over many decades.[6]

Enthusiasm and idealism were rampant not just in Ukraine but across Europe. These were the years when the EU was at the height of its influence and generated much excitement. And to improve the chances of success, both EU and the U.S. had devoted considerable sums to financing NGOs able to mobilize people in Ukraine.[7]

Western Ukraine pressured hard

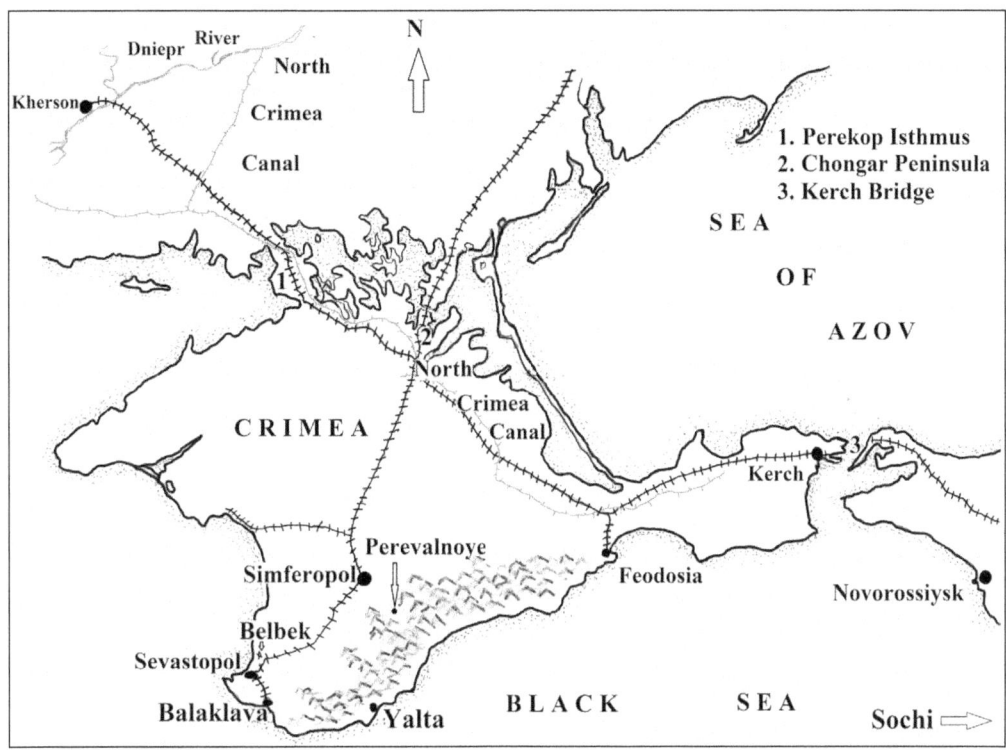

for Yanukovych to conclude the Association Agreement, but Eastern Ukraine and Crimea were opposed. The Ukrainian oligarchs, sensing the immediate loss of profits, were pressuring the president to postpone signing the agreement. Then the EU issued an ultimatum declaring that the Vilnius summit of 29 November 2013 was the deadline for accepting the Association Agreement.[8]

An anxious Yanukovych traveled to Moscow on 9 November 2013 to seek a compromise. President Vladimir Putin explained that if Yanukovych proceeded with the Association Agreement, Russia could no longer provide assistance to Ukraine. Instead, if Ukraine walked away from the EU, then Russia was willing to extend additional loans and assistance. On one level, the generous offer from Putin confirmed that Ukraine was capable of extracting the maximum benefits from the West and from Russia.[9]

Yanukovych then turned to the EU to see if it could top the Russian offer. On 21 November 2013 he declared that Ukraine was delaying action on the Association Agreement until experts could measure its effect on the country's economy. But the EU did not make a counteroffer and reiterated the ultimatum. Yanukovych went in person to the Vilnius summit and humiliated himself by begging German Chancellor Angela Merkel for at least an extension.[10]

With arrogance Merkel and the Europeans ignored the pleas for an extension and were determined to teach a lesson to anyone who dared to defy the institution. Up to this moment the EU had been respectful of Yanukovych and had not criticized his questionable methods of ruling Ukraine because he was the instrument who could deliver the country to the EU. But once he failed to complete his assigned mission, the demonization of the Ukrainian president began, and soon Western media propagated the image of an Oriental despot wallowing in luxury while his people suffered.[11]

The Maidan Protests

Viktor Yanukovych was determined not to use force to crush protests, and this attitude made his regime vulnerable. The announcement on 21 November 2013 that Ukraine postponed signing the Association Agreement with the EU persuaded a journalist to appeal on social media for protestors to gather in Maidan square. In the first days the crowds were sparse, but as the NGOs mobilized their networks through social media, the numbers increased to 300,000 by 24 November. The crowds diminished over the next few days, and the worst seemed to have passed.[12] Protestors had set up tents in Maidan, but when on the night of 29–30 November the police tried to dismantle the camp, the attempt failed. The next day, on 1 December, nearly a million people arrived to support those camping in the square. Demonstrators even seized several government buildings, including city hall.[13]

A standoff ensued for the rest of the month and into early 2014. Yanukovych limited the police to using anti-riot arms such as shotguns and stun grenades but no rifles. The protests turned into a non-stop rally while speakers harangued the crowd in front of live television cameras. High-ranking American officials and U.S. senators supported the demonstrators and distributed food and other supplies in front of cameras. A parade of Europeans likewise came to show their public support for the Maidan protests.[14]

While Yanukovych tried to cling to power, the U.S. was selecting the members of the next provisional government. The U.S. attitude was that the EU had made a mess of things and that it was up to Washington to deliver Ukraine to the West. The U.S. mobilized support at all levels including cooperation from the UN Secretary General.[15] In vulgar language, a female American diplomat stated "that would be great, I think, to help glue this thing and to have UN help glue it and, you know, fuck the EU."[16]

On the ground the situation became more critical, and starting on 22 January 2014 demonstrators seized administrative buildings in western Ukraine. Buses brought people from the western part of the country to Kiev, and demonstrators tried to seize the buildings of the parliament and the presidency in late January 2014. The overwhelming majority of protestors wanted to avoid violence and engaged in talks with the authorities. On 14 February the government released all the demonstrators who had been arrested and received in return control of city hall.[17]

The ongoing talks promised a peaceful solution, an outcome unacceptable to a small group of right-wing extremists who infiltrated the movement. Security forces learned that these radical protestors had acquired weapons. When on 18 February 2014 the Berkut riot police and other units tried to raid the buildings storing these weapons, the defenders escaped by setting one of the buildings on fire and using rifles against the police. In the clashes of 18 February, of the 28 people killed, ten were policemen from the Berkut force. The protestors killed were hit from a distance of only a few meters by hunting ammunition, which the police did not use.[18]

The Ukrainian secret police prepared to storm buildings containing weapons on 19 February, but Yanukovych cancelled the order. On 20 February Berkut riot police received the order to capture Hotel Ukraina, from which snipers were firing. When Berkut police approached, they suffered casualties from rifle fire and could not respond because their anti-riot weapons lacked the range. So far in the 20 February clash only police officers had died, and the armed protestors hiding in buildings including Hotel Ukraina realized that the reputation of the movement was at risk. In a cold and ruthless calculation, they opened fire on the innocent and unarmed demonstrators in

Maidan, so that the Yanukovych regime could be blamed for having slaughtered innocent civilians.[19]

The maneuver worked, and Western officials denounced Yanukovych for his barbaric behavior and for using force to remain in power. The Ukrainian president realized his days in office were numbered, and to secure an honorable exit, he had accepted the mediation of the foreign ministers of Germany, France, and Poland, as well as a Russian representative. Once it became clear that the goal of the talks was to drive Yanukovych from office, the Russian diplomat rejected the mediation.[20]

The 21 February 2014 agreement stripped Yanukovych of his authority and moved the date of the presidential elections forward. The crucial clause was the requirement for the government to withdraw its police from Maidan Square. This single decision left the policemen defenseless, because they lacked similar weapons and they were under orders not to use any force against the demonstrators. The police units melted away and its ethnic Russian members fled to safety in Crimea and in Eastern Ukraine.[21]

Yanukovych had seen the end coming, and even before the clashes of 18 February he was preparing to leave. On the night of 21 February after the agreement had been signed, he left for Kharkov and then with Russian help went to Crimea where he stayed about a week. Crimea was still under Ukrainian control and fearing for his life he asked the Kremlin to take him to safety inside Russia, where he has remained. His sudden departure plunged Ukraine into confusion, but the U.S. was ready with a provisional government willing to support the West.[22]

The Reunification with Crimea

The inhabitants of Crimea watched with dismay the events unfolding during the Maidan crisis. Because many relatives worked for the security forces in Kiev, in particular for the Berkut anti-riot police, the interest was personal. Anti-Maidan protests had been taking place in Crimea since early January 2014, but nobody could have imagined that the Viktor Yanukovych presidency was going to disintegrate so fast. The inhabitants of Crimea faced the choice of either obeying or defying Kiev.[23]

In the most gruesome action, on 19 February right-wing Ukrainian nationalists stopped Crimea-bound buses carrying passengers who had participated in anti-Maidan demonstrations in Kiev. In what has become known as the Korsun pogrom, the Ukrainians beat the passengers, subjected them to humiliations, spread gasoline, and threatened to set them on fire. The nationalists did torch four of the eight buses; at least seven passengers died and more than twenty remain missing.[24]

In late December 2013 inhabitants of Crimea created the first militias. Their organization accelerated when Kiev ordered demolition of the statue of Lenin in the central square of Simferopol. The militias practiced daily drills and took turns guarding the statue around the clock. On 24 February 2014 the militias occupied the Sevastopol and Simferopol airports to prevent Ukrainian extremists from flying in. Likewise, the militias set up road blocks at the Perekop Isthmus and the Chongar Peninsula.[25]

On 23 February the Ukrainian parliament, in one of its first acts after the flight of Yanukovych, passed a bill outlawing the Russian language. Although the bill never became law, this new threat intensified fears in Crimea. Right-wing Ukrainians prepared, on 24 February, to send trainloads of Maidan supporters to gain control of Crimea.[26]

The struggle divided the peninsula into pro-Kiev and pro-Russian sides. Sevastopol took the lead and its city council elected Alexey Chalyi to be the new mayor on 25 February; this was an open act of defiance because only Kiev had the authority to appoint the mayor. In response the provisional government ordered the local police to arrest Chalyi, but its commander defied Kiev and refused to comply.[27]

And it was not just the local police who challenged the provisional government. Berkut was the last remaining security force in Crimea, but when the provisional government abolished this agency on 25 February, this action caused outrage. The inhabitants had just finished giving a hero's welcome to the units returning from Kiev and could not accept making this special police force the scapegoat for the Maidan deaths. Ethnic Russians composed the majority of the personnel, and they feared punishment and contemplated fleeing to Russia to save their lives. But when Kiev officials came to disband Berkut, a crowd prevented them from entering the building, and this show of public support persuaded this police force to revolt against Kiev.[28]

Berkut could spare only 24 officers to join the self-defense militias at the Perekop Isthmus and the Chongar Peninsula. The defenders were still inadequate to hold the positions, and the situation improved with the arrival of 450 Cossack volunteers, who had come with the permission of their ataman or commander. The Cossacks dug trenches but most of them lacked weapons. Because they wore uniforms, the Ukrainians postponed the attack, fearing that they faced the Russian army.[29]

The Ukrainian nationalists could not bring reinforcements by land or air, and instead a steady stream of Russian volunteers was coming to Crimea, not just the Cossacks but also other groups like the motorcycle clubs. To counter the numerical inferiority, the Ukrainian nationalists gambled on a single maneuver. They spread the rumor that Moscow intended to deport the Tatars just as Joseph Stalin had done during World War II. Many Tatars believed the lie, and they joined the pro-Kiev rally in front of the Crimean parliament building. The Ukrainian nationalists also applied all the skill they had gained in clashing with the Berkut police in Maidan to the demonstration in front of the parliament building.[30]

On 26 February Ukrainian nationalists gathered according to plan in front of the Simferopol parliament building to manifest their support for the Kiev-appointed governor of Crimea. They overwhelmed the pro-Russian supporters, and in a surprise sally a group of Tatars broke through one of the doors and entered the parliament building. By then the word had spread in the city that the Ukrainian nationalists were about to capture the parliament building, and pro-Russian supporters arrived in large numbers to drive away the pro-Kiev protestors. Many people were injured and at least several individuals died in the clashes, including an old man trampled by the raging crowds. The few Tatars who had penetrated into the lobby did not know what to do and after a while left, while the pro-Russian supporters established control over the entire area. Later many Tatars realized that they had been duped and joined the self-defense militias.[31]

The Kremlin watched these developments and concluded that the provisional government was certain to use maximum force to crush the local inhabitants. The Kremlin also maintained the hope that Yanukovych could return to power. At a long meeting in the Kremlin on the night of 22–23 February, most of the discussion centered on how to extricate Yanukovych. Putin stated months later that he also concluded the meeting by stating that "we must start working on returning Crimea to Russia,"[32] but the vague language still left open many possibilities.

After the meeting of 22–23 February the Kremlin confirmed its fundamental goal of avoiding a bloodbath in Crimea. But before taking any action, the government conducted a poll to see if the inhabitants of Crimea wished to join Russia. Of those surveyed, 75 percent answered in the affirmative, a figure consistent with the 73-percent approval pro–Russian leader Yuri Meshkov had received in January 1994. But the Ukrainian military worried the Kremlin, and the uniformed personnel of 25,000 more than doubled the 12,000 soldiers Russia stationed in Sevastopol under the lease arrangements. The 1997 agreement prohibited Russia from placing heavy weapons in Crimea, and instead Ukraine possessed 41 tanks, armored personnel carriers, and heavy artillery.[33]

Facing such adverse odds, the Kremlin's first steps were cautious and modest. At 4:25 a.m. on February 27 around fifty well-armed men wearing either uniforms without insignia or dressed as civilians surrounded the parliament at Simferopol. The nine policemen guarding the building left, and the "little green men" or "polite people" as they came to be called, proceeded to fortify the building. Pro-Kiev officials called the police the next day to drive out the intruders, and a bloody clash seemed inevitable when hundreds of police surrounded the building. But before any shooting could take place, thousands of pro–Russian supporters surrounded the police and convinced them that the intruders were part of the self-defense militias. Later that day deputies came to the parliament, elected a new pro–Russian governor to replace the Kiev appointee, and then authorized a referendum to decide whether Crimea should reunify with Russia. Only the Ukrainian military units remained outside the control of pro–Russian supporters.[34]

The defeat at the parliament showed the Ukrainian nationalists that they were outnumbered. The majority of Berkut units were pro–Russian, but one detachment remained loyal to Kiev and made a desperate attempt to retake control of Simferopol airport so that Ukrainian reinforcements could fly into Crimea. But the arrival of marines from Sevastopol naval base made the pro–Kiev Berkut detachment vanish, and Simferopol airport remained under the control of pro–Russian supporters.[35]

Pro-Kiev forces suffered major defeats on 27 February both at the Simferopol airport and at the Crimean parliament, but the response of the Ukrainian troops in the peninsula still remained an open question. The decisive test came at 0300 hours on 28 February when in their boldest move so far, Russian Special Forces attempted to seize Belbek military airport, where Ukraine stationed its MIG fighters. Special Forces again dressed as civilians or with unmarked uniforms took control of the main installations and blocked the runway and the tarmac so that the warplanes could not take off. In less than an hour Ukraine lost control of all its combat planes in Crimea.[36]

Gaining control of Belbek airport still left the possibility that warplanes from the Ukrainian mainland could attack Russian forces. Some Ukrainian planes did fly over the peninsula, and at any moment Kiev could reverse its policy and order its units with heavy weapons to attack the Russian light infantry. The threat became real when aerial surveillance revealed that Ukrainian Grad multiple rocket launchers and 80 mm mortars were on their way to Crimea. President Vladimir Putin turned to the upper house of the legislature on 1 March 2014 to seek authorization to deploy troops in Ukraine until conditions normalized. The Russian upper house after a few hours of debate unanimously granted the authority, even though the heavy formations were not available to start crossing via the Kerch ferries until days later.[37]

The Kiev provisional government declared on 1 March, that the new government in Crimea was illegal. On 28 February, in an attempt to drive a wedge between the inhabitants and the leadership, the provisional president vetoed the bill outlawing the use of the Russian language, but this conciliatory measure came too late. On 5 March Kiev increased the pressure by ordering the start of criminal proceedings against the new officials in Simferopol. Meanwhile enthusiasm was manifest in the streets of Simferopol and other cities in the peninsula. The inhabitants could not hide their excitement and were shouting "Russia, Russia" every time they saw the "polite people" pass on foot or on vehicles. Russian flags were everywhere on display.[38]

In response to the threats from Kiev, the Crimean government on 6 March moved forward the date for the referendum on Crimea's political future from 30 to 16 March. The ballots printed in the Russian, Ukrainian, and Tatar languages asked the voters to answer two questions. "Are you in favor of restoring the 1992 Constitution and the status of Crimea as a part of Ukraine?" It should be noted that Kiev had blocked the adoption of 1992 Constitution as too separatist. The other question was "Are you in favor of reunification with Russia as part of the Russian Federation?" On 16 March huge lines formed outside the polls even before they opened. Of the voters 96.7 percent expressed their preference for reunification with Russia.[39]

The Kremlin conducted another poll on 14 March to determine this time whether Russians supported the unification. The toughest questions was whether to unify even in the face of Western opposition, but even here 83 percent of the 40,000 surveyed from Kaliningrad to Kamchatka answered in the affirmative. With Russian public opinion supporting unification, the Kremlin felt confident about taking decisive action to expel the remaining Ukrainian garrisons still in Crimea.[40]

An unprepared Russian Defense Ministry scrambled to find forces to send to Crimea, and the heavy weapons indispensable for any successful defense were far away. On 14 March batteries of 155 mm cannon and multiple rocket launchers arrived by the Kerch ferries, and the deployment of these heavy weapons on the Perekop Isthmus and the Chongar Peninsula at last blocked any Ukrainian invasion.[41]

The final step was the arrival on 15 March of surface to air missiles able to block Ukrainian airplanes from flying over the peninsula. The momentum to return Crimea to Russia was unstoppable, and on 18 March the regional government signed the Accession Treaty with Russia. On 21 March 2014 the Russian parliament approved the treaty, and the reunification of Crimea with Russia was complete.[42]

Up to this moment the self-defense militias and the Russian troops had been patient with the remaining Ukrainian garrisons in the well-founded assumption that most of the uniformed personnel did not want to fight for Kiev. The transition to Russian rule became easier when in a decree on 20 March Putin guaranteed the same rank and privileges to all uniformed personnel who swore loyalty to Moscow. In a small way, Russia in Crimea was compensating for the humiliating loss of the nearly one million Soviet soldiers who in January 1992 shifted their loyalty from Moscow to Kiev.

Because most conscripts were local, about three-quarters of the military personnel pledged allegiance to Moscow; the percentage was higher among the police and security forces almost all natives of Crimea. The last major holdouts were the Belbek air base and the Ukrainian marines at Feodosia. Russian Special Forces had neutralized the warplanes on 28 February without firing a shot, but the Ukrainian garrison remained defiant. Many feared a bloody clash when under the glare of television cameras Russian troops burst into the Ukrainian compound on 22 March. Although some shots were fired in the air, the takeover of the base occurred without bloodshed, and the Ukrainian personnel either switched sides or left for Ukraine. Even more dangerous was the face-off with the marines at Feodosia. Kiev had transferred this unit to Crimea in January, and all its members came from Western Ukraine and none were local recruits. A swift operation on 24 March at 0300 seized the armory at the base. Some shots were fired in the air, and the garrison agreed to leave for Ukraine without any loss of life.[43]

A few small units still refused to accept the inevitable, but by the end of March all traces of Ukrainian authority in Crimea had vanished. The reunification with Russia had been a great victory for the Kremlin, but the peaceful outcome for the inhabitants of Crimea did not mean the end of turmoil in Ukraine.

The Revolt in Eastern Ukraine

In spite of repeated false accusations to the contrary from the West, the reason why the Kremlin intervened in Crimea was to prevent a bloody Ukrainian repression. Russian leaders believed that the reunification with Crimea did not change the long-standing policy of promoting sympathetic governments in Ukraine. The economic dependence of Ukraine on Russia gave the Kremlin considerable leverage.[44]

The unfolding events in Crimea had captured the world's attention but the other Russian-speaking areas of Ukraine evoked little interest. In contrast to the activism in Crimea dating back to the late Soviet period, Eastern Ukraine had remained calm and even passive. Coal miners from the Donbass region had made a small contribution to the fall of the Soviet Union, but afterwards disappeared from view.

Eastern Ukraine voted for pro–Russian candidates in the presidential elections, but nobody read into the electoral preference any desire to start a revolt against Kiev. The inhabitants of Eastern Ukraine were themselves torn between a mix of conflicting loyalties and identities and could not agree on a common position. The region was slow to react to the Maidan demonstrations, and only when Viktor Yanukovych fell from power did worries appear about the future.[45]

The decisive event came when the Ukrainian parliament passed a bill restricting the Russian language. The language bill angered many inhabitants of Eastern Ukraine, and in an additional provocation, Kiev also blocked the broadcasts of Russian TV channels in late February. Outraged inhabitants of Eastern Ukraine took to the streets and staged the first protests in March. In an attempt to terrify the citizens, Ukrainian fighter jets flew at low heights over the demonstrators.[46]

The provisional government realized it had gone too far and vetoed the language bill on 28 February, but by then it was too late to reverse the mounting anger in Eastern Ukraine. Seeing an opportunity to play a mediating role, the Russian Foreign Ministry issued a statement on 17 March 2014 calling on Kiev to grant considerable self-rule or autonomy to the provinces and to give permanent status to the Russian language and culture in the regions. In historical terms, the Foreign Ministry was trying to adapt to Ukraine the multinational policies of the former Soviet Union. The proposal aimed to create a "consociational" agreement making impossible changes in language and nationality policy without the approval of the minorities. Similar arrangements existed in countries like Belgium and Switzerland.[47]

The blueprint of the Russian Foreign Ministry was the best way to prevent the crisis from becoming a bloody confrontation, but Kiev, emboldened by the universal support of Western powers, did not even consider the proposal.

Pro-Russian groups took control of the main government buildings in Donetsk and Kharkov on 6 April 2014 and proclaimed People's Republics the next day. The rebels in Kharkov followed the example of Crimea

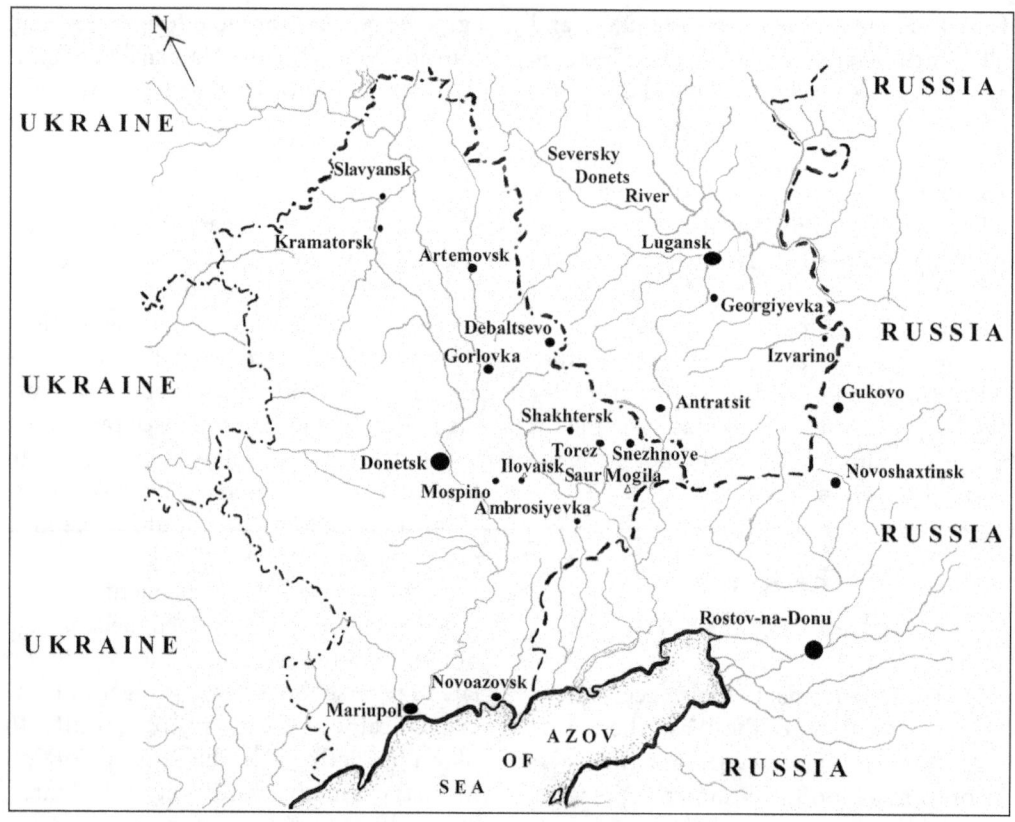

by announcing on 7 April their intention to hold a referendum on whether the city wanted to join Russia. The provisional government rushed security forces and police from Central Ukraine, and on 8 April the reinforcements dislodged the rebels from the government buildings. The rebels had been so successful because of the sympathy they enjoyed among the local police, and in reprisal Kiev purged those units of anyone suspected of pro-Russian feelings.[48]

To replace the purged individuals Kiev brought police and security personnel from Central Ukraine to Kharkov but soon the provisional government exhausted its supply of loyal units. In the rest of the provinces, the Ukrainian authorities were on their own and could count on little support from Kiev. The rebels took over the office of the Ukrainian security service (SBU) in Donetsk on 7 April and on 12 April they seized the police headquarters in that city.[49]

The Rebel Capture of Slavyansk

Another decisive event took place on 12 April 2014. So far Donetsk was the only city under full rebel control, but it was vulnerable to a Ukrainian counterattack as had happened in Kharkov. To prevent the arrival of Ukrainian reinforcements, rebel leader Igor Strelkov (alias Igor Girkin) led 52 men to capture the road junction at Slavyansk on 12 April. Their rifles were old Soviet Kalashnikovs and the unit lacked any heavy weapons or new equipment. Locals provided food, and soon his force swelled to over 200 men. Because a few men wore old Soviet camouflage uniforms, Kiev concluded that these were "little green men" of the type that had participated in the reunification of Crimea.[50]

For the provisional government the rebel seizure of Slavyansk was the start of a war. Kiev was determined to send a strong message to Moscow that no repetition of the scenario in Crimea was possible in Eastern Ukraine. On 13 April the provisional government announced the start of its military campaign against the rebels, and later the elected president Petro Poroshenko ratified the decision.[51]

The Response of Russia

Russia was at a loss as to how to respond to the unfolding events in Eastern Ukraine. The Kremlin was still not yet convinced that the inhabitants of Eastern Ukraine wanted independence from Kiev. The rebels still had not reached a consensus on the future of the region. The fear existed in the Kremlin of falling into the trap of supporting a small faction, as happened during the Soviet occupation of Afghanistan during 1979 to 1989. And although public opinion in Russia supported unification with Crimea no matter what the cost of Western reprisals, many Russian citizens were still undecided about Eastern Ukraine.

The meeting of the Russian Security Council chaired by President Vladimir Putin on 24 April 2014 decided against an intervention in Eastern Ukraine. This momentous decision was disastrous from a military and a humanitarian perspective. The rebel infantry was more than capable of securing the entire region, and all that Russia needed to do was to provide heavy artillery units. Had cannon stood behind the rebel defenders at Slavyansk, Ukraine could not have started its offensive. And the civilian population would have been spared the horrendous suffering of subsequent years.[52]

Ukraine on the Offensive

On 2 May Ukrainian nationalists perpetrated the massacre of nearly 50 pro-Russian sympathizers, including women, in Odessa. The slaughter confirmed the fears in Crimea that the Ukrainians had intended to carry out similar bloodbaths. In Odessa the May massacre foreshadowed the reprisals the Ukrainian nationalists were intent on inflicting on Eastern Ukraine.[53]

Ukraine proceeded with its military campaign in the east, but repeated attacks at Slavyansk failed to drive out the defenders of Strelkov. Kiev scored its first big success when oligarch Rinat Akhmetov turned against the rebels and had his employees assist Ukrainian forces in the recapture of the port city of Mariupol on 13 June.[54]

In an attempt to appease the West, still angry about Crimean reunification, Russia broadcast its intention not to intervene in Eastern Ukraine. On 25 June the Russian parliament repealed the authorization of 1 March 2014 to introduce troops into Ukraine. When Kiev on 1 July began to bomb civilian targets in Eastern Ukraine only then did the Kremlin realize that Kiev was not interested in a peaceful solution.[55]

In response to the bombing of civilians, Russia on 5 July 2014 halted the return of the arsenals captured in Crimea to Ukraine. In a quixotic effort to maintain normal relations with Kiev, Moscow had offered to send the captured weapons and military equipment as a goodwill gesture. Soon the rebels captured many of these returned weapons from Ukrainian forces. And Kiev with Western approval continued the inhuman bombing campaign against civilians.[56]

The Ukrainian aerial bombardment was having two unintended effects. Until July the population of the rebel areas rejected Kiev but had not reached a consensus on the best political alternative. When the bombing reached civilian areas in Donetsk and Lugansk, the West remained indifferent to the large-scale loss of life and the destruction of property. This attitude was in sharp contrast to the indignant condemnations at any hint of using excessive force against the Maidan protestors. The West also had pretended to be very concerned about refugees, but the start of what became the flight of nearly a million refugees to other parts of Ukraine and over a million to Russia failed to evoke humanitarian concerns.[57]

Each bomb and shell landing in the rebel areas of Donetsk and Lugansk brought the inhabitants ever closer to supporting a complete break with Kiev. The indecision of March and April gave way in July to near unanimous consensus on the need for political separation from Ukraine. Once the bombs and shells of Ukraine seared this idea into the minds of the inhabitants, any possibility of a negotiated solution disappeared.[58]

The war became one of national survival for the inhabitants who were motivated to fight to the last. These volunteers dedicated to their cause faced ill-trained Ukrainian conscripts who often considered this colonial war not worth dying for. The courage and determination of the pro–Russian separatists made them formidable on the battlefield. The television images had a dramatic effect on Russian public opinion. Russians had supported the reunification with Crimea but had been ambivalent about Eastern Ukraine, and this lack of concern was a major reason why the Kremlin decided on 24 April not to intervene. But after June public opinion shifted toward the side of the separatists. People could not understand why Kiev was determined to kill people who wanted to speak Russian. A strong wave of sympathy for the separatists swept Russia and private organizations provided assistance and deployed volunteers.[59]

In a paradox, it was the shooting down of the Malaysian Airlines plane on 17 July 2014 that galvanized support in Russia for the rebels. The West condemned Russia for this tragedy, when the exact causes still remain unknown to this day; even the Prime Minister of Malaysia has criticized the rush to condemn Russia rather than carry out a fair investigation.[60] The West had ignored the wanton bombardment of civilians in Eastern Ukraine but all of a sudden gushed with sympathy over the Malaysian Airlines tragedy.

Just as happened in Transnistria, the Caucasus, and in Crimea, volunteers came to help the rebels; recruitment centers appeared in Moscow and other Russian cities to train and ship citizens to fight alongside the rebels. The Kremlin refused to deploy army units, although a small number of personnel with ties to the region received leaves of absences to go fight in Donbass.[61]

The offensive was off to a good start and on 5 July the Ukrainians at last entered Slavyansk and opened the road to Donetsk. Kiev claimed Slavyansk to have been a big victory, when in reality the encircled Strelkov escaped with his fighters, and they joined the defenders in Donetsk. When the Ukrainians reached that city, the resistance was so intense that they decided to bypass the urban area and carry out a massive "pincer" movement from Lugansk to Mariupol with the intention of trapping all the rebels.[62]

Rebel Defiance

The ambitious plans of Kiev proved to be unrealistic, and the summer offensive soon bogged down. Rather than the rebels being trapped in the pincer movement, it was the Ukrainians who were encircled. By late August 2014 the summer offensive ended in catastrophic defeat, and the fleeing Ukrainian troops suffered huge casualties trying to escape. During their panicky retreat the Ukrainians abandoned vast quantities of weapons, equipment, and vehicles. The reversal stunned the West, and ever since the official line has been that only Russian troops could have inflicted such a massive defeat on the Ukrainians. The West refused to believe that the rebel David vanquished the Ukrainian Goliath.[63]

Up to this moment the West rejected

all offers for a negotiated solution and insisted on the destruction or surrender of the rebels. But the rebels had regained the offensive and if not stopped could well reach Kharkov and even further. The West revived the platitude of the Chechen wars that "no military solution" was possible and persuaded Russia to sign a ceasefire in the Minsk I accords on 5 September 2014.[64]

Almost everyone expected the Minsk I agreement to be more of a truce, and the West also hoped that during the lull Ukraine could rebuild its forces. Combat was already frequent in October, and the war resumed on 5 November 2014 when Ukrainian artillery batteries opened fire on Donetsk. The rebels were well prepared to respond because of the piles of weapons and equipment the fleeing Ukrainians had left behind in the panicky retreat of August. Combat raged over the Donetsk airport, and by the end of January 2015 the rebels gained control of the installation.[65]

The rebels were poised to break through the weakened Ukrainian lines and push north to recapture Slavyansk. The West had been very supportive of this second Ukrainian offensive but the possibility of another disastrous defeat made Western diplomats scramble to end the combat once they saw their side losing. Resurrecting their refrain that "no military victory" was possible, Western diplomats obtained another ceasefire in the Minsk II accord of 12 February 2015. The winning rebels were opposed to this premature halt, and as a modest concession to their demands, President Vladimir Putin qualified the ceasefire saying that it would not go into effect in the Debaltsevo area where the rebels had encircled the Ukrainian defenders.[66]

Debaltsevo was the crucial rail and road juncture between Donetsk and Lugansk, and rebel control was indispensable to guarantee the economic survival of the separatist regions. Incessant rebel shelling pounded the town and the demoralized Ukrainian garrison abandoned almost all its equipment and weapons in a hurried night flight on 18 February 2015. After this final rebel victory, large military operations ended in the region, but skirmishing has continued across the front line until today.[67] The separatists had defended their territories, and their success confronted the Kremlin with the need to adopt a policy toward the new entities.

The People's Republics of Donetsk and Lugansk

Ukraine suffered a decisive military defeat but did not abandon the goal of restoring its control over the separatist regions. Kiev rejected Russian offers to broker an arrangement with the separatist regions and insisted on full reintegration before discussing any political modifications. Ukraine pursued a direct and firm policy toward the People's Republics in contrast to the ambivalent Kremlin. The unexpected defeat of Ukraine meant that the problem was not going away, but what action to take remained a matter of deep divergences inside the Kremlin.

The easiest decision was to reject any proposal to introduce Russian troops into the People's Republics. Moscow pressured the rebels to halt their successful offensive and accept the very disadvantageous Minsk I and II accords. The Kremlin believed that the Minsk accords could be the first step toward a comprehensive agreement creating a federalist system in Ukraine with permanent guarantees for the rights of Russian speakers.

Domestic public opinion shaped Russian policy toward the People's Republics. After Ukraine launched the indiscriminate bombing campaign against civilians in July 2014, the suffering of the inhabitants evoked an intense sympathy among Russian citizens. Truck convoys and railway cars wagons delivered much needed foodstuffs and medical supplies, and soon

Russian firms were supplying spare parts and equipment to replace those damaged during the fighting. But when the state enterprises halted delivery of natural gas and petroleum because of non-payment from the bankrupt People's Republics, a desperate delegation went to Moscow to implore help from the only person who could restore the flow of fuel. In a dramatic presentation on live TV, the delegates begged Vladimir Putin not to abandon them. Under immense domestic political pressure, the president agreed to their requests and instructed the state enterprises to make sure that oil and natural gas kept flowing to the People's Republics.[68]

Ukraine tightened its economic and financial blockade of the separatist republics. Kiev planned to bring the rebel regions back under its control through a combination of economic warfare and military harassment. But the inhabitants of the People's Republics were determined to resist no matter how bleak conditions became. The images of their suffering moved Russian public opinion, and the Kremlin searched for ways to help the inhabitants of the People's Republics but short of introducing Russian combat units.

One major step proved easy. The economic warfare of Ukraine deprived the separatist regions of new supplies of paper currency, and the old bills disintegrated through wear and tear. Rubles were already circulating in the rebel zones, but the Kremlin preferred a more discreet solution. After the unification with Russia, Crimea converted all the Ukrainian currency into Russian rubles. The vaults of banks in Crimea bulged with Ukrainian bills, and it was a simple matter to transfer this currency to Donetsk and Lugansk.[69]

After the expulsion of the Ukrainian authorities in April 2014, the People's Republics inherited the routine functions of issuing official documents such as birth and marriage certificates, personal identification papers including passports, and also vehicle registration plates and driver's licenses. In another expression of sympathy, official employees across Russia accepted as valid the legal documents of the People's Republics. For Russian citizens, the inhabitants of those regions were another group of Russians whose rights needed to be respected.

The Kremlin was uncomfortable with this irregular procedure but did not wish to defy the general will of the Russian people. After the most recent round of negotiations ended once again in resounding failure, on 18 February 2017 Vladimir Putin decided to issue a Presidential Executive Order recognizing all official documents of the People's Republic as valid inside the Russian Federation. An anguished howl of protest went up from Kiev and the West, but there was no turning back from recognizing the reality of the existence of the People's Republics.[70]

On 1 March 2017 Russia accepted the request of the People's Republics to make the ruble their official currency. By that date the stocks of Ukrainian paper currency received from Crimea were depleted, and the economy faced paralysis without bills in circulation. Banks in Donetsk and Lugansk began dispensing the rubles, and the People's Republics had entered into a monetary and customs union with Russia.[71]

Russian Citizenship

When the People's Republics commemorated their fifth anniversary of existence the Kremlin decided to simplify the procedures for residents of the People's Republics to acquire Russian citizenship and passports. The decree published on 24 April 2019 waived the exam on Russian language proficiency and also eliminated the five-year residency requirement for inhabitants of Donetsk and Lugansk. In contrast to Ukraine, Russia recognized dual citizenship, so the inhabitants could also keep the passports issued by the People's Republics.[72]

The inhabitants did not have to go to Russia to present the applications for citizenship, and officials had to decide upon the request no later than in three months. The authorities of the People's Republics conveyed the applications to the nearest Russian office in the border. The inhabitants did have to appear in person to take the oath of loyalty and then they received the "internal" passport. Once in possession of the "internal" document the new Russian citizens could then apply for the separate passport for travel abroad.[73]

The first Russian office that opened near the border of Lugansk possessed the capacity to process nearly 50,000 applications each year. Soon a second office appeared to tend to the applicants from Donetsk. By acquiring this citizenship, older persons who moved to Russia qualified to receive the minimum pension payment, even though they had never made contributions to the Russian system.[74]

Ukraine was outraged at the granting of Russian citizenship and declared the new passports to be invalid. Kiev threatened to halt pension payments to those residents who received Russian citizenship. In a petty gesture, Ukraine drew up sanctions lists targeting those Russian officials issuing the passports at the two offices. The reprisals and the threats had no effect, and by 17 July 10,000 inhabitants had already received Russian citizenship, starting with the first new citizens who took the loyalty oath on June 14.[75]

A backlog of applications formed in the two border offices, and the number of applicants grew when Putin signed a new decree on 17 July 2019 extending the process of obtaining Russian citizenship to all the inhabitants of Donetsk and Lugansk and not just to those parts of the provinces under the control of the People's Republics. The fee for a Russian passport equaled the average monthly wage of inhabitants, yet this high price did not deter the applicants. By October 2020, 150,000 residents of Lugansk and 170,000 of Donetsk had obtained Russian citizenship. Demand remained steady, and the total number of passports issued was headed to surpass the half-million mark during 2021.[76]

Ukrainian officials at the United Nations denounced the issuance of Russian passports to the citizens of Donetsk and Lugansk as clear proof of "creeping annexation."[77] The accusation was groundless, because Russia had rejected all the previous opportunities to annex the region. At most the separatist republics were moving closer to the model of Abkhazia but with the major difference that no Russian troops were present in Donetsk and Lugansk. The intransigence of the West and of Ukraine has left the new republics no other option than to move their economies closer to Russia but without a formal unification.

24

Reprisals Over Ukraine

Russia is too big to be isolated.—U.S. Diplomat[1]

The West took many reprisals against Russia in response to its reunification with Crimea. A first set of measures aimed to isolate the country from the international community. The West accompanied these political reprisals with a process to impose harsh economic sanctions on Russia. Some of the sanctions targeted Crimea, and Ukraine went further by trying to blockade the peninsula into submission.

Isolating Russia

Russian troops had not yet finished occupying Crimea when the West launched its reprisals. On 5 March 2014 the West announced the end of military cooperation with Russia and halted the meetings of the NATO-Russia Council. The next day the European Union suspended the ongoing conversations on a new trade treaty to replace the Partnership and Cooperation Agreement with Russia. On 13 March the Organization for Economic Cooperation and Development (OECD) halted negotiations on Russian accession. In early April NATO restricted the access of Russian diplomats to its headquarters. And on 23 July the European Bank for Reconstruction and Development ceased to invest in Russia.[2]

The West took additional steps going beyond the response to the Five Day War with Georgia. On 23 March the Western powers expulsed Russia from the G8, the exclusive club which then became the G7. This action had no practical effect, because the Kremlin long had felt that the periodic gatherings of rulers and cabinet ministers served to pressure Russia rather than engage in meaningful dialogue. Already, Vladimir Putin had declined to attend the G8 in May 2012. On a symbolic level, the West wanted to convey the image that the expulsion of Russia was a public shaming in front of the whole world. Personal dynamics were also at work, and as President Donald Trump afterwards explained, an angry Barack Obama wanted to get even with Putin who had outsmarted the American president.[3]

Because the Russian veto prevented taking any action in the Security Council, the West went to the General Assembly of the United Nations. The resolutions of the General Assembly are non-binding, but the possibility of leaving Russia alone in the world was irresistible to the West, much as had happened to the U.S. when only a couple of countries defended the American trade embargo on the small island of Cuba. The U.S. and its NATO allies launched a vigorous lobbying campaign to bury Russia in negative votes as had happened to the U.S. over the embargo on Cuba. But Russia was not alone, and 11 countries, mainly from Latin America, voted against the resolution, 54 abstained, and others, such as U.S. ally Israel, did not show up for the vote.[4]

The resolution did pass with 100 votes on 27 March 2014, but even then "it is known what shameless pressure up to political blackmail and economic threats was applied on several member states to make them vote for this resolution."[5] The moral outrage the world had shown at U.S. hostile actions in Latin America and Vietnam was missing against Russia.

The high point of the campaign to exclude Russia from international bodies came when the Parliamentary Assembly of the Council of Europe expelled the Duma delegates on 10 April 2014. However, Russia remained a member of the Council of Europe and its other agencies.[6]

Most countries saw the Crimea dispute as an attempt to revive the Cold War. But just as happened during the time of the Soviet Union, countries sometimes found themselves dragged into a struggle that was not theirs. The first opportunity to punish Russia came in the unexpected place of Djibouti on the Horn of Africa. Pirates from neighboring Somalia were raiding shipping on the Indian Ocean, and countries organized naval patrols. Russian warships joined the anti-piracy effort in 2008, but they lacked access to any facilities on land. But when Moscow conducted negotiations with Djibouti to establish warehouses and other installations to service Russian warships in the Indian Ocean, the Obama administration saw an opportunity to strike back. National Security Advisor Susan Rice went to Djibouti to block the Russian deal.[7]

As a person of African ancestry, she seemed suited to deliver the message, but in reality the green of U.S. money was the most important color. She offered to increase the annual rent on an existing American facility to $63 million. Russia refused to play a Cold War bidding game and thus lost the deal for facilities in Djibouti. And after 2013 when relations with Egypt became closer, that country became available for the routine resupply of Russian warships.[8]

Economic Sanctions

On 6 March 2014 the U.S. imposed sanctions on high Russian officials believed to have been involved in the events in Crimea. When the peninsula approved the referendum of 16 March on the return to Russia, the next day the U.S. put sanctions on additional Russian officials and natives of Crimea who had supported the referendum. On 28 April the U.S. put seven additional Russians on the sanctions list and 17 Russian companies, including banks. The next round of sanctions came on 12 September, when the U.S. prohibited extending financial credits to Russian oil and gas firms.[9]

By 31 July the EU had targeted 95 individuals for sanctions and added 24 more on 12 September. The sanctions prohibited the travel of these individuals into Europe and also confiscated their assets in the EU. Some Russian billionaires lost their villas and expensive real estate in Europe, but the reprisals could not affect local officials in Crimea who had never traveled outside the region and possessed paltry savings in a neighborhood bank. Closing the access of Gazprom, Rosneft, and other energy companies to deep-water drilling technology and to easy credit did hinder operations but also deprived Western banks of profit opportunities. The sanctions never crippled any Russian company, because the Kremlin whenever necessary drew on Russia's huge cash reserves to bail out any domestic bank.[10]

For years Gazprom had been trying to secure permission to build the South Stream pipeline through the Black Sea as a way to bypass Ukraine. In June 2014 the EU and the U.S. stopped the project at its weakest link when threats persuaded Bulgaria to withdraw permission to build the pipeline through its territory. This was a real setback for Russia, and it took years of negotiations and work to reroute South Stream through Turkey, Greece, and Italy.[11]

The Mistral Episode

Another bizarre reprisal was the cancellation of the delivery to Russia of two Mistral-class helicopter carriers from shipyards in France. Ever since Russia placed the order in 2010, the U.S. opposed this sale, the first major warship order of Russia in the West. When France announced in June 2014 that it was not delivering the two Mistral helicopter carriers, it was doing Russia a big favor. Russia recovered the payments it had made on these useless vessels, and because the French navy did not want them either, Paris ended up selling the two ships to Egypt at a huge loss. One of the arguments against the sale had been to prevent the transfer of sensitive technology to Russia, so Egypt received stripped down hulks. Russian digital firms made a nice profit by selling the electronics necessary to operate the two Mistral-class helicopter carriers.[12]

The Mistral cancellation confirmed that the reprisals were nuisances. While the American sanctions lacked a set expiration date, the EU sanctions had to be renewed every six months. U.S. and EU representatives roamed the world seeking to enlist other countries into the crusade against Russia. The delegations did persuade Australia and Switzerland to impose sanctions. The biggest success was with Japan, and a naïve Tokyo could not understand why its entreaties about returning the southern Kurile Islands met a stony silence in the Kremlin.[13]

The failure to persuade more countries to join the sanctions weakened their effect. Only a complete and universal embargo on all trade, services, and financing with Russia stood any chance of making the Kremlin reconsider its options. Even then it was far from sure that the Russian people were willing to abandon Crimea. What impacted Russia was the drop in petroleum prices, and the country fell into an economic recession. The Obama administration and Western media emphasized the effect that the sanctions were having, when in reality it was the downturn in the business cycle that was hurting Russia.

In a surprise move, the Kremlin imposed on 5 August 2014 a ban on the import of fruits and vegetables originating in those countries that had imposed sanctions on Russia. The action came so suddenly, that shipments of fresh fruits and vegetables not just from Belgium but as far away as Spain were stopped in the border and ended up rotting away at a tremendous loss to the growers. Because the ban included cheeses and other dairy products, the effect on the agricultural sector of Western Europe was enormous.[14]

The EU could not lose face and had to pay the heavy price of compensating its farmers not just for the damages of one crop but also to the probable permanent loss of the Russian markets. The Kremlin has preferred to avoid protectionist policies, but the remarkable expansion of grain production, which turned Russia into the world's largest exporter of wheat, suggested that a dose of protectionism could give Russian farmers the confidence to expand the cultivation of other crops.

Neither trying to isolate Russia nor imposing economic sanctions was having any effect on changing the behavior of the Kremlin. The sanctions, however, did worsen the relations of Russia with Ukraine.

Blockades Against Crimea and Ukraine

After the collapse of the Viktor Yanukovych presidency on 22 February 2014, Russia closed the credit line of $15 billion to Kiev, and the provisional government fell into a financial crisis. The Kremlin also announced on 1 April that Ukraine had to pay the market price for gas in the future and no longer the discounted price. On 2 April Russia halted payments for the lease on the Sevastopol naval base and in effect repudiated the 2010 Kharkov Accords which had granted an extension until 2042 in exchange for a deep discount on gas prices. The Kiev government had no choice but to raise gas prices to consumers by 56 percent on 1 May. Ukraine was still refusing to pay full price to Gazprom, and the company shut off deliveries on 1 June and resumed them only after receiving payments.[15]

Blockade of Crimea

Prior to the incorporation into Russia, Crimea received 85 percent of its water and three-quarters of its electricity from mainland Ukraine. The water came through the North Crimean Canal from the Dnieper River. Kiev built a dam in the canal 40 kilometers north of the border in late April and ruined the rice harvests in Crimea.[16]

Kiev did restore electricity to exert pressure and also to receive revenue, but Russia was at work laying underwater cables. Their completion became urgent when Ukrainian ultranationalists in November 2015 destroyed the transmission towers bringing electricity to Crimea. By late 2015 the first two underwater power cables were ready and the rest entered into service in early 2016.[17]

Kiev halted all rail, bus, and automobile traffic with Crimea but allowed pedestrians to cross on foot. The normal sight at the border checkpoints was to see individuals dragging a wheeled suitcase while walking the no-man's land of about one kilometer between the last Russian checkpoints and the first Ukrainian outposts. From March 2014 to December 2017 citizens of either country could cross without any border control, but starting on 1 January 2018 Ukraine subjected Russian citizens to strict inspections and demanded biometric passports.[18]

Kiev was trying to do everything possible to impede the movement of people between Russia and Ukraine, yet the Kremlin was slower to respond in kind because it harbored the illusion that some semblance of polite diplomatic relations was still possible. Ukrainian ultranationalists launched attacks on the embassy and consulates of Russia on 14 June 2014, causing considerable damage to the installations, yet Moscow still hesitated to respond. But when the provisional government took concrete steps to use military force to repress the separatists in Eastern Ukraine, the Kremlin halted on 5 July the return of armament, equipment, and vehicles the Ukrainian troops left behind after the hurried evacuation from Crimea.[19]

Association Agreement with EU

The precipitating event that triggered the Maidan revolt had been Viktor Yanukovych's decision to postpone the signing of the Association Agreement with the EU in November 2013. A defiant Kiev joined Georgia and Moldova to sign on 27 July 2014 their association agreements to show Moscow that the three former Soviet republics preferred the EU over Russia.[20]

When on 7 August 2014 the Kremlin announced the ban on the import of fresh fruits and vegetables coming from any of the countries imposing sanctions against Russia, this action turned Ukraine into a smuggling route into Russian markets. The Kremlin, unable to obtain guarantees from Kiev to halt this contraband traffic, extended on 22 October 2014 its ban to all fresh produce originating in Ukraine. This measure was another blow to the Ukrainian economy, which continued to shrink. Just in 2015 its Gross Domestic Product dropped by 9 percent, twice as large as the drop in the preceding year.[21] The Maidan revolt had failed to end corruption, and "Ukraine is the same kleptocracy as it was before."[22]

Ukrainian nationalists in November 2015 vented their anger by blowing up the transmission towers providing Crimea's electricity. In reply, Russian hackers attacked the Ukrainian electricity grid and plunged Kiev into darkness on 23 December 2015.[23]

Combat along the front lines with the separatists never died out, and almost daily shelling and machine gun bursts punctuated most nights and sometimes even the day. In events still not understood, first on 6 August 2016 and then on August 8 groups of Ukrainian ultranationalists tried to regain territory in Crimea. In the resulting clashes, four Russian servicemen lost their lives. The Federal Security Service soon dismantled a subversive network and until the present no similar event has occurred in Crimea.[24]

Starting in 2015 Ukraine joined the West in imposing sanctions on Russia. Because Ukraine was not able to make a real contribution to most of the Western sanctions, it decided to expand its black lists beyond those of the West. Of the 1,228 individuals and 468 firms Kiev sanctioned by the middle of 2017, almost all were Russian (the rest were separatists from Eastern Ukraine). Nothing was too insignificant for Kiev, and even Russian performers wanting to stage shows in the country suffered considerable restrictions. The campaign to remove the Russian language from schools intensified when the State Language Law entered into force on 16 July 2019. The law made Ukrainian the sole language for government, education, and in most areas of social activity, including the media.[25]

Russian Responses

In a first step toward recognizing the independence of Donetsk and Lugansk, on 18 February 2017 the Kremlin accepted as legally valid the personal identification papers and the vehicle registration documents of the two separatist republics. On 1 March Donetsk and Lugansk also declared the Russian ruble the official currency, a decision the Kremlin accepted.[26]

Russia was taking every possible step to deprive Ukraine of any leverage. A great example was the railroad linking two Russian towns but which crossed a bulge of Ukrainian territory. To prevent Kiev from using this stretch of track to blackmail the Kremlin, a battalion of railway troops constructed a bypass of 37 kilometers. The troops completed the stretch one year ahead of schedule, and the new track crossing through Russian territory opened for traffic on 11 December 2017. These and other measures led the *Moscow Times* to observe that "Ukraine faces going from a traditional bridge between east and west to becoming an island."[27]

Russia's most ambitious measure to end Crimea's dependence on Ukraine came with the construction of two bridges linking the mainland with the peninsula at Kerch. The massive undertaking to build the longest bridge in Russia was such a huge engineering challenge that skeptics doubted it could be completed. President Putin inaugurated the four-lane highway bridge on 14 May 2018. Workers completed the first span of the railroad bridge in May 2019 and the first passenger train crossed on 25 December 2019.[28]

The Coal Blockade

Ukraine obtained most of its coal from the separatist regions. The rebels controlled the majority of the mines, but the utilities, factories, and coke plant consuming the coal were on the Ukrainian side. A key figure in this trade was the Ukrainian billionaire Rinat Akhmetov, whose facilities were located on both sides of the front line. As long as he was able to purchase the coal from the rebel areas, the separatist authorities tolerated his activities.[29]

In January 2017 Ukrainian nationalists blocked railway cars bringing coal from the Donbass. By 15 February the shortage of fuel shut down the coal-fired power plants and caused blackouts in Ukraine. On 25 February 2017 Ukrainian nationalists staged major demonstrations across the country and demanded the halt of all coal shipments from the separatist regions. When the utilities tried to import coal from Russia, the protestors blocked those trains. When the Kiev government sent the police to clear the checkpoints, angry crowds gathered in Maidan Square on 13 March and again the next day. Fearing that the protests would spiral out of control, the government on 15 March prohibited all trade with the separatist regions but authorized utilities to import foreign coal, including from Russia. In a parallel action, Russian railroads reduced the rates on transporting coal from the Donbass to symbolic prices, and on 15 March the first 95 railway cars departed for Russia.[30]

The blockade and the symbolic railway rates created a bonanza for merchants in Russia. Ukraine imported coal from Russia to replace the Donbass supplies. Russian merchants then passed the separatist coal through ports such as Azov and Rostov-on-the Don to replace the Russian coal heading to traditional foreign markets such as Turkey. Ukraine even began to import coal from the United States, but the shipping costs were higher than for the nearby Russian supply.[31]

The changed circumstances made Akhmetov superfluous, and on 1 March the separatist republics nationalized all the assets of the billionaire, a measure they had long threatened but delayed while the beneficial coal trade with Ukraine lasted. This nationalization did not stop Ukrainian ultranationalists from ransacking the offices of Akhmetov in Kiev and his properties in other parts of Ukraine. Despite the popular attacks, the grip by billionaires on the Ukrainian government remained strong, and the first demand of Kiev for any negotiations with the separatist republics was the return of the properties to billionaires such as Akhmetov. A sense of loyalty had lingered among employees as long as they were receiving a paycheck from Ukrainian firms, but the end of that financial dependence severed that link.[32]

War Scares

The realization that Ukraine lacked the means to reconquer the separatist republics by a military campaign was a harsh truth to accept, and this frustration had been one of the reasons behind the furious demonstrations of March 2017. But almost on cue, the West revived hopes for a military solution by sending for the first time weapons to Ukraine at the end of 2017. Both sides had used Soviet-era weapons during the intense combat of 2014–2015 until the end of 2017 when the U.S. and Canada began to provide new weapons. The Javelin anti-tank missile system was an odd preference, because it was the Ukrainians who used Soviet-era tanks but the rebels relied on infantry and artillery.[33]

This escalation in weapons coincided with the passage by the Ukrainian parliament of the bill on the Reintegration of the Donbass region on 18 January 2018. The demonstrators in the March 2017 protests had demanded a similar law, and the parliament complied with the bill declaring Russia the aggressor and placing control of the campaign under the Ukrainian military, which until then had carried out an "anti-terrorist" operation.[34]

The bill was in essence a declaration of war on Russia but stopped short of using those words. President Petro Poroshenko used the bill to try to leverage some concessions from the rebels and from Russia but without any success. On 24 February 2018 he signed the bill into law, and many foreign observers watched with concern whether a renewal of large-scale hostilities was imminent.[35]

At this moment a figure from the past appeared on the scene. Readers may remember Mikheil Saakashvili, the former president of Georgia, who had plunged his country into a disastrous war with Russia in August 2008. President Poroshenko gave him Ukrainian citizenship and appointed him governor of Odessa in May 2015, but rather than being grateful, he sought popularity among Ukrainian nationalists. In Neo-Nazi rallies colored with anti–Semitic slogans, the former darling of the West accused Ukrainian officials of corruption and condemned President Poroshenko for being pro–Russian. Demonstrations erupted when a Ukrainian court denied the request of Saakashvili for asylum, and until this political tempest in a teapot played out, Kiev could not take action against Russia or the separatist republics.[36]

Kiev began to harass Russian fishermen in the Sea of Azov after the passage of the Reintegration Law. Ukraine was trying to provoke Russia into launching a military reprisal and then to use this incident to demand crippling sanctions from the West. The Russian Foreign Ministry warned that "Our patience is not unlimited. We reserve the right to take strict response measures."[37] The sanction sure to hurt Russian pride was the boycott of the World Cup games scheduled to take place in June and July of 2018.

Russia still was not taking the bait, so Kiev increased the pressure. In a decree of 25 April 2018 Ukraine prohibited the passage through its territorial waters of any ships owned by Russians. Such a ban violated countless treaties and did not take into account the fact that Russia controlled the longest stretch of coastline on the Sea of Azov. The sole response of the Russian Foreign Ministry was a warning not to Ukraine but to Russian shipping companies about "the real risks of pirate seizure of Russian vessels by the Ukrainian security agencies."[38]

The Kerch Bridge Incident

Ever since the opening of the bridge linking Crimea to the Russian mainland in May 2018, Russia required all ships navigating under the new structure to undergo a very strict inspection. This measure also affected ships heading to Mariupol in the Ukrainian coast of the Sea of Azov.

President Poroshenko considered these inspections to be illegal, and in July he ordered the Ukrainian military to take measures to prevent these Russian actions. A confrontation occurred on 25 November 2018 when two gunboats and one tugboat approached the Kerch Bridge without providing the proper notifications. The Federal Security Service with its patrol craft closed the passage under the bridge and also put an old tanker to block lengthwise the shipping lane, while fighter jets scrambled and patrolled the bridge.[39]

The Ukrainian vessels retreated into Russian territorial waters, and the massive display of force awed the three Ukrainian crews into submission. Russian authorities impounded the three ships, and the 24 Ukrainian sailors went into imprisonment. The Russian Duma awarded decorations to the Russian servicemen who had seized the Ukrainian vessels, while the European Union, not wishing to be outdone, added to its sanction lists the Russian officials who had participated in the operation.[40]

President Poroshenko proclaimed a state of emergency the next day, but soon his political rivals began to suspect that he was trying to create an incident to bolster his chances at the presidential election of April 2019 and possibly also to postpone them because he was trailing in the opinion polls. Poroshenko agreed to limit the state of emergency to those regions bordering Russia and Transnistria, in the latter case under the doubtful assumption that the 1,200 Russian soldiers in that separatist republic were capable of launching an invasion of Ukraine.[41]

Poroshenko lost the presidential elections in April 2019, and his successor, Volodymyr Zelensky, negotiated with President Vladimir Putin a prisoner swap that included the release of the 24 imprisoned Ukrainian sailors on 7 September. Russia closed the incident by returning the three seized Ukrainian vessels on 18 November 2019.[42]

25

Russia on the Offensive

Russia was and will be a sovereign and independent state. It is an axiom, it will either be such or it will not exist at all.—Vladimir Putin[1]

Saving Syria

Russia and Bashar al-Assad

A Russian team under Foreign Minister Sergei Lavrov travelled to Damascus in the first week of February 2012. Although the Russians did not press the Syrian ruler to step down, the team returned disappointed that al-Assad did not make concessions to the rebels. The frustration with al-Assad mounted in Moscow during February, and U.S. officials learned that a Russian contingency plan consisted of pressuring him to make a transition to a provisional government. In the last months of the Medvedev presidency, the Kremlin reduced its actions to supporting efforts to facilitate humanitarian aid to places such as Homs and ignored U.S. suggestions about a no-fly zone over Syria.[2]

Once Vladimir Putin returned to the presidency in May 2012, he waited until the military situation on the ground became clearer. The rebels already occupied a large part of Aleppo, the economic capital of Syria, and they launched an offensive in July 2012 to capture all of that vital city. It is no exaggeration to state that the fate of the regime hung on the outcome of this battle, and even al-Assad readied plans to abandon Damascus. But once it became clear that the rebels were unable to capture Aleppo, Russia rallied behind the Syrian ruler.[3]

The Russian support for al-Assad proved indispensable for the survival of his regime when a nerve gas attack took place on 21 August 2013. Many possible explanations existed for the chemical attack, but the rebels and the West placed all the blame on the Syrian regime. The Obama administration had been under tremendous pressure to intervene military ever since the revolt started in Syria in 2011, but because the involvement in Libya had turned out to be such a mess, the reluctance to open another can of worms was understandable. Nothing could calm the war hawks, and in an attempt to deflect the criticisms, he stated on 20 August 2012 that a chemical attack constituted a red line calling for a U.S. response. And one year later in August 2013 a chemical attack occurred.[4]

When Obama went through the motions of organizing a coalition of allies, the only unconditional supporter willing to commit armed forces was France, and France was not the best calling card because that country had been the former colonial power in Syria. No UN authorization was possible, and the anti–Syrian operation bore a striking resemblance to the war George W. Bush waged against Saddam Hussein. Applying the formula of "Iraq III" when "Iraq II" in Libya had

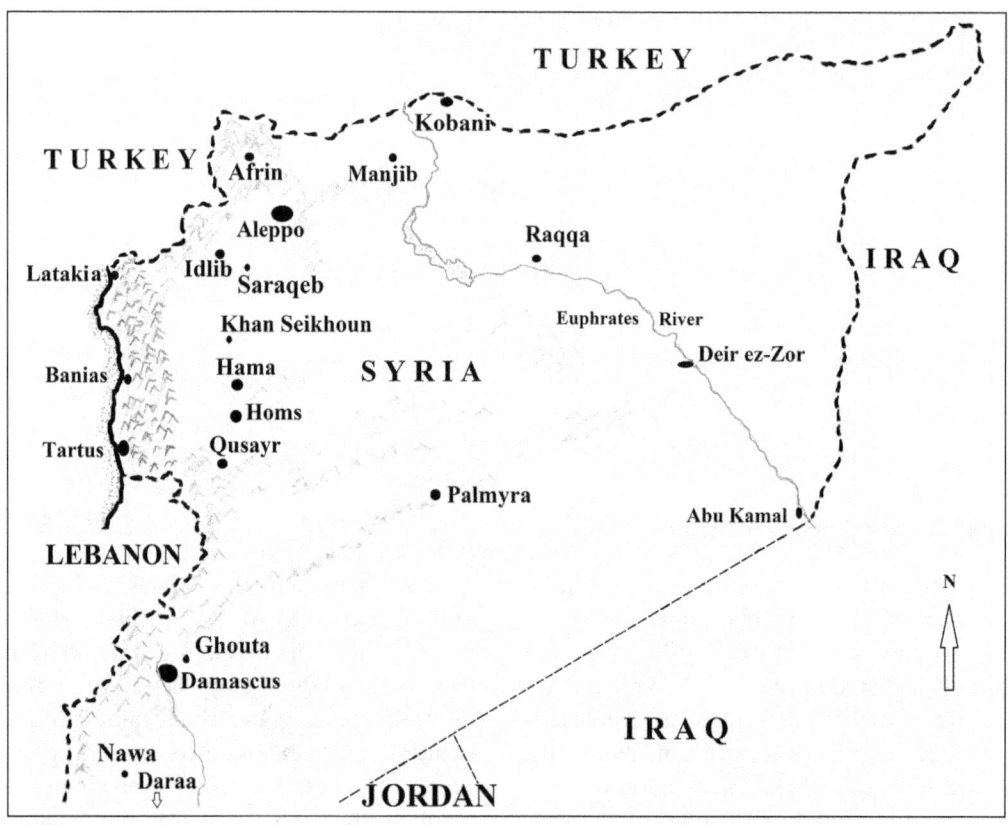

turned out to be a disaster did not seem very promising.⁵

Just a few hours before French warplanes were scheduled to begin their bombing runs against targets in Syria, Obama telephoned French President Nicolas Sarkozy to state that the U.S. was calling off the operation. This left the Obama administration vulnerable to furious political attacks, but at this moment Vladimir Putin appeared with a face-saving formula. The UN Security Council passed a resolution calling for the removal of all chemical weapons in Syria and giving a commission authority and the means to enforce the resolution. Inspectors verified the removal from Syria of all the chemical stockpiles, but the rebels refused to allow inspectors into the one supply dump they had captured.⁶

American support for the Russian initiative to remove chemical weapons did not mean at all that the U.S. had abandoned its original intention to overthrow the Syrian regime. Still feeling the political heat, the Obama administration decided to send arms to the rebels and also went so far as to create its own rebel force. Saudi Arabia and Qatar were supplying funds, equipment, and weapons in abundance to the rebels, but those countries lacked the advanced weapons systems of the U.S. The rebels clamored for surface-to-air missiles to neutralize the Syrian warplanes, but the Pentagon blocked those deliveries because of the bad experience supplying Stinger missiles to Afghan fighters during the Soviet invasion. As a compromise, the U.S. supplied TOW anti-tank missiles, but those too ended up in the hands of Islamic radicals. In response to political pressure, the Obama administration began on 22 September 2014 air operations against Islamic radicals. This was the least effective response on the part of the U.S., and in the initial years the very narrow air campaign achieved few results.⁷

The Russian Military Intervention

The tide started to turn in favor of the rebels, who in a few days broke through the government defenses and occupied Idlib, on 28 March 2015. Idlib was just the first of several provincial capitals the rebels captured, and Russian officials reported that the rebels controlled 70 percent of Syrian territory in the summer of 2015. Events were heading to a turning point, and it became clear to Moscow that the regime of al-Assad was on the verge of collapse. So the Kremlin was not surprised when the Syrian ruler sent an envoy to Moscow reporting on the intention to abandon Damascus and transfer the government to the Alawite homeland near the Mediterranean coast and next to the two Russian military bases.[8]

In a final plea, Putin went to the UN General Assembly on 28 September 2015 to ask other countries to join Russia in a coalition against the Islamic radicals who had taken over the revolt in Syria. The West scoffed at the idea, and Russia was left to proceed alone. The danger for Russia was that a full-scale invasion could well trigger an insurgency just as happened in Iraq to the U.S. In a courageous decision and a bold gamble, Putin decided to risk everything on an air campaign to save the tottering regime of al-Assad.[9]

By late September fighter-bombers were operational in the Hmeymim air base, and all that remained to launch the offensive was to fulfill the constitutional requirement of seeking the approval of the upper house of the Russian parliament. On 30 September 2015 in the morning the upper house unanimously approved the request, and later that same day the first air strikes struck rebel positions in Syria.[10]

The air campaign halted the rebel offensive and ruled out any departure of the Syrian government from Damascus. But as the months passed by, the first naysayers appeared to accuse the Kremlin of having become bogged down in a quagmire like Afghanistan. The military leaders knew that the air campaign was working and tried to reassure the public by showing many videos of planes destroying targets.

Critics of the military intervention in Syrian had a field day when Turkey shot down a Russian fighter-bomber on 24 November 2015. The incident was settled, and the air campaign continued without interruption and achieved its greatest success in Aleppo. Relentless Russian bombardment smashed the rebel strongholds, and the Syrian forces were able to surround the rebel positions in a very slow process. The EU realized that victory in Aleppo meant the survival of al-Assad and tried to persuade Russia to halt the bombing and to press for talks among the warring parties. On 23 December 2016 Defense Minister Sergei Shoigu reported to President Putin in front of television cameras that all of Aleppo was under government control.[11]

The U.S. and Syria

Not everyone in the incoming Donald Trump administration wanted to accept the reality that al-Assad had won the civil war. The new Secretary of State Rex Tillerson went to Moscow on 12 April 2017 to demand that Russia stop its support of al-Assad. The White House may have been blindsided by this ultimatum. At one moment Putin almost refused to see the Secretary of State, a courtesy the Kremlin has extended to all previous holders of that position since World War II. The meeting with the Secretary of State did take place, because the Russian president did not want to embarrass Trump.[12]

Russian patience with the new Trump administration soon brought the first favorable results. Late in June 2017 the U.S. stopped supporting rebels in Syria. In September 2015 the Pentagon revealed that it had spent over half a billion dollars to put in the field a handful of pro–American rebels;

by the middle of 2017 the price tag was a billion dollars with no better results. This program was long overdue for cancellation, but when the decision was leaked to the press, the overwhelming reaction fed into the narrative that Trump was a puppet of Putin and the American president was following the orders of his Kremlin "handler."[13]

Diplomatic Recognition for Syria

One analyst observed in October 2017 with little exaggeration that "al-Assad's enemies are scurrying back to him."[14] The European countries that broke diplomatic relations in 2012 sent one delegation after another to Damascus in late 2017 to try to reestablish contacts. France had been the most insistent in pushing for the overthrow of al-Assad, but in a complete reversal, French diplomats, in desperation, were seeking suggestions from anybody who could help them restore relations. And Hungary was the first EU member to upgrade its diplomatic mission in Damascus in late 2019.[15]

In the Arab world a diplomatic reversal had been gaining momentum since late 2017. The large role the non–Arab states of Iran and Turkey played in Syria offended Arab pride and was a stimulus to repair relations with Damascus. Although Saudi Arabia remained committed to its policy of overthrowing the Syrian government, the majority of Arab countries accepted the victory of al-Assad. Egypt still was reluctant to make a public turnaround and did not publicize its acceptance of al-Assad.[16]

A notable breakthrough came when the United Arab Emirates (UAE) reopened its embassy in Damascus on 27 December 2018 and Bahrain did the same the next day. The UAE did not waste any time trying to restore its influence and was soon distributing humanitarian food packages to needy sectors of the Syrian population. The UAE also saved the Syrian entertainment industry and its many destitute actors by funding the production and then broadcasting at home two soap operas with a conservative religious theme for the holy month of Ramadan. A grateful Syrian government expedited all the permits for the television production and for other investment projects of the rich Gulf States.[17]

A next step was the return of Syria to the Arab League—the organization from which it had been expelled in 2011. Although a majority of countries supported the measure, strong U.S. pressure on Saudi Arabia and Egypt prevented the return of Syria to the Arab League in the initial months of 2019.[18] But this was just a hitch, and on 6 March 2019 the UAE Foreign Minister Sheikh Abdullah bin Zayed explained that the reopening of the embassy in Damascus was "just the start of the journey [...] to ensure that Syria returns to the Arab region."[19] This statement carried even more weight because standing right by him was Foreign Minister Sergei Lavrov who was on a tour of capitals in the region. The Russian diplomat stated that both "Russia and the UAE have the same approaches to resolving conflicts in the region."

Russian Assistance

At no time did al-Assad forget who his real savior had been. Syria was flooded with posters showing Putin standing next to al-Assad, while television emphasized the friendship between Syria and Russia. The close relationship went beyond the military and covered many areas. Bread shortages had contributed to the outbreak of the Arab Spring in 2011, and a scarcity of flour once again in 2017 threatened the stability of the regime. Meanwhile Crimea had succeeded in replacing the water-intensive rice crop with wheat, but Western embargoes blocked sales to almost all export markets. Starting in July 2017 Crimea dispatched wheat shipments to Syria, and ten grain ships delivered their cargoes by June 2018. A grateful Syria reciprocated with shipments of fresh fruit to Sevastopol.[20]

Chlorine Attack

On the ground Syrian forces during 2017 and 2018 continued their offensive. The rebels once again tried to provoke U.S. intervention by staging an attack with chlorine gas (available for civilian use) in eastern Ghouta on 7 April 2018. The rebels recorded the supposed incident, and eager media diffused the video across the world. Without examining the evidence, the U.S., Britain, and France in a knee-jerk reaction launched missile attacks against several installations of the Syrian government.[21]

The missile attack turned out to be the last gasp of the Western campaign against al-Assad. The Syrian forces resumed their offensive to drive out the rebels from southern and eastern parts of the country, and soon Syrian forces reoccupied the border posts facing Israel and Jordan. In a humanitarian action, the Syrian government agreed to allow rebels to leave isolated towns and to find safety in Idlib province, a gesture that postponed the final reckoning.

The Turkish Intervention

The timetable for the final pacification of Syria suffered a long delay when Turkey decided to intervene in the civil war. Turkey was determined to prevent the appearance of an independent Kurdish state in northern Syria. This ethnic group had been responsible for many terrorist attacks inside Turkey. For reasons far from clear President Recep Tayyip Erdogan of Turkey also wanted to overthrow the Syrian ruler. Al-Assad was more than willing to forget past animosity just as he had done with Arab leaders who years before clamored for his removal from office.[22]

On 19 January 2018 Turkish artillery began shelling Kurdish positions in northern Syria, and the next day troops streamed across the border heading toward Afrin. The Kremlin saw the intervention as a powerful incentive for the Kurds to seek reunification with Damascus as their best remaining option. Moscow's approval for the Turkish invasion was indispensable, because under an informal agreement Russia controlled the air space to the west of the Euphrates River, while the U.S. controlled the air space to the east of the Euphrates.[23]

Facing modest resistance from the Kurds, Turkish troops surrounded Afrin at the end of January 2018 but delayed the occupation until Arab rebels could enter the city on March 2018. Turkey changed the nature of the invasion when its troops started to push south in Idlib province and at first they encountered resistance from rebel groups. But then the rebels welcomed the invasion as a lifeline. Syrian forces had been redeploying near Idlib in preparation for the final offensive of the civil war, while Russian warplanes had been pounding rebel targets in that province. As Turkish troops moved south into Idlib, the risk increased that they might clash with either Syrian forces or suffer Russian air strikes.[24]

Putin tried to persuade Erdogan to abandon the Turkish push into Syria but had to settle for an agreement in September 2018 creating a demilitarized zone between the rebels in Idlib and government forces. Turkish troops established twelve observation posts and Russian military police took up positions to patrol this demilitarized zone.[25]

In the Idlib front the ceasefire held and protected the rebels from both Syrian attacks and Russian bombings for the rest of 2018. This relative quiet emboldened those in the U.S. government who still clamored for the overthrow of al-Assad by turning Idlib province into a bulwark to make a rebel comeback across Syria. Articles appeared describing Idlib as an ideal society of equality with respect for the rights of all. Even the Athenian democracy of classical age paled in comparison to the description of these idealized rebels who were fighting to save their enclave from destruction at the hands of a brutal dictator.

These dreams came crashing down when in late December 2018 the Trump administration announced its decision to withdraw all American forces from Syria. The news provoked an outcry in the United States from those who wanted to overthrow al-Assad. The accusations multiplied that Trump took this action to pander to his Kremlin masters. The resignation in protest of the Secretary of Defense confirmed that the desire to use American military force in Syria was widespread among U.S. officials. The backslash was so strong, that President Trump felt obliged to retreat and slowed down the withdrawal of the 2,000 American soldiers and left 500 to defend the oil fields.

In January 2019, in a swift coordinated action, the Islamic Jihadists seized control of the Idlib enclave. The ideal society patterned on Athenian democracy came crashing down. Events in the province paralleled at an accelerated pace the evolution in Syria since the Arab Spring. The pro-Western democratic rebels of 2011 gave way to radicalized Jihadists, a transformation taking place over seven years in Syria but in only seven months at Idlib.[26]

Despite the ceasefire of September 2018, the Jihadists were eager to renew combat and resumed hostilities in April 2019. The jihadists maintained their shelling of civilian areas in Aleppo and also launched several major attacks in May 2019. Once again Russian fighter-bombers retaliated against rebel targets. The jihadists tried to stop the Russian air strikes by launching rockets against the air base of Hmeymim. Russian planners had anticipated such a move, and the air defense system shot down all the incoming missiles.[27]

The real risk existed that the Russian air strikes might by accident hit the Turkish outposts, but then jihadists tried to drive out Turkish troops from one area of Idlib. In response, Turkish officers asked for help from Russia and provided the coordinates of the enemy positions, so that Russian fighter-bombers could deliver a devastating strike. The extensive bombing of the jihadist positions also meant the start of the long-delayed Syrian campaign against Idlib province, and on 20 August 2019 government forces recaptured the town of Khan Seikhoun. The fall of Idlib seemed imminent, but then a new development again postponed the final victory.[28]

The Russian-Turkish Accord

In a telephone call to Erdogan on 6 October 2019, Trump announced his decision to begin a withdrawal from Syria. Trump was impatient to fulfill his campaign pledge to bring American troops back home from foreign wars. He had already made the decision to withdraw in December 2018, but fierce resistance in the U.S. forced him to postpone its implementation.[29]

As the around 2,000 American troops evacuated—sometimes in such haste that they left food on the table and appliances running in the bases—Erdogan saw an opening. On 9 October 2019 Turkish troops invaded Syria and declared their intention to establish a 20-mile safe zone along the border. At first the Kurds attempted to resist, but they soon realized that their light weapons were no match for the NATO equipment of the Turks. Faced with certain defeat, the Kurds turned to al-Assad and agreed to let Syrian troops enter zones under Kurdish control. A race ensued with Syrian troops rushing to occupy territories in the safe zone ahead of the advancing Turkish troops. On 14 October Syrian forces entered Manbij and soon they occupied other towns in northern Syria. Videos even captured the moment when departing American troops crossed paths in the highway with the arriving Syrian troops.³⁰

The real danger existed of clashes between Syrian troops and Turkish forces, and to avoid that risk, Presidents Erdogan and Putin reached an agreement calling for Russian military police to patrol the safe zone. The Russian military police had the primary task of keeping Turkish and Syrian troops separated along the entire long corridor of the safe zone. The Russian military police in many instances settled into the bases the Americans had abandoned in a rush. The rebels continued the sporadic shelling of Aleppo from hidden positions to the north and west of the city, and Syrian forces went on the offensive to eliminate this threat to civilians.³¹

The Syrian advance drove the rebels back and regained territory in January 2020. In early February after the rebels abandoned the town of Saraqeb and its key intersection, Syrian forces reopened the highways leading from Aleppo to Ham and to Latakia. By then the front line had moved to the north and of the twelve Turkish observation posts, ten were surrounded by Syrian forces. The close proximity of troops led to clashes, and at one point artillery barrages killed Turks and Syrians. President Erdogan demanded that Syrian forces abandon their recently occupied territory, and for a few weeks in February 2020 the threat of a war between Syria and Turkey was a possibility. Erdogan feared that Turkey was being squeezed out of Syria and faced an avalanche of refugees should Syria recapture all of Idlib province.³²

Turkey poured more troops into Syria to show al-Assad that the capture of all of Idlib province was not possible at this time. But the lack of support from the West forced Erdogan to turn again to Moscow. In a meeting on 6 March 2020 with Putin, the two presidents agreed to a new ceasefire, with Syria halting its offensive but keeping its territorial gains. The two leaders also ratified the use of Russian military police and Turkish forces to patrol the highways in the remaining rebel area of Idlib.³³ The outbreak of the coronavirus pandemic throughout the world cooled any desires of the participants for combat, and the arrangements have preserved a shaky peace in the last remaining rebel strips of Idlib province.

Target: The United States

Private Russian Hackers

Private Russian hackers had the ability to inflict horrendous damage on the former Soviet republics, but the most elemental analysis showed that trying to repeat this feat against the United States was a proposition of a different magnitude. For profit, criminal, and vanity reasons, Russian hackers had been seeking American targets of opportunity at least since 2010, but the real stimulus for an extensive campaign against the U.S. came after the reunification with Crimea in March 2014. The U.S. was determined to undo the reunification and manifested its anger by imposing sanctions on Russia. This hostile reaction persuaded outraged patriotic individuals to lash out in response. Billionaires targeted by the sanctions also wanted to strike back, and they contributed to finance private hackers. A first option was to provide sympathetic coverage of Russia in social media.³⁴

By the end of 2014 the Internet Research Agency, owned by billionaire Yevgeny Prigozhin, became the main organization targeting social media in the United States. This "troll" farm was one of the smallest of the digital organizations then proliferating in Russia and never had any formal links with the Kremlin. Other private Russians set up accounts in social media, and these sites promoted a variety of views among Americans. The focus came in early 2016 when Hillary Clinton emerged as a candidate in the presidential elections of November 2016. The Russians decided to use their social media accounts to support the Republican candidate Donald Trump. This decision rested on the questionable assumption that Republican presidents had been more willing to engage Russia.[35]

U.S. security agencies in their reports on Russian interference work from the assumption that American democracy is a very fragile creature and that the slightest tampering can send the entire political system crashing down. U.S. security agencies assumed the role of protecting naïve American citizens who can be fooled by subversive foreign influences. For U.S. officials a few postings on Facebook and a RT broadcast could sway millions of voters. This attitude resurrected the policy of the former KGB of trying to isolate Soviet citizens from outside subversive influences. Indignant U.S. officials even went so far as to prevent a handful of Russian diplomats from observing a few polling places. Had these unfounded fears about the fragility of the electoral process and the gullibility of American voters been true, then the U.S. was long overdue for a complete transformation of its political system.[36]

The Russian Campaign in the 2016 Election

Media: RT and Sputnik

These two state-owned agencies have reported on a wide variety of topics. Western media and U.S. official reports dismissed the two agencies as propaganda outlets for the Kremlin. But their effect on the presidential election of 2016 was minimal because of their small audiences in the United States. In a final compelling argument, the Meuller investigation did not file any charges against these state-owned agencies and did not even bother to repeat the accusations contained in previous U.S. reports.[37]

Social Media

Already in 2014 private Russians whether as individuals or working through the Internet Research Agency established a presence in Facebook, YouTube, and Twitter. In 2015 Instagram also witnessed activity when Russians pretending to be Americans opened accounts. And to make the accounts look authentic, Russians traveled to the U.S. to take photographs and obtain additional materials for inclusion in the sites.[38]

To refer users to these accounts, just in Facebook the Russian operators purchased over 3,500 advertisements at a cost of $100,000. The accounts concentrated on creating racial and religious divisions among Americans. Google did not escape the accusations, but it was hard to see how the purchase of $4,700 in adds for the equivalent of 0.0002 of spending in the 2016 campaign in Google could have produced much impact.[39]

Once the presidential campaign began, most of the accounts shifted to promoting Trump and attacking Hillary Clinton. The first Facebook advertisement supporting Trump appeared on 19 April 2016 and many more followed. The Russian sites tried to fan the anti-immigrant rhetoric of the Trump campaign. In a new step, starting in November 2015 the sites also organized demonstrations. Then in June 2016, the gatherings shifted their focus to bolstering support for Trump. The Facebook sites promoted 120 rallies in total. Russian operators had the greatest success in Facebook, and they did manage to attract the attention of 5 million Americans. But this was a small number when 129 million Americans had the opportunity to access the Russian sites, and the 5 million was insignificant among the 33 trillion stories appearing on Facebook pages during the campaign period.

Of the Russian advertising on Facebook, 56 percent was visited only after the election and 25 percent of the ads were never seen.[40]

Easy as it had been for Russian operators to enter Facebook, Twitter, and Google, it was becoming clear that even the strong presence in Facebook was not having any major effect on a public drowning in digital messaging. In the spring of 2016, private Russian hackers concluded that to have a real effect they needed to pursue a more aggressive and illegal approach.

Voting Infrastructure

Starting in June 2016 Russian operators began a reconnaissance of electoral facilities in at least 21 states. In some cases the search did not go beyond looking at the public web sites of state agencies to see what if any vulnerabilities existed for a later possible exploitation. For major states, the Russian hackers from the start sought access to electoral rosters and other voting materials.[41]

In Illinois, the hackers obtained the voter registration records of 200,000 citizens out of a total number 14 million voters. The information obtained included "voter's name, partial social security number, date of birth, and either a driver's license number or state identification number."[42] Without the entire social security number the information was of negligible value for criminal or intelligence purposes. During the reconnaissance phase the operators downloaded only a small fraction of the available voter registration records.[43]

Hacking into DNC Servers

In June 2016 Russians gained access to records of the Democratic National Committee (DNC) and the Republican National Committee. While it seems that hackers obtained the Republican records, the origin of the materials from the DNC still remains under dispute. U.S. security agencies using convoluted and complex arguments have condemned Russian military intelligence (GRU).[44] While proving the charge that private Russians carried out the hacks on the DNC is difficult, confirming the role of the Russian government is almost impossible. Considerable indications exist that disgruntled employees or sympathizers of Bernie Sanders leaked the documents to Wikileaks in reaction to the favoritism of the DNC toward Hillary Clinton.

The Kremlin Reacts

The Kremlin supported RT and Sputnik in the valiant attempts of those agencies to reach Western audiences and breach the information blockade Western media had imposed on Russian news. Those well-run agencies required little supervision, and Kremlin spokesman Dmitry Peskov was their advocate within the Presidential Administration. The Russian Foreign Ministry and the ambassador in Washington Sergei Kislyak supported "the objective of shifting the U.S. political consensus in Russia's perceived interests regardless of who won."[45] A sort of mission creep came into the program, and the Kremlin by early 2016 realized that private Russians were buying advertisements and opening sites in social media in the United States. Because the U.S. prides itself on the free flow of ideas and opinions, Peskov saw this entry into social media to be a natural extension of the public relations activities of RT and Sputnik, both of which already operated extensive on-line services.[46]

The Russian Foreign Ministry and Russian ambassador Kislyak were skeptical. Foreign Minister Sergei Lavrov and other diplomats feared that going beyond supporting RT and Sputnik could be counterproductive and hurt the goals Russia was trying to achieve. Just at the same time, many private Russians sought a more effective channel to influence the U.S.[47]

Somewhere around May 2016 Sergei

Ivanov, the chief of the Presidential Administration, let private individuals know that the Kremlin had no objections to the more ambitious plans of scanning the electoral infrastructure of the U.S. to see what vulnerabilities existed. He also implied that the Kremlin did not object to hacking into e-mail accounts of candidates and political organizations to uncover compromising material (*Kompromat*). But because these were private operators, they lacked the software tools, the expertise, and the technical sophistication of the Russian security agencies. In U.S. official reports the expressions "amateur" and "amateurish" reappear, an indication that they were freelancers rather than skilled professionals.

Someone had to monitor these activities, and Ivanov assigned this task to Mikhail Kalugin in the Russian embassy in Washington. Ivanov was able to do this because of his reputation as a former KGB official and the authority he commanded from his daily contact with President Putin. In the best tradition of spy practice, he intended to keep the president in the dark so as to make possible deniability for any failure.[48]

The operation was too big to keep secret inside the Kremlin for long. In the initial days of August 2016 Putin learned that Ivanov had sponsored an operation to influence U.S. elections. Even worse, it was learned that the presidential aide did not have full control over the campaign. The response of Putin was swift, and on 12 August he announced the replacement of Ivanov with his deputy the much younger Anton E. Vaino, who had not been involved. Such a sudden departure of a high-ranking official had never happened before, because the approach of Putin had been to prepare the public for changes in leadership positions.[49]

In a parallel move, the Foreign Ministry also in early August recalled diplomat Kalugin to Moscow on the argument that his tour of duty abroad had come to an end. The message went out that the Kremlin did not approve of any tampering with the U.S. electoral system. The scanners did not exploit the weaknesses discovered in the reconnaissance phase, and the U.S. electoral infrastructure remained unharmed.[50] None of the 50 states admitted that any tampering had occurred with the voting results in November 2016. The Senate Committee on Intelligence stated that "The Committee has seen no indications that votes were changed, vote-tallying systems were manipulated, or that any voter registration data was altered or deleted."[51]

Reversing course was not always possible, when the first e-mails from the DNC already reached the public in June 2016. Starting in July and lasting through October 2016, Wikileaks released the e-mails.[52] By that time the campaign of Hillary was in such serious problems that the e-mail releases were just another nail in the coffin.

The Russian government never took any direct actions to interfere in the U.S. presidential elections, while the activities of private individuals had little if any effect. And in comparison with the frequent U.S. meddling in elections in Latin America and other parts of the world, the Russian reconnaissance was insignificant.

26

The Russian Diplomatic Campaign

I want you to hear me. We aren't going to attack any country. We don't threaten any state [...] we don't want war.—Deputy Defense Minister Anatoly Antonov[1]

Frankly, Russia should go away and shut up.—British Defense Minister Gavin Williamson[2]

Each year that passed after the reunification of Crimea with Russia in March 2014 undermined the claim that the Kremlin was determined to invade Europe. On the diplomatic front Russia had not remained passive, and on 10 March 2015 it announced the suspension of talks to revive the abrogated Conventional Armed Forces in Europe Treaty (CFE). The reaction of Western powers was rather muted, and in another indicator, the resistance to Russia's formal entry into the Organization for Economic Cooperation and Development (OECD) appeared to be softening. This institution suspended accession talks in March 2014, but technical cooperation continued in 2016. Even more encouraging, the chief and the staff of OECD supported resuming membership negotiations for Russia.[3]

To test the hypothesis that the West might even be willing to reverse its reprisals, on 22 April 2016 Russia submitted to the World Trade Organization (WTO) its adhesion to a protocol inserting the Trade Facilitation Agreement into the founding treaty. Russian diplomats had participated in the negotiation of the new agreement intended to remove barriers from international trade. Russian diplomats could not detect any hostility toward the agreement, and at least in the WTO, it was business as usual for the Kremlin.[4]

Encouraged by the results, the Foreign Ministry decided to take the offensive to restore Russia's position in several regional bodies. The two most important were NATO and the European Union (EU), but the greatest opportunity to make a first breakthrough came in the Council of Europe, the main human rights organization for the region.

The Council of Europe

The Parliamentary Assembly of the Council of Europe suspended the voting rights of the Russian delegation on 10 April 2014. This suspension marked the high point of the Western reprisals against Russia over the reunification with Crimea. In contrast to other international bodies, the Russian representatives to the Parliamentary Assembly were not diplomats but deputies to the Duma. The Russian deputies walked out in protest, and in a fit of anger they wanted to end Russia's membership in the Council of Europe altogether. The Russian legislature has been the most nationalistic body in the government, and the executive had to exert great effort to persuade the legislators that the moment was not ripe for departing.

Sympathy for the Council of Europe inside Russia declined. One of its bodies was the European Court of Human Rights, and angry legislators wanted to remove its authority to hear appeals from the country. In fact, the Russian Constitutional Court took the lead when its ruling of July 2015 stated that the Constitution could prevent the enforcement of a judgment by the European Court of Human Rights. The legal reasoning was that no channel existed to bring those cases for appeal inside Russia. Right on cue, in December 2015 the legislature passed a law creating a special judicial committee to decide whether to refer rulings of the European Court of Human Rights to the Russian Constitutional Court.[5]

These actions also provided a warning to the West that the Kremlin might withdraw from that regional body if the Parliamentary Assembly did not restore the voting rights of Russia.[6] Delegations from both chambers of the Russian legislature traveled to Strasbourg to discuss the return of the deputies to the Parliamentary Assembly of the Council of Europe throughout 2016, and at first it seemed that the Council of Europe might restore voting rights by the end of 2017.[7]

However, the movement toward restoration of normal participation in the Council of Europe suffered a setback when another of its bodies, the Committee of Ministers, issued on 3 May 2017 anti–Russian statements about the treatment of inhabitants in Crimea and in Georgia. In response on 30 June 2017 the Foreign Ministry announced the suspension of Russian contributions to the Council of Europe for the rest of the year. Russia also warned that it might not accept the rulings of the European Court of Human Rights on the grounds that its judges were elected without the participation of the Russian delegation to the Parliamentary Assembly.[8]

The EU and the U.S. (even though not a member) brought all possible pressure on the Council of Europe to prevent a first dangerous crack on the united front against the Kremlin over the reunification with Crimea. The West accused Russia of "blackmail," and the violent campaign persuaded the Kremlin to announce in January 2018 that Russia was suspending all payments to the Council of Europe. Because Turkey had done the same, the loss of around a quarter of its budget plunged the regional institution into a precarious financial state.[9]

The other member states did not jump to cover the shortfall in the budget, and as a result during 2018 the Council of Europe became receptive to Russian concerns. Agencies of the Council discussed the discrimination against Russian speakers in the Baltics, and in turn Moscow stated that for the moment it had no intention of leaving the organization. However, Russia held firm to its refusal to pay contributions until its delegates regained full voting rights.[10]

INTERPOL Episode

Russia seemed to be making progress in its campaign to regain full voting rights in the Council of Europe, but the opposition was looking for a way to strike a counterblow. The opportunity came in late 2018 when the presidency of INTERPOL became vacant. According to the traditions of the highest police agency in the world, a system of rotation regulated the succession to the presidency, and it was the turn of the Russian vice president to become the chief of the organization. The member states each had one vote, and they were expected to confirm the nomination of the very well qualified Alexander Prokopchuk.[11]

The news of his confirmation set off a firestorm in the West, and wild accusations flew that Prokopchuk, a seasoned police veteran, intended to subvert the rule of law. For the first time in recent history, American and European officials lobbied member states to vote against the Russian candidate at the annual conference. The U.S. Congress joined the echo chamber with denunciations of Prokopchuk, and a Kremlin had little time to do damage control.[12]

On 21 November 2018 the country delegates voted to elect a less qualified South Korean official to be the next president. Headlines trumpeted the defeat of the Russian candidate, and the success emboldened the enemies of Russia to launch a campaign to expel Russia from INTERPOL. Unrealistic as this ambitious goal was, the drive to isolate Russia was still strong, and the Kremlin needed to prepare to face even more serious attacks.[13]

The European Union, NATO, the Salisbury Incident, and the G7: Blunting Russia

The substantial financial contributions to the Council of Europe bolstered the Kremlin's position in that institution but nothing similar existed to influence the EU and NATO. In the latter case, the presence of the United States made futile attempts to pressure the military alliance, and Russia concentrated its diplomatic efforts on the EU.

European Union

The EU refused to lift sanctions until Russia returned Crimea to Ukraine and halted all support for the rebels in Eastern Ukraine.[14] These rigid demands clashed with two realities emerging by 2016. First, Russia was not invading any European countries, so the accusations about a military threat became less credible with the passage of time. Second, the sanctions the West had imposed on Russia were not crippling the economy. The sanctions drove the Kremlin to adopt protectionist measures, such as the ban on the import of agricultural products. Russia, which was already the world's largest exporter of wheat, received a powerful stimulus to expand its cultivation of fruits and vegetables. To mention another example, the output of dairy products also increased. The real danger existed that the prolongation of the sanctions could institutionalize protectionism in the country to the detriment of world trade.[15]

Countries such as Italy and Cyprus realized the danger of keeping Russia out of international trade, and in early 2016 they began pressing for the lifting of the sanctions. Other countries felt the same way, for example, both houses of the French parliament passed non-binding resolutions calling on the EU to suspend the sanctions.[16]

The EU renewed the sanctions every six months, and just as the meetings to decide upon renewal were about to take place, the Kiev government launched raids and shelled rebel-held territory in Eastern Ukraine. These incidents then served as proof for those opposed to lifting sanctions that Russia was out of control and on a rampage.

A deeper divergence had been present even before the outbreak of the crisis in Ukraine in 2014. The Partnership and Cooperation Agreement (PCA) of 1997 had governed the commercial relationship with Russia, but the agreement was long overdue for revision. In the first decade of the twenty-first century Russia constructed its own institutional arrangements, and the stage of copying European Union formulas was over. Negotiations to find a replacement for PCA dragged on. Russia and the EU agreed that before a new treaty could regulate their economic relations, the country first had to join the WTO and the OECD. Russia joined WTO in 2012 (a prerequisite for OECD membership), but OECD suspended accession talks in March 2014. The EU also halted negotiations on a new treaty to replace the PCA.[17]

The hostility of the EU toward Russia began to soften in 2017, because the

European Union was facing serious threats. When Britain voted to leave the EU on 23 June 2016, this surprise plunged the institution into a crisis; soon other countries were threatening to withdraw or to renegotiate their relationship. Russia reaffirmed its support for a strong EU, an attitude that encouraged many member states to press harder for the repeal of the sanctions against Russia.

The Salisbury Incident

Any tendency to better relations with Russia has coincided with the appearance of some incident to derail the process.[18] It could not have been otherwise in March 2018, when the Salisbury incident occurred in Britain. The former Russian spy Sergei Skripal and his daughter Anna were the victims of an apparent chemical attack. While both survived, British Prime Minister Theresa May accused the Kremlin of their attempted assassination. Her weak government needed to rally public support and also wanted to obtain favorable terms from the EU over Brexit. Likewise the opponents of lifting EU sanctions against Russia needed something, anything, to bolster the false accusation that Russia still posed a military threat to Europe.[19]

In a panicky reaction, 23 countries, mainly EU members, ordered the departure of over 100 Russian diplomats, and the U.S. expelled the largest number of 60. However, even among NATO and EU members not all countries could be stampeded into expulsing Russian diplomats. A sense of suspense gripped television viewers who could watch on scoreboards the tallies of the countries and the number of diplomats expelled. Britain, sensing a favorable moment to strike, proposed boycotting the World Cup set to take place in Moscow during June and July of 2018.[20]

When a British couple in a town near Salisbury also became sick on 30 June, the Theresa May government jumped at the opportunity to keep the issue alive and claimed that they too were victims of the same nerve attack occurring four months earlier in Salisbury. Dawn Sturgess died and the other partner of the couple was left incapacitated, but finding a direct link with the previous poisoning attempt proved difficult. The furor died down and some semblance of sanity started to return to the relations of Russia with the EU.[21]

NATO

The military alliance joined in the uproar over the Salisbury incident. But because the military wielded weapons and not just commercial and financial instruments as did the EU, the generals were more restrained when it came to action. The goal of NATO was to generate as much fear as possible by going near the brink if necessary but never to cross the line into combat. The resurgence of the Russian military in the 2010s had come at a very convenient time for NATO but was not sufficient to fuel real fears. The Russian military had acquired a formidable defense capacity but only limited offensive potential.

In no way had the Russian military replaced the Soviet and Warsaw Pact armies able to overrun Western Europe. The need for a massive NATO staff and its structure of 33 commands was no longer necessary, and their number shriveled to seven.[22] With talk of a "peace dividend" in the 1990s, the military of NATO countries declined in size, and countries such as France abolished the conscription of their citizens. NATO looked with nostalgia at the Cold War years when huge armies stared at each other for decades without having to fire a shot.

For NATO Russia was the ideal opponent, and the military alliance fueled fears among the civilian population in order to secure ample budget allocations. But at the same time, the hostility could not reach the point of an actual shooting war, so NATO officials had to maintain channels to their Russian counterparts to prevent any escalation that could threaten world peace. NATO has been very successful in pulling off this dangerous balancing act.[23]

The first reaction of NATO to the crisis in Crimea was to suspend meetings of the NATO-Russia Council in February 2014. Russia considered withdrawing from the Council as the best response but upon closer reflection left the door open for meetings in a future. The NATO-Russia Council had devoted most of its efforts to revive the Conventional Armed Forces in Europe Treaty (CFE), which Russia had suspended in November 2007. But when the Russian Foreign Ministry announced on 10 March 2015 the complete withdrawal from the CFE Treaty, in retaliation NATO in April limited Russian personnel in headquarters to thirty and placed their movements under police escort.[24]

The need to communicate with Russia forced the West to convene the NATO-Russia Council for the first time in April 2016. Two other meetings followed that year and in later years.[25] The mounting pressure to improve relations with Russia was evident to a NATO more worried about preserving military budgets. The stories of violations of air space and other incursions were wearing thin and no longer scared civilians, and the time had come for the big lie to terrify the public.[26]

Russia had resumed the practice of holding military maneuvers, but at a small fraction of the scale compared to the Soviet period when hundreds of thousands of soldiers and over a dozen divisions had participated. For Zapad 2017 the Russian Defense Ministry in September deployed 12,700 soldiers. This small figure could not scare anybody, and thus secret information was leaked to the *New York Times* and soon broadcast throughout mass media that 100,000 soldiers and 4,000 train loads of tanks and military equipment were headed to Belarus, within easy striking distance of NATO borders.[27] "We are astonished" at the accusations explained Russian officials, but not even the presence of 548 foreign and domestic journalists and extensive television coverage on the official military channel could dispel the myth of the 100,000 figure belonging to the reconstituted First Guards Army.[28]

What Russian diplomats and generals were too embarrassed to admit was that the country lacked the ability to put 100,000 soldiers into one front line and that the First Guards Army had still not taken shape. NATO well knew the limitations of the Russian army, but the military alliance needed the 100,000 figure to terrify the West.[29]

The scare campaign worked, and NATO received additional funding to restore some of its commands and to reverse the decline in its personnel. Russia tired of the antics, and on 22 January 2018 recalled its ambassador to NATO and left the position unfilled.[30] Relations between Russia and NATO could not return to the condition of before Crimea, but the lack of progress did not exclude cracks in the harsh attitude toward Russia.

G7

The expulsion of Russia from the G8 on 23 March 2014 was a psychological blow. This forum was supposed to be an opportunity for world leaders and their cabinet ministers to meet. It did not have a formal staff, and the host country provided the logistical support. The meetings could help to facilitate contacts and discussions, but G8 resembled more an exclusive club rather than a functioning international organization. Boris Yeltsin had craved admission, but Vladimir Putin had always been skeptical about this group.[31]

The strong hostility the Barack Obama administration felt toward Russia blocked any attempts to reconsider the expulsion of Russia from the G7. In January 2017 the

Foreign Ministry stated that Russia had no intention of seeking the return to the G7 because other international forums provided ample opportunity to discuss trade and other economic issues.[32] It thus came as a complete surprise when on 8 June 2018 on the eve of a summit of the G7 in Quebec, Canada, President Donald Trump announced that Russia should return to this body.

The proposal was all the more striking because before in April 2018 the G7 Foreign Ministers had issued one of the routine condemnations of Russia for its "malign behavior" in the world. The Italian Prime Minister seconded Trump's call, but other countries remained opposed. Because French President Emmanuel Macron has been cultivating close ties with Putin, the readmission of Russia remained a real possibility.[33]

Any attempt to use admission into the G7 as a bargaining chip to extract concessions from Russia was doomed to failure. The Kremlin wanted no repetition of the disastrous deal of Boris Yeltsin who exchanged the withdrawal of Russian troops from the Baltic Republics for membership in the G7. However, a Russian refusal to even consider returning to the G7 made the country look petty and vindictive. The Kremlin wanted to avoid another expulsion in the future, but the West refused to give guarantees. The astute solution of Putin was to state a willingness to return but with the condition that China and India also become members: by this proposal Russia made even more cordial its ties with those two countries and also appeared before the world as flexible and willing to engage in negotiations at all levels.[34]

Breakthrough for Russia in the Council of Europe

The first crack in the wall of post–Crimea reprisals against Russia came in the Council of Europe. Russia here enjoyed the good fortune of having a staunch advocate in Thorbjørn Jagland, the Secretary General of the organization. Serving his second five-year term, the Secretary General took determined action to persuade the member states to restore the voting rights of the Russian delegation to the Parliamentary Assembly of the Council of Europe. He made sure that Russia could participate in the other bodies of the Council of Europe. In partial recognition of his tireless efforts, Russia only reduced that part of its contributions corresponding to the Parliamentary Assembly.[35]

Jagland visited the capitals of each of the member states trying to persuade them to restore Russia's full membership in the Parliamentary Assembly. The referendum of 23 June 2016 approving the withdrawal of Britain from the European Union gave him an additional argument. A "Ruxit" from the Council of Europe following on the heels of Brexit threatened the very idea of Europe.[36] The fears about Russian aggression had proven groundless, and the demonization of Russia was proving hard to sustain.

The Parliamentary Assembly seemed ready to restore voting rights to the Russian delegation when the Salisbury poisoning appeared in March 2018 to unleash another wave of anti–Russian hysteria. But as the months wore by, sustaining the anti–Russian frenzy became more difficult. Britain refused to share its evidence on the supposed poisoning, and the accusations appeared as groundless if not a hoax. Even Salisbury residents expressed doubts about the Russian involvement. The turning point came when the relatives of the sole British fatality turned to the Russian embassy in London and wrote a letter to President Vladimir Putin asking for information on the matter because the British authorities had provided nothing.[37]

The unraveling confidence in the handling of the Salisbury incident further undermined the status of British Prime Minister

Theresa May. Countries repaired their relations with a forgiving Russia, while an unexpected boost came from the World Cup held in Moscow from 14 June to 15 July 2018. The Kremlin lifted visa requirements so that sports fans could travel to the country without any restrictions. Visitors were pleased with the warm reception, and many gained a new appreciation for the country. In response to the wishes of many tourists to return to Russia, the Kremlin extended the exemption on requiring visas until December of 2018. The people-to-people contact showed Europeans that the Russians were friendly individuals just trying to cope with the struggles of daily life.[38]

In an attempt to reverse the trend toward normalizing relations with Russia, hostile EU parliamentarians seized upon the naval incident in the Kerch Strait on 25 November 2018. The EU parliament at one point even threatened to repeal the 1997 Partnership and Cooperation Agreement with Russia, but the proposal was so harmful to the economies of the member states that the idea soon floundered. The Parliamentary Assembly joined the latest anti–Kremlin campaign, and on 24 January 2019 culminated its debates by adopting a resolution condemning Russian actions in the Kerch Strait and in Crimea.[39]

Seeing the resolution coming, the Duma suspended all dues payments to the Council of Europe on 17 January 2019. The Founding Charter stipulated that a country qualified for expulsion if after two years it had not paid in full its dues. Russia had stopped paying in June 2017, and the expulsion deadline was fast approaching. The Kremlin announced that Russia would quit the organization before suffering the humiliation of expulsion. Ruxit loomed as a real possibility and as a threat to the very concept of Europe.[40]

The firm hand Russia played gave Secretary General Jagland and sympathetic countries the arguments to defuse the crisis. Die-hard opponents of Russia's return to the organization tried to mobilize support over the Kremlin's decision on 24 April 2019 to issue Russian passports to citizens in the separatist republics of Eastern Ukraine, but this last-ditch effort failed. Countries such as Italy and Hungary all along had been clamoring for Russia's return, and others such as Germany were sympathetic but did not want to take the initiative. Russia had been a major financial supporter of the Council of Europe, and no other country was willing to compensate with additional contributions. The turning point came when French President Emmanuel Macron early in May 2019 spoke in favor of restoring Russia to full membership in the Council of Europe.[41]

Germany then joined France in pushing the measure through the Committee of Ministers, the highest governing body of the Council of Europe. On 17 May of 47 member states, all but five voted to restore voting rights to Russia. Of these the most vociferous was Ukraine, joined by Finland and Lithuania, and these die-hard holdouts promised a bitter fight when the issue came up for a vote in the Parliamentary Assembly. To try to calm the waters, officials explained that the measure did not mean approval for the events in Crimea but was intended to offer protections to the Russians who otherwise would lose the right to appeal judicial decisions to the European Court of Human Rights.[42]

Just as Ukraine had promised, a bitter fight raged inside the Parliamentary Assembly over the proposal to restore full voting rights to Russia. But in spite of all the outrage the vote on 25 June 2019 was not even close, and 118 voted for and 62 against with 10 abstentions. Of the Russian deputies, four were on the sanctions lists over events in Crimea, and others represented Crimea in the Russian Duma. By giving seats to these Crimean deputies, the Council of Europe had legally acknowledged the reality of the reunification of Crimea with Russia. All that the Ukrainian delegation could do was storm out of the hall, but the futility of these protests influenced the new president of Ukraine, Volodymyr Zelensky, to seek an alternative to confrontation as the best way to settle disputes with Russia.[43]

Russia did have the largest number of appeals on Human Rights as was to be expected for the country with the largest population, but in per capita terms the figures were comparable to those of other European states. The question was not so much the validity of the human rights accusations, but whether the return of Russia to full membership in the Council of Europe meant the dismantling of all sanctions and reprisals after the events in Crimea.[44] Was the Russian victory in the Council of Europe just a leaky crack in the dam or the start of the return of Russia to full participation in the European international system?

27

The Rollercoaster of U.S.-Russia Relations

> *Those are internal political games of the U.S. Don't hold the relationship between Russia and the U.S. hostage to this internal political struggle.*—Vladimir Putin[1]

The overwhelming reach of the United States meant that whenever Russia made a move beyond its borders, the Kremlin ran into a real or perceived U.S. interest. Thus, whatever the topic of the chapters in this book, the U.S. was a major player. The preponderance of power was on the side of the U.S., whose military budget was ten times larger than Russia's. The U.S. stationed troops across the globe, in contrast to Russia whose only foreign bases outside the former Soviet Union were in Syria. The U.S. possessed 11 nuclear-powered attack aircraft carriers compared to Russia's single diesel carrier.

The comparisons could go on, but they never quieted the fears of those in the U.S. who viewed any Russian involvement as a direct challenge, if not threat. The Middle East required immediate action, but the U.S. considered Russian intervention in Syria unacceptable. The assumption in Washington was that any Russian encroachment reduced U.S. influence. This view of international relations as a zero-sum game poisoned relations with Russia.

Scaring the American Public

The Opening Shot

The appearance of leaked e-mails from the Democratic National Committee was the final step in the collapse of the presidential bid of Hillary Clinton. In a desperate attempt to salvage the doomed campaign, the U.S. intelligence chief, on 7 October 2016, blamed the Russians for the leaks, but Clinton still lost the presidential election.[2] Self-recrimination rocked the outgoing Obama administration, and officials sought a scapegoat.

FBI director Jim Comey felt a declaration by the Obama administration was sure to be regarded as a partisan statement. But the political pressure was so strong, that the intelligence committee scrambled to compile *Assessing Russian Activities and Intentions in Recent U.S. Elections* for presentation to the public on 6 January 2017.[3] To the great relief of the intelligence community, an earlier report *Russia—Kremlin's TV Seeks to Influence Politics, Fuel Discontent in U.S.* already existed. Reproduced in its entirety as an annex, its seven pages comprised more than half of *Assessing Russian Activities*. Nobody cared about the logical fallacy of using a report of 11 December 2012, or four years before the alleged interference in the 2016 U.S. elections.[4]

Assessing Russian Activities avoided the need to find proof by stating that "We did not make an assessment of the impact that Russian activities had on the outcome of the 2016 election."[5] But this admission raised the question of whether the activities of RT and Sputnik had any impact. *Assessing Russian Activities* "seemed to struggle to describe what, exactly made the Russian outlets' influence on the election, so nefarious [and] provided no detail about how that might have worked."[6]

The assumption of the intelligence community was that RT and Sputnik had blinded Americans until at last *Assessing Russian Activities* appeared to open their eyes. The report made Margarita Simonyan, the chief editor of RT and Sputnik, into the villain of the movie. A photograph in the report showed her standing before a display resembling a war map as she pointed to an approving Putin how the network has been reaching target audiences.[7]

Because the report did not make predictions, *Assessing Russian Activities* could not join the long list of intelligence failures in U.S. history. But it was no less an embarrassment because of its abject submission to the party line. It was shocking to see independent agencies groveling before a presidency already in the last days of its existence. And the accusations against RT and Sputnik had the unintended effect of sparking the curiosity of Americans who had never heard of those news outlets. The intelligence communities had provided more free advertisement than RT and Sputnik could have ever obtained on their own.[8] "There's a hysteria about RT,"[9] and U.S. officials had to perform damage control on the problem they themselves had created.

Muzzling RT and Sputnik

Assessing Russian Activities exposed RT and Sputnik as the real culprits, but the Constitution limited the power of the government to prevent free speech. The government forced RT and Sputnik to register under the Foreign Agents Registration Act, and as foreign entities, they were prohibited from owning stations in the U.S. but could still lease air time from American owners. Sputnik began live broadcasting on FM radio in the Washington, D.C., and Northern Virginia area in June 2017. Later in November 2017 Sputnik also offered AM radio to the same region. In an abusive interpretation of the law, the government then required the owners of stations transmitting Sputnik to file under the Foreign Agents Registration Act. The Washington, D.C., station complied, and in January 2020 another owner began to broadcast radio from Kansas City, Missouri.[10]

Forcing RT and Sputnik to register as foreign agents provoked an immediate reaction from the Kremlin. Up to that time Russia lacked its own Foreign Agents Registration Act, but the legislature closed the gap by adopting similar legislation. The cost and burden of the Russian registration did not stop large firms such as BBC and CNN from operating inside the country but discouraged any new agencies from opening shop in Moscow.[11]

The materials RT submitted for the filing made available to the public for the first time financial information on the company, but the findings were not what U.S. officials wanted to hear. After all the accusations of a media giant drowning the American public in propaganda and having unlimited funds, "RT's budget is laughably tiny"[12] and the two million dollars it spent each month was the sum major networks such as CBS spent in seven hours. RT squeezed into the bottom of the list of the 100 most watched cable channels in the United State.

In March 2018 U.S. officials scored a major victory in their censorship campaign when they used the threat of having to register as a foreign agent to force a small television cable provider to stop transmitting RT in the Washington area. The owner, rather than engage in an expensive court battle, preferred to sell the service to another company that would not transmit any foreign news. In the case of major cable providers, such as Spectrum, the government reached an accommodation. Spectrum could continue to provide

Russian-language services on the correct assumption that Russian immigrants were the viewers. In exchange Spectrum dropped the English-language programs of RT.

The attempts to censor social media were less successful. Facebook agreed to remove 278 accounts traced to a Russian troll farm, but an absolute prohibition on RT and Sputnik seemed improbable. Google seemed to have found a balanced solution when it announced the "de ranking" of RT articles. Although viewers could still request a specific article, a new algorithm meant that a search pushed the RT articles to the end of the listing.[13]

The Maria Butina Episode

It is hard to prove an espionage case without having a person to accuse. In the Anna Chapman episode of 2010, a group of Russian informants provided an easy target for arrest. But in 2017 authorities could not find anybody to detain. Just when all hope of finding a scapegoat seemed lost, on the screen of federal prosecutors popped up Maria Butina, who was also a redhead like Chapman. But there the coincidences stopped. Chapman was a beautiful woman, a valuable quality for her job of real estate agent. Instead the photographs of Butina revealed the girlish look of a woman and did not fit the stereotype of a gorgeous spy who seduced her unsuspecting male victims. The young Russian female was a native of Siberia, and living in that frontier region Butina became a passionate supporter of gun ownership. In Russia, like in the rest of Europe, the state controlled guns ownership, and she wanted to loosen the restrictions by collaboration with pro-gun groups in Russia.[14]

Her enthusiasm was contagious, and soon she found a private sponsor for her quixotic endeavor. Russian gun advocates decided to turn to the National Rifle Association to see how they might learn ways to soften the ban on gun ownership. After meeting with NRA officials in Moscow, Butina went to the U.S. in 2015 to become a graduate student at the American University. Her outgoing personality and engaging conversation made her popular in NRA circles, and with excessive optimism she believed that she could use gun rights to improve relations between the U.S. and Russia.[15]

Like many Americans, she posted photographs of herself carrying big guns on social media, but the fact that she was a Russian caught the attention of American officials. As anti–Russian hysteria swept the U.S., the FBI was under pressure to find somebody to accuse, and the only available candidate for the scapegoat position was the unfortunate Butina. The Senate Committee on Intelligence grilled her in April 2017, and this summons was the first warning that she needed to leave the country. Later that month the FBI raided her apartment on a fishing expedition to try to discover incriminating evidence. At that moment she did hire a lawyer, but still did not want to realize that the feds were out to get her. She refused to flee and in her innocence trusted the fairness of the American criminal justice system.[16]

In July 2017 she was arrested and detained at a prison facility. Under the threat of facing 15 years in prison she plead guilty on 13 December 2018 to lesser charges; in similar cases the usual sentence had been six months in prison.[17] However, the judge did not limit her sentence to time served and imposed 18 months in prison because she "jeopardized our country's national security."[18] Mounting doubts about her guilt contributed to her early release from prison on 25 October 25 2019 on good behavior. U.S. officials escorted her in secret to an Aeroflot airliner for deportation to Moscow, where a crowd showed up at the airport to welcome her home.[19]

The Kremlin and Russian officials denied any official involvement with Butina, but U.S. analysts insisted on constructing the fantasy that her mission followed past practices of the Soviet-era KBG. Even American University, where she had been a student, could not escape attacks, and critics accused its Carmel Institute of Russian Culture and History for being too sympathetic to Russia. Others speculated that she was part of a broad network of seductive agents, but all efforts to locate the rest of the supposed conspirators came up empty-handed. Cold Warriors longed for the revival of the clash with Russia, and for a while the Butina case helped the media to fuel paranoid and unfounded fears about a threat to the U.S.[20]

Open Skies Treaty

In the supercharged atmosphere of anti–Russian hysteria, the prospects for the Open Skies Treaty were not very favorable. Ever since the war in Georgia of August 2008, arguments inside the Consultative Commission had become heated. Even though the original treaty prohibited flights near a border, the U.S. was angry when Russia did not authorize Open Skies flights within 10 kilometers of the border of Georgia.[21]

Another U.S. demand concerned the Russian enclave of Kaliningrad, a small territory surrounded on land by NATO countries. In 2014 Russia limited flights over Kaliningrad to a maximum itinerary of 500 kilometers. As a Western observer noted, "prior to that, surveillance flights wound their way across Kaliningrad, creating havoc for commercial aviation and stressing the air traffic control system."[22] In a sharp reaction, the U.S. threatened to limit flights over the long Hawaiian archipelago to a route no longer than 900 kilometers and also to exclude Russian personnel from two convenient air bases in the continental U.S.[23]

The U.S. was also worried with Russia's shift from film to digital in the cameras. The Consultative Commission had been discussing this transition since 2008. The guiding principle was that the digital technology for cameras had to be available to any of the 34 members of the treaty. For reasons still not clear, the U.S. and the Pentagon dragged their feet about making the conversion. While almost all civilian use of film in the U.S. had disappeared, the Pentagon maintained the venerable tradition of cumbersome, expensive, and sometimes dangerous film.[24]

In 2014 Russia received authorization to use digital technology on its flights over Europe. In February 2016 Russia requested permission to use digital cameras over the U.S. The effective resolution of the cameras remained unchanged at 30 centimeters, less precise than the 25 centimeters available on commercial satellite services such as Google-Earth.[25]

When a Russian observation plane on 9 August 2017 flew over Washington, D.C., and photographed the Capitol, the White House, and the Pentagon, this was too much for American legislators. The Defense Appropriation Law of August 2018 forbade the expenditures of public funds on the Open Skies program unless the president first certified that Russia complied with all American wishes. In effect the U.S. Congress had given the Trump administration the loaded gun to destroy the treaty. When on 10 September the Pentagon refused to certify the equipment aboard a Russian plane, it seemed that the end of the treaty was at hand.[26]

Less than a week later, on 18 September 2018 the U.S. reversed itself and cleared the Russian plane to conduct overflights. Russia reciprocated and on 21 February 2019 the U.S. conducted its first flight over Russia in over a year. On 25 April 2019 Russia also flew over the U.S.[27] To the dismay of European countries, the U.S. on 21 May 2020 gave the required notification of six months to withdraw. Sensing an opening to continue improving relations with the Europeans, Moscow reaffirmed its commitment to the Open Skies Treaty on the condition that they did not share the photographs with the U.S. Because the Europeans failed to provide guarantees, Russia on 15 January 2021 gave the six months' notice to withdraw. Unless the Joe Biden administration rejoins, the Open Skies Treaty will expire in June 2021.[28]

U.S. Hostility to Russia

Long before Donald Trump was elected president, he had spoken many times in favor of improving relations with Russia. His statements during the electoral campaign encouraged some Moscow officials to believe that should he become president, a slim chance existed of at least halting the deterioration in relations with the United States. The surprise victory of Trump fueled hopes for closer relations, even though scholars such as Stephen Cohen warned that the foreign policy establishment was not going to give the new president any room to maneuver. Even before Trump had taken office insistent rumors already were circulating that he planned to reach a Yalta 2.0 agreement carving up the world into respective spheres of influence.[29]

Many influential circles in the United States have continued to believe that Trump was an agent of Russia and that his "handler" was none other than Vladimir Putin. It was only a small step from that myth to the accusation that he had colluded with the Kremlin to steal the presidential election from an innocent Hillary Clinton. The charge of collusion was so hard to prove that even the Mueller Report could not conclusively say that the Trump campaign had directly conspired with Russia to win the 2016 presidential election.

After Election Day it has been normal practice for representatives of foreign governments to approach influential persons around the president-elect to see what sort of policy their countries could expect in the future. But in the supercharged atmosphere after November 2016, both Democrats and the media depicted any contact between Trump officials and the Russian government in the most sinister light. In these treacherous and uncharted waters Trump's first national security advisor, former General Michael Flynn, was caught in the rip tide, and had to resign on 13 February 2017 even before he could complete his first month in office.[30]

The hope shifted to Rex Tillerson, whom Trump nominated to be his first Secretary of State. The former head of Exxon-Mobil, Tillerson had extensive contacts with Russia through the oil business, and in the past he had made statements sympathetic to the Kremlin. The U.S. Senate would have none of it, and senators grilled him. It became clear that he needed to announce very hostile anti–Russian views if he did not want to put at risk his confirmation.[31]

Once he became Secretary of State, Tillerson forgot all his previous pro–Russian statements and joined the chorus of those demanding the harshest reprisals against the Kremlin. Tillerson clashed with the administration, and the president grew frustrated with him. On 31 March 2018, barely a year after taking office, he stepped down as secretary of state.[32]

Russia became the common enemy for both political parties. Congress felt that the sanctions the outgoing Obama administration had imposed on Russia were too weak and both houses passed a harsher bill. The president had no choice but to sign the bill into law on 2 August 2017, although he did explain that some of the clauses were unconstitutional and pledged court action to halt their implementation.[33]

The normal pattern became to have Congress and Western media press for harsh action against Russia while Trump tried to minimize or delay any hostile steps. It would be wearisome for the reader to run through the full list of reprisals, and some examples suffice to capture the spirit of the moment. The August 2017 law called for the U.S. government to issue a list of wealthy Russians and political figures as a first step toward leveraging those individuals to turn against the Putin presidency. The Treasury

Department complied and issued the "Kremlin list" in the last days of January 2018. A few individuals were already under the U.S. sanctions approved after the reunification with Crimea in 2014, and over the coming year the U.S. Treasury began to impose sanctions on many of these individuals.[34]

While the sanctions caused disruptions in the foreign activities of some Russian firms, the attempt to leverage the Putin administration through the billionaires was a failure. Rather than a source of shame, appearing in the list became a badge of honor and absence from the list could well lead to questioning their loyalty to Russia.[35] Prime Minister Dmitry Medvedev even joked that "in this case not being included on this list provides grounds for resignation."[36]

Western media kept up a steady barrage of anti–Russian news and was on the lookout for any indication that the Kremlin had Trump in its pocket. To the disappointment of the media and Democrats, the Mueller Report found no concrete evidence of a conspiracy between Trump officials and the Kremlin. And in a sharp break with *Assessing Russian Activities* and congressional reports, the Mueller Report of March 2019 no longer blamed RT and Sputnik.

Both Trump and the Kremlin tried to use the Mueller Report to bury the accusations against Russia, but the task was hopeless. The anti–Russian forces did not even allow the American president to have a constructive conversation with Putin when the two world leaders held a private meeting during the G-20 Summit in Osaka, Japan. The media wanted Trump to accuse Putin of having meddled in the U.S. elections, but the media-savvy American president laughed off the matter when, in front of cameras, he told Putin, "don't meddle in the elections."[37]

Again the U.S. Congress was obsessed with imposing additional sanctions on Russia, and President Trump tried to delay as long as possible. On 1 August 2019, under massive congressional pressure, he signed the executive order imposing new sanctions, even though he knew this measure was bad for the United States. To try to soften the blow, he telephoned Putin the day before to offer U.S. assistance in the wildfires raging across vast areas of Siberia. The gracious Russian ruler realized the tightrope his counterpart was having to walk, and rather than say no to the offer of aid, Putin replied that for the moment the agencies in Russia were able to handle the natural disaster, but should some specialized equipment prove necessary, he would contact the American president again.[38]

Anti-Russian hysteria in the foreign policy establishment prevented President Trump from reaching agreement with the Kremlin on many of the world's problems. Europe, because of its proximity to Russia and its large economic ties, has become more receptive to restoring close relations with the Kremlin. The Russian delegation returned to the Parliamentary Assembly of the Council of Europe in June 2019, and this important step marked the start of a long journey toward full reintegration. When the Covid-19 struck the world, the Kremlin dispatched a cargo plane full of much needed medical supplies to New York in April 2020. The hope was that this friendly gesture might persuade the United States to support the efforts of the American president to improve relations with Russia.

The U.S. withdrawal from the Open Skies Treaty was a strong indicator that the Trump administration was no less harsh on Russia than the U.S. Congress. In both Open Skies Treaty and New START the executive branch used its freedom of action to pursue adversarial policies toward Russia.

Since 2010 New START limited nuclear warheads and delivery vehicles of the U.S. and Russia, but the treaty was set to expire on 5 February 2021. Its clauses provided for a five-year renewal, but rather than a fast notification, the Trump administration wanted to score a diplomatic victory to take to the 2020 presidential election and pressed Russia to renegotiate the agreement. When Russia insisted on the five-year renewal, the Trump administration offered a one-year extension. Matters dragged until the new president Joe Biden in a conversation with Putin on 24 January 2021 agreed to the extension for five years. In the U.S. the executive branch on its own could renew the treaty, and in Russia the parliament unanimously gave its approval. Few believed that an era of friendship was about to begin under the new president, but the positive action about New START suggested that the Biden administration wanted to avoid a deterioration of relations with Russia.[39]

Chapter Notes

Chapter 1

1. Robert M. Gates, *Duty: Memoirs of a Secretary at War* (New York: Alfred A. Knopf, 2014), p. 158.
2. Igor S. Ivanov, *The New Russian Diplomacy* (Washington, D.C.: Brookings Institution, 2002), pp. 21–23. For a brief account of the rapprochement with China, See, René De La Pedraja, *The Russian Military Resurgence: Post-Soviet Decline and Rebuilding, 1992–2018* (Jefferson, NC: McFarland, 2018), pp. 43–44.
3. Yevgenia Albats, *Mina zamedlennogo deistviia: politicheskii portret KGB* (Moscow: Russlit, 1992), appendix of KGB documents.
4. Christopher Andrew and Vasili Mitrokhin, *The World Was Going Our Way: The KGB and the Battle for the Third World* (New York: Basic Books, 2005), Ch. 20; Yevgenia Albats, *The State within a State; The KGB and Its Hold on Russia* (New York: Farrar, Straus, Giroux, 1994), pp. 43–49.
5. Yuri M. Baturi, et al., *Epokha Yeltsina: ocherki politicheskoi istorii* (Moscow: VAGRIUS, 2001), p. 469; René De La Pedraja, *The United States and the Armed Forces of Mexico, Central America, and the Caribbean, 2000–2014* (Jefferson, NC: McFarland, 2014), pp. 240–243.
6. Baturi et al., *Epokha Yeltsina*, pp. 467–473; Timothy J. Colton, *Yeltsin: A Life* (New York: Basic Books, 2008), Ch. 9.
7. "Yeltsin Abolishes Soviet Foreign Ministry," 19 December 1991, Reuters; Jeff Checkel, "Russian Foreign Policy: Back to the Future," *RFE/RL Research Report*, 16 October 1992; Suzanne Crow, "Personnel Changes in the Russian Foreign Ministry," Draft Research Report, Radio Free Europe/Radio Liberty, April 1992, John B. Dunlop Collection, Box 6, Hoover Institution Archives, Stanford, California (henceforth Dunlop-Hoover).
8. "Russian Embassy in Washington Still Mostly Soviet," 17 January 1992, NCA/Sonia Winter; Crow, "Personnel Changes in the Russian Foreign Ministry," April 1992; Suzanne Crow, "Russia's Foreign Policy Course," Draft Research Paper, Radio Free Europe/Radio Liberty, 27 January 1992, Box 6, Dunlop-Hoover; "Churkin Says Russia Taking over All Soviet Embassies," 3 January 1992, NCA/AP.
9. Crow, "Personnel Changes in the Russian Foreign Ministry," April 1992; Crow, "Russia's Foreign Policy Course," 27 January 1992; Checkel, "Russian Foreign Policy."
10. Crow, "Personnel Changes in the Russian Foreign Ministry," April 1992; Baturi et al., *Epokha Yeltsina*, pp. 480–481.
11. "Президент Анголы принял Министра Иностранных Дел России," 27 February 1992, Kutschem; "Андрей Козырев выразил удовлетворение итогами визита в Анголу," 27 February 1992, Itar-Tass; Checkel, "Russian Foreign Policy."
12. "Soviet Forces Leaving Camranh Bay," 14 September 1991, AFP; "Russia to Open Talks on Camranh Bay Withdrawal," 23 January 1992, Reuter.
13. De La Pedraja, *Russian Military Resurgence*, p. 237.
14. *Baltimore Sun*, 18 January 1992.
15. "Cuba Slams Russian Betrayal at Rights Commission," 29 February 1992, Reuter; Crow, "Russia's Foreign Policy Course," 27 January 1992.
16. "Warsaw and Moscow Locked in Bitter Dispute about Withdrawal of Soviet Troops," *New York Times*, 23 February 1992.
17. "Poland, Russia Agree on Key Point in Troop Pullout," 21 February 1992, NCA/AP; "Warsaw and Moscow Locked in Bitter Dispute about Withdrawal of Soviet Troops," *New York Times*, 23 February 1992.
18. "Гранданский комитет […] вопрос о возвращении финляндии территорий," 5 February 1992; "De-Finlandizing Finland," 17 February 1992, B-Wire; "Return of Karelia: Not Now, Maybe Later," Cable from U.S. Embassy, Helsinki, 16 October 1991, U.S. State Department, Freedom of Information Act (henceforth State-FOIA); "Most Finns Want Karelia Back—Poll," 10 February 1992, B-Wire.
19. "Return of Karelia: Not Now, Maybe Later," Cable from U.S. Embassy, Helsinki, 16 October 1991, State-FOIA; "Finnish President Halonen's June 7 Meeting with Russian President Putin," Cable from U.S. Embassy, Helsinki, 12 June 2000, Wikileaks.
20. "Виталии Чуркин провел брифинг по текущим вопросам международной политики," 2 March 1992, Pirogovs; Suzanne Crow, "Russia's Foreign Policy Course," 27 January 1992, Radio Free Europe/Radio Liberty.
21. De La Pedraja, *Russian Military Resurgence*, pp. 250–251.
22. "Japanese-Russian Talks on Kuriles," 12 February 1992, A-Wire.
23. Baturi et al., *Epokha Yeltsina*, p. 474; Angela

Stent, *Putin's World: Russia against the West and with the Rest* (New York: Twelve, 2019), pp. 244–246.

24. Ronald D. Asmus, *Opening NATO's Door: How the Alliance Remade Itself for a New Era* (New York: Columbia University Press, 2002), pp. 11, 309.

25. Arms Control Association, "The Conventional Armed Forces in Europe (CFE) Treaty," 1 August 2012; Anne Witkowsky, Sherman Garnett, and Jeff McCausland, *Salvaging the Conventional Armed Forces in Europe Treaty Regime: Options for Washington* (Washington, D.C.: Brookings Arms Control Series, 2010), pp. 1–2.

26. Vojtech Mastny, Malcom Byrne, and Magdalena Klotzbach, eds., *Cardboard Castle? An Inside History of the Warsaw Pact* (Budapest: Central European University Press, 2005), pp. 665–683; "Warsaw Pact Alliance to Dissolve on April 1, Moscow Announces," *Washington Post*, 13 February 1991.

27. Yevgeny Primakov, *Russian Crossroads: Toward the New Millennium* (New Haven: Yale University Press, 2004), pp. 128–130. Primakov stated that with regard to NATO expansion, "unfortunately, Gorbachev and Shevardnadze were indifferent to this issue," Memorandum of Conversation of 15 July 1996, State-FOIA.

28. "NATO Expansion: What Gorbachev Heard," National Security Archive; Pavel Stroilov, "Revealed: The Kremlin Files that Prove that NATO Never Betrayed Russia," *The Spectator*, 6 September 2014, has the same idea but slightly different wording.

29. Primakov, *Russian Crossroads*, pp. 129–130; Stroilov, "Kremlin Files."

Chapter 2

1. Dmitry Volkogonov to Boris Yeltsin, 1 April 1994, Dmitry Volkogonov Papers, Box 7, Library of Congress, Washington, D.C. (henceforth Volkogonov).

2. The signing of the Brasilia Treaty between Peru and Ecuador in 1998 can be interpreted as ending the last of the major territorial disputes among the countries of the former Spanish Empire in America. However, minor disputes still exist, such as Colombia with Nicaragua and Venezuela. For Peru and Ecuador, See, René De La Pedraja, *Wars of Latin America, 1982–2013: The Path to Peace* (Jefferson, NC: McFarland, 2013), pp. 183–188. In a whole different legal category are the still ongoing conflicts over the boundaries between the successor states of the Spanish Empire and foreign powers, most notably Britain.

3. Vicken Cheterian, *War and Peace in the Caucasus: Ethnic Conflict and the New Geopolitics* (New York: Columbia University Press, 2008), pp. 285–289; Thomas de Waal, *The Caucasus: An Introduction* (New York: Oxford University Press, 2010), pp. 87–97.

4. Charles King, *The Moldovans: Romania, Russia, and the Politics of Culture* (Stanford: Hoover Institute Press, 1999), pp. 189–191; René De La Pedraja, *The Russian Military Resurgence: Post-Soviet Decline and Rebuilding 1992–2018* (Jefferson, NC: McFarland, 2018), pp. 91–93.

5. King, *Moldovans*, pp. 191–195; De La Pedraja, *Russian Military Resurgence*, p. 92; "Official-Informal," Secret Cable from Secretary of State, 18 October 2000, U.S. State Department, Freedom of Information Act (henceforth State-FOIA).

6. King, *Moldovans*, pp. 192–194, 196; William H. Hill, *Russia, the Near Abroad, and the West: Lessons from the Moldova-Transdniestria Conflict* (Washington, D.C.: Woodrow Wilson Center Press, 2012, pp. 52–60; De La Pedraja, *Russian Military Resurgence*, pp. 93–94.

7. King, *Moldovans*, pp. 98–102, 181–188; Hill, *Moldova Conflict*, pp. 48–49; De La Pedraja, *Russian Military Resurgence*, pp. 89, 91–92.

8. Hill, *Moldova Conflict*, pp. 53–54; King, *Moldovans*, p. 206.

9. "Official-Informal," Secret Cable from Secretary of State, 18 October 2000, State-FOIA; De La Pedraja, *Russian Military Resurgence*, p. 94; Hill, *Moldova Conflict*, pp. 55–56.

10. "Official-Informal," Secret Cable from Secretary of State, 18 October 2000, State-FOIA; "Transnistria–Life in a Russian Bear Hug," Moments in U.S. Diplomatic History, internet; De La Pedraja, *Russian Military Resurgence*, p. 94; Dov Lynch, *La Russie face à l'Europe* (Paris: Institut d'Études de Sécurité, 2003), p. 42.

11. "The Export of Russian Weapons from Transnistria Will Resume from October 3," 1 October 2002, Grani.Ru; De La Pedraja, *Russian Military Resurgence*, p. 94; Hill, *Moldova Conflict*, pp. 52, 55–56; "Transnistria–Life in a Russian Bear Hug," Moments in U.S. Diplomatic History.

12. This paragraph and the next draw on de Waal, *The Caucasus*, pp. 38–40, 60–66; Frederick Coene, *The Caucasus: An Introduction* (London: Routledge, 2010), pp. 122, 126, 131–134.

13. Richard H. Ullman, *Britain and the Russian Civil War* (Princeton: Princeton University Press, 1968), p. 334.

14. de Waal, *The Caucasus*, p. 67; Ullman, *Britain and the Russian Civil War*, p. 231. The British withdrawal was not unilateral, and in the imperial tradition of negotiating spheres of influence, London in the treaty of 16 March 1921 recognized that Russia was the preponderant power in the former territories of the tsarist empire. In exchange Moscow "refrains from any attempt by military or diplomatic or any other form of action or propaganda to encourage any of the peoples of Asia in any form of hostile action against British interests or the British Empire, especially in India and in the Independent State of Afghanistan." "Trade Agreement between His Britannic Majesty's Government and the Government of the Russian Socialist Federal Soviet Republic," London, 16 March 1921, *The American Journal of International Law* 16(1922): 141–147.

15. "Shevardnadze's Number Two Ioseliani: An Ally, But Is He a Democrat?" Cable from U.S. Embassy, Tbilisi, 2 June 1992, State-FOIA; de Waal, *The Caucasus*, p. 138.

16. War-ravaged Tskhinvali could not receive the refugees, and most ended up at North Ossetia in the Russian Federation; the presence of these refugees

fueled clashes with the Ingush; See, De La Pedraja, *Russian Military Resurgence*, p. 113 and a longer account in Valery Tishkov, *Ethnicity, Nationalism and Conflict in and after the Soviet Union: The Mind Aflame* (Oslo: International Peace Research Institute, 1997), pp. 163–164.

17. "Об обстанобке в Юго-Осетинской автономной области," Moscow, 19 March 1991, Fond 89, Opis 22, Delo 66, Herbert Hoover Institution Archives, Stanford, California; Coene, *Caucasus*, pp. 155–156; de Waal, *The Caucasus*, pp. 134–135.

18. Confidential Report to Boris Yeltsin, 1992, Box 7, Volkogonov; De La Pedraja, *Russian Military Resurgence*, p. 102.

19. Проблемы вывода грузинских войск из Абхазии," *Report*, 7 June 1993, Box 3, folder 14, Joan Eichrodt Papers, Herbert Hoover Institution Archives, Stanford, California (henceforth Eichrodt–Hoover); Cheterian, *War and Peace in the Caucasus*, pp. 187, 191–192; "Battle of Sukhumi (1992)," 29 December 2019, Wikipedia.

20. "Vladislav Ardzinba: Historian Who Became the First President of Abkhazia," *The Independent*, 18 April 2010; "Vladislav Ardzinba, Once Led Abkhazia, Dies at 64," *New York Times*. 5 March 2010.

21. "War in Abkhazia (1992–1993)," 10 April 2020, Wikipedia; "Chronicle: Cease Fire and Its Consequences," Box 8, Eichrodt–Hoover; De La Pedraja, *Russian Military Resurgence*, p. 103.

22. de Waal, *The Caucasus*, pp. 161–162; Cheterian, *War and Peace in the Caucasus*, p. 197; Neal Ascherson, *Black Sea* (New York: Hill and Wang, 1995), pp. 253–255; The Union of the Women of Abkhazia, "War in Abkhazia: Illustrative Examples of Breaching of Principles of Humanity," Gudauta, 23 March 1993, Box 8, Eichrodt–Hoover; Confidential Report to Boris Yeltsin, 1992, Box 7, Volkogonov.

23. Cheterian, *War and Peace in the Caucasus*, pp. 195–196; de Waal, *The Caucasus*, p. 161; Union of Women of Abkhazia, "War in Abkhazia." As late as May 1993 Georgian officials were still talking about the annihilation of the entire Abkhazian people; See, "Speech made by T. Nadareishvili. Broadcasted by the Georgian Radio," 13 May 1993, Box 8, Eichrodt–Hoover.

24. "Abkhaz Leader Ardzinba on Negotiations with Georgia," Cable from Secretary of State, Washington, D.C., 18 March 1994, and "Crisis in Abkhazia; Russian Options and U.S. Interests," Cable from U.S. Embassy, Moscow, 9 October 1992, State-FOIA; Cheterian, *War and Peace in the Caucasus*, pp. 192, 195.

25. "Russia, Georgia, Abkhazia: The View from the South," Cable from U.S. Embassy, Tbilisi, 28 December 1992, State-FOIA; "Battle of Gagra," 10 April 2020, Wikipedia; "War in Abkhazia (1992–1993)," 10 April 2020, Wikipedia.

26. "Crisis in Abkhazia; Russian Options and U.S. Interests," Cable from U.S. Embassy, Moscow, 9 October 1992, State-FOIA; Confidential Report to Boris Yeltsin, 1992, Box 7, Volkogonov.

27. "Crisis in Abkhazia; Russian Options and U.S. Interests," Cable from U.S. Embassy, Moscow, 9 October 1992, State-FOIA; "Russian Ambassador Speaks about Abkhazian Crisis," Cable from U.S. Embassy, Moscow, 22 January 1993, State-FOIA; "War in Abkhazia (1992–1993)," 10 April 2020, Wikipedia.

28. "Crisis in Abkhazia; Russian Options and U.S. Interests," Cable from U.S. Embassy, Moscow, 9 October 1992; "Russian Ambassador Speaks about Abkhazian Crisis," Cable from U.S. Embassy, Tbilisi, 22 January 1993, State-FOIA.

29. "War in Abkhazia (1992–1993)," 10 April 2020, Wikipedia; De La Pedraja, *Russian Military Resurgence*, p. 104.

30. "Abkhaz Leader Ardzinba on Negotiations with Georgia," Cable from Secretary of State, Washington, D.C., 18 March 1994, State-FOIA.

31. "The Russian Ministry of Foreign Affairs on Abkhazia, Yeltsin's Meetings, and Russian-Georgian Relations," Cable from U.S. Embassy, Moscow, 27 August 1993, State-FOIA.

32. "The Russian Ministry of Foreign Affairs on Abkhazia, Yeltsin's Meetings, and Russian-Georgian Relations," Cable from U.S. Embassy, Moscow, 27 August 1993, State-FOIA; Cheterian, *War and Peace in the Caucasus*, pp. 333–334.

33. "The Russian Ministry of Foreign Affairs on Abkhazia, Yeltsin's Meetings, and Russian-Georgian Relations," Cable from U.S. Embassy, Moscow, 27 August 1993, State-FOIA.

34. de Waal, *The Caucasus*, p. 163; "Battle of Gagra," 10 April 2020, Wikipedia; "War in Abkhazia (1992–1993)," 10 April 2020, Wikipedia.

35. "Russian Deputy Foreign Minister Pastukhov on Georgia/Abkhazia," Cable from U.S. Embassy, Geneva, 12 January 1994, State-FOIA; "Проблемы вывода грузинских войск из Абхазии," *Report*, 7 June 1993, Box 3, folder 14, Eichrodt–Hoover.

36. "Russian Deputy Foreign Minister Pastukhov on Georgia/Abkhazia," Cable from U.S. Embassy, Geneva, 12 January 1994, State-FOIA.

37. The State Department even ignored the well-reasoned recommendation of the U.S. Embassy in Moscow to create a peacekeeping force under UN mandate. See "Peacekeeping in the Caucasus," Cable from U.S. Embassy, Moscow, 24 June 1994, State-FOIA.

38. Cheterian, *War and Peace in the Caucasus*, pp. 210, 335; de Waal, *Caucasus*, p. 166; "War in Abkhazia (1998)," 5 January 2020, Wikipedia.

39. Ronald Grigor Suny, *The Revenge of the Past: Nationalism, Revolution, and the Collapse of the Soviet Union* (Stanford: Stanford University Press, 1993), p. 133; Cheterian, *War and Peace in the Caucasus*, pp. 92, 94; Coene, *Caucasus*, pp. 146–147.

40. "Karabakh Is Still the Issue in Yerevan and Baku," Cable from U.S. Embassy, Moscow, 11 April 1989, State-FOIA; Cheterian, *War and Peace in the Caucasus*, pp. 101, 110–111; Coene, *Caucasus*, pp. 146–147.

41. Taline Papazian, "State at War, State in War: The Nagorno-Karabakh Conflict and State-Making in Armenia, 1991–1996," *The Journal of Power Institutions in Post-Soviet Societies*, Issue 8, 2008, par. 25; Cheterian, *War and Peace in the Caucasus*, p. 111; de Waal, *The Caucasus*, pp. 109–110.

42. Paul B. Hanze, *The Transcaucasus in Transition* (Santa Monica, CA: RAND, 1991), p. 9.

43. Suny, *The Revenge of the Past*, pp. 135–136; "Karabakh Is Still the Issue in Yerevan and Baku," Cable from U.S. Embassy, Moscow, 11 April 1989, State-FOIA; Cheterian, *War and Peace in the Caucasus*, pp. 113, 121; Coene, *Caucasus*, p. 147.

44. "Nagorno-Karabakh: The View from Yerevan," Cable from U.S. Embassy, Yerevan, 4 March 1992, State-FOIA; Charles King, *The Ghost of Freedom: A History of the Caucasus* (New York: Oxford University Press, 2008), pp. 213–214; Cheterian, *War and Peace in the Caucasus*, p. 122. The war over Nagorno-Karabakh paralleled the Chaco War in South America: while Bolivia wanted to keep the distant Chaco, for underdog Paraguay the war was a struggle for the survival of its nationality. These two examples of Armenia and Paraguay also help to give meaning to the difficult concept of Jean-Jacques Rousseau about the "General Will." For the Chaco War, See René De La Pedraja, *Wars of Latin America, 1899–1941* (Jefferson, NC: McFarland, 2006), chapters 12 and 13.

45. "Nagorno-Karabakh: Flashpoint yet Again?" Cable from U.S. Embassy, Moscow, 5 September 1991, State-FOIA; "Continuing Caucasus Unrest Threatens Prospects for Development, Cooperation," Cable from U.S. Embassy, Moscow, 13 December 1991, State-FOIA; "Secretary of State Visit to Former Soviet Union: Unrest in the Caucasus," Cable from U.S. Embassy, Moscow, 13 December 1991, State-FOIA; "Armenia-Azerbaijan: Turkey May Enter the Fray," Cable from U.S. Embassy, Moscow, 21 May 1992, State–FOIA; William E. Odom, *The Collapse of the Soviet Military* (New Haven, CT: Yale University Press, 1998), p. 357.

46. Cheterian, *War and Peace in the Caucasus*, pp. 129, 134, 151; de Waal, *The Caucasus*, pp. 113–114; "Nagorno-Karabakh: The View from Yerevan," Cable from U.S. Embassy, Yerevan, 4 March 1992, State-FOIA; "Armenia-Azerbaijan: Turkey May Enter the Fray," Cable from U.S. Embassy, Moscow, 21 May 1992, State–FOIA.

47. "Continuing Caucasus Unrest Threatens Prospects for Development, Cooperation," Cable from U.S. Embassy, Moscow, 13 December 1991, henceforth State-FOIA; Henze, *Transcaucasus in Transition*, p. 9.

48. "Secretary of State Visit to Former Soviet Union: Unrest in the Caucasus," Cable from U.S. Embassy, Moscow, 13 Dec 1991, State-FOIA; Papazian, "Nagorno-Karabakh Conflict," par. 25; Cheterian, *War and Peace in the Caucasus*, pp. 135, 145; de Waal, *The Caucasus*, p. 114.

49. "Current Situation in Nagorno-Karabakh," Cable from U.S. Secretary of State, Washington, D.C., 3 March 1992, State-FOIA; "Nagorno-Karabakh: The View from Yerevan," Cable from U.S. Embassy, Yerevan, 4 March 1992, State-FOIA; King, *History of the Caucasus*, p. 216; Cheterian, *War and Peace in the Caucasus*, pp. 88, 126–128.

50. "Current Situation in Nagorno-Karabakh," Cable from U.S. Secretary of State, Washington, D.C., 3 March 1992, State-FOIA; "Nagorno-Karabakh: The View from Yerevan," Cable from U.S. Embassy, Yerevan, 4 March 1992, State-FOIA; Papazian, "Nagorno-Karabakh Conflict," par. 23; Cheterian, *War and Peace in the Caucasus*, pp. 87–88, 127–128, 133–134.

51. "CSCE Involvement in Nagorno-Karabakh," Cable from U.S. Embassy, Vienna, 5 February 1992, State-FOIA; "Nagorno-Karabakh Crisis: Following up on the CSCE Agreement," Cable from Secretary of State, Washington, D.C., 28 March 1992, State-FOIA; "History of the Nagorno-Karabakh Conflict," 2000, State-FOIA; Cheterian, *War and Peace in the Caucasus*, p. 321; William H. Hill, *No Place for Russia: European Security Institutions since 1989* (New York: Columbia University Press, 2018), p. 70.

52. "Ter-Petrosyan Fights Uphill Battle for Moderate Policy on Nagorno-Karabakh," Cable from U.S. Embassy, Yerevan, 10 July 1992, State-FOIA; Cheterian, *War and Peace in the Caucasus*, pp. 137–138

53. Papazian, "Nagorno-Karabakh Conflict," par. 20–21; Cheterian, *War and Peace in the Caucasus*, pp. 129, 137; De La Pedraja, *Russian Military Resurgence*, pp. 12–14.

54. Cheterian, *War and Peace in the Caucasus*, pp. 141–142; de Waal, *The Caucasus*, pp. 122–123.

55. Cheterian, *War and Peace in the Caucasus*, pp. 141–142; de Waal, *The Caucasus*, pp. 122–123; Coene, *Caucasus*, p. 147.

56. Dmitry Volkogonov to Boris Yeltsin, 21 February 1994, Box 7, Volkogonov; "Ambassador Meets with Acting Foreign Minister," Cable from U.S. Embassy, Yerevan, 29 May 1993, and "Peacekeeping in the Caucasus," Cable from U.S. Embassy, Moscow, 24 June 1994, State-FOIA; Cheterian, *War and Peace in the Caucasus*, p. 142; de Waal, *The Caucasus*, p. 124.

57. "Relations with Turkey and Internal Socio-Economic Problems," Cable from U.S. Embassy, Yerevan, 16 November 1992, State-FOIA; "Scene Setter for CODEL Levin's Visit to Armenia," Cable from U.S. Embassy, Yerevan, 11 November 1998, State-FOIA; Congressional Research Service, "Armenia: Unexpected Change in Government," 5 May 1998, Wikileaks; Cheterian, *War and Peace in the Caucasus*, p. 88.

58. "Scene Setter for CODEL Levin's Visit to Armenia," Cable from U.S. Embassy, Yerevan, 11 November 1998, State-FOIA; Congressional Research Service, "Armenia: Unexpected Change in Government," 5 May 1998, Wikileaks; "Armenia Leader's Candle Fades," *New York Times*, 9 February 1998; Cheterian, *War and Peace in the Caucasus*, pp. 324–325.

59. Papazian, "Nagorno-Karabakh Conflict," par. 25; See chapter 18.

60. "Scene Setter for CODEL Levin's Visit to Armenia," Cable from U.S. Embassy, Yerevan, 11 November 1998, State-FOIA; Papazian, "Nagorno-Karabakh Conflict," par. 25; See chapter 18.

Chapter 3

1. Niccolò Machiavelli, *Discorsi sopra la prima deca di Tito Livio* (Milan: Biblioteca Universale Rizzoli, 1984), p. 316. Translation by Beatriz De La Pedraja.

2. This paragraph and the next draw on Vicken Cheterian, *War and Peace in the Caucasus: Ethnic Conflict and the New Geopolitics* (New York: Columbia University Press, 2008), pp. 109–110, and Frederick Coene, *The Caucasus: An Introduction* (London: Routledge, 2010), p. 142. For a full scholarly account of the origins of the war, See, John B. Dunlop, *Russia Confronts Chechnya: Roots of a Separatist Conflict* (New York: Cambridge University Press, 1998.

3. This paragraph and the next draw on Cheterian, *War and Peace in the Caucasus*, pp. 245–246, René De La Pedraja, *The Russian Military Resurgence: Post-Soviet Decline and Rebuilding, 1992-2018* (Jefferson, NC: McFarland, 2019), p. 110, and Timothy J. Colton, *Yeltsin: A Life* (New York: Basic Books, 2008), p. 226.

4. This paragraph and the next draw on Cheterian, *War and Peace in the Caucasus*, pp. 245–246; De La Pedraja, *Russian Military Resurgence*, p. 112.

5. Cheterian, *War and Peace in the Caucasus*, pp. 246–247; De La Pedraja, *Russian Military Resurgence*, pp. 113–114; Coene, *Caucasus*, p. 142; Colton, *Yeltsin*, pp. 288–289.

6. Cheterian, *War and Peace in the Caucasus*, pp. 245–246.

7. De La Pedraja, *Russian Military Resurgence*, p. 114; Cheterian, *War and Peace in the Caucasus*, pp. 251–252; Colton, *Yeltsin*, p. 290.

8. Andrei Saldatov and Irina Borogan, *The New Nobility: The Restoration of Russia's Security State and the Enduring Legacy of the KGB* (New York: Public Affairs, 2010), pp. 15–17; De La Pedraja, *Russian Military Resurgence*, pp. 114–116.

9. Cheterian, *War and Peace in the Caucasus*, pp. 256–247; De La Pedraja, *Russian Military Resurgence*, pp. 116–117.

10. "Guidance for Discussion of the Vice President's Visit to Russia," Cable from Secretary of State, Washington, D.C., 21 December 1994, U.S. State Department, Freedom of Information Act (henceforth State-FOIA).

11. Strobe Talbott, *The Russia Hand: A Memoir of Presidential Diplomacy* (New York: Random House, 2003), pp. 149–151; Thomas Reeve Pickering, Oral History, April 2003, pp. 178, 401.

12. Letter of Bill Clinton to Boris Yeltsin, 6 January 1995, Washington, D.C., State-FOIA.

13. Talbott, *The Russia Hand*, pp. 150–152; Letter of Bill Clinton to Boris Yeltsin, 6 January 1995, Washington, D.C., State-FOIA.

14. "Preparing for Geneva," Memorandum of Strobe Talbott, 12 January 1995, Washington, D.C., State-FOIA.

15. "U.S. Sharply Rebukes Russia for Its Offensive in Chechnya," *New York Times*, 12 April 1995; De La Pedraja, *Russian Military Resurgence*, pp. 120–122.

16. P. Terrence Hopmann, "The Organization for Security and Cooperation in Europe: Its Contribution to Conflict Prevention and Resolution," in Paul C. Stern and Daniel Druckman, eds., *International Conflict Resolution after the Cold War* (Washington, D.C.: National Academies Press, 2000), pp. 586–588; Letter of Bill Clinton to Boris Yeltsin, 6 January 1995, Washington, D.C., State-FOIA; Talbott, *The Russia Hand*, pp. 152–154.

17. "Russia's Sustainable Cost of War Conflict," *Los Angeles Times*, 22 July 1995; "Speedup Is Charged in Chechnya," *Washington Post*, 11 April 1995.

18. Cheterian, *War and Peace in the Caucasus*, pp. 264–266; De La Pedraja, *Russian Military Resurgence*, pp. 120–122.

19. "OSCE and Chechnya," Cable from U.S. Mission, Vienna, 8 May 1995, State-FOIA; "Chechen Leader Rejects Russia Truce," *Los Angeles Times*, 30 April 1995; "Lingering Chechen Fight Embarrasses the Kremlin," *Los Angeles Times*, 8 May 1995; Hopmann, "OSCE," pp. 588–589.

20. Accounts of the war agree on the decisive role played by the media, a conclusion that already contemporary observers noted. See for example, "Chechens Hit at Grozny as Yeltsin Talks Peace," *Washington Post*, 8 March 1996.

21. De La Pedraja, *Russian Military Resurgence*, p. 128; Hopmann, "OSCE," pp. 588–589.

22. De La Pedraja, *Russian Military Resurgence*, pp. 128–129; Colton, *Yeltsin*, pp. 371–373.

23. Hopmann, "OSCE," pp. 589–590; De La Pedraja, *Russian Military Resurgence*, p. 131.

24. Hopmann, "OSCE," pp. 589–590; De La Pedraja, *Russian Military Resurgence*, pp. 130–131.

25. Cheterian, *War and Peace in the Caucasus*, pp. 271–273; De La Pedraja, *Russian Military Resurgence*, p. 132.

Chapter 4

1. Igor S. Ivanov, *The New Russian Diplomacy* (Washington, D.C.: Brookings Institution Press, 2002), p. 41.

2. Strobe Talbott, ed., *Khrushchev Remembers* (Boston: Little, Brown, 1970), p. 292.

3. Steven Weber, "Origins of the European Bank for Reconstruction and Development," *International Organization* 48 (1994): 33.

4. "ERBB and the Progress of Transition," 7 June 2000, Parliamentary Assembly of the Council of Europe; "The Contribution of EBRD to Economic Development in Central and Eastern Europe," 4 June 2002, Parliamentary Assembly of the Council of Europe.

5. Weber, "Origins," pp. 30–31; "History of the EBRD," 2019.

6. Weber, "Origins," p. 22.

7. Weber, "Origins," pp. 21n63, 30n32; Steven Weber, "Origins of the European Bank for Reconstruction and Development," Working Paper, Harvard University Center for European Studies, 1992, p. 124 n.220. Of the original 60,000 shares of the Soviet Union, in January 1992 the Russian Federation received 40,000 and also retained its meaningless seat in the board of directors; the other former Soviet republics distributed among themselves the remaining 20,000 shares. See Weber "Origins," Working Paper, p. 123 n214.

8. "The EBRD and Russia," 19 April 2016; "EBRD and the Progress of Transition," 7 June 2000, Parliamentary Assembly of the Council of Europe; Weber, "Origins," Working Paper, pp. 60, 69–70, 121 n206; "Russia Small Business Fund," 2019.

9. "ERBB and the Progress of Transition," 7 June 2000, Parliamentary Assembly of the Council of Europe; "The EBRD and Russia," 19 April 2016; "Russia Small Business Fund," 2019.

10. Marina Lazareva, "The European Union and Russia: History of the Relationship and Cooperation Prospects," *Studia Juridica et Politica Jaurinensis* 1 (2014): 38; William H. Hill, *No Place for Russia: European Security Institutions since 1989* (New York: Columbia University Press, 2018), pp. 84–86; "Secretary Christopher's February 25 Meeting with Russian Foreign Minister Kozyrev," Secret Cable from Secretary of State, 4 March 1995, Freedom of Information Act (henceforth State-FOIA).

11. "Secretary Christopher's February 25 Meeting with Russian Foreign Minister Kozyrev," Secret Cable from Secretary of State, 4 March 1995, State-FOIA.

12. Anastasia Chebakova, "Exposing the Limits of EU-Russia Autonomous Cooperation: The Potential of Bakhtin's Dialogic Imagination," Ph.D. Dissertation, University of Victoria, 2015, p. 92; "Joint Political Declaration on Partnership and Cooperation between the Russian Federation and the European Union," 9 December 1993.

13. Lazareva, "The European Union and Russia," 1 (2014): 39; Chebakova, "The Limits of EU-Russia Cooperation," pp. 92, 98; "Joint Political Declaration on Partnership and Cooperation between the Russian Federation and the European Union," 9 December 1993.

14. Chebakova, "The Limits of EU-Russia Cooperation," pp. 94–96; Dov Lynch, *La Russie face à l'Europe* (Paris: Institut d'Études de Sécurité, 2003), p. 57.

15. Lazareva, "The European Union and Russia," 1 (2014): 38; Chebakova, "The Limits of EU-Russia Cooperation," pp. 96–98; Lynch, *La Russie face à l'Europe*, pp. 57–58.

16. "Russia-EU Partnership and Cooperation Agreement Turns 20," and "Russia—EU Summits," Permanent Mission of the Russian Federation to the European Union; Lazareva, "The European Union and Russia," 1(2014): 39; Lynch, *La Russie face à l'Europe*, p. 57; Sami Adoura, "Assessment of the Cooperation between the EU and Russia," 28 March 2006; "European Community-Russian Federation: Trade and Trade-related Matters/ Interim Agreement," 17 July 1995.

17. "Council of Europe" Website; Katlijn Malfliet and Stephan Parmentier, eds., *Russia and the Council of Europe 10 Years after* (London: Palgrave Macmillan, 2010), pp. 7–9.

18. Jean-Pierre Massias, *Russia and the Council of Europe: Ten Years Wasted?* (Paris: IFRI, 2007), p. 5; "Препятствия для вступления в Совет Европы," 8 October 1993, *Независимая газета*; Rudolf Bindig, "Russia's Accession to the Council of Europe," in Malfliet and Parmentier, eds., *Russia and the Council of Europe*, p. 35.

19. Mark Entin and Ekaterina Entina, "Russia and the Council of Europe," 17 April 2019, p. 9; "Препятствия для вступления в Совет Европы," 8 October 1993, *Независимая газета*.

20. "Russia's Request for Membership in the Light of the Situation in Chechnya," Resolution of the Parliamentary Assembly of the Council of Europe, 2 February 1995; Massias, *Russia and the Council of Europe*, p. 5; Bindig, "Russia's Accession to the Council of Europe," pp. 35–36.

21. "Procedure for an Opinion on Russia's Request for Membership of the Council of Europe," 26 September 1995, Parliamentary Assembly; "Council of Europe and Russian Federation," 2019, Website of Moscow Office of Council of Europe; Bindig, "Russia's Accession to the Council of Europe," pp. 35–38.

22. Mark Entin and Ekaterina Entina, "Russia and the Council of Europe," 17 April 2019; "Council of Europe and Russian Federation," 2019, Website of Moscow Office of Council of Europe.

23. Entin and Entina, "Russia and the Council of Europe," pp. 7, 10; Massias, *Russia and the Council of Europe*, p. 16.

24. Arms Control Association, "START I at a Glance," February 2019; Lawrence D. Freedman, "Strategic Arms Reduction Talks," Britannica.com; "Russian Strategic Forces under START II," National Intelligence Council Memorandum, 19 January 1993, CIA declassified reports.

25. Arms Control Association, "Brief Chronology of START II," March 2019; Strobe Talbott, *The Russia Hand: A Memoir of Presidential Diplomacy* (New York: Random House, 2002), pp. 34, 42–43, 374–375; Angela E. Stent, *The Limits of Partnership: U.S. Russian Relations in the Twenty-First Century* (Princeton: Princeton University Press, 2015), p. 29.

26. Elena Kropatcheva, "The Evolution of Russia's OSCE Policy: From the Promises of the Helsinki Final Act to the Ukrainian Crisis," *Journal of Contemporary European Studies* 23(2015): 10; International Democracy Watch, *The Organization for Security and Cooperation in Europe (OSCE)* (Brussels: European Union, 2018), p. 6.

27. P. Terrence Hopmann, "The Organization for Security and Cooperation in Europe: Its Contribution to Conflict Prevention and Resolution," in Paul C. Stern and Daniel Druckman, eds., *International Conflict Resolution after the Cold War* (Washington, D.C.: The National Academies Press, 2000), pp. 576–577; David J. Galbreath, *The Organization for Security and Co-operation in Europe* (London: Routledge, 2007), pp. 39–64; Kropatcheva, "The Evolution of Russia's OSCE Policy," 23(2015): 10–11; OSCE, "Secretariat Established in Vienna," 29 November 1993.

28. "OSCE Involvement in Nagorno-Karabakh," Cable from U.S. Embassy, Vienna, 5 February 1992, U.S. State Department, State-FOIA; Hopmann, "OSCE," pp. 576–578; Galbreath, *The Organization for Security and Co-operation in Europe*, pp. 39–64.

29. Hopmann, "OSCE," pp. 576–577; Kropatcheva, "The Evolution of Russia's OSCE Policy," 23(2015): 11; International Democracy Watch, *The Organization for Security and Cooperation in Europe (OSCE)*, p. 6; Galbreath, *The Organization for Security and Co-operation in Europe*, pp. 39–64.

30. "NATO Summit—The Substantive Framework," Memorandum, 2 July 1993, State-FOIA.

31. "Poland Free of Russian Combat Troops," 13 November 1992, RFE/RL Research Report.

32. "NATO Summit—The Substantive Framework," Memorandum, 2 July 1993, State-FOIA.
33. "Expanding and Transforming NATO," Memorandum, 13 August 1993, State-FOIA.
34. "Strategy for NATO's Expansion and Transformation," 7 September 1993, State-FOIA; "Your October 6 Lunch Meeting with Secretary Aspin and Mr. Lake," 5 October 1993, State-FOIA; Ronald D. Asmus, *Opening NATO's Door: How the Alliance Remade Itself for a New Era* (New York: Columbia University Press, 2002), pp. 37–39.
35. "Your Deputies' Committee Meeting on the NATO Summit," 13 September 1993, State-FOIA; "Your October 6 Lunch Meeting with Secretary Aspin and Mr. Lake," 5 October 1993, State-FOIA; Asmus, *Opening NATO's Door*, p. 68; Talbott, *Russia Hand*, pp. 97–99.
36. "Expanding and Transforming NATO," Memorandum, 13 August 1993, State-FOIA; Asmus, *Opening NATO's Door*, pp. 92–93; Talbott, *Russia Hand*, pp. 130–131, 138–139. The pandering by the Clinton administration to Eastern European voters proved futile, and the Republican Party swept the elections of November 1994.
37. This quotation and the one in the next paragraph from Asmus, *Opening NATO's Door*, p. 66.
38. Talbott, *Russia Hand*, pp. 125–126; Asmus, *Opening NATO's Door*, pp.125–130.
39. Talbott, *Russia Hand*, pp. 233–234; Asmus, *Opening NATO's Door*, pp.125–130.
40. Talbott, *Russia Hand*, p. 129; Asmus, *Opening NATO's Door*, pp. 125–130.
41. "Prime Minister Horn Welcomes NATO Expansion Plans and Asks That Russia's Concerns Be Considered," Cable from U.S. Embassy, Budapest, 3 March 1995, State-FOIA; Asmus, *Opening NATO's Door*, pp. 66–69.
42. Talbott, *Russia Hand*, pp. 164–165.
43. Yevgeny Primakov, *Russian Crossroads: Toward the New Millennium* (New Haven: Yale University Press, 2004), pp. 122–123, 125; Yuri M. Baturin, *et al.*, *Epokha Eltsina: ocherki politicheskoi istorii* (Moscow: BAGRIUS, 2001), pp. 481–485.
44. "NATO Report Summarized," 26 November 1993, *Foreign Broadcast Information Service*.
45. Letter of Bill Clinton to Boris Yeltsin, 8 February 1996, State-FOIA.
46. "Ambassador's May 1 Meeting with President Chirac," Cable from U.S. Embassy, Paris, 2 May 1996, and "NATO-Russia: Objectives, Obstacles, and Work Plan," 29 July 1996, State-FOIA.
47. "Secretary Christopher's Meeting with Ukrainian Foreign Minister Udovenko, March 19, 1996, Kiev, Ukraine," Cable from Secretary of State, Washington, D.C., 15 April 1996, State-FOIA.
48. Memorandum of Conversation of 15 July 1996, State-FOIA. In general the contemporary documents reveal a much harder attitude of Strobe Talbott toward Russia than his memoir *The Russia Hand*. The harsh tone of the documents also help to solve the riddle in his memoirs of why despite his great expertise on Russia he was not a forceful opponent of the eastern march of NATO. Instead he went with the flow and followed the group think that put the U.S. on a path to confrontation with Russia during the early decades of the twenty-first century.
49. Primakov, *Russian Crossroads*, pp. 137–138; Memorandum of 15 July 1996, State-FOIA.
50. "NATO Enlargement—Turkish Take on Russian Views," Cable from U.S. Embassy, Ankara, 8 January 1997, Wikileaks; Primakov, *Russian Crossroads*, p. 139.
51. "NATO Enlargement—Turkish Take on Russian Views," Cable from U.S. Embassy, Ankara, 8 January 1997, Wikileaks.
52. Primakov, *Russian Crossroads*, pp. 160–161; Founding Act between NATO and the Russian Federation, Paris, 27 May 1997.
53. "Initial Russian Reactions to PJC Upbeat," Cable from U.S. Embassy, Moscow, 29 September 1997, State-FOIA; Talbott, *The Russia Hand*, pp. 247–248; Congressional Research Service, "NATO: Congress Addresses Expansion of the Alliance," 24 May 1999, Wikileaks; NATO, *NATO–Russia Council; Rome Summit 2002*, p. 5.
54. "INR Viewpoint," Eurasian Foreign Policy Update," Cable from Secretary of State, 20 June 1997, State-FOIA; "Initial Russian Reactions to PJC Upbeat," Cable from U.S. Embassy, Moscow, 29 September 1997, State-FOIA; Primakov, *Russian Crossroads*, pp. 161–162; Talbott, *The Russia Hand*, p. 242.

Chapter 5

1. "Secretary Christopher's Meeting with Russian Foreign Minister Kozyrev," Secret Cable from Secretary of State, 4 March 1993, U.S. State Department, Freedom of Information Act (henceforth State-FOIA).
2. Andrew Wilson, *The Ukrainians: Unexpected Nation* (New Haven, CT: Yale University Press, 2000), p. 215.
3. René De La Pedraja, *The Russian Military Resurgence: Post-Soviet Decline and Rebuilding, 1992–2018* (Jefferson, NC: McFarland, 2018), pp. 96–99; "Ukrainian Parliament Votes for Transitional Army," 31 January 1992, B-Wire.
4. Steven Pifer, *The Eagle and the Trident: U.S.-Ukraine Relations in Turbulent Times* (Washington, D.C.: Brookings Institution, 2017), pp. 31–32; De La Pedraja, *Russian Military Resurgence*, pp. 100–101.
5. Richard Sakwa, *Frontline Ukraine: Crisis in the Borderlands* (London: I. B. Tauris, 2016) p. 68; Serhy Yekelchyk, *Ukraine: Birth of a Modern Nation* (New York: Oxford University Press, 2007), p. 196; *Eagle and Trident*, pp. 38–44; De La Pedraja, *Russian Military Resurgence*, p. 97.
6. Sakwa, *Frontline Ukraine*, p. 68; Yekelchyk, *Ukraine*, p. 196; Pifer, *Eagle and Trident*, pp. 44–47.
7. Andrew Wilson, *Ukraine's Orange Revolution* (New Haven, CT: Yale University Press, 2005), p. 38; Sakwa, *Frontline Ukraine*, pp. 68–69; Yekelchyk, *Ukraine*, p. 196; "Memorandum on Security Assurances in Connection with Ukraine's Accession to the Treaty on the Non-Proliferation of Nuclear Weapons," Budapest, 5 December 1994. Ukraine has often accused Russia of having violated the Budapest

Memorandum of 5 December 1994. Washington has echoed but not championed the accusations, because the U.S. record is far from spotless. A pertinent example is the ratified treaty the U.S. signed with Colombia guaranteeing the latter's territorial integrity, but then Washington supported the separatists of Panama against Colombia in 1903—a great precedent for Russian actions over Crimea in 2014.

8. "Ukrainian Parliament Votes for Transitional Army," 31 January 1992, B-Wire; "Kravchuk Demands Dismissal of Black Sea Fleet Admiral," 31 January 1992, B-Wire; John W. R. Lepingwell, "The Black Sea Fleet Agreement: Progress or Empty Promises?" 9 July 1993, *RFL/RL Research*.

9. "Ukrainian Parliament Votes for Transitional Army," 31 January 1992, B-Wire; Lepingwell, "Black Sea Fleet Agreement," 9 July 1993, *RFL/RL Research*; "Ukraine Is Accused by Russian Admiral of Snatching Ships," 22 July 1992, Associated Press.

10. Lepingwell, "Black Sea Fleet Agreement," 9 July 1993; "Адмирал Касатополъ," 13 March 2015, RIA Novosti.

11. Marvin Kalb, *Imperial Gamble: Putin, Ukraine, and the New Cold War* (Washington, D.C.: Brookings Institution, 2015), p. 191; "Ukrainian Parliament Votes for Transitional Army," 31 January 1992, B-Wire; Yekelchyk, *Ukraine*, pp. 194–195; Pifer, *Eagle and Trident*, p. 29.

12. Sakwa, *Frontline Ukraine*, p. 58; Yekelchyk, *Ukraine*, pp. 200–201; Wilson, *Ukrainians*, pp. 209, 220.

13. Roman Solchanyk, "Ukrainian-Russian Confrontation over Crimea," 11 February 1992, RFE/RL Research Institute; Sakwa, *Frontline Ukraine*, pp. 58–59; Kalb, *Imperial Gamble*, p. 117; Yekelchyk, *Ukraine*, pp. 200–201; Wilson, *Ukrainians*, pp. 207–208.

14. For a full discussion of events of Crimea in the last years of the Soviet Union, see chapter 6 of Gwendolyn Sasse, *The Crimea Question: Identity, Transition, and Conflict* (Cambridge, MA: Harvard Ukrainian Research Institute, 2007). See also, Jane I. Dawson, "Ethnicity, Ideology, and Geopolitics in Crimea," *Communist and Post-Communist Studies* 30 (1997): 436–437.

15. Sasse, *The Crimea Question*, pp. 142–146; Dawson, "Ethnicity, Ideology, and Geopolitics in Crimea," pp. 432–444, 437.

16. Sasse, *The Crimea Question*, pp. 142–146; Dawson, "Ethnicity, Ideology, and Geopolitics in Crimea," p. 437; Pifer, *Eagle and Trident*, p. 22.

17. Sasse, *The Crimea Question*, pp. 146–148; Dawson, "Ethnicity, Ideology, and Geopolitics in Crimea," p. 437.

18. Sasse, *The Crimea Question*, pp. 146–148; "Crimea Oks Constitution Declaring Its Independence from Ukraine," 21 May 1994, *Los Angeles Times*.

19. "Separatist Winning Crimea Presidency," 31 January 1994, *New York Times*; Sasse, *The Crimea Question*, pp. 141–142, 153; Dawson, "Ethnicity, Ideology, and Geopolitics in Crimea," pp. 436–437.

20. Sasse, *The Crimea Question*, pp. 156–157.

21. "Separatist Winning Crimea Presidency," 31 January 1994, *New York Times*; Sasse, *The Crimea Question*, pp. 155–158, 162–163; "Prickly Nationalists Squeeze Crimea's New Leader: Victorious Yuri Meshkov Is Already Toning down His Secessionist Rhetoric," 1 February 1994, *Independent*.

22. "Separatist Winning Crimea Presidency," *New York Times*, 31 January 1994; "Yuri Meshkov," 2 January 2020, Wikipedia; Sasse, *The Crimea Question*, p. 161; "Prickly Nationalists Squeeze Crimea's New Leader: Victorious Yuri Meshkov Is Already Toning down His Secessionist Rhetoric," *Independent*, 1 February 1994.

23. "Yuri Meshkov," 2 January 2020, Wikipedia; Sasse, *The Crimea Question*, pp. 135–136, 140, 155–156; "Crimea's President a Prisoner of His Own Separatist Revolt," 23 May 1995, *Los Angeles Times*.

24. "Crimea: Yuri Revels in Reversal of Fortune," 23 March 2014, BBC; Sasse, *The Crimea Question*, p. 164; Wilson, *Ukrainians*, p. 215.

25. "Crimea Oks Constitution Declaring Its Independence from Ukraine," *Los Angeles Times*, 21 May 1994; Sasse, *The Crimea Question*, p. 165.

26. "Crimea's President a Prisoner of His Own Separatist Revolt," 23 May 1995, *Los Angeles Times*; Sasse, *The Crimea Question*, pp. 165–166, 170; Wilson, *Ukrainians*, p. 215.

27. "Crimea's President a Prisoner of His Own Separatist Revolt," *Los Angeles Times*, 23 May 1995; Sasse, *The Crimea Question*, pp. 166–167; "Prickly Nationalists Squeeze Crimea's New Leader: Victorious Yuri Meshkov Is Already Toning down His Secessionist Rhetoric," *Independent*, 1 February 1994; Dawson, "Ethnicity, Ideology, and Geopolitics in Crimea," pp. 438–439.

28. Yekelchyk, *Ukraine*, pp. 201–202; Sasse, *The Crimea Question*, p. 171; Wilson, *Orange Revolution*, p. 38.

29. Pifer, *Eagle and Trident*, p. 98; P. Terrence Hopmann, "The Organization for Security and Cooperation in Europe: Its Contribution to Conflict Prevention and Resolution," in Paul C. Stern and Daniel Druckman, eds., *Conflict Resolution after the Cold War* (Washington, D.C.: National Academies Press, 2000), pp. 583–584.

30. "Crimea's President a Prisoner of His Own Separatist Revolt," *Los Angeles Times*, 23 May 1995; Hopmann, "OSCE," pp. 583–584.

31. "Информационно-аналитическая справка о военно-политической ситуации на Украине," circa July 1994, Box 13, Vitalii L. Kataev Papers, Hoover Institution Archives, Stanford, California (henceforth Kataev-Hoover); Yekelchyk, *Ukraine*, p. 202.

32. "Crimea's President a Prisoner of His Own Separatist Revolt," *Los Angeles Times*, 23 May 1995; Sasse, *The Crimea Question*, pp. 178–179; Dawson, "Ethnicity, Ideology, and Geopolitics in Crimea," p. 438.

33. "Crimea: Yuri Revels in Reversal of Fortune," 23 March 2014, BBC; Sasse, *The Crimea Question*, p. 179; Dawson, "Ethnicity, Ideology, and Geopolitics in Crimea," pp. 438–439; Wilson, *Ukrainians*, p. 215. Only in July 2011 did Yuri Meshkov return to Crimea to settle family matters. When asked in a press conference, he reaffirmed his support for the

1992 Crimean Constitution. The statement angered Ukrainian officials who deported him just eleven days after his arrival. In addition, Kiev banned him from returning to Ukraine for five years or until 2016.

34. Wilson, *Ukrainians*, pp. 198, 215, 274.

35. "Информационно-аналитическая справка о военно-политической ситуации на Украине," circa July 1994, Box 13, Kataev-Hoover; Wilson, *Ukrainians*, pp. 253–262; Dale B. Stewart, "The Russian-Ukrainian Friendship Treaty and the Search for Regional Stability in Eastern Europe," Thesis, Naval Postgraduate School, Monterey, California, 1997.

36. "Russia and Ukraine Divide Long-Suffering Black Sea Fleet," 29 May 1997, RIA–Novosti; Kalb, *Imperial Gamble*, p. 123; Pifer, *Eagle and Trident*, pp. 99–100.

37. Pifer, *Eagle and Trident*, pp. 100–101; Treaty of Friendship, Cooperation, and Partnership between Ukraine and the Russian Federation, Kiev, 31 May 1997, United Nations Treaty Series. In contrast, when on 16 July 2001 Russia signed with China the Treaty of Good Neighborliness and Friendly Cooperation, the text cited many specific cases and situations for enhancing existing ties between the two countries. See De La Pedraja, *Russian Military Resurgence*, pp. 237, 239–245.

38. Wilson, *Ukrainians*, pp. 216–217; Kalb, *Imperial Gamble*, pp. 123–124.

Chapter 6

1. William H. Hill, *No Place for Russia: European Security Institutions since 1989* (New York: Columbia University Press, 2018), p. 169.

2. "Insurgency in Kosovo (1995–1998)," 19 March 2020, Wikipedia; John Norris, *Collision Course: NATO, Russia, and Kosovo* (Westport, CT: Praeger, 2005), pp. xix, xxii; "Albanian Civil War," 30 March 2020, Wikipedia.

3. Madeleine Albright, *Madam Secretary: A Memoir* (New York: Miramax Books, 2003), pp. 492, 500; Strobe Talbott, *The Russia Hand: A Memoir of Presidential Diplomacy* (New York: Random House, 2003), p. 302; Norris, *Collision Course*, pp. xx–xxi; Elena Kropatcheva, "The Evolution of Russia's OSCE Policy: From the Promises of the Helsinki Final Act to the Ukrainian Crisis," *Journal of Contemporary European Studies* 23(2015): 12.

4. Norris, *Collision Course*, pp. xxii, 9; "Kosovo War," 10 April 2020, Wikipedia.

5. "Secretary's Meeting with French Foreign Minister Vedrine," Cable from Secretary of State, Washington, D.C., 30 March 1998, State Department, Freedom of Information Act (henceforth State-FOIA).

6. Talbott, *The Russia Hand*, p. 301.

7. "Secretary's Meeting with French Foreign Minister Vedrine," Cable from Secretary of State, Washington, D.C., 30 March 1998, State-FOIA; "Secretary's Meeting with Russian Foreign Minister Yevgeny Primakov," Secret cable from Secretary of State, Washington, D.C., 1 September 1998, State-FOIA;

Albright, *Madam Secretary*, p. 490; Talbott, *Russia Hand*, p. 313.

8. Albright, *Madam Secretary*, pp. 498, 517; "Kosovo War," 10 April 2020, Wikipedia.

9. Both Norris, *Collision Course*, p. 6 and Talbott, *Russia Hand*, p. 304 state that Serbia was assembling forces to launch the offensive; instead Albright, *Madam Secretary*, pp. 503, 516–517, 520 claimed that the Serbian offensive was underway before NATO began its bombing campaign.

10. Yevgeny Primakov, *Russian Crossroads: Toward the New Millennium* (New Haven, CT: Yale University Press, 2004), pp. 265–269; Norris, *Collision Course*, p. 3.

11. "Telephone Conversation with Russian President Yeltsin," Memorandum of 24 March 1998, State-FOIA; Norris, *Collision Course*, pp. 4–5.

12. Talbott, *Russia Hand*, pp. 304–306; Norris, *Collision Course*, p. 14.

13. Albright, *Madam Secretary*, pp. 518–519; Talbott, *Russia Hand*, p. 303; Norris, *Collision Course*, p. 8.

14. CNN broadcasts, March-May 1999; Albright, *Madam Secretary*, p. 523; Talbott, *Russia Hand*, p. 307; Norris, *Collision Course*, pp. 21–23; "Kosovo War," 10 April 2020, Wikipedia.

15. Talbott, *Russia Hand*, pp. 311, 328–329; Norris, *Collision Course*, pp. 18–19.

16. Albright, *Madam Secretary*, pp. 327–328, 533; Norris, *Collision Course*, pp. 70–10; "Kosovo War," 10 April 2020, Wikipedia; "Secretary Albright's April 12 Meeting with UK Foreign Secretary Cook in Brussels," Cable from Secretary of State, Washington, D.C., 23 April 1999, State-FOIA.

17. Albright, *Madam Secretary*, pp. 525–526, 537–538; Talbott, *Russia Hand*, pp. 301, 315; "Kosovo War," 10 April 2020, Wikipedia.

18. Talbott, *Russia Hand*, pp. 308–309, 335–336; Norris, *Collision Course*, pp. 42–43; Primakov, *Russian Crossroads*, p. 278.

19. Timothy J. Colton, *Yeltsin: A Life* (New York: Basic Books, 2008), pp. 427–428; Talbott, *Russia Hand*, p. 315.

20. Albright, *Madam Secretary*, p. 532; Talbott, *Russia Hand*, pp. 317, 348.

21. Norris, *Collision Course*, pp. 104–105; Albright, *Madam Secretary*, p. 530.

22. Norris, *Collision Course*, pp. 216–217; Albright, *Madam Secretary*, p. 534; Talbott, *Russia Hand*, pp. 330–331; "Kosovo War," 10 April 2020, Wikipedia.

23. Norris, *Collision Course*, pp. 216–217; Albright, *Madam Secretary*, pp. 535–536; Talbott, *Russia Hand*, p. 330.

24. Norris, *Collision Course*, pp. 218–219; "Pristina Stand-off: How Moscow Blindsided NATO with Secret Kosovo Airport Raid 20 Years ago," 11 June 2019, RT.

25. Norris, *Collision Course*, pp. 244–245; René De La Pedraja, *The Russian Military Resurgence: Post-Soviet Decline and Rebuilding, 1992-2018* (Jefferson, NC: McFarland, 2018), p. 140.

26. Norris, *Collision Course*, pp. 243–246; "Confrontation over Pristina Airport," 9 March 2000, BBC.

27. Norris, *Collision Course*, pp. 237, 243; Talbott,

Russia Hand, pp. 337, 342; "Pristina Stand-off: How Moscow Blindsided NATO with Secret Kosovo Airport Raid 20 Years ago," 11 June 2019, RT.

28. "General Sir Mike Jackson: My Clash with NATO Chief," *The Telegraph*, 4 September 2007; Norris, *Collision Course*, p. 247.

29. "General Sir Mike Jackson: My Clash with NATO Chief," *The Telegraph*, 4 September 2007; Norris, *Collision Course*, p. 239.

30. "General Sir Mike Jackson: My Clash with NATO Chief," *The Telegraph*, 4 September 2007. Same idea but slightly different wording in Norris, *Collision Course*, p. 278 and "U.S. General Was Overruled in Kosovo," *New York Times*, 10 September 1999.

31. Norris, *Collision Course*, pp. 241–242, 247–248, 251; "U.S. General Was Overruled in Kosovo," *New York Times*, 10 September 1999.

32. Norris, *Collision Course*, pp. 243, 248, 252, 286; Talbott, *Russia Hand*, pp. 346–347; Albright, *Madam Secretary*, p. 539; "Confrontation over Pristina Airport," 9 March 2000, BBC.

33. "General Sir Mike Jackson: My Clash with NATO Chief," *The Telegraph*, 4 September 2007; Talbott, *Russia Hand*, p. 347; "Pristina Stand-off: How Moscow Blindsided NATO with Secret Kosovo Airport Raid 20 Years ago," 11 June 2019, RT.

34. "Secretary's Meeting with Russian First Deputy Foreign Minister Aleksandr Avdeyev," Cable from Secretary of State, Washington, D.C., 25 February 1999, State-FOIA.

35. Kropatcheva, "The Evolution of Russia's OSCE Policy," 23(2015): 11–12. A typical example of those Russians who became disillusioned with the West because of the NATO bombing of Serbia was the future editor in chief of RT television, Margarita Simonyan; See, Jim Rutenberg, "The Disruption," 17 September 2017, *New York Times Magazine*, p. 53.

Chapter 7

1. "Italian/Council of Europe Discussions with Government of Russia on Chechnya," Cable from U.S. Embassy, Moscow, 29 June 2000, U.S. State Department, Freedom of Information Act (henceforth State-FOIA).

2. Vicken Cheterian, *War and Peace in the Caucasus: Ethnic Conflict and the New Geopolitics* (New York: Columbia University Press, 2008), p. 341.

3. René De La Pedraja, *The Russian Military Resurgence: Post-Soviet Decline and Rebuilding, 1992–2018* (Jefferson, NC: McFarland, 2018), p. 145. The Organization for Security and Cooperation in Europe (OSCE) supervised the elections of 27 January 1997.

4. Cheterian, *War and Peace in the Caucasus*, p. 343.

5. "Your Meeting with Chechen President Maskhadov," Briefing Memorandum, Washington, D.C., 7 August 1998, State-FOIA; "OSCE/Chechnya Activity Report for July 16–31," Cable from U.S. Mission OSCE, Vienna, 19 August 1998, State-FOIA; Cheterian, *War and Peace in the Caucasus*, pp. 344–345.

6. "Your Meeting with Chechen President Maskhadov," Briefing Memorandum, Washington, D.C., 7 August 1998, State-FOIA; Cheterian, *War and Peace in the Caucasus*, pp. 341–342.

7. "Your Meeting with Chechen President Maskhadov," Briefing Memorandum, Washington, D.C., 7 August 1998, State-FOIA.

8. Cheterian, *War and Peace in the Caucasus*, pp. 345–346; "Your Meeting with Chechen President Maskhadov," Briefing Memorandum, Washington, D.C., 7 August 1998, State-FOIA.

9. "Sharia Law in Chechnya: The Veil of Extremism," Cable from U.S. Embassy, Moscow, 4 February 1999, Wikileaks; "Your Meeting with Chechen President Maskhadov," Briefing Memorandum, Washington, D.C., 7 August 1998, State-FOIA; "OSCE/Chechnya Activity Report for July 16–31," Cable from U.S. Mission OSCE, Vienna, 19 August 1998, State-FOIA; "Egypt: New Terrorist Group, Al-Wa'Ad (the Promise) Faces Military Tribunal," Cable from U.S. Embassy, Cairo, 10 December 2001, Wikileaks.

10. "Sharia, Shura, and Statehood in Chechnya," Cable from U.S. Embassy, Moscow, 26 February 1999, Wikileaks; "INR Assessment: Russia: Chechnya and Dagestan on the Edge," Cable from Secretary of State, Washington, D.C., 2 September 1998, State-FOIA; Cheterian, *War and Peace in the Caucasus*, 346–348; De La Pedraja, *Russian Military Resurgence*, p. 146.

11. "INR Assessment: Russia: Chechnya and Dagestan on the Edge," Cable from Secretary of State, Washington, D.C., 2 September 1998, State-FOIA.

12. "INR Assessment: Russia: Chechnya and Dagestan on the Edge," Cable from Secretary of State, Washington, D.C., 2 September 1998, State-FOIA; "INR Assessment: Russia/Central Asia/Afghanistan: Verbal Volley," Cable from Secretary of State, Washington, D.C., 23 May 2000, State-FOIA.

13. "INR Assessment: Russia: Chechnya and Dagestan on the Edge," Cable from Secretary of State, Washington, D.C., 2 September 1998, State-FOIA; "Putin Rattled by Memories, Recalling Terrorist Invasion of Dagestan and Bravery of Militia Defenders," 20 June 2019, RT; Cheterian, *War and Peace in the Caucasus*, pp. 347–348.

14. "Putin Rattled by Memories, Recalling Terrorist Invasion of Dagestan and Bravery of Militia Defenders," 20 June 2019, RT; Steven Lee Myers, *The New Tsar: The Rise and Reign of Vladimir Putin* (New York: Vintage Books, 2015), p. 155.

15. De La Pedraja, *Russian Military Resurgence*, pp. 147–148; Strobe Talbott, *The Russia Hand: A Memoir of Presidential Diplomacy* (New York: Random House, 2003), p. 359.

16. This paragraph and the next rely on De La Pedraja, *Russian Military Resurgence*, pp. 148–151.

17. "Digging In on the Chechen Front," *Washington Post*, 5 October 1999; "Russia's New Chechnya Battle," *Los Angeles Times*, 22 November 1999; "In Occupied Chechnya, Order without Allegiance," *New York Times*, 22 November 1999; De La Pedraja, *Russian Military Resurgence*, p. 150.

18. Talbott, *Russia Hand*, p. 360; De La Pedraja, *Russian Military Resurgence*, p. 149.

19. Congressional Research Service, "Russia's Chechnya Conflict: An Update," 16 April 2003, p. 11;

Congressional Research Service, "Renewed Chechnya Conflict: Developments in 1999-2000," 3 May 2000, pp. 2, 11, Wikileaks; Myers, *Vladimir Putin*, p. 181; Cheterian, *War and Peace in the Caucasus*, pp. 350.

20. "Secretary's February 2 Meeting with Russian Acting President Putin," Cable from Secretary of State, Washington, D.C., 17 February 2000, State-FOIA; Talbott, *Russia Hand*, pp. 357-358; "Chechnya: An Update," p. 3, Wikileaks; Dov Lynch, *La Russie face à l'Europe* (Paris: Institut d'Études de Sécurité, 2003), p. 41.

21. "Secretary's February 2 Meeting with Russian Acting President Putin," Cable from Secretary of State, Washington, D.C., 17 February 2000, State-FOIA; "Russian Troops Take Chechnya's Second Largest City," *Los Angeles Times*, 13 November 1999; Madeleine Albright, *Madam Secretary: A Memoir* (New York: Miramax Books, 2003), p. 556; Myers, *Vladimir Putin*, p. 182.

22. Talbott, *Russia Hand*, pp. 361-362; "Russian Troops Take Chechnya's Second Largest City," *Los Angeles Times*, 13 Nov 1999; "Boris to Bill: Butt Out," *Newsweek*, 29 Nov 1999.

23. Talbott, *Russia Hand*, p. 361-362; "Boris to Bill: Butt Out," 29 November 1999, *Newsweek*; Angela E. Stent, *The Limits of Partnership, U.S.-Russia Relations in the Twenty-First Century* (Princeton: Princeton University Press, 2015), p. 45.

24. Talbott, *Russia Hand*, pp. 362-363; Albright, *Madam Secretary*, p. 556.

25. "IMF Head Links Loan Money and Chechnya," *RFE/RL Newsline*, 29 November 1999; "IMF Lending to Russia Is Effectively Suspended," *Monitor*, 14 December 1999; "Moscow Finds Deep Pockets for War," 10 December 1999, *Christian Science Monitor*; Congressional Research Service, "Renewed Chechnya Conflict: Developments in 1991-2000," 3 May 2000, pp. 15, 17, Wikileaks; "INR Assessment: Russia/Central Asia/Afghanistan: Verbal Volley," Cable from Secretary of State, Washington, D.C., 23 May 2000, State-FOIA; "Conflict in Chechnya," Resolution of Parliamentary Assembly of Council of Europe, 4 November 1994.

26. "Moscow Finds Deep Pockets for War," 10 December 1999, *Christian Science Monitor*; "Memorandum of Conversation—Meeting between the Deputy Secretary and Russian Prime Minister Putin, Moscow, 22 December 1999," State-FOIA; "Renewed Chechnya Conflict," p. 15; Lynch, *La Russie face à l'Europe*, pp. 62-64.

27. Stent, *The Limits of Partnership*, pp. 26-27, 35-36, 47-48; "Chechnya: An Update," p. 14.

28. "Renewed Chechnya Conflict," pp. 15-17, 19-20; Stent, *The Limits of Partnership*, pp. 75-78.

29. "Chechnya—Political Aspects," Cable from U.S. Embassy, Moscow, 23 January 2001, State-FOIA; "Memorandum of Conversation—Meeting between the Deputy Secretary and Russian Prime Minister Putin, Moscow, 22 December 1999," State-FOIA; "Renewed Chechnya Conflict," p. 15; Igor S. Ivanov, *The New Russian Diplomacy* (Washington, D.C.: Brookings Institution, 2002), p. 101.

30. "Italian/Council of Europe Discussions with Government on Chechnya," Cable from U.S. Embassy, Moscow, 29 June 2000, State-FOIA; "Renewed Chechnya Conflict," p. 15.

31. Quotation and paragraph from "Demarche Request: EU Sponsorship of an UNGA Resolution on Chechnya," Cable from Secretary of State, 18 October 2000, State-FOIA.

32. "Credentials of the Delegation of the Russian Federation," 25 January 2001, Parliamentary Assembly of the Council of Europe; "Chechnya: An Update," p. 4.

33. This quotation and the next from "Chechnya," Memorandum circa mid-2001, State-FOIA. This document disproves the claim in Talbott, *Russia Hand*, page 404 that before 9/11 the Bush administration "went easier on the Russian government over Chechnya than we had done."

34. "Chechnya—Political Aspects," Cable from U.S. Embassy, Moscow, 23 January 2001, State-FOIA; "Chechnya," Memorandum circa mid-2001, State-FOIA.

35. "Displeased by Russian's Resistance to Reform and War in Chechnya," 21 January 21, *New York Times*; De La Pedraja, *Russian Military Resurgence*, pp. 157-158.

36. Peter Baker and Susan Glasser, *Kremlin Rising: Vladimir Putin's Russia and the End of Revolution* (Washington, D.C.: Potomac Books, 2007), pp. 121-122.

37. "Chechnya: An Update," p. 14; Stent, *The Limits of Partnership*, pp. 64-66.

38. "Chechnya: An Update," p. 3; Elena Kropatcheva, "The Evolution of Russia's OSCE Policy: From the Promises of the Helsinki Final Act to the Ukrainian Crisis," *Journal of Contemporary European Studies* 23 (2015): 13; Myers, *Vladimir Putin*, p. 230.

39. "Chechnya: An Update," pp. 5, 18.

Chapter 8

1. "Current State of Play in U.S./NATO Russia Security Relations," Memorandum by Hilary Driscoll, 15 January 2002, Michael McFaul Papers, Box 7, Hoover Institution Archives, Stanford, California (henceforth McFaul-Hoover).

2. Angus Roxburgh, *The Strongman: Vladimir Putin and the Struggle for Russia* (London: I. B. Tauris, 2014), p. 36; Angela E. Stent, *The Limits of Partnership: U.S.-Russian Relations in the Twenty-First Century* (Princeton: Princeton University Press, 2015), pp. 63-64; Peter Baker and Susan Glasser, *Kremlin Rising: Vladimir Putin's Russia and the End of Revolution* (Washington, D.C.: Potomac Books, 2007), p. 122.

3. Stent, *The Limits of Partnership*, pp. 64-65; Baker and Glasser, *Kremlin Rising*, p. 121.

4. Roxburgh, *Strongman*, pp. 36-39; Congressional Research Service, "Russia's Chechnya Conflict: An Update," 16 April 2003, p. 14; Baker and Glasser, *Kremlin Rising*, pp. 129-133.

5. "Current State of Play in U.S./NATO Russia Security Relations," Memorandum by Hilary Driscoll, 15 January 2002, Box 7, McFaul-Hoover; Roxburgh, *Strongman*, p. 42.

6. "NATO-Russia: Negotiating the NATO-Russia Council," Secret Cable from Secretary of State, Washington, D.C., 17 January 2002, U.S. State Department, Freedom of Information Act (henceforth State-FOIA); Congressional Research Service, "NATO Enlargement," 5 May 2003, p. 5; James A. Baker, "Russia in NATO?" *The Washington Quarterly*, 25 (2002): 101.

7. "NATO Enlargement," Memorandum of early 2001, Washington, D.C., State-FOIA; Roxburgh, *Strongman*, pp. 96–97.

8. "Current State of Play in U.S./NATO Russia Security Relations," Memorandum by Hilary Driscoll, 15 January 2002, Box 7, McFaul-Hoover; Baker and Glasser, *Kremlin Rising*, pp. 219–220; Stent, *The Limits of Partnership*, p. 67.

9. "Fact Sheet: The Treaty on Open Skies," 1 February 2017, Center for Arms Control and Non-Proliferation; "Open Skies Treaty Mission in Russian Far East," Cable from Secretary of State, Washington, D.C., 24 February 2009, Wikileaks; George M. Reynolds, "Taking Stock of the Treaty on Open Skies," 3 November 2017, Council on Foreign Relations.

10. "Open Skies: Lift Off! 500 Flight Commemoration Plenary and Balloon Release," Cable from U.S. Mission to European Union, 6 May 2008, Wikileaks; "The Open Skies Treaty at a Glance," October 2012, Arms Control Association; "Open Skies Treaty Mission in Russian Far East," Cable from Secretary of State, Washington, D.C., 24 February 2009, Wikileaks; Reynolds, "Taking Stock of the Treaty on Open Skies."

11. "Open Skies Treaty: May 5 OSCC Plenary: Russian Accusation of Double Standard," Cable from U.S. Mission to European Union, 6 May 2008, Wikileaks.

12. "Open Skies Treaty: UK to Cease Active Flights Due to MOD Budget Cuts," Confidential/NoForn, Cable from U.S. Mission to European Union, 18 April 2008, Wikileaks; "Open Skies Treaty: April 14 Plenary—U.S. Chairmanship Takes Off," Cable from U.S. Mission to European Union, 18 April 2008, Wikileaks.

13. "Open Skies Treaty: UK to Cease Active Flights Due to MOD Budget Cuts," Confidential/NoForn Cable from U.S. Mission to European Union, 18 April 2008, Wikileaks.

14. Arms Control Association, "START II and its Extension Protocol at a Glance," March 2019; Lawrence D. Freedman, "Strategic Arms Reduction Talks," Britannica.com.

15. Arms Control Association, "START II and its Extension Protocol at a Glance," March 2019; Stent, *The Limits of Partnership*, pp. 73–74; Freedman, "Strategic Arms Reduction Talks," Britannica.com.

16. Carnegie Endowment for International Peace, "SORT of a Treaty," 14 May 2003; "Strategic Offensive Reductions Treaty," 17 June 2019, Wikipedia; Arms Control Association, "START II and its Extension Protocol at a Glance," March 2019; Steven Pifer, "SORT vs. New START: Why the Administration Is Leery of a Treaty," Brookings Institution, 15 March 2013.

17. "After U.S. Scraps ABM Treaty, Russia Rejects Curbs of START II," *New York Times*, 15 June 2002; "Strategic Offensive Reductions Treaty," 17 June 2019, Wikipedia; Arms Control Association, "START II and its Extension Protocol at a Glance," March 2019.

18. "After U.S. Scraps ABM Treaty, Russia Rejects Curbs of START II," *New York Times*, 15 June 2002; Stent, *The Limits of Partnership*, pp. 72–73; Freedman, "Strategic Arms Reduction Talks," Britannica.com; Michael McFaul, *From Cold War to Hot Peace: An American Ambassador in Putin's Russia* (Boston: Houghton Mifflin Harcourt, 2018), p. 65.

19. Congressional Research Service, "NATO Enlargement," 5 May 2003, pp. 1–2, Wikileaks.

20. Roxburgh, *Strongman*, p. 86.

21. "NATO Enlargement," Memorandum of early 2001, Washington, D.C., State-FOIA. The U.S. State Department also complained about "the particularly combative attitude" of Russian ambassador to NATO Sergei Kislyak, who later became ambassador to the U.S. Washington believed that "an open-minded ambassador would be more helpful to Russia's interaction with the alliance." *Ibid*.

22. "Current State of Play in U.S./NATO Russia Security Relations," Memorandum by Hilary Driscoll, 15 January 2002, Box 7, McFaul-Hoover; Roxburgh, *Strongman*, pp. 41, 85–86; Baker, "Russia in NATO?" 25 (2002): 96, 101; McFaul, *Cold War to Hot Peace*, p. 60.

23. Stent, *The Limits of Partnership*, pp. 75–76; Baker, "Russia in NATO?" 25 (2002): 95–103.

24. Roxburgh, *Strongman*, pp. 31–33; Baker and Glasser, *Kremlin Rising*, pp. 125, 127; Myers, *Vladimir Putin*, p. 205; Robert M. Gates, *Duty: Memoirs of a Secretary at War* (New York: Alfred A. Knopf, 2014), p. 409.

25. "Readout of Berlusconi-Putin Summit," Cable from U.S. Embassy, Rome, 5 April 2002, Wikileaks; Roxburgh, *Strongman*, p. 86.

26. "Readout of Berlusconi-Putin Summit," Cable from U.S. Embassy, Rome, 5 April 2002, Wikileaks; Don Lynch, *La Russie face à l'Europe* (Paris: Institut d'Études de Sécurité, 2003), pp. 36–37.

27. "NATO-Russia: Russia Tables Its Own Paper for New NATO-Russia Council," Cable from U.S. Mission to NATO, 15 February 2002, State-FOIA.

28. Baker, "Russia in NATO?" 25 (2002): 98.

29. "Ambassador Burns Brief Italians on NATO Issues," Cable from U.S. Embassy, Rome, 13 February 2002, Wikileaks; "Readout of Berlusconi-Putin Summit," Cable from U.S. Embassy, Rome, 5 April 2002, Wikileaks; "Berlusconi Seeks Support for Bush-Putin Meeting in Rome," Cable from U.S. Embassy, Rome, 8 April 2002, Wikileaks; Roxburgh, *Strongman*, pp. 86–87; NATO, *NATO—Russia Council: Rome Summit 2002*, pp. 12, 14.

30. Roxburgh, *Strongman*, p. 87; Lynch, *La Russie face à l'Europe*, pp. 38–41.

31. "Ambassador Burns Brief Italians on NATO Issues," Cable from U.S. Embassy, Rome, 13 February 2002, Wikileaks; "NATO-Russia: Ministry of Foreign Affairs Thoughts on Next Steps," Cable from U.S. Embassy, Moscow, 4 June 2002, State-FOIA; "NATO Enlargement," p. 2; Roxburgh, *Strongman*, pp. 94–95; NATO, "Prague Summit Declaration," 21 November 2002.

Chapter 9

1. Condoleezza Rice, *No Higher Honor: A Memoir of My Years in Washington* (New York: Crown Publishers, 2011), pp. 212-213.
2. Peter Baker and Susan Glasser, *Kremlin Rising: Vladimir Putin's Russia and the End of Revolution* (Washington, D.C.: Potomac Books, 2007), pp. 218, 224; Angela E. Stent, *The Limits of Partnership: U.S.-Russian Relations in the Twenty-First Century* (Princeton: Princeon University Press, 2015), pp. 87-88.
3. Angus Roxburgh, *The Strongman: Vladimir Putin and the Struggle for Russia* (London: I. B. Tauris, 2014), pp. 101-102; Folders of the 1960s and 1970s in Archives de Ministère des Affaires Étrangères, Paris, France.
4. Stent, *The Limits of Partnership*, pp. 88-89; Baker and Glasser, *Kremlin Rising*, pp. 214-215.
5. "Berlusconi-Putin Meeting: Italian Readout," Secret Cable from U.S. Embassy, Rome, 17 October 2002, Wikileaks.
6. "Tariq Aziz: Iraq Punishes Lukoil for Trying to Get U.S. Support," 18 December 2002, Grani.Ru; Baker and Glasser, *Kremlin Rising*, p. 224; Roxburgh, *Strongman*, pp. 100-101.
7. "Histoire des Services Secrets français," 2010, Episode 4, France TV 5.
8. Congressional Research Service, "NATO Enlargement," 5 May 2003, p. 4, Wikileaks; Stent, *The Limits of Partnership*, pp. 89-90.
9. Baker and Glasser, *Kremlin Rising*, p. 225; Stent, *The Limits of Partnership*, pp. 90-92.
10. Roxburgh, *Strongman*, p. 102; Stent, *The Limits of Partnership*, p. 90.
11. Baker and Glasser, *Kremlin Rising*, pp. 224-225; Roxburgh, *Strongman*, p. 102.
12. Baker and Glasser, *Kremlin Rising*, p. 224. Several books give the mistaken impression that during the visit to Paris Vladimir Putin, one step above a country bumpkin, was swept away by the pomp and circumstance of the spectacle. Nothing could be farther from the truth, because the Kremlin had long before reached its firm conclusion on opposing the war, and Putin was trying to use the visits to advance other Russian goals.
13. Roxburgh, *Strongman*, pp. 103-104; Baker and Glasser, *Kremlin Rising*, pp. 224-225.
14. "Yevgeny Primakov Completed His Trip to Iraq," 23 February 2003, Grani.Ru; Roxburgh, *Strongman*, pp. 104-105.
15. This paragraph and the next draw on Baker and Glasser, *Kremlin Rising*, p. 227, Roxburgh, *Strongman*, pp. 105-106, and Stent, *The Limits of Partnership*, p. 91.
16. Baker and Glasser, *Kremlin Rising*, p. 227.
17. Stent, *The Limits of Partnership*, p. 95; Baker and Glasser, *Kremlin Rising*, p. 228.

Chapter 10

1. Russian Federation, *Foreign Policy Concept*, 28 June 2000.
2. President Vladimir Putin "said that in his personal opinion, Stalin had made a mistake by invading Finland during the Winter War [...] but nonetheless, in his view, what was done was done and the territorial border between Finland and Russia could not now be undone." "Finish President Halonen's June 7 Meeting with Russian President Putin," Cable from U.S. Embassy, Helsinki, 12 June 2000, Wikileaks.
3. "NATO Ambassador Nicholas Burns' Visit to Finland, November 29-30," Cable from U.S. Embassy, Helsinki 26 November 2004, Wikileaks; "Translation of Putin September 1 Interview with Finnish Daily, *Helsingin Sanomat*," Cable from U.S. Embassy, Helsinki, 10 September 2001, Freedom of Information Act, U.S. State Department.
4. "Finns Find Putin Frustrated, Anxious," Cable from U.S. Embassy, Helsinki, 29 December 2004, Wikileaks; "Finland: Putin Warms Up in Latest Meeting with Vanhanen," Cable from U.S. Embassy, Helsinki, 29 October 2009, Wikileaks.
5. "Finland: Halonen Assumes Traditional Posture towards Russia," Cable from U.S. Embassy, Helsinki, 28 September 2009, Wikileaks.
6. "Finns Find Putin Frustrated, Anxious," Cable from U.S. Embassy, Helsinki, 29 December 2004, Wikileaks.
7. "Finnish President Halonen's June 7 Meeting with Russian President Putin," Cable from U.S. Embassy, Helsinki, 12 June 2000, Wikileaks.
8. "NATO Ambassador Nicholas Burns' Visit to Finland, November 29-30," Cable from U.S. Embassy, Helsinki, 26 November 2004, Wikileaks; "Finland: NATO Debate Heats Up," Cable from U.S. Embassy, Helskinki, 19 December 2006, Wikileaks.
9. "Russia Finland Hungary," 19 June 2007, Stratfor, Wikileaks; "Russian-Hungarian Summit in Moscow, on the 22nd of March," 24 March 2007, Stratfor, Wikileaks.
10. "Russia's Hungarian Offensive," Cable from U.S. Embassy, Budapest, 1 June 2007, Wikileaks; "Hungarian Foreign Policy Drifting to the East," Secret cable from U.S. Embassy, Budapest, 17 August 2007, Wikileaks.
11. "Russia-Hungary: Warming Trend," Cable from U.S. Embassy, Moscow, 12 April 2007, Wikileaks.
12. "Russian-Hungarian Summit in Moscow, on the 22nd of March," 24 March 2007, Stratfor, Wikileaks; "Russia-Hungary: Warming Trend," Cable from U.S. Embassy, Moscow, 12 April 2007, Wikileaks.
13. "Russian-Hungarian Summit in Moscow, on the 22nd of March," 24 March 2007, Stratfor, Wikileaks; "Russian Investments," 10 June 2007, Stratfor, Wikileaks.
14. "Nineteenth-Century Nervous Breakdown: Shades of the Past as Hungary Regards Twenty-First Century Europe?" Cable from U.S. Embassy, Budapest, 26 November 2007, Wikileaks.
15. Quotes and paragraph draw on "Russia's Hungarian Offensive," Cable from U.S. Embassy, Budapest, 1 June 2007, Wikileaks.
16. "Opening Doors and Opening Eyes: Prime Minister Gyurcsany on Relations with the U.S. and

Russia," Cable from U.S. Embassy, Budapest, 18 June 2007, Wikileaks.

17. "Prime Minister's Policy Advisor on Kosovo, Azerbaijan," Cable from U.S. Embassy, Budapest, 31 January 2008, Wikileaks.

18. "Hungary's Russia Policy: Rethinking or Rephrasing?" Cable from U.S. Embassy, Budapest, 22 July 2008, Wikileaks.

19. "Hungary—Where They Stand on Russia-Georgia Crisis," Cable from U.S. Embassy, Budapest, 22 August 2008, Wikileaks.

20. "Putin Visits Turkey: Russia Bids to Turn Turkey from West," Secret Cable from U.S. Embassy, Ankara, 10 December 2004, Wikileaks.

21. "Former President Demirel Tells Ambassador Turkey Must Mend Fences with United States," Cable from U.S. Embassy, Ankara, 22 April 2003, Wikileaks.

22. "Turkey: MFA Discusses Armenia, Caucasus Issues," Cable from U.S. Embassy, Ankara, 21 July 2003, Wikileaks; Author's Trip to Turkey, July 2002; "Former President Demirel Tells Ambassador Turkey Must Mend Fences with United States," Cable from U.S. Embassy, Ankara, 22 April 2003, Wikileaks.

23. "Turkey-Russia Relations: Into the Bear's Den?" Cable from U.S. Embassy, Ankara, 21 May 2007, Wikileaks.

24. Oliver Stone, *The Putin Interviews* (New York: Hot Books, 2017), p. 133; "New Era in Turkish Russian Economic Relations?" Cable from U.S. Embassy, Ankara, 10 December 2004, Wikileaks; Author's Study Trip to Russia, July-August 2007; "Turkey-Russia Relations: Into the Bear's Den?" Cable from U.S. Embassy, Ankara, 21 May 2007, Wikileaks.

25. Author's trip to Turkey, February-March 2011; Turkish Brochure of 2011 "Вам лучше видеть куда вы ныряете."

26. "Turkey-Russia Relations: into the Bear's Den?" Cable from U.S. Embassy, 21 May 2007, Wikileaks. For a rare case when President Vladimir Putin implies that he could have questioned President Recep Tayyip Erdogan, See Stone, *Putin Interviews*, pp. 134–136.

27. "Putin Visits Turkey: Russia Bids to Turn Turkey from West," Secret Cable from U.S. Embassy, Ankara, 10 December 2004, Wikileaks.

28. "Анкара обвинила Москву в фашизме," 27 July 2000, *Nezavisimaia gazeta*; "У Анкары кончилось терпение," 29 November 2001, *Nezavisimaia gazeta*.

29. "Montreux Convention: Military Limits on the Turkish Straits," Cable from U.S. Embassy, Ankara, 23 May 2006, Wikileaks. Warships from non-littoral states could not stay longer than 21 days in the Black Sea, and no single non-littoral state could have more than 30,000 tons in warships at one time. Because the total tonnage allowed to states from outside the region could not exceed 45,000 tons, this often forced a warship of one NATO country to have to wait off Istanbul until the warship of another member state exited the Black Sea. U.S. officials made public complaints about these burdensome restrictions. See, "Another Look at Turkey's Black Sea Maritime Security Policy," Cable from U.S. Embassy, Ankara, 27 March 2006, Wikileaks. On a practical level, for NATO to try to repeat the Crimean War of 1854–1856 but without using the Turkish Straits was a logistical nightmare.

30. "What Is Behind Turkey's Black Sea Policy?" Cable from U.S. Embassy, Ankara, 4 October 2005, Wikileaks; "Montreux Convention: Military Limits on the Turkish Straits," Cable from U.S. Embassy, Ankara, 23 May 2006, Wikileaks.

31. "What Is Behind Turkey's Black Sea Policy?" Cable from U.S. Embassy, Ankara, 4 October 2005, Wikileaks; "Mare Nostrum? Black Sea Maritime Security and Turkish Leadership Ambitions," Cable from U.S. Embassy, Ankara, 13 April 2007, Wikileaks.

32. "Putin Visits Turkey: Russia Bids to Turn Turkey from West." Secret Cable from U.S. Embassy, Ankara, 10 December 2004, Wikileaks; "New Era in Turkish Russian Economic Relations?" Cable from U.S. Embassy, Ankara, 10 December 2004, Wikileaks; ""Russian Defense Minister Ivanov's Extra Day in Ankara," Cable from U.S. Embassy, Ankara, 15 December 2004.

33. "Turco-Russian Rapprochement: Seven Hours of Erdogan-Putin Talks in Sochi," Secret Cable from U.S. Embassy, Ankara, 12 August 2005, Wikileaks; "Turkey: Gul's Historic Visit to Russia," Cable from U.S. Embassy, Ankara, 24 February 2009, Wikileaks.

34. "Turkey on Russia's CFE Concerns," Cable from U.S. Embassy, Ankara, 4 June 2007, Wikileaks; "Turkey Prepared to Recognize Kosovar Independence and Will Seek to Calm Moscow," Cable from U.S. Embassy, Ankara, 15 February 2008, Wikileaks; "Turkey/NATO: Turkey and Our Bucharest Summit Priorities," Cable from U.S. Embassy, Ankara, 26 March 2008, Wikileaks; "Turkey-Russia Relations: Into the Bear's Den?" Cable from U.S. Embassy, Ankara, 21 May 2007, Wikileaks.

35. "Influencing Turkey's Approach to Addressing Threats in the Black Sea Region," Cable from U.S. Embassy, Ankara, 26 March 2009, Wikileaks.

36. "Let's Make a Deal (or Twenty): Putin in Ankara," Cable from U.S. Embassy, Ankara, 7 August 2009, Wikileaks.

37. "Turkey-Russia: Lavrov Visit Heavy on Good Will, Light on Substance," Cable from U.S. Embassy, Ankara, 5 July 2008, Wikileaks; "Let's Make a Deal (or Twenty): Putin in Ankara," Cable from U.S. Embassy, Ankara, 7 August 2009, Wikileaks; Angela E. Stent, *The Limits of Partnership: U.S.-Russian Relations in the Twenty-First Century* (Princeton: Princeton University Press, 2015), pp. 200–201.

38. "Russia Plays Its Cards in Armenia, Azerbaijan, Turkey," Cable from U.S. Embassy, Moscow, 14 January 2010, Wikileaks.

Chapter 11

1. "Russia Seeks, and Finds, a Role in the Middle East Peace Process," Cable from U.S. Embassy, Moscow, 8 February 2008, Wikileaks.

2. René De La Pedraja, *The Russian Military Resurgence: Post-Soviet Decline and Rebuilding, 1992–2018* (Jefferson, NC: McFarland, 2018), p. 287; Angela

Stent, *Putin's World: Russia against the West and with the Rest* (New York: Twelve, 2019), pp. 262–264.

3. "Planned February Visit of Putin to the Kingdom," Secret Cable from U.S. Embassy, Riyadh, 14 January 2007, Wikileaks; "У Анкары кончилось терпение," 29 November 2001, *Nezavisimaia gazeta*.

4. "Planned February Visit of Putin to the Kingdom," Secret Cable from U.S. Embassy, Riyadh, 14 January 2007, Wikileaks; "Russia Seeks, and Finds, a Role in the Middle East Peace Process," 8 February 2008, Cable from U.S. Embassy, Moscow, 8 February 2008, Wikileaks.

5. "Russian President Putin's First Visit to Egypt Falls Short on Substance," Cable from U.S. Embassy, Cairo, 12 May 2005, Wikileaks; "Mubarak's Visit to Russia and China: Diversifying Relations, Assessing Opportunities," Cable from U.S. Embassy, Cairo, 30 October 2006, Wikileaks; De La Pedraja, *The Russian Military Resurgence*, pp. 287–288.

6. "Russian President Putin's First Visit to Egypt Falls Short on Substance," Cable from U.S. Embassy, Cairo, 12 May 2005, Wikileaks.

7. "Russia Keeps up the Pace in Middle East Diplomacy," Cable from U.S. Embassy, Moscow, 27 November 2006, Wikileaks; "Mubarak's Visit to Russia and China: Diversifying Relations, Assessing Opportunities," Cable from U.S. Embassy, Cairo, 30 October 2006, Wikileaks.

8. "The Russian Arms Deal with Algeria: A Model for Expanding the Market?" Cable from U.S. Embassy, Moscow, 31 March 2006, Wikileaks; "Exchange of Harsh Words between Algeria and France: Sign of Increasingly Tense Relationship," Cable from U.S. Embassy, Algiers, 24 April 2006, Wikileaks; Louis-Marie Clouet, *Rosoboronexport, Spearhead of the Russian Arms Industry* (Paris: Russia/NIS Center, 2007), p. 8.

9. "The Russian Arms Deal with Algeria: A Model for Expanding the Market?" Cable from U.S. Embassy, Moscow, 31 March 2006, Wikileaks; "Putin Visits Accentuates Bilateral Cooperation," Cable from U.S. Embassy, Rabat, 13 September 2006, Wikileaks; "Ministry of Foreign Affairs Downplays Results of Putin's Trip to Libya," Cable from U.S. Embassy, Moscow, 23 April 2008, Wikileaks; "Russian NSC Delegation to Visit Libya June 22–24," Cable from U.S. Embassy, Tripoli, 17 June 2009, Wikileaks; Clouet, *Rosoboronexport*, p. 8.

10. "Russo-Tunisian Business Council Created," Cable from U.S. Embassy, Tunis, 10 April 2006, Wikileaks; "Putin Visits Accentuates Bilateral Cooperation," Cable from U.S. Embassy, Rabat, 13 September 2006, Wikileaks.

11. "Putin Pays a Call on UAE Leadership," Cable from U.S. Embassy, Abu Dhabi, 11 September 2007, Wikileaks; "Russia Seeks Improved Ties with Gulf States," Cable from U.S. Embassy, Moscow, 3 December 2007, Wikileaks.

12. "Lavrov's Middle East Diplomacy," Cable from U.S. Embassy, Moscow, 18 September 2006, Wikileaks; "Russia Keeps up the Pace in Middle East Diplomacy," Cable from U.S. Embassy, Moscow, 27 November 2006, Wikileaks.

13. "Russian Views on Engagement with Iraq and Iran," Cable from U.S. Embassy, Moscow, 8 April 2008, Wikileaks.

14. "Russia Seeks and Finds a Role in the Middle East Peace Process," Cable from U.S. Embassy, Moscow, 8 February 2008, Wikileaks; Stent, *Putin's World*, pp. 291–292. The U.S. placed itself at a disadvantage by rejecting talks with many players in the Middle East and by refusing to have embassies in key countries such as Iran and later Syria. In a surprising and illogical reversal, when the civil war began in Syria in 2011, the U.S. changed its definition of radicalism. In a desperate and futile search to find local Syrian allies, the U.S. gave the label of "pro–Western" to many rebel groups that Russia and other countries identified as radical Islamic fundamentalists.

15. "Russia's Concept of the Greater Middle East, Tinged by Racism," Cable from U.S. Embassy, Moscow, 17 November 2008, Wikileaks.

16. "Planned February Visit of Putin to the Kingdom," Secret Cable from U.S. Embassy, Riyadh, 14 January 2007, Wikileaks; "Russia-Saudi Ties Remain Firm but Puzzling," Cable from U.S. Embassy, Moscow, 13 June 2008, Wikileaks; "Russian Influence in Saudi Arabia Defies Limited Presence," Cable from U.S. Embassy, Riyadh, 3 November 2008, Wikileaks; "Russian Arms Sale to Saudi—Delayed," Secret Cable from U.S. Embassy, Riyadh, 24 June 2008, Wikileaks.

17. "Russia/Iran: Convergent Interests," Intelligence Assessment, 5 January 2001, U.S. State Department, Freedom of Information Act (henceforth State-FOIA); Christopher Andrew and Vasili Mitrokhin, *The World Was Going Our Way: The KGB and the Battle for the Third World* (New York: Basic Books, 2005), pp. 183–187, 191–192.

18. "Thoughts on Iran—The Lion and the Cage," Cable from U.S. Embassy, Abu Dhabi, 21 May 1997, Wikileaks; "Russia/Iran: Convergent Interests," Intelligence Assessment, 5 January 2001, State-FOIA; "Russian Views on Engagement with Iraq and Iran," Cable from U.S. Embassy, Moscow, 8 April 2008, Wikileaks.

19. "Russia/Iran: Convergent Interests," Intelligence Assessment, 5 January 2001, State-FOIA; "Putin Tells Berlusconi All Cooperation on Bushehr Halted," Cable from U.S. Embassy, Rome, 1 August 2003, Wikileaks.

20. "Russian Ambassador Argues Russia Can't Support Iran Sanctions Because of Possible Iranian Retaliatory Moves," Secret Cable from U.S. Embassy, Algiers, 14 November 2005, Wikileaks.

21. "Russia-Iran Relations Driven by Regional Political and Economic Interests," Cable from U.S. Embassy, Moscow, 6 November 2008, Wikileaks.

22. "Iran: Putin Frustrated with Teheran," Cable from U.S. Embassy, Moscow, 11 April 2007, Wikileaks.

23. "Russia and Iran: Moscow's Shifting Views," Cable from U.S. Embassy, Moscow, 13 July 2007, Wikileaks.

24. "Insight—Russia and Iran," 19 October 2007, Stratfor, Wikileaks.

25. "Russia and Iran: Moscow's Shifting Views," Cable from U.S. Embassy, Moscow, 13 July 2007, Wikileaks; "Russia-Iran Relations Driven by Regional

Political and Economic Interests," Cable from U.S. Embassy, Moscow, 6 November 2008, Wikileaks.

26. "Moscow's Increasing Frustration with Teheran," Cable from U.S. Embassy, Moscow, 14 December 2009, Wikileaks.

27. Angela E. Stent, *The Limits of Partnership: U.S.-Russian Relations in the Twenty-First Century* (Princeton: Princeton University Press, 2015), pp. 232–233.

28. "Информация о деятельности российских компаний на рынке САР, " 1999, Fond 10213, Opis 1, Delo 309, State Archive of the Russian Federation (henceforth GARF); Andrew and Mitrokhin, *The World Was Going Our Way*, pp. 162–166, 210–213; De La Pedraja, *The Russian Military Resurgence*, p. 288.

29. "Russia Keeps up the Pace in Middle East Diplomacy," Cable from U.S. Embassy, Moscow, 27 November 2006, Wikileaks; "Time for Talking Points to Counter Syria's Charm Offensive," Cable from U.S. Embassy, 10 July 2008, Wikileaks; De La Pedraja, *The Russian Military Resurgence*, pp. 288–289; "Bashar El-Assad: Le Pouvoir ou la Mort," December 2017, French Television Documentary.

30. "Syria-Iran Relations Flourishing: Is Further Improvement Inevitable?" Cable from U.S. Embassy, Damascus, 16 March 2006, Wikileaks; "Russia Keeps up the Pace in Middle East Diplomacy," Cable from U.S. Embassy, Moscow, 27 November 2006, Wikileaks; De La Pedraja, *The Russian Military Resurgence*, p. 289.

31. "Syrian Government Trumpets Burgeoning Economic Ties with Russia," Cable from U.S. Embassy, Damascus, 22 March 2006, Wikileaks; "The Russian Arms Deal with Algeria: A Model for Expanding the Market?" Cable from U.S. Embassy, Moscow, 31 March 2006, Wikileaks; "On Russian Naval Base in Syria," 9 August 2007, Stratfor, Wikileaks; "Syrian Civil Aviation Authorities Desperate," Cable from U.S. Embassy, Damascus, 8 September 2009, Wikileaks;"Информация о деятельности российских компаний на рынке САР," 1999, Fond 10213, Opis 1, Delo 309, GARF.

32. "On Russian Naval Base in Syria," 9 August 2007, Stratfor, Wikileaks; "Syria's Calculation of Russia's Naval Strategy," 10 August 2007, Stratfor, Wikileaks; De La Pedraja, *The Russian Military Resurgence*, p. 289. Russia did have bases in several countries of the near abroad but those in Syria were the only ones outside the former Soviet Union.

33. "Syrian Government Trumpets Burgeoning Economic Ties with Russia," Cable from U.S. Embassy, Damascus, 22 March 2006, Wikileaks; "Russia Keeps up the Pace in Middle East Diplomacy," Cable from U.S. Embassy, Moscow, 27 November 2006, Wikileaks.

Chapter 12

1. Steven Lee Myers, *The New Tsar: The Rise and Reign of Vladimir Putin* (New York: Vintage Books, 2015), p. 229.

2. Charles King, *The Moldovans: Romania, Russia, and the Politics of Culture* (Stanford: Hoover Institution Press, 1999), p. 162; William H. Hill, *Russia, the Near Abroad, and the West: Lessons from the Moldova-Transdniestria Conflict* (Washington, D.C.: Woodrow Wilson Center Press, 2012), pp. 60–6l; Congressional Research Service, "Moldova: Basic Facts," 26 June 2001, Wikileaks.

3. Hill, *Moldova Conflict*, pp. 53–64; "Russian Deputy Foreign Minister on Moldova," Cable from U.S. Embassy, The Hague, 2 October 2003, Wikileaks; Congressional Research Service, "Moldova: Basic Facts," 26 June 2001, Wikileaks.

4. Hill, *Moldova Conflict*, p. 64; Congressional Research Service, "Moldova: Basic Facts," 26 June 2001, Wikileaks; William H. Hill, *No Place for Russia: European Security Institutions since 1989* (New York: Columbia University Press, 2018), p. 228.

5. Hill, *Moldova Conflict*, pp. 64–65.

6. Congressional Research Service, "Enlargement Issues at NATO's Bucharest Summit," 18 April 2008, Wikileaks; Hill, *Moldova Conflict*, pp. 70, 148.

7. Congressional Research Service, "Moldova: Basic Facts," 26 June 2001, Wikileaks; "Kozak Memorandum," 19 February 2020, Wikipedia.

8. Hill, *Moldova Conflict*, pp. 69–73; Congressional Research Service, "Moldova: Basic Facts," 26 June 2001, Wikileaks.

9. Hill, *Moldova Conflict*, pp. 95, 96.

10. *Ibid.*, pp. 69–73, 104–105.

11. "Russian Deputy Foreign Minister on Moldova," Cable from U.S. Embassy, The Hague, 2 October 2003, Wikileaks.

12. Hill, *Moldova Conflict*, p. 107.

13. "Russian Deputy Foreign Minister on Moldova," Cable from U.S. Embassy, The Hague, 2 October 2003, Wikileaks.

14. "Kozak Memorandum," 19 February 2020, Wikipedia. The two drafts of the Kozak Memorandum are in Hill, *Moldova Conflict*, pp. 197–220; the final version is also available on the internet. The veto authority falls under the concept of "consociation" agreements.

15. Hill, *Moldova Conflict*, p. 142.

16. Hill, *No Place for Russia*, p. 229; Hill, *Moldova Conflict*, pp. 147–148.

17. "Italy's Response to Russian Effort to Resolve Transnistrian Conflict," Cable from U.S. Embassy, Rome, 25 November 2003, Wikileaks; Hill, *Moldova Conflict*, p. 141.

18. *Ibid.*, p. 152.

19. "Italy's Response to Russian Effort to Resolve Transnistrian Conflict," Cable from U.S. Embassy, Rome, 25 November 2003, Wikileaks; Hill, *Moldova Conflict*, pp. 147–149, 152. In a recent example, the military orchestra of Saudi Arabia experienced considerable difficulties playing the Russian national anthem; "Sounds Grate! Saudi Military Orchestra Welcomes Putin with Russia's Anthem … or at Least It Tries to," 14 October 2019, RT.

20. "Moldovan President Voronin Terms Kozak Plan Unacceptable," Cable from U.S. Embassy, Rome, 3 December 2003, Wikileaks; Hill, *No Place for Russia*, p. 229.

21. "EU on Expanded Transnistria Visa Ban: Need to Persuade Member States," Cable from U.S. Em-

bassy, Brussels, 19 July 2004, Wikileaks; Hill, *No Place for Russia*, p. 229.
  22. "EU Update on Georgia, Moldova, Ukraine," Cable from U.S. Embassy, Brussels, 18 June 2004, Wikileaks.
  23. "U.S.-EU OSCE Consults Focus on Russia," Cable from U.S. Embassy, Brussels, 30 September 2004, Wikileaks.
  24. "Italy's Response to Russian Effort to Resolve Transnistrian Conflict," Cable from U.S. Embassy, Rome, 25 November 2003, Wikileaks; Hill, *No Place for Russia*, p. 231.
  25. de Waal, *Caucasus*, pp. 189–190; Lincoln A. Mitchell, *The Color Revolutions* (Philadelphia: University of Pennsylvania Press, 2012), p. 58.
  26. de Waal, *Caucasus*, p. 191; Mitchell, *Color Revolutions*, pp. 3, 48.
  27. de Waal, *Caucasus*, pp. 190–191; Mitchell, *Color Revolutions*, p. 57; Michael McFaul, *From Cold War to Hot Peace: An American Ambassador in Putin's Russia* (Boston: Houghton Mifflin Harcourt, 2018), p. 68.
  28. de Waal, *Caucasus*, p. 192; Mitchell, *Color Revolutions*, p. 58.
  29. Angus Roxburgh, *The Strongman: Vladimir Putin and the Struggle for Russia* (London: I. B. Tauris, 2014), pp. 128–130; de Waal, *Caucasus*, pp. 192–193.
  30. Roxburgh, *Strongman*, pp. 128–130; Vicken Cheterian, *War and Peace in the Caucasus: Ethnic Conflict and the New Geopolitics* (New York: Columbia University Press, 2008), pp. 210–211.
  31. Roxburgh, *Strongman*, pp. 128–130; René De La Pedraja, *The Russian Military Resurgence: Post-Soviet Decline and Rebuilding, 1992-2018* (Jefferson, NC: McFarland, 2018), pp. 105–106, 192.
  32. Roxburgh, *Strongman*, pp. 128–130; De La Pedraja, *Russian Military Resurgence*, p. 192.
  33. Roxburgh, *Strongman*, p. 112.
  34. De La Pedraja, *Russian Military Resurgence*, p. 192; de Waal, *Caucasus*, pp. 194, 234; Roxburgh, *Strongman*, p. 112.
  35. Mitchell, *Color Revolutions*, p. 49; Roxburgh, *Strongman*, pp. 131–132; Andrew Wilson, *Ukraine's Orange Revolution* (New Haven: Yale University Press, 2005), Chapter 5; Richard Sakwa, *Frontline Ukraine: Crisis in the Borderlands* (London: I. B. Tauris, 2016), p. 151.
  36. Mitchell, *Color Revolutions*, p. 51; Peter Baker and Susan Glasser, *Kremlin Rising: Vladimir Putin's Russia and the End of Revolution* (Washington, D.C.: Pentagon Books, 2007), p. 377.
  37. Mitchell, *Color Revolutions*, pp. 78–79, 83–84, 86, 88; Roxburgh, *Strongman*, pp. 130–132; Baker and Glasser, *Kremlin Rising*, p. 377.
  38. White, *Orange Revolution*, pp. 145–146; Roxburgh, *Strongman*, pp. 135–136; "Poisoning that Shaped 15 Years of Ukraine Politics Never Happened—Prosecutor on Yushchenko Case," 30 July 2019, RT.
  39. Serhy Yekelchyk, *Ukraine: Birth of a Modern Nation* (New York: Oxford University Press, 2007), p. 215.
  40. Wilson, *Orange Revolution*, Chapter 6; Mitchell, *Color Revolutions*, p. 59. In the 21 November 2004 runoff, the 96 percent in Donetsk and the 93 percent in Lugansk for Viktor Yanukovich even exceeded his 89 percent in Sevastopol and the 82 percent in Crimea. In Western Ukraine Viktor Yushchenko ran up similar majorities, for example 92 percent in Lvov and the more modest 76 percent in Kiev.
  41. Wilson, *Orange Revolution*, Chapter 7; Sakwa, *Frontline Ukraine*, p. 52; Yekelchyk, *Ukraine*, pp. 216–217.
  42. Mitchell, *Color Revolutions*, p. 60.
  43. Wilson, *Orange Revolution*, Chapter 7; Sakwa, *Frontline Ukraine*, p. 52.
  44. U.S. Congress, Commission on Security and Cooperation in Europe, *Kyrgyzstan's Revolution: Causes and Consequences* (Washington, D.C.: Government Printing Office, 2007), p. 29; Julia Gerlach, *Color Revolutions in Eurasia* (London: Springer, 2014), pp. 12–13; "Kyrgyz Private Sector Frustrated by Government Corruption," Cable from U.S. Embassy, Bishkek, 30 March 2006, Wikileaks; Carnegie Endowment for International Peace, "Kyrgyzstan after the Events of March 24," 14 June 2004.
  45. Stent, *U.S.-Russian Relations*, p. 117; Carnegie Endowment for International Peace, "Kyrgyzstan after the Events of March 24," 14 June 2004; "Kyrgyz Private Sector Frustrated by Government Corruption," Cable from U.S. Embassy, Bishkek, 30 March 2006, Wikileaks.
  46. Carnegie Endowment for International Peace, "Kyrgyzstan after the Events of March 24," 14 June 2004.
  47. Mitchell, *Color Revolutions*, pp. 53, 55, 61; Gerlach, *Color Revolutions in Eurasia*, p. 13; Erica Marat, *The Tulip Revolution: Kyrgyzstan One Year After, March 15, 2005–March 24, 2006* (Washington, D.C.: The Jamestown Foundation, 2006), pp. 8, 123.
  48. Mitchell, *Color Revolutions*, p. 62; U.S. Congress, *Kyrgyzstan's Revolution*, p. 10; Marat, *The Tulip Revolution*, p. 12.
  49. Gerlach, *Color Revolutions in Eurasia*, pp. 13–14; Mitchell, *Color Revolutions*, p. 62; Marat, *The Tulip Revolution*, p. 8.
  50. Gerlach, *Color Revolutions in Eurasia*, p. 14; Marat, *The Tulip Revolution*, p. 12; Mitchell, *Color Revolutions*, p. 63.
  51. Marat, *The Tulip Revolution*, pp. 9, 124; Mitchell, *Color Revolutions*, p. 62.
  52. Marat, *The Tulip Revolution*, pp. 13, 124–125.
  53. U.S. Congress, *Kyrgyzstan's Revolution*, pp. 13, 27; Stent, *U.S.-Russian Relations*, p. 117; Gerlach, *Color Revolutions in Eurasia*, p. 14; Marat, *The Tulip Revolution*, pp. 13–15, 125.
  54. "Government of Armenia Defers to Putin Comments on Kyrgyzstan," Cable from U.S. Embassy, Yerevan, 24 March 2005, Wikileaks; Mitchell, *Color Revolutions*, pp. 4, 63–64.
  55. Carnegie Endowment for International Peace, "Kyrgyzstan after the Events of March 24," 14 June 2004; Stent, *U.S.-Russian Relations*, p. 118.

Chapter 13

  1. Lincoln A. Mitchell, *The Color Revolutions* (Philadelphia: University of Pennsylvania Press, 2012), p. 2.

2. "Assistant Secretary Lowenkron Discusses NGO Law with State Duma Deputy Andrey Makarov," Cable from U.S. Embassy, Moscow, 27 January 2006, Wikileaks.

3. "NGO Draft Legislation: Still Unsigned by Putin," Cable from U.S. Embassy, Moscow, 11 January 2006, Wikileaks; "Assistant Secretary Lowenkron Discusses NGO Law with State Duma Deputy Andrey Makarov," Cable from U.S. Embassy, Moscow, 27 January 2006, Wikileaks. Typical of the reaction of the West to the NGO bill was Canada's: "Russia cannot afford to pass restrictive or capricious legislation that constrains the activities of domestic or international organizations." "Russia Also Concerned about Russian Draft NGO Law," Cable from U.S. Embassy, Ottawa, 30 November 2005, Wikileaks.

4. "Putin Signs NGO Legislation," Cable from U.S. Embassy, Moscow, 17 Jan 2006, Wikileaks.

5. "NGOs Chilled by Spy Allegations," Cable from U.S. Embassy, Moscow, 27 Jan 2006, and "Putin Signs NGO Legislation," Cable from U.S. Embassy, Moscow, 17 Jan 2006, Wikileaks.

6. "New Restrictive Russian Electoral Legislation," Cable from U.S. Embassy, Moscow, 18 July 2006, Wikileaks; "Extremism Law Signed by Putin," Cable from U.S. Embassy, Moscow, 31 July 2006, Wikileaks.

7. "Dutch NGO Refused Re-Registration," Cable from U.S. Embassy, Moscow, 27 November 2006, Wikileaks; "Russian-Chechen Friendship Society Ordered Liquidated," Cable from U.S. Embassy, Moscow, 23 January 2007, Wikileaks.

8. "NGOs: Silver Lining but a Looming Dark Cloud," Cable from U.S. Embassy, Moscow, 16 February 2007, Wikileaks; "Russia: The Case for Limited U.S. Funding of RFFE," Cable from U.S. Embassy, Moscow, 27 February 2007; "The Russian NGO Law One Year Later," Cable from U.S. Embassy, Moscow, 20 December 2007, Wikileaks; "Provocations from Russian Security Services," Secret Cable from U.S. Embassy, Moscow, 30 January 2009, Wikileaks.

9. "A Russian Take on OSCE Elections/Other Issues," Cable from U.S. Mission to European Union, Brussels, 3 April 2006, Wikileaks; "Organization for Security and Cooperation in Europe (OSCE)," 23 February 2020, Wikipedia.

10. "OSCE," 23 February 2020, Wikipedia; Igor S. Ivanov, *The New Russian Diplomacy* (Washington, D.C.: Brookings Institution, 2002), pp. 96–99.

11. "Whiter Goest OSCE: A Departing Personal View," Cable from U.S. Mission to European Union, Brussels, 12 June 2006, Wikileaks; Steven Lee Myers, *The New Tsar: The Rise and Reign of Vladimir Putin* (New York: Vintage Books, 2015), p. 230.

12. "U.S.-EU Consults Focus on Russia," Cable from U.S. Mission to European Union, Brussels, 30 September 2004, Wikileaks; "Whiter Goest OSCE: A Departing Personal View," Cable from U.S. Mission to European Union, Brussels, 12 June 2006, Wikileaks; "French Discuss OSCE Issues with Russian Diplomat," Cable from U.S. Embassy, Paris, 8 March 2005, Wikileaks.

13. "Russian Reaction to OSCE Madrid Ministerial," Cable from U.S. Embassy, Madrid, 7 December 2007, Wikileaks; "OSCE," 23 February 2020, Wikipedia.

14. "Moscow Views on Ministerial," Cable from U.S. Embassy, Moscow, 26 November 2007, Wikileaks.

15. "French Explain and Reassure on Trip to Russia," Cable from U.S. Embassy, Paris, 3 January 2005, Wikileaks.

16. "Whiter Goest OSCE: A Departing Personal View," Cable from U.S. Mission to European Union, Brussels, 12 June 2006, Wikileaks.

17. "French Discuss OSCE Issues with Russian Diplomat," Cable from U.S. Embassy, Paris, 8 March 2005, Wikileaks.

18. "Russians on Spanish OSCE Chairmanship," Cable from U.S. Embassy, Madrid, 22 May 2007, Wikileaks.

19. "French Complain about Russian Actions in OSCE, Call for Close Quad Consultations," Cable from U.S. Embassy, Paris, France, 8 June 2006, Wikileaks; "Russians on Spanish OSCE Chairmanship," Cable from U.S. Embassy, Madrid, 22 May 2007, Wikileaks. As one European diplomat explained, "it should be an EU policy goal not to let gaps between the U.S. and EU emerge—particularly on difficult issues. It is important, she said, not to let third countries exploit U.S.-EU differences." "U.S.-EU Consultations on OSCE," Cable from U.S. Mission to European Union, Brussels, 14 May 2004, Wikileaks.

20. "Whiter Goest OSCE: A Departing Personal View," Cable from U.S. Mission to European Union, Brussels, 12 June 2006, Wikileaks.

21. Vladimir Putin, Munich Speech, 10 February 2007; "Government of Russia: Unrelenting but Measured Criticism," Cable from U.S. Embassy, Moscow, 7 September 2007, Wikileaks.

22. "A Russian Take on OSCE Elections/Other Issues," Cable from U.S. Mission to European Union, Brussels, 3 April 2006, Wikileaks; "Russian DFM Grushko on OSCE Dues," Cable from U.S. Embassy, Moscow, 28 December 2007, Wikileaks; "OSCE," 23 February 2020, Wikipedia.

23. "CSTO: Russia's Counter to NATO," Cable from U.S. Embassy, Moscow, 14 March 2007, Wikileaks; "Russia: Using CSTO to Claim Influence in the Former Soviet Union," 23 February 2009, Stratfor.com; Richard Weitz, *Assessing the Collective Security Treaty Organization: Capabilities and Vulnerabilities* (Carlisle, PA: Strategic Studies Institute, 2018), pp. 53–58.

24. "CSTO Rapid Reaction Force Becoming a Reality," Cable from U.S. Embassy, Moscow, 4 June 2009, Wikileaks; "CSTO: Russia's Counter to NATO," Cable from U.S. Embassy, Moscow, 14 March 2007, Wikileaks.

25. "CSTO to Funnel Russian Aid to Afghanistan," Cable from U.S. Embassy, Moscow, 17 December 2007, Wikileaks; "CSTO: Russia's Counter to NATO," Cable from U.S. Embassy, Moscow, 14 March 2007, Wikileaks; "Russia: Using CSTO to Claim Influence in the FSU," 23 February 2009, Stratfor.com.

26. "Defense Minister Reviews CSTO, Russia, Regional Security," Cable from U.S. Embassy, Yerevan, 17 February 2009, Wikileaks; "CSTO: Russia's Counter to NATO," Cable from U.S. Embassy, Moscow, 14 March 2007, Wikileaks; "Russia: The Nuclear

Umbrella and the CSTO," 25 February 2010, Stratfor, Wikileaks.

27. Condoleezza Rice, *No Higher Honor: A Memoir of My Years in Washington* (New York: Crown Publishers, 2011), p. 578. See also, "NATO Secretary General Ready to Reach Out to CSTO?" Cable from U.S. Mission to NATO, 10 September 2009, Wikileaks.

28. Yevgeny Primakov, *Russian Crossroads: Toward the New Millennium* (New Haven: Yale University Press, 2004), pp. 5–7; "Is the Kremlin Really Losing the Information War? Only in the West," Cable from U.S. Embassy, Moscow, 14 August 2008, Wikileaks; Jim Rutenberg, "The Disruption," 17 September 2017, *New York Times Magazine*, p. 50; Ivanov, *The New Russian Diplomacy*, p. 175.

29. Rutenberg, "The Disruption," pp. 52–53; Simon van Zuylen-Wood, "At RT, News Breaks You," 4 May 2017, *Bloomberg Business Week*; Julia Ioffe, "What Is Russia Today?" *Columbia Journalism Review*, September-October 2010; "RT (TV Network)," 5 April 2020, Wikipedia.

30. Rutenberg, "The Disruption," pp. 49, 52–53; Ioffe, "What is Russia Today?" "RT (TV Network)," 5 April 2020, Wikipedia.

31. Rutenberg, "The Disruption," p. 53; "What is RT?" 8 March 2017, *New York Times*; "Russia—Kremlin's TV Seeks to Influence Politics, Fuel Discontent in U.S.," 11 December 2012, p. 8; Open Source Center, *Russia—Kremlin's TV Seeks to Influence Politics, Fuel Discontent in the U.S.*, 11 December 2012.

32. "Is the Kremlin Really Losing the Information War? Only in the West," Cable from U.S. Embassy, Moscow, 14 August 2008, Wikileaks; Ioffe, "What Is Russia Today?"

33. Simon van Zuylen-Wood, "At RT, News Breaks You," 4 May 2017, *Bloomberg Business Week*; Ioffe, "What Is Russia Today?"

34. Rutenberg, "The Disruption," p. 53.

35. van Zuylen-Wood, "At RT, News Breaks You." Rutenberg, "The Disruption," p. 53; Ioffe, "What Is Russia Today?"

36. van Zuylen-Wood, "At RT, News Breaks You"; "RT (TV Network)" 5 April 2020, Wikipedia.

37. Rutenberg, "The Disruption," p. 69; van Zuylen-Wood, "At RT, News Breaks You"; "RT (TV Network)" 5 April 2020, Wikipedia.

38. The main source for these paragraphs is Angus Roxburgh, *The Strongman: Vladimir Putin and the Struggle for Russia* (London: I. B. Tauris, 2014), pp. 184–191.

39. "Is the Kremlin Really Losing the Information War? Only in the West," Cable from U.S. Embassy, Moscow, 14 August 2008, Wikileaks.

40. This paragraph and the next draw on Roxburgh, *Strongman*, pp. 193–196; Angela E. Stent, *The Limits of Partnership: U.S.-Russian Relations in the Twenty-First Century* (Princeton: Princeton University Press, 2015), pp. 85–86, 181–193, 309.

41. "Russia's Institute for Democracy and Cooperation," Cable from U.S. Embassy, Moscow, 30 January 2008, Wikileaks; Roxburgh, *Strongman*, pp. 195–196.

42. "Russia's Institute for Democracy and Cooperation," Cable from U.S. Embassy, Moscow, 30 January 2008, Wikileaks.

43. "Institut de la Démocratie et de la Coopération," Paris, 5 July 2018; "Russia's Institute for Democracy and Cooperation," Cable from U.S. Embassy, Moscow, 30 January 2008, Wikileaks; "The Birth of Putin's Institute of Democracy and Cooperation," 25 June 2018, thesternfacts; Roxburgh, *Strongman*, p. 196.

44. "Russia's Institute for Democracy and Cooperation," Cable from U.S. Embassy, Moscow, 30 January 2008, Wikileaks; "In the Heart of New York, Russia's Soft Power Arm Gaining Momentum," 15 February 2009, RadioFreeEurope/RadioLiberty; "The Birth of Putin's Institute of Democracy and Cooperation," 25 June 2018, thesternfacts.

45. "The Birth of Putin's Institute of Democracy and Cooperation," 25 June 2018, thesternfacts; "Pro-Putin Think Tank Based in New York Shuts Down," 30 June 2015, BuzzFeed News.

46. "Itar-TASS," *Encyclopedia Britannica*; "TASS," 25 September 2019, Wikipedia; "Russian Media Continues to Push Anti-U.S., Anti-Georgian Message," Cable from U.S. Embassy, Moscow, 13 August 2008, Wikileaks.

47. "Sputnik (News Agency)," 7 April 2020, Wikipedia; "About Us," 2020, Sputnik Web Page.

48. Rutenberg, "The Disruption," p. 64.

49. "Sputnik (News Agency), 7 April 2020, Wikipedia.

50. "About Us," 2020, Sputnik Web Page.

Chapter 14

1. Angus Roxburgh, *Strongman: Vladimir Putin and the Struggle for Russia* (London: I. B. Tauris, 2014), p. 99.

2. Richard Sakwa, *Frontline Ukraine: Crisis in the Borderlands* (London: I. B. Tauris, 2016), pp. 52–53; "Yulia Tymoshenko," 31 March 2020, Wikipedia.

3. "Ukraine on the Road to NATO: A Status Report," Cable from U.S. Embassy, Kiev, 15 February 2006, Wikileaks; Sakwa, *Frontline Ukraine*, p. 53; Steven Pifer, *The Eagle and the Trident: U.S.-Ukraine Relations in Turbulent Times* (Washington, D.C.: Brookings Institution, 2017), p. 280.

4. "Moscow Comfortable with Ukrainian Developments," Cable from U.S. Embassy, Moscow, 30 January 2006, Wikileaks; "Ukraine: Party of Regions Election Strategy: A New Approach," Cable from U.S. Embassy, Kiev, 15 March 2006, Wikileaks; "Manafort on Election Problems," Cable from U.S. Embassy, Kiev, 24 March 2006, Wikileaks; Sakwa, *Frontline Ukraine*, p. 53.

5. "Ukraine: Prime Minister Yanukovych Advances Relations with EU," Cable from U.S. Embassy, Kiev, 18 September 2006, Wikileaks; "Prime Minister Yanukovych Tells Assistant Secretary Fried: Ukraine's European Choice Has Been Decided," Cable from U.S. Embassy, Kiev, 17 November 2006, Wikileaks.

6. "Ukraine: Engaging the New Ukrainian Reality after 50 Days of Prime Minister Yanukovych," Cable from U.S. Embassy, Kiev, 28 September 2006, Wikileaks.

7. "Ukrainian Crisis: Initial Reactions from

Moscow," Cable from U.S. Embassy, Moscow, 3 April 2007, Wikileaks; "Ukrainian Crisis: No Sharp Movement from Moscow," 6 April 2007, Wikileaks; Sakwa, *Frontline Ukraine*, pp. 53–54.

8. "Russia's Sober Outlook on Ukrainian Parliamentary Elections," Cable from U.S. Embassy, Moscow, 26 October 2007, Wikileaks; Sakwa, *Frontline Ukraine*, pp. 53–54.

9. "Ukraine and Russia April 13," 2007, Stratfor, Wikileaks; Angela E. Stent, *The Limits of Partnership: U.S.-Russian Relations in the Twenty-First Century* (Princeton: Princeton University Press, 2015), pp. 200–201; de Waal, *The Caucasus*, pp. 168, 177.

10. "Government of Russia Not Disappointed with Tymoshenko's Comeback," Cable from U.S. Embassy, Moscow, 18 December 2007, Wikileaks; "Russia Ukraine—Energy and Elections," 27 June 2007, Stratfor, Wikileaks.

11. "Government of Russia Not Disappointed with Tymoshenko's Comeback," Cable from U.S. Embassy, Moscow, 18 December 2007, Wikileaks.

12. "Ministry of Foreign Affairs Official on the Threat of Secession in Georgia," Cable from U.S. Embassy, Ankara, 3 December 2003, Wikileaks; "Turkey/Georgia: Some Bumps in the Road," Cable from U.S. Embassy, Ankara, 24 March 2006, Wikileaks; Thomas de Waal, *The Caucasus: An Introduction* (New York: Oxford University Press, 2010), p. 146.

13. Roxburgh, *Strongman*, p. 118.

14. "Turkey/Georgia: Some Bumps in the Road," Cable from U.S. Embassy, Ankara, 24 March 2006, Wikileaks.

15. René De La Pedraja, *The Russian Military Resurgence: Post-Soviet Decline and Rebuilding, 1992–2018* (Jefferson, NC: McFarland, 2018), p. 194; de Waal, *The Caucasus*, pp. 200–201.

16. Roxburgh, *Strongman*, p. 120.

17. Stent, *U.S.-Russian Relations*, p. 168; Ronald D. Asmus, *A Little War that Shook the World: Georgia, Russia, and the Future of the West* (New York: Palgrave Macmillan, 2010), pp. 57–58; de Waal, *The Caucasus*, pp. 203–204.

18. De La Pedraja, *The Russian Military Resurgence*, p. 195; "Russia-Georgia: Deputy Assistant Secretary Bryza Conversation with Russian Deputy Foreign Minister Karasin," Cable from U.S. Embassy, Moscow, 19 October 2006, Wikileaks.

19. "Bulgaria Consults on Arms Transfer to Georgia," Secret/NoForn Cable from U.S. Embassy, Sofia, 28 September 2006, Wikileaks; "Czechs Request U.S. Information on Georgia's Military Buildup," Secret Cable from U.S. Embassy, Prague, 24 October 2005, Wikileaks.

20. "Azerbaijan's Intention Ambiguity toward NATO," Cable from U.S. Embassy, Baku, 17 January 2008, Wikileaks. American diplomats stated that "Azerbaijan always tries to stay a step behind Georgia on issues related to Euro-Atlantic Integration, letting the Georgians test the waters in terms of Russia's response." See, "Azerbaijan's Relationship with Russia in the Lead Up to Medvedev's Visit," Cable from U.S. Embassy, Baku, 2 July 2008, Wikileaks.

21. "Georgia Arrests Russians for Spying, Planning Provocation," Secret/NoForn Cable from U.S. Embassy, Tbilisi, 28 September 2006, Wikileaks; Andrei Illarionov, "The Russian Leadership's Preparation for War, 1999–2008," in Svante E. Cornell and S. Frederick Starr, eds., *The Guns of August 2008* (2009), pp. 61–62; "Armenians Worried about Effects of Georgia-Russia Relations," Cable from U.S. Embassy, Yerevan, 6 October 2006, Wikileaks.

22. "Not War, but Close: Russian Reaction to Georgia Arrests of Russian Soldiers," Cable from U.S. Embassy, Moscow, 28 September 2006, Wikileaks; "NATO Allies Give Georgia Constructive Criticism in Handling of Russian Spy Case," Secret/NoForn Cable from U.S. Mission to NATO, 16 October 2006, Wikileaks.

23. "Georgian Arrests Update—September 29," Cable from U.S. Embassy, Tbilisi, 29 September 2006, Wikileaks; "Russia Reacts to Arrests of Soldiers in Georgia," Cable from U.S. Embassy, Moscow, 29 September 2006, Wikileaks; "NATO Allies Give Georgia Constructive Criticism in Handling of Russian Spy Case," Secret/NoForn Cable from U.S. Mission to NATO, 16 October 2006, Wikileaks.

24. "Georgia Releases Russian Officers," Cable from U.S. Embassy, Tbilisi, 2 October 2006, Wikileaks; "Russia-Georgia: No Let Up," Cable from U.S. Embassy, Moscow, 9 October 2006, Wikileaks; Illarionov, "The Russian Leadership," 63–64.

25. "Georgia-Russia: Some Positive Steps—and Some Red Lines," Cable from U.S. Embassy, Moscow, 4 April 2006, Wikileaks; "Russia Transfer Akhalkalaki Military Base to Georgia," Cable from U.S. Embassy, Tbilisi, 29 June 2007, Wikileaks; "Another Train with Russian Military Hardware Leaves Georgia Base," 26 July 2007, RIA Novosti.

26. "Russia-Georgia: No Let-Up," Secret Cable from U.S. Embassy, Moscow, 9 October 2006, Wikileaks; "Russia-Georgia: Backlash against the Backlash?" Cable from U.S. Embassy, Moscow, 12 October 2006, Wikileaks; Illarionov, "The Russian Leadership," p. 62; Asmus, *Little War*, p. 72.

27. "Russia Reacts to Arrests of Soldiers in Georgia," Cable from U.S. Embassy, Moscow, 29 September 2006, Wikileaks; "Georgian Arrests Update—September 29," Cable from U.S. Embassy, Tbilisi, 29 September 2006, Wikileaks; "Georgia Releases Russian Officers," Cable from U.S. Embassy, Tbilisi, 2 October 2006, Wikileaks; "Russian Sanctions on Georgia to Stay for Now," Cable from U.S. Embassy, Tbilisi, 3 October 2006, Wikileaks; "Impact of Russian Sanctions on Georgian Economy," Cable from U.S. Embassy, Tbilisi, 23 August 2007, Wikileaks; Illarionov, "The Russian Leadership," pp. 62–63; Asmus, *Little War*, p. 72.

28. "Georgia-Russia: FM Bezhuashvili Gets Russia's Message," Cable from U.S. Embassy, Moscow, 2 November 2006, Wikileaks.

29. Stent, *U.S.-Russian Relations*, pp. 153–154.

30. "U.S. Joseph-Russian DFM Kislyak Meeting on Strategic Security Dialogue: Part I," Secret Cable from U.S. Embassy, Moscow, 9 March 2007, Wikileaks; "NATO-Russia: Missile Defense Playing out as Debate between U.S. and Russia," Cable from U.S. Mission to NATO, 2 May 2007, Wikileaks; Stent, *U.S.-Russian Relations*, p. 154; Roxburgh, *Strongman*, pp. 200–201.

31. Stent, *U.S.-Russian Relations*, pp. 155–156; Roxburgh, *Strongman*, pp. 200–207.
32. Luis-Marie Clouet, *Rosoboronexport, Spearhead of the Russian Arms Industry* (Paris: Russia/NIS Center, 2007), pp. 7–9.
33. "Russian Firms Decry U.S. Sanctions," 5 August 2006, Associated Press; "U.S. Puts Sanctions on 7 Foreign Companies Dealing with Iran," *New York Times*.
34. "Russian Deputy Foreign Minister Kislyak: Bilateral Relations Update," Cable from U.S. Embassy, Moscow, 9 November 2006, Wikileaks.
35. "U.S. Sanctions Rosoboronexport over Deals with Iran," 8 January 2007, *Eurasia Daily Monitor*; "Russian Deputy Foreign Minister Kislyak: Bilateral Relations Update," Cable from U.S. Embassy, Moscow, 9 November 2006, Wikileaks; "Russian Anger over New U.S. Sanctions," 5 January 2007, *Sydney Morning Herald*.
36. "U.S. Sanctions Rosoboronexport over Deals with Iran," 8 January 2007, *Eurasia Daily Monitor*; "Russia Reacts Negatively to Imposition of ISNPA Sanctions," Cable from U.S. Embassy, Moscow, 10 January 2007, Wikileaks; "Russian Anger over New U.S. Sanctions," 5 January 2007, *Sydney Morning Herald*.
37. "Russians Defend Arms Transfers to Iran, Syria," Cable from U.S. Embassy, Moscow, 31 January 2007, Wikileaks; "U.S. Imposes Sanctions on Arms Suppliers to Iran, Syria," 6 January 2007, The Age.
38. "Russians Defend Arms Transfers to Iran, Syria," Cable from U.S. Embassy, Moscow, 31 January 2007, Wikileaks; "Russia Reacts Negatively to Imposition of ISNPA Sanctions," Cable from U.S. Embassy, Moscow, 10 January 2007, Wikileaks.
39. "Russians Defend Arms Transfers to Iran, Syria," Cable from U.S. Embassy, Moscow, 31 January 2007, Wikileaks.
40. "Putin Says Russia Won't Be Dictated to over Arms Purchases," 31 October 2007, RIA Novosti; "Russians Defend Arms Transfers to Iran, Syria," Cable from U.S. Embassy, Moscow, 31 January 2007, Wikileaks.
41. Roxburgh, *Strongman*, p. 196.

Chapter 15

1. "Putin in Munich: Sharp Tone, but Familiar Complaints," Cable from U.S. Embassy, Moscow, 12 February 2007, Wikileaks.
2. Remarks of President Vladimir Putin at the 43rd Munich Conference, 10 February 2007.
3. This paragraph and the next draw on "Putin and Gates Dominate Munich Security Conference," Cable from U.S. Consulate, Munich, 12 February 2007, and "Putin's Munich Speech: One Week Later," Cable from U.S. Embassy, Moscow, 16 February 2007, Wikileaks, Robert M. Gates, *Duty: Memoirs of a Secretary at War* (New York: Alfred A. Knopf, 2014), pp. 155–157.
4. Ronald D. Asmus, *A Little War That Shook the World* (New York: Palgrave Macmillan, 2010), p. 128. For a sample of U.S. anger at Putin's Munich Speech, See, Michael McFaul, *From Cold War to Hot Peace: An American Ambassador in Putin's Russia* (Boston: Houghton Mifflin Harcourt, 2018), pp. 72–73.
5. "Estonia's Bronze Soldier: Excavation Begins," Cable from U.S. Embassy, Tallinn, 26 April 2007, Wikileaks; "Reactions to Removal of Estonia's Bronze Soldier," Cable from U.S. Embassy, Tallinn, 27 April 2007, Wikileaks.
6. "Estonia's Bronze Soldier: Excavation Begins," Cable from U.S. Embassy, Tallinn, 26 April 2007, Wikileaks; "Reactions to Removal of Estonia's Bronze Soldier," Cable from U.S. Embassy, Tallinn, 27 April 2007, Wikileaks.
7. "Estonia: Demonstrators Quit Estonian Embassy as Ambassador Returns to Tallinn," Cable from U.S. Embassy, Moscow, 4 May 2007, Wikileaks; "Update on Russia-Estonia Standoff," Cable from U.S. Embassy, Moscow, 11 May 2007, Wikileaks.
8. "Estonia's Cyber Attacks: World's First Virtual Attack against Nation State," Secret Cable from U.S. Embassy, Tallinn, 4 June 2007, Wikileaks.
9. "Russian Bear Hug Squeezes Estonian Economy," Cable from U.S. Embassy, Tallinn, 29 May 2007, Wikileaks.
10. "Estonia's Cyber Attacks: World's First Virtual Attack against Nation State," Secret Cable from U.S. Embassy, Tallinn, 4 June 2007, Wikileaks; "Russian Bear Hug Squeezes Estonian Economy," Cable from U.S. Embassy, Tallinn, 29 May 2007, Wikileaks.
11. This quotation and the next from "Estonia's Cyber Attacks: World's First Virtual Attack against Nation State," Secret Cable from U.S. Embassy, Tallinn, 4 June 2007, Wikileaks.
12. "Russian-Estonian Relations: Inching toward Normalcy," Cable from U.S. Embassy, Moscow, 7 September 2007, Wikileaks.
13. "Putin's Munich Speech: One Week Later," Cable from U.S. Embassy, Moscow, 16 February 2007, Wikileaks.
14. "Putin's State of the Federation Address," Cable from U.S. Embassy, Moscow, 26 April 2007, Wikileaks.
15. "CFE and Putin's April 26 Remarks," Cable from U.S. Embassy, Paris, 3 May 2007, Wikileaks.
16. "NATO Russia Council/CFE, Russia Wants Complete Elimination of Flank Regime," Cable from U.S. Mission to NATO, 27 July 2007, Wikileaks.
17. "State Duma Votes Unanimously to Suspend CFE Treaty," Cable from U.S. Embassy, Moscow, 9 November 2007, Wikileaks; "CFE Impasse: How Did We Get Where We Are?" Cable from U.S. Mission to EU, 15 April 2009, Wikileaks.
18. "NATO Russia Council/CFE: Russia Wants Compete Elimination of Flank Regime," Cable from U.S. Embassy, Moscow, 27 July 2007, Wikileaks; "CFE Impasse: How Did We Get Where We Are?" Cable from U.S. Mission to EU, 15 April 2009, Wikileaks; "CFE," 21 May 2007, Stratfor, Wikileaks.
19. "CFE Impasse: How Did We Get Where We Are?" Cable from U.S. Mission to EU, 15 April 2009, Wikileaks; "The Conventional Armed Forces in Europe (CFE) Treaty and the Adapted CFE Treaty at a Glance," 1 August 2012, Arms Control Organization.
20. "Putin's State of the Federation Address," Cable from U.S. Embassy, Moscow, 26 April 2007,

Wikileaks; "France Shares U.S. Views on CFE and Putin's April 26 Remarks," Cable from U.S. Embassy, 30 April 2007, Wikileaks; "Russia and a CFE Moratorium," Cable from U.S. Embassy, Moscow, 11 May 2007, Wikileaks; "Russia: No Flexibility on CFE Redlines," Cable from U.S. Embassy, Moscow, 8 June 2007, Wikileaks.

21. "State Duma Votes Unanimously to Suspend CFE Treaty," Cable from U.S. Embassy, Moscow, 9 November 2007, Wikileaks; "CFE: The Day after," Cable from U.S. Embassy, Moscow, 7 December 2007, Wikileaks.

22. "Russia and Kosovo: The Politics of Delay," Cable from U.S. Embassy, Moscow, 19 September 2006, Wikileaks; Asmus, *Little War*, pp. 88–95.

23. "D'Alema/Kosovo: Can't Let Russia Impose Will on Europe," Cable from U.S. Embassy, Rome, 26 July 2007, Wikileaks; Asmus, *Little War*, pp. 94–99.

24. "Ministry of Foreign Affairs Official Rethinks Putin's Abilities, Urges Discretion on Options for Kosovo," Secret Cable from U.S. Embassy, Paris, 9 March 2005, Wikileaks; "Kosovo: Hardline Russian Deputy Foreign Minister Titov Urges Phased Approach," Cable from U.S. Embassy, Moscow, 16 March 2007, Wikileaks; "Kosovo: U.S. Special Representative Wisner Briefs Austrian Political Director," Cable from U.S. Embassy, Vienna, 24 April 2006, Wikileaks. The possibility cannot be ruled out that spies of either military intelligence (GRU) or the foreign intelligence service (SVR) uncovered the Western proposal to negotiate a swap with Russia over Kosovo. However, with the available evidence I have found more plausible the explanation that when a proposal was circulating during several years among countless diplomats of many countries, inevitably someone blurted out the idea to a Russian diplomat.

25. "D'Alema/Kosovo: Can't Let Russia Impose Will on Europe," Cable from U.S. Embassy, Rome, 26 July 2007, Wikileaks.

26. "Ukraine: MFA Official Worries that Kosovo Independence Could Complicate Transnistria," Cable from U.S. Embassy, Kiev, 14 September 2006, Wikileaks; "D'Alema/Kosovo: Can't Let Russia Impose Will on Europe," Cable from U.S. Embassy, Rome, 26 July 2007, Wikileaks.

27. "Russia-France Relations: After Kouchner, Before Sarkozy," Cable from U.S. Embassy, Moscow, 20 September 2007.

28. Quotation and rest of paragraph from "Russia-France Relations: After Kouchner, Before Sarkozy," Cable from U.S. Embassy, Moscow, 20 September 2007.

29. "Deputy Assistant Secretary Bryza's January 19 Meeting with Georgian Prime Minister Gurgenidze," Secret Cable from U.S. Embassy, Tbilisi, 24 January 2008, Wikileaks.

30. "Russia Prepares for a Kosovo Collision," Cable from U.S. Embassy, Moscow, 19 January 2008, Wikileaks; Asmus, *Little War*, pp. 98–104.

31. "Russia Continues to Resist Kosovo CDI," Cable from U.S. Embassy, Moscow, 30 January 2008, Wikileaks; "Turkey Prepared to Recognize Kosovar Independence and Will Seek to Calm Moscow," Cable from U.S. Embassy, Ankara, 15 February 2008, Wikileaks.

32. "Kosovo: Russia Reacts Predictably, Stops Short of Recognition of Frozen Conflicts," Cable from U.S. Embassy, Moscow, 18 February 2008, Wikileaks.

33. "NATO: The Day after Kosovo Independence," Cable from U.S. Mission to NATO, 18 February 2008, Wikileaks; "Russia Attempts to Frame Kosovo Discussion as a Breach of International Law," Cable from U.S. Embassy, Moscow, 5 March 2008, Wikileaks; Web sites of World Bank and International Monetary Fund.

Chapter 16

1. "Russia Continues to Overplay Hand with Georgia: Warns of Dangers of War," Cable from U.S. Embassy, Moscow, 7 May 2008, Wikileaks.

2. "Russia Cautiously Approaches Improvement in Ties with Georgia," Cable from U.S. Embassy, Moscow, 13 February 2008, Wikileaks; "Georgia Strongly Protests Russia's Withdrawal from CIS Sanctions on Abkhazia," Cable from U.S. Embassy, Tbilisi, 7 March 2008, Wikileaks.

3. "Duma Links Kosovo and NATO MAP to Frozen Conflicts' Recognition," Cable from U.S. Embassy, Moscow, 24 March 2008, Wikileaks; Ronald D. Asmus, *A Little War that Shook the World: Georgia, Russia, and the Future of the West* (New York: Palgrave Macmillan, 2010), p. 146.

4. Condoleezza Rice, *No Higher Honor: A Memoir of My Years in Washington* (New York: Crowne Publishers, 2011), pp. 671–672; Asmus, *Little War*, pp. 115–117, 124–125.

5. Rice, *No Higher Honor*, pp. 671–675; Asmus, *Little War*, pp. 118–125.

6. "Russia Loses Bucharest," Cable from U.S. Embassy, Moscow, 18 April 2008 and "Georgia Reacts Positively to NATO Summit Outcome," Cable from U.S. Embassy, Tbilisi, 4 April 2008, Wikileaks; Asmus, *Little War*, pp. 133–137; Rice, *No Higher Honor*, pp. 673–675.

7. "Russia's Expectations for NATO Summit Depend on MAP for Ukraine and Georgia," Cable from U.S. Embassy, Moscow, 25 March 2008, Wikileaks; "Russia Loses Bucharest," Cable from U.S. Embassy, Moscow, 18 April 2008, Wikileaks; Asmus, *Little War*, pp. 128, 135–136; Rice, *No Higher Honor*, pp. 675–676.

8. "Russia Loses Bucharest," Cable from U.S. Embassy, Moscow, 18 April 2008, Wikileaks.

9. "Russia's Reaction to Saakashvili's New Abkhazia Proposal," Cable from U.S. Embassy, Moscow, 8 April 2008, Wikileaks.

10. "Russian Deputy Foreign Minister Denisov on Georgia-Abkhazia," Cable from U.S. Embassy, Moscow, 15 April 2008, Wikileaks.

11. "Putin's Instructions on Abkhazia and South Ossetia," Cable from U.S. Embassy, Moscow, 16 April 2008, Wikileaks.

12. "Russia Unmoved by Concerns over Presidential Instructions," Cable from U.S. Embassy, Moscow, 18 April 2008, Wikileaks; "Georgia Freezes Negotiations with Russia on WTO Membership," Cable from U.S. Embassy, Moscow, 30 April 2008, Wikileaks.

13. "Georgian Ambassador to Armenia Gives His Views," Secret/NoForn Cable from U.S. Embassy, Yerevan, 26 February 2010, Wikileaks. For more discussion of this extraordinary cable, See Chapter 18 note 30.
14. "Georgia Reacts to Russian Peacekeeping Increase," Cable from U.S. Embassy, Tbilisi, 30 April 2008, Wikileaks; "Russia Completes Peace Keeper Force Reinforcement," Cable from U.S. Embassy, Tbilisi, 5 May 2008, Wikileaks; René De la Pedraja, *The Russian Military Resurgence: Post-Soviet Decline and Rebuilding, 1992-2018* (Jefferson, NC: McFarland, 2018), p. 198.
15. "Russia: Not Seeking Conflict with Georgia but Will Defend Interests," Cable from U.S. Embassy, Moscow, 6 May 2008, Wikileaks.
16. "Deputy Assistant Secretary Bryza Visit with Defense Minister Kezerashvili," Cable from U.S. Embassy, Tbilisi, 2 June 2008, Wikileaks; "Germany/Russia: Chancellery Views on MAP for Ukraine and Georgia," Cable from U.S. Embassy, Berlin, 6 June 2008, Wikileaks.
17. "Russia-Georgia Relations: A Small Thaw?" Cable from U.S. Embassy, Moscow, 25 January 2008, Wikileaks; Angus Roxburgh, *The Strongman: Vladimir Putin and the Struggle for Russia* (London: I. B. Tauris, 2004), pp. 296–300.
18. "Georgia: Russian Reaction to UNOMIG Report," Cable from U.S. Embassy, Moscow, 28 May 2008, Wikileaks; "Getting Germany on Board for MAP for Georgia and Ukraine," Cable from U.S. Embassy, Berlin, 5 June 2008, Wikileaks.
19. Rice, *No Higher Honor*, pp. 678–680; De La Pedraja, *Russian Military Resurgence*, pp. 198–199.
20. Rice, *No Higher Honor*, pp. 684–686; De La Pedraja, *Russian Military Resurgence*, p. 201.
21. This paragraph and the next draw on Asmus, *Little War*, pp. 168–170 and De La Pedraja, *Russian Military Resurgence*, pp. 201–203.
22. The discussion in this section draws on Independent International Fact-Finding Mission on the Conflict in Georgia, *Report*, 3 vols. (Brussels: European Union, 2009) and De La Pedraja, *Russian Military Resurgence*.
23. Rice, *No Higher Honor*, pp. 687–688.
24. Asmus, *Little War*, pp. 188–210; De La Pedraja, *Russian Military Resurgence*, pp. 211–212.
25. "Press Statement Following Negotiations with French President Nicolas Sarkozy," 12 August 2008, the Kremlin, Moscow.
26. Asmus, *Little War*, pp. 188–210; De La Pedraja, *Russian Military Resurgence*, pp. 212–213.
27. Asmus, *Little War*, p. 206.
28. Fact-Finding Mission, *Report*, 2: 219; Asmus, *Little War*, p. 212.
29. De La Pedraja, *Russian Military Resurgence*, pp. 213–214.
30. Fact-Finding Mission, *Report*, 2:175–184; Asmus, *Little War*, p. 211.
31. "Pressuring Russia Economically: Difficult Choices," Cable from U.S. Embassy, Moscow, 29 August 2008, Wikileaks; Asmus, *Little War*, pp. 212–213.
32. "French View OSCE Monitors in Georgia as Emergency Step Only," Cable from U.S. Embassy, Paris, France, 21 August 2008, Wikileaks.
33. *Ibid.*
34. "Russia Pockets EU Council Statement on Georgia," Cable from U.S. Embassy, Moscow, 5 September 2008, Wikileaks.
35. "New Sarkozy-Medvedev Agreement: Questions Remain," Secret/NoForn Cable from U.S. Embassy, Moscow, 9 September 2008, Wikileaks.
36. "Press Conference Following Talks with President of France Nicolas Sarkozy," 8 September 2008.
37. Asmus, *Little War*, pp. 212–213.

Chapter 17

1. "French View OSCE Monitors in Georgia as Emergency Step Only," Cable from U.S. Embassy, Paris, 21 August 2008, Wikileaks.
2. "NATO Allies Lack Cohesion during First Meeting on Georgia Crisis," Secret/NoForn Cable from U.S. Mission to NATO, 11 August 2008, Wikileaks; "For Peter: Black Sea Key for Russia," August 2008, Stratfor, Wikileaks.
3. "NATO Allies Lack Cohesion during First Meeting on Georgia Crisis," Secret/NoForn Cable from U.S. Mission to NATO, 11 August 2008, Wikileaks; "Ukraine, MAP, and the Georgia-Russia Conflict," Cable from U.S. Mission to NATO, 14 August 2014, Wikileaks.
4. "Russian Media Continues to Push anti-U.S., Anti-Georgian Message," Cable from U.S. Embassy, Moscow, 13 August 2008, Wikileaks.
5. "Russian Online Opinions Largely Anti-American, Pro-Russia," Cable from U.S. Embassy, Moscow, 12 August 2008, Wikileaks; "Youth-Dominated Russian Blogosphere Critical of U.S., Georgia," Cable from U.S. Embassy, Moscow, 14 August 2008, Wikileaks.
6. "Union of Soldiers' Mothers Says Government of Russia Should Have Acted Sooner in South Ossetia," Cable from U.S. Embassy, Moscow, 14 August 2008, Wikileaks.
7. "Russian Moderates' Views on the Conflict and What It Means for Russia and U.S.-Russian Relations," Cable from U.S. Embassy, Moscow, 20 August 2008, Wikileaks.
8. "Russia-Georgia: Anti-U.S. Backlash," Cable from U.S. Embassy, Moscow, 12 August 2008, Wikileaks; "Democratic Opposition Test Drives Unity, Opposition to War," Cable from U.S. Embassy, Moscow, 26 August 2008, Wikileaks.
9. "Russia Defiant," Cable from U.S. Embassy, Moscow, 14 August 2008, Wikileaks; Independent International Fact-Finding Mission on the Conflict in Georgia, *Report*, 3 vols. (Brussels: European Union, 2009), 1: 18.
10. "Russia on New Monitors, Relations with West," Cable from U.S. Embassy, Moscow, 12 September 2008, Wikileaks; "Russian Leadership Continues Offensive," Cable from U.S. Embassy, Moscow, 12 September 2008, Wikileaks.
11. "South Ossetia, Abkhazia Leaders Seek Independence and Russian Guarantees against Georgia,"

Cable from U.S. Embassy, Moscow, 14 August 2008, Wikileaks.

12. "Medvedev Will Recognize South Ossetian, Abkhaz Independence," Cable from U.S. Embassy, Moscow, 26 August 2008; "Medvedev's Letter of Recognition," Cable from U.S. Embassy, Moscow, 26 August 2008, Wikileaks; René De La Pedraja, *The Russian Military Resurgence: Post-Soviet Decline and Rebuilding, 1992–2018* (Jefferson, NC: McFarland, 2018), p. 213.

13. "Embassy Action to Block Austria-Russia Gas Pipeline Negotiations," Cable from U.S. Embassy, Vienna, 29 August 2008, Wikileaks.

14. "Russia Pockets EU Council Statement on Georgia," Cable from U.S. Embassy, Moscow, 5 September 2008, Wikileaks.

15. "Russia Halts Military Cooperation with NATO Countries," Cable from U.S. Mission to NATO, 22 August 2008, Wikileaks.

16. "NATO-Russia: Putting No Business as Usual into Practice," Cable from Secretary of State, Washington, D.C., 2 September 2008, Wikileaks.

17. "CSTO Summit Hailed as Victory for Russian Diplomacy," Cable from U.S. Embassy, Moscow, 10 September 2008; Congressional Research Service, "U.S.-Russian Civilian Nuclear Cooperation Agreement: Issues for Congress," 9 September 2008, Wikileaks.

18. "Open Skies September 23 Plenary: Russia Cites Safety for Restrictions," Cable from U.S. Mission to European Union, Brussels, 25 September 2008, Wikileaks.

19. "Germany/Georgia: Status of EU Observer Mission and Other Initiatives," Cable from U.S. Embassy, Berlin, 12 September 2008, Wikileaks.

20. "Russia Confident at Parliamentary Assembly of Council of Europe," Cable from U.S. Embassy, Moscow, 24 September 2008, Wikileaks; "Reconsideration on Substantial Grounds of Previously Ratified Credentials of the Russian Federation," 1 October 2008, Parliamentary Assembly of the Council of Europe.

21. "Government of Turkey Urged to Demand Russian Withdrawal from Gori; Erdogan Goes to Moscow and Tbilisi," Cable from U.S. Embassy, Ankara, 14 August 2008, Wikileaks.

22. "Belarussian Embassy: No Government of Russia Pressure to Recognize Republics," Cable from U.S. Embassy, Moscow, 2 October 2008, Wikileaks; "India Not Taking Sides on Russia—Georgia," Cable from U.S. Embassy, New Delhi, 4 September 2008, Wikileaks.

23. "Russia Campaigns for International Support on Georgia," Cable from U.S. Embassy, Moscow, 3 September 2008, Wikileaks.

24. "Georgia Disappointed with China's Response to Russia-Georgia Conflict," Cable from U.S. Embassy, Beijing, 14 August 2008, Wikileaks; "China Maintains Consistent Position; Will Not Recognize South Ossetia and Abkhazia, Says MFA," Cable from U.S. Embassy, Beijing, 18 March 2009, Wikileaks; De La Pedraja, *Russian Military Resurgence*, p. 213.

25. "Nicaragua Recognizes Independence of South Ossetia and Abkhazia," Cable from U.S. Embassy, Managua, 4 September 2008, Wikileaks.

26. "Belarussian Embassy: No Government of Russia Pressure to Recognize Republics," Cable from U.S. Embassy, Moscow, 2 October 2008, Wikileaks.

27. "Russian Leadership Continues Offensive," Cable from U.S. Embassy, Moscow, 12 September 2008, Wikileaks.

28. "French Presidency Reacts to Geneva Meeting on Georgia," Cable from U.S. Embassy, Paris, 17 October 2008, Wikileaks.

29. "Russia Confident at PACE," Cable from U.S. Embassy, Moscow, 24 September 2008, Wikileaks.

30. "Ossetians Refuse Access to OSCE," Cable from U.S. Embassy, Tbilisi, 12 September 2008, Wikileaks; "Georgia: Military Moves from Abkhazia on the Horizon?" Cable from U.S. Embassy, Tbilisi, 23 December 2008 Wikileaks; "Next Steps on an OSCE Field Mission Mandate for Georgia," Cable from U.S. Mission, Brussels, 1 January 2009, Wikileaks; Ronald D. Asmus, *A Little War that Shook the World: Georgia, Russia, and the Future of the West* (New York: Palgrave Macmillan, 2010), pp. 211–212.

31. "UN Secretariat Considers Changes to Georgia Mission," Cable from U.S. Mission, New York, 18 December 2008, Wikileaks; "Russia Receptive to OSCE/UNOMIG Compromise," Cable from U.S. Embassy, Moscow, 14 January 2009, Wikileaks; "Georgia: Security Council Extends UNOMIG Mandate," Cable from U.S. Mission, New York, 14 February 2009, Wikileaks; "Russia Vetoes UN Observer Mission," 15 June 2009, Hillary Clinton E-Mails, Wikileaks; Asmus, *Little War*, pp. 211–212.

32. "Berlusconi's Comments on Missile Defense and Kosovo Create Firestorm in Italy," Cable from U.S. Embassy, Rome, 13 November 2008, Wikileaks.

Chapter 18

1. "Azerbaijan: Presidential Advisor Fears Russia's New Era in South Caucasus," Cable from U.S. Embassy, Baku, 2 September 2008, Wikileaks.

2. Thomas de Waal, *The Caucasus: An Introduction* (New York: Oxford University Press, 2010), pp. 129, 181.

3. "President Aliyev Looks to the Future of Azerbaijan," Cable from U.S. Embassy, Baku, 21 March 2006, Wikileaks.

4. Angela E. Stent, *The Limits of Partnership: U.S.-Russian Relations in the Twenty-First Century* (Princeton: Princeton University Press, 2015), pp. 199–200; de Waal, *The Caucasus*, pp. 168–171.

5. "Azerbaijan and Russia: Can Baku Maintain the Balance?" Cable from U.S. Embassy, Baku, 10 February 2009, Wikileaks; Stent, *U.S.-Russian Relations*, pp. 198–200; de Waal, *The Caucasus*, pp. 172, 172–181; Artyom Tonoyan, "Rising Armenian-Georgian Tensions and the Possibility of a New Ethnic Conflict in the South Caucasus," *Demokratizatsiya*, 2010, p. 290.

6. "Azerbaijan's Increasingly Confident Foreign Policy," Cable from U.S. Embassy, Baku, 3 January 2008, Wikileaks; "Armenia: Views on Russia, U.S., Turkey, Azerbaijan," 1 December 2010, Stratfor, Wikileaks; "Russian Pundit Views Responsibility for Failure of Latest Nagorno-Karabakh Talks," 28 June 2011,

BBC; Laurence Broers, *The Nagorny Karabakh Conflict: Defaulting to War* (London: Chatham House, 2016), p. 6.

7. "Azerbaijan's Evolving Approach to Relations with Russia," Cable from U.S. Embassy, Baku, 20 February 2007, Wikileaks.

8. "Russia-Azerbaijan Dyspepsia: Eat Tomatoes and Get Gas," Cable from U.S. Embassy, Moscow, 8 February 2007, Wikileaks; "Russia-Azerbaijan Relations Back on Track despite Irritants," Cable from U.S. Embassy, Moscow, 14 March 2008, Wikileaks; "Azerbaijan's Relationship with Russia in the Lead Up to Medvedev's Visit," Cable from U.S. Embassy, Baku, 3 July 2008, Wikileaks.

9. "Russian Defense Minister Ivanov's Visit to Azerbaijan: Heating up the Courtship?" Cable from U.S. Embassy, Baku, 3 February 2006, Wikileaks.

10. "Azerbaijan's Increasingly Confident Foreign Policy," Cable from U.S. Embassy, Baku, 3 January 2008, Wikileaks.

11. "Azerbaijan's Intentional Ambiguity toward NATO," Cable from U.S. Embassy, Baku, 17 January 2008, Wikileaks.

12. "Azerbaijan's Relationship with Russia in the Lead Up to Medvedev's Visit," Cable from U.S. Embassy, Baku, 2 July 2008, Wikileaks.

13. "Azerbaijan: Presidential Advisor Fears Russia's New Era in South Caucasus," Cable from U.S. Embassy, Baku, 2 September 2008, Wikileaks.

14. de Waal, *The Caucasus*, p. 180; "Azerbaijan: Presidential Advisor Fears Russia's New Era in South Caucasus," Cable from U.S. Embassy, Baku, 2 September 2008, Wikileaks.

15. "Azerbaijan: Presidential Advisor Fears Russia's New Era in South Caucasus," Cable from U.S. Embassy, Baku, 2 September 2008, Wikileaks.

16. "Azerbaijan and Russia: Can Baku Maintain the Balance?" Cable from U.S. Embassy, Baku, 10 February 2009, Wikileaks.

17. "Despite Hot Spring in Armenia, Revolution Unlikely to Bloom," Cable from U.S. Embassy, Yerevan, 5 April 2005, Wikileaks; "Armenia's Upcoming Protest and Russia's Position," 17 March 2011, Stratfor, Wikileaks; de Waal, *The Caucasus*, pp. 128–129.

18. Gaïdz Minassian, *Armenia, a Russian Outpost in the Caucasus?* (Paris: Russia/NIS Center, 2008), pp. 11–13; "Reaffirming Ties with Armenia," Cable from U.S. Embassy, Yerevan, 7 April 2004, Wikileaks.

19. "Rail Blockade: Tightening the Noose around Armenia," Cable from U.S. Embassy, Yerevan, 10 December 2004, Wikileaks; "Russia Plays Its Cards in Armenia, Azerbaijan, Turkey," Cable from U.S. Embassy, Moscow, 14 January 2010, Wikileaks; "Defense Minister Reviews CSTO, Russia, Regional Security," Cable from U.S. Embassy, Yerevan, 17 February 2009, Wikileaks; Minassian, *Armenia*, p. 11; Tonoyan, "Rising Armenian-Georgian Tensions," p. 290.

20. "Armenia: Increasing (But Still Modest) Trade with Russia," Cable from U.S. Embassy, Yerevan, 12 February 2004, Wikileaks; "Russia Plays Its Cards in Armenia, Azerbaijan, Turkey," Cable from U.S. Embassy, Moscow, 14 January 2010, Wikileaks; Minassian, *Armenia*, pp. 8–10; "Nothing New under the Sun: Armenian Politicos Stick Close to Long-Held Positions," Cable from U.S. Embassy, Yerevan, 5 April 2004, Wikileaks. The economic growth actually surpassed official estimates: "in off-the record conversations with local businessmen they admit that their businesses' incomes are considerably higher than what they report officially," *ibid.*

21. "Rail Blockade: Tightening the Noose around Armenia," Cable from U.S. Embassy, Yerevan, 10 December 2004, Wikileaks; "Saakashvili Makes First State Visit to Armenia," Cable from U.S. Embassy, Yerevan, 17 March 2004, Wikileaks.

22. "Turkey Takes a Small Step in Dealing with Armenia," Secret cable from U.S. Embassy, Ankara, 23 February 2005, Wikileaks; Minassian, *Armenia*, pp. 6–7.

23. "Deciphering the Armenian-American Diaspora," Cable from U.S. Embassy, Yerevan, 1 June 2004; Minassian, *Armenia*, pp. 8–9.

24. "Russia-Armenia Relations," Cable from U.S. Embassy, Moscow, 9 October 2007, Wikileaks.

25. "Russia, Armenia, and Azerbaijan," 11 August 2008, Stratfor, Wikileaks.

26. "Armenian PM Raises Alarm on Fuel, Grain Shipments through Georgia," Cable from U.S. Embassy, Yerevan, 14 August 2008, Wikileaks; "Armenia Not to Recognize South Ossetia and Abkhazia, Will Seek to Remain Neutral," Cable from U.S. Embassy, Yerevan, 28 August 2008, Wikileaks; "Georgia's Vital Railway Link to Armenia Reopens," Cable from U.S. Embassy, Yerevan, 17 September 2008, Wikileaks.

27. "Turkey: Putin Tells Erdogan Not to Link Armenian Rapprochement with Nagorno-Karabakh," Cable from U.S. Embassy, Ankara, 22 May 2009, Wikileaks; "Russia-Turkey in the South Caucasus: No Zero-Sum," Cable from U.S. Embassy, Moscow, 2 April 2009, Wikileaks.

28. "Turkey: Putin Tells Erdogan Not to Link Armenian Rapprochement with Nagorno-Karabakh," Cable from U.S. Embassy, Ankara, 22 May 2009, Wikileaks; "Armenia: on the Negotiations with Azerbaijan and Turkey," 20 April 2009, Stratfor, Wikileaks.

29. "Bringing Ilham along: How to Convince Azerbaijan to Stop Undermining the Turkey-Armenia Process," Cable from U.S. Embassy, Baku, 2 July 2009, Wikileaks; "Economic Projects Ready to Go—Even without Turkey Border Opening," Cable from U.S. Embassy, Yerevan, 2 September 2009, Wikileaks; "Reaping Benefits of Truce," 13 October 2009, RBC Daily; de Waal, *The Caucasus*, pp. 130, 187, 225; Tonoyan, "Rising Armenian-Georgian Tensions," p. 292.

30. The quotes in this paragraph and the next come from "Georgian Ambassador to Armenia Gives His Views," Secret/NoForn Cable from U.S. Embassy, Yerevan, 26 February 2010, Wikileaks. This extraordinary cable deserves more analysis. The contents were so shocking, that the U.S. Embassy in Yerevan sent the draft of the cable to the U.S. Embassy in Tbilisi for review before submission to the State Department. The American diplomats in Tbilisi claimed that they never heard similar comments before, and if that was true, then they indirectly confirmed that U.S. reporting from Georgia had been seriously flawed

and deficient for years. Since the 1990s the marching orders to the U.S. Embassy in Tbilisi had been to do everything possible to drive Russia back behind its borders; reporting on the aggressive intentions of Georgia to launch an invasion did not fit under this mandate. The 26 February 2010 cable thus provides an invaluable window to understand the origins of the Five Day War in August 2008.

31. "Azerbaijan-Turkey: Still One Nation, Two States?" Cable from U.S. Embassy, Baku, 13 March 2008, Wikileaks; de Waal, *The Caucasus*, pp. 130, 187; "Deciphering the Armenian-American Diaspora," Cable from U.S. Embassy, Yerevan, 1 June 2004, Wikileaks.

32. "Bringing Ilham along: How to Convince Azerbaijan to Stop Undermining the Turkey-Armenia Process," Cable from U.S. Embassy, Baku, 2 July 2009, Wikileaks.

33. "Russia Plays Its Cards in Armenia, Azerbaijan, Turkey," Cable from U.S. Embassy, Moscow, 14 January 2010, Wikileaks; "Bringing Ilham along: How to Convince Azerbaijan to Stop Undermining the Turkey-Armenia Process," Cable from U.S. Embassy, Baku, 2 July 2009, Wikileaks.

34. "Haut-Karabakh," 10 November 2020, *Le monde*.

35. "Roots of War," 27 October 2020, *New York Times*; "Les filières turques de mercenaires syriens en Azerbaïjan," 19 October 2020, *Le monde*; "Reordering of Regional Powers," 10 November 2020, *New York Times*.

36. "Haut-Karabakh," 2020 November 9, *Le figaro*.

37. "Haut-Karabakh," 18 October 2020 *Le figaro*; "At Front Lines of a Brutal War," 18 October 2020, *New York Times*; "Armenia Knew the War Was Coming," 14 October 2020, RT.

38. "Haut-Karabakh," *Le figaro*, 18 October 2020; "Reordering of Regional Powers," *New York Times*, 10 November 2020; "Haut-Karabakh," 10 November 2020, *Le monde*.

39. "Russian Foreign Ministry Appreciates Azerbaijan's Admission of Guilt," 9 November 2020, RT.

40. "Reordering of Regional Powers," 10 November 2020, *New York Times*.

41. "Haut-Karabakh," 9 November 2020, *Le figaro*; Novosti television news broadcasts, 2020 December.

Chapter 19

1. Russian Federation, *Foreign Policy Concept*, 28 June 2000.

2. Oleg Kalugin, *Spymaster: My Thirty-Two Years in Intelligence and Espionage against the West* (New York: Basic Books, 2009), pp. 71–72; 252; Pete Earley, *Comrade J: The Untold Secrets of Russia's Master Spy in America after the End of the Cold War* (New York: Berkley Books, 2009), pp. 106, 186–187.

3. "The Russian Ministry of Foreign Affairs: An Anachronism Creeping toward the Twenty-First Century," Cable from U.S. Embassy, Moscow, 10 March 2009, Wikileaks.

4. Odd Arne Westad, *The Global Cold War: Third World Interventions and the Making of Our Times* (New York: Cambridge University Press, 2007), pp. 316–326 and René De La Pedraja, *The Russian Military Resurgence: Post-Soviet Decline and Rebuilding, 1992–2018* (Jefferson, NC: McFarland, 2018), pp. 27–29.

5. Kalugin, *Spymaster*, pp. 250–254; Interview with Galina Vasilevna Tikhonova, former professor at MGIMO, 13 September 1998, Box 67, David E. Hoffman Papers, Hoover Institution Archives, Stanford, California (henceforth Hoffman-Hoover). On the frustration of KGB officials at not being able to investigate corrupt and sexually abusive diplomats: See also Vladimir Kuzichkin, *Inside the KGB: My Life in Soviet Espionage* (New York: Pantheon Books, 1990).

6. Kalugin, *Spymaster*, pp. 243–246. For the Soviet ambassador who defected: See his account, Arkady N. Shevchenko, *Breaking with Moscow* (New York: Ballantine Books, 1985).

7. Serhii Plokny, *The Last Empire: The Final Days of the Soviet Union* (New York: Basic Books, 2014), pp. 31–32; "Об обстановке в партийной организации советский учреждений в г. Женеве," 7 June 1991, Fond 89, Opis 22, delo 75, Hoover Institution Archives.

8. "Yeltsin Abolishes Soviet Foreign Ministry," 19 December 1991, Reuters; Jeff Checkel, "Russian Foreign Policy: Back to the Future," RFE/RL 16 October 1992; Suzanne Crow, "Personnel Changes in the Russian Foreign Ministry," Draft Research Report, Radio Free Europe/Radio Liberty, 1992 April, John B. Dunlop Collection, Box 6, Hoover Institution Archives, Stanford, California.

9. Igor S. Ivanov, *The New Russian Diplomacy* (Washington, D.C.: Brookings Institution, 2002), pp. 36–37; Earley, *Comrade J*, pp. 21–23, 186–187; Crow, "Personnel Changes in the Russian Foreign Ministry," 1992 April; De La Pedraja, *Russian Military Resurgence*, pp. 74–75.

10. Andrei Soldatov and Irina Borogan, *The New Nobility: The Restoration of Russia's Security State and the Enduring Legacy of the KGB* (New York: Public Affairs, 2010), pp. 13, 17; Earley, *Comrade J*, pp. 189, 279–271; De La Pedraja, *Russian Military Resurgence*, pp. 71–72.

11. Interview of Ambassador Thomas R. Pickering, 18 April 2003, p. 368, Foreign Affairs Oral History Project; "Sexism, Low Pay, and Real Estate: Russian Diplomats on Working at the MFA," Cable from U.S. Embassy, Moscow, 20 October 2008; "The Russian MFA: An Anachronism Creeping toward the Twenty-First Century," Cable from U.S. Embassy, Moscow, 10 March 2009, Wikileaks. It is not known whether the FSB recruited agents among diplomatic personnel or whether FSB officials continued to serve under diplomatic cover in the departments but with the acquiescence of the senior leadership as had been the custom during the Soviet period. This last practice had been routine under KGB because its agents needed to return to Moscow before taking another posting in an embassy abroad in order to preserve their diplomatic cover. After 1991 the existence of two separate agencies—SVR and FSB—obviously complicated this type of arrangement, and it probably disappeared at least for the FSB. The SVR and GRU

just like CIA continue the nearly universal practice of placing their personnel under diplomatic cover.

12. "МГИМО: На всех языкак мира" 24 October 2019, Russian Television Channel 1; "Sexism, Low Pay, and Real Estate: Russian Diplomats on Working at the MFA," Cable from U.S. Embassy, Moscow, 20 October 2008, Wikileaks.

13. De La Pedraja, *Russian Military Resurgence*, pp. 81–82; "Sexism, Low Pay, and Real Estate: Russian Diplomats on Working at the MFA," Cable from U.S. Embassy, Moscow, 20 October 2008, Wikileaks; Crow, "Personnel Changes in the Russian Foreign Ministry," 1992 April.

14. In contrast to the many web sites both official and private trying to attract candidates for the Foreign Service in the United States, even the Russian language site of the Foreign Ministry has been skimpy on recruitment information. Actually, the announcements were superfluous, because almost all candidates came from the Moscow region and could rely on personal or family contacts to obtain the necessary information. "Sexism, Low Pay, and Real Estate: Russian Diplomats on Working at the MFA," Cable from U.S. Embassy, Moscow, 20 October 2008, Wikileaks.

15. "Information of Russia's Afghanistan Policy Makers," Cable from U.S. Embassy, Moscow, 11 June 2009, Wikileaks; De La Pedraja, *Russian Military Resurgence*, pp. 211, 323–324. American diplomats repeatedly complained about the failure of Foreign Ministry personnel to answer e-mails or heaven forbid sometimes not to have e-mail accounts, as if digital communications could magically make disappear the rivalries between Russia and the West.

16. "Yeltsin's Defense Policies: Competing Influences, Drift at the Top," SECRET cable from U.S. Embassy, Moscow, 5 March 1992, U.S. State Department, Freedom of Information Act; "Inside the Federal Service for Military-Technical Cooperation," SECRET cable from U.S. Embassy, Moscow, 28 March 2008, Wikileaks; Louis-Marie Clouet, *Rosoboronexport, Spearhead of the Russian Arms Industry* (Paris: Russia/NIS Center, 2007), pp. 6, 16.

17. "Interview with Tikhonova," Hoffman-Hoover; "Sexism, Low Pay, and Real Estate: Russian Diplomats on Working at the MFA," Cable from U.S. Embassy, Moscow, 20 October 2008, Wikileaks. This cable estimated that "approximately two-thirds of the new diplomats hired" came from the Moscow State Institute of International Relations (MGIMO). A compilation by the author of career paths for nearly 50 Russian diplomats shows that the percentage of MGIMO graduates was over 80 percent. However, because the sample is skewed toward the higher echelons of the Foreign Ministry and includes such dignitaries as Foreign Minister Sergei Lavrov and famous ambassadors such as Sergei Kislyak, I have settled on three-fourths as a more representative estimate.

18. Biographies of diplomats in Web Page of Ministry of Foreign Affairs of the Russian Federation June 2018; Author's sample of career biographies of Russian diplomats.

19. Angus Roxburgh, *Strongman: Vladimir Putin and the Struggle for Russia* (London: I. B. Tauris, 2014), pp. 188–189; "Putin Pays a Call on UAE Leadership," Cable from U.S. Embassy, Abu Dhabi, 11 September 2007, Wikileaks; "Yuri Ushakov," 8 November 2019, Wikipedia. The media and scholars constantly talk and write about the supposed dominance of "*siloviki*," the former members of the security services, in the Russian government. Former diplomats did not fit into this narrative, and even U.S. diplomats inexcusably ignored the function of the Foreign Ministry as a recruitment ground for promotion to other high offices.

20. This paragraph and the next draw on "Sexism, Low Pay, and Real Estate: Russian Diplomats on Working at the MFA," Cable from U.S. Embassy, Moscow, 20 October 2008, Wikileaks and "The Russian Ministry of Foreign Affairs: An Anachronism Creeping toward the Twenty-First Century," Cable from U.S. Embassy, Moscow, 10 March 2009, Wikileaks.

21. Earley, *Comrade J*, pp. 16, 19; "Sexism, Low Pay, and Real Estate: Russian Diplomats on Working at the MFA," Cable from U.S. Embassy, Moscow, 20 October 2008, Wikileaks. A few Russian embassy schools have accepted tuition-paying children of other diplomats and even of locals. This trend could well be the beginning of the establishment of a network of Russian schools across the world. All major capitals already have English (in both American and British variants), French, Italian, and German schools serving primarily elite families in those countries and only secondarily diplomats' children. See the convenient "List of Ministry of Foreign Affairs of Russia Overseas Schools," 20 March 2020, in Wikipedia.

22. "Information of Russia's Afghanistan Policy Makers," Cable from U.S. Embassy, Moscow, 11 June 2009, Wikileaks; Roxburgh, *Vladimir Putin*, pp. 188–189; Galina Vasilevna Tikhonova Interview, 13 November 1998, Hoffman-Hoover. U.S. Government Accountability Office (GAO), "Department of State: Foreign Language Proficiency Has Improved, but Efforts to Reduce Gaps Need Evaluation," March 2017 is the latest in a series of reports and hearings about an endemic problem dating back to the twentieth century. Their inevitable conclusion may be paraphrased: although some progress has been made in improving language proficiency, much remains to be done.

23. GAO, "Foreign Language Proficiency," pp. 10, 15; Biographies in web site of Russian Foreign Ministry; Tikhonova Interview, Hoffman-Hoover. In Spanish-speaking countries, on television Russian representatives were usually more fluent in Spanish than American diplomats.

24. GAO, "Foreign Language Proficiency," pp. 3, 10, 12, 23; Biographies in web site of Russian Foreign Ministry.

25. "Government Has Foreign-Language Deficit," 21 May 2012, *Washington Post*; GAO, "Foreign Language Proficiency," pp. 1–3.

26. "Sexism, Low Pay, and Real Estate: Russian Diplomats on Working at the MFA," Cable from U.S. Embassy, Moscow, 20 October 2008, Wikileaks. GAO, "Foreign Language Proficiency," p. 5. Conclusions about the relative size of the U.S. State Department and the Russian Foreign Ministry can only be approximate because most of the available statistics are not comparable. On the Russian side it is not clear how

the figures reflect the practice of hiring wives and children of diplomats for many routine duties. On the U.S. side the large number of locals employed at embassies and consulates (by the way one of the most effective instruments of U.S. foreign policy) complicates calculations. Both countries placed intelligence officials under diplomatic cover, and it is not clear when they were counted as "clean" diplomats.

Chapter 20

1. William Shakespeare, *Henry VI*, Part III Act 4, Scene 3, Playshakespeare.com.
2. Michael McFaul, *From Cold War to Hot Peace: An American Ambassador in Putin's Russia* (Boston: Houghton Mifflin Harcourt, 2018), pp. 98–99; Angela E. Stent, *The Limits of Partnership: U.S.—Russian Relations in the Twenty-First Century* (Princeton: Princeton University Press, 2015), pp. 211–212, 321; Robert M. Gates, *Duty: Memoirs of a Secretary at War* (New York: Alfred A. Knopf, 2014), p. 404.
3. Angus Roxburgh, *Strongman: Vladimir Putin and the Struggle for Russia* (London: I. B. Tauris, 2014), p. 265.
4. Lawrence D. Freedman, "Strategic Arms Reduction Talks," Britannica.com; "SORT vs. New START: Why the Administration Is Leery of Treaty," 15 March 2013, Brookings; Stent, *Limits of Partnership*, pp. 222–224. For a full discussion of New START, See, McFaul, *Cold War to Hot Peace*, chapter 9; for a shorter account, See Gates, *Duty*, pp. 406–409.
5. "U.S.-Russia Consultation on Afghanistan," Cable from U.S. Embassy, Moscow, 19 February 2009, Wikileaks; Stent, *Limits of Partnership*, p. 230; "Pressuring Russia to Assist Us in Afghanistan," Cable from U.S. Embassy, Moscow, 17 April 2009, Wikileaks; "U.S. Strategy, Pakistani Threat to Karachi Supply Line," 3 December 2009, Stratfor, Wikileaks.
6. "Kyrguz Demand over $2 Billion to Keep Manas Open," Cable from U.S. Embassy, Bishkek, 2 February 2009; Stent, *Limits of Partnership*, p. 117. Kyrgyzstan was trying to extort the U.S. over the rent payments for the Manas base. As a way to evoke sympathy, the Kyrgyz said they were under immense Russian pressure to close the U.S. base at Manas.
7. "Russia to Allow U.S. Arms Shipments to Afghanistan," 4 July 2009, Associated Press; Stent, *Limits of Partnership*, p. 231; McFaul, *Cold War to Hot Peace*, pp. 106, 123–124; Press Conference by President Obama and President Medvedev of Russia, 6 July 2009.
8. Stent, *Limits of Partnership*, pp. 243–244; Roxburgh, *Strongman*, pp. 232–233; McFaul, *Cold War to Hot Peace*, pp. 163–171; Gates, *Duty*, pp. 404–405. As a way to attack the Obama administration, a number of articles appeared claiming that Russia agreed to vote for UN sanctions on Iran in exchange for lifting the sanctions on Russian firms and allowing Russia to sell the S-300 anti-aircraft weapon system. The critics claimed the Obama administration had made a bad deal because "Russia is extracting a huge price for its cooperation." "U.S. Makes Concessions to Russia for Iran Sanctions," 21 May 2010, *New York Times*. In reality, Russia made no such deal and has never been willing to "sell" its vote like so often happens with banana republics. As the text indicated, the discovery that Teheran had been lying persuaded the Kremlin to support tough sanctions against the Iranian nuclear program.
9. Stent, *Limits of Partnership*, pp. 233, 321; Steven Lee Myers, *The New Tsar: The Rise and Reign of Vladimir Putin* (New York: Vintage Books, 2016), p. 371.
10. Quotation and paragraph from McFaul, *Cold War to Hot Peace*, pp. 173–174. This is one of the most interesting revelations in McFaul's memoirs.
11. Gates, *Duty*, pp. 159–167; Stent, *Limits of Partnership*, pp. 226–228.
12. "U.S., Russia: Washington's Latest Offer to Moscow," 18 June 2009, Stratfor, Wikileaks; "Russia's Latest Move to Stymie U.S. Efforts in Central Europe," 23 November 2011, and "Russia's Plan to Disrupt U.S.-European Relations," 13 December 2011, Stratfor, Wikileaks; Stent, *Limits of Partnership*, pp. 228–229.
13. "Joint Report by the Coordinators of the U.S.-Russia Presidential Commission," 25 May 2011; Stent, *Limits of Partnership*, pp. 243–244.
14. "Russia and NATO after Georgia," Cable from U.S. Embassy, Moscow, 3 March 2009, Wikileaks; Congressional Research Service, "Georgia Republic and NATO Enlargement: Issues and Implications," 7 March 2008, Wikileaks.
15. "Russia's Hardening Views on Sphere of Influence," Cable from U.S. Embassy, Moscow, 14 May 2009, Wikileaks.
16. William H. Hill, *No Place for Russia: European Security Institutions since 1989* (New York: Columbia University Press, 2018), p. 292; "Russia's Hardening Views on Sphere of Influence," Cable from U.S. Embassy, Moscow, 14 May 2009, Wikileaks; Congressional Research Service, "NATO Enlargement," 5 May 2003, Wikileaks.
17. "Biden Says Weakened Russia Will Bend to U.S.," 25 July 2009, *Wall Street Journal*.
18. "Deputy Foreign Minister Grushkho on Georgia, Energy Security, and European Security," Cable from U.S. Embassy, Moscow, 13 February 2009, Wikileaks; "Russia and NATO after Georgia," Cable from U.S. Embassy, Moscow, 3 March 2009, Wikileaks; "New Biden Criticism Surprises Russia," 25 July 2009, *New York Times*; Stent, *Limits of Partnership*, p. 217
19. "Russia and NATO after Georgia," Cable from U.S. Embassy, Moscow, 3 March 2009, Wikileaks.
20. Statement preceding the draft of the European Security Treaty, 29 November 2009, web site of the Presidency of the Russian Federation; Hill, *No Place for Russia*, p. 288.
21. "Draft of the European Security Treaty," 29 November 2009, web site of the Presidency of the Russian Federation; Hill, *No Place for Russia*, pp. 288–291.
22. "Medvedev's Proposed European Security Treaty: How to Respond," Cable from U.S. Embassy, Moscow, 2 December 2009, Wikileaks.
23. "Russian Initiative Regarding a Treaty on European Security," 5 December 2008, OSCE.

24. "Medvedev's Proposed European Security Treaty: How to Respond," Cable from U.S. Embassy, Moscow, 2 December 2009, Wikileaks; Richard Weitz, "The Rise and Fall of Medvedev's European Security Treaty," May 2012, *On Wider Europe*.
25. "Medvedev's Proposed European Security Treaty: How to Respond," Cable from U.S. Embassy, Moscow, 2 December 2009, Wikileaks.
26. Hill, *No Place for Russia*, pp. 292–293; Stent, *Limits of Partnership*, p. 239; "Medvedev's Proposed European Security Treaty: How to Respond," Cable from U.S. Embassy, Moscow, 2 December 2009, Wikileaks; Stent, *Limits of Partnership*, p. 239.
27. "U.S. Lifts Sanctions on Russian Arms Exporter," 22 May 2010, Reuters; "U.S. Makes Concessions to Russia for Iran Sanctions," 21 May 2010, *New York Times*; "Policy Advisor to Become U.S. Ambassador to Russia," 29 May 2011, *New York Times*; McFaul, *Cold War to Hot Peace*, p. 172. The Obama administration had good intentions in appointing Michael McFaul to be the ambassador to Russia, but in retrospect it selected the wrong candidate. His commitment to creating an ideal political system in Russia and his refusal to accept any Russian concerns in the near abroad—not even remotely resembling the hegemony the U.S. has exercised over the Caribbean—doomed his mission to failure.
28. Roxburgh, *Strongman*, p. 270; Myers, *Vladimir Putin*, p. 372; McFaul, *Cold War to Hot Peace*, pp. 194–195, 197.
29. "Russia—Spy Round-up Theory II," 30 June 2010, and "Russian Spy Round Up," 2 July 2010, Stratfor, Wikileaks; Myers, *Vladimir Putin*, p. 372; "FBI Arrests 10 Accused of Working as Russian Spies," 29 June 2010, *Washington Post*.
30. "Russia—Spy Round-up Theory II," 30 June 2010, Stratfor, Wikileaks; Myers, *Vladimir Putin*, p. 372; McFaul, *Cold War to Hot Peace*, pp. 201–202.
31. "Russian Spy Round Up," 2 July 2010, Stratfor, Wikileaks; "Spying Suspects Seemed Short on Secrets," 29 June 2010, *New York Times*; Roxburgh, *Strongman*, p. 270; "Couples Accused as Spies Were the Suburbs Personified," 29 June 2010, *New York Times*. Readers interested in spy stories will enjoy learning that U.S. officials had trouble getting their story together. The CIA at first claimed that four of the couples were agents of military intelligence GRU (a largely male operation), but in the indictments the FBI decided to blame the Foreign Intelligence Service. The CIA also claimed that it needed to extricate ("exfiltrate" in spy jargon) their agent who had exposed the sleeper spy ring. That a source in Moscow could have revealed in 2010 the existence of the spies already identified at least since 2000 because of their careless behavior remains a glaring contradiction. At the very least, Alexandr Poteyev, the spy the CIA extricated from Moscow, could not have been providing very valuable information. To thicken the plot, Poteyev, who was sentenced to 25 years of prison in absentia, was reported to have died in the U.S. in July 2016. Moscow suspected a fake death, and the *New York Times* confirmed that the former spy was still alive in 2019. See, Gates, *Duty*, pp. 409–410; "Russian Traitor Who Exposed Anna Chapman's Spy Ring Dead in U.S.," 7 July 2016, RT; "CIA Informant Extracted from Russia Had Sent Secrets to U.S. for Decades," 9 September 2019, *New York Times*.
32. McFaul, *Cold War to Hot Peace*, p. 203; "Anna Chapman" 5 April 2020, Wikipedia; Stent, *Limits of Partnership*, p. 242; Gates, *Duty*, pp. 410–411.

Chapter 21

1. "Multilateral Efforts to Keep Georgia Intact and Independent," Cable from U.S. Embassy, Tbilisi, 3 November 1993, U.S. State Department, Freedom of Information Act.
2. "Impact of Closing the OSCE Mission to Georgia," Cable from U.S. Embassy, Tbilisi, 30 December 2008, Wikileaks.
3. "Georgia: Russian Veto Forces Expiration of UNOMIG Mandate," Cable from U.S. Mission to United Nations, New York, 16 June 2009, Wikileaks.
4. "Under Secretary Alain Le Roy Tells Quad Russia and UN Controller Are Obstacles to High-Level UN Envoy," Cable from U.S. Mission to UN, New York, 12 November 2009, Wikileaks.
5. "Georgia: Good and Bad News from EU Monitoring Mission," Cable from U.S. Embassy, Tbilisi, 6 April 2009, Wikileaks.
6. "Georgian Military Coup," 5 May 2009, Stratfor, Wikileaks; "Foreign Minister Briefs on Mutiny," Cable from U.S. Embassy, Tbilisi, 7 May 2009, Wikileaks.
7. "Russia Denies Involvement in Failed Georgian Coup Attempt," Cable from U.S. Embassy, Moscow, 6 May 2009, Wikileaks.
8. "NATO Exercises in Georgia—The Facts," Cable from U.S. Mission to NATO, 21 April 2009, Wikileaks; "Serbia Pulls out of NATO Exercise in Georgia," Cable from U.S. Embassy, Belgrade, 4 May 2009, Wikileaks; "NATO Pullout Part of Larger Picture," Cable from U.S. Embassy, Moldova, 8 May 2009, Wikileaks; "Georgian Military Coup," 5 May 2009, Stratfor, Wikileaks; Roger N. McDermott, *The Reform of Russia's Conventional Armed Forces: Problems, Challenges, and Policy Implications* (Washington, D.C.: The Jamestown Foundation, 2011), pp. 31, 69, 229–239.
9. Independent International Fact-Finding Mission on the Conflict in Georgia, *Report*, 3 vols. (Brussels: European Union, 2009).
10. "Georgia: Additional Guidance on Successor to SRSG Verbeke," Cable from Secretary of State, Washington, D.C., 25 November 2009, Wikileaks; "Heidi Tagliavini," 1 July 2019, Wikipedia.
11. René De La Pedraja, *The Russian Military Resurgence: Post-Soviet Decline and Rebuilding, 1992-2018* (Jefferson, NC: McFarland, 2018), p. 215; "Georgian Coast Guard Cracks Down on Abkhazia Shipments," Cable from U.S. Embassy, Tbilisi, 24 August 2019, Wikileaks.
12. "QUAD Demarche on Georgian Ship Seizures," Cable from Secretary of State, Washington, D.C., 11 September 2009, Wikileaks; "MFA on Russia-Georgia," Cable from U.S. Embassy, Moscow, 8 October 2009, Wikileaks; De La Pedraja, *Russian Military Resurgence*, pp. 215–216.

13. "Georgia: Risky Situation in the Black Sea," Cable from U.S. Embassy, Tbilisi, 19 Nov 2009, Wikileaks; "Georgia Seizes Ukrainian Ship near Abkhazia," 29 July 2010, Tbilisi Kavkas-Press.

14. "Russian Ministry of Foreign Affairs Downplays Discord with Ukraine," Cable from U.S. Embassy, Moscow, 13 July 2009, Wikileaks.

15. Steven Pifer, *The Eagle and the Trident: U.S.-Ukraine Relations in Turbulent Times* (Washington, D.C.: Brookings Institution, 2018). p. 7; Richard Sakwa, *Frontline Ukraine: Crisis in the Borderlands* (London: I. B. Tauris, 2016), pp. 72–73.

16. "Nyet Means Nyet: Russia's NATO Enlargement Redlines," Cable from U.S. Embassy, Moscow, 1 February 2008, and "Duma Resolution Calls for Withdrawal from BIG Treaty," Cable from U.S. Embassy, Moscow, 5 June 2008, Wikileaks; "Ukraine Update," 30 June 2006, Stratfor, Wikileaks.

17. "Russian Analyst Dmitry Trenin Warns of Consequences if Ukraine Joins NATO," Cable from U.S. Embassy, Moscow, 24 June 2008, and "Merkel Trip Communicates Staunch Opposition to Quick NATO and EU Accession," Cable from U.S. Embassy, Berlin, 24 July 2008, Wikileaks.

18. "Ukraine, MAP, and the Georgia-Russia Conflict," Secret/NoForn Cable from U.S. Mission to NATO, 14 August 2008, Wikileaks.

19. "Yushchenko Disappointed by Italy's Tepid Support for MAP," Cable from U.S. Embassy, Rome, 16 October 2008, Wikileaks; "Ukraine, MAP, and the Georgia-Russia Conflict," Secret/NoForn Cable from U.S. Mission to NATO, 14 August 2008, Wikileaks.

20. "Russia Demands Ukraine Pay Its Gas Debt, or Else," Cable from U.S. Embassy, Kiev, 24 November 2008, Wikileaks; Angela E. Stent, *The Limits of Partnership: U.S.-Russian Relations in the Twenty-First Century* (Princeton: Princeton University Press, 2015), pp. 195–196; Pifer, *Eagle and Trident*, p. 289.

21. "Russia Cuts off Gas to Ukraine," Cable from U.S. Embassy, Kiev, 1 January 2009, Wikileaks; "Ukraine-Russia: Political Aspects of the Gas Crisis," Cable from U.S. Embassy, Kiev, 30 January 2009, Wikileaks; Pifer, *Eagle and Trident*, p. 289.

22. "Ukrainian-Russian Relations after Yushchenko: A Preview," Cable from U.S. Embassy, Kiev, 2 February 2010, Wikileaks.

23. "Ukrainian-Russian Relations after Yushchenko: A Preview," Cable from U.S. Embassy, Kiev, 2 February 2010, Wikileaks.

24. "Update on Ukraine Election Situation," 9 February 2010, Hillary Clinton E-Mails, Wikileaks; Sakwa, *Frontline Ukraine*, pp. 55–56.

25. Stent, *Limits of Partnership*, p. 236; Marvin Kalb, *Imperial Gamble: Putin, Ukraine, and the New Cold War* (Washington, D.C.: Brookings Institution Press, 2015), pp. 138–139.

26. "Moves towards Russia (Part I)," 26 July 2010, Stratfor, Wikileaks; Taras Kuzio, Russianization of Ukrainian National Security Policy under Viktor Yanukovych," *Journal of Slavic Military Studies* 25(2012): 572–573; Pifer, *Eagle and Trident*, p. 292.

27. "Russian Envoy to Ukraine Sets out Antonov Aircraft Joint Venture, Warship Plans," 13 June 2010, BBC; "Russia Renews An-70 Military transport Plane Funding to Ukraine," 12 May 2010, Stratfor, Wikileaks; Pifer, *Eagle and Trident*, p. 32.

28. "Russia Resumes Orders for Military Equipment Repairs at Ukrainian Enterprises," 10 December 2010, Stratfor, Wikileaks; "Russia, Ukraine Restore Full-Scale Military Cooperation," 25 June 2010, BBC.

29. "Incorporating Ukraine into U.S.-Russia Policy," Cable from U.S. Embassy, Moscow, 21 September 2009, Wikileaks.

30. Stent, *Limits of Partnership*, p. 236; Sakwa, *Frontline Ukraine*, pp. 70–71.

31. "Ukraine-Russia: Is Military Conflict no Longer Unthinkable?" Cable from U.S. Embassy, Kiev, 8 October 2009, Wikileaks.

32. "MFA on Russian and American Roles in Central Asia," Cable from U.S. Embassy, Moscow, 24 November 2008, Wikileaks; "Russia Watches U.S. with a Wary Eye in Central Asia," Cable from U.S. Embassy, Moscow, 24 November 2008, Wikileaks.

33. Congressional Research Service, "Unrest in Uzbekistan: Context and Implications," 8 June 2005, Wikileaks; Congressional Research Service, "Central Asia: Regional Developments and Implications for U.S. Interests," 13 November 2008, Wikileaks.

34. Congressional Research Service, "Unrest in Uzbekistan"; Congressional Research Service, "Central Asia."

35. "Islam Karimov and the Massacre in Uzbekistan that the World Forgot," 2 September 2016, *Washington Post*; Congressional Research Service, "Unrest in Uzbekistan"; Congressional Research Service, "Central Asia."

36. "Islam Karimov and the Massacre in Uzbekistan that the World Forgot," 2 September 2016, *Washington Post*; Congressional Research Service, "Unrest in Uzbekistan"; "Tajikistan Not Overly Pleased by New Russia-Uzbekistan Alliance," Cable from U.S. Embassy, Dushanbe, 21 November 2005, Wikileaks.

37. "Karimov Urges Closer Cooperation with U.S.," Cable from U.S. Embassy, Tashkent, 2 November 2000, Wikileaks; Congressional Research Service, "Central Asia."

38. Congressional Research Service, "Unrest in Uzbekistan"; Congressional Research Service, "Central Asia."

39. "Karimov Urges Closer Cooperation with U.S.," Cable from U.S. Embassy, Tashkent, 2 November 2000, Wikileaks; "Russia-Uzbekistan Relationship: Complex but Growing," Cable from U.S. Embassy, Moscow, 27 March 2008, Wikileaks; Congressional Research Service, "Uzbekistan: Current Developments and U.S. Interests," 27 August 2008, Wikileaks.

40. "Ministry of Foreign Affairs on Russian and American Roles in Central Asia," Cable from U.S. Embassy, Moscow, 6 October 2006, Wikileaks.

41. Lincoln A. Mitchell, *The Color Revolutions* (Philadelphia: University of Pennsylvania Press, 2012), pp. 4, 63–65; Erica Marat, *The Tulip Revolution: Kyrgyzstan One Year After* (Washington, D.C.: The Jamestown Foundation, 2006), pp. 46–52.

42. De La Pedraja, *Russian Military Resurgence*, p. 246; Marat, *The Tulip Revolution*, pp. 46–52.

43. Michael McFaul, *From Cold War to Hot Peace: An American Ambassador in Putin's Russia* (Boston: Houghton Mifflin Harcourt, 2018), pp. 185–186; De La Pedraja, *Russian Military Resurgence*, p. 247; Annete Bohr, "Revolution in Kyrgyzstan—Again" April 2010, Chatham House; "Kyrgyzstan and the Russian Resurgence," 3 April 2010, Stratfor, Wikileaks.

44. De La Pedraja, *Russian Military Resurgence*, p. 247; Bohr, "Revolution in Kyrgyzstan."

45. De La Pedraja, *Russian Military Resurgence*, pp. 247–248; McFaul, *Cold War to Hot Peace*, pp. 183–184.

46. "Moscow Caught Unprepared by the Carnage in the Ferghana Valley," 17 June 2010, *Eurasia Daily Monitor*, No. 117; De La Pedraja, *Russian Military Resurgence*, p. 248; McFaul, *Cold War to Hot Peace*, p. 195.

47. "BBC Monitoring Alert," 15–20 June 2010, Stratfor, Wikileaks; De La Pedraja, *Russian Military Resurgence*, p. 248; McFaul, *Cold War to Hot Peace*, p. 195.

48. "After Competing for Influence in Kyrgyzstan, Big Powers Step Aside," 19 June 2010, *New York Times*; De La Pedraja, *Russian Military Resurgence*, p. 249.

Chapter 22

1. "Middle East: Ministry of Foreign Affairs on Lebanon, Syria, and Iraq," Cable from U.S. Embassy, Moscow, 26 December 2006, Wikileaks.

2. "Rebuilding an Empire While It Can," 31 October 2011, Stratfor, Wikileaks; Catherine Putz, "Remember the Eurasian Economic Union: Oh Yeah, That … How's That Going," 13 January 2018, *The Diplomat*; Evgeny Vinokurov, "Eurasian Economic Union: Current State and Preliminary Results," p. 56; "Eurasian Economic Community," 10 April 2020, Wikipedia.

3. "Karimov Urges Closer Cooperation with U.S.," Cable from U.S. Embassy, Tashkent, 2 November 2000, Wikileaks; Vinokurov, "Eurasian Economic Union," p. 56; "Eurasian Economic Community," 10 April 2020, Wikipedia.

4. "Karimov Urges Closer Cooperation with U.S.," Cable from U.S. Embassy, Tashkent, 2 November 2000, Wikileaks; Vinokurov, "Eurasian Economic Union," p. 56; "EAEU," 2 January 2015, Global Edge.

5. Vinokurov, "Eurasian Economic Union," p. 56; "EAEU," 2 January 2015, Global Edge.

6. "The Customs Union and a Unified WTO Accession Process," Cable from U.S. Embassy, Moscow, 23 December 2009, Wikileaks; Vinokurov, "Eurasian Economic Union," p. 56; "EAEU," 2 January 2015, Global Edge; Dominic Fean, *Decoding Russia's WTO Accession* (Paris: Russia/NIS Center, 2012), pp. 10–11.

7. "What Russia's Trade Negotiators Accomplished in Six Months: Structure and Operation of the Russia, Belarus, Kazakhstan Customs Union," Cable from U.S. Embassy, Moscow, 23 December 2009, Wikileaks; "The Customs Union and a Unified WTO Accession Process," Cable from U.S. Embassy, Moscow, 23 December 2009, Wikileaks.

8. "Russia Becomes WTO Member after 18 Years of Talks," 16 December 2011, BBC; "Russia Deal with Georgia Clears Way to Join WTO," 3 November 2011, *Wall Street Journal*; Fean, *Decoding Russia's WTO Accession*, pp. 10, 16; "Russia's Plan to Disrupt U.S.-European Relations," 13 December 2011, Stratfor, Wikileaks; Angela E. Stent, *The Limits of Partnership: U.S.-Russian Relations in the Twenty-First Century* (Princeton: Princeton University Press, 2015), p. 208; Michael McFaul, *From Cold War to Hot Peace: An American Ambassador in Putin's Russia* (Boston: Houghton Mifflin Harcourt, 2018), p. 196.

9. "Russia Becomes WTO Member after 18 Years of Talks," 16 December 2011, BBC; "Russia Deal with Georgia Clears Way to Join WTO," 3 November 2011, *Wall Street Journal*; "Context of Russia's WTO Accession," 23 December 2011, and "Press Release on Acceptance of the WTO Trade Facilitation Agreement," 22 April 2016, Russian Ministry of Foreign Affairs; McFaul, *Cold War to Hot Peace*, p. 172.

10. "Eurasian Economic Union," 10 April 2020, Wikipedia; "EAEU," 2 Jan 2015, Global Edge.

11. Vinokurov, "Eurasian Economic Union," p. 59; "Eurasian Economic Union," 10 April 2020, Wikipedia.

12. Vinokurov, "Eurasian Economic Union," pp. 60–62, 67; Putz, "Eurasian Economic Union."

13. Vinokurov, "Eurasian Economic Union," p. 65.

14. "China to Sign Free Trade Agreement with Eurasian Economic Union on May 17," 15 May 2018, *China Briefing*; Gregory Shtraks "Next Steps in the Merger of the Eurasian Economic Union and the Belt and Road Initiative," *China Brief*, 19 June 2018.

15. McFaul, *Cold War to Hot Peace*, pp. 222–223; Myers, *Vladimir Putin*, pp. 381–382.

16. McFaul, *Cold War to Hot Peace*, pp. 223–225; René De La Pedraja, *The Russian Military Resurgence: Post-Soviet Decline and Rebuilding, 1992–2018* (Jefferson, NC: McFarland, 2018), p. 290; Myers, *Vladimir Putin*, pp. 382–383.

17. McFaul, *Cold War to Hot Peace*, pp. 225–227; De La Pedraja, *Russian Military Resurgence*, p. 290; Myers, *Vladimir Putin*, pp. 383–384; Stent, *Limits of Partnership*, pp. 248–249.

18. McFaul, *Cold War to Hot Peace*, pp. 191–193, 226–227; Robert M. Gates, *Duty: Memoirs of a Secretary at War* (New York: Alfred A. Knopf, 2014), p. 530.

19. De La Pedraja, *Russian Military Resurgence*, pp. 291–293; David W. Lesch, *Syria: The Fall of the House of Assad* (New Haven: Yale University Press, 2012), pp. 136–140; Stent, *Limits of Partnership*, p. 249; McFaul, *Cold War to Hot Peace*, p. 332.

20. This quotation and the next from "Russia Is Writing off the Syrian Regime?" 5 August 2011, Stratfor, Wikileaks.

21. Angus Roxburgh, *Strongman: Vladimir Putin and the Struggle for Russia* (London: I. B. Tauris, 2014), p. 340.

22. De La Pedraja, *Russian Military Resurgence*, p. 293; Lesch, *Syria*, pp. 160–161; Stent, *The Limits of Partnership*, p. 249.

23. De La Pedraja, *Russian Military Resurgence*, p. 293; Lesch, *Syria*, pp. 138–140.

24. Julia Gerlach, *Color Revolutions in Eurasia* (New York: Springer, 2014), pp. 21–22; Lincoln A. Mitchell, *The Color Revolutions* (Philadelphia: University of Pennsylvania Press, 2012), pp. 161–162.
25. Roxburgh, *Strongman*, pp. 316–318; Myers, *Vladimir Putin*, pp. 387–391.
26. Gerlach, *Color Revolutions in Eurasia*, pp. 22–23; Roxburgh, *Strongman*, pp. 317–319; McFaul, *Cold War to Hot Peace*, pp. 117–119, 245.
27. Gerlach, *Color Revolutions in Eurasia*, p. 22.
28. Mitchell, *Color Revolutions*, pp. 3–5; Gerlach, *Color Revolutions in Eurasia*, p. 23; McFaul, *Cold War to Hot Peace*, p. 243.
29. Roxburgh, *Strongman*, pp. 322–325. The prevailing interpretation holds that harsh measures against the demonstrators were the result of pressure from Vladimir Putin, while a soft approach to the protests reflected the camp of Dmitry Medvedev. The text reflects the more nuanced response of the authorities to weaken and then reduce the protest movement to insignificance.
30. "Russia—More—Moscow Protests," 10 December 2011, Stratfor, Wikileaks; "Moscow Demos Update 3:50 P.M.," 10 December 2011, Stratfor, Wikileaks.
31. "Russia Digs in Heels on Syria Resolution," 17 January 2012, Reuters; "Russia and China Veto Resolution in Favor of Demonstrations in Russia," 4 February 2012, *New York Times*; Security Council, Resolution S 2012/77 of 4 February 2012; McFaul, *Cold War to Hot Peace*, p. 244.
32. Roxburgh, *Strongman*, pp. 325–328.
33. Myers, *Vladimir Putin*, pp. 405–406; Roxburgh, *Strongman*, pp. 330–331.
34. "Protest in Moscow, Russia Update," Cable from U.S. Embassy, Moscow, 6 May 2012, Freedom of Information Act; "Russia—Moscow Demonstrations Update 3:50 P.M.," 10 December 2010, Stratfor, Wikileaks; McFaul, *Cold War to Hot Peace*, p. 257.
35. Myers, *Vladimir Putin*, pp. 409–412; Roxburgh, *Strongman*, pp. 328–329.
36. "Russia—More—Moscow Protests," 10 December 2011, Stratfor, Wikileaks; "Russia—Who Are the Protestors?" 16 December 2011, Stratfor, Wikileaks; Gerlach, *Color Revolutions in Eurasia*, p. 23.
37. De La Pedraja, *Russian Military Resurgence*, pp. 65–67.
38. Gerlach, *Color Revolutions in Eurasia*, p. 24; Roxburgh, *Strongman*, pp. 331–332, 338; Myers, *Vladimir Putin*, p. 422; McFaul, *Cold War to Hot Peace*, pp. 258, 361–363.
39. Roxburgh, *Strongman*, pp. 340–341; Stent, *Limits of Partnership*, pp. 210–252.
40. Roxburgh, *Strongman*, pp. 341–342; Myers, *Vladimir Putin*, pp. 422–423; Stent, *Limits of Partnership*, p. 252; McFaul, *Cold War to Hot Peace*, pp. 364–368.
41. "Russian Media, Often Critical of Foreign Adoptions, Now Turns Gaze Toward Domestic Abuse," Cable from U.S. Embassy, Moscow, 25 June 2009, Wikileaks; Stent, *Limits of Partnership*, pp. 252–253; McFaul, *Cold War to Hot Peace*, pp. 368–371.

Chapter 23

1. "Deputy Foreign Minister Grushko on NATO-Russia and European Security," Cable from U.S. Embassy, Moscow, 9 June 2009, Wikileaks.
2. Richard Sakwa, *Frontline Ukraine: Crisis in the Borderlands* (London: I. B. Tauris, 2016), p. 106.
3. "How the EU Lost Ukraine," 25 November 2013, *Spiegel*; Sakwa, *Frontline Ukraine*, pp. 73–74; Steven Pifer, *The Eagle and the Trident: U.S.-Ukraine Relations in Turbulent Times* (Washington, D.C.: Brookings Institution, 2017), pp. 297–298.
4. Sakwa, *Frontline Ukraine*, p. 74; Oliver Stone, *The Putin Interviews* (New York: Hot Books, 2017), p. 64; "How the EU Lost Ukraine," 25 November 2013, *Spiegel*.
5. Sakwa, *Frontline Ukraine*, p. 78; Stone, *The Putin Interviews*, p. 64.
6. "How the EU Lost Ukraine," 25 November 2013, *Spiegel*; Sakwa, *Frontline Ukraine*, p. 75; Stone, *The Putin Interviews*, p. 64.
7. Sakwa, *Frontline Ukraine*, p. 86; Stone, *The Putin Interviews*, p. 71.
8. "How the EU Lost Ukraine," 25 November 2013, *Spiegel*; Sakwa, *Frontline Ukraine*, pp. 77–79; Melvin Kalb, *Imperial Gamble: Putin, Ukraine, and the New Cold War* (Washington, D.C.: Brookings Institution, 2015), p. 139; Pifer, *Eagle and Trident*, p. 297.
9. "How the EU Lost Ukraine," 25 November 2013, *Spiegel*; Sakwa, *Frontline Ukraine*, p. 57; Stone, *The Putin Interviews*, p. 64.
10. Sakwa, *Frontline Ukraine*, p. 57; Stone, *The Putin Interviews*, p. 63; Pifer, *Eagle and Trident*, p. 299.
11. Sakwa, *Frontline Ukraine*, pp. 57, 79; Pifer, *Eagle and Trident*, pp. 299–201.
12. Sakwa, *Frontline Ukraine*, pp. 81–82; Kalb, *Imperial Gamble*, p. 141; Stone, *The Putin Interviews*, p. 73. Viktor Yanukovych confessed that he refused to sign an order to use weapons, "I could not lift my hand to do it." "Crimea, the Way Home," television documentary by Andrey Kondrashev, posted on YouTube on 15 March 2015. Yanukovych was the direct spiritual heir of Mikhail Gorbachev who also refused to use force to save the Soviet Union. And both men fell from power because their opponents had no hesitation about using force.
13. Ivan Katchanovski, "The Snipers' Massacre on the Maidan in Ukraine," 2015, p. 61; Sakwa, *Frontline Ukraine*, p. 82; Stone, *The Putin Interviews*, p. 73; Kalb, *Imperial Gamble*, pp. 142, 151.
14. Ministry of Foreign Affairs of the Russian Federation, *White Book on Violations of Human Rights and the Rule of Law in Ukraine, November 2013–March 2014* (Moscow: Ministry of Foreign Affairs, 2014), pp. 31–32; Sakwa, *Frontline Ukraine*, pp. 86–87; Katchanovski, "The Snipers' Massacre," p. 17; Stone, *The Putin Interviews*, pp. 71, 73.
15. "Ukraine Crisis: Transcript of Leaked Nuland-Pyatt Call," 7 February 2014, BBC; Sakwa, *Frontline Ukraine*, pp. 79–80.
16. "Ukraine Crisis: Transcript of Leaked Nuland-Pyatt Call," 7 February 2014, BBC.
17. Ministry of Foreign Affairs, *White Book November 2013–March 2014*, p. 10; Katchanovski,

"The Snipers' Massacre," pp. 61, 63; Sakwa, *Frontline Ukraine*, pp. 83–86; Kalb, *Imperial Gamble*, p. 151.

18. Katchanovski, "The Snipers' Massacre," p. 61; Sakwa, *Frontline Ukraine*, p. 87; Kalb, *Imperial Gamble*, p. 151; "Crimea, the Way Home," YouTube; "Berkut (Special Police Force)," 2 March 2020, Wikipedia.

19. Katchanovski, "The Snipers' Massacre on the Maidan in Ukraine," pp. 46, 48–49, 63–64; Sakwa, *Frontline Ukraine*, pp. 87–88.

20. Pifer, *Eagle and Trident*, pp. 300–301; Kalb, *Imperial Gamble*, pp. 151–152.

21. Sakwa, *Frontline Ukraine*, pp. 88–89; Pifer, *Eagle and Trident*, p. 302; Kalb, *Imperial Gamble*, p. 152.

22. "Crimea, the Way Home," YouTube; "Ukraine Crisis: Transcript of Leaked Nuland-Pyatt Call," 7 February 2014, BBC.

23. "Crimea, the Way Home," YouTube; René De La Pedraja, *The Russian Military Resurgence: Post-Soviet Decline and Rebuilding, 1992-2018* (Jefferson, NC: McFarland, 2018), pp. 261–262.

24. Ministry of Foreign Affairs, *White Book November 2013–March 2014*, pp. 12–13; "Crimea, the Way Home," YouTube.

25. Sakwa, *Frontline Ukraine*, p. 93; "Crimea, the Way Home," YouTube; De La Pedraja, *Russian Military Resurgence*, p. 263.

26. Ministry of Foreign Affairs, *White Book November 2013–March 2014*, p. 17; "Crimea, the Way Home," YouTube; Sakwa, *Frontline Ukraine*, p. 86.

27. "Crimea, the Way Home," YouTube; De La Pedraja, *Russian Military Resurgence*, p. 263.

28. "Crimea, the Way Home," YouTube; De La Pedraja, *Russian Military Resurgence*, pp. 263–264; "Berkut (Special Police Force)," 2 March 2020, Wikipedia.

29. "Crimea, the Way Home," YouTube; De La Pedraja, *Russian Military Resurgence*, p. 263.

30. Ministry of Foreign Affairs, *White Book November 2013–March 2014*, pp. 37–40; "Crimea, the Way Home," YouTube; Kalb, *Imperial Gamble*, p. 158.

31. Ministry of Foreign Affairs, *White Book November 2013–March 2014*, pp. 17–18; "Crimea, the Way Home," YouTube; Kalb, *Imperial Gamble*, p. 158.

32. "Crimea, the Way Home," YouTube.

33. Gwendolyn Sasse, *The Crimea Question: Identity, Transition and Conflict* (Cambridge, MA: Harvard University Press, 2007), pp. 159–160; "Crimea, the Way Home," YouTube; De La Pedraja, *Russian Military Resurgence*, p. 263.

34. "Crimea, the Way Home," YouTube; Sakwa, *Frontline Ukraine*, p. 103; De La Pedraja, *Russian Military Resurgence*, p. 264.

35. "Crimea, the Way Home," YouTube.

36. De La Pedraja, *Russian Military Resurgence*, pp. 264–265; "Crimea, the Way Home," YouTube; "No Bloodshed in a Standoff at Airport in Ukraine," 15 March 2015, *New York Times*.

37. Kalb, *Imperial Gamble*, p. 159; "Crimea, the Way Home," YouTube; De La Pedraja, *Russian Military Resurgence*, p. 266.

38. Sakwa, *Frontline Ukraine*, p. 96; "Crimea, the Way Home," YouTube; De La Pedraja, *Russian Military Resurgence*, p. 267; "Timeline of the Annexation of Crimea by the Russian Federation," 20 February 2020, Wikipedia.

39. Sakwa, *Frontline Ukraine*, pp. 104–105; "Crimea, the Way Home," YouTube; Pifer, *Eagle and Trident*, p. 303.

40. "Crimea, the Way Home," YouTube.

41. De La Pedraja, *Russian Military Resurgence*, p. 267; "Crimea, the Way Home," YouTube.

42. Sakwa, *Frontline Ukraine*, pp. 105, 107. For Yuri Meshkov, the reunification of Crimea with Russia vindicated his failed attempt in 1994 and 1995. He returned to Crimea in early July 2011 to take care of family matters, and just eleven days after his arrival the Ukrainian authorities deported him on 13 July 2011 and banned him from entering Ukraine for five years. When the rule of Kiev ended in the peninsula so did the prohibition, and he was among the first to visit Crimea in March 2014, to a hero's welcome. He and Admiral Igor Kasatonov were very fortunate to have lived to witness the realization of their dreams.

43. "No Bloodshed in a Standoff at Airfield in Ukraine," 15 March 2015, *New York Times*; "For Ukraine Military in Crimea, Glum Capitulation," 23 March 2014, *New York Times*; De La Pedraja, *Russian Military Resurgence*, p. 268; "Crimea, the Way Home," YouTube.

44. Mikhail Barabanov, "Viewing the Action in Ukraine from the Kremlin's Windows," in Colby Howard and Ruslan Pukhov, eds. *Brothers Armed: Military Aspects of the Crisis in Ukraine*, 2nd. ed. (Minneapolis: East View Press, 2016), pp. 188–189.

45. Sakwa, *Frontline Ukraine*, p. 89; "Behind the Masks in Ukraine, Many Faces of Rebellion," 3 May 2014, *New York Times*.

46. Sakwa, *Frontline Ukraine*, pp. 96, 150; "Behind the Masks in Ukraine, Many Faces of Rebellion," 3 May 2014, *New York Times*.

47. Barabanov, "From the Kremlin's Windows," pp. 190–192; Sakwa, *Frontline Ukraine*, p. 96.

48. "Kharkov Settles down, While Pro-Russian Separatists Still Hold Buildings in Lugansk, Donetsk," 8 April 2014, *Kyiv Post*; "Ukraine's Second City Holds Firm," 27 October 2014, *Bloomberg Business News*; Sakwa, *Frontline Ukraine*, p. 150.

49. "Kharkov Settles down, While Pro-Russian Separatists Still Hold Buildings in Lugansk, Donetsk," 8 April 2014, *Kyiv Post*; Sakwa, *Frontline Ukraine*, p. 150; De La Pedraja, *Russian Military Resurgence*, p. 273;"Behind the Masks in Ukraine, Many Faces of Rebellion," 3 May 2014, *New York Times*.

50. Sakwa, *Frontline Ukraine*, p. 150; De La Pedraja, *Russian Military Resurgence*, pp. 273–274; "Origins of the War in Donbass," 14 September 2016, Irrusianality.

51. Sakwa, *Frontline Ukraine*, p. 151; De La Pedraja, *Russian Military Resurgence*, p. 274.

52. Barabanov, "From the Kremlin's Windows," pp. 193–194; De La Pedraja, *Russian Military Resurgence*, p. 275.

53. Sakwa, *Frontline Ukraine*, pp. 98–99; De La Pedraja, *Russian Military Resurgence*, p. 275.

54. Anton Lavrov, "Civil War in the East: How the Conflict Unfolded before Minsk I," in Howard and Pukhov, eds. *Brothers Armed*, p. 213; "Tragedy in Odessa," in Ministry of Foreign Affairs of the Russian Federation, *White Book on Violations of*

Human Rights and the Rule of Law in Ukraine, April 2014–Mid-June 2014 (Moscow: Ministry of Foreign Affairs, 2014), pp. 51–60.

55. De La Pedraja, *Russian Military Resurgence*, p. 276; Barabanov, "From the Kremlin's Windows," p. 196.

56. De La Pedraja, *Russian Military Resurgence*, p. 276; Lavrov, "Civil War in the East," in Howard and Pukhov, eds. *Brothers Armed*, p. 203.

57. Chris Kaspar de Ploeg, *Ukraine in the Crossfire* (Atlanta: Clarity Press, 2017), pp. 140–142, 145; Sakwa, *Frontline Ukraine*, pp. 152–153; Lavrov, "Civil War in the East," pp. 211–212.

58. Sakwa, *Frontline Ukraine*, pp. 153–154; "Origins of the War in Donbass," 14 September 2016, Irrusianality.

59. Sakwa, *Frontline Ukraine*, pp. 155–156; De La Pedraja, *Russian Military Resurgence*, p. 276.

60. "MH17 Probe Did Not Look for Causes of Tragedy, Opted to Impulsively Blame Russia—Malaysian Prime Minister," 24 July 2019, RT; Sakwa, *Frontline Ukraine*, pp. 168–169.

61. "Behind the Masks in Ukraine, Many Faces of Rebellion," 3 May 2014, *New York Times*; Sakwa, *Frontline Ukraine*, pp. 153–154.

62. De La Pedraja, *Russian Military Resurgence*, p. 277; "Pro-Russian Fighters Routed from Stronghold, Ukraine Says," 5 July 2014, *New York Times*.

63. "Ukraine's Deadliest Day: The Battle of Ilovaisk, August 2014," 29 August 2014, BBC; De La Pedraja, *Russian Military Resurgence*, pp. 278–280; "Ukraine Troops Suffer Catastrophic Defeat in Novorossiya," 30 August 2014, Global Research News.

64. Lavrov, "Civil War in the East," pp. 224–225; De La Pedraja, *Russian Military Resurgence*, pp. 279–280.

65. "Second Battle of Donetsk Airport," 28 March 2020, Wikipedia; De La Pedraja, *Russian Military Resurgence*, pp. 282–283.

66. de Ploeg, *Ukraine in the Crossfire*, pp. 204–205; De La Pedraja, *Russian Military Resurgence*, p. 283.

67. "City of Debaltseve Emerges as a Tipping Point in Ukraine's War," 9 February 2015, *Financial Times*; De La Pedraja, *Russian Military Resurgence*, pp. 283–284; "Comment on the Deteriorating Situation in Southeastern Ukraine," 18 August 2015, Ministry of Foreign Affairs of the Russian Federation.

68. BBC Television news broadcasts, July–December 2014.

69. "Russia's Ruble Conquers Eastern Ukraine," 2015 May, *Bloomberg Business Week*; De La Pedraja, *Russian Military Resurgence*, p. 286.

70. "Putin Quietly Detaches Ukraine's Rebel Zones as U.S. Waffles," 19 April 2017, *Bloomberg News*; "On Recognition of Documents and Vehicle Registration Plates in Certain Districts of Ukraine's Donetsk and Lugansk Regions," 20 February 2017, Ministry of Foreign Affairs of the Russian Federation.

71. "Putin Quietly Detaches Ukraine's Rebel Zones as U.S. Waffles," 19 April 2017, *Bloomberg News*; "Ukraine's Breakaway Lugansk Republic Declares Ruble Official Currency," 27 February 2017, *Moscow Times*.

72. "Жителям ЛНР ДНР облегчили получение российских паспортов. Что это значит?" 24 April 2019, BBC in Russian; "Putin Signs Decree Making It Easier for Eastern Ukraine Residents to Obtain Russian Passports," 24 April 2019, RT.

73. "Жителям ЛНР ДНР облегчили получение российских паспортов. Что это значит?" 24 April 2019, BBC in Russian; "В Ростовской области открылся центр выдачи паспортов для жителей ЛНР," 29 April 2019, BBC in Russian.

74. "Россия облегчила получение паспортов для жителей Донбасса. Во сколько это обойдется?" 26 April 2019, BBC in Russian; "В Ростовской области открылся центр выдачи паспортов для жителей ЛНР," 29 April 2019, BBC in Russian; "Жителям Донбасса начали выдавать российские паспорта," 14 June 2019, BBC in Russian. Russian companies operating in the People's Republics witheld sums from salaries for remittance to the Russian pension system. It was expected that all firms in the rebel republics would do the same, thereby reducing the additional expenses the 24 April 2019 decree placed on the Russian pension system.

75. "Путин расширил выдачу паспортов жителям Украины," 17 July 2019, and "Украина может лишит пенсий получивших паспорта России," 8 May 2019, BBC in Russian.

76. "Жителям Донбасса начали выдавать российские паспорта," 14 June 2019, and "Путин расширил выдачу паспортов жителям Украины," 17 July 2019, BBC in Russian; "Moscow Pressures Ukrainian Authorities," *Eurasia Daily Monitor*, 1 July 2020; TASS announcements of 2020 October 1 and November 4. The difficulty of obtaining copies of legal documents from the war ravaged regions often required the longer process of taking depositions to certify the civil status of individuals seeking Russian passports.

77. "Russian and Ukrainian Envoys Clash at UN Security Council over Passports Decree," 26 April 2019, RT.

Chapter 24

1. "Russia Downplays Isolation Post-SCO Summit," Cable from U.S. Embassy, 2 September 2008, Moscow, Wikileaks.

2. "Comment […] regarding NATO's Decision to Restrict Access," 8 April 2014, Russian Ministry of Foreign Affairs; "OECD Suspends Russia Accession Talks while Moscow Vows Symmetrical Sanctions," 13 March 2014, DW; "Grushko Warns that Moscow May Withdraw from NATO-Russia Founding Act," 10 June 2013, Atlantic Council; "EBRD Statement on Operational Approach in Russia," 23 July 2014.

3. *Daily Mail*, 24 March 2014; Television news, 24 March 2014, CNN; "Trump Says Russia Should Be Readmitted to G7," 20 August 2019, *New York Times*; Steven Pifer, *The Eagle and Trident: U.S.-Ukraine Relations in Turbulent Times* (Washington, D.C.: Brookings Institution, 2017), pp. 303–304. American officials thought they were doing Russia such a big favor by letting its president attend the G8 that they were dumbfounded when Putin declined to attend in May 2012. See Michael McFaul, *From Cold War to Hot Peace*:

An American Ambassador in Putin's Russia (Boston: Houghton Mifflin Harcourt, 2018), pp. 326–327.

4. Richard Sakwa, *Frontline Ukraine: Crisis in the Borderlands* (London: I. B. Tauris, 2016), pp. 113–114.

5. "Comment Regarding the Voting on the Draft Resolution 'Territorial Integrity of Ukraine' in the UN General Assembly, 28 March 2014, Russian Ministry of Foreign Affairs.

6. "Russian Delegation Suspended from Council of Europe over Crimea," 10 April 2014, *The Guardian*; "Situation Following the Stripping of the Russian Delegation of its Right to Vote in the Parliamentary Assembly of the Council of Europe, 30 January 2015, Russian Ministry of Foreign Affairs.

7. "U.S. Signs New Lease to Keep Strategic Military Installation in the Horn of Africa," 5 May 2014, *New York Times*; "Djibouti: Playing the Great Game," 6 January 2016, *The Africa Report*.

8. "U.S. Signs New Lease to Keep Strategic Military Installation in the Horn of Africa," 5 May 2014, *New York Times*; "U.S. Wary of Its New Neighbor in Djibouti: A Chinese Naval Base," 25 February 2017, *New York Times*; "In Snub to U.S., Russia and Egypt Move Toward Deal on Air Bases," 30 November 2017, *New York Times*.

9. Sakwa, *Frontline Ukraine*, pp. 187–188, 191.

10. "EU Restrictive Measures in Response to the Crisis in Ukraine," 29 March 2019, European Union.

11. Sakwa, *Frontline Ukraine*, pp. 192–193; "EU Restrictive Measures in Response to the Crisis in Ukraine," 29 March 2019, European Union.

12. "Confirmed: France Canceled Mistral Deal with Russia under Pressure from NATO," 29 September 2015, RT; "France Hands First ex–Russian Mistral Ship to Egypt," 2 June 2016, RT.

13. Sakwa, *Frontline Ukraine*, p. 197; "Comment regarding the introduction of additional sanctions by Australia," 22 May 2014, "Comment regarding the Swiss Government's decision," 28 August 2014, Ministry of Foreign Affairs of the Russian Federation.

14. "Пармезан навсегда как чиновники закупают запрещенные продукты," 5 August 2016, BBC in Russian; BBC TV News Broadcasts, August-September 2014.

15. Sakwa, *Frontline Ukraine*, pp. 107, 140–141, 173; René De La Pedraja, *The Russian Military Resurgence: Post-Soviet Decline and Rebuilding* (Jefferson, NC: McFarland, 2018), p. 262.

16. "Crimea Feels the Pain of Joining Russia," 2 March 2015, *Bloomberg Business News*; Sakwa, *Frontline Ukraine*, pp. 110–111.

17. "Russia to Spend over $800 Million on Electricity Cable to Crimea," 17 July 2015, *Moscow Times*; "How Hackers Took Down a Power Grid," 18 January 2016, *Bloomberg Business Week*; "Dreams in Isolation: Crimea Two Years after Annexation," 18 March 2016, *Moscow Times*.

18. "Crimea Feels the Pain of Joining Russia," 2 March 2015, *Bloomberg Business Week*; "Comment by the Information and Press Department on Ukraine's New Entry Procedure for Russian Nationals," 26 December 2017, Russian Ministry of Foreign Affairs; Videos on YouTube, 2015–2016. It was later discovered that a major reason why Ukraine instituted strict border controls was to take prisoner any person suspected of involvement in the uprisings in Crimea, Donetsk, and Lugansk against Kiev. Many of these hostages obtained their freedom with the prisoner swap of 7 September 2019 for Ukrainian sailors.

19. "Statement by the Russian Ministry of Foreign Affairs regarding the Aggravation of the Situation around Russian Foreign Institutions in Ukraine," 16 June 2014 and "Suspension of the Measures to Transfer Armaments, Military Equipment, and Material Supplies of Ukrainian Armed Forces from the Territory of the Republic of Crimea of the Russian Federation," 5 July 2014, Russian Ministry of Foreign Affairs.

20. "Comment by the Information and Press Department of the Russian Ministry of Foreign Affairs regarding the Signing of European Union Association Agreements with Ukraine, Georgia, and Moldova," 27 June 2014; Sawka, *Frontline Ukraine*, pp. 142, 261. In a great irony, the benefits the people expected the Association Agreements with the EU of 27 July 2014 to bring have failed to materialize until the present.

21. "Пармезан навсегда как чиновники закупают запрещенные продукты," 5 August 2016, BBC in Russian; BBC TV News Broadcasts, August-September 2014; Sakwa, *Frontline Ukraine*, pp. 140, 142.

22. "Something's Rotten in the State of Ukraine," 22 February 2016, *Bloomberg Business Week*.

23. "How Hackers Took Down a Power Grid," 18 January 2016, *Bloomberg Business Week*; "The Next Hack Will Turn Your Lights Off," 6 November 2017, *Bloomberg Business Week*.

24. "Upping the Ante: Putin Dismisses Diplomacy after Alleged Ukrainian Incursion," 10 August 2016, *Moscow Times*; "Statement by the Foreign Ministry of Russia," 11 August 2016.

25. "Comment by the Information and Press Department on the Latest Ukrainian Sanctions against Russia," 16 May 2017 and "Comment by the Information and Press Department on another Round of Anti-Russian Initiatives by the Ukrainian Authorities," 6 October 2017, Russian Ministry of Foreign Affairs; "Council of Europe's Experts Criticize Ukrainian Language Laws," 7 December 2019, *RadioFreeEurope/RadioLiberty*.

26. "Recognizing a Problem," *Moscow Times*, 20 February 2017; "Comment by the Information and Press Department on the Presidential Executive Order," 20 February 2017, Russian Ministry of Foreign Affairs; "Ukraine's Breakaway Luhansk Republic Declares Ruble Official Currency," 27 February 2017, *Moscow Times*.

27. *Moscow Times*, 11 December 2017.

28. "Why Kerch May Prove a Bridge Too Far for Russia," 17 June 2016, *Moscow Times*; Joshua Yaffa, "Oligarchy 2.0," 29 May 2017, *New Yorker*; De La Pedraja, The *Russian Military Resurgence*, p. 271; "Connecting Russia: First Railroad Span across Crimean Bridge Complete," 14 June 2019, RT; Novosti Television news, 27 to 29 December 2019. The tickets for the first passenger train crossing over the Kerch Bridge had sold out months before.

29. "Beneath the Front Lines," 23 February 2015, *Time*; "Ukraine Rebels Seize Billionaire Akhmetov's Enterprises in Donbass," 1 March 2017, bneintellinews; "Maidan 2.0: Ukrainian Nationalist Provoking Political Crisis with Coal Blockade," 25 February 2017, RT; Chris Kaspar de Ploeg, *Ukraine in the Crossfire* (Atlanta: Clarity Press, 2017), p. 167.

30. "Ukraine's House Divided Counts the Cost of the Donbass Blockade," 18 January 2018, *Newsweek*; "How Ukraine Shot Itself in the Foot with Its Own Blockade of Donbass," 24 February 2017, Sputnik; "Maidan 2.0: Ukrainian Nationalist Provoking Political Crisis with Coal Blockade," 25 February 2017, RT; "Ukraine Blockaders Try to Cut off Rail Traffic from Rebel Areas," 2 March 2017, *New York Times*; "Donetsk People's Republic Starts Coal Exports to Russia," 15 March 2017, Sputnik; "Protests Held Nationwide against Crackdown on Blockade Activists," 14 March 2017, *Kyiv Post*; "Kiev and the Kremlin Face Narrowing Options in Ukraine, 3 April 2017, *Time*; "Putin Quietly Detaches Ukraine's Rebel Zones as U.S. Waffles," 19 April 2017, *Bloomberg News*.

31. "Ukraine's House Divided Counts the Cost of the Donbass Blockade," 18 January 2018, *Newsweek*; "Coal Smuggled from Ukraine's Occupied Donbass Ends up in Poland," 12 October 2017, *Eurasia Daily Monitor*; "Kiev and the Kremlin Face Narrowing Options in Ukraine, 3 April 2017, *Time*.

32. "Ukraine Rebels Seize Billionaire Akhmetov's Enterprises in Donbass," 1 March 2017, bneintellinews; "Infographics: Not Only Akhmetov," 9 March 2017, 24-my-info; "Protesters Attack Akhmetov's Office," 15 March 2017, *Kyiv Post*; "Zelensky Has Ultimatum for Donbass, But Is He in a Position to Talk?" 9 July 2019, RT.

33. "Comment by Foreign Ministry Spokesperson Maria Zakharova on American and Canadian Weapons Deliveries to Ukraine," 14 December 2017 and "Comment by Deputy Foreign Minister Sergey Ryabkov on U.S. Arms Deliveries to Ukraine," 23 December 2017, Russian Ministry of Foreign Affairs.

34. "Ukraine Moves to Restore Control over Separatist-Held Areas," 18 January 2018, Radio FreeEurope/Radio Liberty; "Comment by the Information and Press Department in Connection with Ukraine Adopting the So-Called Law on Re-Integration and De-Occupation of Donbass," 18 January 2018, Russian Ministry of Foreign Affairs; "Protests Held Nationwide against Crackdown on Blockade Activists," 14 March 2017, *Kyiv Post*.

35. "Comment by the Information and Press Department on the Signing of the Donbass Reintegration Law," 24 February 2018, Russian Ministry of Foreign Affairs.

36. "A Foreign Reformer Takes on Odessa," 27 July 2015, *Bloomberg Business Week*; Peter Zalmaev and Lincoln Mitchell, "The Rise and Fall of Mikheil Saakashvili," 20 February 2018, Aljazeera; "In Ukraine, Ultranationalist Militia Strikes Fear in Some Quarters," 30 January 2018, Radio Free Europe/RadioLiberty.

37. "Press Release on the Situation with the Crew of the *Nord* Vessel," 19 April 2018, Russian Ministry of Foreign Affairs.

38. "Press Release on Threats from Ukrainian Authorities to Russian Shipping," 28 April 2018, Russian Ministry of Foreign Affairs.

39. "Weekly Report of the EU Delegation to Ukraine," 20 July 2018, diplomatic cable of European Union, *New York Times*; "Kerch Strait Standoff: Ukrainian Navy Consciously Ignored Orders to Stop, FSB Says," 27 November 2018, RT; "Russia-Ukraine Fight over Narrow Sea Passage Risks Wider War," 26 November 2018, *New York Times*; "La Russie capture trois navires ukrainiens, escalade de tensions entre Kiev et Moscou," 26 Nov 2018, *Le figaro*.

40. "Russia Ukraine Incident: Duma to Honour Ship Seizure Troops," 3 December 2019, BBC; "ЕС ввел санкции против восьми россиян из-за инцидента в Кечеcком проливе," 15 March 2019, BBC in Russian; "La Russie capture trois navires ukrainiens, escalade de tensions entre Kiev et Moscou," 26 Nov 2018, *Le Figaro*.

41. "Kerch Strait Standoff: Ukrainian Navy Consciously Ignored Orders to Stop, FSB Says," 27 November 2018, RT; "Russia-Ukraine Fight over Narrow Sea Passage Risks Wider War," 26 November 2018, *New York Times*.

42. "Moscow Releases Ukrainian Navy Boats Seized during Violation of Russian Territorial Waters near Crimea in 2018," 18 November 2019.

Chapter 25

1. "Russia Can't Exist without Being Independent," 20 February 2018, RT.

2. "Syria Update—Russian Team back in Moscow," Message from Joseph Kruzick, 7 February 2012, State-FOIA; "Syria; for Hillary from Sid," 24 February 2012, Hillary E-mails, Wikileaks; "Burns-Denisov," Message from Jacob J. Sullivan, 25 February 2012, Hillary E-mails, Wikileaks.

3. "View from the Field on Emerging Arguments for a Syria No-fly Zone," Message from Tom Malinowski, 21 August 2012, Hillary E-mails, Wikileaks; René De La Pedraja, The *Russian Military Resurgence: Post-Soviet Decline and Rebuilding, 1992–2018* (Jefferson, NC: McFarland, 2018), p 293; "Assad's Plans; for Hillary from Sid," 18 September 2012, Hillary E-mails, Wikileaks.

4. De La Pedraja, *Russian Military Resurgence*, p. 294; Steven Lee Myers, *The New Tsar: The Rise and Reign of Vladimir Putin* (New York: Vintage Books, 2015), p. 442.

5. "Syria/France: Hollande Weighs Options Following Parliament Debate," Cable from U.S. Embassy, Paris, 13 September 2013, State-FOIA; Myers, *Vladimir Putin*, pp. 442–443; Michael McFaul, *From Cold War to Hot Peace: An American Ambassador in Putin's Russia* (Boston: Houghton Mifflin Harcourt, 2018), pp. 350–352.

6. De La Pedraja, *Russian Military Resurgence*, p. 295; Myers, *Vladimir Putin*, pp. 443–444; Angela E. Stent, *The Limits of Partnership: U.S.-Russian Relations in the Twenty-First Century* (Princeton: Princeton University Press, 2015), pp. 280–281; McFaul, *Cold War to Hot Peace*, pp. 352–356.

7. "Behind the Sudden Death of a $1 Billion Secret CIA War in Syria," 2 August 2017, *New York Times*; De La Pedraja, *Russian Military Resurgence*, pp. 295–297.

8. "Syria, Turkey, Israel, Iran," 24 July 2012, Hillary E-mails, Wikileaks; De La Pedraja, *Russian Military Resurgence*, pp. 297–298.

9. "By Focusing on Syria, Putin Is Catering to an Audience at Home," 27 September 2015, *New York Times*; "Putin's Syria Gamble,"26 October 2015, *Time*; De La Pedraja, *Russian Military Resurgence*, p. 298.

10. "Putin's Syria Gamble," 26 October 2015, *Time*; De La Pedraja, *Russian Military Resurgence*, p. 299.

11. "Informal Meeting of Foreign Affairs Ministers," Amsterdam, 5–6 February 2016, diplomatic cable of European Union, released by *New York Times* on 18 December 2018; De La Pedraja, *Russian Military Resurgence*, pp. 300–303.

12. "The Trump-Putin Reset Is Dead—But Don't Rule Out an Amicable Settlement," 24 April 2017, *Time*; "Trump Officials Tell Russia to Drop Its Support for Syria's Assad," 10 April 2017, *Washington Post*; "U.S.-Russia Reset Screeches to a Halt," 12 April 2017, *New York Times*. In contrast to the hostility in the State Department, a quiet supporter of the Russian intervention in Syria was Israel. In a private conversation a high-ranking official of the Israeli Foreign Ministry admitted that "the situation in Syria would have been even more complex without the Russian presence." See, "Political Consultations between Slovakia and Israel," Jerusalem, 12 June 2018, diplomatic cable of European Union, released by *New York Times* on 18 December 2018.

13. "Trump Ends Covert CIA Program to Arm Anti-Assad Rebels in Syria," *Washington Post*, 19 July 2017; "Behind the Sudden Death of a $1 Billion Secret CIA War in Syria," 2 August 2017, *New York Times*; De La Pedraja, *Russian Military Resurgence*, p. 295.

14. "The Syrian Civil War Is Decided," 26 October 2017, Stratfor.

15. "Syria: A Hungarian Step Towards Diplomatic Normalization?" 11 September 2019, BBC; The Syrian Civil War Is Decided," 26 October 2017, Stratfor.

16. "Arab League Set to Readmit Syria Eight Years after Expulsion," 26 December 2018, *The Guardian*; "The Syrian Civil War Is Decided," 26 October 2017, Stratfor; "Why Did the UAE and Bahrain Reopen their Embassies in Syria?" 8 January 2019, Aljazeera.

17. "UAE Reopens Syria Embassy in Boost for Assad," 27 December 2018, Reuters; "Why Did the UAE and Bahrain Reopen their Embassies in Syria?" 8 January 2019, Aljazeera; "UAE Using Soft Power in Syria after 7-Year Frost," 31 May 2019, Asia Times; "Syria Should Recover Its Place in the Arab World, Says UAE Minister," 6 March 2019, *The National*.

18. "Arab League Set to Readmit Syria Eight Years after Expulsion," 26 December 2018, *The Guardian*; "UAE Reopens Syria Embassy in Boost for Assad," 27 December 2018, Reuters; "U.S. Stands in Way of Assad Rejoining Arab Fold," 3 March 2019, *Washington Post*.

19. This quotation and the next from "Syria Should Recover Its Place in the Arab World, Says UAE Minister," 6 March 2019, *The National*.

20. "Syria Begins to Rebuild," 5 December 2017, *El País*; "Crimea's Lifeline to Syria: Damascus Gets Grain Supplies from Russia's Black Sea Peninsula," 21 June 2018, RT; "What Victory Looks Like: A Journey through Shattered Syria," 21 August 2019, *New York Times*.

21. "In Moscow, a Sense of Relief after a Limited Syrian Attack," 14 April 2018, *New York Times*; "BBC Producer Says Hospital Scenes after 2018 Douma 'Chemical Attack' were staged," 16 February 2019, RT.

22. "Assad Must Go, Erdogan Says, as Syria War Winds Down," 27 December 2017, *New York Times*; "Turkey Charges into Syria, Threatening its Alliance with Russia," 5 February 2018, *Time*; "The War in Syria Has Become a Global Battlefield," 26 February 2018, *Time*.

23. "Turkey Begins Operation against U.S.-Backed Kurdish Militias in Syria," 19 January 2018, *New York Times*; "As Turkey Attacks Kurds in Syria, U.S. Is on the Sideline," 22 January 2018, *New York Times*; "Turkey's Worst Day Yet in Syria Offensive: At Least 7 Soldiers Killed," 4 February 2018, *New York Times*; "Turkey Charges into Syria, Threatening its Alliance with Russia," 5 February 2018, *Time*.

24. "The Fall of Afrin," 2 April 2018, *Time*; "Битва в Идлибе," 2 August 2019, BBC in Russian.

25. "Liberate Syria's Idlib, Precisely for the Civilians that America Fakes Concern over," 25 May 2019, RT; "Битва в Идлибе," 2 August 2019, BBC in Russian.

26. "Syria War: Jihadist Takeover in Rebel-Held Idlib Sparks Alarm," 26 February 2019, BBC; "Syria War: Unexplained Blast Kills 15 in Rebel-held Idlib," 24 April 2019, BBC.

27. "Битва в Идлибе," 2 August 2019, BBC in Russian; "Russian Military Repels 12 Rockets Fired in New Attack on Hmeymim Airbase in Syria," 8 May 2019, RT; "Russia Says Syrian Troops repelled Three Big Militant Attacks in Syria's Idlib," 22 May 2019, *Moscow Times*; "Missiles Fired at Russian Hmeymim Airbase in Syria amid Massive Militant Offensive," 23 May 2019, RT; "Russia's Hmeimim Airbase in Syria Repels Militant Drone Attacks," 2 February 2020, RT; Новости, 20 February 2020, Russian Television 1.

28. "Russian Air Force Targets Militants in Syria's Idlib at Request of Turkish Military," 14 June 2019, RT; "Syrian Forces Move into Strategic Town, Tightening Grip on Rebels," 20 August 2019, *New York Times*; "Khan Sheikhoun: Syrian Rebels Pull out of Key Town after Five Years," 20 August 2019, BBC.

29. "Trump's First Mistake in Syria Was Ever Trusting Erdogan," 17 October 2019, *Washington Post*; "Trump Went off Script during Call with Erdogan, Senior Military Source Reveals," 9 October 2019, Fox News.

30. "Syrian Army Enters City of Manbij at the Height of Turkish Offensive against Kurds," 15 October 2019, RT; "Syrie: résistance des forces kurdes, patrouilles russes après le retrait américain," 15 October 2015, *Le Figaro*; "One out, Another One in: Retreating U.S. Military Meets Advancing Syrian Army," 14 October 2019, RT; "In Syria, Russia Is Pleased to Fill an American Void," 16 October 2019, *New York Times*.

31. "Turkey and Russia to Start Patrolling Kurdish Areas in Northern Syria Together on Friday–Erdogan,"

30 October 2019, RT; "In Syria, Russia Is Pleased to Fill an American Void," 16 October 2019, *New York Times*. Russian bombardment had been ineffective, because the rebels dug an underground bunker several kilometers long for storage of the weapons and 115 mm ammunition for shelling Aleppo, Новости, 20 February 2020, Russian Television 1.

32. "Erdogan Says Turkey Will Not Withdraw from Syria's Idlib until Attacks by Damascus Stop," 21 February 2020, RT; "Turkey Faces Strategic Defeat in Idlib," 19 February 2020, RT; Новости, 14 February 2020, Russian Television 1.

33. "Russian Military Police Deployed to Strategic Town of Saraqeb," 2 March 2020, RT; "U.S. Blocks UN from Supporting Russian-Turkish Ceasefire," 6 March 2020 RT; "How Russia's Putin Became the Go-to Man on Syria," 5 March 2020, BBC.

34. "Inside a 3-Year Campaign to Influence U.S. Voters," 16 February 2018, *New York Times*. U.S. official reports did not even consider the possibility that the actions of private Russian citizens were in response to the U.S. sanctions over Crimea.

35. Robert S. Mueller, III, *Report on the Investigation into Russian Interference in the 2016 Presidential Election*, 2 vols. (Washington, D.C.: U.S. Department of Justice, 2019), 1: 14–19; House Permanent Select Committee on Intelligence, *Report on Russian Active Measures*, 22 March 2018, pp. 3, 13, 31–32, 35.

36. Senate Committee on Intelligence, *Report on Russian Active Measures Campaigns and Interference in the 2016 U.S. Election* Vols. 1–5, 2019–2020, 1: 31–33, 2: 1–12.

37. House, *Russian Measures*, pp. 31–32, appendix C; *Mueller Report*, table of contents.

38. House, *Russian Measures*, pp. 13, 32–33; *Mueller Report*, 1: 21; Senate Committee on Intelligence, *Report*, 2: 30.

39. *Mueller Report*, 1: 25; House, *Russian Measures*, p. 35.

40. "Our Pain for their Gain: The American Activists Manipulated by Russian Trolls," 21 October 2017, *The Guardian*; House, *Russian Measures*, pp. 33–35; *Mueller Report*, 1: 29–31; Senate Committee on Intelligence, *Report*, 2: 46–47; "Inside a 3-Year Campaign to Influence U.S. Voters," 16 February 2018, *New York Times*.

41. Senate Committee on Intelligence, *Report*, 1: 14–15; *Mueller Report*, 1: 50–51.

42. Senate Committee on Intelligence, *Report*, 1: 22.

43. *Mueller Report*, 1: 50; Senate Committee on Intelligence, *Report*, 1: 15–21.

44. House, *Russian Measures*, pp. 28–30. U.S. security agencies were convinced that Russian military intelligence (GRU) was behind the hacking of the DNC, but they have refused to share any of their evidence. See Murray Palmer, "Why I have Still Got My Doubts that the Russians Hacked the DNC," 4 September 2018, HNN. The Veteran Intelligence Professionals for Sanity, who rejected the Weapons of Mass Destruction false accusations of the George W. Bush administration, also argued that the DNC e-mails came from internal leaks, though their methodology and conclusions have been called into question.

45. "Company Intelligence Report 2016/111," 14 September 2016, Christopher Steele Dossier, BuzzFeed News.

46. "Company Intelligence Report/100," 5 August 2016 and "Company Intelligence Report 2016/111," 14 September 2016, Christopher Steele Dossier, BuzzFeed News; Jim Rutenberg, "The Disruption," 17 September 2017, *New York Times Magazine*, pp. 52–53.

47. "Company Intelligence Report 2016/111," 14 September 2016 and "Company Intelligence Report 2016/130," 12 October 2016, Christopher Steele Dossier, BuzzFeed News.

48. "Company Intelligence Report 2016/111," 14 September 2016, Christopher Steele Dossier, BuzzFeed News; "Putin Dismisses Sergei Ivanov, a Longtime Ally, as Chief of Staff," 12 August 2016, *New York Times*.

49. "Company Intelligence Report 2016/111," 14 September 2016, and Company Intelligence Report 2016/135, 19 October 2016, Christopher Steele Dossier, BuzzFeed News; "Putin Dismisses Sergei Ivanov, a Longtime Ally, as Chief of Staff," 12 August 2016, *New York Times*; "Why Putin Fired His Chief of Staff and Longtime Ally," Reuters, 12 August 2016.

50. Senate Committee on Intelligence, *Report*, 1: 10–11, 35, 38; "Trump-Russia Dossier—Bridge Project," 2 October 2917, pp. 30–31.

51. Senate Committee on Intelligence, *Report*, 1: 38 and also p. 3.

52. *Mueller Report*, 1: 1, 48; House, *Russian Measures*, pp. 30–31.

Chapter 26

1. "More Than 100 Military Attachés Visited the Russian Centre for State Defense Control for the First Time," 21 March 2015, Ministry of Defense of the Russian Federation.

2. "Russia Should Go Away and Shut up, UK Defense Secretary Gavin Williamson Says (video)," 16 March 2018, RT.

3. "Russia Completely Ending Activities under Conventional Armed Forces in Europe Treaty," 10 March 2015, RT; Magdelena Lachowicz, "Russia and the Prospects of OECD Membership: between De Jure and De Factor Modernization," *Yearbook of the Institute of East-Central Europe*, October 2016, pp. 166-167; "OECD Maintains Technical Work with Russia despite Postponed Accession Talks, 17 June 2016 and "OECD Wants Russia to Enter despite Some States' Objections,," 29 August 2017, Sputnik International.

4. "Press Release on Acceptance of the WTO Trade Facilitation Agreement," 22 April 2016, Ministry of Foreign Affairs.

5. "Russian Federation: Constitutional Court Allows Country to Ignore ECHR Rulings," 18 May 2016, Global Legal Monitor of Library of Congress.

6. In a first case on 19 April 2016, the Russian Constitutional Court ruled that the clause in the 1993 Constitution denying inmates the right to vote prevailed over the decision of the European Court of Human Rights to allow voting by all inmates. See, "Russian Federation: Constitutional Court Allows

Country to Ignore ECHR Rulings," 18 May 2016, Global Legal Monitor of Library of Congress.

7. "Deputy Foreign Minister Alexey Meskov's Interview with the TASS News Agency," 30 September 2016, Russian Ministry of Foreign Affairs.

8. "Comment by the Information and Press Department on the Decision on Crimea Adopted by the Council of Europe's Committee of Ministers," 5 May 2017, and "Statement of the Ministry of Foreign Affairs of the Russian Federation Concerning the Suspension of Payment of Russia's Contribution to the Council of Europe," 30 June 2017, Ministry of Foreign Affairs of the Russian Federation; "Russia Tests Council of Europe in Push to Regain Vote," 26 Nov 2018, *Financial Times*; "Russian Lawmakers Vote to Keep Up Council of Europe Boycott," 17 Jan 2019, DW.

9. "Russia to Extend Suspension of Payment to Council of Europe—Source," 12 January 2018, TASS; "Human Rights Body Faces Cash Crisis after Clash with Russia," 16 March 2018, *The Guardian*; "Russia Withholds Payments to the Council of Europe," 1 March 2018, DW.

10. "Press Release on the Participation of Deputy Foreign Minister Alexander Gurshko in the 128th Ministerial Session of the Committee of Ministers of the Council of Europe," 18 May 2018, Ministry of Foreign Affairs of the Russian Federation; "Press Release on the Meeting of the Interdepartmental Commission Concerning the Council of Europe, 29 March 2018; "Human Rights Body Faces Cash Crisis after Clash with Russia," 16 March 2018, *The Guardian*.

11. "Leading Candidate to Head Interpol Is Russian, Drawing Western Objections," 20 November 2018, *New York Times*.

12. "There Is a Wolf at Interpol's Door," 22 November 2018, RT; "Leading Candidate to Head Interpol Is Russian, Drawing Western Objections," 20 November 2018, *New York Times*.

13. "Interpol Presidency Vote: Russia in Surprise Loss to South Korea," 21 November 2018, BBC; "There Is a Wolf at Interpol's Door," 22 November 2018, RT.

14. "Deputy Foreign Minister Alexey Meshkov's Interview with the TASS News Agency," 30 September 2016, Ministry of Foreign Affairs of the Russian Federation.

15. "Comment by the Information and Press Department on the Extension of EU Sectoral Sanctions against Russia," 1 July 2016, Ministry of Foreign Affairs of the Russian Federation; "Dining under Putin: How Sanctions are Fueling a Russian Food Revolution," 29 November 2016, CNN; "Russia to Retain Crown as World's Top Wheat Exporter," 13 May 2019, RT; "Russian Economic Growth Hit 6-Year High in 2018 despite Sanctions—World Bank," 5 June 2019, RT.

16. "Comment by the Information and Press Department on the Cypriot Parliament's Vote against anti-Russia EU Sanctions," 7 July 2017, Ministry of Foreign Affairs of the Russian Federation.

17. Anastasia Chebakova, "Exposing the Limits of EU-Russia Autonomous Cooperation: The Potential of Bakhtin's Dialogic Imagination," PhD Dissertation, University of Victoria, 2015, pp. 183–189, 192–196; Fyodor Lukyanov, "Life after Sanctions: What Kind of Future Awaits Russia and the EU?" 4 February 2016, *Russia Beyond*.

18. A similar observation is in Robert M. Gates, *Duty: Memoirs of a Secretary at War* (New York: Alfred A. Knopf, 2014), pp. 409–410.

19. "Comment by the Information and Press Department on the Statement of the EU Foreign Affairs Council of March 19, 2018 on the Incident in Salisbury," 19 March 2018 and "Foreign Ministry Statement," 23 March 2018, Ministry of Foreign Affairs of the Russian Federation. The former Russian spy had been doing consulting work for Eastern European countries about the activities of organized crime groups. An alternate explanation for the attempted murder was that it had been a botched Mafia hit.

20. "Britain to Expel 23 Russian Diplomats after Poisoning of Ex-Spy," 14 March 2018, *Washington Post*; "Spy Poisoning: Russian Diplomats Expelled across U.S. and Europe," 26 March 2018, BBC. In a good illustration of horse trading for votes in international fora, Hungary agreed to expel one Russian diplomat. In exchange, the British government of Theresa May ordered the Conservative Party representatives in the European Parliament to vote against sanctions on Hungary. The understanding Kremlin sympathized with the predicament of Hungary, and after the furor over the Salisbury incident receded, Russia resumed very close relations with its traditional ally.

21. "Salisbury Poisoning: One Year on, Still No Evidence of Novichok Nerve Agent Use Disclosed to Public," 4 March 2019, RT; "Kept in the Dark: Novichok Poisoning Survivor Tells Russian Ambassador He Got NO Info from UK Govt," 6 April 2019, RT.

22. "Facing Russian Threat, NATO Boosts Operations for the First Time since the Cold War," 8 November 2017, *Washington Post*.

23. "NATO Kicks out Russian Spies but Revives Kremlin Hotline amid Ukraine Tensions," 10 May 2015, *The Guardian*.

24. "NATO Kicks out Russian Spies but Revives Kremlin Hotline amid Ukraine Tensions," 10 May 2015, *The Guardian*; "NATO-Russia Council: From High Hopes to Broken Dreams," 12 July 2016, RadioFreeEurope/Radio Liberty; "How Putin Killed NATO's Agreement with Russia," 3 June 2016, *Newsweek*; "Grushko Warns that Moscow May Withdraw from NATO-Russia Founding Act," 10 June 2014, Atlantic Council.

25. "NATO-Russia Council Talks Fail to Iron out Differences," 20 April 2016, *The Guardian*; "NATO-Russia Council: From High Hopes to Broken Dreams," 12 July 2016, RadioFreeEurope/Radio Liberty; "NATO-Russia Council," 16 June 2017, North Atlantic Treaty Organization.

26. "The NATO-Russia Founding Act: A Dead Letter," 29 June 2017, Carnegie Europe.

27. "Russia's Military Drills near NATO Border Raise Fears of Aggression," 31 July 2017, *New York Times*.

28. "Russian Defense Ministry Commented on Upcoming Zapad 2017 Exercise," 9 September 2017, Ministry of Defense of Russian Federation.

29. "How Putin Killed NATO's Agreement with Russia," 3 June 2016, *Newsweek*; "Russian Defense Minister Summed up Zapad 2017 Exercise," 10 October 2017, Ministry of Defense of Russian Federation.

30. "Facing Russian Threat, NATO Boosts Operations for the First Time since the Cold War," 8 November 2017, *Washington Post*; "NATO Chief Plans to Discuss NATO-Russia Council Activities with Lavrov," 15 February 2018, TASS.

31. "U.S., Other Powers Kick Russia out of G-8," 24 March 2014, CNN; "G8 Becomes the G7," 24 March 2014, *Daily Mail*.

32. "Russia Announces Plan to Permanently Leave G-8 Group of Industrialized Nations," 13 January 2017, *The Independent*.

33. "G7 Unite to Condemn Russia for Behavior That Has Undermined International Law," 23 April 2018, *The Independent*. "Russia Should be in G7," 8 June 2018, RT; "End of Western Hegemony: Why Does Macron Want Russia at Europe's Side?" 27 August 2019, RT.

34. "Trump Says Russia Should be Readmitted to G7," 20 Aug 2019, *New York Times*; "West's Leading Role Is Ending: G7's No Good without India and China, Putin Says," 5 Sept 2019, RT.

35. "Foreign Minister Sergei Lavrov's Opening Remarks at Talks with Council of Europe Secretary General Thorbjørn Jagland," 20 October 2017, Ministry of Foreign Affairs of the Russian Federation; "We Won't Pay for Thin Air: Moscow Responds to Council of Europe Expulsion Threats," 11 October 2018, RT.

36. "Russia Tests Council of Europe in Push to Regain Vote," 26 November 2017, *Financial Times*; "We Won't Pay for Thin Air: Moscow Responds to Council of Europe Expulsion Threats," 11 October 2018, RT.

37. "Human Rights Body Faces Cash Crisis after Clash with Russia," 16 March 2018, *The Guardian*; "Feeling Betrayed by UK, Says Novichok Victim's Son in Letter to Putin," 3 March 2019, RT; "Kept in the Dark: Novichok Poisoning Survivor Tells Russian Ambassador He Got NO Info from UK Govt," 6 April 2019, RT.

38. The overwhelming majority of sports fans visiting Russia for the World Cup of June-July 2018 were Europeans, although Americans comprised the single largest nationality.

39. "The European Parliament Will Consider the Suspension of the Partnership and Cooperation Agreement with Russia in March 2019," 1 December 2018, Unian.info/world; "The Escalation of Tensions around the Sea of Azov and the Kerch Strait," Resolution of 24 January 2019.

40. "Russian Lawmakers Vote to Keep Up Council of Europe Boycott," 17 January 2019, DW; "Russian MPs Prolong Payments Freeze to Council of Europe," 18 January 2019, Euractiv; "Russia May Leave Council of Europe and European Court of Human Rights," 15 March 2019, *The Japan Times*.

41. "Bring Russia back in from the Cold, Says Council of Europe Chief," 7 April 2019, *Financial Times*; "President Deeply Concerned by Russia's Decision to Offer Russian Citizenship to Donbass Residents," 30 April 2019, Parliamentary Assembly of the Council of Europe; "Macron Says Would Like Russia to Remain Council of Europe Member," 6 May 2019, TASS.

42. "Council of Europe Votes to Maintain Russia's Membership," 17 May 2019, *The Guardian*; "Council of Europe Ministers Agree Way for Russia to Rejoin," 17 May 2019, RadioFreeEurope/RadioLiberty; "Russia to Stay in PACE, European Ministers Say despite Anger from Ukraine," 18 May 2019, RT.

43. "Council of Europe Restores Russia's Voting Rights," 25 June 2019, *New York Times*; "Le Conseil de L'Europe lève ses sanctions contre la Russie," 25 June 2019, *Le Monde*; "Ukraine Exits in Protest," 26 June 2019, RT; "ПАСЕ подтвердила полномочия российских делегатов," 26 June 2019, BBC in Russian.

44. Entin and Entina, "Russia and the Council of Europe."

Chapter 27

1. "Five Takeaways from Putin's Fox Interview," 17 July 2018, RT. Slightly different translation in "Chris Wallace Interviews Russian President Vladimir Putin," 18 July 2018, Fox News.

2. "U.S.-Russia Tensions Reach Dangerous New Level," 14 October 2016, *Time*.

3. Office of the Director of National Intelligence, *Intelligence Community Assessment: Assessing Russian Activities and Intentions in Recent U.S. Elections*, ICA 2017–01D, 6 January 2017; "The Troublemaker,"16 January 2017, *Time*, p. 26.

4. Open Source Center, *Russia—Kremlin's TV Seeks to Influence Politics, Fuel Discontent in U.S.*, 11 December 2012; "Russia's RT Network: Is It More BBC or KGB?" 8 March 2017, *New York Times*. Even the anti–Russian Senate Committee on Intelligence admitted that the 2012 report should have been updated. See *Report on Russian Active Measures Campaigns and Interference in the 2016 U.S. Election* Vols. 1–5, 2019–2020, 4: 132–133.

5. *Assessing Russian Activities*, p. i.

6. Jim Rutenberg, "The Disruption," 17 September 2017, *New York Times Magazine*, p. 67.

7. *Assessing Russian Activities*, pp. 7–9.

8. "Russia's RT Just Isn't Worth Attacking," 15 November 2017, *Bloomberg News*.

9. "Russia's RT Network: Is It More BBC or KGB?" 8 March 2017, *New York Times*.

10. "U.S. Orders Sputnik News Agency to Register as Foreign Agent," 10 January 2018, *Moscow Times*; "Sputnik (News Agency)," 7 April 2020, Wikipedia; "Playing on Kansas City Radio,"13 February 2020, *New York Times*.

11. "Russia's RT Just Isn't Worth Attacking," 15 November 2017, *Bloomberg News*; "Kremlin TV Network RT Registers as Foreign Agent in U.S.," 13 November 2017, *Moscow Times*.

12. Quotation and paragraph from "Russia's RT Just Isn't Worth Attacking," 15 November 2017, *Bloomberg News*.

13. "Facebook Takes Down over 200 Accounts and Pages Run by the IRA, a Notorious Russian Troll Farm," 3 April 2018, Business Insider; "Google Will

De-rank RT Articles to Make Them Harder to Find—Eric Schmidt," 22 November 2017, RT.

14. "Beyond the NRA: Maria Butina's Peculiar Bid for Russian Influence," 4 August 2018, *New York Times*; Photographs of Maria Butina on Google.

15. "Russian Spy Maria Butina Pleads Guilty to Conspiracy against U.S.," 13 December 2018, *The Guardian*; "NRA Seeks Distance from Russia as Investigations Heat Up," 28 January 2019, *New York Times*.

16. "Beyond the NRA: Maria Butina's Peculiar Bid for Russian Influence," 4 August 2018, *New York Times*; "Maria Butina: Russian Agent Sentenced to 18 Months in Prison," 26 April 2019, BBC.

17. "Russian Spy Maria Butina Pleads Guilty to Conspiracy against U.S.," 13 December 2018, *The Guardian*; "Comment by the Information and Press Department on the Latest U.S. Allegations regarding Russia," 15 January 2019, Ministry of Foreign Affairs of Russian Federation.

18. "Maria Butina: Russian Agent Sentenced to 18 Months in Prison," 26 April 2019, BBC.

19. Russian Language TV News Broadcasts, October 25 to 30, 2019. Butina's lawyer commented on the heavy guard of her deportation from the U.S.: "They tend to do these things like they are moving a nuclear bomb, and they are not." See, "Maria Butina: Russian Agent Released from U.S. Prison," 25 October 2019, BBC.

20. "Inside the Decade-Long Russian Campaign to Infiltrate the NRA and Help Elect Trump," 2 April 2018, *Rolling Stone*; "Has a U.S. College Given Russia Too Friendly a Platform?," 6 November 2019, *New York Times*; "American U Program Inspired by a Russian Ambassador," 8 November 2019, Inside Higher Ed; "The Russia-AU Connection: University's Russian Cultural Institute Stirs Controversy," 23 May 2017, *AU Classifieds*; The Maria Butina story became an almost daily fixture on the talk shows of networks such as CNN and to a lesser degree on BBC America.

21. "Open Skies Treaty Mission in Russian Far East," Cable from Secretary of State, 24 February 2009, Washington, D.C., Wikileaks; "Fact Sheet: The Treaty on Open Skies," 1 February 2017, Center for Arms Control and Non-Proliferation.

22. Gary Wetzel, "Why Killing the Open Skies Treaty Would Be a Mistake for the Trump Administration," 29 September 2017, FoxtrotAlpha.

23. George M. Reynolds, "Taking Stock of the Treaty on Open Skies," 3 November 2017, Council on Foreign Relations; Wetzel, "Why Killing the Open Skies Treaty," 29 September 2017, FoxtrotAlpha.

24. "Open Skies: December 14 Plenary, Revcon, and Sensors," Cable from U.S. Mission to European Union, Brussels, 21 December 2009, Wikileaks; Wetzel, "Why Killing the Open Skies Treaty," 29 September 2017, FoxtrotAlpha.

25. Reynolds, "Taking Stock of the Treaty on Open Skies," 3 November 2017, Council on Foreign Relations; "Fact Sheet: The Treaty on Open Skies," 1 February 2017, Center for Arms Control and Non-Proliferation.

26. "Russia to Limit U.S. Military Flyovers in Tit-for-Tat Response," 27 December 2017, Bloomberg; Reynolds, "Taking Stock of the Treaty on Open Skies," 3 November 2017; "U.S. Reverses Course, Certifies Russian Open Skies Aircraft," 20 September 2018, www.defense.news.com. "The U.S. Freezes Open Skies Treaty with Russia," 14 August 2018, UAWire.

27. "U.S. Reverses Course, Certifies Russian Open Skies Aircraft," 20 September 2018, www.defense.news.com; "Open Skies Treaty Flights Resume in 2019," 1 April 2019, Arms Control Association; "Upgraded Russian Spy Plane Makes Maiden Flight over U.S. Nuclear and Military Sites," 28 April 2019, RT.

28. "U.S.-Russia Surveillance Flights Treaty under Threat," 30 October 2019, BBC; "U.S. Plans to Withdraw from Open Skies Treaty Increase Risk of Nuclear War—Russian Senior Official," 11 November 2019, Sputnik; *Le monde*, 21 May 2020; *Новости*, 22 May 2020; "Russia May Pull Out of Open Skies Treaty," 26 December 2020, RT; "Russia to Exit Open Skies Treaty," 15 January 2021, *New York Times*.

29. "For Russia and Putin, a Surprise Gift from America," *New York Times*, 9 November 2016; Stephen Cohen, "If Trump Moves to Heal Ties with Russia, Establishment will Oppose Him Fiercely," 11 November 2016, RT.

30. "Michael Flynn," 16 March 2020, Wikipedia. In May 2020 the Justice Department dropped the charges against Flynn, and President Trump pardoned him on 24 November 2020.

31. "Rex Tillerson's Special Friend in the Kremlin," *New York Times*, 22 December 2016; Televised Confirmation hearings before U.S. Senate.

32. "On Russia, Trump and his Top National Security Aides Seem to be at Odds," *Washington Post*, 18 April 2017; Dexter Filkins, "The Breaking Point: Will Donald Trump Let Rex Tillerson Do His Job?" 16 October 2017, *New Yorker*; "Rex Tillerson," 29 March 2020, Wikipedia.

33. "Trump Signs Russia Sanctions Bill, But Makes Clear He's Not Happy about It," *Washington Post*, 2 August 2017.

34. "U.S. Releases Oligarchs List and Opts against New Sanctions on Russia," 30 January 2018, National Public Radio; "Putin Laughs off Washington's Kremlin List," 31 January 2018, News24 News. For the full list of names, See, "Report to Congress […] Regarding Senior Foreign Political Figures and Oligarchs in the Russian Federation and Russian Parastatal Entities," 29 January 2018.

35. "The Kremlin List: Why Russian Oligarchs Shrugged," 30 January 2018, *Washington Post*.

36. "Russian Prime Minister Jokes that Cabinet Members on U.S. Kremlin List Should Step Down," 30 January 2018, TASS.

37. "A Daunting Agenda … Sprinkled with Wisecracks: Highlights from the Trump-Putin G20 Talks," 28 June 2019, RT.

38. "Trump Calls Putin, Offers Help Putting out Siberia Wildfires," 31 July 2019, RT; "Trump Adds to Sanctions on Russia over Skripals," 1 August 2019, *New York Times*.

39. "Trump thought he had a nuclear deal with Putin," *New York Times*, 14 October 2020; "Dangerous delusions," RT 14 October 2020; "Putin and Biden Confirm Extension of New START Treaty," 27 January 2021, AP.

Annotated Bibliography

Asmus, Ronald D. *A Little War that Shook the World: Georgia, Russia, and the Future of the West.* New York: Palgrave Macmillan, 2010. This diplomatic history is based on inside information from the West. Chapters 4 to 7 are lively and perceptive.

———. *Opening NATO's Door: How the Alliance Remade Itself for a New Era.* New York: Columbia University Press, 2002. This basic source for the expansion of NATO contains many fascinating details, although it is not easy reading.

Cheterian, Vicken. *War and Peace in the Caucasus: Ethnic Conflict and the New Geopolitics.* New York: Columbia University Press, 2008. Best read after Thomas de Waal, this thoughtful book is full of interesting details and valuable insights.

Coene, Frederik. *The Caucasus: An Introduction.* London: Routledge, 2010. The many maps are the distinguishing trait of this book which nicely complements Thomas de Waal.

Colton, Timothy J. *Yeltsin: A Life.* New York: Basic Books, 2008. The standard biography of Boris Yeltsin is extremely useful to anyone interested in this period. Clearly written and covering a lot of material, this study judiciously evaluates Yeltsin.

"Crimea. The Way Home." 15 March 2015, 144 minutes. This documentary film directed by journalist Andreiy Kondrashov gathers testimonies of participants and presents televised footage about the reunification of Crimea with Russia against the backdrop of the scenery of the peninsula. Translated into the major languages of the world and posted on many sites including YouTube, this documentary has been watched by millions of viewers; it has been condemned in Ukraine.

De La Pedraja, René. *The Russian Military Resurgence: Post-Soviet Decline and Rebuilding, 1992–2018.* Jefferson, NC: McFarland, 2018.

de Waal, Thomas. *The Caucasus: An Introduction.* New York: Oxford University Press, 2010. A great starting point for beginners, this well-written and carefully structured book also remains a great tool for scholars. Should be followed by Cheterian, Vicken.

Dunlop, John B. *Russia Confronts Chechnya: Roots of a Separatist Conflict.* New York: Cambridge University Press, 1998. This meticulous work of scholarship is indispensable reading for understanding the origins of the First Chechnya War.

Gates, Robert M. *Duty: Memoirs of a Secretary at War.* New York: Alfred A. Knopf, 2014.

Hill, William H. *No Place for Russia: European Security Institutions since 1989.* New York: Columbia University Press, 2018. A very rare dissident voice within the U.S. foreign policy establishment questions the policy of relentless hostility toward Russia.

———. *Russia, the Near Abroad, and the West: Lessons from the Moldova-Transdniestria Conflict.* Washington, D.C.: Woodrow Wilson Center Press, 2012. An observer-participant has written a revealing and perceptive study of this conflict.

Ivanov, Igor S. *The New Russian Diplomacy.* Washington, D.C.: Brookings Institution, 2002.

McFaul, Michael. *From Cold War to Hot Peace: An American Ambassador in Putin's Russia.* Boston: Houghton Mifflin Harcourt, 2018. This book about the diplomatic experiences of a Stanford University professor does for the Obama administration what Strobe Talbott did for the Clinton years. See also Ch.20n27.

Mitchell, Lincoln A. *The Color Revolutions.* Philadelphia: University of Pennsylvania Press, 2012. The best scholarly coverage of the movements that swept some of the former Soviet republics. Good analysis of the participants.

Norris, John, *Collision Course: NATO, Russia, and Kosovo.* Westport, CT: Praeger, 2005.

Pifer, Steven. *The Eagle and Trident: U.S.-Ukraine Relations in Turbulent Times.* Washington, D.C.: Brookings Institution, 2017. A former U.S. ambassador provides valuable information on the relations of Ukraine with Russia.

Primakov, Yevgeny. *Russian Crossroads: Toward the New Millennium.* New Haven: Yale University Press, 2004. The memoirs of this foreign minister and prime minister provide invaluable insights into the foreign relations of Russia in the 1990s. A good English translation makes the text accessible to many readers.

Roxburgh, Angus. *The Strongman: Vladimir Putin and the Struggle for Russia.* London: I.B. Tauris, 2014. This British journalist and consultant to the Kremlin provides important details on Russian foreign relations.

Sakwa, Richard. *Frontline Ukraine: Crisis in the Borderlands.* London: I.B. Tauris, 2016. This book covers most issues in relations between Russia and the West. Judiciously written and encyclopedic in its coverage, this is an indispensable guide.

Sasse, Gwendolyn. *The Crimea Question: Identity, Transition, and Conflict.* Cambridge, MS: Harvard Ukrainian Research Institute, 2007.

Stent, Angela E. *The Limits of Partnership: U.S.-Russian Relations in the Twenty-First Century*. Princeton: University Press, 2015. A careful scholarly study.

_____. *Putin's World: Russia Against the West and with the Rest*. New York: Twelve, 2019.

Stone, Oliver. *The Putin Interviews: Oliver Stone Interviews Vladimir Putin*. New York: Hot Books, 2017. Readers are fortunate to have this very revealing account, which continues the story of Putin's *First Person* into the presidential years. This book is indispensable to understand the personality and policies of the Russian president.

Talbott, Strobe. *The Russia Hand: A Memoir of Presidential Diplomacy*. New York: Random House, 2003. A scholar recounts his experiences with Russia during the time when Bill Clinton took advantage of a weak Boris Yeltsin. The book is a companion to Michael McFaul's memoirs covering the Obama years. On Talbott, See also Ch.4n48.

Wilson, Andrew. *Ukraine Crisis: What It Means for the West*. New Haven: Yale University Press, 2014.

_____. *Ukraine's Orange Revolution*. New Haven: Yale University Press, 2005.

_____. *The Ukrainians: Unexpected Nation*. New Haven, CT: Yale University Press, 2000. The leading Western scholar on Ukraine produced a book packed with information on post–Soviet Ukraine.

Yekelchyk, Serhy. *Ukraine: Birth of a Modern Nation*. New York: Oxford University Press, 2007. The best introduction to the sweep of Ukraine's turbulent history. The pages on independent Ukraine are particularly perceptive.

Index

Abashidze, Aslan 101, 115
Abkhazia and Abkhazians 5, 19–21, 115–116, 203; and CFE 124; and EU 173; and Five Day War 129–135; and Georgia 239n23; and Kosovo 52, 126; merchant shipping 173–174; and UNOMIG 172; and WTO 182
Abu Dhabi 90–91
Adjara 101, 115, 135, 144; and Armenia 151; and Russia 86, 99
adoptions 188
aerial surveillance 71–72, 195, 232
Aeroflot 231
Afghanistan 62, 65, 67, 69; and Britain 238n14; and Russia 108, 165–166, 168; Soviet invasion of 32, 158, 199, 213; and U.S. 9, 104, 177, 179, 212
Africa 9, 110, 125
Afrin (Syria) 215
Agreement on Partnership and Cooperation 35
agriculture 16, 157, 206, 223
Ahtisaari, Martti 55
air space 215
airborne forces 130–131, 134
aircraft carriers 108, 229; see also Mistral
airlines 94
airports 28, 56–57, 135; in Armenia 150–151; in Crimea 193, 195; of Moscow 144; in Ukraine 201
Akayev, Askar 103–104
Akhalgori (South Ossetia) 137
Akhalkalaki (Georgia) 117
Akhmetov, Rinat 199, 208
Al-Qaeda 69, 71
Alawite 213
Albania 51
Albright, Madelaine 53, 64
alcoholism 158
Aleppo 211, 213, 217
Alexander I 79
Algeria 90, 118
algorithm 231
Aliyev, Heidar 26, 147, 148, 153–154
Aliyev, Ilham 147, 149
American University 231
anarchists 187
Andijon 177–178

Andorra 46
Andover 71
Angola 9
anthem, national 45, 99, 252n19
anthropologists 132
Anti-Ballistic Missile Treaty 72–73, 118
anti-Communism 10
anti-Semitic 210
Antonov, Anatoly 221
apartments 161, 162
apology 83
appeasement 99, 199
Arab League 214
Arab Spring 183–185
Arabic language 108, 111–112, 163
Arabs 214
archives 20–21
Ardzinba, Vladislav 20–21, 23
Armenia 18–19, 23–27; and CSTO 108; and Eurasian Economic Union 182; and pipeline 148; and railroads 131, 135, 137; and Russia 149–153
arms sales 90–91, 93, 108; and Georgia 130; of Russia 118, 161
arrogance 57; of European officials 34, 36, 85–86, 190–191; of U.S. officials 55, 78, 84, 86
arsenals 29, 199, 207
artillery 63, 116, 124; and Georgia 130, 132, 136, 149; in Syria 215–217; in Ukraine 195, 199, 201, 208
Aspin, Les 39
al-Assad, Bashar 94, 183–185, 211–217
al-Assad, Hafez 94
assassinations 61
Assessing Russian Activities and Intentions 229–230, 234
Association Agreement 190–192, 207, 271n20
ataman 194
Atatürk, Kemal 86
atheism 6
August 1991 coup attempt 7, 8–9, 188
Australia 206
Austria 88, 125; neutrality of 14, 81–82, 167; and South Stream 142
autonomy 23, 197

Azerbaijan 18–19, 23–27; and Georgia 116, 256n20; and Russia 147–149, 151; and Turkey 153–154

Bahrain 214
bait and switch 166, 184
Baker, James 14, 73
Bakiyev, Kurmanbek 104, 179
Baku 18, 24, 147–148
Baltic Republics 5, 8, 38, 40, 122; and G7 226; and NATO 70, 75
banana republics 84, 144, 275n8
bands 108
Bank of New York 119
banks 122, 205
Basayev, Shamil 61–63
bases 95, 103, 179; of Russia 184, 252n32; of U.S. 177, 264n6
Batumi 18, 115, 117, 144, 174
BBC 108, 230, 277n20
Belarus 43, 44, 48, 105; and Eurasian Economic Union 181–183; and Zapad 2017 225
Belbek (Crimea) 195–196
Belgium 197, 206
Benghazi 183
Berkut 192–195
Berlusconi, Silvio 74–75, 77, 87, 93, 125; and Georgia 130–131; and response to Five Day War 146; and Ukraine 175
Bible 123
Biden, Joe 168–169, 233–235; and Libya 183–184
billionaires 217, 234; see also oligarchs
Bishkek 103–104, 179
Black Sea 84, 86–87; and NATO 128–129, 140, 143–144, 178, 250n29; and pipelines 205
Black Sea Fleet 44–46, 49, 174
blackmail 124, 130, 203, 208, 222
Blair, Tony 73, 77
blockade 30, 62, 117, 123; on Abkhazia 128; on Crimea 204; on Eastern Ukraine 208–209
Blue Stream 88, 114, 152; 175
Bolivia 240n44
Bolotnaya Square (Moscow) 186–187
Bolsheviks 18–19, 159

281

bombing 53–54, 63, 66; of Georgia 136; of Iraq 80; in Libya 183; of Serbia 141; in Syria 213, 215; in Ukraine 199–200
Border Monitoring Operation (OSCE) 107
Bordyusha, Nikolay 108
Bosporus 128, 148
Botlikh 63
"bots" 123
brandy 150
Brasilia Treaty 238n2
bread 27, 47, 214
Brexit 224, 226
bribery 79
bridges 208
Britain 18, 64, 71–72, 106; and European Security proposal 169; and Iraq invasion 77; response to Five Day War 140; and Salisbury incident 224; and Syria 215
British Council 106
Bronze Soldier Statue 122–123, 140
Bucharest Summit 121, 128–129, 175
Budapest Memorandum 44, 243n7
budgets 224–225, 229
Bulgaria 57, 75, 81, 116, 125; and pipelines 88, 205
bullying 78; see also ultimatums
bunker 274n31
buses 193, 207
Bush, George H.W. 14, 72, 73
Bush, George W. 66–69, 121, 146; and Caucasus 174; and Chechnya 247n33; and Five Day War 175; and Georgia 116, 128–130, 142; and Iran 94; and Iraq invasion 75–90, 211; and missile defense 167; and nuclear weapons 72–73; and sanctions 118; and Sarkozy mission 125–137; and Ukraine 128–129
business 182, 188, 206

Cairo 165
Caliphate in the Caucasus 62
cameras 232
Camranh Bay (Vietnam) 9, 69
Canada 209, 254n3
capitalism 7
Caribbean 265n27
Carmel Institute of Russian Culture and History 232
Caspian Sea 5, 87, 178, 147
casus belli 149, 153
Catalonia 126
Caucasus 18–27, 62, 135; and CFE 124; and U.S. 174, 177
Caucasus 2008 132–133
Caucasus 2009 173
CBS 230
ceasefire: in Abkhazia 23; in Chechnya 31–32, 65–66; in Georgia 135; in Moldova 16; in Nagorno-Karabakh 27; in South Ossetia 20, 133; in Ukraine 201

Central Asia 5, 67, 69, 104, 166, 177–180; and Eurasian Economic Union 181
Ceyhan (Turkey) 149
CFE see Conventional Forces in Europe
Chaco War 240n44
Chalyi, Alexey 193–194
chambers of commerce 84, 90
Chapman, Anna 170–171, 231
Chechnya and Chechens 21; and Central Asia 177, 178; and CFE 124; and Council of Europe 36; and EU 35; First Chechnya War 28–32, 41, 48, 63, 66; and Five Day War 134; and France 125; and Iran 93; and Iraq invasion 79; and media 241n20; and NGOs 106; and OSCE 246n3; Second Chechnya War 61–70, 80, 89; and Transnistria 97; and Turkey 86, 89
cheese 206, 223
Cheeseburger Summit 169–170
chemical weapons 13, 211–212
Chernobyl 44
Chernomyrdin, Victor 54–55
children 162–163
China 5–6, 10, 13, 245n37; and arms sales 118; and Eurasian Economic Union 183; and Five Day War 144; and G7 226; and Iraq invasion 78–79; and Kosovo 54; and Russian diplomats 164; in Russian Far East 148; and Syria 185; and Uzbekistan 178; and Vietnam 9–10; and White Revolution 187
Chinese language 163
Chirac, Jacques 78–79
Chisinau 98–99
chlorine gas 215
Chongar Peninsula (Crimea) 193–194, 196
Christians 21, 52, 147, 149
Churchill, Winston 18
CIA 160, 265n31
citizens and citizenship 45, 47, 117; Eastern Europe 202–203; protection of 137, 141
Clark, Wesley 56–57
Clinton, Bill 58; and Chechnya 31, 106; and Kosovo 53–55, 57; and NATO expansion 38–39, 243n36; and Yeltsin 40–41, 64–65, 70, 121
Clinton, Hillary 165, 169, 179; and U.S. election 109, 217, 229, 233; and White Revolution 187
CNN 52, 54, 56, 230, 275n20
coal 197, 208–209
"coalition of the willing" 77
Coast Guard 174
coat of arms 45
Cohen, Stephen 233
coke plant 208
Cold War 6, 13–14, 33, 37, 39; and

Black Sea 140; and Iran 93; and Iraq 77; nostalgia for 224; relics of 188; revival of 205; and Turkey 84, 86–88; and use of force 120
Cold Warriors 53, 66, 71, 167–168, 232; and Georgia 174; and NATO 70, 73–75
Collective Security Treaty Organization see CSTO
Color Revolutions 105–108, 178, 185–186
Comey, Jim 229
Committee of Ministers of Council of Europe 222, 227
Committees of Soldiers' Mothers 141
Commonwealth of Independent States (CIS) 43–45, 181
Communism 5–7, 4, 1875; in Russian Foreign Ministry 9
Communist Party of Georgia 100
Communist Party of the Russian Federation 32, 36
Communist Party of the Soviet Union 6, 24 186; and Chechnya 28; and Foreign Ministry 158–159, 161
compensations 43, 82
computers 122–123
condominium status 46–47
Conference for Security and Cooperation in Europe see CSCE
conscripts 200, 224; in Crimea 46, 196; in Russia 141, 187
Conservative Party (Britain) 275n20
"consociational" 197, 252n14
Constitutional Court of Russia 222, 274n6
constitutions: of Crimea 46–48, 196; of Moldova 97
consulates (Russian) 9, 160, 162, 164, 207
consumerism 158
contacts 170
containment 13, 70
Conventional Forces in Europe Treaty (CFE) 13–14, 87, 96; repeal of 123–125, 221, 225
coronavirus 217, 234
corruption 29–30; in Georgia 100; in Kyrgyzstan 103, 179; in Soviet Foreign Ministry 158–159; in Ukraine 207, 210
Cossacks 194
Council of Europe 35–37, 38; and Chechnya 65–66, 106; and Crimea 205; and Five Day War 143, 145; and Russia 221–222, 226–228
counterintelligence 158, 160, 170
coup attempt 173
crime 13, 61–62, 64, 91
Crimea 80, 95, 102; currency of 202; and Russia 174; and Syria

Index

214–215; and Transnistria 99; unification with Russia 193–197, 221; U.S. reprisals 111, 204–206, 217, 274*n*34
Crimean War of 1854–1856 140, 250*n*29
CSCE (Conference for Security and Cooperation in Europe) 13, 26, 36–38, 168
CSTO (Collective Security Treaty Organization) 107–108, 168, 176; and Armenia 149, 152, 154; and Uzbekistan 178
Cuba 6, 15, 69–70, 97, 163; and U.S. 118, 204; and Yeltsin 7, 10
cultural genocide 19, 21
currency 202, 208
Customs Union 182–183
Customs Union Treaty of 1995 181
cyberwar 140–141
Cyprus 88, 139, 223
Czech Republic 39, 42, 116; and European Security proposal 169; and missile defense 118, 119, 167
Czechoslovakia 10, 13

Dagestan 62
dam 207
Daraa (Syria) 184
Debaltsevo (Donetsk) 201
deception 166
defense industry 114, 157
demilitarized zone 215
Democratic National Committee (DNC) 219, 229, 274*n*44
demonstrators 102–104, 173, 179, 268*n*29; in Ukraine 192–193
Department of New Threats and Challenges 160
despot 191
diamonds 91
Diensthier, Jiri 13
digital 206, 232
Dima Yakovlev Act 188–189
diplomacy 30, 78, 132; classical 138; Russian 128
Diplomatic Academy 161–162
diplomats 76, 79–80, 107; Russian 90, 98, 109–110, 125, 218; U.S. 83–85, 105, 132, 133, 163, 169, 170
Distributed Denial of Service attacks 122
Djibouti 205
Dnieper River 48, 207
Dr. Strangelove 56
dollar zone 119
Donbass 197, 200, 208–209; *see also* Eastern Ukraine
Donetsk 102, 113–114, 197–203, 208
double standards 66, 71, 107, 141, 143; *see also* morality
drones 133
drugs 108
drunkenness 55, 121
Dudayev, Dzhokhar 28–32, 61
Duma 69, 72, 80, 105; and

Abkhazia 128, 142; and Council of Europe 205, 221–222, 227; and Crimea 210; and Kosovo 126; and South Ossetia 142
"Dutch Disease" 148

Eastern Europe 36, 39, 70, 97; currency of 202; and EU 34; and European Security proposal 169; languages of 163; and Mafia 275*n*19; and NATO expansion 13, 129, 243*n*36; and Soviet Union 6, 10
Eastern Ukraine 50, 102, 113–114, 193; passports for 227; revolt of 197–202
EBRD (European Bank for Reconstruction and Development) 33–35; and Parliamentary Assembly 36; sanctions on Russia 204; and Soviet Union 241*n*7
economic crisis of August 1998 67
economy 49, 61, 76, 85; of Armenia 150; of Eastern Ukraine 202; of Georgia 100, 117, 137; of Kyrgyzstan 103; of Russia 118, 157, 160, 183; of Ukraine 49–50, 114, 174–176, 207
Ecuador 238*n*2
Egypt 9, 89–90, 94, 183; and *Mistral* 206; and Syria 214
elections 32, 41–42, 65, 70, 107; in Chechnya 61, 246*n*3; in Crimea 46–47; in Finland 83; in Georgia 100; in Kyrgyzstan 103–104; in Russia 186–187; in Ukraine 48–49, 102–103, 113–114, 210; in U.S. 37, 217–219, 229–230
electricity 16, 27, 48; in Crimea 207; in Ukraine 208–209
embassies 9, 54, 74, 96, 122; in Abkhazia 120; in Kyrgyzstan 102–103; of Russia 158–164, 207, 220; *see also* United States embassies
Emmy awards 109
energy sector 150
engineers 162
English language 108, 111–112; in Georgia 116; and Russian diplomats 163–164
enthusiasm 196
envy 98
epidemics 47
Erdogan, Recep Tayyip 87, 144; and Armenia 151–154; and Putin 250*n*26; and Syria 215–217
Ergneti market 115
Estonia 70, 83, 122–123, 140
ethnic cleansing 19, 24, 52, 54; in Kyrgyzstan 179–180
ethnic groups 103–104
EU (European Union) 13, 34–36, 168, 254*n*19; and Association Agreement 190–192; and Azerbaijan 149; and Chechnya 65–66; and Council of Europe 222; and

Eurasian Economic Union 181–183; and Five Day War 135–139; and Georgia 172–173; and Hungary 83–84; reprisals on Russia 204–206, 210, 223–224; and response to Five Day war 142–143, 144–146, 173; and Russia 74–75, 78; and Transnistria 99; and Turkey 84–86; and Ukraine 101, 113, 172, 175, 271*n*20; and use of force 120; and Uzbekistan 178; *see also* Partnership and Cooperation Agreement
Euphrates River 215
Eurasian Economic Community 181–182
Eurasian Economic Union 152, 176, 181–183; and Azerbaijan 149
Euro zone 119
Eurocentrism 34, 86
Europe 81
European Bank for Reconstruction and Development *see* EBRD
European Community (EC) 13
European Court of Human Rights 36, 37, 221–222, 227–228
European Security Treaty draft 167–169
European Union *see* EU
extremism 107
Exxon-Mobil 233

Facebook 218–219, 231
"failed state" 29
fait accompli 132
Farsi language 163
fatigue 66, 138, 173
FBI 160, 170, 229, 231; and spies 265*n*31
Federal Register 119
Federal Security Service (FSB) 27, 63, 105–106, 160; and Abkhazia 174; and Armenia 149; and Crimea 208, 210; and Kyrgyzstan 179
Federal Service for Military-Technical Cooperation 161
federalism 98, 201
Federation Council 142, 195, 199
Feodosia (Crimea) 196–197
ferries 195–196
film 232
financial crisis 136, 138–139, 143, 145; of August 1998 174
Finland 10–11, 14, 81–83, 167; and Council of Europe 227
Finno-Ugrian peoples 83
First Guards Army 225
fishermen 210
Five Day War with Georgia 128–139, 168; and Armenia 151; and Azerbaijan 149; and Bush administration 175; and CFE 124; and Hungary 84; and Lake Valdai 110; and media 109, 111; and Middle East 91; and NGOs 106;

and OSCE 172–173; response of the West 140–146; and Turkey 87
flags 45, 135, 196
"flank" regime 124
Flynn, Michael 233, 277n30
food 151, 152, 214
Foreign Agents Registration Act 109, 111, 230
Foreign Intelligence Service (SVR) 41, 76, 160, 258n24
Foreign Ministry (France) 158
Foreign Ministry of the Russian Federation 8–9, 96–97, 115, 157–164; and CFE 225; and Council of Europe 221–222; and Eastern Ukraine 197; and Five Day War 143–144; and Georgia 131–132, 135, 174; and G7 226; and Libya 183–184; and NATO expansion 129; and neutrality 168; and Ukraine 210; and U.S. elections 219–220
Foreign Ministry of Soviet Union 8–9
Foreign Trade Ministry 158, 159, 161
Founding Act 42
Fourteenth Army (Russia) 16–18, 46, 97
Fox network 109
fragility 218
France 41–42, 81, 224; and CFE 123; and Council of Europe 227; and European Security proposal 169; and Five Day War 135–140; and G7 226; and Kosovo 125–126; and Libya 184; and *Mistral* 206; and NATO expansion 129; and Syria 94, 118, 211–212, 214; and Ukraine 193; and U.S. invasion of Iraq 76–80
free-market fanatics 187
free trade area 35, 79, 81, 190; in near abroad 181–183
"Freedom Agenda" 121, 130
"freedom" fries 81
French language 109, 111, 163
friends 131
Friendship, Cooperation, and Partnership Treaty 49
fruits 206, 207, 215, 223; from Azerbaijan 148–149

G7 225–226
G8 40, 42, 55, 204, 270n3
G20 234
Gaddafi, Muammar 183–184
Gagra (Abkhazia) 20, 21
Gali (Georgia) 20, 23, 134
Gamzakhurdia, Ziad 19–20, 30
gas, natural 83, 113, 149, 157; and Crimea 205; and Ukraine 175–176, 202, 206–207
Gates, Robert M. 5, 121, 275n18
Gazprom 82, 83; and Ukraine 113–114, 175, 203, 207

General Assembly of United Nations 66, 204–205; and Syria 213
General Will 18, 27, 202, 240n44
genocide 19–21, 25, 239n23
Georgia 18–23, 114–118, 125, 128–139, 172–174; and Abkhazia 239n23; and Azerbaijan 256n20; and Chechnya 30, 61–62; and CSTO 108; and EU 207; independence of 25; and Kosovo 52, 87, 126; and NATO 75, 127, 165, 167, 172, 175, 178; and Open Skies Treaty 143, 232; and OSCE 107; railway in 27; Rose Revolution 98–103; and Transnistria 96–98; and Turkey 86–87; and WTO 182
Georgian language 19, 101
German language 109
Germany 10, 14, 31, 73–74, 76–81; and Council of Europe 227; and European Security proposal 169; and Kyrgyzstan 103–104; and NATO expansion 129, 131; and North Stream 114; response to Five Day War 140; and Turkey 85; and Ukraine 193
Ghouta (Syria) 215
Girkin, Igor *see* Strelkov, Igor
Google 218–219, 231
Google-Earth 231
Gorbachev, Mikhail 8, 55, 122; and Chechnya 28; and China 6; and Five Day War 141; and Iraq 77; and Japan 12; and nationalities 15, 19; and NATO 14, 73, 238n27; and Putin 121; and Soviet Union 268n12; and Yeltsin 7
Gore, Al 30, 53
Gori (Georgia) 134
GPlus 109–111
Grachev, Pavel 30
Great Recession 136, 139, 145–146, 182
Greece 88, 121, 125, 205
Grozny 28, 30, 32, 61
GRU (Russian Military Intelligence) 76, 116, 258n24, 262n11; and Foreign Ministry 158–159; and hacking 219, 274n44; and spies 265n31
Grushko, Alexander 190
Gudauta (Abkhazia) 20
Gudermes (Chechnya) 61
guerrillas 23, 32
Gulf War 76
Gumista River 21
gun ownership 231
Gyumri (Armenia) 150
Gyursany, Ferenc 84

hackers 122, 140–141, 208; and U.S. 217–219
Hamas 91
Hanssen, Robert P. 74
harassment 158

hate groups 106
hegemony 265n27
helicopters 25, 56, 67, 206
Helsinki meeting 170
Hezbollah 91
Hill, William H. 51
Hindi language 163
historians 20, 25, 162, 163
Hitler, Adolf 86
Hmeymim air base (Syria) 213, 216
Hobbes, Thomas 19
Homo sovieticus 187
Homs (Syria) 211
Hoover Institution Archives 2
horse-trading 125, 275n20
hostages 271
hotels 109, 192
human rights 106, 122, 125
humanitarian 184, 199
Hungary 10, 41, 57, 83–84, 88, 121; and Council of Europe 227; and EU 275n20; and European Security proposal 169; and NATO 39, 41–42; and Syria 214
hunger 13, 35; in Abkhazia 128; in Foreign Ministry 9
Hussein, Saddam 30, 76–80, 184, 211
hysteria 81, 83, 84, 226, 230–231, 234
idealism 190
ideology 121–123
Idlib (Syria) 213, 214–217
Illinois 219
illusions 57–58, 141, 128, 170
Ilyushin- 76 56, 153
"Immediate Response" 132
immigration 148, 157
imperial overreach 104, 174
imperialism 86
impertinence 126
import substitution 183
independence 28, 32; of Abkhazia 128, 137, 142; of Armenia 25; of Kosovo 52–53, 125–127; of South Ossetia 128, 137, 142; of Spanish America 15
India 18, 93, 118, 133, 238n14; and English language 163–164; and Five Day War 144; and G7 226
India-Pakistan border 133
Indo-European language family 83
industry 16
inflation 160
informants 158, 160, 179, 231
Ingori River (Georgia) 23, 142, 174
Ingush 239n16
inmates 274
inspections 37, 76, 124, 212
Instagram 218
Institute of Democracy and Cooperation 111
intelligence 130, 158; failures 78, 230
Intensified Dialogue (ID) 117
International Atomic Energy Agency 94

international law 132–134
International Monetary Fund (IMF) 65, 126, 176
internationalism 7
internet 112, 140–141, 193
Internet Research Agency 217–218
INTERPOL 222–223
invasion 83, 84, 221
Iran 27, 76, 91, 93–95, 118; and Azerbaijan 147; and Chechnya 89; and hostage crisis 132; and missile defense 167; and Russia 166; sanctions on 119, 169–170, 264n8; and Syria 184, 214; see also Persia
Iraq 72, 75–80, 82, 121; and Obama 183; and Turkey 85
Iraq-II 184, 211
Iraq-III 184, 211
Iron Curtain 113
Islam and Muslims 6, 21, 52, 149; in Azerbaijan 147; in Foreign Ministry 161; and Iran 93; in Kosovo 126; in Pakistan 166; and Russia 89, 93, 161, 166; and Turkey 84, 86; in Uzbekistan 177–178
Islamic extremists and fundamentalists 61–63, 65–67, 69, 71, 76, 86, 89; in Libya 184; in Syria 185, 212, 216, 251n14
isolation 126
isolationism 7
Israel 88, 91, 188, 215; and Crimea 204; and Syria 273n12
Istanbul 18, 64–65, 250n29
Italy 74–75, 87–88, 125; and Council of Europe 227; and European Security proposal 169; and Libya 184; and pipelines 205; and sanctions on Russia 223; and Ukraine 174
ITAR-TASS see TASS
Ivanov, Igor S. 33, 52, 106; and Georgia 101, 115, 117; and U.S. elections 219–220

Jackson, Mike 56
Jackson-Vanik Law 188
Jagland, Thorbjørn 226–227
Jalalabad (Kyrgyzstan) 104, 179
Japan 11–12, 146, 164; and Crimea 206
Javelin missile 209
jews 86, 91, 188; see also Israel
jihad 62, 216
"Joint Political Declaration on Partnership and Cooperation" 35
Jordan 215
journalists 110, 192, 225

Kalashnikovs 198
Kaliningrad 11, 167, 232
Kalugin, Mikhail 220
Karasin, Grigory 128

Karelia 10–11, 82
Karimov, Islam 177–178
Karshi Khanabad 177–179
Kasatonov, Igor 44, 269n42
Kazakhstan 44, 48, 108, 173; and Eurasian Economic Union 181–183
Kazimirov, Vladimir 26
Kerch (Crimea) 195–196
Kerch Bridge 210, 271n28
Kerch Strait incident 227
Ketchum 109–110
KGB 6, 158–159, 262n11
Khan Seikhoun 216
Kharkov (Ukraine) 197–198, 201
Kharkov Agreement 176, 207
Khasavyurt Agreement 32, 66
Khasbulatov, Ruslan 20
Khrushchev, Nikita 6, 65
kidnappings 61–62, 64, 91
King, Larry 109
Kislyak, Sergei 219, 248n21, 263n17
Kocharian, Robert 27
Kodori River 23
Kompromat 97, 220
Korson massacre (Ukraine) 193
Kosovo 51–58, 125–127, 141; and Five Day War 142, 144, 145; and Hungary 84; and Syria 181
Kouchner, Bernard 125
Kozak, Dmitry 97–99
Kozak Memorandum 97–99, 168, 252n14
"Kozak II" 99
Kozyrev, Andrei 8–10, 31, 35, 41, 43
Kravchuk, Leonid 43–45, 47
Kremlin list 234
Kuchma, Leonid 44, 48–49; and Orange Revolution 101–103
Kurds 184, 215–217
Kurile Islands 11–12, 206
Kyrgyzstan 103–104, 108, 166, 177–180; and Eurasian Economic Union 181–183

labor 182–183
Lachin road (Armenia) 25
Lake Valdai International Discussion Club 110
languages 162–164, 165
Latakia (Syria) 95, 217
Latin America 6, 15, 109, 110; and Crimea 204–205
Latvia 70, 71
Laughland, John 111
launch codes 44
Lavrov, Sergei 55, 58, 120, 125, 126; and Five Day War 135, 139, 141, 145; and Georgia 107, 117; and MGIMO 263n17; and reset 165; and Syria 211, 213–214; and U.S. elections 219
leaks of news 110
Lebanon 94
Lebed, Alexander 16, 32

lectures 93
Lehman Brothers 138–139, 145
Lenin, Vladimir 191
Lesin, Mikhail 106
libraries 20–21
Libya 90, 182–183, 211
"line of contact" 26
Lisbon protocol 44
literature 163
Lithuania 11, 227
loans 9, 34, 65, 94, 191
Lourdes (Cuba) 69
luck 176, 178
Lugansk 102, 200–203, 208
Lukhoil 77
lying and liar 53, 139

Machiavelli, Niccolò 28
machine guns 208
Macron, Emmanuel 226–227
Mafia 91, 275n19
Magnitsky Act 188–189
Maidan Square (Kiev) 102, 192–193, 209
Malaya 64
Malaysian Airlines 200
Manafort, Paul 113
Manas air base 103, 166, 264n6
Manbij (Syria) 216–217
MAP see Membership Action Plan Marines
Mariupol (Ukraine) 199, 200, 210
marriages 19
Marxism 76, 79, 85
Maskhadov, Aslan 61–62
massacres 193, 199
Matta Hari 170
May, Theresa 224, 275n20
mayors 193–194
McFaul, Michael 170, 264n10, 265n27
media 21, 108–112; and Chechnya 28, 32, 64, 67–69, 241n20; and Libya 183; and spies 170; and Syria 185; and Ukraine 191; Western 219
Medvedev, Dmitry 165–171, 185; and demonstrators 268n29; and Five Day War 135–138, 142, 144; and Libya 183–184; and sanctions 234
Membership Action Plan (MAP) 87, 117, 128–130, 175
mercenaries 30
merchant ships 86, 173
Merkel, Angela 129, 131, 175; and Ukraine 191
Meshkov, Yuri 46–49, 195, 269n42
MGIMO (Moscow State Institute of Foreign Relations) 111, 160–163, 263n17
middle class 187
Middle East 1, 6, 76, 89–95, 123, 183–185; see also Syria
MIG 195
Migranyan, Andranick 111

military 157, 159–160; and Islam 161; of Ukraine 195–201; *see also* GRU
military districts 43–44
military maneuvers 99, 108, 132–133, 173, 225
military police 217
militias 63; in Abkhazia 20–21, 145; in Armenia 25, 26; in Crimea 193–196; in South Ossetia 19–20
military attaché 55
military districts 97
military solution 66, 68
Milošević, Slobodan 51–55
Ministry of Interior 62–63
Ministry of Internal Affairs (MVD) 160
Minsk I accords 201
Minsk II accords 201
Minsk conference 26–27
missile defense 166–167, 169
Mistral 206
Mitchell, Lincoln A. 105
Moldova 5, 15–18, 96–99, 173; and EU 207; and neutrality 167
Molotov cocktails 20
monarchies 183
Montreux Convention 86, 140
morality 51, 52, 199–200; *see also* double standards
Morocco 90
mortars 195
Moscow 158, 160, 161–162, 164; construction in 85; protests in 186–187; trip to 165, 183
Moscow State Institute of International Relations *see* MGIMO
Moscow Times 208
motorcycle clubs 194
Mubarak, Hosni 89–91, 183
Mueller report 233–234
Munich Speech 119–122, 128–129, 169
museums 20
Myers, Steven Lee 96

Nabucco pipeline 83, 88, 149
Nagorno-Karabakh 24–27, 38, 149–154; and pipeline 148
Napoleon 79
Narabayev, Nursultan 181
Narochnitskaya, Natalia 111
National Liberation Movements 6
National Rifle Association 231
nationalists 16, 45, 49, 52, 186, 188; Russian 140–142, 187–188, 221–222; Ukrainian 192–194, 207–210
NATO (North Atlantic Treaty Organization) 12–14, 37, 145, 190; and Azerbaijan 147–149; and Black Sea 86, 140, 250n29; and candidate states 78; and Caucasus 18; and CFE 124; and Crimea 225; and CSTO 108; and European Security proposal 168–169; expansion of 21, 38–42, 66, 238n27; and Finland 81–83; and Georgia 117–118, 128–132, 165, 167, 178; and Hungary 83–84; and Kosovo 51–58, 72; and missile defense 118; response to Five Day War 140–143, 145; and Russia 73–75, 79, 204, 224–225; and Soviet Union 77; and Transnistria 96–97; and Turkey 84–87; and Ukraine 113, 128–131, 175; and use of force 120; and Uzbekistan 178
NATO-Russia Council 81, 107, 121, 142, 145; creation of 74–75; suspended 204, 225
Nazis 70, 82, 122; invasion of Russia 133, 140; neo-Nazis 210
"Near Abroad" 1, 9, 36, 157; and bases 252n32; and free trade area 181–183; and NGOs 105; and Obama administration 171–180, 265n27
nepotism 158–159
Netherlands 106
neutralization 14, 82, 83, 167–168; of Ukraine 176
New Caledonia 32
New START Treaty 165, 167–169; *see also* START
New York Times 225
newspapers 123
NGOs (Non-Governmental Organizations) 64, 98, 122, 126; in Georgia 100; in Kyrgyzstan 103–104; in Russia 105–106, 140–141, 185–186, 188; and spying 106; in Ukraine 101, 190, 192
Nicaragua 144, 163
9/11 attacks 63, 67, 69–72, 77, 85; and Russia 165
no-fly-zone 183, 185, 211
Nobel Peace Prize 8
nomenklatura 28
non-aggression pact 131
non-use-of-force pledge 131
Noriega, Manuel 121
North Crimea Canal 48, 207
North Korea 93, 118, 167
North Ossetia 238n16
North Stream 82, 114, 175
Northern Alliance 69
Norway 81
nuclear reactors 93, 143
nuclear umbrella 108
nuclear weapons 13, 35, 37, 44, 54, 57, 72–73, 108; and Iran 94, 119, 155, 169–170; *see also* START

Obama, Barack 264n8; and reprisals over Crimea 111, 204–206; and reset 165–171; and Syria 211–212
Obamamania 165
observation posts 215, 217
Ochamchira (Abkhazia) 20
Odessa 17, 44, 209
Office for Democratic Institutions and Human Rights 106

old people 21, 187
oligarchs 58, 191, 199, 205
Olympics *see* Sochi
102nd base (Armenia) 150
125 mm tank shells 97
"one inch to the east" 14, 185
Open Skies Treaty 71–72, 232–233; and Five Day War 143
Orange Revolution (Ukraine) 101–103, 113–114, 176, 182
Organization for Economic Cooperation and Development 85, 204, 221, 223
Organization for Security and Cooperation in Europe *see* OSCE
orphans 188
Ortega, Daniel 144
Orthodox Church 6
OSCE (Organization for Security and Cooperation in Europe) 37–38, 71, 167; and Armenia 27; and Baltic Republics 70; in Chechnya 31–32; and Crimea 48–49; and English language 163; and Five Day War 145–146; and Georgia 128–139, 172; and Kosovo 126; in Kyrgyzstan 103; and NGOs 106 and Russia 106–107; and Transnistria 18, 96–99
OSCE Assistance Group in Chechnya 31, 64, 66–68
Osh (Kyrgyzstan) 104, 179
Ossetia 5

Pakistan 133, 166
paper industry 82
paper tiger 127, 134
parade 115; *see also* Victory in Europe
"parade of sovereignties" 28; *see also* independence
Paraguay 240n44
Paris 111
parliament (Crimea) 46–49, 194–195
Parliamentary Assembly of the Council of Europe (PACE) 33, 35–36, 65–66; and Crimea 205; and Five Day War 143; and Russia 221–222, 226–227, 235
parties, political 57, 73
Partnership and Cooperation Agreement 35, 81, 138, 204; revision of 142–143, 145, 223, 227
"Partnership for Peace" 39–41
passports 47, 129, 137, 141; in Ukraine 174, 207, 227
payments 222, 227
peacekeepers: in Abkhazia 21, 23, 130–131, 239n35; in Georgia 136; in South Ossetia 131, 133–134, 141; in Yugoslavia 56
Pearl Harbor attack 78
pensions 203, 270n74
Pentagon 39, 56, 62, 67; and Open

Skies Treaty 232; and Syria 212–214
People's Republics 201–203
Perekop Isthmus (Crimea) 193–194, 196
Permanent Joint Council 42, 73–75
Permanent Normal Trade Partner (PNTP) 188
Permanent Partnership Council 35
Perry, William 39
Persia 18–19; *see also* Iran
"Person of the Year" 121
Peru 238*n*2
Peskov, Dmitry 162, 219
Peter the Great 18
petroleum 29–30, 85, 202, 206; and Azerbaijan 147–148; and Crimea 205; in Iraq 77, 80
Ph.D.s 162
pipelines 5, 27, 114, 135, 175; and Turkey 148, 149
pirates 203
plebiscites 142
pogrom 193
poisoning 102, 226
poker game 144
Poland 10, 38–39, 42; and European Security proposal 169; and Five Day War 145; and missile defense 118, 119, 167; and Ukraine 193
police: in Chechnya 28, 29, 62–63; in Crimea 47–48, 194–196; and CSTO 108; in Estonia 122; in Kyrgyzstan 104; in Moscow 186–187; in Ukraine 192–193, 197–198; in Yugoslavia 51; *see also* INTERPOL
Policy Planning Staff 73
Polikovskaya, Anna 125
Politburo 158–159, 186
polling places 218
polls 195, 196
population 157
Poroshenko, Petro 199–202, 209–210
posters 214
Poteyev, Alexandr 265*n*31
Poti 174, 150–151
Powell, Colin 66, 78, 115–116, 136
Prague Summit 74–75
presidential commission on U.S.-Russia relations 167
press briefings 110
Prigozhin, Yevgeny 217
Primakov, Yevgeny 41–42, 53, 54, 57, 162; and Hungary 84; and Iraq invasion 79; and Middle East 90
Pristina (Kosovo) 55–57
profits 119, 191
Prokopchuk, Alexander 222
proprietary information 119
prostitution 91
protectionism 183, 206, 223
protectorates 142

pseudonym 119
public opinion 199–201
public relations 109–110, 112
Puerto Rico 15
pundits 133
puppets 37, 112
purges 9
Putin, Vladimir 105, 119, 268*n*29; and Armenia 151–154; and arms sales 161; and Azerbaijan 147; and Chechnya 65, 67; and China 6, 10; and CIS 181; and Crimea 194–196, 204; and Donald Trump 229, 233–235; and Eastern Ukraine 199, 201–203; and Egypt 89–90; and Finland 82–83; and G7 225–226, 270*n*3; and Georgia 100–101, 114–118, 144, 146; and Iran 93–94; and Iraq invasion 77–80; and Kosovo 54, 58; and Lake Valdai 110; and Libya 183; and media 108–111; and Middle East 90–91; and Munich Speech 120–121, 123; and NATO 73–75, 128–129; and NGOs 105; and nuclear weapons 73–73; and OSCE 107; and reset 165, 168–170; and sanctions 118; and Syria 211–217; and Transnistria 96–99; and Turkey 87, 250*n*26; and Ukraine 101–102, 191, 210; and U.S. elections 220, 230; and West 69–70; and White Revolution 185–188

Qaddafi, Muammar 90, 94–95
Qatar 212
quid pro quo 30, 62, 67, 71, 188
quixotic 199, 231

radio 111, 230
railroads 18, 93; in Abkhazia 20; and Armenia 150–152; and Azerbaijan 149, 150; and Crimea 271*n*28; in Georgia 27, 131, 149; in Ukraine 201, 207, 208
railway battalion 131, 208
Ramadan 214
rankings 109, 230
rapes 20, 25, 179
rations 27
real estate 170
Realpolitik 130
red hair 170, 231
"red lines" 42, 127, 165, 167, 172, 175–176; and Iraq 77; in Syria 211
referendum 32, 46, 198; in Britain 226; in Crimea 195–196, 205
refugees 238*n*16; in Abkhazia 20, 23; in Armenia 150; in Syria 217; in Ukraine 200; in Yugoslavia 51–52
regime change 105, 126; in Libya 184; in Russia 182
Reintegration of the Donbass Law 209–210
remittances 104, 117, 174

rent 166, 177–178; on bases 103, 205–207, 264*n*6
Report of the Independent Fact-Finding Mission on the Conflict with Georgia 132–134, 173
Republican National Convention 219
Republican Party 243*n*36
reset in relations with Russia 165–182, 185
restaurants 100–101
retirement 164
RIA Novosti 109–111
rice 207
Rice, Condoleezza 116, 129, 131, 135
Rice, Susan 205
riots 179
rocket launchers 25, 116, 132–133; and Crimea 195, 196
Roki tunnel (Russia) 132–133
Roman Empire 52
Rome 74–75
Rose Revolution (Georgia) 98–103, 114
Rosneft 205
Rosoboronexport 118–119, 169
Rossiya Segodnya 111
Rostov-on-the-Don 209
round wood 82
Rousseau, Jean Jacques 27, 240*n*44
Roxburgh, Angus 113
RT (Russia Today) 91, 108–109, 112, 230; and U.S. elections 218–219
ruble 47, 208
Rumania 57, 75, 169
Russia Today television *see* RT
Russian Chamber of Trade and Industry 84
Russian Civil War 18–19
Russian General Staff 131, 133, 135
Russian language 43, 45, 96, 102, 111, 165; in Azerbaijan 148; in Baltic Republics 222; in Bucharest Summit 129; in Georgia 116; schools 162; in Ukraine 193, 195–197, 201, 208; in U.S. 231
Russian navy 95
Russian Railways 152
Russian Revolution 18, 82
Russian troops: in Chechnya 29, 61; in Eastern Europe 10, 14; in Poland 10; in Transnistria 17–18, 96–99; in Yugoslavia 56–57
Russians, ethnic 5, 16, 28, 40, 70, 97; in Baltic Republics 122; in Ukraine 174, 193–194; in U.S. 109, 231
Russo-Finnish War 82
Russo-Tunisian Business Council 90
Ruxit 226–227
Ryabov, Andrey 121

S-300 170, 264*n*8
Saab 71

Saakashvili, Mikheil "Misha" 100–101, 114–118; and Azerbaijan 148; and coup attempt 173; and Five Day War 130–136, 142; and Ukraine 209–210
Sadat, Anwar 94
Safanov, Aleksandr 119
Saimaa Canal (Russia) 82
St. Petersburg 10–11, 70, 106; and CFE 124
Sakharov Avenue (Moscow) 186
Sakwa, Richard 190
Salisbury incident (Britain) 224, 226
San Francisco Peace Treaty of 1951 11
sanctions: on Abkhazia 128; over Crimea 217, 233–234; and Eurasian Economic Union 183; on Georgia 117; on Iran 93–94, 119, 166; on Russia 118–119, 142, 145–146, 204–206; on Syria 94–95, 185; on Uzbekistan 178
Sanders, Bernie 219
Sarkozy, Nicolas 125; and Five Day War 132–139, 173; and Syria 212
satellites 77–78, 166
Saudi Arabia 93, 94, 252n19; and Chechnya 89; and Syria 212
Sawka, Richard 190
schools 45, 90, 162–163; of embassies 263n21; in Ukraine 208
Schröder, Gerhard 73, 78–79
Sea of Azov 21
2nd Brigade (Georgia) 134
secular 85–86, 147
Security Council (Russia) 194, 199
Security Council (U.N.) 13, 37, 119, 169; and Abkhazia 23; and Georgia 116, 146, 172; and Iran 119, 166; and Iraq invasion 77–78; and Kosovo 55, 126; and Libya 183–184; and Syria 95, 185, 212; and White Revolution 187
Seleznyov, Gennady 80
Senaki (Georgia) 134
separatists 46–49
Serbia 7, 51–56, 66, 72, 125–127; bombing of 141, 245n9; and Georgia 173
Sevastopol 45, 95, 102, 193–196; naval base 176, 207; and Syria 215
Seven Sisters 158, 160
sex trade and practices 91, 158
Shakespeare, William 165
Shalikashvili, John 39
Sharia Law 62
Shevardnadze, Eduard 14, 20–21, 23, 114; and NATO 238n27; and Rose Revolution 100–101, 103
ship repair and shipyard 95, 176
Silicon Valley 170
Simferopol 46–48, 193–196
Simonyan, Margarita 108–109, 111, 230
Skripal, Sergei 224

Slavyansk (Donbass) 198–200
sloppiness 119
Slovakia 75
Slovenia 75
small business 34
Smirnov, Igor 96–99
smuggling 62, 207
soap operas 214
Sochi 67, 69; Olympics in 82, 126
social media 105, 112, 140–141; in Russia 186–188; in Ukraine 192; in U.S. 217–219, 231
socialism 5–7, 54
Somalia 205
South Africa 9
South Ossetia 15, 18–20, 23, 115; and CFE 124; and EU 173; and Five Day War 131–132; and Kosovo 126; and OSCE 172; and WTO 182
South Stream 83, 88, 142
Soviet invasion of Hungary 83, 84
Soviet Union 5–7, 8–9, 15, 45, 98; and CFE 123; and EBRD 33–34; establishment of 19; fall of 268n12; and Finland 82; Foreign Ministry of 157–159; and Georgia 100; and Iran 93; and Middle East 89–91, 94; and NATO 13–14; and Nicaragua 144; resurrection of 181; and shipyards 176; and TASS 111; and Turkey 86
Spain 125–126, 206; and NATO expansion 129
spam 122
Spanish language 108–109, 111–11; and Russian diplomats 261n23
Special Forces 195–196
Spectrum 230
spheres of influence 238n14
Sputnik news organization 111–112, 230–231; and U.S. elections 218–219
spy and spying 74, 220; and Cheeseburger Summit 169–170; in Georgia 116–117
Stalin, Joseph 33, 82, 194
START I 37, 72–73
START II 37, 72–73; see also New Start Treaty
statues 83, 122–123, 193
status quo ante bellum 133, 135
Stepanakert (Nagorno-Karabakh) 24–25, 153
Stinger missiles 212
Strategic Offensive Reductions Treaty (SORT) 72–73
Strelkov, Igor 198–200
strikes 24
Sturgess, Dawn 224
suitcases 207
Sukhoi 118–119
Sukhumi (Abkhazia) 20, 21, 23
Sumgait (Azerbaijan) 24
superficiality 163
Supreme Court of Ukraine 103

surface-to-air missiles 196, 212; see also S-300
Sweden 14, 81–82, 167; and North Stream 82
Switzerland 14, 82, 167, 173, 206; and WTO
Syria 91, 94–95, 118; and reset 189; and Russia 166, 181, 183–185, 211–217
Syrian-Russian Permanent Commission on Economic Cooperation 94

Tagliavini, Heidi 173
Tajikistan 108, 181
Talbott, Strobe 42, 243n48
Taliban 62, 65, 67, 69, 166, 177, 179
tankers 148
tanks 124, 136, 195, 209
tariffs 176, 182
Tartus naval base (Syria) 91, 95
TASS 111
Tatars 194, 196
Tbilisi 99–100, 115, 135; protests in 173
television 64, 67; in Crimea 196; in English 163; and Georgia 99–100; and Kyrgyzstan 179; and Libya 183; in Russia 185–186, 213, 224–225; and Syria 185, 214; and Tskhinvali 140, 143; in Ukraine 101, 192, 197; in U.S. 108–109, 112, 230–231; see also media
temper tantrum 131
Tenet, George 78
tents 102, 186, 192
Ter-Petrosyan, Levon 25–27
Terek River 18, 62–64, 69
territorial integrity 141–142, 175
terrorists 13, 51, 63, 86, 215
theocracy 93, 147
Third Army (Turkish) 108, 150
Tiananmen Square (China) 118
Tillerson, Rex 212, 233
Time 121
time zone 47
tolerance 93
torture 20–21
tourism 85, 89, 91
TOW anti-tank missiles 212
trade 145, 176, 209; of Armenia 150, 152
Transnistria 12, 16–18, 48, 96–99; and CFE 124; and Duma 128; and Kosovo 125–126; and Ukraine 210
Treaty of European Union 34
tribalization 52
Tripoli 183
"troll" farm 217, 231
troops, Ukrainian 47
Trump, Donald 204; and Putin 170, 214, 226, 233–235; and Syria 213–214, 216; and U.S. elections 218–219
tsars 8, 82, 151, 157; acquisitions of 18, 142, 238n14

Index

Tskhinvali 19, 115, 238n16; shelling of 132–134, 140, 143
Tulip Revolution 103–104, 177, 179
Tunisia 90, 183
Turkey 19, 42, 84–88; and Abkhazia 173; and Armenia 25, 26, 27, 151–152; and Black Sea 140; and Blue Stream 114; and Chechnya 86, 89; and coal 209; and Council of Europe 222; and Five Day War 140, 143–144; and Georgia 115; and Kosovo 87, 126; pipelines 148, 205; and Syria 214–217
Twitter 218–219
Tymoshenko, Yulia 113–114, 175–176

U-turn 53, 57
Ukraine 8, 43–50, 171, 190–208, 204–210; and Council of Europe 227; and ethnic Russians 137; and Eurasian Economic Community 182; and Georgia 174; and Kosovo 57, 125; and NATO 75, 87, 127, 165, 167, 172; and Orange Revolution 101 103, 113–114; and pipelines 88; and reset 174–176; and sanctions on Russia 223; and Transnistria 18, 125
Ukrainian language 45, 208
ultimatums 8, 42, 55, 191, 213
underwater cables 207
unilateralism 169
United Arab Emirates 90–91, 214
United Nations 13, 51, 120–121, 168; and Abkhazia 144, 239n37; and English language 163; and European Security proposal 168–169; and Georgia 133, 137; and Iran 264n8; and Kosovo 126, 144; and Russian diplomats 164; and South Ossetia 144
United Nations Comptroller 172
United Nations High Commissioner to Georgia 172–173
United Nations Human Rights Commission 10, 66, 68, 70
United Nations Observer Mission in Georgia (UNOMIG) 23, 145–146, 172
United Nations Secretary General 192
United Russia 185–186
United States 121–122; and Armenia 150–151; and Azerbaijan 147, 149; and Chechnya 62, 67, 69; and coal 209; and Council of Europe 222; and EU 34–35, 37, 254n19; and Finland 82; fragility of 218; and Georgia 115–117; and Hungary 83–84; and Iran 93–94; and

Iraq 91; and reset 165–171; response to the Five Day War 140–146; and Russian diplomats 164; and Salisbury incident 224; and Sarkozy mission 135–139; and Syria 211–217; and Turkey 84–87; and unilateralism 121–123
United States Congress 37, 62, 66, 188, 232–233
United States Department of State 158, 161, 165, 263n26
United States embassies 106, 120, 239n35, 251n14
United States Foreign Service 163–164, 263n14
United States Senate 71, 72, 192, 233
United States Senate Committee on Intelligence 220, 231, 276n4
United States Treasury 40, 119, 234
Upper Kodori Gorge 116, 141, 174
USAID 101, 106, 188
Ushakov, Yuri 120, 162
Uzbekistan 108, 177–179

Vaino, Anton E. 220
vegetables 206, 207, 223; from Azerbaijan 148, 149
Venezuela 118, 144, 163
veto 98
victor's peace 138
Victory in Europe (V-E) parade 31, 41, 122, 123
videos 213, 215
Vietnam 6, 64, 69–70, 205; and Eurasian Economic Union 183; Russian withdrawal 9, 97
Villa, Pancho 121
violence 104
visas 117, 188; and Armenia 150
Voice of Russia 111
Volkogonov, Dmitry 15
Voloshin, Alexander 79
volunteers 16, 21, 194
Vorodin, Vladimir 96–99
Vostok battalion 134
Vostok 2010 176
voter fraud 102–103, 186
votes 274n6
voting infrastructure 219–220

Wall Street Journal 110
war games 124
war lords 29–31, 61–63
warnings 115, 117, 125, 131; from South Ossetia 122
warplanes 29, 99; and Five Day War 131; and Syria 184; and Ukraine 197
Warsaw Pact 13–14, 37–38, 108; and CFE 124; and NATO 83
warships 86, 205–206, 250n29
weapons 29, 97, 118; of Georgia

115–116; of mass destruction 76–77
weather 71
web cameras 186–187
West Qurna oil fields (Iraq) 77
wheat 157, 174, 206; and Syria 214–215
White Revolution 185–188
Wikileaks 1–2, 219
Williamson, Gavin 221
Wilson, Andrew 43
wives 160–162
women 18, 97, 160, 162; *see also* marriages; rapes
World Bank 126
World Cup 210, 224, 227, 276n38
world power 95, 108
World Trade Organization (WTO) 79, 81, 85, 93; and Georgia 130, 182; and Jackson-Vanik Law 188; and Russia 182, 221, 223; and Ukraine 113
World War I 127, 169
World War II 43, 82, 140, 169

Yakovlev, Dima 188
Yalta 78, 233
Yanukovych, Viktor 113–114, 176, 178, 206–207; and Eastern Ukraine 197; and elections 101–102, 253n40; and EU 190–194; fall of 268n12
Yeltsin, Boris 7–8, 36; and Abkhazia 21; and Baltic Republics 11; and Chechnya 28, 30–32, 64–65, 106; and CIS 181; and Crimea 47–48; and Foreign Ministry 159–160; and G7 40, 42, 225; and Japan 11–12; and Kosovo 53–55; and Nagorno-Karabakh 25–27; and nationalities 15; and NATO 14; and NATO expansion 38–39; and nuclear weapons 72; and pipelines 148; and Serbia 7; and television 108; and Ukraine 43–45, 49
Yerevan 150, 153
You-Tube 109, 218
youths 187
Yugoslavia 7, 13, 38, 51; collapse of 125; as deterrent 21, 23; and OSCE 106
Yushchenko, Viktor 102–103, 113–114, 253n40; and NATO 175

Zapad battalion 134
Zapad 2017 225
Zayed, Abdullah bin 215
Zelensky, Volodymyr 210, 228
zero-sum game 229

www.ingramcontent.com/pod-product-compliance
Lightning Source LLC
Chambersburg PA
CBHW060337010526
44117CB00017B/2858